ATLAS
OF
AMERICA

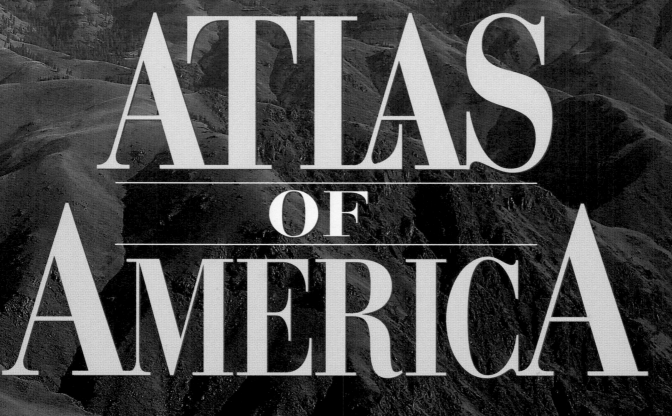

READER'S DIGEST

ATLAS
OF
AMERICA

OUR NATION IN
MAPS, FACTS, AND PICTURES

Reader's
Digest

THE READER'S DIGEST ASSOCIATION, INC.
Pleasantville, New York/Montreal

STAFF

Project Editor
Suzanne E. Weiss

Project Art Editor
Irene Ledwith

Associate Editor
Audrey Peterson

Designer
Tomaso Milian

Associate Designers
Patrizia Bove, Bruce R. McKillip,
Todd Victor

Research Editors
Susan Howard Biederman, Barbara
Guarino Lester, Sandra Streepey

Editorial/Research Assistant
Claudia Kaplan

Special Thanks
Susan Bronson, Louise DiBerardino,
Melissa Endlich, Nancy Mace, Bryce Walker

CONTRIBUTORS

Chief Writer
Justin Cronin

Writers
Joanne Barkan, Jack El-Hai, Dwight Holing,
Tod Olson, William G. Scheller, Nancy
Shepherdson, Scott Weidensaul

Copy Editors
David Fleischmann (cartography)
Gina Grant

Indexer
Rose Bernal

Researcher
Denise Lynch

Cartographers
Hammond Incorporated

Ortelius Design, Inc.

Illustrator
Ian Worpole

Picture Research
PhotoSearch, Inc.

Consultants:
Col. John Elting
U.S. Army (Retired)

The Flag Research Center

Douglas E. Heath
Professor of Geography and Geology
Northampton Community College

Charles R. McNeil
Museum of Florida History

Helen Hornbeck Tanner
Senior Research Fellow
The Newberry Library, Chicago

**READER'S DIGEST
GENERAL BOOKS**

**Editor-in-Chief, Books and
Home Entertainment**
Barbara J. Morgan

Editor-in-Chief, U.S. General Books
David Palmer

Executive Editor
Gayla Visalli

Managing Editor
Christopher Cavanaugh

Editorial Director
Edmund H. Harvey, Jr.

Design Director
Irene Ledwith

Address any comments about Atlas of America
*to Editor-in-Chief, U.S. General Books, Reader's
Digest, 260 Madison Avenue, New York, NY 10016.*

To order additional copies of Atlas of America,
call 1-800-846-2100.

You can also visit us on the World Wide Web at
http://www.readersdigest.com

◀ **Endpaper:** *Wheat grows in
abundance in the Palouse Hills
region of Washington's Columbia
Plateau. Huge areas of fertile
soil and advanced farming
methods are responsible for making the United States one of the
world's largest food producers.*

◀ **Page 1:** *A solitary person is
dwarfed by the vastness of the
pristine St. Elias mountain
range in southeastern Alaska.*

◀ **Pages 2–3:** *Hell's Canyon
on the Idaho-Oregon border is
the deepest gorge (1¹/₂ miles) in
North America. The Snake River
winds through it.*

The credits and acknowledgments that appear on pages 209–210 are
hereby made a part of this copyright page.

Copyright © 1998 The Reader's Digest Association, Inc.
Copyright © 1998 The Reader's Digest Association (Canada) Ltd.
Copyright © 1998 Reader's Digest Association Far East Ltd.
Philippine Copyright 1998 Reader's Digest Association Far East Ltd.

Hammond maps copyright © 1998 HAMMOND INCORPORATED,
Maplewood, NJ.

All rights reserved. Unauthorized reproduction, in any manner,
is prohibited.

Reader's Digest and the Pegasus logo are registered trademarks of
The Reader's Digest Association, Inc.

Printed in the United States of America

Library of Congress Cataloging in Publication Data

Reader's Digest Association.
    Atlas of America : our nation in maps, facts, and pictures.
        p.   cm.
    Includes index.
    ISBN 0-7621-0072-9
    1. United States—Maps.   I. Title.   II. Title: Our nation in
maps, facts, and pictures.
G1200 .R380 1998 <G&M>
912.73—DC21   97-50458
                                                                            CIP
                                                                         MAPS

About This Book

There is a special kind of magic in an atlas. It shows us our position in the world—where we are and where we might go. As a reference tool, it crams an astonishing wealth of information into each square inch of map space. Only a dictionary, perhaps, is consulted more often. Would you like to know the height of Mount McKinley? The capital of West Virginia? An atlas will tell you. It can also help you plan a trip, settle an argument — or take you on an armchair adventure to faraway places you have only dreamed about.

ATLAS OF AMERICA is a comprehensive visual fact book about the nation and its 50 states. Containing more than 200 maps, along with text, graphs, and vivid color photographs, it is a treasure trove of fascinating and valuable information about this country — its geology and climate, plant forms and animal life, agricultural and mineral resources, historic sites, national parks, wilderness areas, and centers of population.

The atlas is divided into two main parts. First comes "The Nation," a 66-page overview of the land and its people, beginning with a two-page, coast-to-coast satellite image of the 48 contiguous states. Subsequent pages explore important topics in vivid detail. The climate section, for example, describes jet-stream patterns, cloud formations, tornado-prone areas, and regional weather makers, such as the Alberta Clipper and the Bermuda High. Other sections cover America's transportation networks, power resources, demographic patterns, timber and agricultural reserves, and much more. One 10-page sequence features thumbnail portraits of the country's national parks, from Acadia in Maine to Zion in Utah. Another segment offers fascinating biographical sketches of notable men and women.

An important element of this first part is a 22-page series of maps, pictures, and narrative texts that summarize the country's remarkable human history. The story begins more than 11,000 years ago, when America's first inhabitants reached Alaska from nearby Siberia, and it continues through three centuries of European colonization, the birth of the world's first modern democracy, and the nation's subsequent rise to greatness as the world's reigning superpower.

The heart of ATLAS OF AMERICA is "The Fifty States," a 134-page section that presents each state in all its glory. Along with the state map — prepared by Hammond Incorporated, using the very latest in satellite and computer technology — a concise text portrait relates the state's history and pinpoints its special character. Each state's presentation is accompanied by a time line, an almanac of vital statistics, an economic summary, a list of major towns and cities, and a weather chart. Often, metropolitan-area or city-street maps zoom in even closer. In addition, occasional special feature maps reveal unique

aspects of particular states: Alaska's 100,000 glaciers, Nevada's ghost towns, Indian mounds in Ohio, the 118 lighthouses of Michigan, and the 138 colleges in Massachusetts, to name just a few.

Every portrait is, by definition, a visual image, and ATLAS OF AMERICA contains some 500 full-color photographs of scenic landscapes, wildlife, wilderness, important buildings, and monuments. In addition, a 6-page general index and a 40-page geographic index (which lists some 35,000 place names) offer easy reference to the wealth of information ATLAS OF AMERICA provides.

▲ **The Statue of Liberty,** *proud lady of welcome for millions of newly arrived Americans, stands atop her pedestal in New York Harbor on a snowy winter's day. A gift from the French, the statue was set in place in 1876.*

Table of Contents

The Nation

▲ *America's wetlands* support a huge array of wildlife, including many species of birds. This egret is flying above the marshes of Georgia's Sea Islands.

The Fifty States

◀ *Large Midwestern farms* like this one in Iowa raise a substantial portion of the nation's crops and livestock.

▶ *Pages 8–9:* This satellite image of the 48 contiguous states reveals geologic features and vegetation patterns.

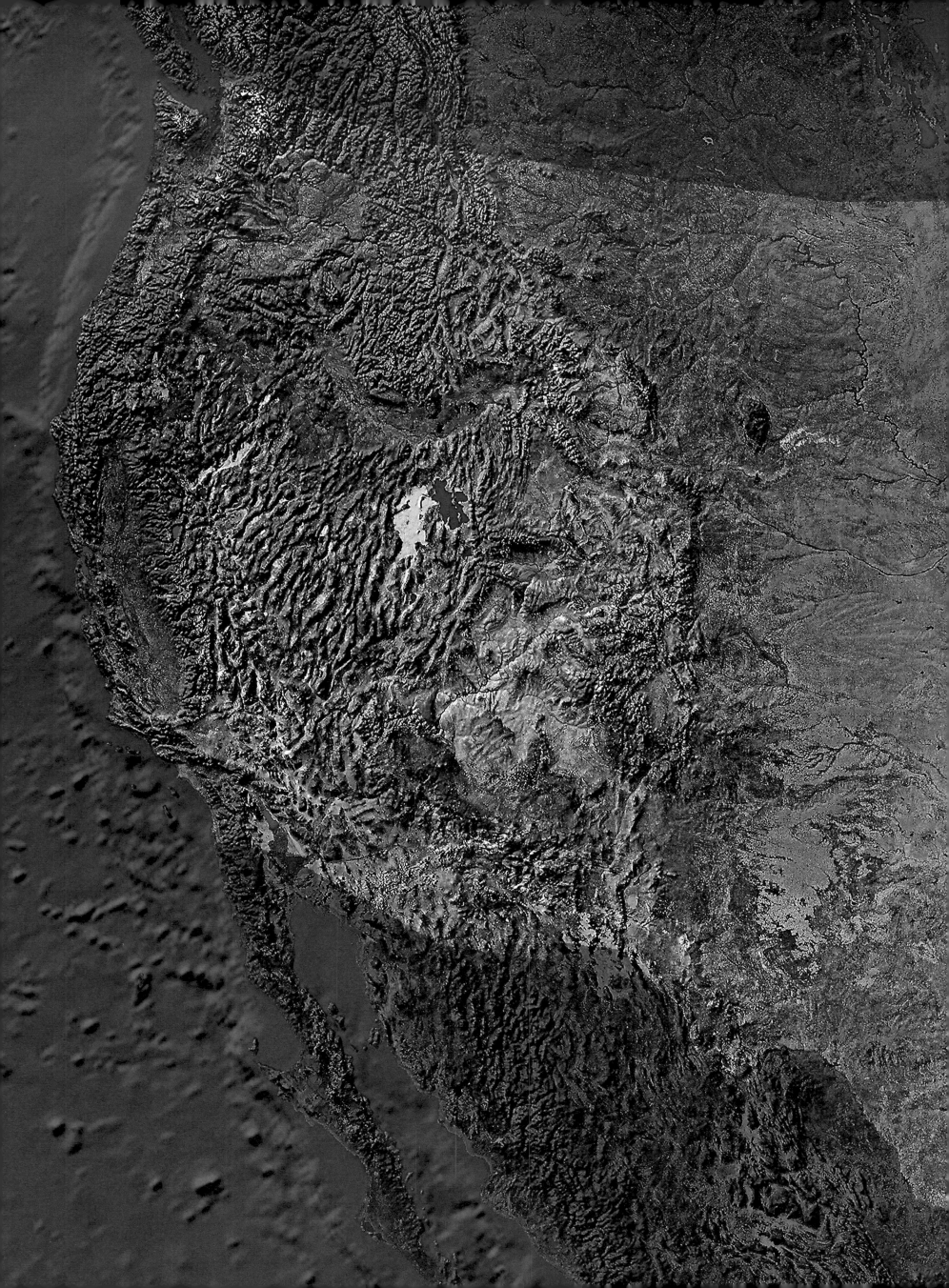

Inside the Earth
This view of the earth's layers shows the solid inner core, made of iron; the liquid outer core, composed of molten nickel and iron; the lower mantle, upper mantle, asthenosphere, and lithosphere—all believed to be igneous rock—and the oceanic and continental crusts, composed of basalt and granite.

Upper mantle (mostly solid, some liquid) about 290 miles thick

Lower mantle (solid) about 1,365 miles thick

Outer core (liquid) about 1,300 miles thick

Inner core (solid) about 1,520 miles in diameter

Crust (solid) Continental—up to 30 miles thick Oceanic—about 4 miles thick

Asthenosphere (part of upper mantle) about 65 miles thick

Lithosphere (includes crust) about 60 miles thick

The Moving Continents
Once part of a giant landmass called Pangaea, the continents began to drift apart because of the constant movement of the tectonic plates beneath them.

225 million years ago

180 million years ago

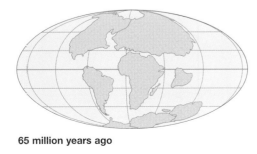

65 million years ago

Present day

Forces That Shaped the Land

We live on a restless planet, a ball of stone and metal wrapped in a thin skin of solid rock, a crust that breaks and shifts with time and the unimaginable heat down below. Over hundreds of millions of years, continents spin and dance, welding together and splitting apart; the epic force of their collision spawns mountains, which erode to dust that spreads out across plains and valleys. Volcanoes push to the surface, reshaping the terrain—or forging new land where once there was only vast ocean. Other forces are subtler, scarcely noticeable except in the great sweep of geologic time. Windblown grit chisels away at the most obstinate rock; water nibbles and smooths, digging a mile-deep canyon here, sculpting the graceful curves of barrier islands there. And in the deep freeze of an ice age, continental glaciers carve their mark with slow violence, plowing up lakes as large as inland seas, scraping off the tops of mountains, and rearranging the land.

MAKEUP OF THE EARTH
From the earth's outer edge to its inner core is a trip of almost 4,000 miles, and humans, even with mines thousands of feet down, have barely scratched its surface. To puzzle out what the interior of the planet is like, geophysicists must decipher the way energy, such as sound and shock waves, moves through rock of different temperatures and consistencies. The seismic rumble of earthquakes provides one test; so do man-made blasts.

The outermost membrane is the crust, up to 30 miles thick, which carries the continents and the seafloor. Rapid seismic waves indicate that the earth remains fairly rigid down to the base of the lithosphere, a depth of approximately 60 miles; there the waves suddenly slow down as they enter the warmer, more supple asthenosphere. Below about 125 miles, the mantle is composed of solid rock, although its high temperature and pressure make it nonrigid and subject to slow, internal movement. Finally, at about 1,800 miles down, there is the core, a sphere of liquid iron-nickel alloy surrounding a ball of solid iron. Temperatures within the core are almost as high as those on the surface of the sun,

and this planetary furnace is stoked by the power of nuclear decay in radioactive elements like uranium. At one time, scientists believed that these components of the earth's interior nested together in a series of concentric rings, like those of an onion, each layer distinct in its composition and temperature. Today, thanks to sophisticated analysis of subterranean shock waves, geophysicists realize that the planet is far more complex than that. Earth, they now believe, is more like a marble cake than an onion, as plumes of hotter material mingle with tongues of denser, cooler rock.

CONTINENTAL DRIFT
Like the pieces of a jigsaw puzzle, the east coast of South America and the west coast of Africa mirror each other's shape, a fact that mapmakers noticed as early as the 16th century. In 1912 German meteorologist Alfred Wegener proposed that this was more than coincidence; Africa and South America, he claimed, had once been a single landmass. But the idea that continents could move around the earth's surface was considered absurd by other scientists, and Wegener's idea was ridiculed—until the 1960s, when evidence convinced them that Wegener had been right all along.

That proof came from several different sources. Geologists have traced similarities in rock strata between places like New England and the Scottish Highlands, and Brazil and Nigeria, while paleontologists have found identical fossils in widely separated parts of the globe. But the most compelling findings came from the seafloor. Running the length of the Atlantic Ocean, the Mid-Atlantic Ridge is a seam from which magma oozes out, forming new ocean crust at a rate of an inch or so a year and pushing the Old World farther away from the New. The Atlantic Ocean is already roughly a dozen feet wider than it was when Christopher Columbus crossed it in 1492. Similar ridges crisscross the world's

other oceans, and at each one scientists have found the same thing: the youngest rock is near the rift, while the oldest is near the edges of the continents.

PLATE TECTONICS
Mapping the ocean floor, scientists have discovered that the planet is covered by 15 medium to large crustal plates, most of which have continents floating on top of them. Floating? It may seem odd, but continental bedrock like granite is

---

Tectonic Plates in Motion
Supported by 15 major tectonic plates that are in constant motion, the earth's crust is subject to its own never-ending metamorphosis. Plate action—whether diverging, converging, or shearing—occurs at the plate boundaries, along which the products of plate tectonics—earthquakes and volcanoes—are strongly concentrated.

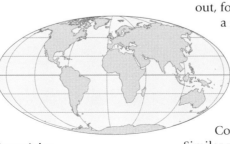

ARABIAN PLATE

AFRICAN PLATE

INDIAN OCEAN

INDO-AUSTRALIA

Major Earthquakes Since 1900 Indicated by Number
(R = Richter Scale Intensity)

1 Armenia 1988, 6.9R	14 Southern Alaska 1964, 8.4R
2 Rasht 1990, 7.7R	15 San Francisco 1906, 8.3R
3 Tabas 1978, 7.7R	1989, 6.9R
4 Quetta 1978, 7.7R	16 Los Angeles 1994, 6.6R
5 Gansu 1920, 8.6R	17 Mexico City 1985, 8.1R
6 Tangshan 1976, 7.8R	18 Guatemala 1976, 7.5R
7 Sakhalin 1995, 7.5R	19 San José 1991, 7.4R
8 Kuril Islands 1994, 7.9R	20 Chimbote 1970, 7.8R
9 Tokyo 1923, 8.3R	21 Valparaiso 1906, 8.6R
10 Kobe 1995, 7.2R	22 Naples 1980, 7.2R
11 Cabanatuan 1990, 7.7R	23 El Asnam (Chlef) 1980, 7.5R
12 Guam 1993, 8.1R	24 Agadir 1960, 5.7R
13 Flores 1992, 7.5R	

lighter than the very dense basalt that makes up the ocean crust, and so it rides on top of the plate, carried along like an object on a conveyor belt. This is the concept known as plate tectonics.

At oceanic ridges, new ocean floor is created as molten magma seeps to the surface; this expansion pushes continents apart. Elsewhere, in extremely deep trenches, the old ocean crust is drawn down into the earth, a process known as subduction, which pulls continents together. The old crust melts and is recycled, but the heat generated sometimes leaks to the surface as volcanoes. As the Juan de Fuca Plate is subducted

beneath the American Plate off Washington and Oregon, it fuels such volcanoes as Mount St. Helens and Mount Rainier; likewise, the Pacific Plate is diving beneath the Aleutian Islands, part of the volcano- and earthquake-prone "Ring of Fire" that circles the north Pacific. As the plates subduct, any continental crust riding on top is scraped off, piling up along the plate edge in dramatic mountains like the Coast Range of the Pacific Northwest. A much older plate collision that started 65 million years ago raised the Rocky Mountains.

Plates don't always meet head-to-head. Where they slide past one

another, in what geologists call a transform fault, the result can be massive earthquakes. The San Andreas, the most famous transform fault of all, runs 750 miles from near the Mexican border to northern California. Sometimes the plates slip past each other with little effect, but when stresses build up over long periods, the plates can snap free with astounding force, as happened during the legendary San Francisco earthquake of 1906.

VOLCANOES
Ordinarily, the earth's hard crust provides a shield from the infernal heat far

▲ *Earth's changing surface.*
The Blue Ridge Mountains in the Appalachian system (left) were once much higher than they are now; 280 million years of erosion have greatly reduced their size. A more drastic change occurs in only seconds when tectonic plates grind against each other, causing earthquakes in such fault zones as San Francisco, California (center). The Utah Cliff (right) near the San Juan River is a classic example of a slow process called sedimentation, by which organic debris is deposited by water and air over millions of years to form stratified rock.

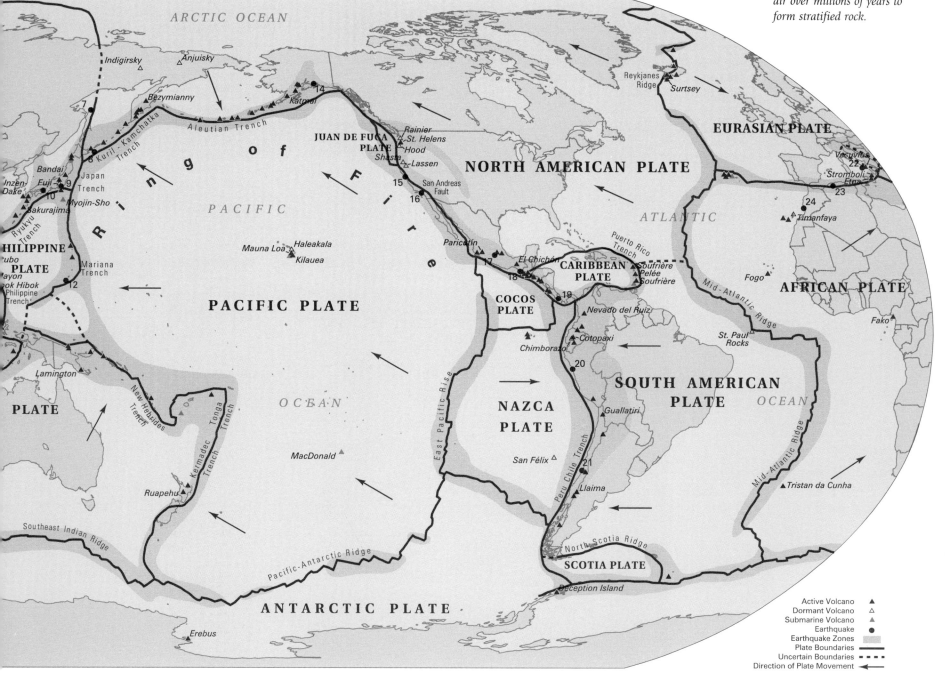

Active Volcano	▲
Dormant Volcano	△
Submarine Volcano	▲
Earthquake	●
Earthquake Zones	
Plate Boundaries	
Uncertain Boundaries	▬ ▬ ▬
Direction of Plate Movement	←

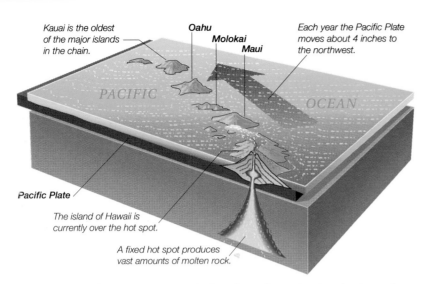

Kauai is the oldest of the major islands in the chain.

Oahu
Molokai
Maui

Each year the Pacific Plate moves about 4 inches to the northwest.

PACIFIC

OCEAN

Pacific Plate

The island of Hawaii is currently over the hot spot.

A fixed hot spot produces vast amounts of molten rock.

Hawaii's Hot Spots

The slow northwestward drift of the Pacific Plate over a stationary hot spot has created the Hawaiian islands over the past 5 to 6 million years. The hot spot spews lava, building a volcano that later emerges from the sea as an island. The plate then moves on, taking the island with it and making room for a new island to be formed. The island of Hawaii is presently over the hot spot.

The Great Lakes

About 15,000 years ago lobes of the last Pleistocene glacier gouged the basins of the Great Lakes (below, top). Some 10,000 years ago the melting ice sheet filled the basins of Lakes Michigan and Erie (center). Further melting filled the other basins to create the world's largest system of freshwater lakes (bottom).

below, but where that barrier is weak, the earth's molten innards may squeeze through—with dramatic effect. Volcanoes, with their explosive eruptions and fiery lava flows, can rapidly reshape the land, even creating it out of the ocean's depths. As the earth's tectonic plates have shifted over time, volcanoes have cropped up in many parts of what is now the United States. In the Four Corners region of the Southwest, volcanic landforms like Shiprock dominate the scene—places where lava pushed to the surface through one deep pipe and a few wide cracks, hardened, and now stand as gigantic spikes and slabs against the horizon, the softer rock around them having been eroded away.

Surprisingly, Mount St. Helens in Washington, which exploded in 1980, was not the most violent volcanic eruption in the United States this century. That distinction goes to Novarupta, a volcano 10 times more powerful that exploded in southwest Alaska in 1912 with a blast heard hundreds of miles away and covered vast areas with ash. An expedition to the region four years later found a moonlike landscape. The group dubbed the area the Valley of Ten Thousand Smokes, and it is now part of Katmai

Retreating ice sheet

11,000 B.C.

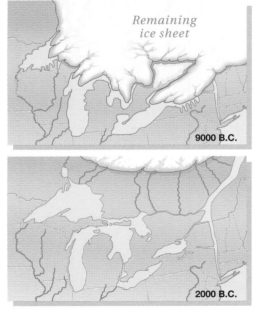

Remaining ice sheet

9000 B.C.

2000 B.C.

▶ *The five Great Lakes* captured in a satellite mosaic image. The largest one, Lake Superior, is at the top; Lake Michigan, Lake Huron, Lake Erie, and Lake Ontario are pictured from left to right.

▲ *The Hawaiian Islands chain,* as seen from space. From bottom right to top left are the islands of Nihau, Kauai, Oahu, Molokai, Lanai, Maui, Kahoolawe, and Hawaii.

National Park, which boasts 15 active volcanoes within its boundaries.

Deep beneath the Pacific Ocean, volcanoes have built the greatest mountains on the earth, capped by the Hawaiian Islands. At 32,000 feet (most of it below sea level), Mauna Kea, on the island of Hawaii, is far more massive than Mount Everest. The island chain, strung out like pearls across the ocean, was born of volcanoes created by a persistent plume of heat rising from a hot spot deep in the underlying mantle. As the Pacific Plate drifts northwest across the hot spot, new volcanoes boil up, create islands, then become dormant when the island slides off the hot spot a million or so years later. The outermost islands, like Kauai and Oahu, are the oldest. The newest

Hawaiian Island, the Loihi seamount, is still submerged but inching toward the surface 3,000 feet away.

Far from Hawaii, another hot spot is a time bomb waiting to explode. Deep beneath Yellowstone National Park, fueling its showy geysers and steam vents, lies a hot spot that erupted with unimaginable fury in the past, carpeting thousands of miles of the West with ash and lava and creating a crater that encompasses 1,300 square miles. Its last eruption was 600,000 years ago; the next, say scientists, could be at any time.

GLACIERS

Volcanoes alter the land in seconds; glaciers do the same over millennia. Rivers of ice, glaciers today are restricted

to the highest mountains in Alaska and the West, where snowfall accumulates but does not melt; compressed into ice by the growing weight, the sheet is forced downhill, its underside an abrasive sandpaper of boulders and debris that cuts away the hills through which it flows. Glacier-carved valleys have a distinctive U-shaped profile with sheer, steep walls. The head of the glacier also gnaws at the crowns of mountains, forming the bowl-shaped valleys known as cirques, divided by knifelike ridges that separate the "drainages" of different glaciers. (Even without glaciers, ice can conquer rock; when water seeps deep into a crack, then freezes and expands, it can split even the hardest boulder.)

Most glaciers today are in retreat; in Alaska's Glacier Bay National Park, the ice has withdrawn 65 miles in a mere two centuries. But approximately 2 million years ago, a continental ice sheet crept down from Canada, moving as far south as Pennsylvania, Illinois, Nebraska, and Washington State, only to melt then advance three more times. In places, the ice was more than a mile thick, and its effect on the face of North America was profound. The ice cut the graceful valleys and cirques of the White Mountains in New Hampshire, and it rearranged many of the rivers in the eastern two-thirds of the country, which until the ice ages had flowed north; their waters were forced south, cutting new channels to the sea. The ice also moved millions of tons of dirt and gravel, dropping boulders in its retreat like so much litter. The glaciers carved myriad small lakes and ponds, bogs and marshes, but the grandest markers of their passing are the Great Lakes, the largest group of freshwater lakes in the world, which were gouged out of intractable rock by the sheer force of grinding ice. The last retreat of the ice front occurred between 20,000 and 10,000 years ago.

WATER
When the Appalachians were first formed, more than 200 million years ago, they would have rivaled the

▲ **The Colorado River** *cuts a dramatic serpentine pattern called The Loop into the sedimentary rock at Canyonlands National Park, Utah. Eventually, the river will wear away the thin barriers of stone forming the S-curve, leaving two islands.*

Himalayas in size—craggy, snaggle-toothed peaks rising into the heavens. Today the highest is Mount Mitchell in North Carolina, at 6,684 feet tall a shadow of its past glory, thanks to water.

Water can move mountains—and cut valleys, reshape cliffs, rearrange shorelines, and much more. Over 30 million years, the Colorado River in Arizona has chewed through layers of rock to create the Grand Canyon, 277 miles long and more than a mile deep; the river has cross-sectioned time as well as stone, exposing strata that date back almost 2 billion years. In fact, rivers and streams have been the most potent force in shaping the face of America. Seen from space, the nation's system of rivers and streams branches across the land like the roots of great trees, each contributing to the character of the land: rushing torrents or placid bayous, dramatic water gaps in mountains, meandering oxbows through lowlands. The oceans' incessant waves mold the shoreline, from the gen-

tle beaches of white quartz sand along the Gulf Coast to the granite cliffs of New England and the monolithic sea stacks standing guard against the Pacific, ultimately doomed to topple by the corrosive action of swirling water.

Barrier islands, which shield much of the Atlantic and Gulf shores, are an ephemeral union between sea and land yet not entirely the realm of one or the other. Along the Virginia and Maryland coasts, for example, 30-mile-long Assateague Island began as a long spit, pulled south like warm taffy by ocean currents, which deposited sand at the southern tip. Eventually, a storm breached the link with the mainland, leaving Assateague free to move at the whim of water and wind.

WIND
Compared to water, wind has only a minor role in shaping the land, but in places its presence is sweeping. Much of the fertile soil of the Great Plains, the nation's breadbasket, is loess—fine silt picked up by the wind from glacial riverbanks during the Ice Age and deposited across thousands of square miles in blankets more than 60 feet thick.

Along the coast, wind fashions sand into shifting dunes that march across the barrier islands, covering forests or revealing the stumps of trees buried for centuries. Nor are dunes found only along the ocean; in northern Michigan, the giant Sleeping Bear Dunes stand between Lake Michigan and the mainland while other dune fields are scattered across the West, relics of earlier times when seas and rivers ran differently. Yet even these pale beside the Sand Hills of north central Nebraska. Between 5,000 and 7,000 years ago, this area became the Western Hemisphere's largest dune field, covering some 19,000 square miles; today the sand is fixed in place by grasslands freckled with lakes and marshes—a reminder of the power of wind to transform the landscape.

▲ *The Atlantic Ocean pounds away at a New Jersey beach. Shorelines from Maine to Florida are robbed of tons of sand by tropical storms, hurricanes, and northeasters, brutal storms that attack the East often during the winter months.*

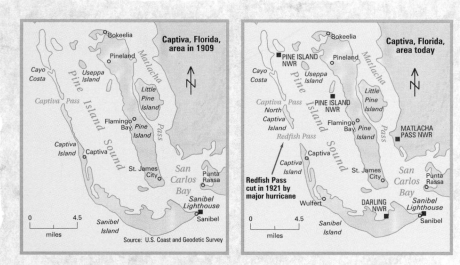

Captiva, Florida, area in 1909

Captiva, Florida, area today

Redfish Pass cut in 1921 by major hurricane

Source: U.S. Coast and Geodetic Survey

When Weather Splits the Earth
The aptly named barrier islands are usually the first line of defense against violent storms. In October 1921, however, the Florida barrier island of Captiva fell victim to the elements when a hurricane swept away a piece of land called the Narrows that linked Captiva to Upper Captiva. A passageway called Redfish Pass now separates the two islands.

▲ *A dust storm kicks up a menacing cloud of fine dirt and organic debris into the Texas air. Aside from reducing visibility, dust storms, which can cover hundreds of miles and reach heights of 10,000 feet or more, can also erode thousands of tons of loose soil.*

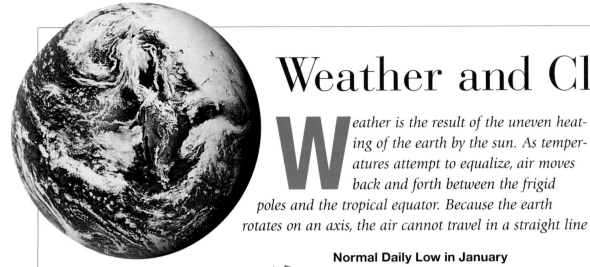

Weather and Climate

Weather is the result of the uneven heating of the earth by the sun. As temperatures attempt to equalize, air moves back and forth between the frigid poles and the tropical equator. Because the earth rotates on an axis, the air cannot travel in a straight line and is forced to move horizontally from one sector of the planet to another. When observed in a particular region on a daily basis, this movement of air—and any resultant clouds and precipitation—is referred to as an area's weather. Measured over a period of time, the weather that a region typically experiences is called its climate.

▲ **Cloud patterns,** as viewed from space, tell meteorologists about global atmospheric conditions, which are responsible for their formation.

▲ **Cumulus clouds**—often called fair-weather clouds because they generally don't bring precipitation—appear in all U.S. climate zones throughout the year.

▲ **Snowfall** is the winter watchword on the northern Plains. As a general rule, it takes 1 inch of water to produce 10 inches of snow.

▲ **Much hotter than the sun's surface,** a lightning bolt's average temperature is 50,000°F. Lightning can result from regional weather phenomena, such as Texas's Dry Line, which creates severe summer storms.

Normal Daily Low in January

Wet and cloudy
Heavy mountain snow
Heavy snow and bitter cold
Frequent snowfalls
Occasional ice storms
Dry
Mild and pleasant

- ☐ Below 0°F
- ☐ Zero to 9°F
- ☐ In the teens
- ☐ In the 20's
- ☐ In the 30's
- ☐ Warmer than 40°F

Normal Daily High in July

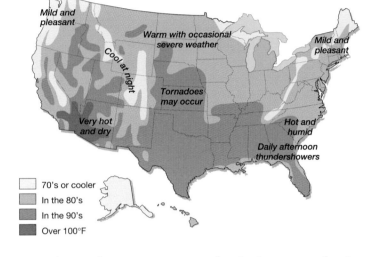

Mild and pleasant
Warm with occasional severe weather
Mild and pleasant
Cool at night
Tornadoes may occur
Very hot and dry
Hot and humid
Daily afternoon thundershowers

- ☐ 70's or cooler
- ☐ In the 80's
- ☐ In the 90's
- ☐ Over 100°F

U.S. CLIMATE ZONES

The United States is subject to a wide array of weather conditions because it covers such a broad portion of the globe. Its landmass lies close enough to both the North Pole and the equator to be influenced by their extremes of temperature. In addition, the country has large mountain ranges and expansive plains, and it is bordered on its eastern, western, and southern flanks by ocean. This geographical diversity has a measurable effect on local weather. The Pacific Coast, for instance, enjoys mild temperatures year-round because of the moderating influence of the Pacific Ocean.

On the maps above, the United States is divided into climate zones based on historically recurring winter and summer temperature patterns. General seasonal weather conditions that have been observed within these zones, such as heavy snowfall for the Great Lakes in the winter and daily thundershowers for the Southeast in the summer, are also noted.

REGIONAL WEATHER SHAPERS

Meteorologists have observed certain recurring phenomena that have a major influence on regional weather in the United States. As seen on the map at right, these weather shapers include the following:

Jet Stream: A fast-moving (150- to 200-mile-per-hour) "river" of air that forms at an altitude of roughly 30,000 feet. It separates warm, subtropical air from colder, polar air. Its position varies with the time of year, and it

can be a strong influence on the weather of the entire United States.

Alberta Clipper: A fast-moving winter storm system that travels southeastward out of Alberta, Canada, across the northern Plains and into New England. These storms can bring high winds, heavy snows, and bitter cold.

Chinook Winds: Warm winds that blow down the eastern slopes of the Rocky Mountains during the winter. These warm winds can cause the temperature to increase as much as 20°F to 40°F in as little as 15 minutes.

Monsoonal Flow: A flow of moist air from the Pacific Ocean off the southwestern coast of the United States that is responsible for bringing rain to this usually dry region. A monsoonal flow

occurs most often in the summer, but it has also happened at other times of year.

Dry Line (Marfa Front): A weather feature that separates the hot, dry air of western Texas from the hot, moist air of eastern Texas. A normal summer occurrence, the Dry Line migrates eastward and can be the cause of severe weather.

Bermuda High: An area of high pressure that occurs each summer near the island of Bermuda. The clockwise flow of air around this high-pressure system causes warm, humid air to be drawn north from the Gulf of Mexico all the way up the East Coast. This feature is responsible for the high heat and humidity experienced throughout the eastern region of the United States in the summer months.

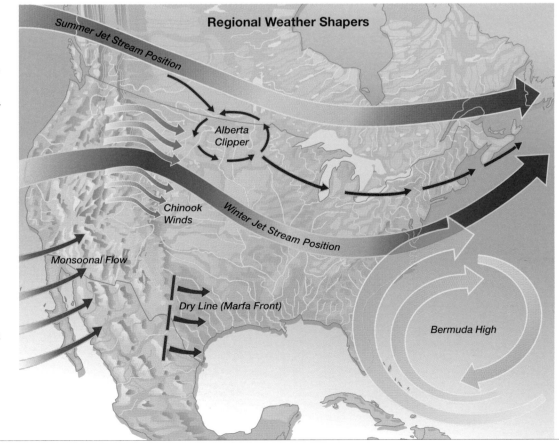

Regional Weather Shapers

Summer Jet Stream Position
Alberta Clipper
Chinook Winds
Winter Jet Stream Position
Monsoonal Flow
Dry Line (Marfa Front)
Bermuda High

EXTREME WEATHER

Most sections of the United States are prone to some form of extreme weather throughout the year. Two of the most common forms in summer are hurricanes and tornadoes.

The hurricanes that affect the United States grow primarily out of complexes of thunderstorms in the tropical Atlantic Ocean. The annual season for these immense storms is from June 1 to November 30, with the majority of occurrences in August, September, and October. The areas most prone to hurricanes are the East and Gulf coasts, in particular the state of Florida.

Tornadoes are violent, funnel-shaped vortices of wind that can reach speeds greater than 300 miles an hour. They originate from severe thunderstorms and can take extremely erratic paths. Recent advances in Doppler radar technology now allow meteorologists to peer inside violent thunderstorms to detect the formation of tornadoes, in order to better forecast their occurrence.

When the potential exists in a particular area for the onset of severe weather (a hurricane, tornado, flash flood, or major winter storm), the National Weather Service issues a watch. When the severe condition has already formed, will definitely form, or is heading toward the watch area, the National Weather Service issues a warning. Both should be taken very seriously.

*▲ **The earth** is constantly being monitored by spacecraft, ranging from weather satellites to the Space Shuttle. The information they provide enables meteorologists to track large, remote storms, such as hurricanes (top), and forecast when and where they will strike. In the photo above, Hurricane Andrew is observed just before it made landfall in Palm Beach, Florida, in August 1992.*

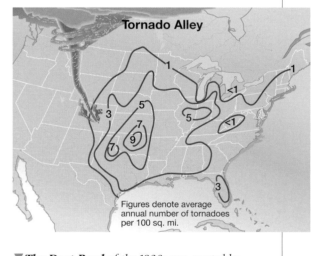

Tornado Alley

Figures denote average annual number of tornadoes per 100 sq. mi.

*◀ **When a white tornado** touches down on the ground, the dirt and debris it churns up turn its funnel-shaped cloud dark and ominous.*

*▼ **The Dust Bowl** of the 1930s was created by prolonged drought, as seen below in the Oklahoma Panhandle. In that decade, some regions of the country had record annual rainfall, while other areas received next to none.*

America's Plant Kingdom

As the sun arcs over the United States, its rays illuminate distinct bands of vegetation. A mixed forest of beech, sugar maple, and birch lines the East Coast before giving way to pine, hickory, and live oak that stretch to the Mississippi River. Grass savanna blankets the Great Plains, while conifers follow the length of the Rocky Mountains. Sagebrush and cactus dot the desert states, and a dense forest of cedar fir, pine, hemlock, and redwood borders the West. Soft tundra muffles the wilds of Alaska, and before setting in the Pacific, the last sunbeams of the day shine on the tropical blooms of the Hawaiian Islands.

▲ **The flowering dogwood,** a native tree of the East, as engraved by naturalist William Bartram in 1817.

American Vegetation

Many factors, including physical geography, determine which types of vegetation will grow in a region. While the hot, dry Southwest mainly supports shrubs, brush, and cacti, the moist coastal states contain evergreen and deciduous trees. But boundaries are not rigid; deciduous trees like willows do grow along rivers that flow through what are mostly Midwestern grasslands.

TREES

The plants that grow in the great bands of vegetation that stripe the United States are as diverse as the country's people and cultures. The nation's immense size and huge mix of soil types, climates, rainfall amounts, and elevations nurture an incredible array of plant types that boggles the botanist's mind and amazes the weekend gardener.

About 750 different species of trees—including 60 kinds of oaks, some 35 pines, and more than 12 maples—can be found growing wild. Scientists link them with seven types of forest, which are, geographically, Northern, Pacific Coast, Western Mountain, Northeastern, Central, Southeastern, and Subtropical.

Among America's trees are many notable species. The coast redwood that grows in California ranks as the tallest tree in the world. Another California species, the giant sequoia, is considered the largest tree in the world, as measured by total wood volume. The United States also boasts the world's oldest living species, the bristlecone pine; some in Nevada are more than 5,000 years old.

▲ **Densely leaved horse-chestnut trees** shade streets and parks in the Northeast.

▲ **The American, or white, elm** grows in moist land throughout the East.

▲ **The white oak** grows up to 100 feet tall and flourishes in moist or dry Eastern soils.

The Western states are dominated by conifers—trees that have needles and produce their seeds in cones—while the East is known mainly for its deciduous species—trees that shed their leaves before the onset of winter. Each autumn the forests from the Adirondack and Appalachian mountain ranges west to the Mississippi River put on a fiery show as the leaves of the sugar maple, sycamore, and hickory turn to yellow, orange, or red (depending on the weather and the amount of pigment they contain) before dropping.

WILDFLOWERS AND GRASSES

The United States is also brightened by more than 20,000 species of native flowering plants. No matter the time of year, something is always blooming someplace in the nation. Between December and June speckled red-and-yellow dancing-girls shimmy on their stems to attract pollinating bees in the moist

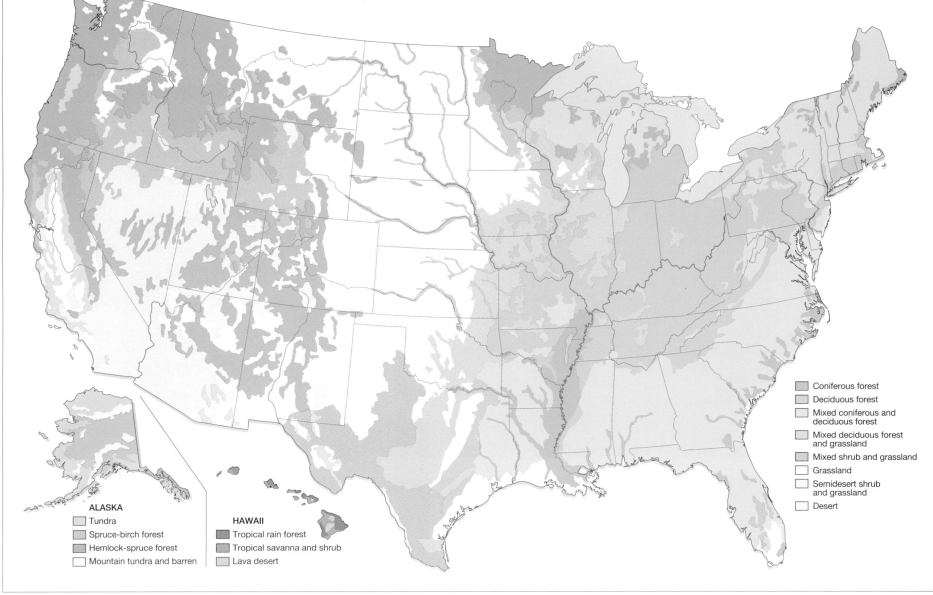

ALASKA
- Tundra
- Spruce-birch forest
- Hemlock-spruce forest
- Mountain tundra and barren

HAWAII
- Tropical rain forest
- Tropical savanna and shrub
- Lava desert

- Coniferous forest
- Deciduous forest
- Mixed coniferous and deciduous forest
- Mixed deciduous forest and grassland
- Mixed shrub and grassland
- Grassland
- Semidesert shrub and grassland
- Desert

southeastern swamps of Florida and Louisiana. Purple sand verbena and yellow desert sunflowers cover the desert floors in California like an Oriental carpet after the March rains. Like tiny patches of pure snow, the petals of white trillium bloom in North Carolina in April, when winter loosens its icy grip. Bluebonnets brighten Texas throughout the spring. Pink fireweed blazes across Alaska in summer. Black-eyed Susans blossom everywhere in the United States from June to October. Fringed gentians bloom from Maine to Michigan to the southern coastline of the country from August to November.

Along with wildflowers grow some 1,100 species of grass, including such food grasses as wheat, barley, oats, millet, and sugarcane. One of the most important grasses is maize, or corn. Native Americans began farming this indigenous plant more than 3,000 years ago, and it is currently cultivated on every continent but Antarctica. Now this most traditional of American foods is a staple around the world.

▲ **The giant saguaro cactus** *thrives in the desert valleys, slopes, and rocky hills of the Southwest. It can reach 50 feet in height.*

▲ **Indian rice** *grows in shallow lakes, ponds, and swamps throughout most of the country.*

▲ **Fragile ferns** *sprout through rock crevices in most parts of the United States.*

▲ **These shaggy mane mushrooms** *will melt into an inky liquid as they age.*

▲ **Goldenrods** *can be spotted in fields, marshes, woods, prairies, and beaches.*

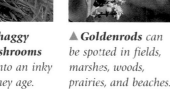

▲ **The Indian paintbrush** *has pale, tubular flowers; color is found in the leaves.*

▲ **The carnivorous Venus's-flytrap** *is native to the sandy coastal savannas of the Carolinas.*

▲ **The rosebay rhododendron,** *or great laurel. blooms in moist regions in the East.*

▲ **Giant sequoias** *grow only on the western slopes of the Sierra Nevada range in California. Some of these massive trees are more than 3,000 years old.*

America's Animal Kingdom

▲ *The majestic bald eagle, which is found only in North America, has a wingspan of up to 7¹/₂ feet. These white-headed birds usually mate for life and build nests that can weigh 1,000 pounds. Above, a 1723 sketch by colonial naturalist Mark Catesby.*

From bald eagles that symbolize freedom to herds of buffalo that represent the untouched West, America's distinctive collection of wildlife captures the essence of the nation's heritage and reflects our common spirit. Imagine all the strange and wondrous creatures seen by those who first explored these shores. Species like raccoons, beavers, and armadillos had never been imagined before. While America has undergone monumental change since the days of the early settlers, wild animals are still sometimes close at hand. Mountain lions prowl within earshot of cities and towns in the West. Grizzly bears, the largest of their kind on Earth, roam the wilds of Montana and Alaska. Alligators, a living link to the age of the dinosaur, cruise the Florida swamps. And moose are frequent sights in New England.

MAMMALS

America owes its variety of animal life to the country's size and geographical diversity. A wide spectrum of climatic zones allows for habitats that support many types of wildlife.

Approximately 400 species of mammals live in the United States. They range in size from the tiny but venomous American short-tailed shrew that weighs in at just a half an ounce to the 40,000-pound gray whale. In between are a host of amazing creatures, some more unusual than others. The manatee, for instance, is a docile, cowlike marine mammal that spends its time feeding on aquatic plants in the warm waters off Florida. Armadillos, which range across the South from Florida to Texas, are armor-shelled relatives of the anteater, although their heavy coat of mail often leads them to be mistaken for reptiles. America is home to two types of wolf, the gray and the red; the former lives mainly in Alaska, and the latter is restricted to the Ozark Mountains. Their cousin, the coyote, is commonly seen and heard throughout the West.

Many of America's animals have suffered greatly as the result of human settlement. American bison, commonly called buffalo, are a prime example. They once roamed the Great Plains in vast herds numbering in the millions. Hunters armed with rifles slaughtered them, along with deer, elk, and pronghorn (often wrongly referred to as "antelope"). While a number of species are still threatened with extinction, wildlife conservation laws have served to protect many, including the moose, bobcat, and grizzly bear.

BIRDS

Because of their numbers, color, and movement, birds are America's most readily visible wildlife. Scientists have identified 645 different species of birds that nest in the United States. The total bird population is estimated to be about 20 billion. Of these, fewer than 6 billion are year-round residents; the rest depart

▲ *Black-tailed prairie dogs are rodents that live in underground "towns" in the west central part of the country.*

◄ *White-tailed deer, the most abundant hoofed mammals in North America, inhabit forests and swamps.*

▲ *The solitary mountain lion—also known as the puma, cougar, panther, painter, and catamount—hunts deer and other mammals in the West and the South.*

▲ *A male wild turkey displays its impressive plumage during mating season. Capable of flying short distances, these birds live in deciduous woodlands, bottomlands, and brushy areas in the South, the Southwest, and the East.*

North American Flyways

Each spring and fall billions of birds migrate across North America. While some species, such as American robins and song sparrows, may fly only a few hundred miles, others go much farther. For instance, the American golden plover flies from the Arctic to Argentina, a trip of more than 8,000 miles. Ducks and geese tend to concentrate along four of the distinct routes shown, known as flyways (see map at right), but each of the more than 500 species of migratory birds in North America has its own unique route.

◀ *Great horned owls* *have adapted to virtually every environment in the Americas. They prey on medium-size mammals and birds.*

▲ *American robins* *dwell in forests, farmlands, suburbs, and city parks.*

▲ *Prothonotary warblers* *nest in tree cavities near rivers and swamps.*

⋯⋯ Pacific flyway
⋯⋯ Central flyway
⋯⋯ Mississippi flyway
⋯⋯ Atlantic flyway

in the fall and return in the spring. Most wing their way to the warmer climes of Central and South America, following four principal migration routes.

Each region of the United States is associated with a particular group of birds. Texas is known for whooping cranes, the East Coast for colorful warblers; the desert states play host to the snake-eating roadrunner. Hawaii is noted for its colorful honeycreepers, while California is the home of the condor, a seriously endangered carrion eater with an 8- to 10-foot wingspan.

REPTILES, AMPHIBIANS, FISH, AND INSECTS

An array of cold-blooded creatures lives in the United States. Although the poisonous snakes—corals, rattlers, water moccasins, and copperheads—surely attract the most attention, there are other fascinating reptiles as well. One, the horned lizard, is unique to the United States and Mexico. It dwells in the desert, and if attacked by a predator, it shoots blood out of its eyes as a defense.

Nearly 50 species of turtles call North America home. They range from the alligator snapper of the

◀ *Grizzly bears* *can grow up to 7 feet long. Their diet consists mainly of rodents, fish, and plants.*

Southeastern swamps to the desert tortoise of California, which traces its ancestry back 2 million years.

More than 3,000 types of frogs, toads, and salamanders, collectively known as amphibians, hop and crawl all over the United States. One of the best known is the bullfrog; the male of the species is noted for its ability to disrupt the silence of a spring evening with its loud, deep mating call.

Approximately 2,000 species of fish, ranging from tiny desert pupfish to five types of salmon that travel up Pacific Coast rivers each year to spawn, to the whale shark (the largest fish), swim in American waters.

One class of American creatures far outnumbers all the others combined. An estimated 90,000 species of insects are found north of the Mexican border. Although often annoying, and rarely appreciated, each plays an important role in maintaining the nation's rich biological diversity.

▶ *The brown trout,* *Atlantic cod, and large-mouth bass (top to bottom) are among the most plentiful of fish species populating the lakes and coastal waters of the United States.*

▲ *Monarch butterflies* *often travel up to 1,800 miles to winter in Mexico or California.*

▲ *The black widow spider's* *venom can be fatal to humans.*

◀ *The poisonous western diamondback rattlesnake* *(far left) coils in the prairies, deserts, and rocky foothills of the Southwest. The barking tree frog (left) makes its home in the Southeast.*

▲ *The Bering Strait, which separates Alaska from Russia, is 53 miles wide at its narrowest point. Its formation in about 8000 B.C. ended the first large-scale migration to the Americas. This view is from Little Diomede Island (U.S.), looking toward Big Diomede Island (Russia) and the Siberian coast.*

▼ *The remains of 12 mammoths were exposed in the 1930s in a gully near Dent, Colorado, where 11,000 years ago Paleo-Indian hunters stampeded and killed the huge animals with boulders and Clovis-point spears.*

The Peopling of the Americas

Long before the days of Columbus or the Spanish conquistadores, the North American continent was inhabited by the descendants of nomadic Ice Age hunters who migrated across Beringia, the region linking Siberia and Alaska, between 40,000 and 8000 B.C. Traveling south and east, some of these early Americans reached the southern tip of South America by 13,000 B.C. Along the way, they established rich and diverse cultures—hunting game, cultivating the land, building towns and villages, forging trade routes, erecting monuments to their dead, and communicating in some 2,000 different languages and dialects.

THE CLOVIS PERIOD

No one can say for certain when the first groups of Asiatic peoples—the ancestors of modern-day Native Americans—crossed the area known as Beringia, now located beneath the shallow Bering Sea. Nomadic hunters of such giant Stone Age animals as mammoths, mastodons, and ground sloths, they probably followed game, migrating from one continent to the next and crossing the 1,000-mile-wide wilderness laid bare during the last great Ice Age, when sea levels dropped as much as 300 feet.

Although it has been thought that the first human inhabitants of North America arrived around 10,000 B.C., some archaeologists believe that sites in Pennsylvania, California, Florida, and Chile support the theory that humans arrived as early as 40,000–30,000 B.C. or that some early Stone Age peoples may have crossed the Bering Strait in primitive boats. In any event, people and animals, including the camel and the horse, traveled back and forth between the continents. By 8000 B.C., when sea levels rose and flooded Beringia, the first great migration to the Americas came to an end. The last people to cross from Siberia were ancestors of the Inuit (or Eskimo) and Aleut peoples.

In North America the new settlers—the Paleo-Indians—followed two major routes south, migrating along the coast or between the massive ice sheets that covered present-day Canada. Moving in small bands, they followed the herds of wild game that sustained them, hunting their prey with stone weapons known as Clovis points (named for the site in New Mexico where this type of tool was first found). Between 9500 and 8500 B.C., the use of the Clovis point spread across virtually all of North America, from Mexico to eastern Canada. So successful were these early hunters that some scientists theorize that overhunting contributed to the extinction of several species of giant mammals.

PATTERNS OF SETTLEMENT

Once these first immigrants were far enough south of the ice, they fanned out in all directions, quickly populating the continent and forming a number of dis-

▶ *Projectile points used by early Americans for hunting.*

40,000 B.C.	9500 B.C.		5500 B.C.	
40,000–8000 B.C. Hunters arrive in America from Siberia either by crossing ice-free land or by sailing across the Bering Sea, and spread as far	as South America. **9500–8500 B.C.** Clovis stone points are used for hunting big game by Paleo-Indians. **9200 B.C.** Folsom arrow points are first used in what is now New Mexico. **8000 B.C.** Giant game animals,	including mastodons, dire wolves, and woolly mammoths, have become extinct in North America. Plano (Plainview) culture emerges. **6000 B.C.** Coahuiltecan hunting and gathering	lifestyle flourishes in Big Bend region of Texas. **5500 B.C.–A.D. 1000** Encinitas culture flourishes along California coast. **5000 B.C.** Northern Archaic people hunt caribou, elk, deer, and moose. **4000 B.C.** Ocean Bay culture	develops on Kodiak Island in Alaska. **3000 B.C.** On Umnak and other Aleutian Islands, hunters of seals, sea lions, and whales construct villages with small oval houses. The Picosa culture of

tinct cultural groups. Some remained nomadic, moving seasonally with bison and caribou herds; others settled in fishing communities on the northwestern coast. Regardless of their pursuits, they all sustained themselves on the abundant fruits, nuts, and berries.

The beginnings of systematic agriculture some 3,500 years ago provided a reliable food source that permitted higher population densities. The growth of permanent settlements led to stratified social orders in distinctive local or tribal societies. Permanence also encouraged trade and the development of a trading economy that was based on such nonessential goods as decorated pottery, jewelry, and other crafted items.

Many of early America's most successful cultures appeared in some of its most inhospitable climes. In the semi-arid region of the Sonoran desert, the Hohokam constructed apartmentlike complexes from earthen bricks and irrigated crops of corn, squash, avocados, and beans with a system of canals. Still greater achievements were made by the nearby Anasazi. Builders of the great cliff dwellings at the pueblo cities of New Mexico's Chaco Canyon (about A.D. 900) and Mesa Verde (A.D. 1000), the Anasazi commanded a thriving turquoise-based trade economy that reached far into the Rockies, south into Mexico, and east into present-day Texas.

had pursued the great Ice Age beasts.

At the same time (known as the Woodland Period east of the Mississippi), the dense forests of the eastern third of North America were home to various tribal groups. Many settled along rivers, coastal inlets, and lakes, establishing permanent centers that lasted for generations and were sustained by fishing, hunting, and small plot farming.

Like the cliff dwellers of the Southwest, these early Americans also left behind evidence of their ingenuity and rich spiritual traditions—in this case, gigantic heaps of sculpted earth known as mounds. These spectacular earthworks, also called the Hopewell phenomenon (after Capt. Mordecai Hopewell, a farmer and the owner of the major mound site in Ohio), were first constructed as tombs for tribal chiefs, who were usually buried with a lavish array of valuable and sacred objects: ceramic pots and figurines, carved pipe bowls, copper ornaments, and gemstones. Among the most striking of the Hopewell-era creations are the animal effigy mounds—for example, the Great Serpent Mound, which winds nearly 1,300 feet along a river bluff near Chillicothe, Ohio.

MISSISSIPPIAN ERA

Hopewellian mounds, found throughout the eastern United States and Canada, testify to a stage in Indian life that flourished between 1000 B.C. and A.D. 500. Not a single tribe or even a confederation, these Native Americans were an agglomeration of various peoples sharing similar traits—a deep reverence for the dead, an interest in trade, and a reasonably stable society.

The people of the next Native American era proved even more adept at large-scale engineering and social planning. Corn, probably imported from Mexico, became a staple around A.D. 500. At the same time, the Mississippian peoples began to organize themselves into larger, more stable communities, governed by a ruling clan or chieftain and often centered on a single large ceremonial mound site. At Moundville, Alabama,

4 million cubic feet of earth were moved to erect an earthen platform that housed the tribe's ruling elite, symbolically placing them in close proximity to the sky. A similar structure can be found in Cahokia, Illinois, across the Mississippi River from St. Louis. At this site, which dates to A.D. 1300, a mound covering approximately 15 acres once stood at the center of an urban and suburban area of some 40,000 residents—a metropolis to rival anything found on other continents. No less than the Europeans who would arrive later, America's original inhabitants were inventors, explorers, builders, and discoverers, driven by the inexorable human impulse to conquer new worlds.

▲ **Cliff Palace,** *the largest of the multistoried Anasazi villages at Mesa Verde, Colorado, has more than 200 rooms.*

OTHER CULTURES

During the period from 1000 B.C. to A.D. 1000, other early Native American cultures developed. In the Pacific Northwest, the Chinook and Kwakiutl people built a stable way of life based on the abundant resources of the coastal inlets, rivers, and maritime rain forests. In the Great Basin's arid expanse, bands of Paiute roamed, following game and foraging for food. On the vast Great Plains, hunters adopted bows and arrows to chase herds of bison and antelope, much as their ancestors

▼ **Cahokia, Illinois,** A.D. 1100. *More than 100 mounds from this prehistoric city remain today.*

Map labels:

Polar Ice

SIBERIA

BERINGIA

c. 40,000–8,000 B.C. Land exposed at intervals

Bering Sea

ALASKA

PACIFIC OCEAN

Cordilleran Ice Sheet

Laurentide Ice Sheet

Columbia

Rocky Mountains

Wilson Butte Cave

Dent

Schaefer

Meadowcroft Rock Shelter

Domebo

Sandia

Murray Springs

Clovis

Lehner

Naco

Levi Rock Shelter

Mississippi

Little Salt Spring

Gulf of Mexico

Legend:
- Ice sheets c. 14,000 B.C.
- Ice sheets c. 10,000 B.C.
- → Possible migration routes
- ■ Archaeological sites
- Modern coastline
- Ancient coastline

Our Ancestors' Arrival

Scholars have long believed that Asian hunters entered North America from Siberia by land. But some now think that many may have come by boat along the coast. It would probably have been faster and helps to explain how these pioneers could have reached Pennsylvania—where a rock shelter was found—16,000 years ago.

2000 B.C.		1000 B.C.		700 B.C.	
Archaic Period hunter-gatherers develops in the Southwest.	Copper mining begins in Lake Superior region.	Hopewell, and Mississippian peoples, develops throughout the Midwestern and Eastern regions.		sippi Basin area of New Mexico cultivate the "three sisters": maize, beans, and squash.	many small mounds in eastern Great Plains.
2000 B.C. Earliest pottery north of Mexico is crafted at sites in Georgia and Florida. Arctic Small Tool tradition emerges in Alaska.	**1400 B.C.** Poverty Point and other planned communities that center around the building of mounds are established. **1100 B.C.** Woodland culture, which includes Adena,	**1000 B.C.** People in Missis-		**700 B.C.** Dorset Inuit culture emerges in region north of Hudson Bay. **500 B.C.–A.D. 1000** Plains Woodland people build	**400 B.C.** Adena people in Ohio build 1,254-foot-long Serpent Mound. **100 B.C.** Societies of Hopewell mound builders develop in Ohio and Illinois regions.

▶ **A Hopewell** *burial offering made of sheet mica.*

Native Americans at Contact

▲ *An Iroquois comb carved from bone more than four centuries ago. Iroquois women used combs both for decoration and to keep their hair in place.*

▼ *John White, governor of the failed Roanoke Island colony of 1585–87, based this watercolor, called* Indians Fishing, *on his observations.*

At the time of Columbus and the Spanish con-quistadores, when Europeans first came to North America, an estimated 6 million people were living here. Although their ancestors may all have come from Siberia, the native inhabitants—who had been living on the continent for centuries—spoke several hundred languages and were settled throughout the land in many different types of communities. There were sophisticated confederations of tribes, some more democratic than others. Some Native Americans lived as nomads, following game and foraging for food, while others lived in settled societies as farmers, builders, and tradesmen. They occupied the most livable regions of the country as well as marginal areas where existence was hazardous. For all their cultural and political differences, however, the Native Americans would share a common fate: the extinction of their town sites and their way of life with the coming of the Europeans.

INDIANS OF THE EAST

Although would-be immigrants were told that the New World was "spacious and void," the East Coast was densely settled by Native Americans, with many separate villages located on sheltered coastal and island harbors, inland lakes, and rivers and streams.

In much of the Northeastern section of the country, as well as the Great Lakes area, Indians lived according to the seasons in a pattern of migration called the "annual round." The long summer days provided a time for neighboring tribes to visit with each other, participate in festivals, play games, run races, observe rituals, and reap the last fruits of the late-summer harvests. In the fall tribe members dried and smoked fish.

Come winter, the community broke up into small kinship groups to hunt game. With the first sign of spring, the tribes moved to the sugaring camp to tap maple trees and boil sap into syrup—sometimes their only food until the weather warmed up and the ice broke for fishing. Finally, it was time to return to the village for planting and perhaps a warriors' expedition—a type of war party during which men tested their skill and bravery by making forays into enemy territory.

Counter to the popular notion that a "big chief" lorded it over an entire tribe, the smaller Eastern communities tended to be strongly egalitarian. The leader, identified by Europeans as "chief," had no real control over his people. He could ask them to do his bidding, but ultimately he was obligated to carry out the decisions reached by consensus, which often involved lengthy meetings.

Some Eastern tribes, however, did maintain a hierarchy. The Five Nations of Iroquois, centered in the northern part of present-day New York, gave the highest power to honored elder women and traced their lineage through the female line. On the western shores of Chesapeake Bay, an Indian named Powhatan established a supreme chief-dom during the late 16th and early 17th centuries, exacting tributes in the form of gifts and payments from allied and conquered towns and acting as the sole spokesperson for his tribes when the English began to settle in the area.

MIDWEST TO SOUTHWEST

No less sophisticated than the Eastern tribes were the tribes of the lower Missis-sippi River valley—a region of organized city-states, each with temple mounds, a priestly ruler, administrative staff, and an army of archers. Although the major center of Cahokia, across the river from modern-day St. Louis, was largely deserted by A.D. 1400, some 70 other temple-mound city-states still existed throughout the Appalachians and in what is now Arkansas, eastern Texas, and Florida when the Europeans arrived.

Other Indian urban centers existed in the present states of Arizona, New Mex-ico, Utah, and Colorado. Here in the canyons and on the cliffs of the Ameri-can Southwest, ancestors of the Pueblo people had built multistoried apart-mentlike dwellings and fortresslike structures from stone, masonry, and adobe. Some structures were as high as five stories, with room for some 1,000 people. Because of their thick walls, the buildings, or pueblos, provided cool relief from the harsh heat of the day and warm shelter from bitter-cold nights. The Pueblo Indians irrigated their parched land to produce corn and other vegetables and became masters at the art of fine pottery.

By contrast, bands of roving hunters in the thinly populated western plains sought buffalo and other game follow-ing a centuries-old lifestyle. These semi-nomadic peoples kept their possessions to a minimum and erected portable structures, such as the tentlike tepee. By the 18th century the Plains Indians' lives had changed drastically with the intro-duction of the horse, brought to North America 200 years earlier by the Span-iards. The horse had become not only a status symbol but a highly prized trad-ing commodity, as well as a faster, more efficient means to hunt buffalo.

THE PACIFIC NORTHWEST

Perhaps the clearest examples of a class system among Native American tribes were found in the fishing communities of the Pacific Northwest—the land of abundant seafood, cedar houses, and elaborately carved and painted totem poles. Elite tribe members—warriors, chiefs, shamans—controlled the wealth, and they often established their status through an elaborate giveaway ceremony called the potlatch. During this event the

The manner of their fishing

Tribal Lands Before the White Man Came

Most of America's main Indian groups dwelled either along the seacoast or in river and lake country, which sustained a prosperous mixed economy of fishing, hunting, and farming. Life was more difficult for the nomadic hunter-gatherers of the northern regions and mountainous areas like the Rockies and the Appalachians; there the growing season was short, and places like the arid Great Plains were virtually uninhabited.

Legend:
- Northwest coast marine economy
- Plains hunter-gatherers
- Plains horticulturalists
- Nonhorticultural peoples
- Peoples with low-intensity horticulture
- Peoples with intensive horticulture
- Pueblos with intensive horticulture
- Seacoast foragers
- Marginal horticultural hunters
- River-based horticultural chiefdoms
- Orchard-growing alligator hunters
- Horticulturalists-hunters-fishers
- Fishers and wild-rice gatherers
- Sparsely populated
- ▲ Town with temple mound

wealthy hosts showered gifts on the common people. The elite, whose stations were determined by birthright, were served by commoners or slaves, often captured in raids on other tribes.

THE COMING OF THE WHITE MAN

North American tribes maintained contact with one another through trade, diplomacy, and warfare on trails, rivers, and even on the open ocean. (Florida Indians paddled out to the Bahama Islands and traded with Cuba until 1840.) But the arrival of Europeans, beginning in the Southeast

with the Spanish explorers and conquistadores, changed things drastically. Hernando DeSoto's expedition, which began in 1541 brought about the destruction of 85 percent of the native population of the temple-mound states through warfare and epidemics of such

European diseases as smallpox, measles, and influenza. Of the towns east of the Mississippi River, only that of the Natchez survived, and their town was destroyed by the French in 1735. Tragically, it was the beginning of the end for the Native Americans.

▼ *The Taos Pueblo in northern New Mexico was probably built around 1350. This five-story communal dwelling, which today looks much as it did when the Spaniards first saw it in 1540, is home to about 150 Taos Indians.*

◄ *This Crow Indian tepee, as illustrated by George Catlin in 1851, is covered by buffalo hides.*

▲ *The Native American town of Pomeiockt in North Carolina, as painted by John White.*

---

plains and Southwest.
880 At Spiro Site, in Oklahoma, Caddoans build series of large, square ceremonial buildings around a plaza.
900 Mississippian lifestyle emerges in eastern U.S. In Alaska, Thule Inuit

(Eskimo) culture begins to spread east, replacing Dorset groups.
900–1180 Chaco Canyon, a 32-square-mile area in New Mexico, is center of Anasazi culture.
1000 Vikings attempt unsuccessfully to establish

colony in an area they call Vinland, which was probably present-day Newfoundland or Labrador.
1000–1300 Anasazi in Mesa Verde, Colorado, build elaborate cliff dwellings.
1025 Ancestral Navajo

migrate to Southwest.
1100–1804 Shell money becomes widely used in California region.
1250 Pima-Papago pueblo builders in Arizona replace Hohokam.
1300–1600 Great Temple Mound (Middle Missis-

sippian) civilizations flourish. Caddoans build village societies in the Texas-Louisiana-Arkansas-Oklahoma border region.
1350 In eastern Great Basin, Paiute, Ute, and Shoshone peoples

replace Fremont culture.
1400s Iroquois Confederacy is established.
1450 Groups related to the Pawnee travel north to Missouri River in South Dakota. These people are ancestors of the Arikara.

Discovery and Settlement

Scholars may debate Christopher Columbus's place in history, but there can be no doubt that his transatlantic voyage in 1492 represented a turning point in global history. Dozens of explorers—English, Spanish, Portuguese, Dutch, Italian, French—would follow, tracing the coastlines, sailing inland along America's rivers, and setting out across its forests, deserts, and plains. Their motives were varied— some came seeking riches to plunder, others, souls to save. Many came in search of the elusive Northwest Passage to the Far East. Often they simply came to answer the question: What is this New World?

Christopher Columbus

Giovanni da Verrazano

THE NEW WORLD IN 1492
Christopher Columbus no more "discovered" America than did the legions of explorers who followed him. That credit goes to the Siberian Paleo-Indians, America's first human inhabitants. Nor was Columbus the first European to visit North American shores; historians now know that Norsemen from Greenland sailed along the Atlantic coasts of modern-day Labrador and Newfoundland, perhaps reaching as far south as New England, as early as the 11th century.

Columbus was a navigator, and like most explorers of his day, his interests lay in finding a sea route to Asia, the great trading prize of the period. Convinced that the world was round, Columbus calculated that a voyage of 30 days across the Atlantic would bring him within range of the island of Cipangu, as Japan was then known, which he believed was just 2,400 miles away.

But the world is more than four times as large as Columbus imagined. In October 1492, after a month and a half at sea, Columbus, with his three ships, the *Niña*, *Pinta*, and *Santa Maria*, made landfall on the Bahamian island of Guanahani, which he called San Salvador ("Holy Savior"). Believing that he was in the East Indies (Asia), Columbus called the inhabitants of the island Indians. He explored Hispaniola (now Haiti and the Dominican Republic) and Cuba—before heading home in triumph.

EARLY EXPLORATION
Columbus's discoveries were met with great enthusiasm in Europe, and over the next century, other explorers followed the trail that he had blazed, many of them searching for a shortcut to Asia that came to be known as the Northwest Passage. Explorer John Cabot led the first British-backed expedition to North America in 1497, landing somewhere along the coast of Newfoundland or Cape Breton Island.

An Italian named Amerigo Vespucci made three voyages to South America between 1499 and 1504, exploring what is now Brazil. (It was Vespucci whose name was adopted by a German cartographer as the name of the New World: America.) Two Frenchmen, Jacques Cartier (1535) and Samuel de Champlain (1603), and Englishman Henry Hudson (1609 and 1610) explored much of the Northeast, from New York to the

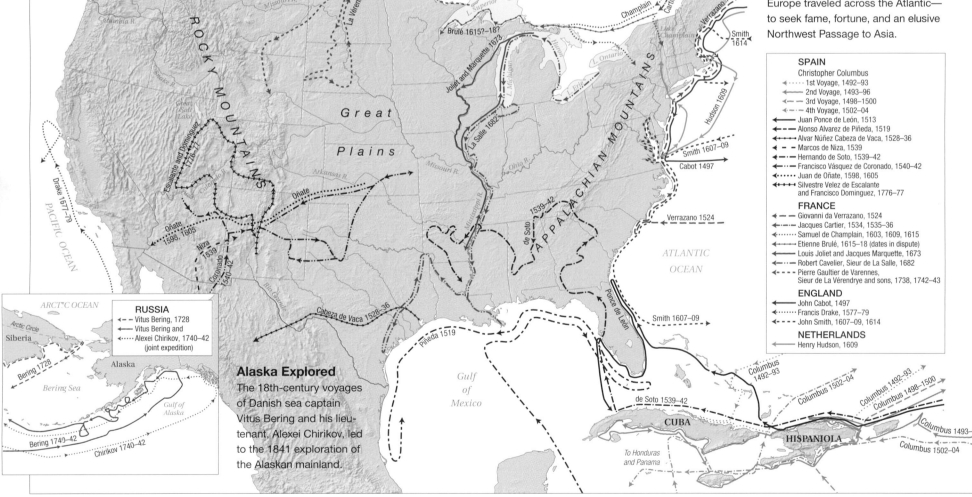

New World Exploration
Spurred by Columbus's successful voyages, explorers from all over Europe traveled across the Atlantic— to seek fame, fortune, and an elusive Northwest Passage to Asia.

SPAIN
Christopher Columbus
◄······ 1st Voyage, 1492–93
◄——— 2nd Voyage, 1493–96
◄— — 3rd Voyage, 1498–1500
◄—— 4th Voyage, 1502–04
◄—— Juan Ponce de León, 1513
◄—— Alonso Alvarez de Piñeda, 1519
◄— — Alvar Núñez Cabeza de Vaca, 1528–36
◄— - ■ Marcos de Niza, 1539
◄—— Hernando de Soto, 1539–42
◄—— Francisco Vásquez de Coronado, 1540–42
◄—— Juan de Oñate, 1598, 1605
◄+++◄ Silvestre Velez de Escalante
        and Francisco Dominguez, 1776–77
FRANCE
◄— — Giovanni da Verrazano, 1524
◄···· Jacques Cartier, 1534, 1535–36
◄······ Samuel de Champlain, 1603, 1609, 1615
◄—— Etienne Brulé, 1615–18 (dates in dispute)
◄—— Louis Joliet and Jacques Marquette, 1673
◄—— Robert Cavelier, Sieur de La Salle, 1682
◄— - - Pierre Gaultier de Varennes,
        Sieur de La Vérendrye and sons, 1738, 1742–43
ENGLAND
◄—— John Cabot, 1497
◄—— Francis Drake, 1577–79
◄— - - John Smith, 1607–09, 1614
NETHERLANDS
◄—— Henry Hudson, 1609

RUSSIA
◄- ·- Vitus Bering, 1728
◄—— Vitus Bering and
◄······ Alexei Chirikov, 1740–42
        (joint expedition)

Alaska Explored
The 18th-century voyages of Danish sea captain Vitus Bering and his lieutenant, Alexei Chirikov, led to the 1841 exploration of the Alaskan mainland.

1492			1570	1576	

1492 Christopher Columbus lands on Bahama island of Guanahani, thinking that he has found Asia.

1497 John Cabot reaches North American coast.

1513 Ponce de León looks for Fountain of Youth in Florida and claims

region for Spain.

1539 Hernando de Soto lands in Florida and leads expedition through Tennessee, Georgia, Alabama, and Arkansas in search of gold.

1565 The Spanish city of St. Augustine, Florida,

becomes first permanent European settlement in North America.

1570 Iroquois nation is formed from the Indian nations of the Five

► **A mariner's compass,** *probably from Italy, c.1570.*

Finger Lakes and Mohawk Valley.

1576 English begin sending expeditions to North America to search for Northwest Passage to Asia.

1578 Sir Francis Drake takes possession of California

region for England.

1581 First black slaves land at St. Augustine.

1582–1604 Spanish explore American Southwest.

1607 Jamestown, Virginia, becomes first permanent English colony in North America.

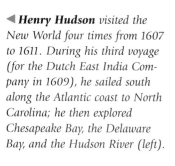

◀ **Henry Hudson** *visited the New World four times from 1607 to 1611. During his third voyage (for the Dutch East India Company in 1609), he sailed south along the Atlantic coast to North Carolina; he then explored Chesapeake Bay, the Delaware Bay, and the Hudson River (left).*

Sir Francis Drake

Hernando de Soto

St. Lawrence Seaway and Hudson Bay. In the 1570s, another Englishman, Sir Francis Drake, explored the coast of what is now California.

SPANISH CONQUESTS
Based on Columbus's early claims for the Spanish Crown, Spanish explorers focused their energies in the South. Conquistador Juan Ponce de León led his army across Florida in 1513, paving the way for Hernando de Soto (1539), whose futile search for gold led him on a harrowing three-year trek as far east as North Carolina and as far west as Arkansas. From their bases in New Spain (present-day Mexico), Spanish expeditions in the West mapped much of what is now Arizona, New Mexico, southern California, Texas, Oklahoma, Arkansas, and Kansas.

THE GREAT MIGRATION
By the mid-17th century, the commercial potential of North America had begun to reveal itself, setting the stage for settlement and, later, the first war between European powers on American soil. French interests in the New World centered on Quebec and Montreal, both established as trading outposts in the early 1600s. In the process of traveling the rivers to trade with Indians, French traders played a key role in the exploration of the continent's interior.

British efforts at settlement were at first more tentative—and sometimes disastrous. In 1587 a poorly supplied expedition, organized by Sir Walter Raleigh,

deposited colonists on present-day Roanoke Island, Virginia; when a supply ship returned three years later, all 117 settlers had vanished. Nearly two more decades passed before the British established their first permanent colony at Jamestown in 1607. In New England, meanwhile, Puritan colonies at Plymouth (1620) and Massachusetts Bay (1630) attracted members of England's persecuted religious minorities, and by 1640 trading settlements at Fort Orange (now Albany) and New Amsterdam (New York City) had given the Dutch control of the Hudson River valley.

THE FIRST GLOBAL WAR
European incursion in the Northeast proved devastating for Native American tribes who had lived there for generations. As settlers cleared the forests to grow crops, they disrupted the ecological balance on which these tribes depended. To worsen matters, competition for the European fur trade sparked ruinous intertribal wars. Exposure to European diseases decimated half of New England's Algonquins and three-quarters of the Abenaki in one epidemic alone.

Eastern America's European population, meanwhile, increased fivefold between 1700 and 1750 to more than 1 million. Britain's 13 Colonies (the British had ousted the Dutch in 1664, seizing New Amsterdam and renaming it New York) represented a burgeoning new civilization with a thriving economy. By the mid-18th century,

American products—wheat, tobacco, sugar, rice, and lumber—accounted for fully a third of Britain's export trade.

Inevitably, competing colonial powers came to loggerheads. Anglo-French rivalry in America reached a crisis in 1754, resulting in the French and Indian War, which lasted until 1763. When the smoke cleared, France was forced to cede all of Canada and all lands east of the Mississippi except for New Orleans. By 1763 nothing stood in the way of British domination of the New World—except for Americans themselves.

Shifting European Claims in the New World
After the French and Indian War (1754–63), the defeated French lost their land in Canada and their territory east of the Mississippi River (except New Orleans) to the British. Spain, which had been France's ally, gave Florida to the British but received New Orleans and the land west of the Mississippi in return.

- ■ British
- ■ Spanish
- ■ French
- ■ Russian
- ■ Unexplored

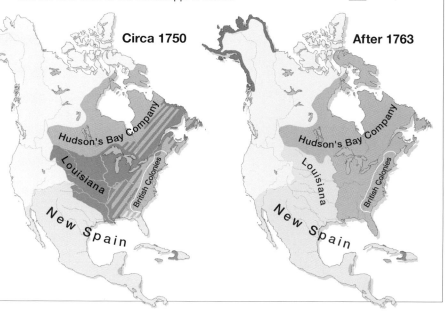

Circa 1750

After 1763

1609

1609 Henry Hudson explores Chesapeake Bay, Delaware Bay, and Hudson River.
1610 Santa Fe is established as capital of Spanish New Mexico.
1616 Smallpox epidemic wipes out most of Indi-

ans in New England.
1620 Plymouth Colony is established by Pilgrims in Massachusetts.
1624 Colony of New Netherland is established by the Dutch.
The Dutch buy Manhattan island from Indians.

1628

1628 Puritans settle at Salem, Massachusetts.
1664 England takes over New Netherland and New Sweden.
1676 New England colonists defeat Wampanoag Indians and four other Indian tribes in King

Philip's War.
1681 Robert Cavelier, sieur de La Salle of France, claims Mississippi River valley region from Quebec to Gulf of Mexico for France. He names it Louisiana after King Louis XIV.

1718

English Quaker William Penn is granted charter for Pennsylvania area. He founds city of Philadelphia.
1718 French settlers from France and Canada establish New Orleans. A Franciscan mission

and military post is built in San Antonio, Texas.
1733 James Oglethorpe founds Savannah in Georgia.
1754–63 French and Indian War is fought in Europe and America. It ends in British victory.

The Making of a Nation

Battles of the Revolution
From the opening salvos at Lexington and Concord to the British surrender at Yorktown, Revolutionary War battles pitted scrappy colonials against the well-oiled British military machine.

Victory in the French and Indian War left Britain the undisputed colonial superpower in Eastern America. Burdened by the expense of the protracted war on two continents, and facing the tremendous challenges of policing its vast new colonial holdings, the Crown turned to the Colonies themselves to carry much of the cost—only to find that America's colonists, accustomed to managing their own affairs, were unwilling to foot the mother country's bills. Thus, the stage was set for an escalating conflict, a philosophical debate about the very nature of government that would lead to a war of rebellion and the birth of a new nation.

CAUSES OF THE REVOLUTION

Britain's imperial war debt may have been the spark that lit the fires of revolution, but the causes of the American War of Independence had been smoldering for decades. With more than a million people, Britain's 13 Colonies were by 1763 so prosperous that they were already a hotbed of independent thinking. Although the Colonies had long relied on British forces for protection from the Indians and other European nations along the frontier, the end of hostilities in 1763 seemed to make this no longer necessary. Britain's victory over France actually promoted colonial self-confidence, making the government in London seem remote and irrelevant.

The ink was barely dry on Britain's treaty with France when the British government tried to reassert its authority over the Colonies—and met swift resistance. Despite a royal proclamation forbidding colonists to spread westward past the Appalachian Mountains, speculators and frontiersmen, including the legendary Daniel Boone, began to move west into what is now Kentucky and Tennessee. At the same time, parliamentary acts to tap colonial revenue deepened the colonists' resentment of the government in London. New taxes on East Indian sugar, and on newspapers, marriage licenses and other legal documents, as well as imported lead, paper, and tea enraged many colonists, who organized boycotts and openly criticized the Crown.

It wasn't just money at stake. Inspired by the writings of Enlightenment-age philosophers, colonial lawyers like John Adams issued passionate complaints that such "taxation without representation" was in violation of British law and contravened Americans' "essential rights as British subjects."

As anti-British sentiment spread across the Colonies, British troops were sent in to demonstrate the Crown's resolve. In March 1770, taunted by an angry crowd of Bostonians, British troops opened fire, killing five people and wounding several more. This event, known as the Boston Massacre, left no doubt as to the seriousness of the growing crisis. Three years later, Boston's rebellious citizenry responded to new regulations on tea by dressing up as Indians and dumping East India Company tea into the harbor. In response, the British passed a sweeping packet of repressive legislation, known as the Intolerable Acts of 1774, that sharply limited the Colonies' right of self-government and allowed British troops to commandeer inns and unoccupied buildings for housing.

A "SHOT HEARD ROUND THE WORLD"

Although anti-British sentiment was far from uniform across the Colonies, the standoff with London inspired colonial leaders to organize the First Continental Congress, which assembled in Philadel-

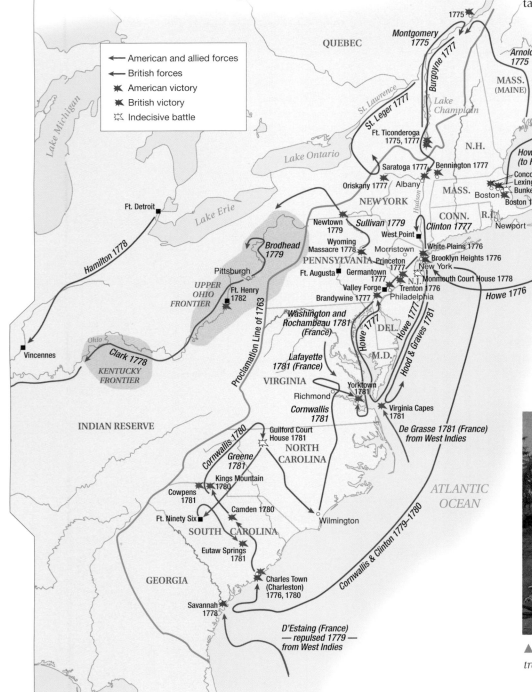

▲ **The Battle of Germantown**, on October 4, 1777, ended in defeat for Washington's troops. An American victory at Saratoga 13 days later reinvigorated the Revolution.

1763 Britain draws a Proclamation Line, declaring Indian lands west of Appalachian Mountains off-limits to colonial settlement.

▶ *A revenue stamp, as required by the 1765 Stamp Act.*

1770 British soldiers kill five colonists in Boston Massacre.
1773 Colonists dump 342 cases of British tea into Boston Harbor during Boston Tea Party.
1774 First Continental Congress convenes in Philadelphia.
1775 Colonial Minutemen and British clash in battles at Lexington and Concord, beginning Revolutionary War. Second Continental Congress convenes in Philadelphia. It

appoints George Washington commander in chief of the Continental Army.
1776 Congress adopts Declaration of Independence. Capt. James Cook charts Alaskan coast and is first European to

▲ *The first American flag flew from 1775 to 1777.*

We the People of the United States, in order to form a more perfect Union, establish Justice, insure domestic Tranquility, provide for the common defence, promote the general Welfare, and secure the Blefsings of Liberty to ourselves and our Posterity, do ordain and establish this Constitution for the United States of America.

phia in September 1774. Many delegates still believed that a peaceful settlement with London was possible, but in the meantime, colonists were preparing themselves for armed conflict. The crisis reached its fateful turning point in the spring of 1775, when British general Thomas Gage, the royal governor of Massachusetts, ordered soldiers to seize a cache of weapons stored by the Massachusetts militia at Concord. Forewarned of the British troop advance by patriots like Paul Revere and William Dawes, the Americans met them across the green in the Massachusetts town of Lexington. No one knows who fired first, but the resulting "shot heard round the world," as it came to be known, brought an end to all hope of peaceful resolution. The American Revolution had begun.

A month later American delegates gathered for the Second Continental Congress. For nearly a year Congress debated the wisdom of war with Britain while it simultaneously organized for a wider conflict. As Loyalist voices struggled to be heard, patriots like Thomas Paine, whose pamphlet *Common Sense* became a rallying point for armed resistance, argued that a complete break with Britain was inevitable. A committee was finally convened to draw up a document

of formal separation; adopted on July 4, 1776, America's Declaration of Independence, largely penned by Thomas Jefferson, proclaimed America to be a free and independent nation.

A LONG WAR

Despite its massive naval power, Britain entered the war at a disadvantage. The Colonies' remoteness, combined with their sheer size, made waging a successful ground war difficult, especially for Britain's small professional army. On the American side, Gen. George Washington's troops—a ragtag group at best, underfed, poorly supplied, and plagued by desertion—had challenges of their own to surmount. But every year that Washington could keep pressure on the British had the effect of weakening imperial resolve.

Major early victories went to the British, who captured New York late in 1776 and Philadelphia the next year, forcing the temporary evacuation of the Continental government to York, Pennsylvania. But a stunning defeat at Saratoga by American forces under the command of Horatio Gates in 1777 did much to improve American morale and persuaded the French, eager to avenge their own defeat 14 years earlier, to enter the war on the American side.

With most of New England and eastern and central New York in American hands, the focus of the war then shifted southward. Following the long, hard winter encampment at Valley Forge (1777–78)—a low point for the Americans—the British were forced to evacuate Philadelphia, while American victories in the West continued to make the war a costly and dispiriting proposition for the British. In Parliament the war had become so unpopular that members of the opposition Whig party had taken to wearing blue and buff, the colors of Washington's uniform. A Southern campaign, initiated in late 1778, gave the British control of Savannah and, in 1780, Charleston, but British lieutenant general Lord Charles Cornwallis's trek across the Carolinas, beleaguered by guerrilla attacks, gave him little that was positive to report to his commanders back home. After moving his troops to

Yorktown, Virginia, in early August 1781, the exhausted Cornwallis found himself caught between a French fleet under Adm. François-Joseph Paul de Grasse and Washington's troops. On October 19 Cornwallis was forced to surrender his army, effectively ending the war.

AN INFANT NATION

With the signing of the Treaty of Paris in September 1783, the United States formally joined the company of world powers. Retaining Canada, Britain surrendered all other claims to territory east of the Mississippi and returned Florida to Spain, which also kept its vast holdings to the west. The original 13 Colonies became the first states, while lands west of the Appalachians were divided into territories awaiting settlement and, eventually, statehood. Running unopposed, the popular Washington became the first federal president, taking the oath of office in the nation's new capital of New York in 1789.

The Articles of Confederation had given Congress the power to manage foreign affairs and oversee the war with Britain but otherwise left governing, including the levying of taxes and the regulation of trade, to the states themselves. For the infant republic—badly in debt, with great challenges still to come—a stronger federal government was needed. A Constitutional Convention was held in Philadelphia between May and September 1787; five months of intense bargaining resulted in a document that stands apart from all other documents of its kind as a blueprint for democratic government, dividing federal powers among a bicameral legislature, an executive branch, and a federal judiciary. By 1790 each of the 13 states had ratified it; a year later it was amended to include the Bill of Rights, which safeguarded fundamental personal freedom of speech, assembly, petition, and worship as the core of American life. The great American experiment was under way.

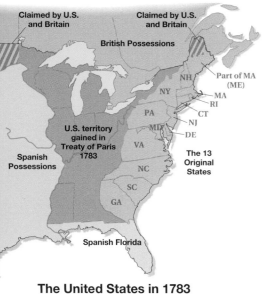

The United States in 1783
Achieving independence, the 13 Colonies became states; Vermont was part of New York, and Maine belonged to Massachusetts. Few people lived in the Western territories.

▲ *The Constitution of the United States* was drafted in order to establish the structure of the government and the basic laws of the new nation. Signed by delegates at the Constitutional Convention on September 17, 1787, the much-debated document describes the government's intentions and how they can be realized. While it defines federal powers, it also protects the rights of states and individuals.

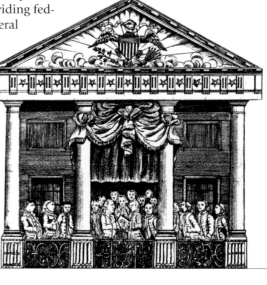

▼ *George Washington* was inaugurated as the first president of the United States on the balcony of Federal Hall in New York City on April 30, 1789. Washington had been unanimously elected by the 69 delegates of the first Electoral College. Although he was enormously popular, the 57-year-old statesman and former general accepted the appointment with great reluctance.

The Growth of a Nation

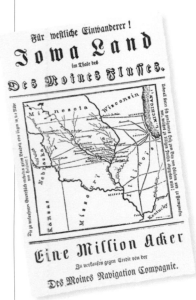

Finally free from Britain, a newly independent America struggled to find its footing. The nation's economy, still tied to Britain's, was in chaos, and its government was untested. All but bankrupted by the Revolution, the federal government had no resources to police the nation's borders or to pro-

tect new Western lands against aggressors. Many observers of the day found scant reason to believe that the United States would survive. Yet America rapidly became one of the world's most prosperous and powerful nations. By the end of the 19th century, its population had grown to outstrip that of any European country.

WESTWARD EXPANSION

In 1791 American territory comprised approximately 800,000 square miles, stretching from the Atlantic Ocean to the Mississippi River and from the Great Lakes to Florida. Except for the coasts, most of this land was thinly settled. Past the frontier, marked by the Appalachian Mountains, lay a wilderness of unpopulated forests.

Westward expansion began almost immediately, as speculators and settlers traveled over the mountains into the Ohio River valley. Many journeyed on foot or horseback on the Wilderness Road, a dirt track first opened by Daniel Boone in 1775; later they came by wagon on the

▲ *An advertisement for land.* *Companies that owned land in the West would frequently offer to sell plots to immigrants. This poster, from the Des Moines Navigation Company, sought to lure German settlers to the Des Moines River valley in Iowa. The advertisement promises access to good-quality, plentiful, and inexpensive lumber for farm supplies and houses.*

much-improved National Road, which followed a similar route through the narrow Cumberland Gap. By 1800 some 200,000 pioneers had made the journey.

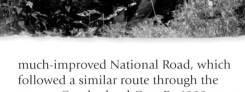

◄ *These pioneers passing through Kansas were among the hundreds of thousands who ventured westward in covered wagons.*

A MANIFEST DESTINY

It wasn't long before the nation itself expanded. The same year that Ohio became a state—1803—American territory doubled when President Thomas Jefferson authorized the purchase of land covering more than 800,000 square miles west of the Mississippi River from the French government for $15 million. To investigate these lands, Jefferson sent a military detachment west, led by former frontier army officers Meriwether Lewis and William Clark. Starting in St. Louis, they followed the Missouri River and its tributary as far as they could into what is now Montana, then crossed the Continental Divide and continued to the Pacific Ocean. The Lewis and Clark party spent two years in the wilderness and returned to the East in 1806 with a wealth of information about the lands and peoples west of the Mississippi.

During the first half of the 1800s, Americans' appetite for land found them pushing deeper into the continent's interior. The opening of the Erie Canal in 1825, connecting Albany with Buffalo and the Great Lakes, sped the migration of many settlers from crowded New England, as well as newcomers from Europe, to the central and upper Midwest. By this time riverboats were becoming an important mode of transportation for goods and settlers. Following the route taken by Lewis and Clark, the boats plied the Missouri River north from St. Louis—dubbed the Gateway to the West—bringing settlers to the Northwestern territories. Other pioneers loaded their wagons and headed out across the Santa Fe, Old Spanish, Oregon, Mormon, and California trails to the central plains and deserts. Bad

The Nation Expands

From 1783 to 1803, the country's territorial expanse increased dramatically; with the Oregon Country cession in 1846, the United States stretched, for the first time, from "sea to shining sea."

Oregon Country cession 1846
Red River cession 1818
Louisiana Purchase 1803
Mexican cession 1848
Texas annexation 1845
Gadsden Purchase 1853
Addition of 1783
The 13 Colonies 1776
Florida cession 1819

Oregon Trail
California Trail
Mormon Trail
Old Spanish Trail
Santa Fe Trail
National Cumberland Rd.

Portland, OR, WA, MT, ID, NV, CA, UT, AZ, NM, CO, WY, ND, SD, NE, KS, OK, TX, MN, IA, MO, AR, LA, WI, IL, MI, IN, KY, TN, MS, AL, GA, OH, WV, VA, NC, SC, FL, PA, NY, VT, NH, MA, CT, RI, ME, NJ, MD, DE

Salt Lake City, Sacramento, Los Angeles, Santa Fe, Independence, Vandalia, Nauvoo, Cumberland

ALASKA
Alaska Purchase 1867 (Canada's claims on southeastern panhandle settled 1903)

HAWAII
Hawaii annexation 1898

1793 Fugitive Slave Act makes it illegal to help or prevent arrest of runaway slaves.
1800 National capital moves from Philadelphia to Washington, D.C.
1803 Purchase of Louisiana Territory from France

▲ *The 15 stars and stripes reflect the 15 states of 1795.*

doubles size of the U.S.
1804–06 Meriwether Lewis and William Clark lead expedition to explore lands between Mississippi River and Pacific Ocean.
1807 Embargo Act is passed to try to stop Britain

and France from interfering with U.S. trade.
1808 Congress bans importation of slaves, but slaves continue to be

◄ *Lewis and Clark recorded their observations in journals that were later published.*

weather, disease, accidents, poor planning, and Indian attacks took many lives along the way. But the tide was inexorable—a "manifest destiny," as it was called, to occupy the continent from coast to coast. The passage of the Homestead Act in 1862, which made 160-acre plots of land in underpopulated Western states available to the public at no cost, substantially quickened the pace of immigration along the frontier.

American territory also continued to enlarge. Ceded by Spain (under threat of occupation), Florida joined the country, first as a territory in 1819, then in 1845 as the 27th state. The second great period of territorial expansion began in 1845 when war with Mexico led first to the annexation of the Texas Republic and, three years later, to the Mexican Cession—together adding nearly 1 million square miles to the nation. The same year negotiations with Great Britain over the Oregon Country in the Pacific Northwest concluded with Great Britain turning over its claims south of the 49th parallel. In 1853 the Gadsden Purchase

▲ *This sod house, photographed in 1886, was the home of the J. C. Cram family of Nebraska. It was typical of houses built by homesteaders settling the treeless plains.*

settled a dispute with Mexico over lands in southern New Mexico and Arizona.

Although in just over half a century America had gone a long way toward fulfilling its "manifest destiny," the nation was not yet complete. In 1867 Secretary of State William Seward persuaded the federal government to buy Alaska from Russia for $7.2 million—a purchase that skeptics derided as "Seward's folly," believing it to be a

frigid wasteland. Much warmer but no less remote, the Hawaiian Islands were formally annexed in 1898, giving the United States a strategic presence in the Pacific Basin.

TO AMERICAN SHORES

By the mid-19th century, America's national character was being shaped by a very important factor: fewer and fewer Americans were native-born citizens. Between 1790 and 1820 European immigration accounted for just 8,000 new Americans; doubts about the long-term prospects of the infant republic and the Napoleonic Wars in Europe discouraged and prevented many would-be Americans from making the trip. But this was to change in the 40 years that followed, when Europe sent 120,000 immigrants annually to America's shores; by 1860 nearly one out of eight Americans—some 4 million people—was foreign-born.

Among early immigrants, by far the single largest group came from Ireland, where overpopulation and a repressive tenant-farming system created abject poverty. Between 1845 and 1848 a blight on the Irish potato crop—known as the Great Famine—killed nearly a million Irish and inspired a million more to brave the transatlantic crossing and an unknown future in America. Once here, a majority of the Irish immigrants crowded into the port cities, such as Boston, Philadelphia, and New York.

The second-largest group followed a somewhat different course. America's German immigrants—shopkeepers, farmers, and craftsmen from the Rhine region—often arrived with more resources at their disposal. Many did not linger in the East but instead headed out to the frontier, traveling to Minnesota, Wisconsin, Iowa, and Michigan. Others settled in Midwestern cities, especially Chicago, St. Louis, Milwaukee, and Cincinnati, where a growing industrial base promised employment. At the peak,

in 1854, some 215,000 Germans arrived here, outnumbering even the Irish.

America's new arrivals stood at the center of the country's growth as a global industrial power, providing the muscle to fire its furnaces, construct its cities, mine its hills, and build its railroads. In the post–Civil War period, from 1880 to 1920, the nation saw a second, larger surge of new arrivals, when immigrants from Italy and the politically volatile regions of central and eastern Europe—especially Poles, Czechs, Hungarians, Serbs, and Russians—traveled in great numbers to American shores. California attracted Italians, Germans, and Russians, as well as immigrants from Asia, most notably China and Japan. At the peak, between 1904 and 1914, more than a million newcomers were arriving each year.

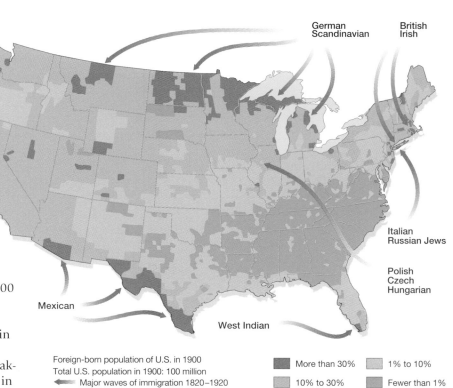

Foreign-born population of U.S. in 1900
Total U.S. population in 1900: 100 million
◀— Major waves of immigration 1820–1920

■ More than 30%	■ 1% to 10%
■ 10% to 30%	■ Fewer than 1%

Patterns of Immigration

U.S. population rose from 50 million to 105 million between 1880 and 1920, largely owing to immigration. The largest influx was from Europe, Russia and the Baltic States, and Canada.

Waves of Secession

Abraham Lincoln's election as president in November 1860 convinced South Carolina to secede from the Union, and six other states quickly followed suit. The rebel attack on the federal garrison at Fort Sumter, South Carolina, marked the beginning of the Civil War. Within two months after Union troops surrendered the fort, on April 14, 1861, four more states seceded.

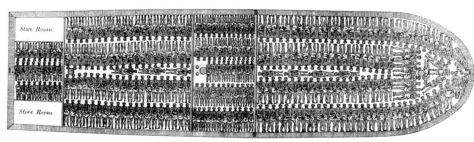

▲ *A plan for the stowage of slaves under the Regulated Slave Trade Act of 1788. Amazingly, slaves were often crammed in even more tightly than shown above, with one being chained between the legs of another.*

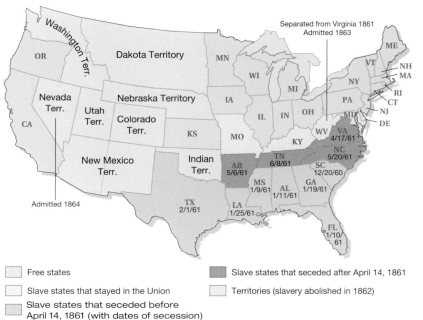

☐ Free states	■ Slave states that seceded after April 14, 1861
☐ Slave states that stayed in the Union	☐ Territories (slavery abolished in 1862)
■ Slave states that seceded before April 14, 1861 (with dates of secession)	

imported illegally.
1811 Gen. William Henry Harrison defeats Indian tribes in Battle of Tippecanoe.
1812–14 War of 1812 between Britain and the U.S. ends in U.S. victory.
1817–25 Erie Canal is built.

▲ *The flag of 1818 had 20 stars for the 20 states.*

1819 Spain cedes Florida to the U.S.
1820 The Missouri Compromise is passed.
1822 Stephen Austin establishes first legal Anglo-American settlement in Texas.
1823 President Monroe

announces Monroe Doctrine, which emphasizes U.S. isolationism.
1825 Congress adopts policy of moving Eastern Indian tribes to lands west of the Mississippi.
1829 The Baltimore & Ohio, first commercial

railroad in U.S., begins operation.
1830 Under Removal Act, Eastern Indians are forced to resettle in Oklahoma Territory.
1831 Nat Turner leads unsuccessful slave revolt in Virginia.

1835 Seminole Indians massacre U.S. troops when they are ordered to leave Florida and move west of the Mississippi.
1836 Republic of Texas is established with Texan defeat of Mexican army at San Jacinto.

Large-scale immigration to America continued with scant interruption until 1924, when new laws slowed the flow by setting quotas based on country of origin. By then, however, America was already a "nation of nations"—over 100 million strong and enriched by a cultural and ethnic diversity.

A NATION TORN

American expansion did not come without grave cost, as a growing breach between North and South led inexorably to armed strife. Although popular lore says that the Civil War was a fight to emancipate the South's enslaved African-American population, historians agree that, at bottom, the conflict of 1861–65 was a cultural war: an inevitable confrontation between an agrarian South and a rapidly growing industrial North.

Tension between North and South mounted in the decades leading to the war,

▶ *Richmond, Virginia, was one of many Southern cities that lay in ruins at the end of the Civil War.*

focusing on the slave or free status of new states admitted to the Union. Southern leaders argued that a balance needed to be maintained, while in the North a growing Abolitionist movement, repelled by the inhumanity of slavery, hoped to outlaw the practice. A series of federally engineered compromises linking the admission of free and slave states forestalled open rebellion. But it was increasingly clear that the Southern way of life could not endure the withering censure of the world. Nor could the nation, in the words of Abraham Lincoln, remain "half-slave, half-free."

Civil War

Full-scale civil war did not begin until 1862. The North's strategy was to cut off resources by naval blockade and gain control of the forts and river routes in the West. Southern general Robert E. Lee defended the Confederate capital of Richmond and mounted offensives as far north as Gettysburg. But the West was lost to the Confederacy by the summer of 1863, leaving the South wide open for Gen. Ulysses S. Grant's invasion of Virginia and Gen. William Tecumseh Sherman's march through Georgia and South Carolina to the sea, effectively crushing the Southern army.

◀ *Gen. Ulysses S. Grant, as photographed by Mathew Brady. During the Civil War, Grant led the Union Army to victory with aggressive tactics and decisive actions. He later served as U.S. president (1869 to 1877).*

On December 20, 1860, South Carolina was the first to leave the Union, followed by Mississippi, Georgia, Alabama, Louisiana, Florida, and Texas. Meeting in Montgomery, Alabama, delegates from each state united to form the Confederate States of America, with Jefferson Davis as president. Virginia, Arkansas, North Carolina, and Tennessee subsequently joined up as well, although four slave states—Missouri, Kentucky, Maryland, and Delaware—remained in the Union. The war began on April 12, 1861, when Confederate forces attacked a Union garrison stationed at Fort Sumter in Charleston Harbor. After 34 hours of shelling, Fort Sumter finally surrendered.

At the outset Southern leaders forecast a quick victory against the North, and early gains seemed to confirm Southern optimism. Under the command of masterful tactician Gen. Robert E. Lee, Southern forces repelled three Union advances against the Confederate capital of Richmond, Virginia. Northern resolve flagged, and Lincoln's popularity sank.

◀ *Gen. Robert E. Lee was admired by both Northerners and Southerners.*

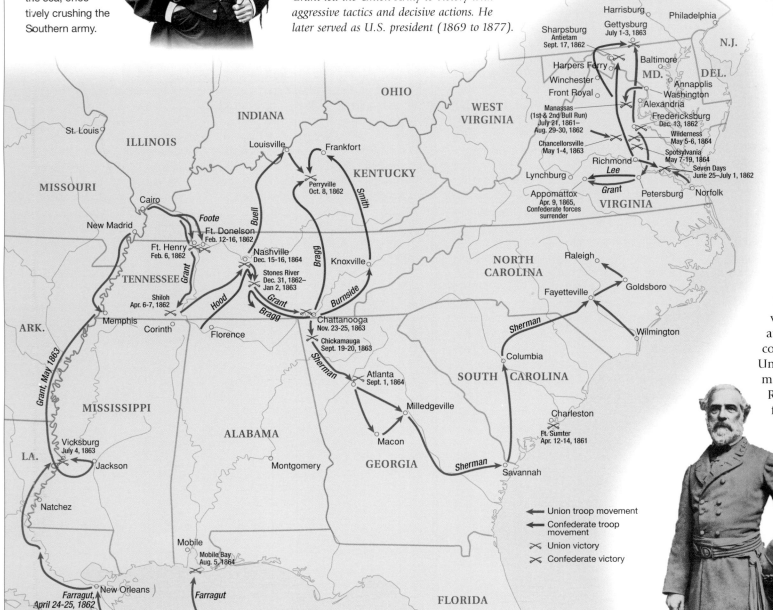

- ← Union troop movement
- ← Confederate troop movement
- ✕ Union victory
- ✕ Confederate victory

1838 Forced removal of 16,000 Cherokee from Georgia to eastern Oklahoma, known as the Trail of Tears, results in 4,000 Indian deaths. Underground Railroad is formed in the South to help slaves escape.

1843 Great migration westward begins over Oregon Trail.

1848 At end of Mexican War, Mexico cedes to the U.S. California, Nevada, Utah, Arizona, and parts of Colorado, Wyoming, and New Mexico.

First U.S. women's rights convention is organized by Lucretia Mott and Elizabeth Cady Stanton at Seneca Falls, New York.

1857 In Dred Scott decision, Supreme Court rules that a slave who has

been brought temporarily into free territory is still a slave and that the Missouri Compromise is unconstitutional.

1859 Abolitionist John Brown leads raid on U.S. arsenal at Harpers Ferry, West Virginia, in an

attempt to free slaves. He is captured and hanged.

1860 Abraham Lincoln, a Republican, is elected president. South Carolina secedes from the Union and takes control of U.S.

▲ *The flag of 1861 had 34 stars for the 34 states.*

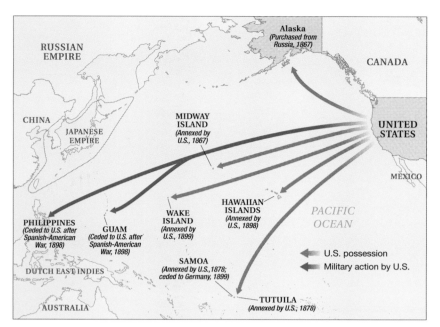

Reaching for Power Across the Oceans

After buying Alaska in 1867, the United States continued to expand overseas through a mixed policy of purchase, treaty, and military conquest. The Spanish-American War (1898) yielded Pacific Ocean naval bases at Guam and in the Philippines; Hawaii joined the United States after local American businessmen overthrew the native monarchy. The capture of Cuba and Puerto Rico from Spain in 1898 began a long history of American intervention in the Caribbean.

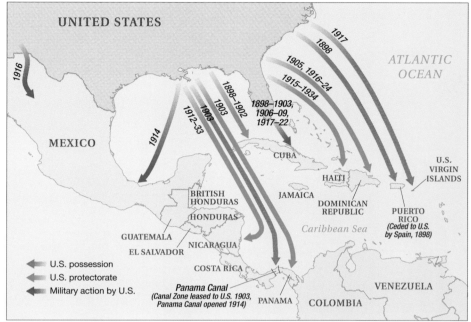

But the Union had won several decisive battles in the West, including the capture of Forts Henry and Donelson and victories at Shiloh, New Orleans, and Vicksburg, one of Gen. Ulysses S. Grant's great victories. The turning point came in July 1863, when news reached Washington of a stunning upset. Driving north across the Maryland panhandle, Lee's army had been stopped by Union forces near the small town of Gettysburg, Pennsylvania. Losses were heavy on both sides; 28,000 Confederate and 23,000 Union soldiers were killed, wounded, or missing. But the Union line had held, and Lee's army had been forced to retreat to Virginia.

Two more bloody years ground the South down, eclipsing all hopes of victory. A naval blockade had left it in virtual economic quarantine, and a Northern advance across the Deep South —culminating in Union general William Tecumseh Sherman's ruinous March to the Sea from Atlanta to Savannah— blackened the landscape with ashes and littered the ground with the dead. Short of men and supplies, and bitterly dispirited, Lee's army could not defend Richmond but watched in retreat as the Confederate capital went up in flames. Surrounded on all sides, Lee surrendered his army to Union forces under Grant's command at the Virginia village of Appomattox Court House on April 9, 1865. Five days later Abraham Lincoln was felled by an assassin's bullet.

INDUSTRY AND EMPIRE

The Civil War left America a fundamentally changed nation. Some 600,000 men had perished—about one-third at the hands of fellow Americans, the rest from disease. The Southern economy lay in ruins, with neither the men nor the money to repair the damage. On the Northern side, deep grievances over the

war's losses found shape in postwar policies that would hamstring a Southern recovery for decades. Emancipation, although morally satisfying to abolitionists, offered little practical help to the South's population of freed slaves, who found themselves the targets of bigotry and further exploitation.

The decades that followed saw a resumption of American expansion to the West and the rapid growth of America's industrial economy. With new railroad lines bringing the four corners of the continent within reach, the population west of the Mississippi more than quadrupled, from 6 million to 26 million, between 1870 and 1910. While industrialists like Andrew Carnegie, J. P. Morgan, and John Rockefeller made huge fortunes in steel, oil, finance, and railroads, they sometimes did so at the expense of their employees, who were frequently forced to live in appalling squalor.

The postwar period was also a time of increasing American interest abroad. In search of new markets for America's industrial output, the United States had already begun to tip its foreign policy toward acquisition, beginning with the purchase of Alaska and the annexation of Hawaii. The Spanish-American War (1898) increased American influence in the Pacific and in the Caribbean as well, giving Americans control of both Cuba and the Philippines.

From the Spanish-American War also emerged a new national figure of tremendous importance: the tough-talking Teddy Roosevelt, a former assistant secretary of the navy whose charge up Cuba's Kettle Hill in 1898 would propel him into the White House. In both regulating business and conducting foreign policy, Roosevelt's mantra—"Speak

softly, and carry a big stick"—was the anthem of an era. As a statesman, he was unabashedly expansionist, mixing bellicose rhetoric with a nuanced, negotiator's touch to expand America's influence in the Western Hemisphere. His greatest triumph, the acquisition of the Panama Canal Zone and the construction of a canal there, showed how far American influence could extend itself on behalf of its strategic and economic interests. Like it or not— and many did not—America was ready to assume a new role of leadership on the world stage.

*▼ **Lt. Col. Theodore Roosevelt** and his Rough Rider regiment strike a victorious pose after American troops won the battles of Kettle Hill and San Juan Hill in 1898. As a result of the four-month-long Spanish-American War, Cuba gained its independence. The United States annexed Guam, Puerto Rico, and the Philippines—and became for the first time a world power.*

1861		**1865**		**1867**	
arsenal at Charleston. **1861** The Confederate States of America is formed, with Jefferson Davis as president. Confederate forces attack Fort Sumter, beginning the Civil War. **1863** Lincoln delivers Gettys-	burg Address at Gettysburg military cemetery. **1863** Lincoln issues Emancipation Proclamation, freeing all slaves. He also offers amnesty to Southerners who take a loyalty oath. **1864** Union general William	Tecumseh Sherman burns Atlanta and marches through Georgia to the sea, causing mass destruction. Cheyenne and Arapaho Indians are massacred at Sand Creek, Colorado. **1865** Confederate general	Robert E. Lee surrenders to Union general Ulysses S. Grant at Appomattox Court House, Virginia, ending Civil War. Lincoln is shot and killed by John Wilkes Booth in Ford's Theater	in Washington, D.C. Andrew Johnson becomes president. Slavery is abolished by 13th Amendment to the Constitution. **1867** The U.S. purchases Alaska from Russia for $7.2 million.	**1868** Fourteenth Amendment grants citizenship to blacks, ensuring them the rights of "due process" and "equal protection." **1870** Fifteenth Amendment grants suffrage to black males 21 and older.

▶ *The Huron Belt* memorializes the 1683 meeting of Jesuit missionaries with the Hurons to plan for the building of the first wooden church on Indian land. Indians, Jesuits, and the church are represented on the belt.

Native Americans on the Defensive

P ropelled by a "manifest destiny," America expanded westward, but as settlers moved west, Native Americans were compelled to give up their homelands. Entire tribes were forcibly relocated to unfamiliar territory. Millions died of disease and starvation and in military conquest. A period of white-Indian conflict ensued following the Civil War, when the Homestead Act, new agricultural technologies, and the expansion of the nation's railway system opened the Great Plains to settlement. By the end of the century, most of America's aboriginal inhabitants lived on reservations, their population reduced to about 250,000.

▲ *This Comanche shield* and cover, dating from around 1875, is decorated to symbolize and pay homage to the powers of the sun and the stars.

American Bison

Prized by Indians for their meat and hides, American bison (buffalo) numbered 60 million in 1800. By the end of the century, they had been hunted to near extinction by white settlers, with only about 1,000 left by 1898.

1600
1800
1875

EARLY CLASHES

The Indian wars of the post–Civil War period were the last in a 400-year history of conflict. Early explorers and settlers had skirmished with the native inhabitants. Eight "major" wars—including war with Virginia's Chief Powhatan and his tribes (1622), New England's Pequot and King Philip's wars (1637 and 1675–77), South Carolina's Westo and Yamanese wars (1680 and 1715), and North Carolina's Tuscarora War (1711–12)—were fought during the early colonial period. British—and, later, American—intrusion on Indian lands west of the Pennsylvania frontier sparked clashes during the French and Indian War (1754–61) and Pontiac's Rebellion (1763), in which an Indian confederation staged a year-long campaign of raids on British forts and villages from the Straits of Mackinac and Detroit to western Pennsylvania. After the Revolution Native Americans resisted the influx of white settlers into the Indian territory northwest of the Ohio River; not until Shawnee chief Tecumseh's defeat at the Battle of the Thames (1813) did the region fall under the white man's control.

INDIAN REMOVAL

During the 19th century, the American government steadily appropriated

▲ *The forced Cherokee relocation of 1838* was the cruelest of those authorized under the Indian Removal Act. The harsh Trail of Tears from Georgia to Oklahoma claimed more than 4,000 lives.

Indian land through various treaties. Specific Native American lands would be purchased in exchange for "just" compensation, often two cents an acre. Frequently, the treaties were little more than a formality because white settlers had already encroached on the land. Between 1788, when the Continental Congress negotiated its first treaty with a native tribe—the Delaware—and 1871, when Congress ended treaty making with individual tribes, some 389 such deals were struck.

The Louisiana Purchase of 1803, which gave America a vast area west of the Mississippi, led to the final evacuation of most of the Eastern Indian tribes. In 1830 Congress passed the Indian Removal Act, mandating the relocation of some 10,000 Northern and 60,000 Southern Indians, including the Five Civilized Tribes—the Creek, Chickasaw, Seminole, Choctaw, and Cherokee—to

what is now Oklahoma. Thousands perished on these forced marches—one of the most notorious being the Cherokee Trail of Tears—yet many Indians evaded removal or returned to their homelands.

WESTERN WARS

Although Indians still dominated the West at the outbreak of the Civil War, the flood of white settlers after 1860 created conflict. As the competition for land and resources increased, federal troops first fought to confine Western Indians to reservations, then later fought to keep them there.

The bitter and protracted Sioux wars began in 1862, when food supplies were withheld from starving Indians awaiting long-overdue treaty payments. The Sioux attacked settlers throughout the Minnesota Valley area, but the uprising was quickly put down. Hundreds of whites and Indians were killed—and 39 Indi-

1871 Indian Appropriation Act nullifies all Indian treaties and makes all Indians wards of the U.S.

1872 San Juan Islands between Washington and Vancouver become part of the U.S.

1876 Chiefs Sitting Bull and Crazy Horse lead Sioux and Cheyenne Indians in their defeat of Lt. Col. George A. Custer at the Battle of Little Bighorn in Montana.
Alexander Graham Bell patents the telephone.

1877 Chief Joseph and his group of Nez Perce are captured by U.S. troops in Montana Territory, 40 miles from Canada. Last of federal troops leave the South, ending Reconstruction.

1879 Thomas Edison invents

incandescent lamp.
Ute Indians are moved from Colorado to Utah.

1884 The Supreme Court rules that interfering with a citizen's right to vote is a federal offense.

1885 Large-scale immigration from eastern and south-

ern Europe begins.

1886 Apache chief Geronimo surrenders, ending Apache Indian wars in the Southwest.
The Statue of Liberty, donated by France, is dedicated in New York Harbor.

1889 White settlers swarm into Oklahoma to homestead lands that were previously Indian territory.

1890 Sioux Indians are massacred by U.S. troops at Battle of Wounded Knee in South Dakota.

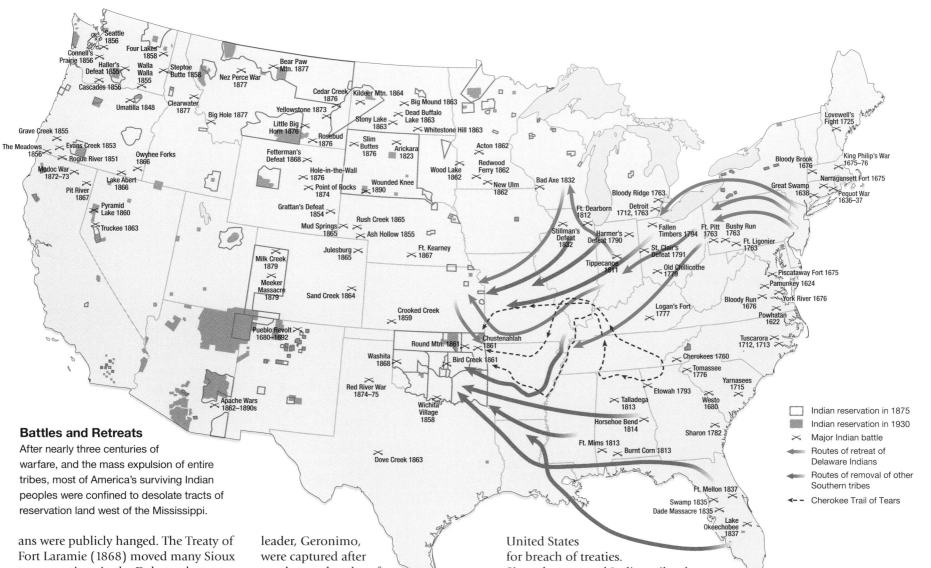

Battles and Retreats

After nearly three centuries of warfare, and the mass expulsion of entire tribes, most of America's surviving Indian peoples were confined to desolate tracts of reservation land west of the Mississippi.

Legend:
- ☐ Indian reservation in 1875
- ■ Indian reservation in 1930
- ✕ Major Indian battle
- ← Routes of retreat of Delaware Indians
- ← Routes of removal of other Southern tribes
- ◀-- Cherokee Trail of Tears

ans were publicly hanged. The Treaty of Fort Laramie (1868) moved many Sioux to reservations in the Dakotas, but a gold rush in the Black Hills, considered sacred by the Sioux and other tribes, reignited the conflict in 1874. Ordered back to the reservation after leaving it to challenge the white men, the Sioux refused to return. Two federal forces sent to corral a Sioux party under warrior chief Sitting Bull failed to do so. The second force, led by Lt. Col. George Armstrong Custer, was completely destroyed at the Little Bighorn River on June 25, 1876, in a battle known thereafter as "Custer's Last Stand." A final Sioux conflict occurred in 1890, when dancing inspired by the religious cult of the "Ghost Dance" was misunderstood as a hostile demonstration, and U.S. Army troops massacred 300 Sioux, including women and children, at South Dakota's Wounded Knee Creek.

Between 1865 and 1898, fighting between Indians and U.S. Army troops flared from Texas to Montana in some 900 engagements. On the southern Plains the slaughter of sleeping Cheyenne by Colorado militia in 1864, in an infamous event known as the Sand Creek Massacre, provoked an uprising of Arapaho and Cheyenne and culminated in the Red River War of 1874–75. In the Southwest the Apache and their great

leader, Geronimo, were captured after nearly two decades of resistance in 1886. In the Northwest the Modoc War (1872–73) and the Nez Perce War (1877) were bloody struggles to round up Indian peoples onto ever smaller parcels of land.

No less devastating for the Native Americans was the destruction of the buffalo, a vital source of food, clothing, and shelter for Indians of the western Plains. By 1885 nearly the entire herd was destroyed by the U.S. Army and professional hide hunters.

INDIANS IN THE MODERN ERA

By the dawn of the 20th century, the frontier had been declared closed for a decade, with the Indians confined to some 200 reservations, and Native American culture languished. By the 1930s total land under Native American control had dwindled from 138 million acres in 1887 to just 48 million.

The near extinction of many Indian tribes was slowed in 1934 with the Indian Reorganization Act, which halted the contraction of Native American lands and the suppression of Indian language and culture. The establishment of the Indian Claims Commission in 1946 allowed Indian tribes the right to sue the

United States for breach of treaties. Since then, several Indian tribes have won formal recognition and compensation for the theft of their lands.

The Indian population of the United States has rebounded and now stands at nearly 1 million. Unemployment, poverty, and other social ills continue to plague Native Americans, yet efforts like the Red Power movement of the 1960s and 1970s and the recent legalization of gambling on reservations has brought some long-awaited relief and hope to the descendants of the first Americans.

▼ *The Mashantucket Pequot Child Development Center* operates on income generated by the Foxwoods Casino, which opened in Ledyard, Connecticut, in 1992. The casino has become a source of enormous wealth for the tribe.

1892 Ellis Island opens.
1896 Supreme Court, in *Plessy* v. *Ferguson* case, rules that "separate but equal" railroad coaches are constitutional.
1898 After its defeat in Spanish-American War, Spain abdicates its

claim to Cuba and relinquishes Puerto Rico, Guam, and the Philippines to the U.S. U.S. annexes Hawaii.
1899 Filipinos try unsuccessfully to drive U.S. from the Philippines.
1901 Members of the Five

Civilized Tribes are given U.S. citizenship.
1903 Orville and Wilbur Wright fly an airplane for 12 seconds at Kitty Hawk, North Carolina.
1906 Most of San Francisco is destroyed by an earthquake and a fire.

1908 Ford introduces Model T automobile.
1909 The National Association for the Advancement of Colored People (NAACP) is organized in New York. Commodore Robert E. Peary, black explorer

Matthew Henson, and four Inuits—Ooqueah, Egingwah, Seegloo, and Ootah—are the first to reach the North Pole.
1913 The 16th Amendment permits federal government to collect income taxes.

▲ *The 48-star flag waved from 1912 to 1959.*

From World War I to World War II

▼ *The first U.S. troops to fight in World War I began landing in France at such ports as Bordeaux, Brest, and Saint-Nazaire (below) in June 1917. By October, they had arrived on the western front. Almost 5 million Americans were in uniform; of these, more than half went overseas.*

The outbreak of war in Europe in 1914 found the United States on the sidelines. To most Americans, the cobweb of alliances that drew nation after nation into the fray seemed arbitrary and arcane. For three years President Woodrow Wilson tried to keep the country out of the war, but it was not to be; America was drawn into the conflict and assumed a new role as a leader in world affairs. Then, a generation later, it happened a second time. Throughout the 1930s America watched as Europe lumbered once again toward all-out war. By the end of World War II, 60 nations had become involved, and battles had been fought in nearly every region of the world, from the jungles of Asia and the streets of Europe to the deserts of North Africa and the snowfields of the Soviet Union. More destructive than any other war in history, World War II ushered in an era dominated by the United States and the Soviet Union as competing global superpowers.

Major American Victories in World War I

American troops won their first big triumph in May 1918, when the U.S. First Division seized Cantigny in a rapier-sharp, 35-minute assault. Other divisions hit the southern sector of the German line, starting at Château-Thierry and building up to the massive Meuse-Argonne offensive at the war's end. Smaller American units aided British and French forces at Ypres and elsewhere.

THE GREAT WAR

Although most Americans privately supported Anglo-French democracy over German militarism, they were not at all willing to have their own country embroiled in a European conflict. President Woodrow Wilson's greatest fear was that anything less than strict neutrality would divide the country. Seeking reelection in 1916, his backers stated his case to the American people with the slogan: "He Kept Us Out of War."

Neutrality may have been the safest course for the nation, but American commercial interests abroad made it a practical impossibility. Most precarious of all was the neutral status of the American shipping industry, which was soon ferrying arms and supplies to the Allies. During the first three years of the war, German U-boats waged submarine campaigns to seal off the British Isles from commercial shipping traffic, which resulted in the loss of American lives. This led, in the winter of 1917, to a diplomatic break between the United States and the Central Powers of Germany and Austria-Hungary. Upon the discovery of a German plot to involve Mexico in the conflict and allow it to reconquer the southwestern United States, the nation was roused to an indignant fury. Wilson then sought a formal declaration of war on April 2, 1917, which he signed on April 6.

America's late entry into the war came not a moment too soon. Three years of murderous warfare had badly depleted the Allies' morale, troop strength, and supplies. The first members of the American Expeditionary Force (AEF) departed almost immediately. Nearly another year would pass, however, before adequate American forces would be available to radically affect the course of the war. Under AEF commander Gen. John J. Pershing, American troops led a series of counteroffensives in the summer of 1918 that helped check the Germans' final effort and drove them eastward. The final battle in which American troops were engaged—fought between the Meuse River and the Argonne Forest from late September to November—involved nearly a million American troops. At the same time, Allied victories in southern Europe and the Middle East

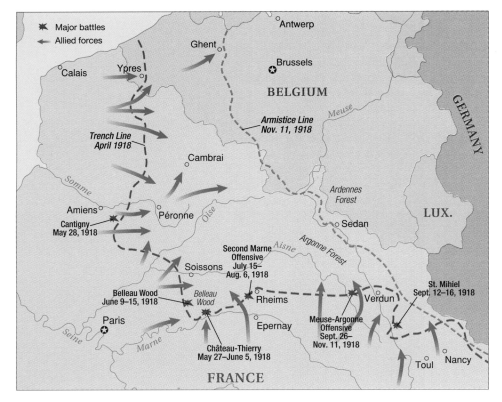

▲ *Hearing of Germany's surrender* on November 11, 1918, members of the U.S. Sixth Infantry Division near the Meuse River in France rejoice.

1914	1918	1919

1914 Panama Canal opens. President Wilson proclaims U.S. neutrality in World War I.

1915 Many Americans are killed when British passenger ship *Lusitania* is sunk by a German U-boat.

1916 The U.S. signs a treaty to buy the Virgin Islands from Denmark for $25 million.

1917 Puerto Rico becomes a U.S. territory, and under the Jones Act its inhabitants become American citizens.

The U.S. declares war on Germany.

1918 Wilson outlines his Fourteen Points for world peace. Kaiser abdicates; Germany surrenders; armistice goes into effect.

Influenza outbreak spreads from Europe to the U.S. By the following year, nearly 500,000 people have died in U.S. (Pandemic kills 20 million people worldwide.)

1919 Treaty of Versailles is signed at Paris Peace

Conference. Wilson's plan for a League of Nations is accepted. U.S. Senate rejects both the treaty and the League of Nations. Eighteenth Amendment, prohibiting production, sale, and transportation of liquor, is ratified.

1920 Nineteenth Amendment grants suffrage to women.

1924 All American-born Indians are granted U.S. citizenship.

1926 U.S. Marines are sent to Nicaragua to stop

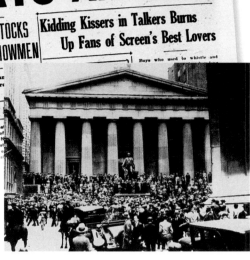

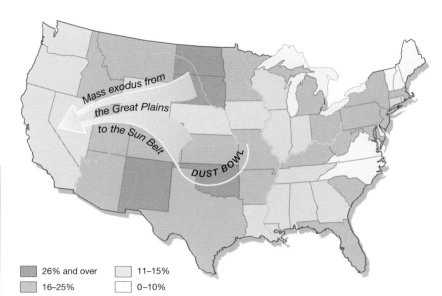

| 26% and over | 11–15% |
| 16–25% | 0–10% |

▶ **When the stock market collapse was reported,** *a huge crowd gathered on the steps of the Treasury Building across from the New York Stock Exchange.*

had brought Bulgaria, Turkey, and Austria-Hungary to the negotiating table. Isolated, short of supplies, and facing Allied advances on the western and southern fronts, Germany petitioned for peace and signed the armistice on November 11, 1918.

A NEW ISOLATIONISM
Victory in the Great War was an Allied victory, but the cost of the war was largely Europe's. Nearly 10 million soldiers had been killed, with more than twice that number wounded. It is unknown how many civilians lost their lives from disease, starvation, or other war-related causes, but some historians think that as many died as soldiers.

Across the Atlantic the United States emerged from the conflict as the world's undisputed economic power. But public opinion turned away from further foreign entanglements. Rejecting membership in the League of Nations and Wilson's and the Democrats' international vision, voters turned out in record numbers in 1920 to elect little-known Republican candidate Warren G. Harding over Democrat James M. Cox.

The junior senator from Marion, Ohio, Harding promised a "return to normalcy," setting the tone for a decade of isolationist foreign policy supported by a rapidly expanding economy. Successors Calvin Coolidge and Herbert Hoover likewise concerned themselves with domestic issues. After a brief postwar recession, the economy had rebounded with gusto; for the first time in history, many Americans had a surplus of money to bet on the stock market, which raced to record highs. Even Prohibition, effected by the 18th Amendment in 1920, did little to dull the "Jazz Age" mood. Quaffing bootleg

liquor and dancing the Charleston while they watched stock prices rise, Americans celebrated their good fortune.

BLACK THURSDAY
The party ended on October 24, 1929—Black Thursday—when the stock market, sliding for a month, went into a tailspin. A consortium of bankers managed to steady the Dow with an infusion of purchase orders, but the following Tuesday, October 29, the market dove again. By the end of the day, $15 billion had vanished from the American economy.

The depths to which the nation would sink in the years to come revealed seri-

▲ **President and Mrs. Woodrow Wilson** *at the 1919 Paris Peace Conference. The U.S. Senate would ultimately reject the resulting Treaty of Versailles.*

ous weaknesses in the American economy. By 1933 nearly a quarter of America's workers were unemployed. Mother Nature did little to help. In the Midwest the worst drought in U.S. Weather Bureau history and the ensuing dust storms deepened the misery; during the height of the Dust Bowl period, some 350,000 people from the hardest-hit states packed up and headed west.

A "NEW DEAL"
For a time, no one seemed to know what to do about the crisis. Responding to public pleas, the Hoover administration initiated several programs to spur the economy but fell short of offering direct federal aid. As the breadlines grew, most Americans began to think that direct government intervention was necessary.

The 1932 election of New York governor Franklin D. Roosevelt to the presidency marked a vital shift in the role of the federal government. Promising a "new deal for the American people," Roosevelt guided a flurry of new initiatives into law during his first 100 days in office. New agencies—such as the National Recovery Administration (NRA), the Civilian Conservation Corps (CCC), and the Public Works Administration (PWA)—dispensed relief funds to unemployed Americans and put others to work building roads, dams, and schools. To stabilize crop prices and revive agriculture, the federal government began to pay farmers for leaving some of their land fallow. Additional New Deal initiatives included the creation of the Federal Deposit Insurance Corporation (FDIC) and the Social Security Administration.

Slowly the economic picture began to brighten. But the glimmer of hope on the horizon would soon be overshadowed by a growing threat across the Atlantic: a mustachioed orator with a dark vision to restore the broken German fatherland to its former greatness.

Unemployment
In the 1930s destitute Americans abandoned the drought-stricken Midwest and Plains states, seeking jobs in the West. The tints above indicate the percentage of a state's population on unemployment in December 1934.

▼ **A migrant worker** *plods along a California highway. The drought that hit the central and southern Plains between 1933 and 1935 caused many to leave their homes in search of work.*

1929	**1934**	**1936**

the fighting and support the existing government after civil war breaks out.
1929 Stocks plummet in October. By the end of the month $15 billion is lost, spurring the Great Depression.

Comdr. Richard E. Byrd flies over South Pole.
1932 Franklin D. Roosevelt is elected president and promises "New Deal" program of federal support for social programs and the economy.
1933 Prohibition is repealed.

In the special "100 days" Congressional session, many social and economic programs are enacted to combat the Depression and to aid citizens.
1934 President Roosevelt begins "Good Neighbor

Policy" with Latin American countries.
1935 Social Security Act sets aside monies for old-age pensions and unemployment compensation.
The Works Progress Administration (WPA)

employs more than 8 million people for public projects.
Soil Conservation Service is formed to control Dust Bowl erosion.
1936 Anti-Fascist Americans fight with Spanish Loyalists in the Spanish

Civil War.
1937 The airship *Hindenburg* explodes over its dock in Lakehurst, New Jersey, killing 35 people.
Third Neutrality Act includes ban on exportation of arms to nations that are at war.

▲ **Pearl Harbor** *was attacked by Japanese planes attempting to cripple the U.S. Pacific Fleet in order to prevent it from blocking Japan's expansion in Asia. The assault on December 7, 1941, sank four of the eight battleships anchored in the harbor. Of the vessels shown burning above, the* West Virginia *(left) and the* Tennessee *(center) were repaired. The* Arizona *remains on the ocean floor.*

EARLY RUMBLINGS

Trouble brewed around the world. Resentments were festering, especially in Germany, which was forced to pay large reparations to the Allies for World War I. The League of Nations proved ineffective at stopping the expansionist ambitions of nationalist movements in Italy, Japan, and Germany. Virtually unimpeded, all three nations embarked on programs of systematic military conquest.

Japan was the first nation to push beyond its borders, invading Manchuria in 1931 and occupying most of eastern China in 1939. Italian Fascist Party leader Benito Mussolini, having established himself as dictator of Italy in 1922, overran Ethiopia in 1935–36.

BLITZKRIEG IN EUROPE

The major architect of war in Europe was a fanatic nationalist, German Führer Adolf Hitler. Calling for "racial superiority," Hitler led both a brutal internal purge of the nation's Jewish minorities and a war of conquest on his neighbors. After invading Poland in 1939 (which brought Britain and France into the war), Hitler's troops moved quickly against Denmark and Norway. In May 1940 German tanks stormed into Belgium, crushing the French and British forces there. A month later German troops occupied Paris, and Britain stood alone against German bombs. In June 1941 Hitler invaded the Soviet Union.

THE U.S. ENTERS THE WAR

Again, the United States hesitated to involve itself directly in a European war, but its sympathies were clear. In March 1941 the Lend-Lease Act became law; it permitted any nation fighting the Axis powers to borrow or lease raw materials and supplies from the U.S. government. All told, the United States sent some $50 billion in aid to the Allies.

As bad as it was, by late 1941 World War II was still a group of regional conflicts confined to Europe. Then, on the morning of December 7, the Japanese attacked the U.S. Pacific fleet stationed at Pearl Harbor, bringing devastating results: in just a few hours, 18 U.S. ships and 342 aircraft were destroyed or badly damaged, and 2,403 U.S. servicemen and 68 civilians were killed. Declaring it "a date which will live in infamy," Roosevelt asked Congress and the entire nation to declare war on Japan. Canada and Great Britain followed within hours, and China, the next day. Italy and Germany declared war on the United States on December 11. By the end of the week, virtually all of the industrialized world had gone to war.

CAPTURING A CONTINENT

To stem German and Italian aggression, military planners used a two-pronged approach: bombing raids against Germany from the British Isles to pave the way for an Allied invasion of France and a ground war to root out the Axis powers from North Africa, thus opening the door to an invasion of Italy via Sicily.

The American invasion of North Africa began in November 1942. In con-

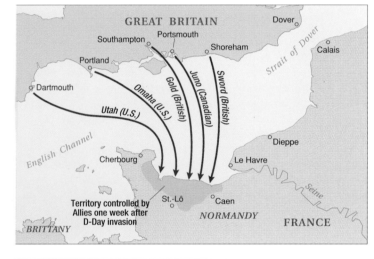

World War II in Europe

After three years of desperate battle, most of continental Europe lay under Axis control; but an early Allied victory in North Africa, followed by invasions throughout Italy and France, as well as Soviet advances in the East, effectively turned the tide of the war.

▲ **D-Day**—*June 6, 1944, Normandy, France. Allied troops stormed 60 miles of coastline in history's largest seaborne invasion.*

1938 The U.S. and Germany recall ambassadors.

1939 Supported by Eleanor Roosevelt, Marian Anderson sings before 75,000 people at Lincoln Memorial. She had not been allowed to sing in Constitution Hall because she was black. World's Fairs are held in New York City and San Francisco, drawing millions of visitors.

1940 The U.S. sends surplus war materials to Britain. Congress initiates first peacetime draft.

1941 After Japan's December 7 attack on U.S. base at Pearl Harbor, the U.S. declares war on Japan on December 8. Germany and Italy declare war on the U.S. on December 11; the U.S. reciprocates against Germany and Italy later the same day. Manhattan Project facilities are set up to develop atomic bomb.

1942 The U.S. sends Japanese-Americans to detention camps. Gasoline rationing is extended to all states. First self-sustained, controlled nuclear chain reaction is produced by a team of scientists under Enrico Fermi. General MacArthur is named Supreme Commander of Allied forces in southwest Pacific. Nazis begin mass slaughter of Jews in gas chambers.

1943 General Eisenhower is made Supreme Commander of Allied forces in French North Africa and Sicily; later,

cert with British forces from Egypt, Allied forces under Gen. Dwight D. Eisenhower subdued the Axis forces there in just six months; in July 1943 they swept north into Sicily and then Italy, reaching Rome on June 4, 1944.

Two days later, on June 6, or D-Day, the long-anticipated Allied invasion of France began. Some 155,000 men waded ashore at France's Normandy beaches. Losses were heavy, but within two months the Allies had broken through. Paris was liberated on August 25; by early fall most of France and Belgium were under Allied control.

Italy had capitulated, and in the east Hitler's troops had been stopped by the Russians. Despite a German counter-attack in December 1944 (the Battle of the Bulge), Allied troops moved into Germany, which by then had been bombed to ruins. American troops crossed the Rhine in March 1945, but Eisenhower agreed to let Soviet troops take Berlin itself, which they did on May 2. On May 7 Germany surrendered.

IN THE PACIFIC

While the war in Europe was an Allied effort, the war with Japan was led largely by America. It began with devastating setbacks. Hours after the air strike on Pearl Harbor, Japanese bombers also attacked the British colony of Hong Kong, the Philippines, and the U.S. islands of Guam and Wake. The Japanese continued to overrun Southeast Asia, and by mid-1942 a quarter of the globe was under Japanese control.

Three events in 1942 turned the tide of the Pacific war. The first was the Doolittle Raid, a surprise attack by U.S. aircraft

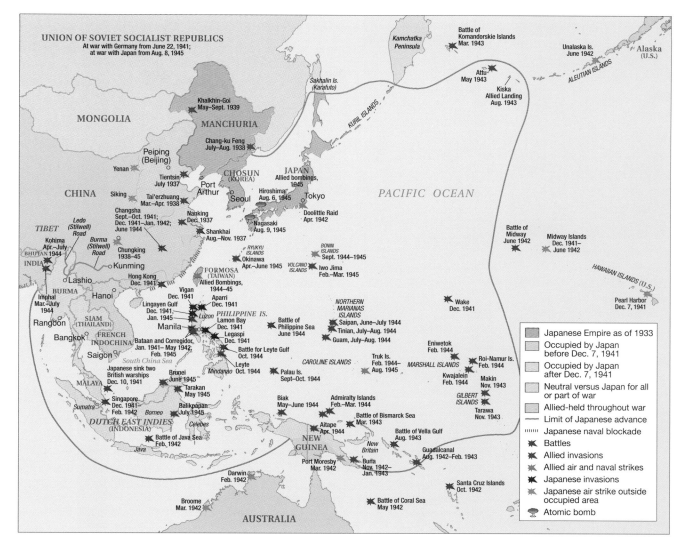

on the Japanese home islands. A month later, in May, the Battle of the Coral Sea ended the Japanese threat to Australia. Most decisive of all was the contest for Midway Island, a three-day air-and-sea battle that cost Japan four of its nine aircraft carriers—and gave the United States its first clear victory in the Pacific theater.

Over the next three years, American forces inched across the Pacific. Losses were often heavy in the face of fierce Japanese resistance, and few Japanese prisoners were taken, since many fought to the death or committed ritual suicide to avoid capture. By late 1944 American forces had control of most of the south and central Pacific, bringing the Japanese home islands within easy reach of U.S. B-29 bombers. American Marine victories on Iwo Jima (March 1945) and Okinawa (July 1945) brought the United States to Japan's very doorstep. Despite a devastating air war, Japan refused to surrender, and

◄ *The bombing of Nagasaki, Japan, on August 9, 1945, brought about a quick end to World War II.*

American military planners began to formulate an invasion of Japan.

DAWN OF THE NUCLEAR AGE

That day never came. On the morning of August 6, 1945, the American B-29 *Enola Gay* flew over the Japanese city of Hiroshima. In the plane's belly was a new kind of weapon. Moments later, the city was engulfed by an atomic fireball. Five square miles of Hiroshima simply vanished; 70,000 to 100,000 Japanese died, and thousands more would perish from radiation poisoning.

When the destruction of Hiroshima failed to elicit a Japanese surrender, a second bomber flew over the city of Nagasaki on August 9, dropping an even larger atomic device; another 40,000 Japanese died. Five days later, on August 14, at the urging of Japanese emperor Hirohito, Japan's military leaders agreed to give up the fight. A world war had ended, and a new nuclear age had begun.

The War in the Pacific

In the war's early years, mastery of the seas allowed Japan to expand across half the Pacific Ocean. The retreat began with U.S. victories at Midway and the Coral Sea and ended in atomic fire over Hiroshima and Nagasaki.

▼ *Crowds celebrate the end of the war in New York City's Times Square on August 15, 1945. Japan had surrendered the day before. The official statement of surrender was signed September 2 on the U.S. battleship* Missouri *in Tokyo Bay.*

The United States as Superpower

▲ **Border patrols** *are stationed all along the 2½-mile-wide demilitarized zone that serves as a buffer between North and South Korea. In the foreground, two members of the U.N./South Korean military police guard the gate on the South Korean side.*

▲ **After the Cuban missile crisis,** *President John F. Kennedy toured the U.S. Air Force Base in Homestead, Florida, and thanked the troops. Above, Kennedy confers with an air force general.*

Even before Europe's guns fell silent, Allied leaders began to formulate plans for peace. But an uneasy partnership between Communist East and Democratic West soon turned sour. *Following a divisive conference at Potsdam in July and August of 1945, Soviet leader Joseph Stalin moved to* extend the umbrella of Soviet influence over the nations of Eastern Europe; the West, led by the United States, rebuilt its own defenses, establishing the North Atlantic Treaty Organization, or NATO, in 1949. For 40 years these two great powers engaged in a political and ideological struggle that defined the postwar era.

AN "IRON CURTAIN"

Speaking at Westminster College in Fulton, Missouri, on March 5, 1946, Winston Churchill warned of the dire threat of Soviet expansion in Europe: "From Stettin in the Baltic to Trieste in the Adriatic, an iron curtain has descended across the Continent." Unofficially, the Cold War had begun.

Facing down the Soviets became the centerpiece of American foreign policy in the postwar period. The second task was containing Communist influence around the globe. Under a 1947 policy that came to be known as the Truman Doctrine, the United States sent aid to such countries as Turkey and Greece, where Communist insurgencies and terrorism threatened to increase the Soviet sphere of influence.

For most Americans, the idea of renewed war in Europe hit home in April 1948, when the Soviet Union surprised the West by closing all routes to Allied-controlled West Berlin, 110 miles inside East Germany. In June the Berlin Airlift began. For over a year American and British planes airlifted more than 2 million tons of vital supplies across the Russian zone of Germany to West Berlin, continuing even after the Soviets finally lifted the blockade in September 1949.

The Berlin Airlift cemented the leadership role of the United States in postwar Europe. But the sense of relief was short-lived. In September 1949 President Harry Truman learned that an American B-29 taking routine scientific measurements detected an atomic blast in Soviet Siberia. A new arms race had begun.

ARMING FOR ARMAGEDDON

Despite the United States' four-year lead, the Soviets quickly narrowed the gap, detonating their first hydrogen "super-bomb" just nine months after the United States tested its bomb at Eniwetok Atoll in November 1952. Then in 1957 the Soviet Union startled the West by successfully launching the world's first man-made satellite, called *Sputnik,* into orbit. Within months American scientists launched the first U.S. Earth satellite. Then, in August 1961, a cement and barbed-wire barrier suddenly appeared in Berlin, dividing the city and blocking a major escape route for refugees fleeing Communist East Germany.

Most seriously, in October 1962 aerial photographs detected the presence of Soviet offensive ballistic missile installations under construction in Communist Cuba, just 90 miles off the coast of Florida. Addressing

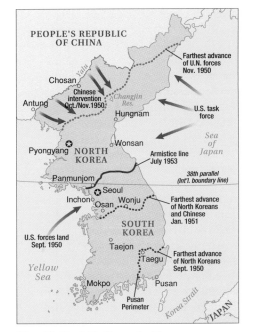

The United Nations in Korea
North Korea's surprise attack in June 1950 drove United Nations (U.N.) and South Korean defenders toward Pusan. Hitting back, U.N. forces pushed up to the Chinese border, where 300,000 Red Army troops sent them reeling.

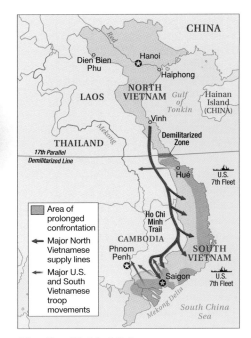

The Conflict in Vietnam
U.S. and South Vietnamese troops battled Communist soldiers and guerrillas from Vietnam's northern highlands to the Mekong Delta's marshes, and thrust into Cambodia and Laos to wipe out enemy bases there.

◀ **The final American evacuation of Vietnam** *took place over the course of 19 hours on April 29, 1975, and included about 1,000 Americans and more than 5,500 South Vietnamese. The last of the 81 Air America helicopters (left) lifted off from the rooftop of the American Embassy in Saigon. The next day, the government of South Vietnam surrendered to that of the North.*

1946

1946 The U.S. initiates atomic testing at Bikini Atoll in the Marshall Islands.
1950 North Korea invades South Korea. The U.N. Security Council demands fighting stop. Sixteen member nations, including the U.S., form U.N. Allied Forces.
1952 Puerto Rico becomes a U.S. commonwealth.
1957 Congress passes first Civil Rights Act since Reconstruction, which sets up a separate division in the Department

1958

of Justice to enforce laws and regulations.
1958 NASA is established; *Explorer I* is first U.S. Earth satellite.
1959 Alaska and Hawaii become 49th and 50th states, respectively.
1960 Soviets down a U.S. U-2 spy plane. John F. Kennedy, at age 43, becomes youngest person and first Roman Catholic to be elected president of the United States.
1961 U.S. and Cuba sever relations. C.I.A.-backed

1962

Bay of Pigs invasion to overthrow Castro fails.
1962 Cuban missile crisis occurs when U.S. discovers Soviet missile bases in Cuba.
1963 President Kennedy is assassinated in Dallas. His alleged killer, Lee

▲ **The 50-star U.S. flag** *has been flying since 1960.*

the nation, President John F. Kennedy warned of the danger and ordered a naval quarantine to prevent further shipment of offensive military equipment to the island. For days the world hovered at the brink of war until, on October 26, Soviet president Nikita Khrushchev wrote Kennedy to say that the Soviet Union would remove its missiles if the United States pledged not to invade Cuba. Kennedy agreed, and on October 28 Khrushchev ordered the missile sites destroyed. By November 2 the crisis was over, although the nuclear stalemate continued for nearly two more decades.

CONTESTS FOR ASIA

In Asia the problem of global Communist aggression was compounded by the emergence of a third world power. The 1949 victory of Communist Mao Tsetung's revolutionary army over nationalist forces led by Western-leaning Chiang Kai-shek created the ominous prospect of a Communist Sino-Soviet alliance, a possibility that drew the United States into two protracted military interventions in Asia.

The Korean War (1950–53) was not technically a U.S. war but a U.N.-authorized military intervention, begun after North Korean troops, with some Soviet-built tanks, crossed the 38th parallel into South Korea on June 25, 1950. In all, 16 U.N. member nations sent troops; by early fall, recovering from initial reversals, American-led U.N. forces had regained the 38th parallel, with the ultimate goal of destroying the North Korean army. Beginning in October, however, China gradually began moving troops across the Yalu River into North Korea, and on November 25–26, the Chinese attacked and sent U.N. forces scrambling back south of the 38th parallel. Thereafter, the war settled into a bloody, two-year stalemate that ended in armistice in 1953. The boundary between Communist North Korea and Democratic South Korea remains one of the most armed borders in the world.

The conflict in Vietnam proved to be an even deeper quagmire. Direct U.S. involvement in the former French colony of Vietnam began with a few hundred "military advisers" sent to the country in 1961 to aid the South Vietnamese government against a Communist North Vietnamese–backed Vietcong guerrilla insurgency force. By spring of 1969, 543,000 U.S. ground forces were "in country"; the fighting spread into Cambodia and Laos, where Communist forces had bases. Despite American military superiority, Vietnam's jungle terrain and the hit-and-run tactics of the North Vietnamese and Vietcong made decisive victory elusive. As the death toll rose,

sentiment at home tipped in favor of an American withdrawal of ground forces, which began in 1969 and was complete by 1973. Although the United States still provided air and sea support, South Vietnam was unable to defend itself from attacks by the North Vietnamese army. The country was reunified under Communist control in 1976.

DÉTENTE AND *PERESTROIKA*

The 1970s, known as the era of détente, saw a general thawing of superpower relations. Beginning in 1969, the United States and the Soviet Union embarked on negotiations to slow the production of both nations' nuclear arsenals. Tensions resurfaced following a Soviet invasion of Afghanistan in late 1979 and early 1980, but by the mid-1980s the East-West dialogue had resumed. The architect of what would be sweeping changes was the new Soviet president, Mikhail Gorbachev; under *glasnost* (candor in admitting problems), Gorbachev began to open the doors of official state secrecy, while his policy of *perestroika* (reforming the economic, political, and social structure) introduced free-market practices to the state-controlled Soviet economy.

By loosening the party's grip on many aspects of Soviet life, Gorbachev inadvertently sparked a reformist wave across the Eastern bloc. Borders were opened, and the Berlin Wall was dismantled by joyous throngs. By 1990 all 15 Soviet republics had declared themselves at least partly autonomous. In the end, the reforms outlived the reformer. In 1991, following a failed military coup by Communist hard-liners that substantially weakened his power, Gorbachev resigned and turned power over to the Russian president Boris Yeltsin.

"A NEW WORLD ORDER"

The collapse of Communism meant that the Cold War was over; in its place, however, arose a number of regional conflicts—Grenada (1983), Lebanon (1982–84), Panama (1989), Somalia (1992), and Haiti (1994–95)—in which the United States involved itself directly, sometimes under the aegis of the United Nations. The greatest test of all came in the summer of 1990, when Iraqi leader Sad-

Global Flash Points
From the Berlin Airlift in 1948 to civil war in Bosnia in 1995, Uncle Sam flexed his military muscle time and again to defend freedom or protect the peace.

▲ *Numerous oil fields* in Kuwait were set afire by Iraqi troops fleeing the Desert Storm attack. In the foreground, an American soldier stands guard.

dam Hussein ordered the invasion of neighboring Kuwait, a major oil-producing nation. In response, U.S. president George Bush assembled a 39-nation coalition, of which 28 nations sent troops to contain the Iraqi threat and force Saddam out of Kuwait. The Persian Gulf War—"Operation Desert Storm"—began on January 17, 1991, with an air attack on Iraqi positions. The 100-hour ground war commenced on February 24 and met little resistance; Bush ended it on February 27. Saddam remained decisively in power.

The victory in the Gulf War left little question as to the importance of American leadership around the world. The United States would again find itself called upon to act as a global watchdog, a role that sometimes earned it mixed reviews. Although the United States stepped into war-torn Bosnia in 1995, the world watched as "ethnic cleansing" recalled the mass murders of the Nazi era. Questions remained as well about the future of Russia, beset by ethnic and economic turmoil, and of China, home to nearly a quarter of the world's people and still under Communist rule.

▲ *The Berlin Wall,* a concrete and barbed-wire barrier that had divided Communist East Berlin from Democratic West Berlin for 28 years, was torn down in November 1989 amid joyful celebrations.

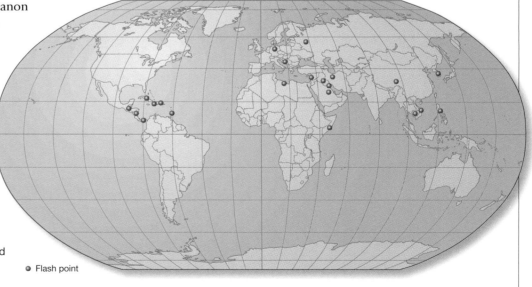

● Flash point

1965

Harvey Oswald, is slain by Jack Ruby. Vice President Lyndon Baines Johnson is sworn in as president.
1965 After Congress passes the Tonkin Gulf Resolution, the first U.S. ground combat troops

are sent to Vietnam to guard U.S. installations.
1967 Washington is the scene of antiwar protests.
1968 Dr. Martin Luther King, Jr., and Robert F. Kennedy are assassinated. At Democratic Convention in Chicago, Vice

1968

President Hubert Humphrey is nominated, despite protests from those supporting antiwar candidate Eugene J. McCarthy. Republican Richard M. Nixon wins the presidential election.

1969

1969 Neil A. Armstrong and Edwin E. Aldrin, Jr., of the U.S. are first men to walk on the moon. President Nixon begins

◄ *Edwin E. Aldrin, Jr.,* takes moon steps as Neil A. Armstrong photographs.

to withdraw U.S. troops from Vietnam.
1970 National Guard units fire on students protesting the Vietnam War at Kent State University in Ohio. Four are killed, and nine are wounded.

The United States at Home

▲ **Levittown,** *a housing devel-opment that began in a potato field on Long Island, New York, in 1946, marked the beginning of the suburban age. Veterans could buy these reasonably priced homes with no down payment.*

▼ **Red Cross nurses** *gave par-enting classes to the increasing population of mothers-to-be. In this 1958 photograph a nurse (using a doll) teaches young women in Queens, New York, how to properly bathe an infant.*

▼ **In 1965 Dr. Martin Luther King, Jr.,** *helped to organize a march from Selma, Alabama, to Montgomery, Alabama, to protest unfair voting barriers for black citizens. Police officers dispersed the protesters with tear gas and clubs. Soon afterward, the Voting Rights Act of 1965 was passed to eradicate voting restrictions.*

From the baby-booming 1950s and the restless '60s and '70s, to the '80s era of excess and the decade before the millennium—no other period of American life has seen such sweeping social, economic, and demographic transformations as the five decades since the end of World War II. At the heart of postwar change was the nation's economic expansion—one of the greatest in world history. Bolstered by an expanded middle class, cities yielded to suburbs— supporting a culture of plenty but leaving some segments of the population behind. African Americans, Hispanics, Asians, and other minorities, long kept on the sidelines of prosperity, would challenge the prevailing social order and stake their rightful claim to the Ameri-can dream, while women would fight for full participa-tion in America's economic and political life. The result was nothing short of a revolution—a reinvention of what it means to be an American.

POSTWAR PROSPERITY

After the war America wasted no time returning to a civilian footing. By the end of 1945, American GI's were stream-ing home at the rate of 1.25 million a month. No event was as important to the postwar era as the "baby boom," a name given to the post–World War II period (1946–64) in which 76 million Americans were born, a period that also encompasses a host of related changes to the American social fabric.

Throughout the 1950s the marriage rate soared, and by 1957 a new baby was born every seven seconds. By decade's end the population had increased by 30 million, becoming the largest single generation in American history.

These new American families lived differently than their parents had. The chief differ-ence was that there were more of them. They were also younger when they mar-ried; the average age at first marriage for men dropped to 22; for women, to 20. But the most significant difference was where these families lived—not in cities or towns but in the new "instant" communities that sprang up in between. Of the 13 million homes built in the 1950s, 11 million had been built on the fringes of city limits across the country.

Suburban life had all the earmarks of the "affluent society." Most suburbanites were middle class and owned their own homes. High employment and elevated wage levels kept consumer confidence high, and this stimulated the economy even more. By 1960, 85 million televi-sion sets were in American homes and three-quarters of the world's automo-biles were owned by Americans.

THE STRUGGLE FOR EQUALITY

Postwar America was on the whole a more affluent America, but pockets of grueling poverty persisted, especially among minorities. Often this was sup-ported by centuries-old strictures that kept nonwhite Americans on the fringes of American life, particularly in the seg-regated South, where African Americans endured withering discrimination in housing, employment, and education.

Perhaps the greatest of all social movements of the period, the civil rights movement of the 1950s and '60s, began in December 1955, when seam-stress Rosa Parks was arrested for refusing to give up her seat in a "whites only" section of a Montgomery, Alabama, city bus. In protest, blacks initiated a 381-day boycott of the bus system. Leading the protest was a charismatic preacher named Dr. Martin Luther King, Jr. In the end, the courts ruled against the bus company.

King's message of nonviolent resis-tance defined the early years of the civil rights movement. Eventually, more mili-tant voices joined the fray and called for revolutionary tactics. During the "long, hot summers" of 1964–68, rioting erupted in dozens of major American cities, including the Watts neighborhood of Los Angeles (1965), Chicago, Cleve-land, San Francisco, Milwaukee (1966), and Newark, Tampa, New York, Boston, Atlanta, and Detroit (1967). In 1968 the movement lost its most eloquent advocate for peaceful protest when King was assassinated in Memphis. This event provoked further violence.

A CRISIS OF LEADERSHIP

The racial turbulence of the 1960s and '70s was mirrored in several other, related social movements, including the antiwar movement, the environmen-tal movement, the feminist movement, the Native American AIM (American Indian Movement), and the Gay Liberation movement. Although each differed, often sharply, in its goals, these movements also shared a deep frustration with the exist-ing social order and a desire for a more just and open society.

1972 President Nixon visits China and U.S.S.R. Five men are arrested for burglarizing Demo-cratic National Commit-tee Headquarters in Watergate complex in Washington, D.C.

1973 The U.S. withdraws last troops from Vietnam. Vice President Spiro Agnew resigns amid charges of tax eva-sion; he is replaced by Gerald Ford.

1974 Under threat of impeachment, Nixon resigns.

1975 North Vietnamese and Vietcong overcome South Vietnam and seize Saigon; U.S. Embassy is evacuated.

1977 The U.S. experiences an "energy crisis." Measures are instituted to con-serve energy.

1978 President Carter arranges peace talks between Egypt and Israel at Camp David; a peace treaty is signed the following year.

1979 In Iran, the U.S. Embassy is stormed, and more than 50 Americans are held hostage for 444 days, following a U.S. decision to admit the deposed shah for med-ical treatment.

1980 Massive eruption of Mount St. Helens vol-cano occurs in state of Washington.

1981 Sandra Day O'Connor becomes first woman to be appointed to Supreme Court. Acquired immune defi-ciency syndrome (AIDS) is identified.

1983 The U.S. sends more than 3,000 troops to

The Progress of Civil Rights

By the mid-1950s black Americans had made some small progress in their effort to win equal status with white Americans. The military was integrated, and the "separate but equal" education law was dismantled in a landmark Supreme Court case, *Brown* v. *the Board of Education of Topeka*. But it took a young minister named Dr. Martin Luther King, Jr., to breathe life into the civil rights movement. King and other activists staged nonviolent protests, including marches and lunch-counter sit-ins. The black struggle was not without bloodshed, however; white opposition was often brutal and sometimes deadly. By the late 1960s the violence was no longer one-sided, as some blacks, notably the Black Panthers, turned to militant movements to promote their cause. Nevertheless, the fruits of the struggle—the Civil Rights Act of 1964, the Voting Rights Act of 1965, and the Fair Housing Act of 1968—were a sweet victory for everyone dedicated to equality.

- ■ Civil rights demonstrations
- ● Riots and urban unrest
- ← Freedom Ride route, 1961

The social movements of the period also shared a general suspicion of government and the nation's leaders, and this mood was exacerbated by the Watergate scandal of the early 1970s. When newspapers reported, in June 1972, that

▲ *The antiwar movement* gained momentum in the 1960s as the Vietnam War escalated. Above, in 1967, a protester faces off members of the National Guard in Washington, D.C.

five men had been caught breaking into the Democratic National Committee's headquarters at the Washington, D.C., complex, few readers could have suspected that this action would eventually topple a presidency. But as the scandal widened, it became increasingly clear that the White House had been directly involved. On August 9, 1974, with impeachment imminent, Richard M. Nixon became the first American president to resign from office.

FROM GURUS TO "THE GIPPER"

Post-Vietnam, post-Watergate America was a nation that seemed, in many ways, less unified and unsure of itself. In response, many Americans turned inward. During the late 1970s charis-

matic Christianity, transcendental meditation, EST, and other spiritual movements drew thousands of new devotees searching for answers. Millions of other Americans donned jogging suits, soaked in hot tubs, danced the night away in discos, and filed for divorce. Some observers hailed the period for its experimental bravery; others scoffed, calling it "the me decade."

The 1980s witnessed yet another swing of the pendulum, politically and culturally. Materialism was on the top of the American agenda; to pilot the nation, Americans elected (in overwhelming numbers) the conservative Republican Ronald Reagan, a former California governor and Hollywood actor. By loosening the reins of federal control and dramatically cutting taxes, Reagan's "trickle-down" economic plan temporarily lifted the economy to new highs, while his conservative social agenda warmed the hearts of white, suburban middle-class Americans. Detractors pointed out that the Reagan economic boom was an illusion, supported by deficit federal spending and leaving most Americans—the poor especially—out in the cold. Every day more Americans were falling below the poverty line, and racial tension was on the increase. But for a while most Americans seemed not to mind. When he left the White House in 1989, "the Gipper" enjoyed one of the highest presidential approval ratings in history.

AMERICA AT THE END OF THE CENTURY

The collapse of the Soviet Union in the late 1980s and early '90s left America the world's military and economic superpower. But it was sharply divided at home. Although the country remained generally prosperous, the gap between rich and poor widened. In the cities 50 years of suburban migration had taken its toll; urban violence skyrocketed, as did racial tension and unrest. In Los Angeles the videotaped beating of black motorist Rodney King, and the subsequent acquittal of the officers involved, sparked the worst race riots since the 1960s. After a brief recession in the early 1990s, the economy roared to life again, but real wages remained stagnant. For the first time since the Great Depression, America's middle class was losing ground.

Yet for all its problems, America remains a nation uniquely endowed. History's greatest experiment in constitutional democracy has grown to become the envy of the world—a global colossus, a nation of nations, and a living monument to the human spirit.

▼ *Trump Tower* in *New York City, built by real estate developer Donald Trump in 1983, epitomized an era of big money. The building's condominiums were bought by celebrities. Its retail space was leased by the most exclusive shops, but by the 1990s many of the upscale stores had failed and were replaced by midpriced establishments.*

1986

Grenada to restore order after a coup and to rescue American medical students.
1986 National Security Adviser John Poindexter and his aide, Oliver North, are implicated in Iran-Contra scandal.

U.S. space shuttle *Challenger* explodes, killing all seven crew members.
1987 A major stock market crash takes place on Wall Street in October.
1989 San Francisco is struck by earthquake measuring 7.1 on the

1990

Richter scale.
The U.S. invades Panama and forces Gen. Manuel Noriega's surrender.
1990 Iraqi president Saddam Hussein invades Kuwait. U.S. troops are sent to Saudi Arabia (Operation

Desert Shield).
1991 U.S. and U.N troops drive Iraqi forces from Kuwait in Operation Desert Storm.
1992 Hurricane Andrew kills 13 people and leaves about 250,000 homeless in southern

1993

Florida and Louisiana.
1993 Six people are killed and more than 1,000 are injured in terrorist bombing of the World Trade Center in New York City.
1994 Los Angeles is struck by earthquake measuring

6.7 on the Richter scale.
1995 The Alfred P. Murrah Federal Building in Oklahoma City is bombed, killing 169 people, in the worst terrorist attack on U.S. soil.
1996 Summer Olympics are held in Atlanta.

Notable Men and Women

America is a land of heroes. In every decade there have been men and women who embody the very best our nation has to offer. The people profiled below represent a sampling of outstanding citizens from all fields of endeavor, whose achievements exemplify the spirit of our nation. They have shown strength in times of adversity, have demonstrated a pioneering spirit, or have found creative solutions to puzzling problems. Whether artist, athlete, or politician; inventor, aviator, or doctor; scientist, businessman, or farmer—their contributions to our nation have helped shape our way of life and enriched our heritage.

▲ Hank Aaron hit his 715th home run in Atlanta Stadium on April 8, 1974.

▲ Abigail Adams was the first First Lady to occupy the current White House.

▲ Susan B. Anthony refused to accept defeat in the battle for a woman's right to vote.

▼ Irving Berlin, who began his musical career singing for pennies on street corners, wrote more than 1,000 songs.

HENRY LOUIS "HANK" AARON (1934–) broke a baseball record many had considered unbreakable: Babe Ruth's lifetime mark of 714 home runs. Aaron spent most of his career with the Milwaukee (later Atlanta) Braves, winning three straight Gold Glove awards for defense. He retired in 1976 with an impressive 755 homers.

ABIGAIL ADAMS (1744–1818), a staunch abolitionist and women's rights advocate, was the wife of John Adams, the second president of the United States, and the mother of John Quincy Adams, the nation's sixth president.

ALVIN AILEY, JR. (1931–1989), a choreographer and the founder of the Alvin Ailey American Dance Theater, brought a new form and meaning to modern dance, often choreographing his pieces to black folk music and jazz.

MARIAN ANDERSON (1902–1993), a contralto, was the first black singer to appear with New York City's Metropolitan Opera. She struck the right note for racial harmony on Easter Sunday 1939, when she sang on the steps of the Lincoln Memorial in Washington, D.C. Several weeks earlier, the Daughters of the American Revolution (DAR) had refused to allow her to perform in nearby Constitution Hall, which the DAR owned.

SUSAN B. ANTHONY (1820–1906), one of the founders of the American woman suffrage movement, labored ceaselessly for women's rights. Her efforts paid off in 1920, when the states ratified the 19th Amendment, which Congress had passed in 1919, giving women the right to vote.

LOUIS ARMSTRONG (1900–1971) virtually defined jazz during the years when it became America's dominant musical form. "Satchmo" was a virtuoso trumpeter whose recordings with his "Hot Five" and "Hot Seven" combos during the 1920s and '30s set a standard rarely equaled. In later years he performed around the world and was famed for his rich, gravelly vocals.

NEIL ARMSTRONG (1930–), an astronaut, became the first person to walk on the moon on July 20, 1969. On first touching the lunar surface, he gave a brief testimonial to a monumental feat, words that would become a permanent part of America's collective memory. Said Armstrong to a worldwide audience of millions, "That's one small step for a man, one giant leap for mankind." Armstrong received the Presidential Medal of Freedom in 1969.

JOHN JAMES AUDUBON (1785–1851), an artist and ornithologist, was famed for his paintings of birds. Discouraged about the prospects for publication of a bird book in the United States, Audubon went to England. His work *Birds of America* was originally published there in a four-volume set.

JAMES BALDWIN (1924–1987), a writer and interpreter of the struggles of African-Americans, was born in New York City's Harlem. Baldwin's first published novel, *Go Tell It on the Mountain*, appeared in 1953. With the release of a book of short stories and the 1962 novel *Another Country*, he established himself as a leading black spokesman and a major figure in American literature.

LUCILLE BALL (1911–1989) combined a talent for slapstick, exaggerated facial expressions, and surefire comic delivery to create the classic television program *I Love Lucy*, which ran from 1951 to 1957 and remains in syndication. With her "Lucy" co-star and real-life husband, Desi Arnaz, the onetime movie comedienne also produced other hit programs in the 1950s and '60s.

CLARA BARTON (1821–1912), founder of the American Red Cross, began her career as a teacher. During the Civil War, Barton carried supplies to soldiers on the front lines and nursed the wounded, who hailed her as the "Angel of the Battlefield."

Alexander Graham Bell

ALEXANDER GRAHAM BELL (1847–1922) was a Scottish immigrant whose work with the deaf led him to study the mechanics of sound waves. In 1876 his research resulted in the transmission of human speech over wires—the first telephone. He established the Bell Telephone Company in 1877; later he was instrumental in founding the National Geographic Society and served as its president from 1896 to 1904.

John James Audubon

JACK BENNY (1894–1974) used a squeaky violin and a fictional age—39—as gimmicks in one of America's longest-running comic routines. Millions who tuned in to Benny's 1932–55 radio show and 1950–65 television program loved his wry, deadpan portrayal of a vain skinflint who tortured the violin. In real life Benny was self-effacing, generous, and an accomplished violinist.

IRVING BERLIN (1888–1989), who wrote the music and lyrics for such beloved works as "God Bless America" and "White Christmas," never learned to read or write musical notation. Berlin composed Broadway show tunes and movie scores, including music for Fred Astaire-Ginger Rogers films of the 1920s and '30s. "There's No Business Like Show Business" was a hit as soon as Ethel Merman belted it out, in 1947.

ALEXANDER CALDER (1898–1976), an internationally recognized artist, became famous as a pioneer of kinetic art. A contemporary artist, Marcel Duchamp, coined the term *mobile* to describe Calder's moving sculptures, which are powered by air currents; the artist Jean Arp coined the term *stabile* for Calder's static artwork.

ANDREW CARNEGIE (1835–1919), a steel manufacturer, believed that the rich are obliged to give away their wealth, and he did just that. He founded institutions devoted to education and world peace and funded some 2,500 public libraries. New York's Music Hall became Carnegie Hall in 1898 in gratitude for his largesse.

Andrew Carnegie

GEORGE WASHINGTON CARVER (1864–1943), born a slave in Missouri, achieved international recognition for his agricultural research. Among the more than 300 products that he made from peanuts were a milk substitute, soap, and printer's ink. In 1896 he became head of the agriculture department at the Tuskegee Institute in Alabama, where he worked on improving the South's farming practices.

CESAR CHAVEZ (1927–1993) gave new hope and dignity to America's neglected migrant farmworkers. Focusing on the table-grape industry, in the 1960s Chavez directed a nationwide boycott against growers, winning recognition of his United Farm Workers Union. American-born but of Mexican descent, Chavez was the first great champion of previously voiceless Latino agricultural laborers.

CRAZY HORSE (1844?–1877), the implacable chief of the Oglala Sioux, spent his life defending the northern Great Plains from white encroachment. His guerrilla campaigns culminated in the 1876 Battle of the Little Bighorn, in which he joined Sitting Bull in annihilating Lt. Col. George Custer and his 7th Cavalry. A year later Crazy Horse was killed while in army custody.

DAVID "DAVY" CROCKETT (1786–1836), a frontier soldier and politician, rose to prominence in Tennessee during the 1820s on the strength of his wit and carefully cultivated bear-and-Indian-fighting persona. After a stint in Congress, Crockett headed for Texas, where he died defending the Alamo during the Texans' 1836 bid for independence from Mexico.

JOHN DEWEY (1859–1952) is regarded as the founder of the progressive-education movement in the United States. A philosopher associated with the theory of pragmatism, Dewey argued that students were not just empty vessels to be filled with facts; instead, he maintained, the schools' role was to give students the tools to grow and the ability to solve problems so that they could lead productive lives.

EMILY DICKINSON (1830–1886), one of America's most brilliant and prolific poets, wrote more than 1,700 poems. Ironically, less than a dozen of these works were published in her lifetime, and those poems that were printed appeared anonymously. In her poetry, she embraced life with gusto; however, the reclusive Dickinson was so shy that for years she rarely left her father's house in Amherst, Massachusetts.

WALT DISNEY (1901–1966) mastered the emerging art of animation to populate movie screens with such lovable characters as Mickey Mouse and Donald Duck. Moving from his "Silly Symphony" series to full-length animated features, Disney changed the film industry. Enduring testimonies of his success are theme parks on three continents and the entertainment conglomerate that bears his name.

FREDERICK DOUGLASS (1817–1895), an abolitionist, orator, and author, published his autobiography, *Narrative of the Life of Frederick Douglass,* in 1845. Born a slave, Douglass became the leading spokesman in the 1800s for the abolition of slavery and the rights of black Americans.

AMELIA EARHART (1898–1937), who in 1932 became the first woman to fly across the Atlantic Ocean alone, was also the first woman to receive the Distinguished Flying Cross. In 1937 Earhart's plane disappeared during an attempted flight around the world.

GEORGE EASTMAN (1854–1932), a businessman and inventor, revolutionized the field of photography. Eastman's low-cost, easy-to-operate camera and its paper-backed flexible roll of film eliminated the need for glass plates, making it possible for amateur photographers to shoot pictures for the first time.

Thomas Edison

THOMAS ALVA EDISON (1847–1931) was a brilliant inventor whose greatest achievements included the invention of the electric lightbulb and the phonograph. Edison also helped to found the motion picture industry and improved the telegraph and telephone.

ALBERT EINSTEIN (1879–1955) set the course of modern physics with his 1905 special theory of relativity. Einstein challenged Newtonian physics through investigation of the relationships among light, gravity, matter, and time; mass and energy, he showed, were two sides of the same coin. Pacifist Einstein helped make possible the atomic bomb, fearing that Hitler might develop the weapon first.

EDWARD KENNEDY "DUKE" ELLINGTON (1899–1974), a bandleader, composer, and pianist, took jazz from its boisterous roots and gave it a sophisticated big-band sheen—all without sacrificing the music's soul and rhythmic drive. A brilliant arranger, Ellington and his bands performed on many of the world's top concert stages.

RALPH WALDO EMERSON (1803–1882) was trained for the ministry but earned fame as a poet, essayist, and lecturer. He was the key figure in transcendentalism, a philosophy proclaiming the essential oneness of God, man, and nature. Emerson had a profound influence on Henry David Thoreau, Nathaniel Hawthorne, Herman Melville, and other writers of his time.

JOHN ENDERS (1897–1985), a microbiologist, helped develop vaccines for polio, typhus, and measles. In 1954 he shared the Nobel Prize in physiology or medicine with two other researchers.

WILLIAM FAULKNER (1897–1962) was a Mississippi author whose novels are imbued with the South's small-town traditions, complex family relationships, and tragic mythology. Master of a richly evocative if sometimes opaque prose style, Faulkner won the 1949 Nobel Prize for literature and two Pulitzer prizes.

GERALDINE FERRARO (1935–) broke the gender barrier at the highest levels of American politics in 1984, when she was chosen as running mate by Democratic presidential nominee Walter Mondale. The first female vice-presidential candidate was a former New York City prosecutor and a three-term congresswoman. The Democrats lost the election to incumbent Ronald Reagan that year.

F. SCOTT FITZGERALD (1896–1940) was the master chronicler of the Jazz Age. Acclaimed at 23 for his first novel, *This Side of Paradise,* Fitzgerald was at the center of the "Lost Generation" whirlwind of expatriates in Paris. His 1925 masterpiece, *The Great Gatsby,* captured the fast living, nervous energy, and unfulfilled promise of his era.

REV. EDWARD FLANAGAN (1886–1948), an Irish-born Catholic priest, believed that there are "no bad boys." He proved it thousands of times over at Boys Town, the self-governing rehabilitative community for homeless and wayward boys he founded in 1917 near Omaha, Nebraska.

HENRY FORD (1863–1947) did more to change the lifestyle of Americans than perhaps anyone else by making cars widely available. His major contribution to the auto industry was overseeing the development of the assembly line.

STEPHEN FOSTER (1826–1864) became America's favorite pre–Civil War songwriter. His music was wildly popular at a time when the only way songs reached the public was through sales of sheet music and live performances. Foster's most enduring songs include "Oh Susanna," "Swanee River," and "Jeanie With the Light Brown Hair."

BENJAMIN FRANKLIN (1706–1790) was a publisher, autobiographer, amateur scientist, and Philadelphia civic leader who participated in the debates leading to the founding of the United States. He also had a long career as a diplomat in France. His inventions include the lightning rod, bifocals, and the Franklin stove.

BETTY FRIEDAN (1921–) fired one of the opening salvos of the modern feminist movement with her 1963 book, *The Feminine Mystique.* To women boxed in by definitions like "wife" and "mother," she recommended seeking new identities and fulfillment through meaningful work.

ROBERT FROST (1874–1963) was a poet whose style reflected the tart, utilitarian speech of the New England Yankees among whom he lived and farmed as a young man.

▲ *Frederick Douglass, a spellbinding orator, decried the injustices of slavery in his lectures and in the newspaper he edited.*

▲ *William Faulkner often told one story from several characters' points of view.*

▲ *Stephen Foster, the most popular songwriter of his day, died forlorn and penniless.*

▼ *Amelia Earhart's uncompleted last flight may forever remain shrouded in mystery.*

▲ *Patrick Henry* exhorted the 13 Colonies to declare themselves a sovereign nation.

▲ *Geronimo* eluded capture for years, using the Sierra Madre as his hilly hideout.

▲ *Helen Keller*, a remarkable role model, overcame twin handicaps: blindness and deafness.

▼ *Martha Graham* used bold costumes and expressive gestures to enhance her dance vocabulary.

He used simple country images to confront both the serious dramas and the small dilemmas of everyday life.

WILLIAM H. GATES (1955–) is the developer and marketer of the software that operates more than three-quarters of the world's computers. Gates founded the Microsoft Corporation with his childhood friend Paul Allen in 1975; within a half dozen years, Microsoft's MS-DOS operating system was an industry standard. By the age of 40, Gates had amassed the largest personal fortune in the world.

LOU GEHRIG (1903–1941), the "Iron Horse" of the New York Yankees, played in 2,130 consecutive games, a record that stood for more than 50 years. In his 15-year career—tragically cut short in 1939 by the neurological disorder that now bears his name—he batted .340 and hit a record 23 grand slams.

GERONIMO (1829–1909) as a young man saw his family killed by Mexican troops; later, the Apache warlord became a scourge of whites on both sides of the border. Before he surrendered in 1886, Geronimo gained renown as a symbol of resistance to the confinement of Native Americans on reservations.

GEORGE GERSHWIN (1898–1937), a songwriter, pianist, and composer, rose to fame with Broadway musicals that included *Funny Face* and *Girl Crazy*. Perhaps his best-known orchestral piece is *Rhapsody in Blue*. His *Porgy and Bess* became the most popular opera ever written by an American.

JOHN GLENN (1921–) was the first astronaut to orbit the earth, on February 20, 1962. Elected to four terms as a U.S. senator from Ohio, Glenn was a candidate for the 1984 Democratic presidential nomination.

CHARLES GOODYEAR (1800–1860), using the substance called India Rubber, accidentally discovered the vulcanization process that made rubber useful for hundreds of industrial products. Some of these, such as automobile tires, were not even invented until well after Goodyear's death.

BILLY GRAHAM (1918–) adapted 19th-century camp-meeting revivalism to the age of radio and television. Graham has taken his staunch evangelical Protestantism around the globe. His popularity and moral authority have made him an unofficial spiritual adviser to U.S. presidents.

MARTHA GRAHAM (1893–1991) gave impetus to the modern dance movement. As a dancer and choreographer, she used her art to express deeply felt emotions. She alternated abstract and abrupt movements with sensuous and fluid dance patterns.

ALEXANDER HAMILTON (1755–1804), a lawyer who served in George Washington's Cabinet as the first U.S. secretary of the treasury, established a national fiscal system. A brilliant leader with a self-destructive bent, Hamilton was killed in a duel with his longtime political foe, Aaron Burr.

OSCAR HAMMER-STEIN II (1895–1960), who wrote the librettos and lyrics for many successful American musicals, first teamed up with Richard Rodgers in 1943 to work on *Oklahoma!*, which became a smash hit. The two went on to write eight other hit musicals together.

JOHN HANCOCK (1737–1793), the president of the Second Continental Congress, is best known as the first person to sign the Declaration of Independence. He later became the first governor of Massachusetts, serving for nine terms.

WILLIAM RANDOLPH HEARST (1863–1951) built a publishing empire on sensationalism, nationalism, and a zeal for reform that was later transformed into archconservatism. Unsuccessful in a bid for the presidency and in New York politics, Hearst in later years spent lavishly on his California estate at San Simeon. He was the model for the newspaper tycoon in Orson Welles's film *Citizen Kane*.

Ernest Hemingway

ERNEST HEMINGWAY (1899–1961), a novelist, short-story writer, and journalist, transformed American literature with his lean, unornamented prose style and his "Hemingway hero"—a man whose adherence to a stoic code helps overcome both physical and mental adversity. A lifelong outdoorsman, Hemingway created a cult of the macho man. *The Sun Also Rises* and *For Whom the Bell Tolls* are among the novels that earned him the Nobel Prize.

PATRICK HENRY (1736–1799), an eminent orator and statesman during the Revolutionary War period, is best remembered for his declaration "Give me liberty or give me death!" in support of independence from England. Henry became governor of the new Commonwealth of Virginia in 1776.

OLIVER WENDELL HOLMES, JR. (1841–1935), one of the greatest and most esteemed Supreme Court justices, was appointed by President Theodore Roosevelt in 1902. Although many of Holmes's most notable opinions were written as dissents, he was still extremely influential in shaping the conscience of the Court.

Oliver Wendell Holmes, Jr.

WINSLOW HOMER (1836–1910), a self-taught artist whose work is revered for its truthfulness and simplicity, is acclaimed for his paintings of the sea, including *The Gulf Stream* and *Northeaster*.

HARRY HOUDINI (1874–1926), born Erich Weiss, was the greatest of all escape-artist showmen. Chains, handcuffs, straitjackets, strongboxes, even underwater bondage—nothing could hold the deft, agile, and superbly fit Houdini. Contemptuous of those who claimed a link with the occult, Houdini worked hard to debunk spiritualist mediums.

ELIAS HOWE (1819–1867), an inventor, was responsible for introducing the first practical sewing machine, which sewed 250 stitches a minute. He patented his idea in 1846.

HENRY JAMES (1843–1916) was arguably the supreme recorder—and critic—of the mores and manners of polite Victorian society. His famously circuitous prose provides a dense framework for his social and psychological observations. Although James spent the latter half of his life in England, the native of New York City set many of his novels in America.

JOHN JAY (1745–1829), appointed the first chief justice of the U.S. Supreme Court in 1789, negotiated the Jay Treaty in 1794, which resolved post–Revolutionary War disputes on borders and commerce between the United States and England. After serving on the Court, Jay was elected governor of New York.

MARY HARRIS "MOTHER" JONES (1830–1930), an important figure in the U.S. labor movement, helped to organize unions, mostly among coal miners. Jones fought for better working conditions, higher wages, shorter hours, and the workers' right to strike.

MICHAEL JORDAN (1963–), called "Air Jordan" for his apparent defiance of gravity on the basketball court, has done more than anyone else to make his sport perhaps America's favorite game. Jordan has led the Chicago Bulls to five NBA championships while claiming four Most Valuable Player titles.

HELEN KELLER (1880–1968), an author and lecturer, grew up blind and deaf. With the help of teacher Anne Sullivan, she learned to read and write and later to speak. Keller earned a college degree and devoted her life to increasing the rights of handicapped people.

MARTIN LUTHER KING, JR.

(1929–1968), a clergyman and civil rights leader, was revered—and demonized—for leading nonviolent civil rights demonstrations. He won the Nobel Peace Prize in 1964. Immortalized by the speech he delivered after a massive march on Washington, D.C., in which he spoke the words "I have a dream," King was assassinated in Memphis, Tennessee, on April 4, 1968.

RAY KROC (1902–1984), who sold milkshake machines to restaurants and diners, took a look at postwar America and saw that it needed food—not just any food but fast food. He bought franchise rights from two brothers named McDonald, who ran a California hamburger restaurant. In 1955 Kroc began to stamp the golden arches onto the national consciousness. That was some 100 billion burgers ago.

ROBERT E. LEE (1807–1870) emerged from the Civil War a hero among victors and vanquished alike. Offered the command of Union forces at the outset of the war, General Lee instead chose loyalty to his native Virginia. Resourceful and imaginative, loved and respected by his men, the man who became the top Confederate commander worked wonders with limited resources and promoted reconciliation after the South's defeat.

MERIWETHER LEWIS (1774–1809) and **WILLIAM CLARK** (1770–1838), army officers, led the first comprehensive exploration of the American West. Sent by President Thomas Jefferson in 1804 to scout the territory obtained in the 1803 Louisiana Purchase, their party traced the Missouri River to its source, traversed the Rockies, and followed the Columbia River to the Pacific. Their journals documented the continent's immense size and the variety of its native inhabitants, flora, and fauna.

ABRAHAM LINCOLN (1809–1865) was the prairie lawyer whose fate was to preserve the American republic in its darkest hour. His Civil War leadership incorporated military savvy, political skill, and masterful oratory. Lincoln overcame a lack of political experience and bouts of severe depression to emerge as a great moral leader. His stewardship confirmed the supremacy of the national government over states' rights. The commitment Lincoln had made to a just reconstruction was largely abandoned after his assassination, just weeks before the war's end.

HENRY ROBINSON LUCE

(1898–1967) laid the foundation of his publishing empire with *Time* magazine (1923), later adding a business journal called *Fortune* and embracing photojournalism with *Life*. Luce's publications reflected his enthusiastic Americanism and staunch anti-Communism; during his tenure, magazine articles seamlessly blended reporting and editorial opinion.

DOUGLAS MACARTHUR

(1880–1964), the Allied supreme commander of U.S. Army forces in the southwest Pacific during World War II, was among the greatest of American soldiers. He fulfilled a promise to liberate the Philippines, accepted Japan's surrender, and, as American occupation chief, engineered Japan's democratization. Removed from a controversial Korean War command by President Harry S. Truman, he retired with five-star honors.

WILLIAM WORRALL MAYO

(1819–1911) was an English-born, American-trained physician who with his surgeon sons William James and Charles Horace Mayo founded the Mayo Clinic in Rochester, Minnesota. A frontier physician who helped organize the Minnesota Territory, Mayo merged the healing practices of the country doctor with the scientific knowledge of the modern medical specialist.

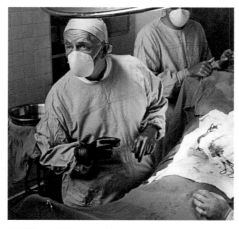

William Worrall Mayo

CYRUS MCCORMICK (1809–1884) revolutionized the harvesting of grain at a time when the Midwestern prairies were becoming the breadbasket of the world. Beginning with a primitive model in 1831, McCormick introduced a series of horse-drawn mechanical reapers that made the scythe obsolete.

MARGARET MEAD (1901–1978) saw the emerging science of anthropology come of age, largely through her own work of exploring cultural influences on personality development. Her research among South Pacific islanders focused on sex roles, adolescence, and interaction with the environment—topics she also explored in her books and lectures on American society and culture.

Margaret Mead

H. L. MENCKEN (1880–1956), the so-called Sage of Baltimore, was the preeminent American literary and social critic of the early 20th century. Through his *Baltimore Sun* newspaper columns and editorship of *Smart Set* and *The American Mercury* magazines, Mencken pilloried parochial tastes in literature, religion, and morality. His book *The American Language* remains perhaps the finest study of our native tongue.

MARGARET MITCHELL

(1900–1949) wrote just one book—a 1,000-page fictional account of her native South in the days of slavery, Civil War, and Reconstruction—yet *Gone With the Wind* remains a best-selling novel, still in print more than 60 years after its debut. The story of the fiery Scarlett O'Hara and the dashing Rhett Butler has become part of American popular culture.

J. P. MORGAN (1837–1913) symbolized Wall Street's enormous power in the winner-take-all business environment of the late 19th century. An investment banker with a genius for reorganization, Morgan put railroads and industrial corporations on a sound footing and aided the U.S. government during financial panics. The rare books and manuscripts he collected are preserved at New York's Morgan Library.

GRANDMA MOSES (1860–1961), born Anna Mary Robertson, took up painting at the age of 78, after a lifetime of farming. Working in the primitive style of an earlier era, Grandma Moses was discovered by the sophisticated art community, and her innocent portrayals of 19th-century rural life received widespread exposure.

JOHN MUIR (1838–1914), a Scottish-born naturalist, had a radical idea—wild places deserve saving for their own sake. Muir left two durable monuments to his abiding love of the great outdoors: the Sierra Club, which he founded in 1892, and the U.S. National Park system, formally organized in 1890, largely as a result of his campaign to save the Yosemite Valley.

EDWARD R. MURROW

(1908–1965) raised radio-news broadcasting to a respected profession. When Murrow covered World War II, the century's biggest story found its greatest reporter. The words "This ... is London" brought the war into American homes. In 1954 his CBS television broadcasts helped topple the demagogue Sen. Joseph McCarthy.

SANDRA DAY O'CONNOR (1930–) breached one of the last domains of male exclusivity in the U.S. government when President Ronald Reagan nominated her to the Supreme Court in 1981. O'Connor maintains a center-right position, moderate on many social issues but conservative on judicial activism.

▲ *The Reverend Martin Luther King, Jr., was a voice of moderation among civil rights leaders.*

▲ *H. L. Mencken was astute and witty but could be savagely scathing to his foes.*

▲ *William Clark, a cartographer and artist, was an ideal partner for Meriwether Lewis.*

▲ *Jesse Owens's* Olympic victory was especially dramatic, with prewar Germany touting so-called Aryan superiority.

▲ *Elvis Presley* rocketed to fame and fortune.

▲ *Sally Ride,* a space pioneer, paved the way for other female astronauts.

▲ *Sacagawea,* the Native American who traveled with Lewis and Clark, as an artist envisioned her.

JESSE OWENS (1913–1980) ran circles around Nazi notions of racial superiority when the African-American athlete won four gold medals in track and field at the 1936 Olympic Games, hosted by Adolf Hitler in Berlin. A record-breaking college star, Owens was repeatedly a victim of racial prejudice, but in the 1960s black activists criticized him for his conservative stance on political issues.

ROBERT E. PEARY (1856–1920), an engineer and naval officer, devoted his life to seeking the North Pole. On his third attempt, in 1909, he achieved his goal of absolute north. His imprecise recordkeeping and a rival's claim to have reached the pole a year earlier have clouded Peary's accomplishment, although it is accepted by most authorities that his claim is authentic.

COLE PORTER (1893–1964) was the epitome of the golden age of American song. Equally gifted as a composer and wordsmith, he combined captivating melodies with superbly crafted lyrics noted for their dry wit and café-society sophistication. His repertoire includes "Night and Day," "Anything Goes," "Begin the Beguine," and "I've Got You Under My Skin."

ELVIS PRESLEY (1935–1977) fused white Southern-ballad and black rhythm-and-blues traditions to become the first star of a new musical genre called rock and roll. An electrifying stage performer, the young Presley personified restlessness and rebellion; later he found a tamer niche in film roles and nightclubs. Since his death in 1977, Presley continues to be venerated by his many fans as "The King." Graceland, his Memphis mansion, has become a major tourist attraction.

JOSEPH PULITZER (1847–1911) almost singlehandedly created the modern newspaper as a vehicle for fact, opinion, community service, and mass advertising. Through his *St. Louis Post-Dispatch* and *New York World,* the Hungarian-born Pulitzer relentlessly pursued reform yet never shrank from tabloid sensationalism, particularly in his rivalry with publisher William Randolph Hearst. His will endowed the Pulitzer Prize, which is given annually to journalists, authors, playwrights, and composers.

SALLY RIDE (1951–) was the first American woman astronaut. Dr. Ride, who holds a Ph.D. in physics, joined the National Aeronautics and Space Administration (NASA) in 1978 and made the first of her two space shuttle flights in June 1983 as a mission specialist, monitoring experiments and helping launch communications satellites. After leaving NASA, Dr. Ride became director of the California Space Institute at the University of California at San Diego.

JOHN RINGLING (1866–1936) was the youngest of five brothers who founded a traveling circus in 1884. Ringling was instrumental in the purchase of the competing Barnum & Bailey Circus. After 1919 the combined troupes billed themselves as "The Greatest Show on Earth." The circus tycoon completed the Ringling Museum of Art in Sarasota, Florida, in 1930.

JACKIE ROBINSON (1919–1972) faced with dignity and poise the tremendous pressure of being Major League baseball's first black player. A college athlete and Negro Leagues talent, Robinson was chosen by Brooklyn Dodgers president Branch Rickey to break baseball's color barrier.

NORMAN ROCKWELL (1894–1978) was an illustrator without peer in capturing the way Americans like to see themselves. Centered around more than 300 covers for *The Saturday Evening Post,* his career celebrated the whimsy and poignancy of everyday life; paintings such as World War II's *The Four Freedoms* put a human face on abstractions.

WILL ROGERS (1879–1935) was a homespun philosopher who proclaimed that "I never met a man I didn't like." Americans liked the part-Cherokee Oklahoma native, who parlayed a rope-twirling-cowboy act into careers as a vaudevillian, radio and film star, and newspaper columnist. Rogers aimed his gentle humor at Jazz Age and Depression-era foibles.

CHARLES M. RUSSELL (1864–1926) painted an American West that he knew firsthand. Heading out to the Montana Territory at 16, Russell hunted, worked as a cowboy, and lived with the Indians. Laced with humor and pathos, his paintings and sculptures depict a struggle with an uncompromising land. Unlike Frederic Remington, an artist who was his contemporary, Russell portrayed Westerners as survivors, not conquerors.

GEORGE HERMAN "BABE" RUTH (1895–1948) was a Baltimore native who grew up to be the greatest baseball player ever. Powerful, ebullient, and given to gargantuan appetites, Ruth endeared himself to fans during his 1920–35 career with the New York Yankees. A onetime star pitcher for the Boston Red Sox, Ruth set season and lifetime home-run records that stood for decades, as he led the Yankees to league titles and World Series victories.

Babe Ruth

SACAGAWEA (1786?–1884?) was a Shoshone woman who accompanied her husband, Canadian trapper Toussaint Charbonneau, on the Lewis and Clark expedition from 1805 to 1806. Toting her newborn son along with her, Sacagawea proved herself invaluable to the explorers as a translator and intermediary among her own people in the northern Rockies.

JONAS SALK (1914–1995) developed a vaccine against poliomyelitis. A medical researcher at work on a World War II campaign against influenza, Dr. Salk introduced his polio vaccine during the height of the 1950s panic over the paralyzing, sometimes deadly disease. Within a short time, millions of American schoolchildren were immunized. Acclaimed a national hero, he later established the Salk Institute, a medical research facility, and attempted to develop an AIDS vaccine.

ALAN B. SHEPARD, JR. (1923–), a naval officer and test pilot, was one of the seven original astronauts selected in 1959 to head up the nation's new space program. Strapped into a cramped capsule, Shepard became the first American to rocket into space. On May 5, 1961, he reached an altitude of 117 miles on his 15-minute suborbital flight. An Annapolis graduate, Shepard commanded the 1971 *Apollo 14* moon landing and resigned from the astronaut program and from the navy as a rear admiral in 1974.

Alan B. Shepard, Jr.

SITTING BULL (1834?–1890) was a visionary chief of the Hunkpapa Sioux who was instrumental in the annihilation of Lt. Col. George A. Custer and his troops at the Battle of the Little Bighorn on June 25, 1876. Sitting Bull surrendered after living five years in Canada and was killed during a struggle with authorities on the reservation where he was confined.

BENJAMIN SPOCK (1903–1998) wrote one of history's best-selling books, *Baby and Child Care.* Despite occasional complaints that the pediatrician was too permissive, "Look it up in Dr. Spock" has been the response of three generations to child-rearing difficulties.

JOHN STEINBECK (1902–1968) was a Nobel Prize- and Pulitzer Prize-winning novelist whose life in Depression-era California produced tales of gentle whimsy, such as *Cannery Row,* as well as *The Grapes of Wrath,* a story of impoverished migrant farmworkers that Steinbeck shaped into an indignant outcry against social injustice.

JIM THORPE (1888–1953) was an outstanding athlete, excelling in football, baseball, and track. A Native American, he capped a superlative college career with 1912 Olympic decathlon and pentathlon victories. Sadly, he had to forfeit his medals because of prior professional experience; the awards were restored posthumously, however. Thorpe went on to successful careers in professional baseball and football.

HARRIET TUBMAN (1821?–1913), born a slave in Maryland, escaped in 1849 to become a leader in the Underground Railroad, the pre–Civil War system of back roads and safe houses that led fugitive slaves to freedom in the North and in Canada. In 19 missions she liberated more than 300 people from bondage. Tubman later worked to advance the cause of black education.

Harriet Tubman

MARK TWAIN (1835–1910), born Samuel Clemens, was a riverboat pilot, gold prospector, and frontier newspaperman who put the American vernacular to its first great literary test. His humor was ingenuously homespun yet freighted with satire and irony. His characters, notably Huck Finn and his riverboat companion Jim, a slave, spoke volumes about the national character.

CORNELIUS VANDERBILT (1794–1877) started his climb to the top of the transportation industry as a Staten Island ferryman. During his career as a steamship magnate, he dismissed newfangled railroads as "them things that go on land." Deciding after all to invest in the rails in the 1860s, "Commodore" Vanderbilt created a vast empire around his New York Central and became the wealthiest American of his day.

GEORGE WASHINGTON (1732–1799), born to Virginia's plantation gentry, risked life and fortune as the commander of American forces during the War of Independence. Seasoned in the French and Indian War, Washington employed surprise attack and strategic retreat to keep the British off balance. He later refused dictatorial power, instead serving with prudence and integrity as the first U.S. president. Reelected in 1792, Washington declined to hold office after his second term, retiring to his farm at Mount Vernon.

JOHN WAYNE (1907–1979) lent the authority of his looming presence and laconic style to dozens of popular Western and war films. As the tough, take-charge American hero, he became one of Hollywood's most enduring icons, cast in some 200 films in a career that stretched nearly a half century. Wayne, whose first starring role was in John Ford's *Stagecoach* (1939), became an off-camera

John Wayne

supporter of conservative causes and an ardent Vietnam war "hawk."

WALT WHITMAN (1819–1892) put lyric poetry to a heroic task: singing the mythic unity of body and soul, life and death, the individual and the democratic ideal. *Leaves of Grass,* which was revised throughout his lifetime, is his poetic monument, a statement of his transcendent yet sensual attachment to the world.

ELI WHITNEY (1765–1825), celebrated as the inventor of the cotton gin, was also important as the developer of a system for manufacturing firearms using interchangeable parts. It was the cotton gin, though, that had enormous socioeconomic repercussions; it made cleaning the crop so easy that the South planted even more cotton, thus reinforcing slavery as an essential element of the plantation economy.

Eli Whitney

FRANK LLOYD WRIGHT (1867–1959), America's most renowned architect, favored open floor plans and the "honest textures" of stone, wood, brick, concrete, and glass. The revolutionary houses of his "Prairie Style" were sheltering horizontal masses that complemented the broad Midwestern earth and sky; in "Fallingwater," in Bear Run, Pennsylvania, Wright integrated a waterfall into the home's design with cantilevered balconies and terraces.

RICHARD WRIGHT (1908–1960), one of America's most distinguished black novelists, wrote *Native Son,* the powerful story of a Chicago youth crushed by racial prejudice and social injustice. Also acclaimed for his vivid autobiographical novel, *Black Boy,* Wright turned to Communism in the 1930s but became disillusioned.

WILBUR WRIGHT (1867–1912) and **ORVILLE WRIGHT** (1871–1948) built the first heavier-than-air craft that worked. Bicycle mechanics who were fascinated with aerodynamics, the brothers experimented with gliders. On December 17, 1903, they achieved flight with a gasoline-powered, propeller-driven airplane at Kitty Hawk, North Carolina.

CHUCK YEAGER (1923–), a decorated World War II fighter pilot, was the first person to travel faster than sound. Flying a Bell X-1 rocket plane, the air force test pilot broke the sound barrier on October 14, 1947. On December 12, 1953, he set a new record of 1,650 miles per hour.

BABE DIDRIKSON ZAHARIAS (1914–1956) was the greatest woman athlete of the 20th century, excelling in track and field, basketball, baseball, and golf. She set world records in javelin and 80-meter hurdles at the 1932 Olympics and was a golf champion in the 1940s.

▲ *Richard Wright's descriptions of racially motivated violence shocked many readers.*

▲ *Frank Lloyd Wright with a model of New York City's cylindrical Guggenheim Museum, which he designed.*

The Presidents of the United States

U.S. presidents have come from all walks of civilian life—farmer, lawyer, salesman, teacher—as well as from the ranks of the military. Whatever their backgrounds, whether their margins of victory were narrow or wide, serving in their nation's highest elected office has often brought out the best in them.

1. George Washington
Apr. 30, 1789–Mar. 3, 1797
2. John Adams
Mar. 4, 1797–Mar. 3, 1801
3. Thomas Jefferson
Mar. 4, 1801–Mar. 3, 1809
4. James Madison
Mar. 4, 1809–Mar. 3, 1817
5. James Monroe
Mar. 4, 1817–Mar. 3, 1825
6. John Quincy Adams
Mar. 4, 1825–Mar. 3, 1829
7. Andrew Jackson
Mar. 4, 1829–Mar. 3, 1837
8. Martin Van Buren
Mar. 4, 1837–Mar. 3, 1841
9. William Henry Harrison
Mar. 4, 1841–Apr. 4, 1841
10. John Tyler
Apr. 6, 1841–Mar. 3, 1845
11. James K. Polk
Mar. 4, 1845–Mar. 3, 1849
12. Zachary Taylor
Mar. 5, 1849–July 9, 1850
13. Millard Filmore
July 10, 1850–Mar. 3, 1853
14. Franklin Pierce
Mar. 4, 1853–Mar. 3, 1857

15. James Buchanan
Mar. 4, 1857–Mar. 3, 1861
16. Abraham Lincoln
Mar. 4, 1861–Apr. 15, 1865
17. Andrew Johnson
Apr. 15, 1865–Mar. 3, 1869
18. Ulysses S. Grant
Mar. 4, 1869–Mar. 3, 1877
19. Rutherford B. Hayes
Mar. 4, 1877–Mar. 3, 1881
20. James A. Garfield
Mar. 4, 1881–Sept. 19, 1881
21. Chester A. Arthur
Sept. 20, 1881–Mar. 3, 1885
22. Grover Cleveland
Mar. 4, 1885–Mar. 3, 1889
23. Benjamin Harrison
Mar. 4, 1889–Mar. 3, 1893
24. Grover Cleveland
Mar. 4, 1893–Mar. 3, 1897
25. William McKinley
Mar. 4, 1897–Sept. 14, 1901
26. Theodore Roosevelt
Sept. 14, 1901–Mar. 3, 1909
27. William H. Taft
Mar. 4, 1909–Mar. 3, 1913
28. Woodrow Wilson
Mar. 4, 1913–Mar. 3, 1921

29. Warren G. Harding
Mar. 4, 1921–Aug. 2, 1923
30. Calvin Coolidge
Aug. 3, 1923–Mar. 3, 1929
31. Herbert C. Hoover
Mar. 4, 1929–Mar. 3, 1933
32. Franklin D. Roosevelt
Mar. 4, 1933–Apr. 12, 1945
33. Harry S. Truman
Apr. 12, 1945–Jan. 20, 1953
34. Dwight D. Eisenhower
Jan. 20, 1953–Jan. 20, 1961
35. John F. Kennedy
Jan. 20, 1961–Nov. 22, 1963
36. Lyndon B. Johnson
Nov. 22, 1963–Jan. 20, 1969
37. Richard M. Nixon
Jan. 20, 1969–Aug. 9, 1974
38. Gerald R. Ford
Aug. 9, 1974–Jan. 20, 1977
39. James Earl Carter
Jan. 20, 1977–Jan. 20, 1981
40. Ronald Reagan
Jan. 20, 1981–Jan. 20, 1989
41. George Bush
Jan. 20, 1989–Jan. 20, 1993
42. Bill Clinton
Jan. 20, 1993–

Thomas Jefferson

Grover Cleveland

Franklin D. Roosevelt

America on the Move

▲ **U.S Route 66,** a 2,400-mile ribbon of highway, once linked Chicago to Los Angeles. Although it was replaced by interstates, segments of the old highway remain.

No other country in the world has transformed itself as the United States has. In little more than two centuries, the nation has grown from a chain of agrarian-based settlements on the Atlantic seaboard to a coast-to-coast network of cities and towns. During that time, America's population has increased more than a hundredfold, and the world's largest economy has been created. This metamorphosis from colonial outpost to superpower is the result of nonstop westward expansion, supported by abundant natural resources, a superior transportation system, industrial ingenuity, and the pursuit of the American Dream.

THE CONTINENT IS OPENED

Americans have always been a mobile people, from the first Pilgrims who crowded aboard tiny wooden ships and sailed across the storm-lashed Atlantic, to the pioneers who pushed through the Western wilderness on foot, by covered wagon, and, later, by railroad.

From the start America needed a unified system of commerce if it was to survive and succeed as a nation. The key to unlocking the door to trade among the original 13 states, as well as opening the vast interior and its bounty of untapped natural resources, was a fully developed transportation system.

Until the early 1800s, trade was restricted to whatever could be carried by flatboats and sailing ships on rivers, lakes, and seas and by pack animals and wagons on rutted dirt trails and roads. With the new century came a technolog-ical revolution in transportation, powered at first by animals and later by steam, petroleum, and electricity.

CANAL TRAVEL

In order to cut the cost of shipping bulk goods, Secretary of the Treasury Albert Gallatin proposed a plan in 1808 to expand the nation's waterways and roads. His scheme included building new roads, improving rivers like the Potomac and the James, and digging a network of canals, including a link between Lake Erie and the Hudson River.

The completion of the 363-mile Erie Canal in 1825 proved to have enormous commercial significance. Because 3,000 boats a year relied on the canal to haul grain and other goods, the more than $7 million it cost was repaid within a decade of its completion. But there were other benefits to the new waterway as well. Freight costs dropped from $100 per ton by wagon to as low as $10 per ton by barge. Passengers traveled for a mere 1½ cents a mile, and the trip took just eight days, instead of the 20 days it had taken by wagon. Not only did the Erie Canal open up the Great Lakes region, but its construction also spurred the building of nearly 4,000 miles of canals in other parts of the country.

STEAMING AHEAD

Even before barges began to travel the Erie Canal, commercial river traffic had been given a huge boost in 1807, when American inventor Robert Fulton proved that his steamboat could operate economically. By 1845 steamboats were in their heyday, chugging along the Mississippi, Missouri, Ohio, Sacramento, and other rivers. The paddle wheelers hauled cotton from Tennessee, iron from Pennsylvania, meat from Ohio, and mining equipment to the goldfields in California. Steamboats also proved to be America's first mass-transit system, ferrying settlers to new territories west of the Appalachians. Some of the vessels were more than just transportation, however. Outfitted with fancy furnishings and art-

▲ **Boats and barges** were pulled along the Erie Canal by horses on towpaths during the early 1800s. The canal was originally built with 18 aqueducts and 83 locks.

▼ **The Santa Fe** was one of four transcontinental rail lines that were built within 30 years of the completion of the first line in 1869. The El Capitan, below, a train powered by a diesel-electric locomotive, ran from Chicago to Los Angeles.

Railroads Link a Sprawling Nation

From 1830, when the first practical steam-powered train made a test run, to 1870, the nation's stock of railroad track soared from almost none to some 53,000 miles. Right: the rail system in 1870.

U.S. Highways

In 1956 Congress authorized the creation of the interstate highway system, the first unified road network linking cities and rural areas from coast to coast. Left: The completion of the last highway in 1992 provided 42,500 miles of roadway.

work, some riverboats were floating hotels that offered the more affluent passengers fine meals, entertainment, and even gambling. By 1855 over 700 riverboats with a combined capacity of more than 170,000 tons were plying the nation's network of navigable waterways.

The steamboat's popularity was short-lived, however, as a cheaper, more reliable use of Fulton's engine was employed to transport goods and people. When it came to changing America and opening new lands to settlers, the train had no rival.

RAILROADS

On Christmas Day 1830, 50 people boarded a train in South Carolina and traveled six miles at speeds of up to 21 miles per hour; with this short trip regularly scheduled passenger train service in the United States was inaugurated. Within three years South Carolina boasted a 135-mile-long railroad, then the longest in the world. Dozens of railroad companies raced to lay track throughout the country. By 1852 rails linked Chicago to the East; eight years later America had more than 30,000 miles of track, nearly as much as the rest of the world combined. On May 10, 1869, in Promontory, Utah, after more than six grueling years of work, the final spike was driven in the nation's first transcontinental railroad track. Overnight, the five-month overland journey across the continent was reduced to eight days. By the end of the 19th century, twin ribbons of steel covered a distance of nearly 200,000 miles.

Trains made the great size of America suddenly seem manageable. Distances between Western mines and Eastern factories no longer appeared so great. Ranchers didn't have to herd their cattle along thousands of miles of trails to deliver them to the Chicago stockyards. And manufacturers found they had a way to distribute their goods to even the most far-flung buyers. These trains did

not just haul goods, however; they also hauled people. With the frontier as close as a few days' ride away, eager settlers poured into the West by the hundreds of thousands.

CAR CULTURE

If you look at a road map of the country today, you'd hardly guess that the network of streets and highways that cover it more intricately than a spider's web is relatively new. In 1904 less than 150 miles of rural roads were paved. By 1920, thanks to manufacturers like Henry Ford and his mass-produced and affordable Model T's, there were more than 9 million motor vehicles in the country. The following year Washington authorized the first system of federally funded roads; in 1924 it established a grid of national highways.

After World War II automobile ownership skyrocketed. Between 1940 and

1960 car registration grew from 27.5 million to 61.5 million. Three out of four American families owned a car in 1960. In 1956 Congress approved the Federal Highway Act, and today there are nearly 4 million miles of paved road in the United States.

Not only has the automobile changed the way Americans live and work, it is also responsible for many distinctive elements of American culture. Suburbs, fast-food restaurants, and traffic jams are all by-products of the automobile.

While the modes of American transportation have evolved over the years, the basic premise remains the same. Waterways and railroads opened the country, and highways helped define it. Today they all help to keep America on the move.

▲ *The car of the future?*
The Bay Area Rapid Transit (BART) electric station car program in San Francisco, California, began testing this non-polluting commuter car in 1995.

◀ *Aviation took off when U.S. airmail delivery began in 1918. By 1957 airplanes carried more people per mile than trains. By the 1960s the roomier interiors and reduced travel time of jet planes made air-freight transport profitable. While the first transcontinental flight in 1930 took 36 hours, the same trip today can take less than 5 hours.*

From Agriculture to Industry

The United States began as a nation of farmers. The original 13 Colonies were founded and populated by people who established small farming communities as well as towns that served as trading posts and service centers. As more pioneers moved west and other parts of the country were settled, the pattern was duplicated. American culture continued to be dominated by family-farm life well into the 1800s. After the Civil War the mass-production techniques used to manufacture battle materials were combined with technological innovations to move America into the modern Industrial Age.

▲ *Apple production* in the United States has nearly doubled in the past quarter century. Almost half of the nation's apples come from Washington State. New York and Michigan alternate as the second- and third-largest producers of apples. The only country that grows more apples than the United States is China.

WESTWARD HO!

Tales of America's abundant farmland were not lost on people living on the other side of the Atlantic. The dream of owning land drew immigrants to this country like moths to a beacon. The hunger for land among the new arrivals appeared insatiable, and it triggered an enormous migration westward.

Settlers cultivated vast portions of the continent's interior, and soon regions became known for their crops. Virginia was famous for its tobacco; the Southern states, for cotton. New York grew apples and grapes. The Midwestern states raised corn and wheat. Citrus fruit came from the sunny climes of Florida and California, and lumber from the virgin forests of the Pacific Northwest.

With such new farm implements as Eli Whitney's cotton gin, invented in 1793, and Cyrus McCormick's grain reaper, patented in 1834, the nation's farmers boosted their output considerably, while improvements in river and rail transportation brought the crops to market cheaply and easily. As a result, by 1850 the United States had become one of the world's leading agricultural nations.

THE RISE OF INDUSTRY

Agriculture remained the backbone of the U.S. economy until the end of the Civil War. At that point the nation's industrial base turned dramatically from cottage industries and small textile factories to large manufacturing plants producing steel and heavy machinery.

When the war broke out, the Northern states had already begun to industrialize. In fact, the War Between the States was mostly a conflict over maintaining a traditional agrarian economy, which was based on slave labor, or supporting an economy based on industry, which would be automated and mechanized.

After the South surrendered in 1865, the fervor that had gone into the mass production of war materials, such as weapons, food, and transportation for the soldiers, was diverted elsewhere. Developments in agricultural production and transportation were combined with raw materials, technological innovations, a huge pool of labor, and large-scale capital investment to further modernize industry.

INCREASED PRODUCTIVITY

Over the next three decades, American industry expanded greatly. Between 1860 and 1890 coal production increased more than tenfold; iron production, nearly elevenfold. Steel production grew from less than 1 million tons in 1879 to more than 4 million tons in 1890. In a mere 15 years, between 1877 and 1892, the nation's factories tripled their output. By 1890 the United States had become the world's agricultural leader; by 1914 it was the leading industrial power as well.

Innovations were made and machines were invented that completely changed the way Americans lived. The typewriter was invented in 1867. In 1876 Alexander Graham Bell patented the telephone. By 1878 Western Union had strung nearly 200,000 miles of telegraph lines across the country. Thomas A. Edison perfected the incandescent lightbulb in 1879; three years later he built the nation's first central electric power station. And in the 1890s America began to manufacture its first automobiles.

MASS PRODUCTION

The industrial boom continued throughout the 20th century. Automobile maker Henry Ford revolutionized the world with his pioneering concept of mass production, and the assembly line was soon being used to make a host of other durable consumer goods.

Small factories gave way to corporate enterprises that made many different products at various locations. Corporations hired workers by the thousands. Assembly-line work enabled factories to produce goods cheaply and quickly. Faster and cheaper meant lower prices; lower prices meant more buyers; and more buyers meant higher sales.

The period following World War II saw more emphasis on sophisticated technology, skilled workers, and scientific research and development, especially in the fields of chemical and electronics production. Later in the century computers and biotechnology came to the fore of American industry. Just as certain regions within the country had

▲ *Modern commercial dairy farms,* such as this one, often have more than 1,000 cows.

▼ *The McCormick reaper* allowed farmers to harvest more than 10 acres of grain in one day. Using a cradle scythe, a farmer could harvest just two or three acres. In the 1920s reapers were replaced by combines (harvester-threshers).

▲ *An early-1900s blast furnace* at the Bethlehem Steel Corporation's plant in Lackawanna, New York. Iron made in blast furnaces is used to produce steel.

▲ *A post–World War II appliance assembly line* in Chicago. Many munitions factories were converted to make consumer products like these ranges.

become known for particular crops, they now became synonymous with the industries they supported. Pittsburgh became home to the largest steel industry in the nation. Detroit became "Motor City," the center for automobile production. Seattle dominated the airplane industry. The movie industry resided in Hollywood, and Silicon Valley nurtured the growth of electronic technology.

MORE CITIES

With the rapid rise of industrialization, the American way of life shifted dramatically. The new factories were drawing people from rural areas to cities in record numbers. Prior to 1870 nearly 75 percent of the population lived in rural areas. By 1916 only half did. The trend continued, until by the late 1980s the nation's entire farm population was just 5 million, or approximately 2 percent of the total. The number of urban areas increased dramatically as a result. The U.S. government defines an urban area as having at least 2,500 people. When the first census was taken in 1790, there were only 24 such areas. By 1890 there were 1,351, and by 1990 there were 8,510.

The growth in population changed the character of America's big cities. Places that were once distinct soon merged with their neighbors to create sprawling metropolitan regions. The small-town way of life that characterized America for much of its history eventually gave way to a complex social system that brought with it a host of opportunities as well as problems. Economic inequality, racial strife, overburdened social services, and job-related stress are just a few of the costs of America's industrialized economy.

Personal Income Nationwide

In 1996 Connecticut ranked number one in the United States in income per person: $28,389. Missouri took middle place ($20,816), and Mississippi came in last with $13,680 per person.

▲ *The Boeing 747,* the world's first jumbo jet, was introduced in 1970. The smaller Boeing 777, which has operated since 1995, has a more spacious interior and is more fuel-efficient.

▲ *The computer industry* has grown by leaps and bounds since the late 1970s. The United States has more computers than any other country. Above, a computer circuit board.

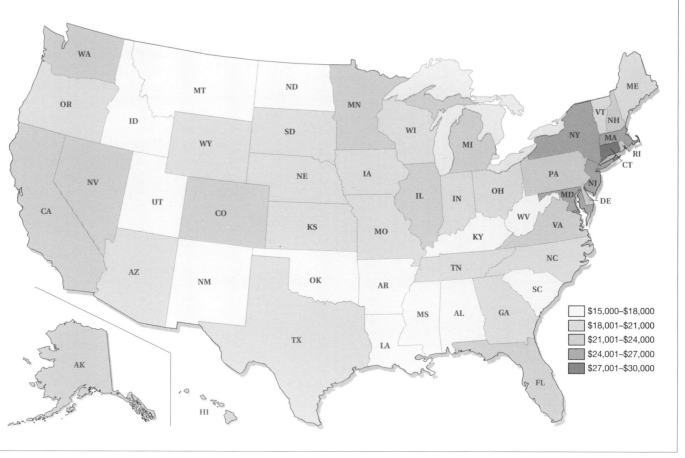

$15,000–$18,000
$18,001–$21,000
$21,001–$24,000
$24,001–$27,000
$27,001–$30,000

The Changing Face of America

Ever since Ice Age nomads came here from Asia tens of thousands of years ago, America's population has undergone a succession of changes. Hunter-gatherers followed the first immigrants, and when the Europeans came to America centuries later, they found hundreds of Native American tribes.

These earliest Americans were overwhelmed by the new immigrants and driven almost to extinction by a policy of submission and eradication. Today Native Americans represent less than 1 percent of the nation's total population and are just one element in a mélange of ethnic groups that represents nearly every region on Earth.

TWO WAVES

Demographers divide the succession of immigrants to America following European discovery of the continent into two waves: "Old Immigration" and "New Immigration." During these two periods more than 30 million immigrants settled in the country.

Old Immigration lasted from 1820 to 1890 and included people from Scandinavia, the British Isles, and Germany. As a result of the potato famine, 1.7 million Irish came over between 1841 and 1860.

Each of these ethnic groups tended to live and work with others of their nationality before assimilating into American society. Many Irish, for example, found work doing manual labor, including building the nation's railroad system. Scandinavians typically headed west to homesteads in Minnesota and the surrounding areas. Germans created their own distinctive communities, such as in Milwaukee.

Old Immigration had a profound impact on the ethnic mix of America. Even today the English, the Germans, and the Irish are the three leading ethnic groups in the country. Nearly one out of five Americans claims German ancestry, and roughly one of eight points to English or Irish heritage.

▲ **Between 1916 and 1970** millions of black Southerners moved to Northern cities in a "Great Migration." Above, children attend a Depression-era art workshop in New York City.

But Northern Europeans weren't the only immigrants to arrive during the country's early days. The slave trade forcibly transferred black Africans to America to toil primarily on Southern plantations. In 1750 there were approximately 200,000 slaves in the Colonies; another 1 million were imported by 1850. From this group emerged the nation's single largest minority group. Today African Americans represent 12.6 percent of the nation's total population.

The United States also experienced a surge in immigration on the Pacific Coast as Chinese were brought to the West chiefly to build railroads. While many of the workers were forced to return home because of new exclusion

▲ **Ellis Island** in New York Harbor was the nation's main entry point from 1892 through the early 1920s for immigrants like this child. The ancestors of 40 percent of all U.S. citizens came through its reception center.

Patterns of Immigration in the 20th Century

Political and religious tolerance and the prospect of financial success made the United States a beacon of hope for millions of people fleeing Western Europe and Western Asia from 1900 to 1940. World War II, however, brought immigration to a virtual standstill for several years. Between 1950 and 1990, the leading sources of emigrants were Eastern Asia and Latin America. There was less significant immigration from Africa (331,932 immigrants) and Australia and New Zealand (176,756 immigrants) between 1901 and 1990.

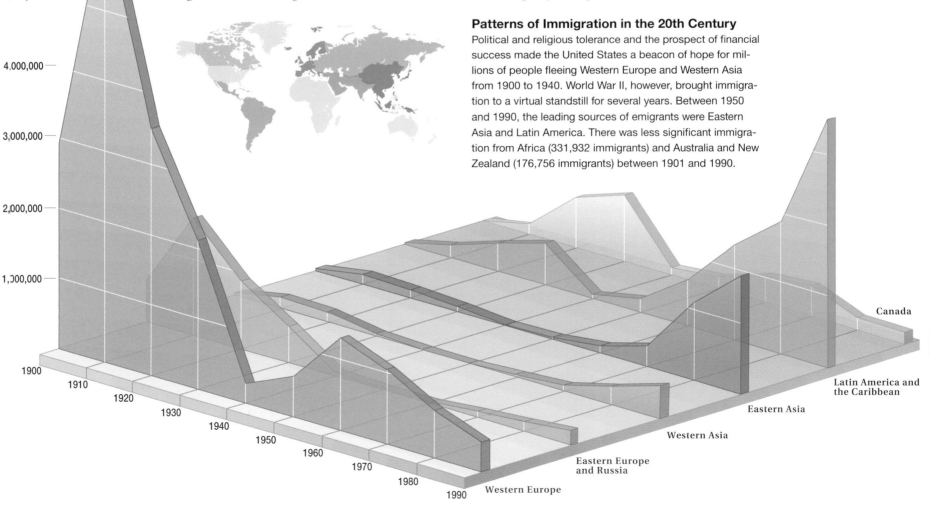

6,000,000 —
5,000,000 —
4,000,000 —
3,000,000 —
2,000,000 —
1,000,000 —

1900
1910
1920
1930
1940
1950
1960
1970
1980
1990

Canada
Latin America and the Caribbean
Eastern Asia
Western Asia
Eastern Europe and Russia
Western Europe

▲ **Chinatown, San Francisco,** *is one of many thriving ethnic communities that have been established by immigrants in major American cities.*

▲ **Some 7,000 people become American citizens during a Los Angeles ceremony.** *While the majority of immigrants who landed at Ellis Island were from Europe, today's new Americans come from countries throughout the world.*

laws that restricted Chinese immigration, nearly 300,000 entered the country between 1850 and 1890.

The New Immigration period extended from 1880 to 1920, and most of the newcomers came from Eastern and Southern Europe. Between 1900 and 1920 America added nearly 14.5 million new residents, most from Italy, Austria-Hungary, and Russia. (Many were Poles and Jews escaping the Russian Empire.) The majority of these new arrivals settled in Northeastern and Midwestern cities and found work in factories.

SETTING QUOTAS

As the result of 1921 legislation that for the first time set an annual quota, immigration declined sharply. Based on the 1910 census, immigration was limited to 3 percent of the number of each nationality present, with a maximum quota of 357,000. Immigration levels dipped for the next several decades, until the laws were abolished with a 1965 act that stipulated an annual ceiling of 170,000 immigrants from the Eastern Hemisphere, with no more than 20,000 from any one country. In 1968 a limit of 120,000 and a per-country maximum was imposed on the Western Hemisphere. In 1995 the cap on all admissions was raised to 675,000.

ASIANS AND HISPANICS

Since 1971 two groups have dominated immigration: more than 6 million people from Asia and 8 million from Latin America and the West Indies have settled in America. Of the 7.3 million people granted immigrant status in the 1980s, 42.9 percent were born in Asia and 41.5 percent in Latin America.

America's Hispanic population is the nation's fastest-growing ethnic group. While Hispanics currently account for 11 percent of the total population, increasing rates of both legal and illegal immigration and a relatively high birthrate have put the group in a position to dis-

place African Americans as the nation's most numerous minority by the year 2010. Hispanics already account for more than 50 percent of the population in many parts of the Southwest.

Increases in the number of ethnic minorities are changing the racial mix of America. By 2050 non-Hispanic whites are expected to constitute a little more than half of the total population, compared to nearly 80 percent in 1980.

GROWING OLDER

Immigration is just one of four factors that have helped push America's post–European-settlement population from 50,000 in 1650 to an estimated 275 million by the year 2000. The three other factors are mortality, fertility, and territorial expansion. The United States has a net gain of one person every 15 seconds.

America boasts one of the sharpest declines in mortality of any of the world's developed countries. Put another way, the average life expectancy in the United States has climbed from 35 years

during colonial times to 76 years today. In addition, Americans have been having children faster than they've been dying. The birthrate has hovered between 15 and 30 births per 1,000 people since 1910, while the death rate has averaged about half that.

Regardless of ethnicity, the fastest-growing segment of the population is the elderly. While the number of Americans under the age of 65 has tripled during the 20th century, the number of those age 65 and older has increased elevenfold. One out of every eight Americans is now considered elderly, compared with only 1 in every 25 in 1900. The rate will continue to rise well into the next century, as the elderly population will more than double between now and the year 2050 to an estimated 80 million.

Simply put, the changing face of America is older and more multicolored than it was when the nation was founded more than 200 years ago.

▼ **Abraham Weintraub,** *one of the growing number of older Americans who remain active, trains for his fifth New York City Marathon at 87. He finished the most recent race in 6:26:05, coming in ahead of hundreds of younger runners.*

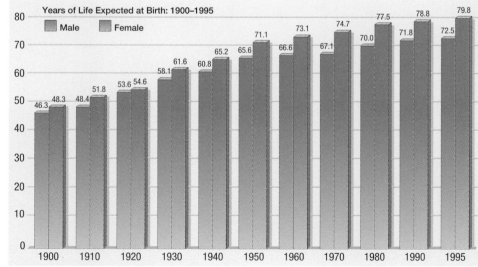

Life Expectancy Among Americans
The steady rise of life expectancy in America is due not only to improved living conditions and health care but also to a lowered mortality rate. In 1996 the mortality rates of some major causes of death, including AIDS, cancer, heart disease, and homicide, reached an all-time low. The overall estimated life expectancy for Americans is now 76.1 years.

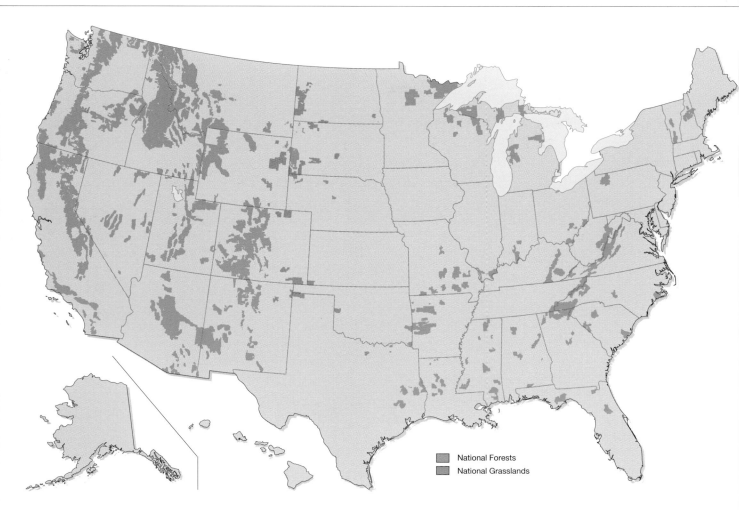

National Forests
National Grasslands

Our National Forests and Grasslands

American Woodlands
Made up of 8.5 percent of the total land area of the United States, national forests and grasslands contain such valuable resources as timber, water, and wildlife. Managed by the U.S. Department of Agriculture's Forest Service, the forests and grasslands feature special sites, which include scenic rivers, wildlife preserves, and wilderness areas—primeval spots that are designated by Congress to remain untouched.

▲ *Maple trees* grow along the Tellico River in Tennessee's Cherokee National Forest, which is bisected by Great Smoky Mountains National Park.

▲ *Frosted grass* blowing in the breeze of Tallgrass Prairie Preserve, which covers 37,000 acres across Kansas and Oklahoma.

▲ *Oglala National Grasslands* in Nebraska supports an assortment of prairie animals. Its Toadstool Geologic Park, above, is filled with mammal fossils.

Trackless hardwood forests replete with streams and wildflowers. Tallgrass prairies beneath a wide-open Great Plains sky. Ancient forests of fir that have stood watch for a millennium in the Pacific Northwest. Orchid-hung subtropical woodlands, Arctic marshes black with waterfowl, Gulf Coast estuaries teeming with fish, Southwestern deserts of arid beauty. Once, all of the country looked like this. Today these glimpses of primeval America are preserved in an unmatched system of national forests and grasslands, thus safeguarding the biological diversity of North America for future generations.

FROM ANCIENT FORESTS TO TIMBER BOOM

Precolonial America was a land of forests. From the Ozarks and the Great Lakes east to the Atlantic, woodlands dominated the landscape, just as they did in the Western mountains. But it was not a uniform blanket of trees; climate, elevation, and soil created a mosaic of forest communities, each adapted to local conditions.

The mountains of the Pacific Northwest, bathed in abundant rain and fog, gave rise to some of the most magnificent forests on Earth. Douglas firs and western hemlocks, some nearly 1,000 years old and more than 200 feet high, rise like steeples, draped in moss and lichens. In the drier Rockies, Ponderosa and lodgepole pines predominate, filling the air with their resinous spice. In the mountainous Southwest and in the Great Basin, the forests are of piñon pine and juniper; subalpine firs stand on the highest peaks—a taste of Canada near the Mexican border.

The Eastern forests were once so thick that the pioneers, trudging beneath the giant oaks and pines, longed to see the sun. Softwoods ruled the coastal plain of the Southeast, especially the noble long-

◄ *Autumn* comes to Nason Ridge in Wenatchee National Forest, Washington.

leaf pine, whose wood was rich with sap that was boiled down to make turpentine. Farther inland stretched the great belt of hardwoods—American chestnuts, maples, oaks, hickories, ashes—that supplied a fledgling nation with everything from cabins to ships. In the colder, wetter Northeast, conifers again held sway, including the white pines, valued for their straight, smooth-grained lumber.

It was along the Atlantic seaboard that the American timber boom began, slowly at first but gathering steam through the 19th and 20th centuries as the virgin trees fell before the ax and saw and railroads moved them to market. Ancient forests were reduced to stump fields. Rivers became choked with logs floating to the mills, and when one area was cleared to the ground, the logging camps simply moved on. An atmosphere of commerce and destruction spread across the Great Lakes region and down the Appalachians, across the Southeast pinelands and up the Rockies and the Pacific Northwest.

CONSERVING AMERICA

Forests were not the only natural communities under assault. Once-lush tallgrass prairies were converted to Midwestern cornfields, while grasslands in the Southwest were badly degraded by heavy cattle grazing. Wildlife was also endangered by the end of the 19th century: formerly abundant species, such as the passenger pigeon and the Carolina parakeet, became extinct, while the number of bison, elk, waterfowl, and many others were drastically reduced.

Around the turn of the 20th century, Americans began to recognize what had happened, and moved to right some of the wrongs. More resilient than anyone had guessed, the land reasserted itself, and forests that had been cut down began to regrow. In 1905, President Theodore Roosevelt, an ardent conservationist, established the U.S. Forest Service, which would maintain vast tracts of federal land and offer guidance on the wise use of woodlands. (He also created, in 1903, the first national wildlife refuge to protect birds being killed for the then-thriving feather trade.)

Today the country's 155 national forests encompass more than 180 million acres, ranging from the spruce-clad fjords of Chugach National Forest in Alaska to the subtropical sand pine woodlands of Ocala National Forest in Florida. Twenty national grasslands, comprising nearly 4 million acres and located mostly in the West, protect grazing land and restored prairie. In all these diverse lands, primeval America shines, a moving reminder of the beauty and tenacity of the natural world.

The Nation's Bounty

The plow followed the ax into the wilderness, creating a nation of farmers in the early days of the republic's history, when 9 out of 10 Americans worked the land. As America spread westward, farmers adapted their crops to the continent's many climates: corn in the Midwest, wheat in the drier Great Plains, cotton across the South, cattle and sheep in the West, on what had recently been the grazing land of bison. Today the number of farmers has fallen to a tiny percentage of the population, but technology allows the few to feed the multitudes, providing a bounty that supports not only this country but much of the world.

▲ **Wheat,** the world's most widely grown food crop, is planted on about one-third of the farms in the United States. While the Great Plains and the Pacific Northwest are the major wheat-producing regions, the grain is cultivated in almost every state in the nation. Altogether, the country's soil yields some 2 billion bushels of wheat per year.

▼ **Soybeans** have been grown in large quantities in the United States only since the mid-20th century. Today the country produces most of the world's supply. The high-protein legume is used in many food and commercial products, including animal feed, margarine, cooking oil, cosmetics, linoleum, and paints. Soybeans are often planted in rotation with other crops, such as corn.

EARLY EFFORTS

Farmers made America blossom in ways that even the greatest optimists could not have foreseen. The rich, loamy soil of the Eastern seaboard supported the early colonists, although they first had to clear the old-growth forest that covered it; many settlers, armed only with crude hand axes, simply cut deep rings in the trees' trunks and killed them, then planted between the leafless stumps, felling the timber later, when they had their first crucial crop in hand.

The colonists brought precious seeds from the Old World—barley and wheat, apples and pears, herbs for seasoning and for medicine. But the crops that first allowed Eastern settlements to thrive were American natives—tobacco and maize, or corn. Helpful Indians had taught the colonists to grow tobacco along the humid mid-Atlantic coastal plain, and the Europeans quickly refined techniques for raising, drying, and shipping the prized leaves to Europe, where pipe smoking had become very popular.

But while tobacco was a cash crop, corn was one of the staples of farm life. Originally domesticated in Mexico or Central America, corn was one of the "three sisters," along with beans and squash, that Native Americans planted together across most of their territory. Among settlers, who learned to cultivate it from the Indians, corn provided sustenance for both humans and livestock. Later, as Americans breached the barrier of the Appalachians and fanned out across the prairies of the Midwest, tidy farmsteads surrounded by great fields of waving corn became a symbol of the fledgling nation's bounty.

▲ **Rice is cultivated** in irrigated paddies in California and some Southern states. The United States is one of the world's leading exporters of the crop.

EXPANSION OF CULTIVATION

Just as climate and soil type once dictated the kinds of forest or grassland in a particular region, so did they determine the type of crops. "King Cotton," for example, grew well in the South. The cultivation of cotton expanded south from Virginia, the Carolinas, and Georgia and westward into Texas by the start of the Civil War. By then the American South supplied three-quarters of the world's cotton fiber. In the 20th century much of the land once farmed in cotton now grows soybeans, an Asian import worth tens of billions of dollars to farmers in the Midwest and the South.

Accustomed to the deep soil and abundant rainfall of the East and the Midwest, pioneers despaired of growing anything on the Great Plains, which for years were known as the "Great American Desert." But the arid climate there was ideal for wheat, as today's expansive fields and abundant grain elevators vividly show.

As cultivation broadened, each region became known for its own specialties—the sugarcane and pineapples of tropical Hawaii, the citrus fruit of Florida, rice in the Gulf states and Arkansas, dairy products in the Northeast and the upper Midwest, and everything from vegetables and fruits to nuts in California, thanks to the long growing season.

ANIMAL HUSBANDRY

Just as the colonists brought seeds with them from the Old World, so too they brought livestock. As early as the 16th century, Spanish conquistadores transported cattle, hogs, and sheep on their ships to America. Other Europeans followed in the 17th and 18th centuries, and when they settled across the country, they took their livestock with them. The corn belt of the Midwest proved perfect for hog farming, and the grasslands of the wide-open plains were ideal for grazing cattle and sheep. Great cattle drives from places like Texas, Montana, and Wyoming brought herds to railroads in Kansas and Illinois and then to Eastern markets. The drives are a thing of the past, but the cattle remain, a mainstay of the Midwest and the Western plains.

Just like the country's interior, America's coasts provide a wealth of their own in the form of fish and shellfish; whether it is salmon and pollock in Alaska, shrimp in the Gulf, or blue crabs in Chesapeake Bay, fishing has been an economic mainstay for generations. But overharvesting has pushed many fish stocks, like bluefin tuna and Atlantic cod, to such low levels that harsh regulations have been needed to protect them.

Aquaculture (the cultivation of fish and shellfish) has made up for a small portion of the loss of wild fish stocks, with farmed salmon and catfish becoming two of the most popular types of fish in the country in the past decade.

▲ **Pecan trees** *in Texas. Georgia is the only state that produces more of the native North American nut than Texas.*

AGRICULTURAL INNOVATION

Farming has always been a difficult way of life, with farmers at the mercy of the weather and the vagaries of the market. But for more than two centuries, the trend has been that fewer farmers produce more and more food. This was the result of a revolution in technology that began in 1793 with Eli Whitney's invention of the mechanical cotton gin, which separated the seeds from the fibers, a job once done by hand. Nearly 40 years later Cyrus McCormick invented a horse-drawn reaper for harvesting wheat.

The biggest advance, however, may have been the steel plow, invented by a blacksmith named John Deere in 1837. Until then, farmers had used cast-iron plows, but damp soil would stick to the rough metal, leaving ragged, collapsed furrows and requiring great effort by both men and draft animals. The steel plow changed all that; it sliced through even the thickest prairie sod with ease, greatly increasing the amount of land one team could cultivate.

In the more than one and a half centuries since then, technology has radically altered the face of American agriculture. Machinery finally replaced the horse and mule in the early 20th century, but other changes have been less obvious. Fertilizers, pesticides, and other agrochemicals have bolstered crop yields considerably, as have such techniques as contour plowing and no-till farming, which protect soil from erosion. An understanding of genetics has led to a host of specialized hybrids and strains, and now selective breeding has moved from the fields to the labs, where genetic engineers tinker with DNA, splicing such attributes as disease resistance directly into crops. The result is phenomenal production, even as the number of American farmers has fallen to an all-time low. In 1850 each farmer produced enough food for four

▼ **Pigs** *are fed a diet that consists largely of corn. Iowa, the state that produces the most corn, also has the most hogs.*

people; today the average farmer produces food for 80 people.

The increasing use of technology has had a dark side, however. The long-term effects of pesticides and genetically engineered food and livestock are not known. Expenses for equipment and chemicals have resulted in financial ruin for some small farms. Since World War II, the number of farms has dropped from 6 million to 2 million, while the average size of a farm has more than doubled—a result of corporate agribusiness buying up failed competitors. Still, many small farmers have adapted—experimenting with different crops and organic farming techniques, even rediscovering old methods like raising chickens free-range—all with a view toward carrying agriculture into the 21st century.

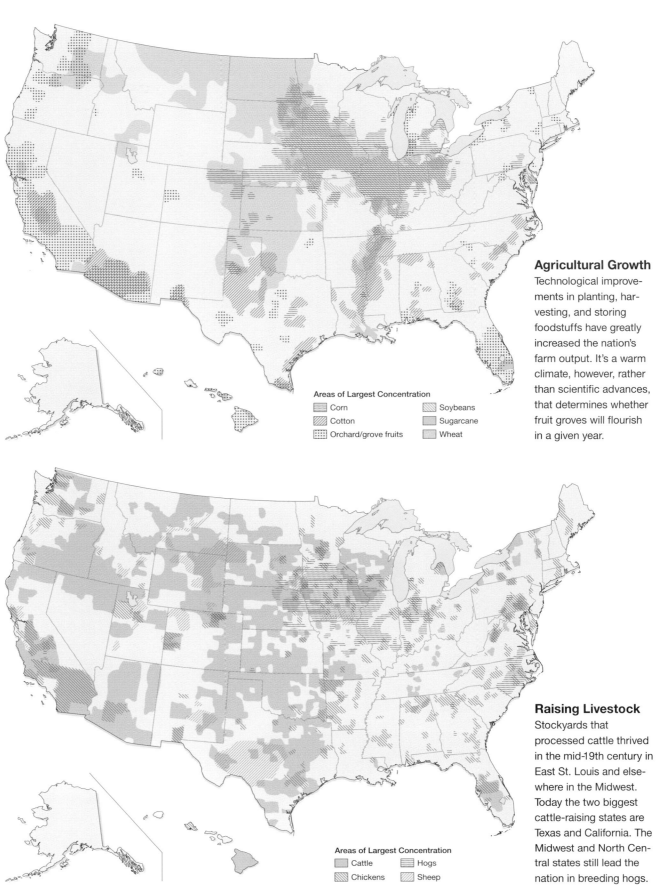

Areas of Largest Concentration

Corn	Soybeans
Cotton	Sugarcane
Orchard/grove fruits	Wheat

Agricultural Growth

Technological improvements in planting, harvesting, and storing foodstuffs have greatly increased the nation's farm output. It's a warm climate, however, rather than scientific advances, that determines whether fruit groves will flourish in a given year.

Areas of Largest Concentration

Cattle	Hogs
Chickens	Sheep

Raising Livestock

Stockyards that processed cattle thrived in the mid-19th century in East St. Louis and elsewhere in the Midwest. Today the two biggest cattle-raising states are Texas and California. The Midwest and North Central states still lead the nation in breeding hogs.

▲ **Poultry production** *in the United States has increased tenfold since 1950, a result of the increasing mechanization of the industry. Today the country produces more than 75 billion eggs and more than 31 billion pounds of poultry per year.*

▶ **Steel** *is refined by blowing oxygen into molten iron and scrap steel at extremely high temperatures. During this process, excess carbon and other impurities are removed and additional elements are added. Large-scale manufacture of steel began in the late 1800s. U.S. steel production today varies according to its demand.*

▲ *Nuggets of gold ore. Nevada is the country's leading gold-producing state, followed by California, Utah, South Dakota, Montana, and Alaska.*

▼ *Because the vast iron-ore deposits of the Mesabi Range are so close to the surface, the technique of open-pit mining (below) is used to extract them.*

The Wealth of the Land

Gold! Time and again in America's history, the cry went up, and the thundering multitudes answered—swarming into the Georgia mountains, the Black Hills, California, and Alaska. But America's landscape conceals mineral wealth of many kinds, and most of them are extracted from the ground only with great effort and at great expense. An automobile requires more than steel; it demands copper for electrical wires, lead for the battery, aluminum for lightweight fixtures, sand for the windshield. And so it is with every aspect of daily life today, which would be impossible without the bounty of the deep earth.

MINING THE LAND

In the language of the Ojibwa, *Mesabi* means "Giant"—a name for the range of mountains in northeastern Minnesota that contains one of the greatest iron-ore deposits in North America. There and elsewhere around Lake Superior—in the nearby Vermilion Range, the Marquette Range, the Menominee, the Gogebic, and other hills—billions of tons of ore have come out of the ground, been hauled to ports and railroads, then sent to mills, in the Midwest and the East, that sat amid coalfields that provided the power to turn ore into finished steel.

Humans have coveted precious metals and rare minerals, such as gold, silver, and gems, since the dawn of civilization. Their discovery can set off stampedes, and create cities almost overnight. But the nation's real mineral wealth is not in precious stones like Arkansas's diamonds or Utah's topaz but in the grit—iron and lead, zinc and bauxite, sulfur and potash, nickel and tungsten, salt and gravel. Mining and transporting minerals has always been difficult, dangerous work, the stuff of legends, like the "20-mule team borax" that came out of California's Death Valley—actually pulled by teams of 18 mules and two horses, dragging wagons weighing 36 tons through the valley's infernal heat.

As early as 5000 B.C., Native Americans in the Great Lakes region were mining "red metal," as they called copper, especially along the southern shore of Lake Superior and on Isle Royale. By heating and hammering the soft metal, a process called annealing, they created knives, spoons, and ornaments that were traded widely across eastern North America. Later, Native American tribes in the Pacific Northwest and Alaska also mastered copperwork, while Indians elsewhere fashioned lead and iron derived from meteorites into tools. In the north central states, a soft, easily worked stone called catlinite was mined for centuries and traded across the continent for use as carved pipe bowls. In the meantime, high-quality Knife River flint from North Dakota was a mainstay of aboriginal commerce as far afield as the Atlantic seaboard.

European settlers also started digging, at places like Mine La Motte, a French lead mine in Missouri established in 1723. (Missouri still leads the nation in lead production.) Ironworks cropped up along the Atlantic coast even earlier: the Falling Creek Ironworks in Virginia in 1619 and the Saugus Ironworks in Massachusetts in 1646. In the New Jersey Pine Barrens, ironworkers used the naturally occurring "bog iron" that came from the damp, peaty soil of the region's marshes. But the biggest iron-ore strikes came from the mountains around Lake Superior, in the Marquette Range in 1844 and in the Mesabi Range in 1892. Low-grade ore from the Mesabi was the mainstay of the American steel industry, supplying more than half of the country's iron needs for more than a century. Other ferrous (ironlike) metals of great importance include molybdenum and vanadium, both of which come from the

◀The Salem Outcrop, in southern Indiana, is just 50 miles long, a few miles wide, and 60 feet deep, but it supplies much of the high-quality limestone used for building exteriors across the country.

is mined by blasting gravel banks with water sprayed at very high pressure.

WEALTH OF A DIFFERENT SORT

At the opposite end of the glamour scale from gold are the everyday mine products on which we build our lives: sand and gravel, cement and crushed stone, produced in Arizona, Nevada, and Texas. No one ever made his fortune in a gravel rush or a sand stampede, but the importance of these mundane substances can hardly be overstated—for over the course of a lifetime, an American is in contact with approximately 3 million pounds of mined material, from high-quality steel to the cement sidewalks underfoot.

▼Miners at work deep in the Homestake gold mine in Lead, South Dakota. The mine, which is the source of most of South Dakota's gold, is the oldest continuously operating gold mine in the world.

Rocky Mountains and, in the case of molybdenum, from Alaska as well. And while copper first came from the area around the Great Lakes, one of the world's richest seams—about 4 billion tons of copper ore—was discovered in 1882 in Montana, while a prospector was exploring the defunct Anaconda silver mine. Other rich deposits were found throughout the Southwest.

THE LURE OF GOLD AND SILVER

It was gold and silver, however, that sparked the great epidemics of mining fever in American history. In the 1830s gold strikes in the mountains of northern Georgia set off a lawless rush that evicted the Cherokee from their homeland. No sooner had that tumult died down than John Sutter's quiet mill in California blazed into history with a discovery in 1849, and thousands of "forty-niners" converged on the state. In Nevada, Arizona, Colorado, and elsewhere in the West, silver was the prize, creating boomtowns like Tombstone,

Carson City, and Silver City. Rock from the fabled Comstock Lode in western Nevada, which set off the greatest silver rush, was worth a fabulous $4,000 a ton in 1859. Acting on orders from the government, in 1874 Lt. Col. George Custer led a treaty-defying expedition to South Dakota's Black Hills, confirming the presence of gold and setting off a rush of prospectors that led to war with the Sioux, who had long considered the mountains sacred. The Homestake Mine, in Lead, South Dakota, opened in 1876 and went on to become the richest single source of gold in the nation.

When the United States purchased Alaska for $7.2 million (2 cents an acre) in 1867, skeptics dubbed the place "Icebergia" and derided the deal as a tremendous waste of money. But in 1880 gold was found in the Gastineau Channel in the southeastern panhandle, the first of several major strikes in Alaska—at Nome, for example, in 1898 and along the Yukon River near Fairbanks in 1902. Thousands of "stampeders" heading for the Klondike and Dawson fields climbed the mountains near Skagway in southern Alaska, loaded like pack animals for the long trip down the Yukon. Today gold still comes from Alaska, and much of it

Underground Riches

Several Eastern and Midwestern states boast deep veins of minerals, but the bulk of the nation's subterranean resources, from asbestos to gold and zinc, is found underground in the West and under the snow and ice in Alaska.

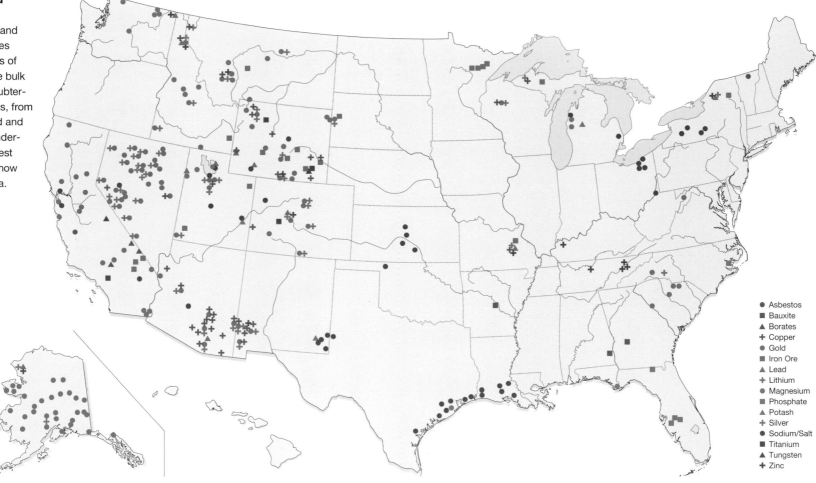

- ● Asbestos
- ■ Bauxite
- ▲ Borates
- ✚ Copper
- ● Gold
- ■ Iron Ore
- ▲ Lead
- ✚ Lithium
- ● Magnesium
- ■ Phosphate
- ▲ Potash
- ✚ Silver
- ● Sodium/Salt
- ■ Titanium
- ▲ Tungsten
- ✚ Zinc

Providing Power for the Nation

Water and wood powered early America, fuel-ing fireplaces and forges, turning water-wheels and millstones. But there was much greater wealth waiting underground—vast fields of coal, ancient deposits of oil and natural gas, and uranium for nuclear power. Without its vast energy reserves, America could never have grown into a world power. The reliance on fossil fuel and nuclear energy, however, brought with it a host of social and environ-mental problems. Today interest in clean, renewable sources of energy, such as solar power, wind power, and biomass power, is being rekindled.

EARLY RESOURCES

Falling water releases energy—it's a simple fact of physics that humans were quick to grasp. Build a large wooden wheel with basins to catch the water, place it upright within a foaming millrace, and the water will turn the device—and anything else attached to its shaft and gears, say, a heavy millstone. Colonial America was dotted with gristmills to which farmers would bring their grain. In the late 18th century, the building of water-powered looms gave birth to New England's thriving textile industry, with mills crowding the banks of rivers like the Merrimack, on which Lowell, Lawrence, and other mill towns became centers of Yan-kee commerce.

The forests provided fuel for homes and industries, in the form of both raw wood and charcoal, which was produced in the mountains and shipped to the cities in a form lighter and more economical than firewood. Charcoal making was a tedious task; wood was stacked in conical mounds, then covered with soil and set afire so that the wood barely smoldered. Tenders watched the fires continuously, damping them down or allowing more oxygen to flow in as needed. As cities grew, nearby forests shrank because of the increasing demand for firewood.

ENTER COAL

In 1790 a Pennsylvania hunter named Necho Allen discovered that his camp-fire had ignited an outcropping of shiny, black rock—anthracite, the hardest, most valuable variety of coal. The anthracite fields of the Appalachians fueled an industrial boom in the East during the 19th and early 20th centuries. But America has far greater deposits of bituminous, or soft, coal beneath the Ohio and central Mississippi valleys, the eastern Plains, and much of the Rockies. Although higher in sulfur compounds that pollute the air, and providing less heat per ton than anthracite, the cheaper, more easily mined bituminous coal became one of the mainstays of energy production, particularly when burned to fire steam-powered electricity-generating plants. Bituminous coal also powered the steel industry where plants converted iron ore from the western Great Lakes into steel for railroads, skyscrapers, and automobiles.

OIL IS STRUCK

Western Pennsylvania also gave the country its first oil well, and people have been using it ever since; in 1859 the first commercial well, in Titusville, Pennsyl-vania, set off a rush of drillers and spec-ulators to rival those of any goldfield. The biggest gushers, however, came in east Texas, at such places as Spindletop in 1901, where wooden derricks crowded cheek by jowl like the skyline of a miniature city. At first oil was refined into kerosene for lamps, a cheap replacement for whale oil; today petro-leum (more than half of which is now imported) satisfies more than 40 percent

▲ *The Trans-Alaska pipeline stretches about 800 miles. It carries oil from a giant oil field in Prudhoe Bay, on the Arctic Ocean in northern Alaska, to Valdez, on the state's southern coast.*

◀ *A derrick at Spindletop oil field, near Beaumont, Texas. This photograph was taken in 1901, the year of its first enormous gush.*

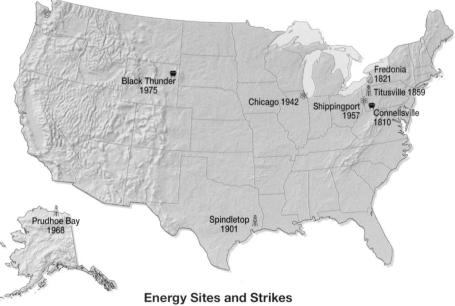

🜚 Coal
🛢 Oil
💧 Natural gas
✴ Nuclear

Energy Sites and Strikes

The map above shows America's first natural-gas well, first com-mercial oil well, and first nuclear reactor. The first nuclear reactor to produce electricity for commercial use (Shippingport) and the nation's largest surface coal mine, in Wyoming, are also included.

Fuels That Supply the Nation's Needs

America has enough coal to last another few centuries. Although there are deposits across the country, the industry is largely reliant on mines in the East and Midwest. The waters off the coasts of Texas, Louisiana, and California are likely sites for new oil and gas reserves (which often occur together), but environmental concerns and expensive permits curtail new mining. Existing U.S. uranium mines could yield about 25 million tons of ore for nuclear-power production.

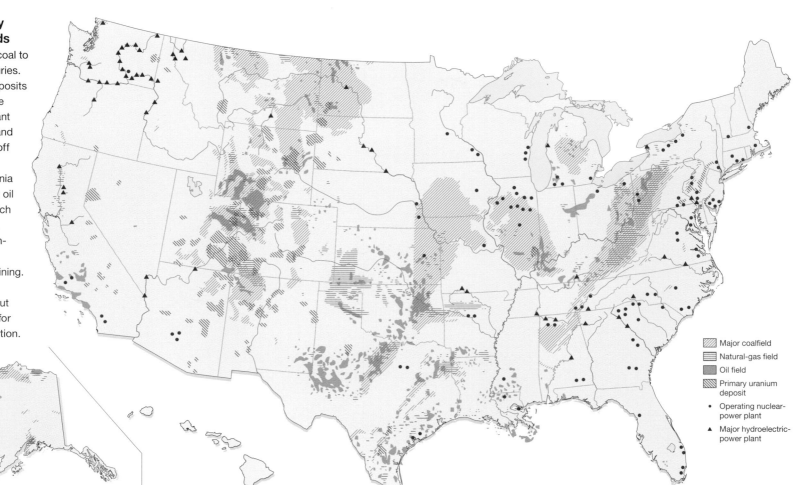

- ▨ Major coalfield
- ▤ Natural-gas field
- ▦ Oil field
- ▨ Primary uranium deposit
- • Operating nuclear-power plant
- ▲ Major hydroelectric-power plant

of America's demands for energy (particularly for gasoline), as well as myriad other uses, from lubricants and synthetic fibers to asphalt. Natural gas, which is found in many of the same geological deposits as oil, was once burned off as a worthless by-product. But as oil supplies shrink, natural gas is gaining importance, especially because it burns more cleanly than oil.

THE COST OF ENERGY

Supplies of fossil fuels like gas, oil, and coal—the compressed remains of swamp forests hundreds of millions of years old—are finite. And use of these resources exacts a heavy toll, both social and environmental. The coalfields of the 19th and early 20th centuries were hell-holes for the men and boys who worked them. By law, the mules that pulled the mine cars had to be given a day off, but no such law protected the workers, mostly poor immigrants. Mine shafts that have been closed for 100 years still blemish the land, leaking poisonous, acid-tainted water that leaves rivers virtually lifeless, while modern strip mines devastate whole valleys, reducing them to scarred rubble.

On March 24, 1989, the nation learned an important lesson on the risks of oil production. The oil tanker *Exxon Valdez*, having been topped off at the Trans-Alaska Pipeline terminal in Valdez, hit a reef in Prince William Sound and dumped nearly 11 million gallons of crude oil into one of the most pristine environments on Earth; the spill polluted more than 1,200 miles, killed thousands of animals, including eagles and sea otters, closed fisheries, and crippled tourism for years. Still, most of the environmental consequences of fossil-fuel use are less dramatic, if no less dire: the smog from car exhaust that blankets

many urban areas, acid precipitation aggravated by coal-fired electrical plants, and the growing suspicion that carbon dioxide from burned fuel has caused a hole in the ozone layer, thus altering the global climate.

NUCLEAR ENERGY

Nuclear power was supposed to be the clean, economical alternative to fossil fuels; proponents in the 1960s claimed that it would one day be too cheap to meter. After all, one pound of uranium produces as much energy as 1,140 short tons of coal. But while nuclear power now supplies about 8 percent of America's energy needs, its development has been stalled by high costs and safety concerns—the latter exacerbated by the 1979 accident at Three Mile Island in Pennsylvania. Few new plants are being planned, and many of the old ones are reaching the end of their useful lives. Nor has the problem of what to do with the highly radioactive waste left over from the fission process been solved. One hope is that scientists can someday harness nuclear fusion—the same process that powers the stars. Using cheap, abundant forms of hydrogen as fuel, and leaving no long-term radioactive waste behind, fusion could potentially provide vast amounts of energy.

A LOOK TOWARD THE FUTURE

Hydropower—the modern equivalent of New England's gristmills—remains an alternative to fossil fuels and nuclear power and is an important source of energy, especially in the Pacific Northwest and the southern Appalachians, where the Tennessee Valley Authority harnessed dozens of rivers in the 1930s.

More recently, renewable energy sources, such as solar power, wind power, and biomass power (fuel created

▲ *Nuclear-power plants produce energy by fission—that is, by splitting the nuclei of atoms (usually of uranium) in two. Fusion, an experimental process that combines two nuclei into one, has so far required more energy than it has created.*

from agricultural products), have caught the public interest. Today sunlight is used to power everything from satellites to water pumps, and passive solar buildings with elements like special south-facing glass and insulation are being built as alternatives to conventional structures. (The U.S. Department of Energy, along with other organizations, hopes to have solar roofs installed in 1 million American buildings by the year 2010.) Each year wind is converted into electricity to provide power for 1 million people, and American farmers grow biomass, or energy crops, that supply vegetation for conversion into gas used in special turbines that generate electricity.

Earth-friendly, virtually inexhaustible, and becoming less expensive to produce every day, renewable energy sources offer some hope for the future of the global environment.

▶ *A lump of anthracite coal from Pennsylvania. Coal is called a fossil fuel because it is formed from the compacted tissue of plants that died between 400 million and 1 million years ago. Anthracite is the hardest and oldest form of coal mined today.*

Our National Parks

From Maine's rocky shores to Hawaii's tropical rain forests and beaches, from Alaskan tundra to Southwestern deserts, America's national parks preserve virtually every type of landscape and seascape on the planet. Volcanic eruptions, tectonic shifts, and glacial movements created their general outlines, while the push and pull of wind, water, and gravity have resculpted their details. The results are dazzling. Coral reefs glow with color under the sea. Wildflowers paint hills and valleys with eye-popping palettes of stunning hues. These 10 pages are an overview of the endless vistas of wonder offered by our 54 national parks.

▲ **Delicate Arch,** sculpted by the interplay of earth, salt, wind, water, and gravity, stands its ground at Arches National Park.

ACADIA

When fog rolls in over Mount Desert Island, which contains the bulk of Acadia National Park, visibility can drop to just a few yards. But sounds intensify—waves smashing on the rocks, seals barking, gulls shrieking, lobster boats sounding their horns. As the fog lifts, the unspoiled wilderness of Maine's coast is revealed in all its glory. The thick woods that blanket the islands push to the Atlantic's edge. Besides offering magnificent ocean views, Acadia's Cadillac Mountain is, at 1,530 feet, the highest elevation on the North Atlantic coast.
Size: 46,998 acres.
Highlights: Jordan Pond, Long Pond, Echo Lake, Eagle Lake, Somes Sound, Park Loop Road, Sand Beach, Thunder Hole, Cadillac Mountain, Seawall, Bass Harbor Head Lighthouse, Isle au Haut.
General information: Some park roads are closed in the winter. Hiking trails, biking (on carriage roads), cross-country skiing, and camping are available.
Location: Maine. See map on page 126.

AMERICAN SAMOA

Located in the South Pacific 2,300 miles southwest of Hawaii and 1,500 miles northeast of New Zealand, America's newest national park may be its most exotic. The park is spread over three volcanic islands in the Samoan archipelago: Tutuila, Ta'u, and Ofu. Its features include some of the tallest sea cliffs in the world, mountains that jut hundreds of feet above the Pacific Ocean, and beaches fringed with palm trees. Besides having the only mixed-species old-world (paleotropical) rain forest, it contains the only Indo-Pacific coral reef in the park system.
Size: 9,000 acres, spread over three islands; 1,000 acres under water.
Highlights: Tutuila: the Cockscomb, villages of Vatia and Afono Pass, Amalau Valley, Mount Alava, Pago Pago Harbor, Rainmaker Mountain, Matafao Peak, Poa Island, and Polauta Ridge. Ta'u: Saua, Lata Mountain, Laufuti Falls. Ofu: coral reefs, pristine beaches.
General information: There are no federal facilities. The park service leases the land from the American Samoan government, which manages the site. Visitors are urged to become familiar with and sensitive to Samoan customs. Guides are needed for hiking in rain forest areas.
Location: American Samoa.

◀ **The play of light** on ancient rock, as viewed from the South Rim in Grand Canyon National Park, creates an ever-changing panoply of color.

ARCHES

Is it a playground for giants or a garden of abstract sculptures strewn across an arid landscape? From any perspective, Arches National Park affords a dramatic backdrop for 2,000 layered salmon- and buff-colored rock formations—the densest collection of natural arches in the world. The largest, Landscape Arch, spans 306 feet. Also protruding from the parched landscape are spires, pinnacles, pedestals, and balanced rocks. A close-up look reveals that a living crust of bacteria, mosses, lichens, algae, and fungi covers much of the parkland. This crust absorbs moisture, protects against erosion, and nourishes such plants as piñon and juniper trees.
Size: 73,379 acres.
Highlights: Devils Garden, Klondike Bluffs, Petrified Dunes, La Sal Mountains Viewpoint, Fiery Furnace, Landscape Arch, Delicate Arch, Double Arch, Sand Dune Arch, Turret Arch, Balanced Rock, Skyline Arch, Broken Arch, Eye of the Whale Arch.
General information: Temperatures can vary by as much as 50°F in a 24-hour period. It is very dry, so visitors should bring lots of water.
Location: Utah. See map on page 190.

BADLANDS

The sharp buttes, steep canyons, spires, gulleys, and pinnacles in Badlands National Park attest to a geologic shudder of major proportions. More than 34 million years ago, marshy plains studded with streams were transformed into a stunning contrast of massive rock formations and grassy lands. The mammals that once roamed the prairie have left their imprint; having been drowned in periodic floods, their carcasses were then embedded in rock. These deposits make up one of the world's richest veins of fossil beds. Native Americans—including the Arikara and the Lakota, or Sioux— have long inhabited the region.
Size: 242,756 acres.
Highlights: Cliff Shelf Nature Trail, Fossil Exhibit Trail, Door Trail, Stronghold Table, Roberts Prairie Dog Town.
General information: Hiking in Sage Creek Wilderness Area. Lodging and camping at Cedar Pass Lodge. Very windy year-round; hot and dry in summer, cold and snowy in winter.
Location: South Dakota. See map on pages 180–181.

BIG BEND

Big Bend National Park straddles the Mexican border with Texas, where the Rio Grande takes a sharp turn as it traverses the southern Rocky Mountains and the Sierra Madre range. Cliff walls that rise 1,500 feet are mirrored in the clear water of the river, an awesome sight for those perched high atop the rocks or aboard a boat passing through the 17-mile-long Santa Elena gorge. The Chihuahuan Desert brushes up against the Chisos Mountains at Big Bend, and such desert vegetation as yuccas, agaves, and some 60 varieties of cactus occupy more than 95 percent of the low-lying areas.
Size: 801,163 acres.
Highlights: The Rio Grande, the Chisos Mountains, Ross Maxwell Scenic Drive to Castolon, Persimmon Gap.
General information: Bring plenty of water and wear sunscreen at all times. Carry tweezers to remove cactus spines. The park is very remote: it is at least 100 miles to the nearest bank, hospital, pharmacy, or supermarket.
Location: Texas. For location in state, see map on page 186.

BISCAYNE

If you're mesmerized by lush tropical beaches and clear, turquoise ocean, you'll understand why Spanish explorer Ponce de León was lured to the area in 1513 in search of the Fountain of Youth. Nestled between Key Biscayne to the north and Key Largo to the south is a park that stretches across 48 islands, plus one swath of shoreline along the mainland. (The strangely contorted mangrove trees near the shoreline protect against hurricanes.) A world-class coral reef burgeons with brilliantly hued tropical fish and other creatures. Manatees, sea turtles, lobsters, shrimp, and fish feed on the rich sea-grass beds.
Size: 172,924 acres, of which about 95 percent is under water.
Highlights: Water sports—swimming, snorkeling, scuba diving, waterskiing,

▲ **The still water** of Acadia's Jordan Pond is a sharp contrast to the waves that crash upon the park's Atlantic shoreline.

▲ **American Samoa's beaches** stretch for miles, affording visitors glorious views of sunset over the South Pacific.

▲ **Badlands National Park** punctures the sky above the Dakota prairie with jagged points. Rocky Mountain bighorn sheep and mule deer flourish here.

▲ **The rim of Crater Lake** is dotted with wildflowers in the spring, but winter brings an average snowfall of 45 feet.

▲ **The coreopsis,** or tree sunflower, is among the 85 native plant species that bloom at Channel Islands National Park. Blue whales, seals, and sea lions inhabit the waters offshore.

▼ **An 830-foot descent** beneath the desert at Carlsbad Caverns National Park brings visitors into the Kings Palace, the Queens Chambers, and other awesome subterranean sites.

and sailing and other types of boating—can be enjoyed year-round. Glass-bottom-boat tours are available, as are scuba and snorkel trips. Boardwalk at Convoy Point; nature trails at Boca Chita Key, Elliott Key, and Adams Key.
General information: Guard against strong sun and biting insects. There are no lifeguards, so don't swim alone. There are campgrounds on Elliott Key and Boca Chita Key.
Location: Florida. See map on page 99.

BRYCE CANYON
Perhaps no other park is as inviting to sci-fi devotees as Bryce Canyon National Park, with its amphitheaters of rock pillars carved in limestone, sandstone, and mudstone. Ancient rivers originally created tall, thin ridges that have been sculpted into shapes called hoodoos. Glowing pastels of purple, pink, and brown are produced by sunlight glinting off rocks that contain iron and magnesium oxide. Those who drive along the road that follows the canyon's plateau are treated to stunning views of Colorado, New Mexico, and Arizona.
Size: 35,835 acres.
Highlights: Fairyland Point, Bryce Amphitheater, Paria View, Farview Point, Natural Bride, Ponderosa Canyon, Agua Canyon, Yovimpa and Rainbow points.
General information: Eighteen-mile park road along plateau rim; more than 50 miles of hiking trails; two campgrounds and backcountry camping.
Location: Utah. See map on page 190.

CANYONLANDS
Located at the convergence of the Colorado and Green rivers, Canyonlands National Park covers a huge expanse of what one writer called "the perfection of [the] silence." This wilderness of rock is divided into three distinct land regions, each with its own geology and wildlife. To the north lies the Island in the Sky, a broad mesa that floats 2,000 feet above the riverbanks; to the southwest, the Maze, a labyrinth of canyons punctuated by spiky rock formations and buttes; and to the southeast, the Needles, filled with sandstone rocks soaring up to 100 feet and with more vegetation and wildlife than elsewhere in the park. The backcountry is accessible to those exploring on foot, in boats, on mountain bikes, or in four-wheel-drive vehicles.

▲ **Capitol Reef** offers miles of desolate, stony landscapes, but there's more to the park: the Hickman Bridge, a 133-foot-long sandstone bridge, as well as cherry orchards.

Size: 337,570 acres.
Highlights: Island in the Sky: Upheaval Dome, Green River Overlook. The Maze: the Maze canyons, the Land of the Standing Rocks, Ernies Country, the Doll House, the Fins, Horseshoe Canyon. The Needles: Devils Kitchen, Angel Arch, Elephant Hill, Caterpillar Arch, Paul Bunyan's Potty, Chesler Park, Horse Canyon, Confluence Overlook. The Rivers: Cataract Canyon rapids.
General information: Two campsites; backcountry camping and boating available by permit. Primitive, rugged hiking trails. Carry at least one gallon of water per person per day.
Location: Utah. See map on page 190.

CAPITOL REEF
Making their own misfortunes the butt of a joke, 19th-century pioneers dubbed this obstacle course a reef. Just as underwater chains of rock could impale ships in the ocean, so the sandstone cliffs and deep canyons halted prairie wagons heading west. For some visitors, the white rock domes recalled the circular structure atop the nation's Capitol Building in Washington, D.C. Capitol Reef National Park preserves the Waterpocket Fold, a 100-mile-long buckling of the earth's surface. The fold was formed 65 million years ago by the same forces that created the Colorado Plateau. Cutting into the deep, twisting canyons and the monoliths of red rock is the verdant Fremont River. Nearby is the art that the Fremont culture etched into sandstone.
Size: 241,904 acres.
Highlights: The Castle, Grand Wash, Capitol Gorge, Cathedral Valley, Halls Creek Narrows, Burr Trail, Hickman Bridge, Old Fruita Schoolhouse.
General information: Trails for hiking and horseback riding. Campgrounds and backcountry camping available.
Location: Utah. See map on page 190.

CARLSBAD CAVERNS
From early spring to October, a million Mexican free-tailed bats migrate to the park to give birth and raise their off-

spring. Each night the skies are filled with massive clouds of bats emerging from the caves on their nocturnal feeding missions. Located in the Chihuahuan Desert of the Guadalupe Mountains, the park contains 83 caves enclosed in a fossil reef that was carved out of an ancient inland sea. The largest cave is Carlsbad Cavern, which provides a type of spectacle entirely different from that of the bat caves—vast underground chambers with exquisitely crafted calcite and aragonite structures decorating a subterranean fantasy land.
Size: 46,766 acres.
Highlights: Natural Entrance, Bat Flight Amphitheater, Bat Cave, Main Corridor, Big Room, Scenic Rooms, Slaughter Canyon Cave.
General information: Temperature inside the caves is about 56°F year-round: bring a sweater or jacket and wear rubber-soled shoes.
Location: New Mexico. See map on page 157.

CHANNEL ISLANDS
Five of the eight California Channel Islands (San Miguel, Santa Rosa, Santa Cruz, Anacapa, and Santa Barbara) that make up the Channel Islands National Park are the tops of submerged mountains that form an underwater link to the Santa Monica Mountains on the mainland. The park waters are home to the blue whale, the largest animal on Earth. On San Miguel, the westernmost island, 20,000 seals and sea lions converge on the beach each winter at Point Bennett.
Size: 249,354 acres, half of which are under the ocean.
Highlights: Arch Rock on Anacapa, Scorpion Anchorage on Santa Cruz, Qenada Canyon on Santa Rosa, Cabrillo's monument on San Miguel.
General information: Hiking trails and backcountry camping are available on Anacapa, Santa Barbara, Santa Rosa, and San Miguel islands. Be prepared for extended periods of wet fog.
Location: California. See map on page 88.

CRATER LAKE

Shimmering, sapphire-blue Crater Lake, the deepest lake in the United States (1,932 feet), owes its remarkable clarity and hue to two natural assets: its depth and the purity of its water, which is rain and melted snow. The lake rests inside the enormous pit formed by the volcanic eruption of Mount Mazama in the Cascade Range. Some 7,700 years ago, a huge explosion spewed enough lava and ash to turn a mountaintop into a crater, and over the years the big hole filled with water. Among the flowers that flourish in this setting is the rare phantom orchid, with its white flowers and paper-thin, nearly transparent leaves.
Size: 183,224 acres.
Highlights: Wizard Island, Phantom Ship, Garfield Peak, the Watchman, Mount Scott, Hillman Peak, Godfrey Glen, Annie Creek Canyon, Rim Drive, the Pinnacles, Pumice Castle.
General information: Some roads are closed in winter. Boat tours and camping are available in summer. Hiking down to the lake is possible only on Cleetwood Trail. Other trails provide spectacular views. Cross-country skiing only on unplowed roadways.
Location: Oregon. See map on page 170.

DEATH VALLEY

Within an 80-mile radius in Death Valley, it is possible to go from the nation's lowest point, 282 feet below sea level, near Badwater, to the peak of Mount Whitney, 14,494 feet high (in Kings Canyon). This divergence is just one of the region's many stark contrasts. In the desert July's daytime temperatures often exceed 120°F, and abandoned mines and animal skulls dot the parched landscape; yet wildflowers bloom after spring rains and date-palm trees thrive at the Furnace Creek oasis. Sunrises and sunsets are extraordinarily colorful; the unpolluted air makes the desert a prime spot for stargazing.
Size: 3,367,628 acres.
Highlights: Badwater, Devil's Golf Course, Artist's Drive, Golden Canyon, Zabriskie Point, Twenty Mule Team Canyon, Dante's View, Sand Dunes, Mosaic Canyon, Salt Creek, Scotty's Castle, Ubehebe Crater, Titus Canyon Narrows, Wildrose Canyon, Charcoal Kilns.
General information: Carry and drink at least one gallon of water a day. Summers are extremely hot and dry. When driving in the summer, remain on paved roads; if your car breaks down, stay with it.
Location: California/Nevada. See maps on pages 87, 89, and 151.

DENALI

Despite winter temperatures that fall below –40°F, the subarctic climate in the sprawling Denali National Park is quite hospitable to the continent's largest land mammals. Caribou outnumber Alaska's human population and spend the summer north of the Brooks Range. Moose wander through the park. Dall sheep, grizzly bears, foxes, and wolverines are among Denali's 37 mammal species. Mount McKinley, the highest mountain in North America (20,320 feet), is the centerpiece of the park. The north boundary offers unsurpassed views of the northern lights in summer.
Size: 4,741,800 acres.
Highlights: The Mount McKinley massif, Savage River, Toklat, Moose's Tooth, Muldrow Glacier, Wonder Lake, Mount Healy Overlook, Taiga Loop Trail, Morino Loop Trail, Rock Creek Trail, Roadside Trail, Horseshoe Lake Trail.
General information: Riley Creek campground is open year-round; other campgrounds are open May to September. Park Road is closed to vehicle traffic in winter. Backcountry is open year-round for snowshoeing, skiing, or dogsledding (obtain permit from park headquarters).
Location: Alaska. See map on page 79.

▲ *A paradise for anglers,* Dry Tortugas National Park also attracts snorkelers: coral formations are submerged only 4 feet deep.

DRY TORTUGAS

Dry Tortugas National Park protects seven islands made of coral reefs and sand as well as the waters around them. The area is called "dry" because it has no fresh water. Ponce de León called the islands "Las Tortugas" (the Turtles), and, indeed, endangered loggerhead, hawksbill, and green sea turtles are among the park's prized residents. Snorkelers glory in the park's colorful tropical fish and coral formations.
Size: 64,700 acres, of which fewer than 40 acres are above-water land.
Highlights: Fort Jefferson, Windjammer Wreck, White Shoal, Loggerhead Key, Brick Wreck, Bird Key Bank, Long Key, Texas Rock, Brilliant Shoal.
General information: Open year-round during the day only, except for Garden Key; however, Fort Jefferson on Garden Key is open only during the day. Bush Key is closed from February to September. No food or water is available. Primitive campsites are available on Garden Key. A Florida saltwater-fishing license is required for fishing. Binoculars are recommended for bird-watching.
Location: Florida. See map on page 92.

EVERGLADES

A watery realm of saw-grass prairies, mangrove swamps, and subtropical jungle, Everglades National Park, the largest subtropical wilderness in the continental United States, supports eight different ecosystems. It is home to more than 700 species of plants, 120 species of trees, and 300 species of birds. Located 38 miles from the main visitor center, Flamingo is the larger of the two sightseeing-boat departure sites (Gulf Coast is the other site); open-air tram tours are available at Shark Valley.
Size: 1,507,850 acres.
Highlights: The road to Flamingo, the Tamiami Trail to Shark Valley, Mahogany Hammock, Mangrove Trail, alligators and crocodiles.
General information: Thunderstorms occur nearly every afternoon. Loose-fitting long-sleeved shirts and long pants are recommended, especially in summer. Insect repellent is a must in all seasons.
Location: Florida. See map on page 92.

GATES OF THE ARCTIC

The only national park located wholly above the Arctic Circle, Gates of the Arctic lies more than 200 miles northwest of Fairbanks, amid the wilderness of the Brooks Range. This vast land—encompassing lakes, rivers, mountain peaks, and valleys—maintains a delicate balance of tundra, plain, and boreal forest. It attracts visitors who enjoy backpacking, river running, mountaineering, and dog mushing—and who crave the ultimate in solitude.
Size: 7,523,898 acres.
Highlights: Wildlife—especially caribou, moose, Dall sheep, wolves, and bears.
General information: Sport hunting is allowed in the preserve areas. No park facilities, established campgrounds, or designated trails.
Location: Alaska. See map on page 79.

GLACIER

Deep in the heart of the Rocky Mountains, Glacier National Park's backbone is the mighty Continental Divide, where coniferous forests, wildflower-laden meadows, shimmering lakes, and icy rivers abound. With its 50 glaciers and

▲ *Among the exotic flora* of the Everglades, cabbage palmetto—a fan-leaved cabbage palm—is found on the Shark River Slough.

▲ *The peaks of the Maidens* make a fitting crown for the virginal backcountry of Gates of the Arctic National Park. In April, when subzero temperatures still prevail, dogsled teams herald the dawning of springtime.

▼ *Beneath a carpet* of summer wildflowers, Logan's Pass marks the spot where Going-to-the-Sun Road crosses the Continental Divide in Glacier National Park.

▲ *Rising abruptly from the valley floor, the majestic Tetons tower above the Snake River in Grand Teton National Park.*

▲ *Amid winter's chill, a trumpeter swan takes wing against a snowy backdrop in Grand Teton National Park.*

▲ *Ancient bristlecone pines, biologically adapted for longevity, mark the timberline of the South Snake Range in Great Basin National Park.*

unique rock formations, Glacier National Park is a walk back into prehistory. Most of the exposed rocks were deposited 800 million to 1,600 million years ago. Such subtle features of sedimentation as ripple marks, mud cracks, raindrop impressions, and fossil algae have withstood the ravages of time.
Size: 1,013,572 acres.
Highlights: Lake McDonald, Trail of the Cedars, Logan Pass, St. Mary Lake, Birdwoman Falls, Jackson Glacier, Hanging Gardens, Grinnel Glacier.
General information: Visitors should dress to protect themselves against strong winds and sudden temperature drops. Snow falls year-round.
Location: Montana. See map on page 146.

GLACIER BAY
The centerpiece of Glacier Bay National Park is Glacier Bay itself—a 65-mile-long fjord—from which fingerlike inlets fan outward. Fewer than 1 percent of park visitors reach the backcountry. Most prefer to stay aboard the ships that cruise the bays, although some visitors view the park in small powerboats or in kayaks. Those who do set out on foot can wend their way past beaches and through a rain forest in the area of Bartlett Cove.
Size: 3,224,794 acres.
Highlights: Muir Inlet, humpback whales, harbor seals, boat tours, birdwatching, kayaking.
General information: The visitor center operates only during the summer. One road, six trails, and one designated campsite at Bartlett Cove.
Location: Alaska. See map on page 81.

GRAND CANYON
About 6 million years ago, the Colorado River began carving a path through the Colorado Plateau of northern Arizona, building up canyon walls and helping to create a gorge that today is 215 miles long, up to 10 miles wide, and in some places a mile deep. The canyon is composed of layers of limestone, sandstone, and shale, and their colors seem to change dramatically from one moment to the next—a sight that never fails to awe visitors. Hikers can follow a trail along the river to Plateau Point, with its commanding view of the Inner Gorge.
Size: 1,217,158 acres.

Highlights: The North and South Rim drives, Mather Point, Bright Angel, South Kaibab and North Kaibab trails, Navajo Falls, Mooney Falls, Point Imperial, Granite Gorge, Marble Gorge.
General information: Mule trips and bus tours offer alternatives to private vehicles and travel on foot. The North Rim is closed half the year because of snow. Reservations are required for camping and lodging (the wait for backcountry permits may be a year), and permits are needed for overnight hiking.
Location: Arizona. See map on page 83.

GRAND TETON
An omnipresent force in Grand Teton National Park is the Cathedral Group—12 spires and pinnacles that soar heavenward at more than 12,000 feet—the tallest peaks in the Teton Mountains of Wyoming. Cutting a serpentine path through the valley below them is the Snake River, flanked from early spring through late autumn by brightly colored wildflowers that blanket mountains and meadows. At higher elevations are sagebrush flats and lodgepole-pine and spruce forests. Each winter herds of elk, seeking refuge from deep mountain snows, converge at the southern end of Jackson Hole.
Size: 309,995 acres.
Highlights: Signal Mountain Overlook, Cathedral Group Turnout, Jenny Lake, Inspiration Point, Jackson Hole Highway, Rockefeller Parkway, Snake River Overlook, Oxbow Bend.
General information: Most park facilities operate only from mid-May to September.
Location: Wyoming. See map on page 206.

GREAT BASIN
Rising dramatically 5,300 feet from the desert floor of the eastern edge of Nevada, the Great Basin offers a virtual checkerboard of deserts and mountains. Thriving amid three groves of bristlecone pines (the earth's oldest living tree species) are trees that have passed their 4,000th birthday. The Lehman Caves are nestled within a pygmy forest of piñon and juniper trees. Twisting and turning, the caves' narrow passageways lead to cavernous chambers. Each room contains elaborate stone sculptures that have been carved by water and carbonic acid seeping through marble bedrock.
Size: 77,180 acres.
Highlights: Lehman Caves, Wheeler Peak Scenic Drive, Bristlecone Pine Forest, Baker and Lehman Creek trails.
General information: Be prepared for sudden weather changes. Hikers should carry an adequate water supply.
Location: Nevada. See map on page 151.

GREAT SMOKY MOUNTAINS
Named for the mantle of haze that often blankets its hills and valleys, Great Smoky Mountains National Park attracts more visitors annually than any other

one in the United States. The park showcases one of the world's most majestic hardwood forests, although conifers predominate along the 6,000-foot crests of its crumpled Appalachian highlands. More than 1,400 species of flowering plants brighten the Smokies, and the summer extravaganza of rhododendrons offers a dazzling display. The park also encompasses log cabins, weathered barns, country churches, and other evocative signposts of pioneer settlements.
Size: 521,621 acres, of which 95 percent is forest.
Highlights: Cades Cove, Cataloochee, Clingmans Dome, Mountain Farm Museum, Newfound Gap, Roaring Fork Nature Trail, Abrams Falls, Ramsay Cascades, Heintooga Overlook.
General information: There are 800 miles of trails for hiking, walking, and horseback riding. Lodging and camping are available.
Location: North Carolina/Tennessee. See maps on pages 162 and 183.

▲ *Columbine, honeysuckle, wild rose, and other brightly colored plants thrive beside springs in the Guadalupe Mountains National Park.*

GUADALUPE MOUNTAINS
Rising abruptly from the vastness of the Chihuahuan Desert, the Guadalupe Mountains ascend to the highest point in Texas, 8,749-foot Guadalupe Peak. These magnificent stark pinnacles are more than they seem, incorporating portions of a 250-million-year-old limestone reef studded with marine fossils. The most dramatic silhouette in the park is that of the 8,085-foot-high El Capitán, whose uppermost 2,000 feet is sheer vertical rock visible 50 miles away.
Size: 86,416 acres.
Highlights: Guadalupe Peak, El Capitán, McKittrick Canyon, The Bowl, The Pinery, Smith and Manzanita springs, Williams Ranch.
General information: Hot summers and cool evenings year-round. High winds and sudden weather changes are common. Watch out for cacti, rattlesnakes, scorpions, and desert centipedes. Do not

climb the mountains. No concessions or supplies are available in the park.
Location: Texas. See map on page 184.

HALEAKALA

Spread like a green apron beneath the stark, 10,023-foot crater rim of the dormant Haleakala volcano, Maui's national park beckons visitors to gaze back through time, to marvel at the forces that created the Hawaiian Islands. Two-thirds of Haleakala, which means "House of the Sun," is preserved as wilderness—a fern-and-forest realm belonging to the nectar-sipping iiwi bird, the dark-rumped petrol, and the rare Hawaiian hoary bat (also known as the peapea), which is one of Hawaii's two native mammals. Views from the park extend more than 100 miles out to sea.
Size: 28,091 acres.
Highlights: Haleakala Crater, the Summit, Kipahulu Valley, 'Ohe'o Gulch, Waimoku Falls, Makahiku Falls, Halemauu Trail, Sliding Sands Trail, Hosmer Grove Nature Trail, White Hill, Leleiwi Overlook, Koolau Gap.
General information: Weather at Haleakala summit is unpredictable, and the oxygen level is lower at high elevations. Kipahulu area is usually warm; flash flooding can be hazardous.
Location: Hawaii. See map on page 107.

HAWAII VOLCANOES

The Kilauea volcano is the volatile centerpiece of this sprawling park on the Big Island, the home of Pele, the folkloric god of volcanic eruptions. To walk the lava fields beneath Kilauea or to drive the crater rim is to witness a landscape perpetually rewritten by fire. To the west is the 13,677-foot Mauna Loa, the world's most massive mountain. It is accessible by an 18-mile trail that meanders through a wilderness of fern forests and hardened lava flows.
Size: 209,695 acres.
Highlights: Kilauea, Mauna Loa, Halema'uma'u Crater and Overlook, Devastation Trail, Thurston Lava Tube, Kilauea Iki trail, Pu'u Huluhulu, Kipuka Puaulu, Crater Rim Drive, Ka'u Desert and tropical rain forest, East Rift, Chain of Craters Road, Sulphur Banks, Steam Vents, Jaggar Museum, Lua Manu and Pauahi craters, Mauna Ulu Lava Shield, Kealakomo Overlook, Holei Sea Arch.
General information: Weather is changeable. Volcanic fumes are hazardous; pay attention to warning signs.
Location: Hawaii. See map on page 107.

HOT SPRINGS

Back in the days when mineral-water cures were held in high esteem by physicians and patients alike, the nation came to bathe at Hot Springs. The popularity of these geothermal springs led to the building of Bathhouse Row, a string of luxury hotels constructed in the early 20th century that offered the latest in hydrotherapy. Laced with supposedly health-enhancing minerals, the water bubbled up from the earth at an average temperature of 143°F. Today's visitors can still relax in warm, mineral-rich waters at the Buckstaff Bathhouse.

▲ **Huge granite boulders** serve as a backdrop for the park's namesake, the spine-covered Joshua tree, and the desert-dwelling yucca.

Adjacent to the city of Hot Springs, the park offers hiking and scenic drives through the surrounding hills.
Size: 5,839 acres.
Highlights: Fordyce Bathhouse, Bathhouse Row, the Grand Promenade.
General information: Hiking trails. Camping is available.
Location: Arkansas. See map on page 84.

ISLE ROYALE

Located 15 miles from the mainland in the cold waters of Lake Superior, Isle Royale is the rugged domain of the timber wolf and its lumbering prey, the moose. The island is a piece of the wild north woods set adrift on the world's broadest freshwater lake, and it is a paradise for anglers, hikers, canoeists, and anyone else seeking silence and solitude.
Size: 571,790 acres.
Highlights: Rock Harbor Lighthouse, Edisen Fishery, Minong Mine.
General information: Open April 16 to October 31. Peak season: late July through the third week of August. More than 165 miles of foot trails. Camping is available. No pets are allowed in the park. No medical services or public telephones on the islands. Bring warm clothing and insect repellent.
Location: Michigan. See map on page 138.

JOSHUA TREE

Named for the weirdly branching Joshua trees that flower gaily in springtime, this park straddles the border between the Colorado and Mojave deserts, and it hosts bobcats, burrowing owls, roadrunners, coyotes, and sidewinder rattlesnakes. At one time the domain of native peoples who left pictographs on rocks, this desert later attracted gold prospectors. Today Joshua Tree is mostly serene and lovely wilderness.

Size: 792,750 acres.
Highlights: Lost Horse and Desert Queen mines, Desert Queen Ranch, Oasis of Mara, Twenty-nine Palms Oasis, Hidden Valley, Barker Dam, Keys View, Ryan Mountain, Geology Tour Road, Cholla Cactus Garden, Cottonwood Spring, Lost Palms Oasis, Transition Zone.
General information: Hiking, interpretive walks, nine campgrounds (bring water and firewood). Drink at least one to two gallons of water daily. Watch out for rattlesnakes and hidden mine shafts.
Location: California. For location in state, see map on page 89.

KATMAI

Katmai National Park is a place of superlatives, a land of high seas, enormous lakes, fierce storms, and, with 15 volcanoes, one of the world's most active volcanic centers. In 1912 it witnessed one of the most violent eruptions in recorded history. In 1916 an explorer dubbed the still-smoldering landscape the Valley of Ten Thousand Smokes, a scattering of which continue to plume upward from the ground more than 80 years later. The park is a favored habitat of North America's largest land predator, the brown bear. Outsize and wild even by Alaskan standards, Katmai boasts nearly 4 million acres of wilderness—and only two hiking trails.
Size: 3,674,541 acres.
Highlights: Brooks River, Takli Island, and Savonoski districts; Katmai coast; Brooks Falls Trail and Platform; Falls Trail; Shelikof Strait Coastline; Valley of Ten Thousand Smokes.
General information: Fishing, hiking, camping available. July and September are the best months for viewing bears. (All visitors must attend "bear etiquette" school.) Bring insect repellent.
Location: Alaska. See map on page 79.

▲ **Haleakala's volcano summit** is accessible by car, but twists and turns add drama to the 38 miles of steep roadway.

▲ **Brown bears** are one of the attractions at Katmai National Park and Preserve. Sharing the huge expanse of land and water are moose, caribou, ducks, loons, and 40 species of songbirds.

▶ *The snowcapped peaks of Alaska's Chigmit Mountains are reflected in the waters of Turquoise Lake, one of the many lakes and rivers scattered throughout Lake Clark National Park and Preserve.*

▲ *Kenai Fjords's Exit Glacier is among the dozens of glaciers that originate at the Harding ice field, which covers 300 square miles. At sea level, the park's 600 miles of coastline are home to more than 60 species of seabirds.*

▲ *A summer sunset on Lake St. Helen conveys a false sense of peace at Lassen Volcanic National Park. The area is a cauldron of steam jets, boiling springs, and gurgling mud holes.*

▲ *Sand dunes meandering across the landscape 45 miles north of the Arctic Circle are an unexpected feature at Alaska's Kobuk Valley National Park.*

KENAI FJORDS

The might of Alaskan glaciers meets a stark and rocky seacoast at Kenai Fjords. The park's landscape was gouged into being by relentless rivers of ice, and its mountain walls are perpetually pulled seaward by the buckling of the earth's crust. Kayakers share fjord waters with Steller's sea lions, harbor seals, and whales, while moose, bears, and mountain goats own the steep slopes above. The glaciers seem alive, "calving" icebergs with a great echoing boom.
Size: 670,643 acres.
Highlights: Exit Glacier, Harding Icefield, Aialik Bay, Nuka Bay, McCarty Fjord, Holgate Arm, Delight Spit, North Arm, Resurrection Bay.
General information: Hiking, camping, fishing, kayaking, boating available.
Location: Alaska. See map on page 79.

KOBUK VALLEY

Straddling the valley of the gently flowing Kobuk River, Kobuk Valley National Park stands at the point where the northern forest gives way to open tundra. The valley's parkland, flanked by mountains to the north and the south, contains the Arctic's largest active dune field—the Great Kobuk Sand Dunes. Here, sand ground by glaciers drifts in ever-changing patterns over 25 square miles; summer temperatures can reach a surprisingly tropical high of 90°F.
Size: 1,750,737 acres.
Highlights: Great Kobuk Sand Dunes, Onion Portage archaeological sites, Kobuk River.
General information: For one month in midsummer, there are 24 hours of daylight; by December, about one hour of daylight. Strong winds at all times; harsh winters. No roads, trails, or visitor facilities in the park. Primitive camping, backcountry hiking, kayaking, rafting, canoeing, boating, and fishing.
Location: Alaska. See map on page 79.

LAKE CLARK

The Aleutian and Alaska ranges meet in a jagged tumble of mountains—the Chigmits, home of two active volcanoes—west of Cook Inlet at the base of the Alaskan peninsula. Adjacent to a federal preserve and largely designated a wilderness, Lake Clark National Park epitomizes the stark grandeur and roadless, trailless character of Alaska's parklands. The 50-mile-long lake that gives the park its name is part of a major sockeye-salmon spawning region.
Size: 2,619,859 acres.
Highlights: Lake Clark, Chigmit Mountains, Mount Redoubt, Mount Iliamna, Cook Inlet, Tanalian Falls, Kontrashibuna Lake, Telaquana Lake, Turquoise Lake, and the Tlikakila, Mulchatna, and Chilikadrotna rivers.
General information: Hiking, camping, boating, and fishing are available, but there are no roads in the park. Wear insect repellent at all times.
Location: Alaska. See map on page 79.

LASSEN VOLCANIC

Lassen is a working museum of volcanism, with all four types of the world's volcanoes represented within its boundaries. Mount Lassen itself, which last erupted over a seven-year cycle beginning in 1914, is the southernmost volcano of the Cascade Range. The terrain surrounding the mountain is a study in the recovery of vegetation after an eruption: areas that were denuded in the 1914–21 blasts are once again mantled in the greens of shrubs and conifers.
Size: 106,372 acres.
Highlights: Lassen Peak, Fairfield Peak, Hat Mountain and Lake, Manzanita Lake, Crater Butte, Boiling Springs Lake, Devil's Kitchen, Terminal Geyser, Chaos Jumbles, Bumpass Hell, Little Hot Spring Valley, Painted Dunes.
General information: Hiking and camping are available. Beware of boiling water under the crust of some thermal features. Rock is unsuitable for climbing.
Location: California. See map on page 86.

MAMMOTH CAVE

The limestone labyrinth that lies beneath central Kentucky constitutes the largest cave system in the world. Some 350 miles of passageways have been mapped, and perhaps another 600 miles await discovery. The caves were formed as water percolating from above dissolved the porous limestone; today surface and subterranean streams continue the sculpting process. Mined for crystals and related salts by Native Americans from 4,000 to 2,000 years ago and rediscovered some 200 years ago, the Mammoth caves are inhabited by eyeless fish, eyeless crickets, and other species that have become acclimated to the darkness.
Size: 52,830 surface acres and hundreds of miles of cave passageways.
Highlights: Mammoth Cave, Green River, Nolin River.
General information: Cave temperature is about 54°F. Make reservations as early as possible for cave tours. Hiking, biking, horseback riding, fishing, boating, canoeing, camping, and lodging are available.
Location: Kentucky. See map on pages 120–121.

MESA VERDE

Some 1,400 years ago the Anasazi, a Stone Age culture, settled at Mesa Verde, which offered protective alcoves in its overhanging cliffs. Probably between

A.D. 1230 and 1260, the Anasazi built the sandstone-block compounds of houses and other structures that still stand. Archaeological digs at Mesa Verde have revealed clues to this once-vibrant society of farmers and hunters who, by 1300, had mysteriously abandoned the site. The tools, basketry, and pottery that have survived intact are exhibited at the park's Chapin Mesa Museum.

Size: 52,122 acres.

Highlights: Cliff Palace, Balcony House, Spruce Tree House, Park Point, Far View, Wetherill Mesa, Chapin Mesa, Petroglyph Point Trail, Spruce Canyon Trail, Square Tower House, Sun Temple, Step House, Long House, Badger House Community, Amphitheater.

General information: Hiking on five trails only. Bicycling on all park roads except those on Wetherill Mesa. Camping is available. Visiting cliff dwellings can be strenuous because of high elevations and uneven trails.

Location: Colorado. See map on page 92.

MOUNT RAINIER

Glacier-girded lord of the Cascades, the 14,410-foot Mount Rainier is a dormant volcano whose present-day impact on its surroundings is not dust and lava but weather patterns. Capturing moisture from Pacific air currents, Rainier receives abundant rainfall, and the winter snowfall averages 630 inches. Many of the more than 300 miles of trails in the park are snow-covered in July. The precipitation helps create rushing streams, lush meadows, and forests that alternately sparkle in sunlight and shimmer, ghost-like, in the mists.

Size: 235,613 acres.

Highlights: Mount Rainier, Columbia Crest, Carbon River rain forest, Grove of the Patriarchs, Wonderland Trail, Mowich Lake, Emmons Glacier, Stevens Canyon, Paradise, Sunrise, Longmire, Ohanapecosh.

General information: The park gets a great deal of rain and snow, especially from October to early May. Hiking trails, mountain climbing (wearing hard hats is encouraged), cross-country skiing, snowshoeing, fishing, camping, and lodging available.

Location: Washington. See map on page 198.

NORTH CASCADES

With its adjacent Ross Lake and Lake Chelan national recreation areas, North Cascades National Park comprises perhaps the most scenic swath of a ruggedly beautiful range. The park includes 318 glaciers, which is more than half of all the glaciers in the lower 48 states. The spiky, unworn Cascade summits seem to have risen yesterday, while below lies the fjordlike grandeur of the region's two long, narrow lakes. At the northern tip of the 1,500-foot-deep Lake Chelan, the starkly beautiful village of Stehekin is accessible only by foot trail, float plane, or a long, slow boat ride through the Cascades—and time itself.

Size: 504,781 acres in North Cascades National Park; 118,000 acres in Ross

Lake National Recreation Area; 62,000 acres in Lake Chelan National Recreation Area.

Highlights: Ross Lake and Diablo Lake overlooks, Goodell Creek, Gorge Lake, Lake Chelan, Stehekin, Happy Creek Forest Walk, Skagit River, Cascade Pass, Rainbow Falls, Buckner Orchard, Sourdough Mountain, Davis Peak, Colonial Peak, Pyramid Peak.

General information: Peak season: mid-June to late September; storms with heavy precipitation during the rest of the year. Hiking trails, camping, canoeing, and boating are available.

Location: Washington. See map on page 198.

OLYMPIC

The dramatic threshold of the Pacific Northwest, Olympic National Park offers three distinct landscapes: a rocky, wave-lashed coast where bald eagles soar; a dripping, somber rain forest where as much as 12 feet of precipitation annually sends Sitka spruce and western hemlock soaring to mossy heights of 300 feet; and the Olympic Mountains themselves, where great glaciers descend from Mount Olympus.

Size: 922,651 acres.

Highlights: Hoh, Quinault, and Queets rain forests; Mount Olympus; Deer Park, Staircase, Graves Creek, Hurricane Ridge; Sol Duc Hot Springs; Rialto and Ruby beaches; Lake Crescent.

General information: Hiking, horseback riding, mountaineering, skiing, snowshoeing, fishing, lodging, camping. Beware of high tides at the coastline.

Location: Washington. See map on page 198.

PETRIFIED FOREST

Ancient tales of geology, botany, and, more recently, human sagas are told in the silent rock records of the Petrified Forest and Painted Desert. The jumbled "forest" of fallen 225-million-year-old trees was created when mineral deposits replaced organic tissue in the sediment-buried boughs; the sediments themselves, exposed by erosion, are striated in vivid shades of red, yellow, and brown. At sites like Newspaper Rock, petroglyphs reveal a native culture that survived until 600 years ago.

Size: 93,533 acres.

Highlights: Painted Desert, Newspaper Rock, Puerco Indian Ruins, Kachina Point, Chinde Point, the Tepees, Blue Mesa, Jasper Forest Overlook, Crystal Forest, the Flattops, Rainbow Forest, Agate House, Giant Logs, Long Logs.

General information: Backcountry camping is allowed only in the Painted Desert Wilderness. A permit is required for overnight wilderness camping.

Location: Arizona. See map on page 83.

REDWOOD

Established to protect the tallest trees in the world from the logging that had drastically reduced their range, Redwood

▶ *Quaking aspens* set Rocky Mountain National Park aglow in shades of gold each fall. These stately trees are by Bear Lake.

National Park and three adjacent state parks preserve magnificent groves of coast redwoods. Along this fog-shrouded coastline, these trees have a lifespan that averages 500 to 700 years. The tree that has gained renown as the world's tallest has been growing here for approximately 2,000 years, and it measures 367 feet at its tip. Yet the redwoods are but one facet of a parkland that includes prairies where elk graze and 40 miles of unspoiled shoreline frequented by pelicans, sea lions, and orca whales.

Size: 110,232 acres.

Highlights: Elk Prairie and Klamath overlooks, Newton B. Drury Scenic Parkway, Gold Bluffs Beach, Howland Hill Road, Tall Trees Grove, Big Tree, Yurok Loop, Enderts Beach, Stout Grove, Simpson-Reed Grove, Redwood Creek Coastal Trail, Smith and Klamath rivers, Elk Prairie, Gold Bluffs Beach, Bald Hills and Davison roads, Crescent Beach, Enderts Beach, Coastal Trail, Tall Trees Grove, False Klamath Cove, Lagoon Creek, Requa Road, Lost Man Creek, Lady Bird Johnson Grove.

General information: Foot, horse, and bicycle trails available, bird-watching, camping. An AYH youth hostel is located in the park.

Location: California. See map on page 86.

ROCKY MOUNTAIN

The bighorn sheep rules this lofty realm, where the Continental Divide separates the waters of East and West along the roofline of North America. The park incorporates the heart of Colorado's Rockies, where some peaks rise more than 14,000 feet and meadows strewn with wildflowers, which reach their peak in late June and July, sit amid towering evergreens. One-third of the park stands above the tree line, assuring uninterrupted vistas along much of the 355-mile trail system and the spectacular 50-mile Trail Ridge Road.

Size: 265,727 acres.

Highlights: Bear Lake, Moraine Park, Sprague Lake, and Tundra nature trails, Longs Peak, Trail Ridge Road, Fall River Road and Pass, Horseshoe Park, Forest Canyon Overlook, Dream Lake, Never Summer Ranch, Lulu City, Wild Basin.

General information: Bicycling, hiking, camping, snowshoeing, skiing, horse-

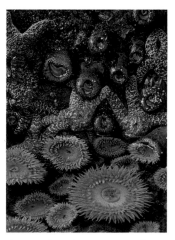

▲ *Deep-hued sea stars* and sea anemones cling to rocks along the 57 miles of coastal wilderness in Olympic National Park.

▲ *Pedestal logs,* whose woody interiors have been replaced by stone in kaleidoscopic colors, perch atop the Blue Mesa in Petrified Forest National Park.

▲ *Rhododendron,* azalea, trillium, and other flowers thrive in the shade of the towering trees in Redwood National Park.

▲ **Petroglyphs** *etched into rock at Signal Hill in Saguaro National Park have been traced to a Native American tribe that lived there from about 500 to 1500.*

▲ **Towering trees** *line the entrance to Kings Canyon National Park at General Grant Grove. The General Grant tree is believed to be the second-largest in the world.*

▲ **White-sand beaches** *attract sunbathers and swimmers alike to Virgin Islands National Park. Coral reefs teeming with a variety of colorful creatures allure scuba divers.*

back riding, mountain climbing. High elevations may trouble those with heart conditions or respiratory ailments. **Location:** Colorado. See map on page 92.

SAGUARO

The Sonoran is biologically the richest American desert, and its greatest living symbol is the saguaro cactus. Split into eastern and western divisions by the city of Tucson, Saguaro National Park is studded with thousands of these stately and imposing plants. Some of them live 150 to 200 years, stand 50 feet tall, and weigh 8 tons, a tribute to the saguaro's survival skills. It thrives despite less than 12 inches of rainfall annually. The saguaro blooms in the late spring, and its brightly colored flowers wait to blossom until after sunset, when the temperature drops. In the east, the lowland desert ascends to the Rincon Mountains, where evergreen forests contrast with cactus stands below.
Size: 91,453 acres.
Highlights: Saguaro West: Bajada Loop Drive, Cactus Garden Trail, Desert Discovery Nature Trail, Valley View Overlook Trail. Saguaro East: Desert Ecology, Tanque Verde Ridge, and Miller Creek trails; Rincon Mountains.
General information: Daytime summer temperatures are extremely high. Carry and drink plenty of water. Hiking, horseback riding, and backcountry camping are available. Be on the watch for cactus spines, rattlesnakes, scorpions, and Gila monsters.
Location: Arizona. See map on page 83.

SEQUOIA AND KINGS CANYON

Earth's largest living thing, a giant sequoia called the General Sherman Tree, has stood in what is now Sequoia National Park for more than 2,300 years. Sequoias grow only on the western slopes of the Sierra Nevada, and many of the surviving groves are protected here. North of the snowcapped peaks of the Great Western Divide in Kings Canyon National Park stands another giant— Mount Whitney, at 14,494 feet the highest mountain in the lower 48 states.
Size: 864,383 acres.
Highlights: Giant Forest (including General Sherman Tree), Lodgepole, General Grant Grove (including General Grant Tree), Mineral King Valley, Ash Mountain, Cedar Grove, Crystal Cave, Mount Whitney, Mount Kaweah, Kern Canyon, Crescent Meadow, Roaring River Falls, Zumwalt Meadow, Grand Sentinel Viewpoint, Don Cedil Trail, Sheep Creek Cascade, Lookout Peak, Hotel Creek Trail, Atwell Grove and Mill, Sawtooth Peak, Monarch Lakes, White Chief Trail, Eagle and Mosquito lakes.
General information: Hiking, camping, lodging, horseback riding, fishing, cross-country skiing, snowshoeing. Watch out for bears, cougars, and rattlesnakes.
Location: California. See maps on pages 87 and 89.

SHENANDOAH

Awash each spring in the flower colors of azaleas and mountain laurels, and in

▲ **Like most waterfalls** *in Shenandoah National Park, Lewis Springs Falls is at its best in spring, when rains melt winter's snow. Rainbows often appear in the afternoon.*

autumn ablaze with the reds and yellows of turning leaves, Shenandoah National Park follows the crest of the Blue Ridge Mountains for more than 100 miles. This rugged terrain once supported hardscrabble farms; today it has mostly reverted to an upland forest habitat for deer, bears, and wild turkeys. Offering magnificent views of Virginia's Piedmont and the Shenandoah Valley, Skyline Drive winds along the entire length of the park (105 miles).
Size: 197,389 acres.
Highlights: Skyline Drive, Big Meadows, Lewis Mountain, Loft Mountain, Skyland, Thornton Gap, Elkwallow, Mathews Arm, Dickey Ridge, Shenandoah Valley Overlook, Gooney Run Overlook, Range View Overlook, Hogback Overlook, Whiteoak Canyon, Crescent Rock, Dark Hollow Falls, Little Stony Man Cliffs, Bearfence Mountain, Rockytop Overlook, Doyles River Trail, Jones Run Falls, Calf Mountain Overlook.
General information: Hiking, fishing; camping, lodging, cabins.
Location: Virginia. See map on page 195.

THEODORE ROOSEVELT

Theodore Roosevelt, America's great conservationist president, first came to Dakota Territory in 1883. As a badlands rancher, he learned the value of protecting natural resources. The park that honors him echoes once again with the thundering hooves of bison and elk, which had to be reintroduced after the original herds were decimated. The badlands, ancient sedimentary deposits that were sculpted into fantastic shapes by water and wind, are still home to the meadowlark and prairie dog.
Size: 70,447 acres.
Highlights: Elkhorn Ranch; North Dakota Badlands, South Unit and North Unit scenic loop drives; Ridgeline, Coal Vein, Caprock Coulee, Squaw Creek, and Little Mo nature trails; Painted Canyon, Jones Creek, Petrified Forest, Lone Tree, Paddock Creek, Talkington, Haah-Daah-Hey, Achenback, North Achenback,

Upper Caprock Coulee, Buckhorn, and Prairie Dog Town trails; Boicourt and Oxbow overlooks; Sperati and Scoria points; Wind Canyon; Peaceful Valley; Petrified Forest, Maltese Cross Canyon.
General information: Hiking, camping, skiing, wildlife viewing. Beware of rattlesnakes and black widow spiders.
Location: North Dakota. See map on page 164.

VIRGIN ISLANDS

Covering more than half the island of St. John, this tropical park offers a kaleidoscopic sampling of the Caribbean environment, both on land and beneath the blue waters. A self-guided snorkeling trail is an introduction to coral reef life, while pathways crisscrossing the island's rugged, forested interior reveal a colorful variety of bird and plant life, pre-Columbian petroglyphs, and ruins of colonial sugar mills. No matter where you are in the park, the island's pristine sugar-sand beaches are never far away.
Size: 14,689 acres.
Highlights: Trunk Bay; Hawksnest Bay; Cinnamon Bay; Salt Pond Bay; Lameshur Bay; Catherineberg, Annaberg, and Reef Bay sugar mill ruins; Reef Bay Valley; Francis Bay Trail.
General information: Hiking on 22 trails, snorkeling, scuba diving (don't touch the coral), self-guided underwater trail, boating, fishing, camping, scenic drives, bird-watching.
Location: U.S. Virgin Islands.

VOYAGEURS

Named for the intrepid couriers of the once-thriving French-Canadian fur trade, Voyageurs National Park is a place where water looms larger than land. Hugging the Canadian border in northern Minnesota, the park encompasses more than 30 lakes, part of the birchbark-canoe trail that linked the far Northwest with the fur-trading depots of Montreal.
Size: 218,035 acres.
Highlights: Rainy, Kabetogama, Namakan, Quill, Elk, Shoepack, and

Sand Point lakes; Kabetogama Peninsula; Oberholtzer Interpretive, Little American Island Gold Mine, Locator Lake, Cruiser Lake, Blind Ash Bay, and Echo Bay trails.
General information: Hiking, boating, fishing, canoeing, kayaking, cross-country skiing, snowshoeing, camping, lodging. Wear insect repellent in summer.
Location: Minnesota. See map on page 140.

WIND CAVE
Beneath the Black Hills of South Dakota lies a secret world where bizarre natural calcite formations—some shaped like snowflakes, others resembling spiky bushes and latticework—ornament chambers with such names as Pearly Gates, Bachelor's Quarters, and Monte Cristo's Palace. Some 77 miles of Wind Cave have been explored since the discovery of the underground treasure in 1881. (Native Americans may have known about it earlier.) Blinking in the sunlight after a cave tour, visitors encounter the vastness of the prairie, where bison and elk graze and pronghorn bound across a fenceless terrain.

▲ *Accustomed to scorching-hot summers* and frigid-cold winters, grasslands and ponderosa pines flourish at Lone Pine Point in Wind Cave National Park.

Size: 28,295 acres.
Highlights: Wind Cave; Cold Brook Canyon; Lookout Tower; Rankin Ridge, Centennial, and Elk Mountain trails.
General information: Cave temperature is about 53°F. Cave touring, hiking, camping. Watch out for rattlesnakes.
Location: South Dakota. See map on page 180.

WRANGELL-ST. ELIAS
Incorporating eastern Alaska's Wrangell, St. Elias, and Chugach mountain ranges—and containing a designated wilderness bigger than Massachusetts and Rhode Island combined—this park and its adjacent preserves form the largest unit in the national park system. It is a land of massive, still-active glaciers, of mighty rivers with intricately braided channels, of waterfalls plummeting down mountain gorges. Despite the terrain, wildlife thrives in the park. Mountain goats and the sure-footed Dall sheep can be found clambering up snow- and ice-covered slopes.
Size: Park is 8,323,618 acres.
Highlights: Mounts St. Elias, Sanford,

Drum, Blackburn, and Wrangell; Chitistone, Chitina, Copper, and Chisana rivers; Chitina, Malaspina, Hubbard, and Logan glaciers; Disenchantment Bay; Bagley Icefield; Kennicott copper mine (privately owned).
General information: Open in winter 8:00–4:30, Monday–Friday; in summer 8:00–6:00 daily. Hiking, camping, fishing, mountaineering, cross-country skiing, rafting, sea kayaking.
Location: Alaska. See maps on pages 79 and 81.

YELLOWSTONE
America's oldest national park is still among its most magnificent. Centered upon a vast volcanic basin, Yellowstone holds most of the world's geysers and hot springs. The justly famed "Old Faithful" is just one of some 300 geysers in the park. The Grand Canyon of the Yellowstone River sluices through ancient lava flows on its way to Yellowstone Lake; the lake's elevation, nearly 8,000 feet, suggests the size and majesty of the mountains that encircle its icy waters. Great stands of lodgepole pine, arid plateaus, subalpine meadows—even the formidable grizzly bear—all contribute to the sum of Yellowstone's grandeur.
Size: 2,219,791 acres.
Highlights: Eagle Peak; Reese Creek; Yellowstone Lake; Mammoth Hot Springs Terraces; Upper Geyser Basin (includes Old Faithful Geyser); Grand Canyon of the Yellowstone; Inspiration, Grandview, and Lookout points; Upper and Lower falls; Uncle Tom's Trail; Artist Point; Norris Geyser Basin; Fountain Paint Pot; Mud Volcano; Dragon's Mouth; West Thumb Geyser Basin; Black Sand Basin; Obsidian Cliff.
General information: Open from mid-April to late October and from mid-December to mid-March (for snowmobiles). Camping, lodging, wildlife viewing, hiking, boating, and horseback riding. Keep a distance of at least 100 yards from bears.
Location: Wyoming/Idaho/Montana. See maps on pages 206, 108, and 147.

YOSEMITE
Crusading naturalist John Muir was but one of countless travelers struck with awe at the sight of Yosemite Valley, where the glacier-scoured channel of the Merced River winds beneath the granite monoliths of Half Dome and El Capitan. Preserved as parkland largely through the efforts of Muir (who proved that the valley was created by glacial erosion), Yosemite National Park extends far beyond the river and its splendid waterfalls to encompass sequoia groves, the flower-strewn Tuolumne Meadows, as well as the 13,000-foot summits of the Sierra Nevada.
Size: 761,236 acres.
Highlights: Yosemite, Bridalveil, Vernal, Nevada, and Illilouette falls, Mariposa Grove of Giant Sequoias, Wawona, Gla-

cier Point, Half Dome, Mirror Lake, Tioga Pass, El Capitan, Cathedral Rock.
General information: Hiking trails, bicycle paths, camping, cross-country and downhill skiing, snowshoeing.
Location: California. See map on pages 86–87.

ZION
Zion National Park is the handiwork of two powerful forces—water and time. Its cliffs, canyons, and lofty mesas were sculpted over millions of years by the North Fork of the Virgin River and the park's lesser streams. As they chiseled deeper into Zion's sediments, the waterways uncovered a spectrum of reddish hues, which each day's sunset burnishes to bronze and gold. Near the park's northwestern corner stands one of its most sublime formations—Kolob Arch, which, at 310 feet, may be the world's largest arch.
Size: 146,598 acres.
Highlights: Great White Throne, Angels Landing, Virgin River, Great Arch of Zion, Checkerboard Mesa, Kolob Terrace and Arch, Weeping Rock, Finger Canyons, Lava Point, Emerald Pools, Hidden Canyon, the Narrows, Canyon Overlook, Riverside Walk, Pairus Trail.
General information: Hiking, biking, horseback riding, camping, and lodging are available. Carry plenty of water.
Location: Utah. See map on page 190.

▲ *Panoramic views* of Yosemite National Park reward intrepid hikers who manage to navigate the 4,900-foot ascent all the way to the top of Half Dome.

▲ *Water gushing* from the Lower Falls into Yellowstone National Park's Grand Canyon makes Artist Point a not-to-be-missed landmark for visitors.

▼ *Checkerboard Mesa,* sculpted in Navajo sandstone, showcases the striking geometry of Zion's ancient petrified dunes, crosshatched by nature's chisel.

LOCATOR MAPS

Adjacent to each state map is a locator map, which highlights the subject state in blue. Certain large states, like Texas, are divided into two sections and have two locator maps. On each of these, a red border marks the section shown.

MILEAGE SCALES

The mileage scale for each map notes either miles per inch or miles per half inch. For easy approximation of mileage, the decorative scale border of each map is divided into half-inch increments.

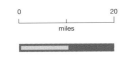

MAP PROJECTION

All state maps, metropolitan-area maps, and city-street maps use the Lambert Conformal Conic projection. Cartographers use projections to depict the three-dimensional world on a flat page. This projection attempts to reduce distortions of distances, direction, and shape with the use of two standard parallels near the top and bottom of the map.

ELEVATIONS

The key at right indicates the elevations that are represented on the state maps. Each tint represents land at a certain number of feet above sea level or below. The shaded area within the elevation key represents the topographic relief shading in the maps.

HEIGHT (ft.)

13,000
9,800
6,500
3,300
1,600
700
330
SEA LEVEL

How to Use the Maps

The next 133 pages of Atlas of America showcase 149 specially commissioned maps, including individual presentations of the 50 states in state-of-the-art satellite relief.

STATE MAPS

From Alabama to Wyoming, each state is represented with an easy-to-read, large-scale full-color map. In the case of a few states, such as California and Texas, the state has been divided into sections in order to make the map more legible.

Each state map is displayed with satellite-image-based topographic relief. Atlas of America is one of the first map collections to show all 50 states with topographic relief based on satellite photos of the land.

Every effort has been made to include all major features—major roadways (such as U.S. interstates and U.S. highways), lakes, and rivers. These maps also include all national and federally administered areas, such as national parks, national historic parks, national recreation areas, military bases, and Indian reservations. In addition, a few state-administered or privately owned points of interest have been included because of their particular significance in the state (for example, major tourist destinations and some state parks).

All cities and towns with populations recorded with the U.S. Bureau of the Census and/or the U.S. Postal Service are identified on the maps. In certain densely populated urban areas, however, it was impossible to fit all towns with recorded populations. (The gold-tinted

State Maps

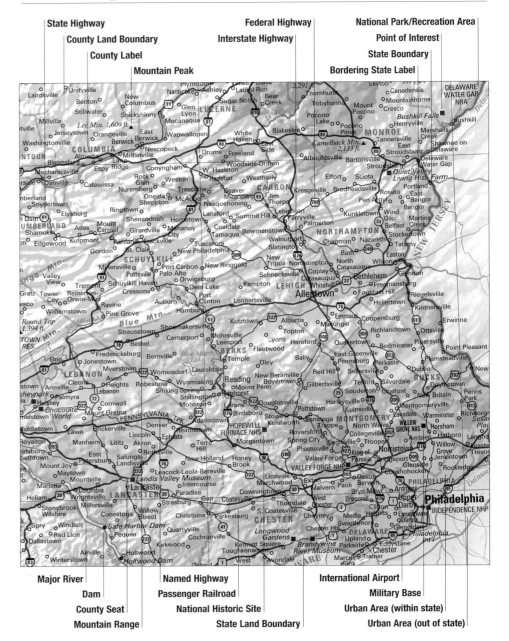

Symbols Used in State, Metropolitan, and City Maps

- National Land Boundary
- National Water Boundary
- State Land Boundary
- State Water Boundary
- County Land Boundary
- County Water Boundary
- Shoreline, River
- Intermittent River
- Canal/Aqueduct
- Continental Divide
- Limited-Access Highway
- Federal or State Highway
- Passenger Railroad
- Urban Area
- National Park/Military Installation/ Indian Reservation
- Lake, Reservoir

- Intermittent Lake
- Dry Lake
- Salt Pan
- Desert/Sand Area
- Swamp
- Lava Flow
- Glacier
- ⊛ State Capital
- ○ County Seat
- ○ Town
- ⤚ Pass
- ● Dam
- ▲ Mountain Peak
- ■ Park/Historic Site/Point of Interest
- ■ Indian Reservation/Government or Military Installation
- ✈ International Airport

Symbols and Type Styles Used in Metropolitan-Area and City-Street Maps

Symbology used in metropolitan-area and city-street maps differs slightly from that used in state maps. The following symbols and type styles are used exclusively in metropolitan and city maps:

- Nonurban Area
- Public Buildings
- City Limits
- Park/Forest/Recreation Area
- City/Local Streets
- Ferries
- Tunnels
- State Land Boundary
- Passenger Railroad
- ⤼ Municipal Airport
- *Brooklyn* Borough
- *Vieux Carré* Neighborhood

Metropolitan and City Maps

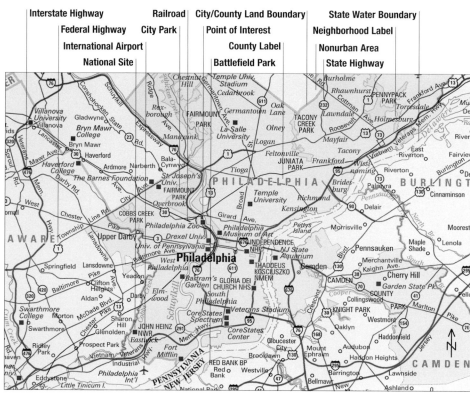

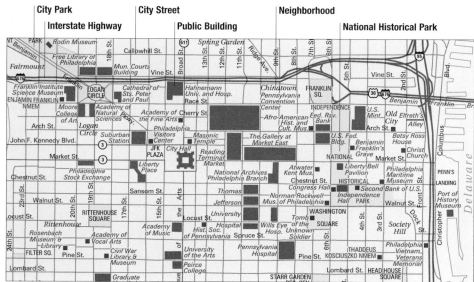

regions on the state maps represent densely populated urban areas.) Some of those towns do appear on metropolitan-area maps, which are rendered in a larger scale.

METROPOLITAN-AREA MAPS

In a number of states, closer-focused metropolitan maps are included; these areas were chosen because of their significant population or their regional importance. On these maps, the gold-tinted area represents the city's municipal boundaries. All the features of the state maps appear on the metropolitan-area maps, with the exception of elevation tints and topographic relief.

The larger scale of the metropolitan maps permits the inclusion of more features—additional towns, almost all state-administered parks, and more privately owned points of interest, such as museums, educational institutions, and nationally known hospitals. Neighborhoods have also been identified, such as Elmwood, Logan, and Kensington in the map of Philadelphia at left.

CITY-STREET MAPS

Occasional street maps are also included and give a close-up view of Boston, Chicago, New York, Philadelphia, and Washington, D.C. These especially dense (and walkable) cities have many points of interest and/or historic sites that are easy to identify on the maps.

THEMATIC MAPS

Some states feature thematic maps that illustrate a unique component of the state's geology, history, or culture. For example, the section on California has a map of the state's irrigation system; one of the pages on New York shows a map of the Erie Canal, while the section on Michigan includes a map of the state's 118 lighthouses.

MAP TYPE STYLES

Atlas of America uses the following type styles to distinguish among features on the maps.

Counties:
LANCASTER

Cities and Towns (by population):

New York	Over 2,000,000
Philadelphia	1,000,000–1,999,999
Cleveland	500,000–999,999
Buffalo	250,000–499,999
Hartford	100,000–249,999
Altoona	30,000–99,999
Plattsburgh	10,000–29,999
Hollidaysburg	1–9,999

Points of Interest:
■ *Museum of the Prairie*

National Parks, Historic Sites, and Recreation Areas:
■ MINUTEMAN NHS
▨ BADLANDS NATIONAL PARK

Government and Military Sites:
■ WRIGHT-PATTERSON AFB
▨ *WHITE SANDS PROVING GROUND*

Indian Reservations:
■ Shoshone IR
▨ *PAIUTE INDIAN RESERVATION*

Bodies of Water and Rivers:
Gulf of Mexico

Capes and Points:
Cape Canaveral

Peaks and Passes:
▲ *Mt. Davis*
⚑ *Donner Pass*

Islands and Peninsulas:
Block Island

Mountain Ranges, Plateaus, Hills:
Allegheny Mountains

Lowlands, Valleys, Canyons:
Sacramento Valley

Abbreviations Used in State, Metropolitan, and City Maps

Natural and Physical Names
Branch — Br.
Brook — Bk.
Canal — Can.
Cape — C.
Channel — Chan.
Creek — Cr.
Fork — Fk.
Harbor — Har.
Head — Hd.
Heights — Hts.
Island, Islands — I., Is.
Lake — L.
Mount — Mt.
Mountain — Mtn.
Mountains — Mts.
Peak — Pk.
Peninsula — Pen.
Point — Pt.
Range — Ra.
Reservoir — Res.
River — R.
Spring, Springs — Spr., Sprs.
Strait — Str.
Valley — Val.

Administrative Names
Air Force Base — AFB
Arsenal — Ars.
Battlefield Park — BP
Capital — Cap.
Coast Guard — CG
Coast Guard Air Station — CGAS
Coast Guard Station — CGS
County — Co.
Department — Dept.
District — Dist.
Fort — Ft.
Indian Reservation — IR
Marine Corps Air Station — MCAS
Military Reservation — MR
National Battlefield — NB
National Battlefield Park — NBP
National Grassland — NG
National Historic Site — NHS
National Historical Park — NHP
National Lakeshore — NL
National Memorial — NMEM
National Monument — NM
National Military Park — NMLP
National Park — NP
National Preserve — NPRSV
National Recreational Area — NRA

National River and Recreational Area — NRRA
National Seashore — NS
Naval Air Station — NAS
Park — Pk.
State Beach — SB
State Historic Park — SHP
State Historic Site — SHS
State Monument — SM
State Park — SP
State Recreational Area — SRA
Township — Twp.
Village — Vil.

Transportation Names
Avenue — Ave.
Boulevard — Blvd.
Bridge — Br.
Drive — Dr.
Expressway — Expwy.
Freeway — Frwy.
Highway — Hwy.
Junction — Jct.
Parkway — Pkwy.
Railroad — RR
Road — Rd.
Square — Sq.
Street — St.
Thruway — Thwy.
Turnpike — Tpk.

Generic Names
Building — Bldg.
Center — Cen.
College — Coll.
East — E.
Federal — Fed.
Historic, Historical — Hist.
Hospital — Hosp.
Institute — Inst.
International — Int'l.
Memorial — Mem.
Military — Mil.
Monument — Mon.
Municipal — Mun.
Museum — Mus.
National — Nat'l.
North — N.
Number — No.
Preserve — Prsv.
Recreation, Recreational — Rec.
Reserve, Reservation — Rsv.
Saint — St.
South — S.
Station — Sta.
Technology — Tech.
United States — U.S.
University — Univ.
West — W.

OUR SOURCES

The U.S. Bureau of the Census and the U.S. Postal Service are the sources of all city and town names. The names and locations of points of interest have been confirmed by official state maps, state tourist publications, or official state Web sites. Land elevations have been provided by the U.S. Geological Survey.

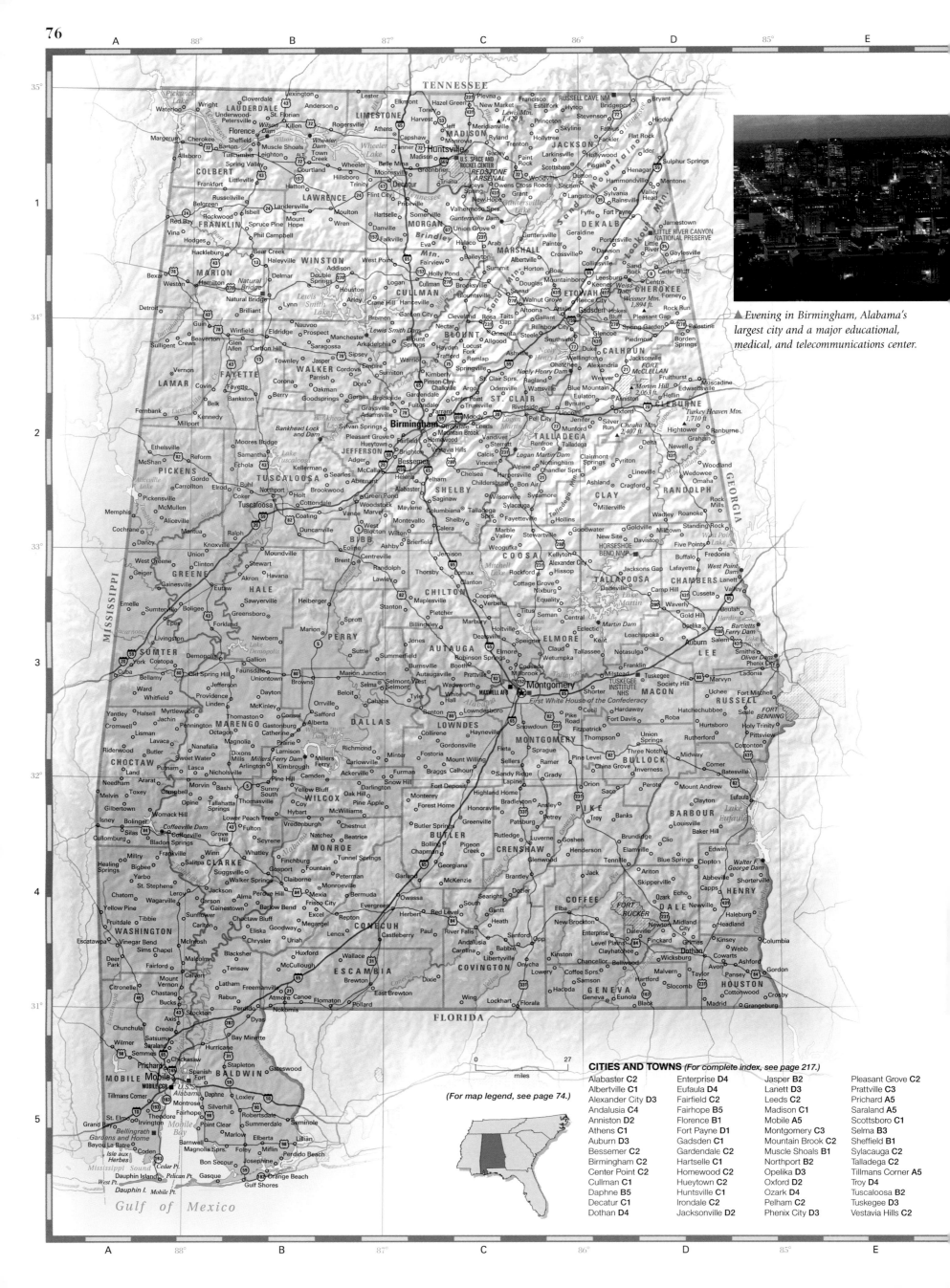

Evening in Birmingham, Alabama's largest city and a major educational, medical, and telecommunications center.

(For map legend, see page 74.)

CITIES AND TOWNS (For complete index, see page 217.)

Alabaster C2	Enterprise D4	Jasper B2	Pleasant Grove C2
Albertville C1	Eufaula D4	Lanett D3	Prattville C3
Alexander City D3	Fairfield C2	Leeds C2	Prichard A5
Andalusia C4	Fairhope B5	Madison C1	Saraland A5
Anniston D2	Florence B1	Mobile A5	Scottsboro C1
Athens C1	Fort Payne D1	Montgomery C3	Selma B3
Auburn D3	Gadsden C1	Mountain Brook C2	Sheffield B1
Bessemer C2	Gardendale C2	Muscle Shoals B1	Sylacauga C2
Birmingham C2	Hartselle C1	Northport B2	Talladega C2
Center Point C2	Homewood C2	Opelika D3	Tillmans Corner A5
Cullman C1	Hueytown C2	Oxford D2	Troy D4
Daphne B5	Huntsville C1	Ozark D4	Tuscaloosa B2
Decatur C1	Irondale C2	Pelham C2	Tuskegee D3
Dothan D4	Jacksonville D2	Phenix City D3	Vestavia Hills C2

Alabama

Home of King Cotton, seat of the Confederacy, and a focal point of the civil rights movement, this Southern state of brooding mountain woods and rolling coastal plains is a place steeped in antebellum tradition but with a mindful eye to a promising future. With vast natural resources at its disposal, a vibrant modern economy, and a more open society committed to racial equality and justice, Alabama is, in every way, a vital part of the New South.

A STATE OF RIVERS

So central are Alabama's rivers to its heritage that their image is featured on the state's great seal. In fact, Alabama contains some 1,350 miles of navigable waterways, more than any other state. Along these waterways—which include the Alabama, the Coosa, the Tallapoosa, the Black Warrior, and the Tombig-bee—steamboats laden with valuable cotton once glided their way downstream to the port of Mobile.

When explorers set foot in Alabama in the 16th century, some 65 percent of the state was heavily forested—about the same percentage as today. The first Spaniard to explore the region thoroughly was the conquistador Hernando de Soto, who found it disappointing: swampy near the coast, thickly wooded and mountainous to the north, and without a trace of gold. In addition, De Soto's encounters with the local Indians proved hazardous, culminating in a bloody battle with the Choctaw, led by Chief Tuscaloosa, in which 2,500 men perished. Such stiff opposition to European, and later American, encroachment lasted nearly three centuries.

COTTON YIELDS TO PEANUTS AND STEEL

The defeat of the Creek Indians by American forces commanded by Andrew Jackson during the War of 1812 effectively ended Indian resistance in the Alabama Territory and opened the doors to settlement. Immigrants poured in from neighboring states, and the population requirement for statehood was met in just two years. The state's central region, known as the Black Belt for its rich, dark soil, became home to huge cotton plantations, the centers of antebellum Southern life.

Cotton held sway over Alabama's agricultural economy until 1915, when the great boll weevil blight decimated the crop and forced growers to diversify. In the state's southeast corner, farmers began growing peanuts; today that region remains a major producer of the nation's peanut crop.

No less vital to Alabama's post–Civil War economy was its steel industry. The east central region of the state, part of the Piedmont Plateau, concealed valuable treasures: huge deposits of iron, coal, and limestone, all in proximity and collectively known as the Big Seam. Here, in the 1880s, the great iron and steel mills of Bir-

▲ *The U.S. Space & Rocket Center's* collection has been hailed by former astronaut John Glenn as the world's finest. Nearby, at NASA's Marshall Space Flight Center, astronauts prepare for weightlessness in a 1-million-gallon tank of water.

▲ *Little River Canyon,* formed more than 300 million years ago, is the deepest gorge east of the Mississippi River.

mingham were born, earning that city the nickname Pittsburgh of the South. Like cotton, steel has long since been dethroned, the victim of a global market that makes domestic steel too expensive to produce. Still, Birmingham has kept pace with the times, and today the city is a leader in the medical field. In addition to its scientific research centers and technological industries, Birmingham is home to 21 hospitals, most prominently the medical center at the University of Alabama.

THE BATTLE FOR EQUALITY

In the mid-20th century, Alabama's struggles centered on the fight for racial justice. Following the Civil War, segregationist policies were enacted that denied virtually all political, educational, and economic opportunity to the state's black minority. The tide began to turn in 1955, when a black woman named Rosa Parks refused to surrender her seat in the all-white section of a Montgomery city bus. Parks's arrest sparked an outcry, and the resulting 381-day bus boycott by black residents, led by civil rights activist Rev. Martin Luther King, Jr., turned national attention to the plight of disenfranchised minorities.

Even though the U.S. Supreme Court had ruled Alabama's segregationist policies unconstitutional in 1954, the state remained a hotbed of civil rights activism. Under the leadership of Gov. George Wallace, an avowed segregationist, change was slow, and such civil rights actions as marches, voter registrations, and sit-ins often resulted in violent suppression by local police. Federal intervention and two major laws—the Civil Rights Act of 1964 and the Voting Rights Act of 1965—helped significantly to bring the state's black residents, roughly a quarter of the state's population, into the network of political and economic power over the next 20 years.

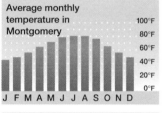

▲ *Adopted in 1895,* the state flag bears the cross of St. Andrew and is modeled after the Confederate flag.

STATE DATA

State bird: Yellowhammer
State flower: Camellia
State tree: Southern pine
State motto: *Audemus jura nostra defendere* (We dare defend our rights)
State song: "Alabama"
Abbreviations: Ala.; AL (postal)
Origin of the name: From the Choctaw word *alibamu,* meaning "I clear the thicket"
Nicknames: Cotton State, Heart of Dixie, Yellowhammer State

AREA AND SIZE

Total area: 51,609 sq. mi.
Rank within U.S.: 29
Extent: 329 mi. north–south; 210 mi. east–west
Highest elevation: Cheaha Mountain, 2,407 ft.
Lowest elevation: Sea level along the Gulf of Mexico

POPULATION

Total: 4,451,000
Rank within U.S.: 22
Ethnic breakdown: White: 72.6%; Black: 25.5%; Hispanic: 0.8%; Asian: 0.7%, Indian: 0.4%
Population density: 87.5 people per sq. mi.

CLIMATE

Average monthly temperature in Montgomery
100°F / 80°F / 60°F / 40°F / 20°F / 0°F
J F M A M J J A S O N D

Average monthly precipitation in Montgomery
10" / 8" / 6" / 4" / 2" / 0"
J F M A M J J A S O N D

ECONOMY

Manufacturing: Pulp and paper, chemicals, textiles, steel
Service industries: Wholesale and retail trade; community, business, and personal services; government
Agriculture: Broiler chickens, cattle, cotton, peanuts, corn

ALABAMA TIME LINE

1519 Spanish explorer Alonso de Piñeda sails into Mobile Bay.

1540 Spain claims lands west and north of Florida.

1629 Charles I deeds Carolinas to Sir Robert Heath. England claims the region.

1783 Britain cedes all lands east of Mississippi except Florida to the U.S.

1819 Alabama joins the Union as 22nd state.

1861 Alabama secedes from the Union. Confederate president Jefferson Davis chooses Montgomery as his capital. (It was moved to Richmond, Virginia, later that year.)

1868 Alabama is readmitted to the Union.

1881 Tuskegee Institute opens; the institute's purpose is to provide black students with a practical education.

1933 Tennessee Valley Authority initiates conservation and flood-control projects in northern Alabama.

1963 In support of voter registration for blacks, Rev. Martin Luther King, Jr., leads a march from Selma to Montgomery.

1972 Gov. George C. Wallace is shot in Maryland while campaigning for the Democratic presidential nomination.

1989 The nation's first civil rights monument is dedicated in Montgomery.

Alaska

▲ **Alaska's flag,** adopted in 1927, shows the Big Dipper and the North Star. The constellation alludes to Alaska's gold resources; the star recalls Alaska's status as the northernmost state.

STATE DATA

State bird: Willow ptarmigan
State flower: Forget-me-not
State tree: Sitka spruce
State motto: North to the future
State song: "Alaska's Flag"
Abbreviations: Alaska; AK (postal)
Origin of the name: From the Aleut word *Alyeska* (The Great Land)
Nicknames: Last Frontier, Land of the Midnight Sun, Great Land

AREA AND SIZE

Total area: 586,412 sq. mi.
Rank within U.S.: 1
Extent: 1,350 mi. north–south; 2,350 mi. east–west
Highest elevation: Mount McKinley, at 20,320 ft. above sea level, the highest peak in North America
Lowest elevation: Sea level

POPULATION

Total: 653,000
Rank within U.S.: 48
Ethnic breakdown: White: 70.6%; Indian: 13.9%; Asian: 6.7%; Hispanic: 4.7%; Black: 4.1%
Population density: 1.1 people per sq. mi.

CLIMATE

Average monthly temperature in Fairbanks
100°F / 80°F / 60°F / 40°F / 20°F / 0°F / -20°F
J F M A M J J A S O N D

Average monthly precipitation in Fairbanks
10" / 8" / 6" / 4" / 2" / 0"
J F M A M J J A S O N D

Average monthly temperature in Juneau
100°F / 80°F / 60°F / 40°F / 20°F / 0°F
J F M A M J J A S O N D

Average monthly precipitation in Juneau
10" / 8" / 6" / 4" / 2" / 0"
J F M A M J J A S O N D

ECONOMY

Service industries: Government, public schools and hospitals, shipping, telephone companies
Mining: Petroleum, gold, zinc, coal, crushed stone
Manufacturing: Food processing, petroleum products, wood products, paper products

---

Cool rain forests drip with moss. Arctic deserts resonate with the sound of howling winds. Snowcapped peaks, some of the tallest in all the 50 states, punctuate this land with their rugged splendor, and remote, fog-enshrouded islands lie at the doorstep of Asia. A portal for human migration since the Ice Age, Alaska, America's "last frontier," is still a land of Inuit and Indian hunters, prospectors, dogsled mushers, and a rough-and-ready frontier spirit.

THE "GREAT LAND"

Nowhere else in America does mankind's imprint rest as lightly as it does in Alaska. Vast stretches of the state are inhabited only by grizzly bears and caribou. More than twice the size of Texas, Alaska has slightly more than 650,000 residents, and half of them live in or around the state's two largest cities, Anchorage and Fairbanks. The state capital of Juneau, set among the spectacular fjords of the southeastern panhandle, is accessible only by boat or airplane.

Alaska is a place of superlatives. While most states have no glaciers at all, Alaska has 100,000 of them. It is also a land of extremes, at once the eastern-most, northernmost, and westernmost state. Because the curving chain of the Aleutian Islands pokes hundreds of miles beyond the 180° meridian, the international date line makes a wide arc so that the archipelago can be in the same day as the rest of the state.

LAND OF MOUNTAINS, LAND OF WATER

The northernmost state is hardly the monotonous, ice-bound expanse most citizens of the "Lower 48" (as Alaskans call the continental United States) imagine it to be. The southeastern panhandle, a stunning archipelago of green islands and ultramarine bays, is a temperate rain forest of astonishing luxuriance. A mild coastal climate and 200 inches of precipitation a year support an ecosystem of towering spruces, red cedars, and western hemlocks. Bald eagles build their huge, car-size nests in old-growth trees, and pods of

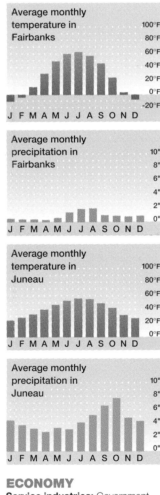

▲ **Mount McKinley** rises from a thick shroud of clouds. Native Athabaskans named the mountain Denali, "The High One."

▲ **The Malaspina Glacier,** which spreads over an area of approximately 850 square miles, is so large it would cover all of Rhode Island.

orcas, or killer whales, patrol the famed glacier-filled Inside Passage. The justly famous Matanuska Valley near Anchorage is known as Alaska's breadbasket; in this area cabbages grow so large in the deep soil and near-endless summer sunlight that they must be cut from their stalks with saws.

Alaska is defined by water and mountains. Bounded on three sides by salt water (the Pacific Ocean to the south, the Arctic Ocean to the north, and the Bering Sea to the west), it has more coastline than the rest of the 49 states combined—some 6,600 miles, not counting islands. Inland, an estimated 3 million lakes cover a staggering 20,000 square miles. Three major mountain systems cross the state. Arching up from the southeastern panhandle is the Coast Range, which includes the rugged, snowcapped St. Elias Mountains, the loftiest coastal peaks in the world, north of Haines. The Alaska Range, with Mount McKinley as its capstone, embraces the milder Cook Inlet region near Anchorage, while the remote Brooks Range walls off the North Slope. In between is the land Alaskans simply call the interior, an area the size of California drained by the almost 2,000-mile-long Yukon River. This is a region of contrasts, where the climate is dry but much of the ground (underlaid with a granitelike permafrost) is perpetually soggy; where temperatures may climb into the 80s during a summer heat wave but drop down to 50 or 60 degrees below zero during winter; where in late June, night lasts only a couple of hours, but in December the sun barely clears the horizon.

THE UNEASY EARTH

Many fathoms below the ocean's surface, hard sections of rock—called plates—make up the Pacific seafloor. Occasionally, one plate will slide under another and create a deep depression. The vast trench that extends thousands of miles along Alaska's southwestern shoreline is a product of this process, called subduction. The friction that results from one plate's sinking beneath another generates heat and sends molten rock bubbling to the surface, fuel for the restless Redoubt Volcano and dozens of others that rumble along the coast. In the Valley of Ten Thousand

◀ **Caribou** migrate extensively in the spring and fall, sometimes traveling more than 600 miles each year.

Chibukak Pt.
Gambell
St. Lawrence Island
Hall I.
Glory of Russia C.
St. Matthew Island
C. Upright
B E R I N G
S E A
St. Paul I.
St. Paul
Pribilof Islands
St. George I.
St. George
A l e u t i
Makushin Volcano 6,680
Dutch H
Umnak I.
Unalaska I.

A   172°   B   168°

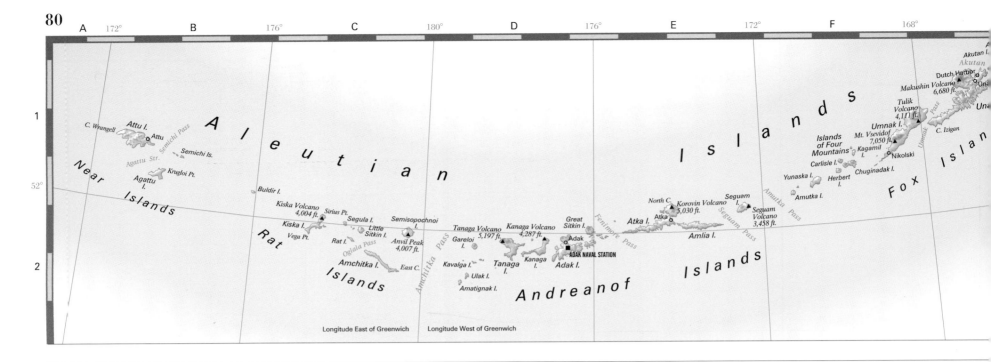

A 172° B 176° C 180° D 176° E 172° F 168°

Longitude East of Greenwich | Longitude West of Greenwich

ALASKA

1741 Vitus Bering, a Dane working for Russia, becomes first European to reach Alaska.

1745–59 Russians, in search of sea otter furs, arrive in Aleutian Islands.

1784 Russians establish base on Kodiak Island.

1804 Sitka becomes capital of Russian Alaska.

1867 U.S. pays $7.2 million for Alaska—less than two cents an acre.

1878 First fish cannery is built on Prince of Wales Island.

1899 Thousands of prospectors flood into Nome after gold is discovered.

1900 Juneau becomes capital.

1912 Alaska becomes a U.S. territory.

1957 Oil is discovered on Kenai Peninsula in southeastern Alaska.

1959 Alaska joins the Union as 49th state.

1964 Earthquake and tsunami kill 115 people and cause severe damage in Anchorage, Kodiak, Seward, and Valdez.

1968 More oil is discovered near Prudhoe Bay in Arctic Circle.

1971 Federal government gives 40 million acres and $962.5 million to Alaska's Eskimos, Indians, and Aleuts.

1977 Eight-hundred-mile Trans-Alaska pipeline from Prudhoe Bay to Valdez is completed.

1989 Prince William Sound is site of largest oil spill in U.S. history.

▲ **Mount Augustine** *belches smoke over Cook Inlet. On October 6, 1883, this volcano split violently in two, bathing the night sky in firelight.*

Smokes, now part of Katmai National Park, steam still rises from a moonlike landscape that was formed by a massive eruption in 1912. Sometimes titanic pressures build beneath the ocean floor and rock the state with earthquakes. The destructive quake of March 1964, which measured higher than 8 on the Richter scale, ravaged shore communities with a deadly tsunami. Lesser quakes regularly rattle Alaska but rarely trouble its residents.

WILDLIFE TREASURES

Furs were Alaska's first wealth, and the state still teems with wildlife, including fish—salmon, halibut, herring, and others—which has been an economic mainstay. Unlike the rest of the United States, Alaska has large populations of the types of animals that require solitude and wide-open spaces—gray wolves, white Dall sheep, trumpeter swans, among many others. Polar bears rule the tundra, while along the coast brown bears, which may weigh 1,600 pounds or more, grow fat on a diet of salmon and berries. Caribou still make their seasonal journeys

of hundreds of miles, filling the silent Arctic air with the odd, castanetlike clicking of their hooves. More than half a million caribou live in Alaska (roughly one for each human resident), including the 170,000-head Porcupine herd, which migrates each spring from the Yukon area, where the Porcupine River meets the Yellow River in northeast Alaska, to the coastal plain of northern Alaska, where the females bear young.

Along the Arctic coast polar bears hunt seals through the frozen, sunless winter, but spring brings a rush of birds to the once-barren tundra. By marshy lakes, sandhill cranes perform elaborate courtship dances, complete with bugling calls that may carry a mile or more; at the same time, waves of other migrants pour in: shorebirds like Hudsonian godwits and yellowlegs back from Argentina, snow geese from California, and Pacific golden plovers from New Zealand. Summer also brings swarms of mosquitoes—so many that pregnant caribou seek the sanctuary of cold, windy snowfields to give birth.

HUMAN TIDES

More than 15,000 years ago, much of the world's water was frozen. Because of this, sea levels were sometimes more than 300 feet lower than they are today, and there was more dry land. Alaska was connected to Siberia by a wide, marshy land bridge that is now under water. This bridge was the entryway for humans into North America, and by the time the bridge sank beneath the encroaching waves, Alaska was peopled with a variety of native cultures that survive to this day. In the Arctic and western Alaska, the Inuit, or Eskimo, had a maritime

Glacier Distribution

Alaska's 100,000 glaciers cover about 29,000 square miles, or only 5 percent of the state.

☐ Existing glaciers

▨ Areas covered by glaciers in the Pleistocene era

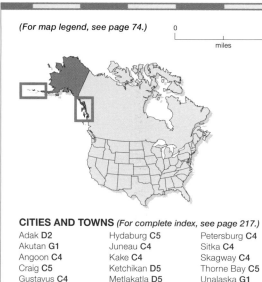

(For map legend, see page 74.)

0 96
miles

CITIES AND TOWNS *(For complete index, see page 217.)*

Adak **D2**	Hydaburg **C5**	Petersburg **C4**
Akutan **G1**	Juneau **C4**	Sitka **C4**
Angoon **C4**	Kake **C4**	Skagway **C4**
Craig **C5**	Ketchikan **D5**	Thorne Bay **C5**
Gustavus **C4**	Metlakatla **D5**	Unalaska **G1**
Haines **C4**	Mountain Point **D5**	Wrangell **C4**
Hoonah **C4**	Pelican **B4**	Yakutat **B4**

▶ *Inuit, or Eskimo, children* learn to adjust to life in the bitter northern and western areas of Alaska, where annual temperatures average only around 25°F.

lifestyle and hunted whales, seals, polar bears, and walrus. The Aleuts of the Aleutian Islands earned the name "brothers of the sea otter" for their skill in handling skin boats. Across the tundra and stunted forests of the interior, Athabaskan Indians hunted the abundant caribou and moose. In the southeastern panhandle, salmon fishing allowed the Haida and the Tlingit to thrive in villages famous for their elaborately decorated wooden houses and totem poles.

This is the world that Russian explorers found in 1741. Czar Peter the Great ordered the admiral Vitus Bering to chart the Siberian and Alaskan coasts, to find out whether they were connected. Instead of a land bridge, however, Bering found the strait that now bears his name and a bonanza of furred animals. By 1784 the Russians had established a permanent settlement on Kodiak Island. Alaska, with its riches of seals, sea otters, and other valuable fur-bearing animals, was a treasure trove for the Russians; more than 15,000 sea otter pelts were shipped out of the village of Sitka in 1804 alone.

BUYING "ICEBERGIA"

The fur traders, or *promishleniks*, enslaved many of the Aleuts as trappers and hunters, and the traders' brutal tactics sparked nearly a half century of warfare. They also exhausted the fur supply, so that in the 1860s Russia offered to sell Alaska to the United States. In 1867 U.S. Secretary of State William H. Seward negotiated the purchase of more than 500,000 square miles for $7.2 million (less than two cents an acre) and was vilified; although Congress supported the purchase, some Americans derided the former Russian colony as "Seward's Folly," "Walrussia," or "Icebergia."

The first official census of the new possession, in 1880, recorded some 33,500 people, all but a few hundred of them natives. That changed almost overnight with the first of several major gold strikes. Thousands of fortune seekers—known as stampeders—turned Skagway from a quiet homestead into a seething, violent, shack-and-tent city of 20,000 people, most of whom were preparing for the dangerous climb over Chilkoot Pass and into the Yukon.

Unfortunately, the gold rush also brought a flood of lawlessness, and the U.S. government, which had largely ignored Alaska for decades, began to reassess the region. In 1884 Congress appointed a governor and established a code of laws; in 1906 it authorized a nonvoting delegate to the House of Representatives. Designation as a territory came in 1912, and politicians who backed Alaska's inclusion in the Union urged its swift admittance. Instead, the issue languished until 1959, when Alaska finally became the 49th state.

WARTIME INDUSTRY, PEACETIME BOOM

Two events dramatically shaped modern Alaskan life: the invasion of the Aleutian Islands by Japanese soldiers during World War II and the discovery of oil and natural gas reserves on the North Slope. Although the Japanese had hoped to use the Aleutians as a springboard for an invasion of the American mainland, they never advanced beyond remote islands like Attu and Kiska, where terrible weather and American resistance stopped them. The war, meanwhile, spurred a huge military buildup in mainland Alaska. Anchorage, once a small supply camp for railroad workers, grew enormously as troops poured into army and air force installations and the number of military personnel skyrocketed from a few hundred to 124,000 statewide.

Realizing that sea routes were vulnerable to attack, in 1942 the government launched the construction of the Alaska Highway, a 1,523-mile road stretching from northern British Columbia to Fairbanks. More than 11,000 soldiers, along with many civilian Alaskans, managed to complete the herculean task in just eight months. Even today, although most of the road is paved and the old wood-and-pontoon bridges have been replaced by sturdier structures, traveling the Alaska Highway—with its ruts, loose rock, and frost heaves (rippled pavement caused by constant freezing and thawing)—remains an adventure.

The discovery of oil beneath the Kenai Peninsula in the 1950s set the stage for Alaska's petroleum boom. Word of large oil and gas reserves in the Arctic at Prudhoe Bay and the construction of the Trans-Alaska pipeline in the 1970s also sparked a new debate in the state—that of economic development versus environmental protection. This reached a crescendo when the *Exxon Valdez* spilled 11 million gallons of oil into Prince William Sound in 1989. The cleanup cost more than $2 billion, and some eight years later, 60,000 acres of the land was turned over to the U.S. and Alaskan governments and given the status of a protected habitat—fitting for a land that John Muir called "as wild and pure as paradise . . . sufficient in kind and quantity for gods and men."

▲ *Two women prospectors* pick their way through an Alaskan mining camp. In all, the Alaskan gold rush produced more than $1 billion worth of the yellow metal.

▼ *Juneau is situated* between Mount Juneau and the Gastineau Channel. It is the only state capital in the nation without road access to the rest of the state.

Arizona

From the awe-inspiring majesty of the Grand Canyon to the barren beauty of the great Sonoran desert, Arizona is a state where nature's power reigns supreme. Carved by the titanic forces of time, this dramatic, arid landscape has long been stamped in the popular imagination as the very essence of the American West. But modern Arizona is a cultural crossroads as well, shaped as much by Hispanic and Native American influences as it is by cowboy culture.

▲ *Sandstone formations pulse with striated color on the Colorado Plateau, which comprises some 50,000 square miles.*

▲ **The state flag** *features 13 red and gold rays, the colors of Spain, which controlled the region from 1540 to 1821. The copper-colored star represents Arizona's chief mineral. The flag was adopted on February 27, 1917.*

STATE DATA

State bird: Cactus wren
State flower: Saguaro cactus flower
State tree: Paloverde
State motto: *Ditat Deus* (God enriches)
State song: "Arizona: The March"
Abbreviations: Ariz.; AZ (postal)
Origin of the name: From a Papago word meaning "small spring"
Nicknames: Grand Canyon State; Copper State

AREA AND SIZE

Total area: 113,909 sq. mi.
Rank within U.S.: 6
Extent: 389 mi. north–south; 337 mi. east–west
Highest elevation: Humphreys Peak, 12,633 ft.
Lowest elevation: 70 ft. above sea level at Colorado River in Yuma County

POPULATION

Total: 4,798,000
Rank within U.S.: 21
Ethnic breakdown: White: 67.8%; Hispanic: 22.3%; Indian: 4.8%; Black: 3.1%; Asian: 1.9%
Population density: 42.2 people per sq. mi.

CLIMATE

Average monthly temperature in Phoenix

	100°F
	80°F
	60°F
	40°F
	20°F
	0°F

J F M A M J J A S O N D

Average monthly precipitation in Phoenix

	10"
	8"
	6"
	4"
	2"
	0"

J F M A M J J A S O N D

ECONOMY

Service industries: Finance, insurance, and real estate; medical facilities; hotels and resorts
Manufacturing: Transportation and electrical equipment, scientific instruments
Agriculture: Beef cattle, cotton, lettuce
Mining: Copper, coal, sand

THREE DISTINCT REGIONS

Visitors to the state will find that in Arizona location is everything. On a summer day the temperature in Phoenix may scrape 110 degrees, while just a few hours' drive north, in Flagstaff, the temperature may be as much as 30 degrees cooler. In fact, Arizona has three distinct geophysical regions.

One region, the Colorado Plateau, is a group of broad table-like structures and valleys that stretch into Colorado, Utah, and New Mexico and make up 40 percent of the state. Lava flows and volcanic mountains punctuate the plateau, as do gorges. Perhaps the most breathtaking of these is the Grand Canyon. It is nine miles wide from the North Rim to the South Rim as the crow flies, but by car the trip is 246 miles. Some 5 million years old, the canyon is a diorama of ages past; its inner walls, at about 2 billion years old, are among the oldest exposed rocks on the planet.

The rest of the plateau region is no less a scenic wonder. East of the canyon, the Painted Desert dazzles with undulating mounds of vividly colored sediments. The skyscraping monoliths of Monument Valley, in the state's lonely northeastern corner, are natural sculptures that resemble everything from wedding cakes to cathedrals.

▲ **Monument Valley Tribal Park,** *in northeastern Arizona, as the 1,000-foot-high Right-hand Mitten (center) casts its long shadow westward.*

Moving southward, the Colorado Plateau comes to an abrupt halt at the Mogollon Rim, a rugged escarpment that signals the beginning of the Mexican Highlands. A temperate climate, a generous supply of timber, and rich deposits of gold, copper, and other minerals concealed within its hills made this region appealing to early settlers.

To the south of the central mountains, the desert asserts itself mile by mile. Pine trees yield to creosote bushes and smoke trees, and the stately profile of the great saguaro cactus looms over boulder-strewn valleys.

▶ **The collared lizard,** *one of 45 species of lizards found in Arizona.*

A LONG HISTORY

Although it is the youngest of the contiguous 48 states—it entered the Union in 1912—Arizona has a history that is ancient. Archeological evidence indicates that human habitation began in the region some 25,000 years ago. Most of these early peoples were cave dwellers; some were nomadic hunters. During the past 2,000 years, four distinct cultures appeared, most notably the agrarian Hohokam and the cliff-dwelling Anasazi. By 1450 both tribes had disappeared, replaced by the nomadic Apache and Navajo.

In 1539 a Franciscan from Mexico, Marcos de Niza, became the first white person to enter Arizona. A permanent European presence was not established, however, until 1692, when Jesuit missionary Eusebio Kino founded a mission at Guevavi, eight miles north of Nogales. More than 20 missions were later established by Father Kino. Incessant warfare with Apache and Comanche Indians, combined with the rigors of Arizona's climate, gradually depleted the white population. By 1821, when Mexico won independence from Spain, along with the Arizona Territory, few white settlers remained to notice.

When the United States acquired Arizona from the Mexicans in 1848, not many Americans held hopes that such a harsh land could be tamed. The discovery of rich deposits of gold, silver, and copper drew prospectors in the 1880s. Others came to graze cattle or farm in the fertile river valleys of the southwestern and central regions. Still, Arizona remained, in most ways, a frontier society until the 1930s, when modern air conditioning, commercial air travel, and the electronics industry spawned the rapid growth for which the state is now known.

A MIX OF CULTURES, OLD AND NEW

Living on more than 20 Indian reservations, Arizona's Native American population is the third largest in the United States and is a powerful cultural presence in the state. Many members of the Hopi tribe live in pueblos built centuries ago on the high mesas of the Navajo reservation. Arizona is also unabashedly bilingual; about one-fifth of its residents claim Hispanic descent. In a state where Western heritage runs deep, many Arizonans are newcomers (only a third of Arizona's residents can claim it as their birth state); they are drawn to the state by its mild weather and vigorous economy. Other people are seasonal residents—the so-called snowbirds who flock each winter to the RV parks and timeshare condos around Phoenix, Tucson, and Tempe.

Such rapid growth as Arizona has seen in recent decades has not come without a cost, and many people wonder when the tide of immigrants to the state will tax its resources to the breaking point. Still, despite the changes people have wrought on the landscape, much of Arizona remains as it always was—a place of spectacular beauty, all but impossible to tame.

ARIZONA TIMELINE

1540 Coronado discovers the Grand Canyon.
1692 Jesuit Eusebio Kino begins missionary work in the area.
1752 First permanent Spanish settlement is established at Tubac.
1821 Arizona passes from Spanish to Mexican rule.
1848 Mexico cedes Arizona north of Gila River to U.S.
1853 U.S. acquires Arizona with Gadsden Purchase.
1858 Gold is discovered at Gila City, on the Colorado River.
1864 Some 9,000 Navajo surrender to U.S. after attack on Canyon de Chelly.
1881 Wyatt Earp and his two brothers gun down three men at O.K. Corral.
1886 Apache chief Geronimo is exiled to Florida; Indian raids on Arizona Territory end.
1889 Capital of Arizona Territory is moved from Prescott to Phoenix.
1912 Arizona joins the Union as 48th state.
1936 Hoover Dam is dedicated.
1950–60 Arizona's population increases faster than that of any other state.
1985 Central Arizona Project directs water from Colorado River to arid rural areas.

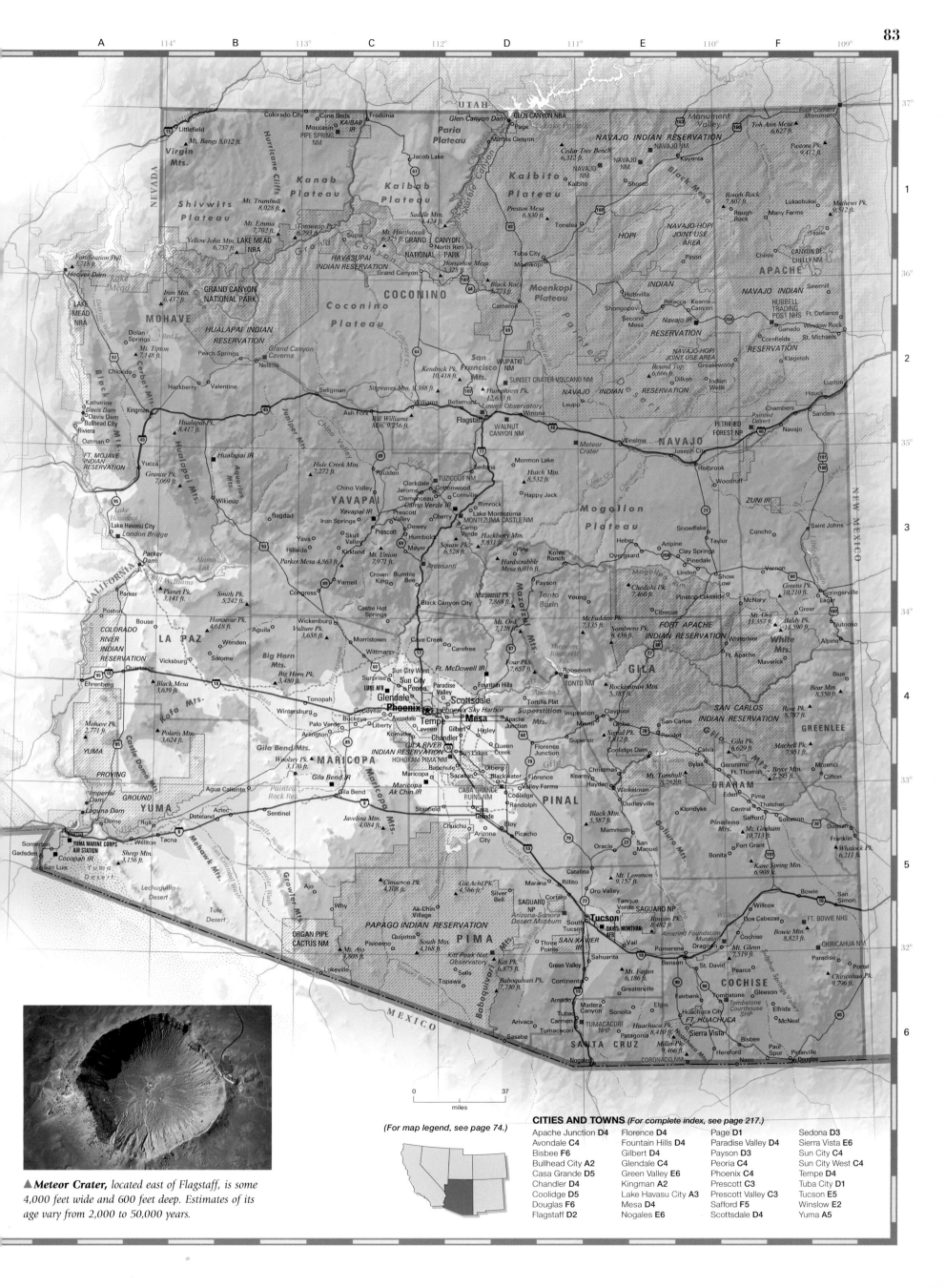

▲ Meteor Crater, located east of Flagstaff, is some 4,000 feet wide and 600 feet deep. Estimates of its age vary from 2,000 to 50,000 years.

(For map legend, see page 74.)

0   37
miles

▲ **A diamond design** recalls
Arkansas's status as the only state
that produces this precious gem.
The flag was adopted in 1913.

STATE DATA
State bird: Mockingbird
State flower: Apple blossom
State tree: Pine
State motto: *Regnat populus* (The
people rule)
State song: "Arkansas"
Abbreviations: Ark.; AR (postal)
Origin of the name: Derived from
the name of a local Indian tribe, the
Quapaw; called Arkansea (south
wind) by other tribes
Nicknames: Land of Opportunity,
Bear State, Wonder State

Arkansas

*Like nowhere else in the United States, Arkansas com-
bines the frontier spirit of the West with the genteel
character of the Old South. Also, few states can claim a
geography that includes such varied features as the flat
Mississippi Delta and the breathtakingly rugged peaks
and gorges of the Ozark and Ouachita mountains.*

THE LURE OF WATER
Just as rivers like the Buffalo, Spring, Illinois, and Strawberry
now draw thousands of canoeing and fishing enthusiasts,
Arkansas's waterways attracted its earliest settlers and explorers,
too. Among the first residents of Arkansas were bluff-dwelling
Indians, who fished, farmed, and hunted by the Mississippi
River. Later, such tribes as the Caddo settled along rivers in the
southwestern part of Arkansas, while the Tunica dwelled in the
southeast; the Quapaw occupied the lower reaches of the
Arkansas River. Arkansas's 9,740 miles of streams and rivers and
more than 500,000 acres of lakes (many of them filled by
water that percolates up from ancient cold springs) made it a
viable area for settlement.

But Arkansas's water was no substitute for riches. In 1541
Spanish fortune seeker Hernando de Soto ventured up the Mississippi River through Arkansas in pursuit of gold. After he left
empty-handed, the region was virtually ignored by the Europeans for decades. Not until 1673 did Père Jacques Marquette
and Louis Jolliet, two Frenchmen traversing the Mississippi,
return, heralding a renewed European interest. Nine years later,
their countryman René-Robert Cavelier, Sieur de La Salle, formally claimed for France a vast region of North America's interior, including Arkansas, and named it Louisiana.

PUTTING DOWN ROOTS
Not surprisingly, Arkansas's first permanent settlement,
Arkansas Post, was established along a major waterway, near
the mouth of the Arkansas River. Arkansas Post, a fort built in
1686 by one of La Salle's aides, Henri de Tonti, was moved several times during periodic flooding of the Arkansas River and
served as a territorial capital until 1821.

France ceded Louisiana to Spain in 1762. Spain never made
much of its possession and secretly ceded the territory back to
France in 1800. With the Louisiana Purchase of 1803, Arkansas
became part of the United States—first attached to the
Louisiana Territory and later to the Missouri Territory. Finally,
Arkansas became a territory in its own right in 1819, and soon
the capital moved up the Arkansas River to another community on its banks, Little Rock. Statehood followed in 1836.

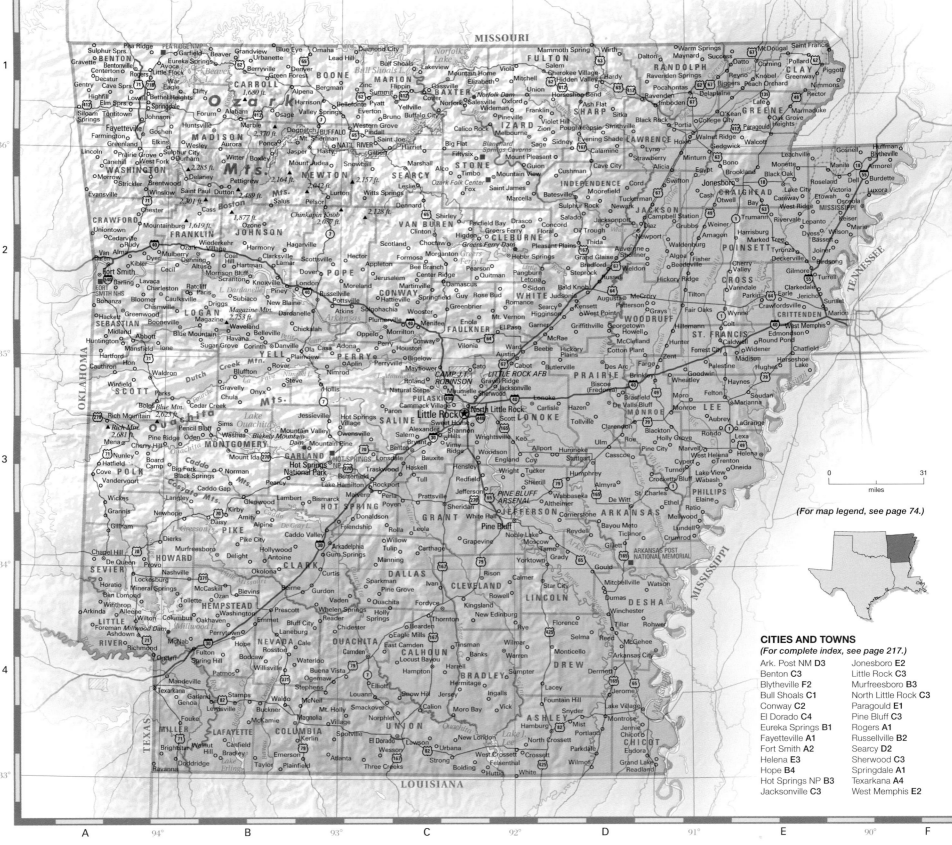

(For map legend, see page 74.)

CITIES AND TOWNS
(For complete index, see page 217.)

▶ *The Buffalo River flows past the Steel Creek Bluffs on its journey through the limestone hills of the central Ozarks. The terrain reminded the pioneers who settled here of their homes back east.*

Since then, water has been crucial to Arkansas's development. At first the swampy tracts along the Mississippi River at the state's eastern edge proved a deterrent to settlement, but the draining of the land and the damming of tributaries opened up a region rich in arable soil. From 1836 to 1860 Arkansas's population swelled tenfold to 500,000, with many people settling on Delta land. The antebellum South thrived in such riverboat towns as Helena, which Mark Twain praised as "one of the prettiest situations on the river."

As lovely as the view may be, living on a river can also be precarious. Arkansas's waterways occasionally display their amazing power—for example, the flooding of the Mississippi River in 1927 left one-fifth of the state under water. Arkansans have been remarkably successful, however, at harnessing nature's waterpower for their benefit. In 1971 a $1.2 billion project to open the Arkansas River to commercial navigation from Mississippi to Tulsa was completed, making Little Rock an inland port. Dams and river engineering have created superb lakes in Arkansas, such as the reservoirs at Bull Shoals, which residents and visitors use for boating and fishing.

Arkansans also know when to leave their waterways alone. The Buffalo River is a prime example. Originating in a remote section of the Ozark Mountains, this river drops 2,000 feet during its nearly 150-mile flow across north central Arkansas. It shimmers beneath 500-foot-high limestone bluffs, joins with smaller spring-fed streams, rolls by box canyons, and provides some of the most spectacular canoeing in the United States. In 1972 the Buffalo River became the country's first watercourse to win designation as a National River.

UP IN THE OZARKS

When people think of Arkansas, they tend to think of the Ozarks, the land of hills, traditional folkways, and independent-minded people. Populated in the 19th century by Easterners of Scotch-Irish descent in search of inexpensive farmland, the Ozarks developed into a region that had no use for slave labor or plantations. Arkansas seceded from the Union in 1861, but the state remained bitterly divided over the issue. In all, about 60,000 Arkansans joined the Confederate cause, and about 14,000—many from the Ozarks, and some 5,000 of them African-Americans—served in the Union Army.

War and division could not stamp out the fierce beauty of the Ozark country. Near Eureka Springs in the highlands, more than 60 natural springs gave birth to a thriving Victorian resort town where heavy mists frequently give the hills a mysterious ghostly visage. Nearby, Pivot Rock balances on a base 15 times smaller than its summit, and Ozark National Forest showcases seemingly endless tracts of hardwood trees.

THE RUGGED OUACHITAS

To the south of the Ozarks lie the Ouachita Mountains and Fort Smith, which offers a glimpse into Arkansas's

▲ *Health seekers at Eureka Springs relax in between taking their water "cures."*

past. Located at the point where the Arkansas River enters the state, this city was an outfitting stop for Mexican War troops and gold seekers heading for California. Fort Smith was the last stop in civilization for outlaws and fugitives. The outpost attracted the likes of Judge Isaac Parker, better known as The Hanging Judge. Determined to establish law and order, Parker handed down about 9,500 criminal convictions and 88 death sentences.

The Ouachitas are best known for their waters. Hot Springs, America's most famous mineral water spa, has been a mecca for health seekers since the early 19th century. Along Bathhouse Row are eight establishments that played host to such guests as Al Capone, Franklin Roosevelt, and Babe Ruth. Only one spa, the Buckstaff, still offers visitors the chance to relax in 143°F water that rises from a source 8,000 feet beneath the earth.

Not too far away, at Murfreesboro, is Crater of Diamonds State Park, the only diamond mine in North America. In 1906 a Pike County farmer named John Huddleston discovered the first diamond at this site. Now a tourist attraction, the volcanic field has yielded hundreds of "finders-keepers" gems to the public, including one 40.23-carat diamond.

▲ *A diamond in disguise? A visitor to Crater of Diamonds State Park examines his find.*

CITIES, TOO

Arkansas has a progressive urban side to it in the form of cities like Helena, where as many as 50,000 people have converged on weekends to attend the King Biscuit Blues Festival or to visit the new Delta Cultural Center, recently an abandoned railroad station. Little Rock, which became a civil rights battlefield in 1957 when President Dwight D. Eisenhower sent federal troops to Central High School to enforce desegregation laws, has plans to refurbish the school and add it to a list of other popular sites, such as the state capitol, a neoclassical structure built in 1915, and the antebellum Old State House, now a museum. Here, in 1992, Arkansan William Jefferson Clinton accepted the 42nd presidency of the United States.

AREA AND SIZE

Total area: 53,104 sq. mi.
Rank within U.S.: 27
Extent: 240 mi. north–south; 276 mi. east–west
Highest elevation: Magazine Mountain, 2,753 ft. above sea level
Lowest elevation: Ouachita River in Ashley and Union counties, 55 ft. above sea level

POPULATION

Total: 2,631,000
Rank within U.S.: 33
Ethnic breakdown: White: 81.9%; Black: 15.5%; Hispanic: 1.3%; Asian: 0.7%; Indian: 0.6%
Population density: 50.4 people per sq. mi.

CLIMATE

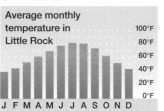

Average monthly temperature in Little Rock

100°F 80°F 60°F 40°F 20°F 0°F
J F M A M J J A S O N D

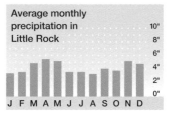

Average monthly precipitation in Little Rock

10" 8" 6" 4" 2" 0"
J F M A M J J A S O N D

ECONOMY

Service industries: Automobile trade; department stores, discount stores; finance, insurance, and real estate; medical facilities
Manufacturing: Animal feeds, cottonseed oil, paper products, fabricated metal products
Agriculture: Broiler chickens, beef cattle, soybeans, rice

ARKANSAS
TIME LINE

1541 Hernando de Soto, a Spaniard, is first European to set foot in Arkansas.

1686 Frenchman Henri de Tonti founds Arkansas Post.

1803 U.S. acquires Arkansas with Louisiana Purchase.

1817 U.S. builds Fort Smith to keep peace between Indian tribes and to protect white settlers moving west.

1836 Arkansas joins the Union as 25th state.

1861 Arkansas secedes. Some 9,000 whites and 5,000 blacks join Union Army.

1868 Arkansas is readmitted to the Union.

1921 Discovery of oil near El Dorado leads to boom; by 1924 Arkansas is fourth among states in oil production.

1927 Flooding of Mississippi River leaves one-fifth of state under water.

1957 In defiance of federal court order, Gov. Orval Faubus blocks integration of Central High School in Little Rock. Federal troops are sent in.

1970 Arkansas River opens to commercial navigation from Mississippi River to Tulsa, Oklahoma.

1985 Arkansas begins a national trend by requiring teachers to pass basic math and reading tests to keep their jobs.

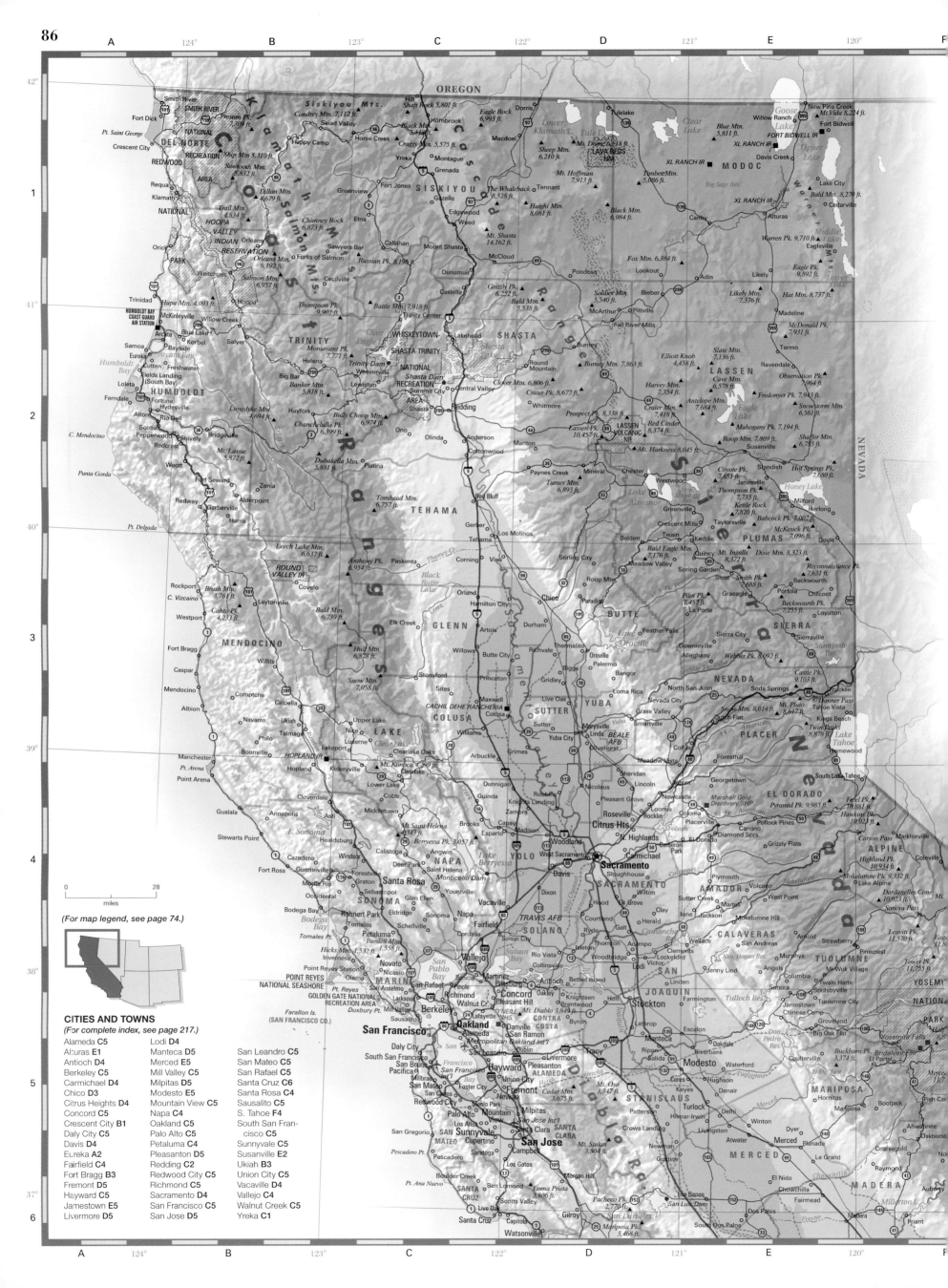

CITIES AND TOWNS
(For complete index, see page 217.)

(For map legend, see page 74.)

▲ *The state flag,* adopted in 1911, is patterned after the one designed and flown by American settlers during their 1846 revolt against Mexico.

◄ *Big Sur extends* 80 miles along California's craggy 3,400-mile coastline—which, with its inlets, is the distance from California to New York.

STATE DATA

State bird: California valley quail
State flower: Golden poppy
State tree: California redwood
State motto: *Eureka!* (I have found it!)—the cry of prospectors during the 1849 gold rush)
State song: "I Love You, California"
Abbreviations: Calif.; CA (postal)
Origin of the name: Named by Spanish explorers for a fictional island called California found in a popular 16th-century romance
Nicknames: Golden State; El Dorado

AREA AND SIZE

Total area: 158,693 sq. mi.
Rank within U.S.: 3
Extent: 646 mi. north–south; 560 mi. east–west
Highest elevation: Mount Whitney, 14,494 ft. above sea level
Lowest elevation: 282 ft. below sea level in Death Valley

POPULATION

Total: 32,521,000
Rank within U.S.: 1
Ethnic breakdown: White: 47.9%; Hispanic: 32.7%; Asian: 12.3%; Black: 6.6%; Indian: 0.5%
Population density: 207.8 people per sq. mi.

CLIMATE

Average monthly temperature in San Francisco
100°F 80°F 60°F 40°F 20°F 0°F
J F M A M J J A S O N D

Average monthly precipitation in San Francisco
10" 8" 6" 4" 2" 0"
J F M A M J J A S O N D

ECONOMY

Service industries: Finance, insurance, and real estate; medical facilities; entertainment companies; wholesale and retail trade; government services; transportation, communication, and utilities
Manufacturing: Transportation equipment, electrical equipment, food processing
Agriculture: Milk, beef cattle, eggs, sheep, turkeys, grapes, almonds, strawberries, walnuts, tomatoes, lettuce, cotton

California

No state boasts more climates, mountain ranges, and species of animals, not to mention freeways, automobiles, and people. A land of superlatives, California has the tallest, oldest, and biggest trees in the country, the nation's largest mountain lake, the lowest point of elevation, and, outside of Alaska, the highest mountain. Above all, California holds the hopes and promise of the many who have come here looking for something better—from the earliest Native Americans who sought its bounty to Spanish explorers in search of new colonies, from forty-niners hoping to strike it rich to countless refugees seeking freedom and prosperity.

THREE GOVERNMENTS

With instructions from the Crown to claim any land for Spain, explorer Juan Rodriguez Cabrillo sailed up the Pacific coast from Mexico in June 1542. Three months later he reached San Diego Bay, then proceeded north, sailing right past the Golden Gate—a deep strait that connects the ocean to the calm waters of San Francisco Bay. Cabrillo went as far as Point Reyes, then sailed past the Golden Gate and San Francisco Bay again on his return to San Miguel. He was not the only one who would miss the magnificent inlet; 37 years later Sir Francis Drake traveled along the coast in his ship *Golden Hind* and claimed all that he discovered for England, calling it New Albion. The San Francisco Bay, however, was not part of Drake's claim—he missed it, too, and it remained uncharted for the next 200 years.

By the time Drake made his discoveries, the Spanish had already named the land on the Pacific coast California, after an island paradise in a popular 16th-century romance. The fictional California was inhabited by Amazons, and Cabrillo found that the real California had its own indigenous population. As many as 300,000 Native Americans—more than 100 different tribes—lived there. Hupa were occupying the northwest and Modoc the northeast; Pomo and Miwok were living around the San Francisco Bay area, Maidu in the Central Valley, and Quechan and Mohave in the south.

Fearing that they might lose California, Spain's monarchs sent more explorers to the west coast of the New World. One was Sebastian Vizcaino, who was so dazzled by what he saw during his 1602 voyage that he urged the Crown to colonize the new land at once.

It would be more than 150 years before Spain followed Vizcaino's advice. In 1769 Captain Gaspar de Portolá led an expedition to present-day San Diego, where he established a *presidio*, or fortress, followed by a second fort in Monterey the next year. Joining Portolá was a Franciscan friar named Junípero Serra. After building a mission in San Diego, Father Serra trekked up the coast of California, establishing 20 more missions along the way, each about a day's walk from the one preceding it. The trail became known as El Camino Real, or the Royal Road, and today its counterpart, Highway 101, is one of the most popular routes used by tourists to explore the state's early Spanish heritage.

▲ *San Diego de Alcalá,* the oldest mission in California, dates to 1769. Missionaries introduced horses, cattle, and wheat to California.

Spanish rule ended in 1821, when Mexico won its independence from Spain. The next year, Mexico took control of California. The land, dotted with sprawling ranches and ancient pueblos, was sparsely populated. Little by little, groups of American settlers, following trails blazed by explorers Jedediah Smith and Kit Carson, began to arrive. Most of the new Californians wanted the territory to be governed by the United States, not by Mexico. In 1846 a ragtag band of American settlers sprang into action; they took over the fort at Sonoma, Mexico's headquarters in northern California, and raised a homemade flag bearing a star and a grizzly bear and the words *California Republic.* Unbeknownst to the leaders of the Bear Flag Revolt, as the rebellion came to be called, the U.S. government had already declared war on its southern neighbor. When Mexico surrendered two years later,

CALIFORNIA
TIME LINE

1542 Juan Rodriguez Cabrillo arrives in San Diego Bay.

1579 Sir Francis Drake lands on California coast and claims land for England.

1769 Junípero Serra founds mission near San Diego.

1781 Los Angeles is founded.

1821 Mexico revolts against Spain and the following year stakes claim on California.

1847 Yerba Buena becomes San Francisco.

1848 Mexico cedes California to U.S. after Mexican War. James W. Marshall finds gold at Sutter's Mill.

1850 California joins the Union as 31st state.

1857 Agoston Haraszthy, a Hungarian immigrant, establishes California's first winery, the Buena Vista, in Sonoma.

1869 California is connected to East with completion of first transcontinental railroad.

1906 A great earthquake and fire devastate San Francisco. Some 3,000 people die, and 300,000 are left homeless.

1910 D. W. Griffith's *In Old California* is first film made in Hollywood.

1937 Golden Gate Bridge opens.

1945 United Nations founded in San Francisco.

1962 California becomes most populous state.

1965 Race riots break out in Watts, resulting in 34 deaths. Cesar Chavez and United Farm Workers organize a strike against grape growers in Delano.

1977 First personal computer, Apple II, is developed in Silicon Valley.

1978 Proposition 13 reduces property taxes by more than half.

1989 Earthquake shakes San Francisco Bay area, causing about 70 deaths and more than $5 billion in damages.

1994 Early-morning earthquake rocks Los Angeles, killing 57 people and causing $20 billion in damages.

California officially became a U.S. territory. Statehood followed in 1850.

THE GOLD RUSH

The same year that California gained independence from Mexico, another event took place that would change the Western territory forever. On January 24, 1848, James Marshall spotted a few shiny flakes of metal flashing in the water at a mill operated by his boss, a Swiss immigrant named John Sutter. It was gold, and Marshall's discovery near the tiny town of Coloma in the Sierra Nevada foothills east of Sacramento touched off the largest mass migration the country had ever seen.

Hundreds of thousands of men and women, collectively known as the forty-niners, poured into the state. Boomtowns sprang up overnight. San Francisco, the principal port of entry and the gateway to gold country—a region aptly called the Mother Lode—grew from a village of barely a few hundred to the nation's 10th-largest city in just two decades.

Only a few of those who came seeking fortune found it, however. Most never made their way past San Francisco or the farming towns in the Central Valley. The promise of a steady job in a store or factory or on a ranch proved more alluring than battling the wilderness, not to mention claim jumpers, robbers, and a host of other unsavory characters who prowled the lawless gold country.

▲ *California grapes* *account for 90 percent of the country's total crop. The state produces wine, table, and raisin varieties.*

POPULATION BOOM

Although the gold strike gradually lost its luster, California remained a shining beacon to immigrants in search of a better life. The completion of the transcontinental railroad in the 1880s drew hundreds of thousands of newcomers. Chinese laborers came all the way across the Pacific Ocean to California to help lay the tracks, while Americans living on the East Coast, as well as Europeans, rode the rails westward across the country. At the turn of the century, thousands of Japanese, eager to cultivate the state's fertile farmlands, arrived.

A once far-flung outpost of the Spanish Empire, El Pueblo de Nuestra Señora la Reina de Los Angeles, received the majority of new arrivals. The discovery of oil in the area during the early 1890s further accelerated the city's growth. An added benefit was its warm climate, which proved ideal for growing citrus fruits—and for making movies. By 1910 D. W. Griffith and other East Coast moviemakers had put southern California on the road to becoming the entertainment capital of the world.

The population boomed once again during the Depression years as more than 1 million desperate farmers left the Dust Bowl for California, hoping for better luck. World War II brought an even bigger wave of immigrants: millions of men and women arrived in California, either as soldiers passing through the state en route to the Pacific or as workers in the state's defense plants. Many were African-Americans who had left their homes in the South.

For more than a century, between 1850 and 1960, California's population virtually doubled every 20 years. In the past 40 years, it has tripled from almost 10 million people to more than 30 million. The state's three largest urban centers—Los Angeles-Long Beach, San Francisco-Oakland, and San Diego—have borne the brunt of the population boom. Nine out of every 10 Californians live in these three areas. While growth has slowed, people still keep coming—making the projected population for the year 2040 an astounding 63 million people.

CULTURAL AND ECONOMIC DIVERSITY

In no other state are there more Mexicans, American Indians, Chinese, Filipinos, Japanese, Koreans, or Vietnamese. California also has the country's second-largest African-American and Asian Indian populations, and it is home to one-fourth of all U.S. immigrants—making the state one of the most culturally diverse places on the planet.

◄ *Universal Studios Hollywood,* *the world's largest film and television studio, contains reusable sets and movie-based amusement rides.*

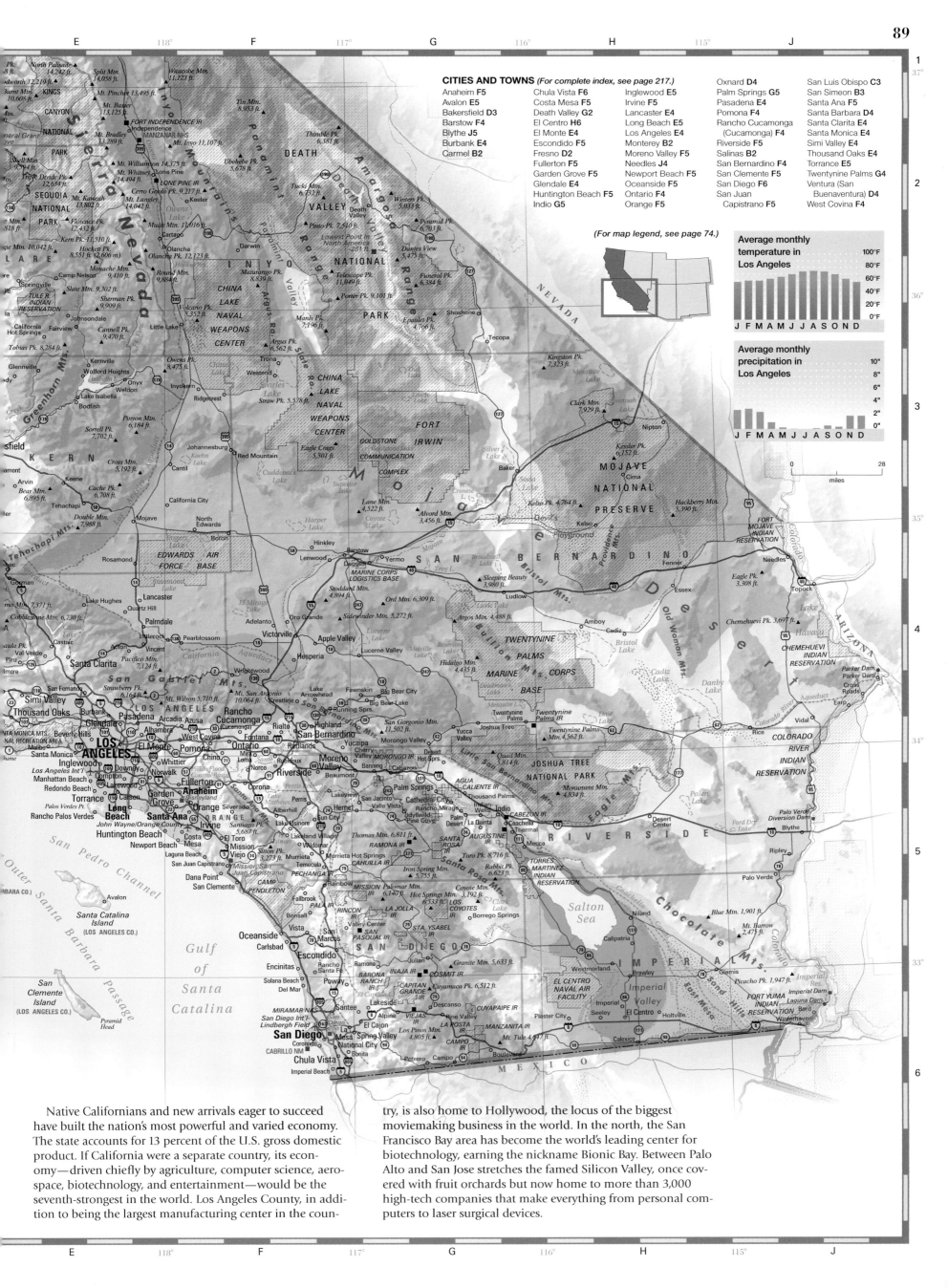

E 118° F 117° G 116° H 115° J

CITIES AND TOWNS *(For complete index, see page 217.)*

Anaheim **F5**	Chula Vista **F6**	Inglewood **E5**	Oxnard **D4**	San Luis Obispo **C3**
Avalon **E5**	Costa Mesa **F5**	Irvine **F5**	Palm Springs **G5**	San Simeon **B3**
Bakersfield **D3**	Death Valley **G2**	Lancaster **E4**	Pasadena **E4**	Santa Ana **F5**
Barstow **F4**	El Centro **H6**	Long Beach **E5**	Pomona **F4**	Santa Barbara **D4**
Blythe **J5**	El Monte **E4**	Los Angeles **E4**	Rancho Cucamonga	Santa Clarita **E4**
Burbank **E4**	Escondido **F5**	Monterey **B2**	(Cucamonga) **F4**	Santa Monica **E4**
Carmel **B2**	Fresno **D2**	Moreno Valley **F5**	Riverside **F5**	Simi Valley **E4**
	Fullerton **F5**	Needles **J4**	Salinas **B2**	Thousand Oaks **E4**
	Garden Grove **F5**	Newport Beach **F5**	San Bernardino **F4**	Torrance **E5**
	Glendale **E4**	Oceanside **F5**	San Clemente **F5**	Twentynine Palms **G4**
	Huntington Beach **F5**	Ontario **F4**	San Diego **F6**	Ventura (San
	Indio **G5**	Orange **F5**	San Juan	Buenaventura) **D4**
			Capistrano **F5**	West Covina **F4**

(For map legend, see page 74.)

Average monthly temperature in Los Angeles

100°F
80°F
60°F
40°F
20°F
0°F

J F M A M J J A S O N D

Average monthly precipitation in Los Angeles

10"
8"
6"
4"
2"
0"

J F M A M J J A S O N D

0   28
miles

Native Californians and new arrivals eager to succeed have built the nation's most powerful and varied economy. The state accounts for 13 percent of the U.S. gross domestic product. If California were a separate country, its economy—driven chiefly by agriculture, computer science, aerospace, biotechnology, and entertainment—would be the seventh-strongest in the world. Los Angeles County, in addition to being the largest manufacturing center in the country, is also home to Hollywood, the locus of the biggest moviemaking business in the world. In the north, the San Francisco Bay area has become the world's leading center for biotechnology, earning the nickname Bionic Bay. Between Palo Alto and San Jose stretches the famed Silicon Valley, once covered with fruit orchards but now home to more than 3,000 high-tech companies that make everything from personal computers to laser surgical devices.

▶ *The Sierra Nevada—the world's largest granite wall—stretches some 400 miles through eastern California. The mountains feature 500 summits more than 12,000 feet high as well as wilderness areas and national and state parks.*

▲ *Death Valley, the hottest spot in North America, is also the lowest point in California. The state's highest point, Mount Whitney, is just 80 miles away.*

Because a variety of produce can be grown in California year-round, the state leads the country in farm income. The Central Valley—a 450-mile-long by 50-mile-wide stretch of farmland—has become the most productive agricultural area in the United States. Fruits, nuts, and vegetables—along with cotton, rice, and wheat—are all grown here. California also leads the nation in wine production. Once just a place of quiet backwoods, the hills and valleys of Napa and Sonoma counties are now home to many of the state's more than 800 wineries.

NATURAL DIVERSITY

Nowhere else in the 48 contiguous states is there a greater variety of plant and animal life. More than 7,850 kinds of vascular plants grow in California, and of the nation's 2,300 vertebrate species, 748 are found in California. Some of the state's wildlife—38 percent of the freshwater fish, 29 percent of the amphibians, and 9 percent of the mammals—can be found no place else in America. No other state in the Lower 48 has such animals as the Coachella Valley fringe-toed lizard and the Delta smelt or plants with such poetic names as large-flowered fiddleneck, Hoover's woolly star, or Sebastopol meadowfoam.

The reason for such diversity lies, in part, with California's variety of habitats: 396 to be exact. About the only type of environment you won't find in California is Arctic tundra. Within the state's borders are some 3,400 miles of coastline, 30,000 miles of rivers and streams, 5,000 lakes, eight major mountain ranges containing more than 100 named mountain chains and 500 peaks, two dormant volcanoes, 40 million acres of forest, and some 27 million acres of desert.

▲ *The San Andreas Fault, which starts in Mexico, is responsible for most of California's seismic upheaval. But it is not the only fault in the state. There are six major fault systems in Los Angeles alone.*

RESTLESS LAND

This panoply of landscapes is a work of art in progress. California is constantly being pushed and pulled from within by a geological force that sends regular reminders of its presence in the form of tremors and earthquakes. The state is the meeting ground of two pieces of the earth's crust called plates. Beneath the state's western shore, the Pacific plate is sliding under the North American plate. The colossal friction causes breaks in the earth's rocky outer shell. The best example of this is the infamous San Andreas Fault, which runs nearly the entire length of the state. (Only 60 miles away from the San Andreas Fault, the Golden Gate Bridge has withstood all tremors without serious damage.)

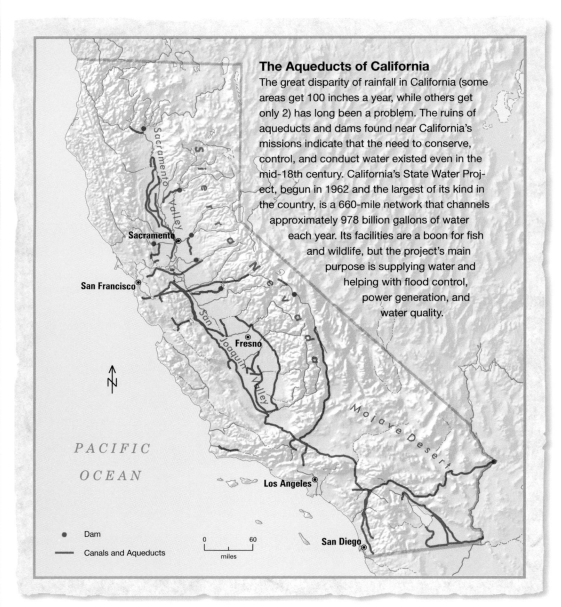

The Aqueducts of California

The great disparity of rainfall in California (some areas get 100 inches a year, while others get only 2) has long been a problem. The ruins of aqueducts and dams found near California's missions indicate that the need to conserve, control, and conduct water existed even in the mid-18th century. California's State Water Project, begun in 1962 and the largest of its kind in the country, is a 660-mile network that channels approximately 978 billion gallons of water each year. Its facilities are a boon for fish and wildlife, but the project's main purpose is supplying water and helping with flood control, power generation, and water quality.

Sacramento Valley

Sacramento

San Francisco

Fresno

San Joaquin Valley

Mojave Desert

PACIFIC OCEAN

Los Angeles

San Diego

N

• Dam

— Canals and Aqueducts

0   60
miles

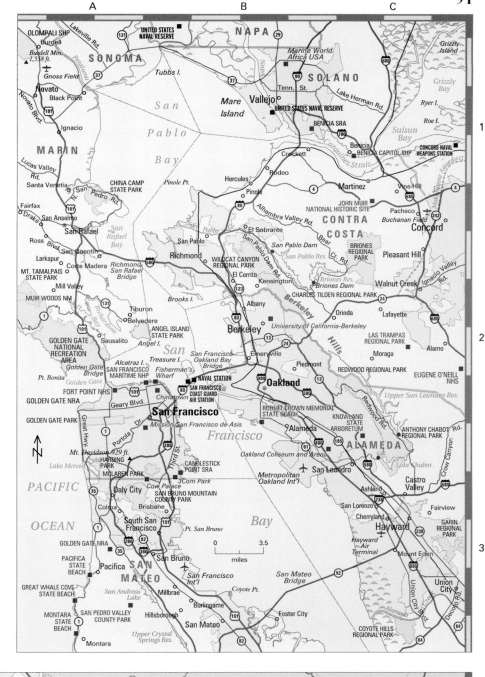

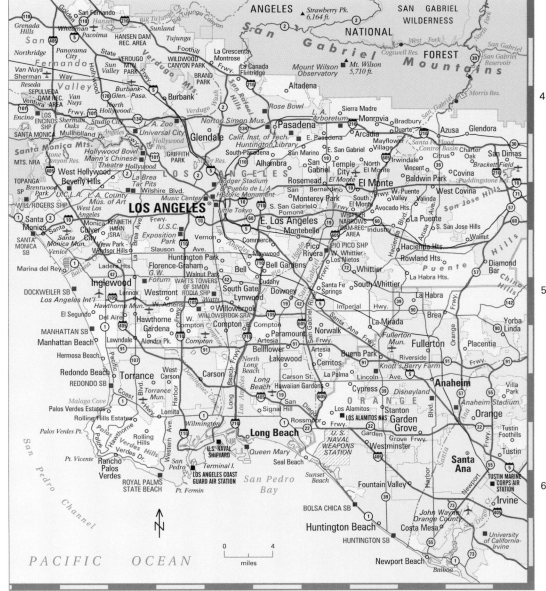

▲ *San Francisco's landlocked harbor, one of the world's most sheltered, has welcomed thousands to the city, currently the 13th largest in the United States.*

Movements of the earth's crust along faults not only trigger earthquakes but slowly and surely push up entire mountain ranges, including the towering 400-mile-long wall of granite that is the Sierra Nevada.

NATURAL WONDERS

Unspoiled nature abounds in California. Nearly 50 percent of its total land area has been protected in the form of parks, preserves, and public lands. There are 17 national forests containing some 20 million acres of land, much of it open to hikers and campers. In addition, there are 24 national wildlife refuges, hundreds of state and county parks, dozens of private preserves, and several huge military reserves.

Another 4.5 million acres fall within the boundaries of the state's six national parks and its 12 national monuments and national recreation areas. Joshua Tree and Death Valley national parks protect desert land in the south, while farther north and west Yosemite, Sequoia, and Kings Canyon national parks showcase the Sierra Nevada and such treasures as the giant sequoia, the earth's tallest tree. Lassen Volcanic National Park offers visitors a glimpse into the state's geological past, as well as a look at one of the most bizarre landscapes in the country. Covered with bubbling mud pots and hissing steam vents, Lassen is a hydrothermal wonderland that bespeaks the restless character of the land; it is also a fitting metaphor for the ever-changing nature of the Golden State.

◀ *Ethnic diversity* has characterized Los Angeles since its founding in 1781 by 11 families of European, African, and Native American heritage.

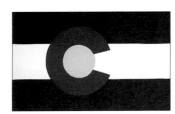

Colorado

With one border stretched across the heartland and another gnarled by the mesas to the west, Colorado straddles the Rocky Mountains at America's watershed, the Continental Divide. Once thought too dry and too mountainous to attract anyone but Indians and fur trappers, the "Roof of America" has become a boom state.

▲ **Colorado's flag,** adopted in 1911, features colors that represent the state: the stripes signify the blue sky and the white snow-capped peaks; the red C stands for Colorado, Spanish for "colored red"; and the golden ball symbolizes the state's gold production.

STATE DATA

State bird: Lark bunting
State flower: Rocky Mountain
   columbine
State tree: Colorado blue spruce

AMERICA'S ALPINE WONDER

In 1869 New England journalist Samuel Bowles called it "The Switzerland of America," a mountainous land where "new and exhilarating scenes" and "an atmosphere of elixir" awaited the adventurous traveler. One such traveler, an English literature professor named Katherine Lee Bates, scaled Pikes Peak in 1893 and was so inspired by the "sealike expanse of fertile country"

below that she began to compose the lines of a hymn she would later call "America the Beautiful." The place that Bowles and Bates both praised was Colorado.

The state's towering landscape, all of which is no less than 3,350 feet above sea level, stretches from a western plateau through the Rockies, which cover nearly half the state, to the arid High Plains of the east, where water is tunneled in from the west to support 80 percent of the state's population. National park land covers one-fourth of the state, and it harbors some of nature's most engaging oddities: the ever-shifting mounds of Great Sand Dunes National Monument; the haphazard domes, pinnacles, and arches hewn from sandstone and shale in Colorado National Monument; the Black Canyon of the Gunnison River, which slices so steeply into the Rockies' western face that the Ute Indians and the settlers alike believed that no one could enter it and come out alive.

BORN OF THE LIVING EARTH

The jewel in the crown of Colorado's stunning landscape, the Rocky Mountains were formed from the ceaseless movement

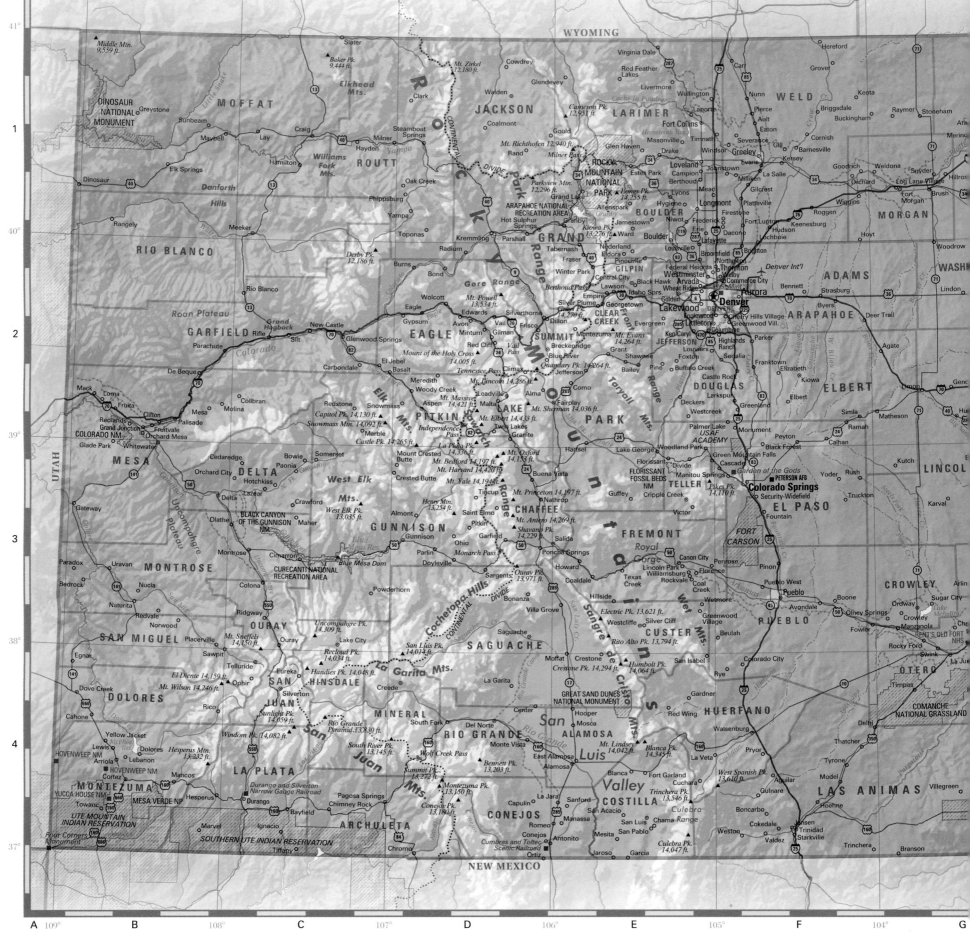

of the earth's crust. About 70 million years ago, a mountain range that was buried beneath an ancient sea began to push its way up, causing the limestone, shale, and sandstone that had been part of the seafloor to crack, fold, and evolve into the Rockies. The San Juan Mountains, in southwestern Colorado, had a more volatile beginning. Scientists have determined that 26 million years ago, the largest volcano in the history of the planet erupted, spewing lava, rock, and ash that eventually accumulated into mountains. The lava flow carried with it precious metals from deep within the earth that were deposited throughout parts of Colorado—a boon for later prospectors.

ROCKY MOUNTAIN WASTELAND

In the early days of the frontier West, this forbidding land managed to hide its future promise well, and until the mid-19th century, only Indians and trappers roughed it in the craggy, rust-colored land that Spanish explorers described as *colorado,* or "red." The first settlers, the Anasazi, arrived some 2,000 years ago and lived in brick villages carved into the jagged cliffs of the Mesa Verde plateau. By A.D. 1300 the Anasazi were gone, pushed out by either drought or nomadic intruders. In their relentless search for gold, Spanish conquistadores crossed corners of the future state in the 16th, 17th, and 18th centuries, as did French fur trappers. In 1803 the Louisiana Purchase placed the High Plains in U.S. hands, and three years later, an inspired 27-year-old army lieutenant named Zebulon Pike plodded west to explore the headwaters of the Arkansas and Red rivers. His party found the site of present-day Pueblo, as well as a snowcapped peak that looked "grand" and now bears Pike's name despite his failure to get to the top.

BROWN AND YELLOW GOLD

In the 1820s a passion in the drawing rooms of Europe for beaver fur brought a rugged breed of pioneer to the Rockies, and their mountaineering skills put Pike's to shame. Trappers like Jim Bridger, Kit Carson, and Louis Vasquez spent years in the mountains battling Indians, bears, and starvation in order to bring home the "brown gold" of beaver pelts. These mountain men surveyed

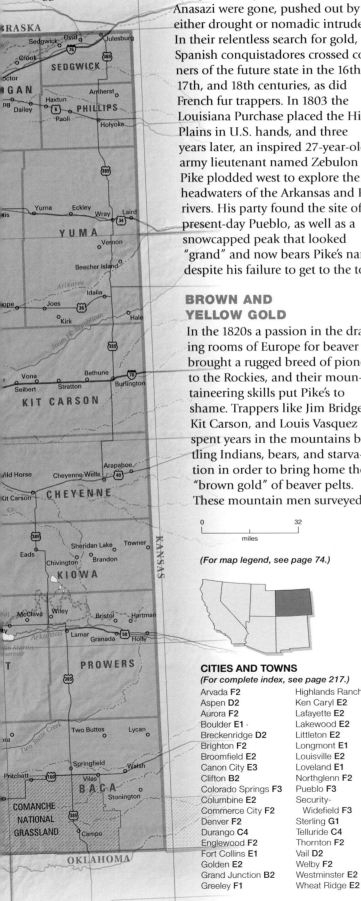

0 ——————— 32
miles

(For map legend, see page 74.)

CITIES AND TOWNS
(For complete index, see page 217.)

Arvada **F2**	Highlands Ranch **F2**
Aspen **D2**	Ken Caryl **E2**
Aurora **F2**	Lafayette **E2**
Boulder **E1**	Lakewood **E2**
Breckenridge **D2**	Littleton **E2**
Brighton **F2**	Longmont **E1**
Broomfield **E2**	Louisville **E2**
Canon City **E3**	Loveland **E1**
Clifton **B2**	Northglenn **F2**
Colorado Springs **F3**	Pueblo **F3**
Columbine **E2**	Security-Widefield **F3**
Commerce City **F2**	Sterling **G1**
Denver **F2**	Telluride **C4**
Durango **C4**	Thornton **F2**
Englewood **F2**	Vail **D2**
Fort Collins **E1**	Welby **F2**
Golden **E2**	Westminster **E2**
Grand Junction **B2**	Wheat Ridge **E2**
Greeley **F1**	

▲ *The Rocky Mountains'* highest summits are concentrated in Colorado, where more than 40 peaks exceed 14,000 feet.

routes that would later be followed by government expeditions, traded with the Cheyenne, Arapaho, and Ute, who hunted in the region, and then told tall tales about their exploits when they returned to civilization.

The area was finally settled when immigrants from New Mexico founded the town of San Luis in 1851, three years after the United States had taken the rest of Colorado in the Mexican War. But towns were still few and far between when, in 1858, a miner named William Russell stumbled across the first traces of the precious metal so treasured by the Spanish.

"THE NEW ELDORADO!!! Gold in Kansas Territory!!!" trumpeted the *Kansas City Journal of Commerce* shortly after Russell pulled $100 worth of nuggets out of Cherry Creek, on the eastern edge of the Rockies. In a matter of months, 100,000 people were on their way west under the slogan "Pikes Peak or Bust." The wife of one hopeful prospector from Nebraska City arrived at Cherry Creek in the summer of 1859 to find "hundreds of families living in wagons, tents, and shelters made of carpets and bedding." In two years this mishmash of a town, with its ragged collection of fortune seekers, would be incorporated as the mile-high city of Denver, so called because it is exactly 5,280 feet above sea level.

THE NEW FRONTIER

Since 1913, when Norwegian Carl Howelson launched the first ski jump at Steamboat Springs, Colorado has developed some of the best slopes in the country at resorts like Aspen, Breckenridge, Telluride, and Vail. Skiing now leads a tourist industry that draws $6 billion a year to the state and employs nearly 10 percent of its workforce.

The 1980s brought tremendous growth to Denver, which has become the financial, manufacturing, and marketing capital of the entire mountain region. With the boom, however, came the downside of modern economic success: pollution, inflation, crime, and rush-hour traffic. Colorado's challenge today is that of the entire modern West: to retain the advantages of civilization in surroundings of natural beauty and to accommodate the new hordes of latter-day pioneers without destroying the lifestyle that lured them west in the first place.

COLORADO TIME LINE

1706 Spain claims Colorado.

1803 After taking control of the territory during Napoleonic Wars, France sells eastern Colorado to U.S. as part of Louisiana Purchase.

1806 Lt. Zebulon M. Pike's expedition sights Rocky Mountains.

1848 U.S. wins western Colorado after Mexican War.

1858 Discovery of gold at Cherry Creek near Denver.

1876 Colorado joins the Union as 38th state.

1906 U.S. Mint in Denver strikes its first coins.

1927 Completion of Moffat Tunnel connects Denver to the transcontinental railroad.

1958 U.S. Air Force Academy opens

near Colorado Springs.

1966 North American Aerospace Defense Command (NORAD) completes its underground headquarters in Cheyenne Mountain.

1985 Frying Pan–Arkansas project is completed, carrying water from the Rockies to Colorado's eastern plains.

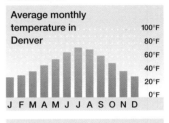

▲ *Prairie sunflowers* add splashes of color to the slopes of the Great Sand Dunes, the tallest in North America.

Connecticut

The Algonquin Indians called the region quinnitukqut, *which means "beside the long tidal river." This remains an apt name, considering that the 407-mile Connecticut River, the longest waterway in New England, divides the state almost in half. Although its western reaches are linked with the New York metropolitan area, Connecticut is a virtual microcosm of New England— a region of tidy seaports, stone-walled farms, and riverside mill towns.*

▲ *Three grapevines adorn a white shield on Connecticut's state flag, adopted in 1895. The state motto is below the shield.*

STATE DATA

State bird: American robin
State flower: Mountain laurel
State tree: White oak
State motto: *Qui transtulit sustinet* (He who transplanted still sustains)
State song: "Yankee Doodle"
Abbreviations: Conn.; CT (postal)
Origin of the name: From the Algonquian word *quinnitukqut*, which means "beside the long tidal river"
Nicknames: Constitution State, Nutmeg State, Land of Steady Habits

AREA AND SIZE

Total area: 5,009 sq. mi.
Rank within U.S.: 48
Extent: 73 mi. north–south; 100 mi. east–west
Highest elevation: Mount Frissell, south slope, 2,380 ft. above sea level
Lowest elevation: Sea level along the Long Island Sound

POPULATION

Total: 3,284,000
Rank within U.S.: 29
Ethnic breakdown: White: 79.8%; Black: 8.9%; Hispanic: 8.8%; Asian: 2.3%; Indian: 0.2%
Population density: 674.3 people per sq. mi.

CLIMATE

Average monthly temperature in Hartford

	100°F
	80°F
	60°F
	40°F
	20°F
	0°F
J F M A M J J A S O N D	

Average monthly precipitation in Hartford

	10"
	8"
	6"
	4"
	2"
	0"
J F M A M J J A S O N D	

ECONOMY

Service industries: Finance, insurance, and real estate; medical facilities; government services; transportation, communications, and utilities; trade in fuel, lumber, and farm products
Manufacturing: Aircraft parts, helicopters, submarines, bearings, computers, medical instruments
Agriculture: Greenhouse and nursery products, milk, eggs, tobacco, hay

THE FOUNDATION FOR FREEDOM

Like the first New England colonies at Plymouth and Massachusetts Bay, Connecticut was settled by religious dissidents— colonists at odds with the rigors of the Puritan theocracy in Massachusetts. Among their leaders was Thomas Hooker, a minister who believed that the election of magistrates was a civil, not a religious, obligation. Historians debate whether Hooker's principles led to America's separation of church and government—but there is no doubt about his status as a Connecticut pioneer: in 1636 he and his followers founded Hartford, destined to become the capital of the state. The first four decades of English settlement in Connecticut saw the newcomers battle native Pequot Indians and chase out Dutch traders who had come north from their own capital at New Amsterdam (later New York) and established a fort.

The farsighted founders of Connecticut built to last. At Guilford stands the Henry Whitfield House; dating back to 1639, it is the oldest stone dwelling in New England. Also created that year was a document called the Fundamental Orders, often regarded as the world's first written constitution. Connecticut yeomen were so fiercely protective of their right to self-government that in 1687, when an unpopular governor was sent from England to rule the Colonies, they stole the precious Connecticut charter and hid it in a hollow tree that became known as the Charter Oak.

Nearly a century later Connecticut stood foursquare for American independence. Although no major battles were fought on Connecticut soil, the state was situated in the crossroads between the vital Revolutionary strongholds of New York and Massachusetts and became known as the Provision State for its role in feeding the Continental Army. At Gov. Jonathan Trumbull's house and the adjacent "war office" on the Lebanon town green, Trumbull and his advisers met to plot the movement of troops and vital supplies with Gen. George Washington and his close friend the French general Marquis de Lafayette.

FROM AGRICULTURE TO INDUSTRY

Connecticut, like the five other New England states, enjoyed its golden age of agriculture during the 50 years following the Revolutionary War. All of the old-growth forest had been cut down for firewood and construction and to make way for pastures and fields. Except for the rich bottomlands of the Central Valley—the portion of the Connecticut River's drainage basin that had at one time been an

◀ **The Connecticut Courant,** *now* The Hartford Courant, *was first printed in 1764. It is the nation's oldest continuously published newspaper.*

enormous glacial lake and where a premium crop of shade-grown tobacco for cigar wrappers thrives today—the state could never really boast that its soil was ideal for farming. Early in the 19th century, Connecticut entrepreneurs discovered that their fortune lay not in the land but in the swift and powerful waters of the Naugatuck, the Shetucket, the Willimantic, and dozens of other rivers that could be put to work turning the wheels of industry.

YANKEE INGENUITY

There was a good reason Hartford resident Mark Twain—who wrote both *The Adventures of Huckleberry Finn* and *The Adventures of Tom Sawyer* while living there—chose a Connecticut fellow as the hero of his novel *A Connecticut Yankee in King Arthur's Court.* This story about a machine-age whiz who brings his expertise back to the court of the legendary British king reflects the status of Connecticut as the Silicon Valley of America's Industrial Revolution, a place where thriving mill towns sprouted in river valleys and Yankee tinkerers dazzled the rest of America with their genius. Near New Haven, Eli Whitney— inventor of the cotton gin—developed a method of manufacturing rifles that foreshadowed mass production. In Thomaston, the young nation was kept on time because of the ingenuity of a clock maker named Seth Thomas. Samuel Colt set up shop in Hartford to manufacture "the world's right arm,"

▲ *Southport, part of the town of Fairfield, is sometimes called the "jewel of Long Island Sound." It is one of many picturesque spots on Connecticut's 253-mile southern coastline.*

the Colt revolver, while the mills of Willimantic and Jewett City turned out cotton cloth and fine linen thread. Lollipops, corkscrews, tape measures, friction matches, cylindrical locks, vulcanized rubber, portable typewriters, sewing machines, vacuum cleaners, and nuclear-powered submarines are just some of the many items that were invented later in the state of Connecticut.

Another key industry in the Constitution State was founded on nothing more tangible than the calculation of risk. Connecticut's first insurance company, Hartford Fire, opened for business in 1794. Several decades later, in 1864, James Goodwin Batterson, president of the Travelers' Insurance Company, sold a $1,000 policy to James Bolter as the two men walked out of the Hartford post office. The policy cost two cents and covered only Bolter's walk back to his home, a distance of just two blocks. Since then, Hartford has become the insurance capital of the nation.

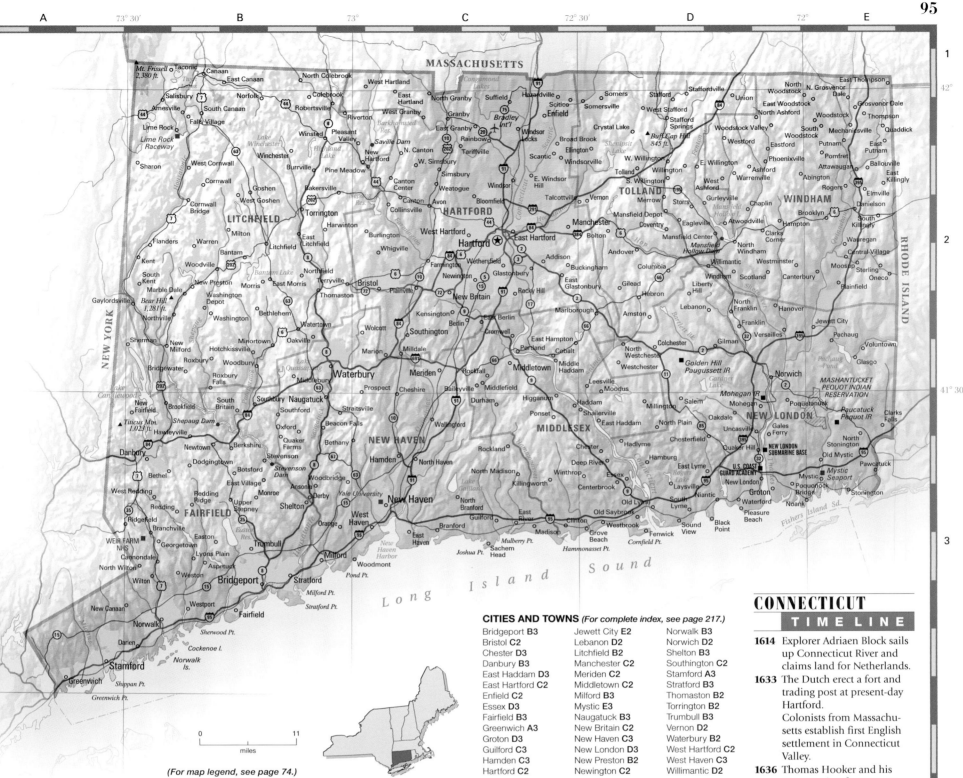

(For map legend, see page 74.)

SUBMARINES AND SCHOLARSHIP

Bolstered by a thriving fishing industry, towns sprang up along the harbor-scalloped coast of calm Long Island Sound. New London, at the mouth of the Thames River, was America's third-largest whaling port during the 19th century. Today it is the home of the U.S. Coast Guard Academy and its tall ship *Eagle*, a sailing vessel used for training cruises. Just across the river, at Groton, the pioneer nuclear submarine U.S.S. *Nautilus* is moored at the Naval Submarine Base. In Mystic, just a few miles east toward the Rhode Island border, the great age of sailing is commemorated at Mystic Seaport. The jewel of the seaport's impressive maritime collection is the *Charles W. Morgan*, the last wooden whaling vessel afloat in the United States.

Connecticut's coastline is studded with lighthouses, but its great intellectual beacon shines from New Haven. Yale University was founded in 1701 as a more conservative alternative to Harvard University in Massachusetts. Today a bastion of secular learning, Yale is renowned for its schools of medicine, architecture, and law.

CONNECTICUT PRESERVED

Although Connecticut bustles with industry no less today than in the 19th century, it would be a mistake to assume that the state has been thoroughly urbanized. Of course, the southeastern corner closest to the New York border has felt the brunt of suburbanization—yet even here green spaces are carefully preserved. Still, the old mill towns are just a few miles away, and hilltop Colonial villages survive virtually untouched. Today industry tends to be centralized around Hartford, Bridgeport, New Haven, New London, and Waterbury.

Certain portions of the state have maintained much of their rural appeal. Among them are the Northwest Highlands, with their lush vineyards and such picture-perfect towns as Litchfield and New Preston, and the less well known area called the Quiet Corner, at Connecticut's northeastern extreme. Another region that is redolent of old Connecticut lies along the final meandering miles of the Connecticut River, which veers to the southeast, after Middletown. Chester and Essex are stunningly restored Colonial shipbuilding towns, and in East Haddam, the mansarded exuberance of the 1876 Goodspeed Opera House contrasts where the plain schoolhouse where a young Yale graduate taught before history and valor sent him on a different mission. His name was Nathan Hale, the great Revolutionary War hero and one of Connecticut's many gifts to the nation.

▲ *Sheldon Tavern was built as a home in 1760 and later served as an inn for the frontier outpost of Litchfield.*

CONNECTICUT
TIME LINE

1614 Explorer Adriaen Block sails up Connecticut River and claims land for Netherlands.

1633 The Dutch erect a fort and trading post at present-day Hartford. Colonists from Massachusetts establish first English settlement in Connecticut Valley.

1636 Thomas Hooker and his congregation from Massachusetts found Hartford.

1639 Representatives of Hartford, Wethersfield, and Windsor meet to adopt Fundamental Orders, or laws—a written constitution establishing popular government.

1647 A young woman named Alse Young is put to death for being a witch. She is the first woman to be executed for witchcraft in New England.

1662 Connecticut receives charter from King Charles II.

1701 Collegiate School, later Yale College, is founded in Branford.

1784 Tapping Reeve establishes America's first law school in Litchfield.

1788 Connecticut becomes fifth state to ratify Constitution.

1806 Noah Webster publishes first American dictionary in New Haven.

1878 First telephone exchange in the world begins operation in New Haven. It has 21 subscribers.

1910 U.S. Coast Guard Academy moves to New London.

1954 *Nautilus*, the first atomic-powered submarine, is launched at Groton.

1979 Connecticut bans building of new nuclear power plants.

▲ *Adopted in 1913, Delaware's flag displays the date it became the first state and shows a farmer and a soldier with a shield bearing agricultural products.*

Delaware

The nation's first state and now home to some 200,000 companies, Delaware has been at the crossroads of history for more than three and a half centuries. Despite being a mecca for big business, however, Delaware retains a bucolic charm—one-half of the state is covered with farmland and one-third with forests. Delaware's southeastern corner fronts the Atlantic Ocean, while the northern tip of the state is nestled in the foothills of the Appalachian Mountains. Delaware is, as Thomas Jefferson once described it, "a jewel among states."

AN INAUSPICIOUS BEGINNING

In 1609, after mistaking the Delaware Bay for a route to the Far East, English explorer Henry Hudson headed north. On his heels was Samuel Argall, a fellow Englishman who happened upon the inlet while seeking shelter from a storm. Before departing, he named the area for Thomas West, Lord De La Warr, the governor of the Virginia colony. Some two decades later, in 1631, the Dutch established a settlement at Zwaanendael (present-day Lewes). Relations with the local Indians soon turned disastrous, however: the colonists were massacred, and their settlement was burned to the ground. It would be another seven years before the Swedes would establish Fort Christina in Wilmington—the first successful settlement in Delaware.

In 1654 a struggle broke out between the Swedes and the Dutch, who had reestablished themselves at Fort Casimir in New Castle. When the Swedes tried to seize the fort, the Dutch fought them off and took control of all the Swedish territory. A decade later, the British settled the question of who owned Delaware when their fleet sailed into Delaware Bay and commandeered the area, making it part of New York.

The territory changed hands for the last time in 1682, when William Penn, concerned that the landlocked colony of

▶ *Thomas Coleman du Pont (1863–1930) lends a helping hand on the Du Pont Highway (Route 13), which he financed for the state.*

Pennsylvania did not have access to the ocean, petitioned King Charles II for a port. He was granted the land south of Pennsylvania on the west side of the Delaware River and Bay. Penn established a representative government for both colonies, but Delawareans became worried that their giant partner would eventually leave them without a voice in government. In response to their demands, the boundary was redrawn in 1701. With the peak of the New Castle courthouse as its center, a circle with a 12-mile radius was drawn; the arc that sliced through Pennsylvania created the only curved border in the United States. Penn granted Delaware its own legislature in 1704.

The British ruled the colony until 1776. Although many citizens of Delaware were loyalists, others bristled under British rule. In the end, the independents won. Two of Delaware's three delegates to the Continental Congress split votes, and it was only after a breathless ride through the night to Philadelphia by the third delegate, Caesar Rodney, that the tie-breaking vote for independence was cast. The one Revolutionary War battle to take place on Delaware's soil was a small skirmish, known as the Battle of Cooch's Bridge, in September 1777. The colonists, outnumbered by the British, were forced to retreat. On December 7, 1787, four years after the end of the Revolution, Delaware led the way to complete independence by being the first state to ratify the United States Constitution.

THE DU PONT LEGACY

The chemical companies in Wilmington are so renowned that the city is known as the Chemical Capital of the World. It all began with the establishment in 1802 of Éleuthère Irénée du Pont's gunpowder mill, an endeavor that led to the creation of E. I. du Pont de Nemours & Company, now one of the world's leading manufacturers of chemicals and synthetic products. More chemical companies have since followed suit, setting up offices, factories, and research labs in Delaware.

CITIES AND TOWNS *(For complete index, see page 217.)*

0   9
miles

(For map legend, see page 74.)

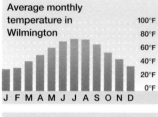

◀ ***Bombay Hook*** *National Wildlife Refuge, on the Atlantic flyway, where thousands of snow geese arrive each autumn to winter in its marshes.*

Still, perhaps the most conspicuous examples of the Du Pont legacy can be found in the area northwest of Wilmington known as Château Country. Here, Du Pont estates dot the landscape. Éleuthère Irénée du Pont's Georgian-style residence, Eleutherian Mills, is now part of the Hagley Museum, which pays tribute to 19th-century industrial life. Pierre S. du Pont's estate, Longwood Gardens, showcases greenhouses, conservatories, and more than 1,000 acres of formal gardens. Alfred du Pont's Louis XVI–style, 102-room mansion, Nemours, has gardens one-third of a mile long. And, not to be outdone by the men in her family, Evelina Gabrielle du Pont Bidermann built Winterthur. Today it features 200 period rooms and possibly the world's most extensive collection of American decorative arts.

Other Du Ponts have left their mark on Delaware as well. In 1911 Thomas Coleman du Pont, long fascinated with the automobile, helped launch Delaware's modern highway system. His paved four-lane highway ran south from Wilmington along the state's entire border and cost $40 million to build. Today Delaware has some 5,500 miles of highway and ranks among the leading states in automobile production. In the post–World War II era, this excellent network of roads allowed Delaware to grow faster than any other state east of the Rockies, with the exception of Florida and Maryland. Delaware also benefited from the altruism of Pierre S. du Pont. His million-dollar gifts built new schools and funded public education.

A PLAIN LAND WITH STRONG CHARACTER

Part of the Delmarva Peninsula, a 180-mile finger of land that includes parts of Maryland and Virginia, Delaware is bounded by the Chesapeake Bay on the west and the Delaware Bay and the Atlantic Ocean on the east. The bay retains some of the finest tidal marshes left in the mid-Atlantic region. Its green coast is furrowed with meandering tidal creeks that play host to hundreds of migrating shorebirds, bald eagles, and snow geese. Below the mouth of the bay, beaches extend for more than 20 miles, offering a summer playground for heat-weary city dwellers.

Inland, the state is a patchwork of subtle landscapes. With the exception of its northern tip, where the land rises to its highest point—442 feet—Delaware is part of the Atlantic Coastal Plain, a flat expanse that stretches along the East Coast from New Jersey to Florida. The state is flat and lies no more than 60 feet above sea level, making it the second-lowest in elevation after Florida. Much of the southern portions of the state remain off the beaten track. It is in this region, stitched together by two-lane back roads that skirt broad fields of rich earth and squared-off woodlots, that modern poultry farming was born. Today broiler chickens are the state's most important agricultural product, accounting for more than one-half of total farm income.

Despite its small size, Delaware is large when it comes to ingenuity and courage. It was at the Battle of Cooch's Bridge that the Stars and Stripes first flew. John Dickinson, one of the drafters of the Articles of Confederation, was a resident of Dover. Nylon, the world's first synthetic fiber, was invented in a Du Pont laboratory in 1935 by Dr. W. H. Carothers. And in 1971 Delaware became the first state to enact strict shore-protection laws. This second-smallest state is, as its nickname says, a "Small Wonder."

▶ ***Wilmington's Holy Trinity*** *(Old Swedes) Church, built in 1698, is the country's oldest continuously operating church.*

▲ ***Rehoboth Beach,*** *called the Nation's Summer Capital, is part of Delaware's 33-mile resort-area coastline. Rehoboth, a biblical term meaning "room enough," is apt considering the area's many vacationers.*

STATE DATA

State bird: Blue hen chicken
State flower: Peach blossom
State tree: American holly
State motto: Liberty and independence
State song: "Our Delaware"
Abbreviations: Del.; DE (postal)
Origin of the name: From Lord De La Warr, the first governor of the colony of Virginia
Nicknames: First State, Diamond State, Small Wonder

AREA AND SIZE

Total area: 2,057 sq. mi.
Rank within U.S.: 49
Extent: 96 mi. north–south; 39 mi. east–west
Highest elevation: 442 ft. above sea level in New Castle County
Lowest elevation: Sea level

POPULATION

Total: 768,000
Rank within U.S.: 46
Ethnic breakdown: White: 75.8%; Black: 18.6%; Hispanic: 3.3%; Asian: 2.0%; Indian: 0.3%
Population density: 387.3 people per sq. mi.

CLIMATE

Average monthly temperature in Wilmington

100°F
80°F
60°F
40°F
20°F
0°F

J F M A M J J A S O N D

Average monthly precipitation in Wilmington

10"
8"
6"
4"
2"
0"

J F M A M J J A S O N D

ECONOMY

Service industries: Banks, insurance companies, investment firms
Manufacturing: Chemicals, food processing, automobile production
Agriculture: Broiler chickens, soybeans, corn, potatoes, peas

DELAWARE TIMELINE

1609 While searching for a trade route to the East, Henry Hudson finds Delaware Bay.
1631 The Dutch establish first European settlement at Zwaanendael (present-day Lewes).
1638 The Swedes establish Fort Christina, which is later seized by the Dutch.
1664 The English take all Dutch holdings.
1682 Delaware is given to William Penn by the Duke of York

and becomes known as the Lower Three Counties of Pennsylvania.
1704 Penn grants Delaware its own legislature.
1787 Delaware is first state to ratify U.S. Constitution.
1802 Éleuthère Irénée du Pont founds gunpowder mill on banks of Brandywine Creek.
1829 The Delaware River and Chesapeake Bay are linked by canal that connects

farmers with city markets.
1861 Delaware supports the Union despite state's pro-slavery stance.
1935 Du Pont chemist Dr. W. H. Carothers develops nylon.
1951 Delaware Memorial Bridge connects Delaware with New Jersey.
1971 Delaware passes Coastal Zone Act for the protection of its wetlands against industrial pollution.

Florida

▲ **The state flag,** adopted in 1899, has a red diagonal cross that frames the state seal. The seal features an Indian woman strewing flowers. In the background is a sabal palm (the state tree) and a steamboat sailing past the rising sun.

STATE DATA

State bird: Mockingbird
State flower: Orange blossom
State tree: Sabal palm
State motto: In God we trust
State song: "The Swanee River" ("Old Folks at Home")
Abbreviations: Fla.; FL (postal)
Origin of the name: Juan Ponce de León explored the northeastern coast of Florida during the 1513 Easter season. He named the land "La Florida" in honor of Pascua Florida, Spain's Eastertime Feast of Flowers.
Nicknames: Sunshine State, Orange State, Alligator State, Everglades State, Peninsular State, Southernmost State

AREA AND SIZE

Total area: 58,560 sq. mi.
Rank within U.S.: 22
Extent: 450 mi. north–south; 465 mi. east–west
Highest elevation: 345 ft. above sea level in Walton County near the Alabama border
Lowest elevation: Sea level

POPULATION

Total: 15,233,000
Rank within U.S.: 4
Ethnic breakdown: White: 68.3%; Hispanic: 15.7%; Black: 14.2%; Asian: 1.6%; Indian: 0.3%
Density: 281.4 people per sq. mi.

CLIMATE

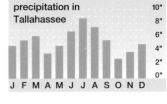

Average monthly temperature in Tallahassee
100°F 80°F 60°F 40°F 20°F 0°F
J F M A M J J A S O N D

Average monthly precipitation in Tallahassee
10" 8" 6" 4" 2" 0"
J F M A M J J A S O N D

ECONOMY

Service industries: Medical offices, law firms, hotels, amusement parks, real estate
Manufacturing: Electrical and communication equipment, food processing, printed materials
Agriculture: Oranges, grapefruits, limes, tangerines, tomatoes, sugarcane, indoor foliage plants

▶ **Dry Tortugas National Park,** 70 miles west of Key West, comprises seven coral islets and showcases Fort Jefferson, America's largest 19th-century coastal fort.

Wrapped in the warm breezes of the Gulf Stream and endless miles of clear coastal water, Florida has been touted from its earliest days as a paradise on Earth. Every year some 40 million visitors and 300,000 new residents flock to the Sunshine State. Giddy with the state's growth, Floridians have struggled to balance the benefits of development with the need to preserve natural resources. Florida is, on the one hand, the land of NASA, Disney World, and Miami Beach; on the other, the land of the manatee, the Everglades, and the Keys.

SOUTHEASTERN SANCTUARY

A long finger of swampy land that points 450 miles into the Atlantic Ocean and the Gulf of Mexico from the southeastern tip of North America, the state of Florida often seems on the verge of being engulfed by water. The nation's geologic "baby" rose from the ocean relatively late and never got very far: its highest point is just 345 feet above sea level. Water fills the maze of passageways in the porous limestone bedrock and rises aboveground into 30,000 lakes and ponds and countless springs. Lake Okeechobee, barely 20 feet deep, is the largest lake in the Southern United States. Its waters drain southward at a pace of half a foot per day, flowing into the exotic 40-mile-wide marsh that is the Everglades.

Florida's terrain is remarkably diverse, with rolling clay highlands in the northwest and dense forests in the east; in the center of the state, large citrus groves bear nearly four-fifths of the nation's orange and grapefruit crop. Still, the Everglades are the state's signature. Shaded by massive mahogany and live-oak trees draped in Spanish moss, the huge marsh shelters a stunning array of wildlife, including blue herons, white ibises, ospreys, bald eagles, and rare Florida panthers. Forests of mangroves, called "walking trees" by the Seminole Indians, line the

◀ **The Caribbean manatee** (Trichechus manatus) grows to 15 feet in length and 1,500 pounds in weight.

coasts. They provide breeding grounds for shellfish and create new land as they trap decaying debris in their tangled roots. Alligators and saltwater crocodiles prowl the waters for prey, while sleepy manatees loll about, devouring one-tenth of their body weight in sea grass every day. The giant, affable sea cows, now endangered by boat propellers and toxins, once left Christopher Columbus terribly disillusioned. The explorer mistook them for mermaids and could not understand why they were so homely.

THE STRUGGLE FOR CONTROL

Throughout its history Florida has endeavored to live up to the hyperbole that accompanies its golden climate. In the early years it failed miserably. Like most explorers of the time, the first European visitors wanted their discovery to sound like Eden itself. When the Spanish adventurer Juan Ponce de León arrived in 1513, he found neither the gold nor the fountain of youth that, legend claims, he was seeking; worse, when he returned eight years later to create a settlement, he was killed by an Indian arrow.

Four decades later the French explorer Jean Ribault described the land as "the fairest, fruitfullest and pleasantest of all the worlds." The 30 settlers he left behind quickly ran out of food and resorted to cannibalism to survive. Ribault subsequently carved out a settlement at the mouth of the St. Johns River, only to have it demolished in 1565 by a Spanish admiral named Pedro Menéndez de Avilés. After killing most of the settlers, sparing only a few Catholics and some women and children, he then had the remaining colonists hanged. Two years later the French retaliated, torching a Spanish fort and executing those who survived the fire.

Between battles, Menéndez found time to build St. Augustine, which since then has managed to withstand skirmishes among the Spanish, British, Americans, and Indians and which has the distinction of being the oldest surviving settlement in the United States. Today its residents welcome the many tourists who come to see the remnants of Florida's Spanish past: Castillo de San Marcos (1672), the oldest masonry fort in the country;

▶ **Wild greater flamingos** exist in very small numbers (no more than 30) on the Florida Bay.

(For map legend, see page 74.)

CITIES AND TOWNS
(For complete index, see page 217.)

Boca Raton **H5**	Fort Myers **G5**
Boynton Beach **H5**	Fort Pierce **H4**
Bradenton **F4**	Gainesville **F2**
Brandon **F4**	Hialeah **H6**
Cape Canaveral **H3**	Hollywood **H5**
Cape Coral **G5**	Jacksonville **G1**
Carol City **H6**	Kendall **H6**
Clearwater **F4**	Key West **G8**
Coral Gables **H6**	Lakeland **G3**
Coral Springs **H5**	Largo **F4**
Davie **H5**	Margate **H5**
Daytona Beach **G2**	Melbourne **H3**
Deerfield Beach **H5**	Miami **H6**
Delray Beach **H5**	Miami Beach **H6**
Deltona **G3**	Miramar **H6**
Fort Charlotte **F5**	North Miami **H6**
Fort Lauderdale **H5**	North Miami Beach **H6**
	Ocala **F2**
	Olympia Heights **H6**
	Orlando **G3**
	Palm Bay **H3**
	Palm Harbor **F3**
	Pembroke Pines **H5**
	Pensacola **A1**
	Pinellas Park **F4**
	Plantation **H5**
	Pompano Beach **H5**
	Port Orange **H2**
	Port Saint Lucie **H4**
	St. Augustine **G2**
	St. Petersburg **F4**
	Sarasota **F4**
	Sunrise **H5**
	Tallahassee **D1**
	Tamarac **H5**
	Tampa **F4**
	Titusville **H3**
	West Palm Beach **H5**

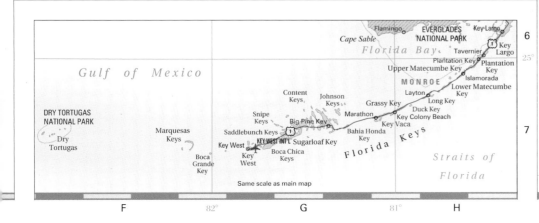

Fragrant blossoms on orange trees that produce 11 billion pounds of fruit annually.

a schoolhouse built in the mid-18th century; and a cathedral from the 1790s.

In 1763 the British captured Florida and divided it into West Florida, which they controlled, and East Florida, which was ruled by the few remaining Spaniards. In 1818 Gen. Andrew Jackson crossed the border with an army of 1,000 men and subdued the Seminole, who were harboring runaway slaves and refusing to leave their land along the boundary of Florida and Georgia. Jackson not only attacked the Indians but moved against the Spanish and executed two British subjects as Indian sympathizers. The renegade general's "unauthorized" war caused a furor in Congress, but, in fact, the United States had coveted Florida for years. In 1819, no doubt thanks to Jackson's rampage, Secretary of State John Quincy Adams got Spain to sign over all its lands east of the Mississippi.

As settlers streamed into northern Florida, they forced a showdown with the Indians. Fiercely independent and firmly entrenched in a labyrinth of swampland, the Seminole lived up to their name, which was derived either from the Creek words *ishti semoli,* meaning "wildmen" or "separatists," or from the Spanish *cimarrón,* meaning "unruly." From 1835 to 1842 Seminole guerrilla raiders locked the U.S. Army into the costliest Indian war it would ever fight.

At the center of the battle were the slaves, who over the course of the past century had been slipping across the border

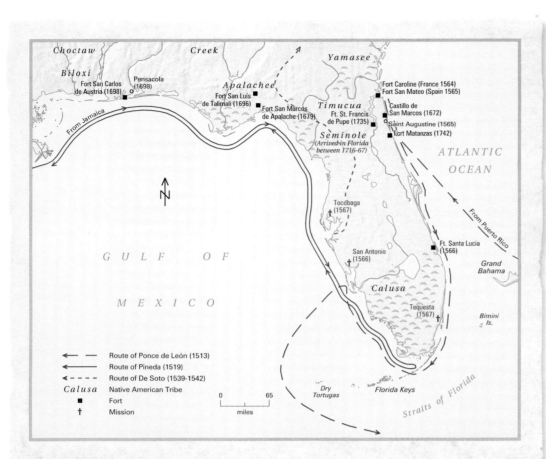

Choctaw — **Creek** — **Yamasee**

Biloxi
Fort San Carlos de Austria (1698)
Pensacola (1698)
Apalachee
Fort San Luis de Talimali (1696)
Fort San Marcos de Apalache (1679)
Timucua
Ft. St. Francis de Pupe (1735)
Fort Caroline (France 1564)
Fort San Mateo (Spain 1565)
Castillo de San Marcos (1672)
Saint Augustine (1565)
Fort Matanzas (1742)
Seminole (Arrived in Florida between 1716-67)
From Jamaica
ATLANTIC OCEAN
From Puerto Rico
Tocobaga (1567)
Ft. Santa Lucia (1566)
Grand Bahama
San Antonio (1566)
Calusa
Tequesta (1567)
Bimini Is.
Dry Tortugas
Florida Keys
Straits of Florida
GULF OF MEXICO

— — ← Route of Ponce de León (1513)
← — Route of Pineda (1519)
◄ - - - - Route of De Soto (1539-1542)
Calusa Native American Tribe
■ Fort
† Mission

0 ————— 65
miles

First in Florida

Florida was the first area in North America settled by Europeans. Other firsts for Florida and the United States took place in St. Augustine in 1565. The birth of Marin de Arguelles, the first European child born in America, occurred 22 years before that of the first English child, Virginia Dare. And Florida's first Thanksgiving predated the celebration in Massachusetts by 50 years. With the Treaty of Paris in 1763, Florida came under British rule, and the First Spanish Period, which had lasted from 1513 to 1763, came to a close. Britain ruled Florida until 1783, when it again came under Spanish rule. All told, Spain ruled Florida for some 300 years—in fact, it will be 2055 before the U.S. flag will have flown over Florida as long as the Spanish flag did.

FLORIDA
TIME LINE

1513 Explorer Ponce de León claims Florida for Spain.

1564 French Huguenots erect Fort Caroline on St. Johns River.

1565 Pedro Menéndez de Avilés routs French and founds city of St. Augustine.

1763 Britain captures Florida and divides it into east and west.

1783 Spain takes Florida from Britain.

1821 Spain cedes Florida to U.S.

1832 Seminole Indians refuse to be relocated to reservations in the West, leading to Seminole Wars.

1845 Florida joins the Union as 27th state.

1920–25 Land speculation leads to a real estate boom and greatly increases the state's population.

1950 New space center at Cape Canaveral sends off its first rocket.

1969 *Apollo 11* astronauts, launched from Kennedy Space Center, become first people to walk on moon.

1971 Walt Disney World opens.

1983–85 Fungus and freezing temperatures ruin the citrus crops.

1986 Space shuttle *Challenger* explodes, killing entire crew.

1988 Space shuttle *Discovery* is launched successfully.

1992 Hurricane Andrew destroys a 60-mile area in southern Florida, causing about $30 billion in damage.

and disappearing into the sanctuary of Seminole villages. Although several bands of Seminole agreed to move west in 1832, they didn't find out until later that no one of African ancestry would be allowed to go with them. After generations of intermarriage, hundreds of families would have been separated. Chief Osceola, whose wife was half black, persuaded several other Seminole leaders to protest at a meeting with Gen. Wiley Thompson in October 1834.

Then, with rifles in hand, Osceola and his braves ambushed U.S. troops, burned plantations, and shot General Thompson, vanishing into the swamps after each raid. A treaty signed in 1837 promised the Seminole "their negroes, their bona fide property," if they would turn in their guns and leave Florida to the whites. When the boats arrived to take them west, however,

▲ **The Florida Keys,** *a 150-mile string of coral and limestone islands, are North America's largest reef system. Divers can encounter hundreds of species of tropical fish under the water.*

▲ **Liftoff from Cape Canaveral,** *the country's center for space operations since 1947. Cape Canaveral was renamed Cape Kennedy in 1963, but 10 years later its original name was reinstated.*

Gen. Thomas Jesup claimed about 90 blacks as runaways and the deal was off. Later that year Jesup seized Osceola during a truce and shipped him off to a federal prison in Charleston, South Carolina, where the Indian chief died a few months later. The Seminole fought on until the army starved them by burning their crops. Most of the remaining Indians left for reservations in Oklahoma Territory, but several bands fled into the swamps. Their descendants today number about 2,000.

Three years after the Seminole were vanquished in 1842, Florida joined the Union as a slave state. In 1850 the white population of 47,000 held about 39,000 slaves and recorded exactly zero popular votes for Abraham Lincoln in the 1860 election. Secession soon followed. During the Civil War the state provided cover for blockade-running ships and supplied the Confederate Army with rations of beef, pork, and cotton.

BEACHFRONT BOOM AND BUST

With the Civil War over, Floridians turned to what would be their main preoccupation for the next half century: development. Phosphate rock—used in fertilizer—was discovered, and the state now churns out 80 percent of the U.S. supply. Cuban cigar magnate Vicente Martinez Ybor fled revolution in his homeland and turned Tampa into the cigar capital of the country. Railroads snaked down both coasts, and by 1900 a New Yorker could breakfast on Florida oranges less than a week after they were picked from the tree.

But the two financiers who had pumped their millions into the railroads had another kind of cargo in mind. For Henry Plant and Henry Flagler, that cargo was people—mainly people with time, lots of disposable income, and a craving for subtropical sun. Plant extended his railroad to Tampa on Florida's west coast, lining it with hotels and resorts. Flagler did the same for Florida's east coast, terminating his line in Palm Beach, a soon-to-be tony resort that got its name when a freighter full of coconuts ran aground, burying its cargo in the sand. When the big freeze of 1894 wiped out the citrus crop and chilled the tourist boom, a landowner in sunny Miami sent Flagler a sprig of orange blossoms and offered him half her property if he would extend the train line. By the turn of the century, even the least adventurous of tourists could explore Florida from top to bottom.

In 1920 Florida's population was nearing the 1 million mark. Henry Ford's Model T brought cars to the masses, and the masses brought their cars to Florida. Even Prohibition was a boon, turning the coastline into a major entry point for bootleg liquor. (By far the most popular rumrunner was Bill McCoy, whose brew was said to be so fine that it may have spawned the expression *the real McCoy.*)

Florida had become the great get-rich-quick scheme of a decade giddy with specu-

▲ **Collins Avenue** *in Miami Beach is named after John Collins, who in the early 1900s had the foresight to promote the island as a residential haven. Today some 250 hotels line its coast.*

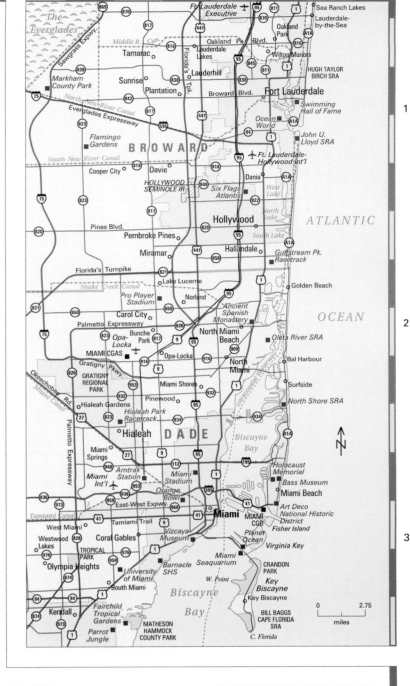

lation fever. Miami had 75,000 people, and one-third of them were said to be real estate agents. The streets were filled with tales of deeds that doubled in value within days. Builders couldn't build fast enough. Motorists clogged the Dixie Highway. Hotels hung out NO VACANCY signs. People slept in tents, train stations, and cars.

There was a fantasy quality to it all. Across the bay from Miami, Carl G. Fisher conjured Miami Beach out of a mangrove swamp, hiding tree stumps under 5 feet of sand and fashioning islands and lagoons out of thin air. George Edgar Merrick dug canals into the swamp at Coral Gables and imported gondolas and gondoliers from Venice. The accompanying rhetoric rivaled anything the wide-eyed entrepreneurs of the 16th century had come up with. "Go to Florida," gushed the *Miamian,* "where you sit and watch at twilight the fronds of the graceful palm, latticed against the fading gold of the sun-kissed sky. . . ." Not to be outdone by places with names like Lake Worth or Hollywood by the Sea, Miami dubbed itself "The Fair White Goddess of Cities" and "The City Invincible."

But with real estate scams almost as plentiful as the graceful palms, the Florida boom was anything but invincible. Investors in a housing complex called Manhattan Estates, in the "fast-growing city of Nettie," found out that Nettie was nothing more than an abandoned turpentine camp. Many people never even saw their property. They simply bought binders that contained blueprints, a description of the land, and a deed, hoping to pass the binder along at a profit. But by early 1926 the binders weren't moving, and Florida's bubble burst with a bang. Buyers defaulted, banks failed, and real estate offices shut their doors. In September of that year, a massive hurricane added to the destruction, flinging yachts onto the streets of Miami and Coral Gables, tearing roofs from shabby cabins, and scattering construction debris like matchsticks. Within a

year lavish developments all across the state lay empty and unfinished behind crumbling gates, prompting Groucho Marx to offer the final word: "You can get stucco. Oh, how you can get stucco."

THE EFFECT OF PROSPERITY

Today Florida's great real estate debacle seems as much a thing of the past as do Marx's jokes about it. Bolstered by military installations during World War II, the space program since the 1950s, and Disney World since 1971, Florida has become one of the most prosperous states in the country. It welcomes 40 million tourists a year, who spend some $33.1 billion. Buoyed by a stream of retirees seeking refuge from cold weather and state taxes (Florida has neither), the state has bypassed Ohio, Illinois, and Pennsylvania to become the fourth most populous in the country.

Success has taken its toll on Florida over the years. Strip malls stretch for miles outside some of the state's most beautiful resort cities. Pollution clouds many once-pristine waterways, erosion wears away the white sand beaches, and logging threatens the pine forests of the north. Less than half of the Everglades's 4,000 square miles are protected by the National Park Service, leaving dozens of rare species to fight for survival. Nonetheless, even while coveting the tourists' dollars, Floridians are well aware that they should protect their home in nature's jewel.

▲ **The Calle Ocho Festival,** *in Miami's Little Havana, has been an annual event since 1978.*

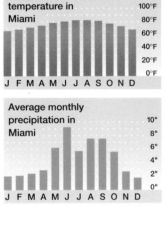

Average monthly temperature in Miami

Average monthly precipitation in Miami

▶ **The Cavalier Hotel,** *in the heart of Miami Beach's Art Deco District, is one of some 800 pastel gems that recall the splendor of the 1920s.*

▲ **The Georgia Dome,** a stadium in downtown Atlanta, was one of the sites for the 1996 Olympic games.

CITIES AND TOWNS (For complete index, see page 217.)

Albany B4	Dublin D3	Marietta B2	Smyrna B2
Americus B3	East Point B2	Martinez D2	South Augusta D2
Athens C2	Forest Park B2	Milledgeville C2	Statesboro E3
Atlanta B2	Fort Benning	Moultrie C4	Thomasville C5
Augusta E2	South B3	North Atlanta B2	Tifton C4
Brunswick E4	Gainesville C1	Plains B3	Tucker B2
Carrollton A2	Griffin B2	Redan B2	Valdosta C5
Columbus B3	Hinesville E4	Rome A1	Vidalia D3
Dahlonega C1	La Grange A2	Roswell B1	Warner Robins C3
Dalton B1	Lawrenceville C2	Sandy Springs B2	Waycross D4
Decatur B2	Macon C3	Savannah E3	West Augusta D2

0   28

miles

(For map legend, see page 74.)

Georgia

Larger than any other state east of the Mississippi, this giant of the South sweeps down from the southern end of the Blue Ridge Mountains, across the Piedmont's red clay hills, to fertile lowlands and the sea. Although the land makes a slow decline, the state certainly has not. A regional leader in manufacturing, agriculture, and service industries, Georgia and its largest city, Atlanta, combine the graciousness of Southern style with the spirit of an economic renaissance.

"FROM RABUN GAP TO TYBEE LIGHT"

Georgians have a saying to explain the state's tilting topography. Georgia, they say, slopes "from Rabun Gap to Tybee Light" on the Atlantic coast. A quick look at a map reveals the story: if you dropped a marble at the top of the state, it might just keep rolling all the way to Savannah.

The rustling palmettos and drooping Spanish moss of Georgia's sultry south are a long way from its mountainous north. Running in a roughly northeastern direction across the state, the Blue Ridge forms a brooding, barely accessible bulk that seems at first glance hardly Southern at all. Laced with scenic byways and dotted with small towns where Appalachian folkways persist, this forested countryside brings a taste of winter to the state each year and brilliant colors in the fall. In many a small northern Georgia town, residents can trace their ancestry straight back to the original Scotch-Irish settlers who came here in the early 1800s.

Much of the Blue Ridge is pristine wilderness, and one of the region's major attractions is its waterways—sparkling rivers that plunge down the mountainsides, carving magnificent canyons and fashioning crystalline waterfalls. Tallulah Gorge, some 1,000 feet from rocky lip to roiling river, is among the state's most breathtaking and oft-visited natural wonders.

The Blue Ridge region is also the seat of Georgia's mining heritage; it was here, near the town of Dahlonega (a Cherokee word for "precious yellow"), that gold was discovered in 1828, spurring the nation's first major gold rush and beating California by some 20 years. (Local lore has it that the expression "There's gold in them thar hills" was first uttered here, not at Sutter's Mill, as is commonly believed.) So much gold was found in the region that the U.S. government established a mint in Dahlonega and more than $6 million in gold coins was pressed here between 1838 and the outbreak of the Civil War. The vein that brought gold fever to the north of Georgia has mostly run its course, but other resources have taken its place. Georgia is the nation's leader in the production of kaolin (a clay), as well as a fine white marble of such clarity that it has been used in monuments around the world, including the Lincoln Memorial in Washington, D.C.

▲ *Dogwoods bloom in the Chattahoochee National Forest along the Appalachian Trail, which stretches 2,050 miles from Maine to Georgia.*

CAPITAL OF THE NEW SOUTH

Georgia's most famous mountain, though, isn't in the Blue Ridge—and it isn't really a mountain at all. Stone Mountain, east of Atlanta, is actually a single piece of rock, the largest isolated block of granite in the world. Nearly a mile and a half long, this megalith rises as a smooth gray dome 825 feet above the red clay hills of the Piedmont Plateau. Scientists believe that most of its bulk actually lies belowground.

▲ *Tallulah Gorge Waterfall, in Tallulah Gorge State Park, has served as the setting for movies and daredevil stunts.*

From the top of Stone Mountain, the lights of Atlanta glimmer to the west, about a half hour's drive away. Burned to the ground by Union forces under the leadership of Gen. William Tecumseh Sherman in 1864, Atlanta was soon being rebuilt, and so far there's no end in sight. Nearly half of all Georgians live in Atlanta's ever-expanding metropolitan area, which serves as the trade, transportation, and telecommunications capital of the Southeast. Among the nationally prominent businesses headquartered here are Time-Warner's Turner Broadcasting and soft-drink giant Coca-Cola, whose secret recipe was first formulated by an Atlanta druggist in 1886.

The past two decades in particular have seen Atlanta grow with astounding vigor. From the air, the city appears as a leafy sprawl, overlaid with a tangled knot of highway interchanges. Glittering glass-and-steel towers soar above the city's vibrant business center, while the ever-widening ring of Atlanta's suburbs reaches farther and farther into the hills of the Piedmont.

Since its birth as a busy crossroads trading depot in the 1830s, Atlanta has always been a regional heavyweight, and the city's muscular modern economy is the source of considerable civic pride. For many residents, Atlanta's selection as host city for the 1996 Centennial Olympic Games only confirmed what they already believed—that theirs is a world-class city.

Twenty-eight percent of Georgia's residents are African-American; in Atlanta, this number increases to 67 percent. Although pockets of inner-city poverty persist, Atlanta's black majority includes many affluent professionals, and African-Americans occupy positions of leadership across the spectrum of government and industry. As a Southern showpiece of black

▶ *The Cable News Network (CNN), based in Atlanta, was founded by businessman Ted Turner. It broadcasts to more countries worldwide than any other cable news channel.*

▲ *The state flag, adopted in 1956, displays the state seal and the Confederate flag. On the seal is a man with a drawn sword.*

STATE DATA

State bird: Brown thrasher
State flower: Cherokee rose
State tree: Live oak
State motto: Wisdom, justice, and moderation
State song: "Georgia on My Mind"
Abbreviations: Ga.; GA (postal)
Origin of the name: After King George II of England
Nicknames: Empire State of the South, Peach State

AREA AND SIZE

Total area: 58,876 sq. mi.
Rank within U.S.: 21
Extent: 318 mi. north–south; 278 mi. east–west
Highest elevation: Brasstown Bald Mountain, 4,784 ft. above sea level
Lowest elevation: Sea level along the Atlantic coast

POPULATION

Total: 7,875,000
Rank within U.S.: 10
Ethnic breakdown: White: 66.9%; Black: 28.7%; Hispanic: 2.4%; Asian: 1.8%; Indian: 0.2%
Population density: 135.3 people per sq. mi.

CLIMATE

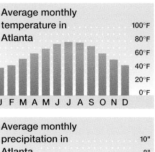

Average monthly temperature in Atlanta

100°F
80°F
60°F
40°F
20°F
0°F

J F M A M J J A S O N D

Average monthly precipitation in Atlanta

10"
8"
6"
4"
2"
0"

J F M A M J J A S O N D

ECONOMY

Service industries: Medical offices, discount stores, real estate, hotels
Manufacturing: Textiles, food processing, transportation equipment, wood and paper products
Agriculture: Eggs, broiler chickens, peanuts, cotton, tobacco, peaches

▲ *Rev. Martin Luther King, Jr.,* at Ebenezer Baptist Church in Atlanta in 1964. King launched his civil rights campaign from this pulpit, where his father, grandfather, and great-grandfather had preached before him.

achievement, the city owes much to its most famous black resident, the Reverend Martin Luther King, Jr. Born in Atlanta, King made the city a center of civil rights activism in the 1950s and '60s, turning back the tide of centuries of oppression. After he was assassinated in Memphis in 1968, King's body was returned to Atlanta for burial; his tombstone is etched with the words of an old slave spiritual that later became an anthem in the struggle against racism: "Free at Last, Free at Last, Thank God Almighty I'm Free at Last."

PEACHES, PEANUTS, PECANS, AND MORE

Visitors to Atlanta frequently complain that half the streets are named "Peachtree." It's an exaggeration, although barely; at last count, 32 street names contained the word.

In fact, Georgia's mild climate and long growing season make it ideal for a wide variety of crops. South of the Piedmont Plateau, the land slopes once again, falling sharply to the coastal plains and the agricultural heart of the state. Before boll weevil blights early in the 20th century

▲ *Peaches and Vidalia onions,* two well-known Georgia crops. The secret of the onions' sweetness is the low-sulfur soil and mild climate.

forced farmers to diversify, this land was planted almost entirely with cotton; today cotton is just one of Georgia's many crops. Around Vidalia—which calls itself The Sweet Onion City—farmers grow an onion of such sweetness, it can be picked and eaten raw like an apple. Enormous poultry farms produce 12 million eggs daily and broilers by the ton. Tobacco grows beside sweet potatoes, squash, soybeans, watermelons, and fruit trees. Peach orchards line the flatlands south of Macon. (Surprisingly, Georgia ranks only third in U.S. peach production.) In the south and west, pecans and peanuts—locally known as "goobers," a West African word brought to the New World by the slaves who once worked these fields—fill mile after mile of farmland. Georgia is the number one producer of both. Without a doubt, Georgia's most famous peanut farmer is former Georgia governor Jimmy Carter, whose folksy style helped propel him to the White House in 1976 and focused world attention on the tiny town of Plains, the site of the Carter family farm.

Agriculture is just part of rural Georgia's economic picture. From the Piedmont to the Plains, dense forests of loblolly, slash, shortleaf, and longleaf pine provide an abundance of wood for harvesting, and the state ranks as the nation's largest source of wood pulp and paper products, as well as other wood by-products like gum resins and turpentine. Wood processing—including sawmills and engineered wood plants—is a major industry, as is food processing. Georgia's textile industry is gigantic, amassing $14 billion in sales every year and employing nearly one-fifth of all the factory workers in the state; fully half of the nation's carpets are made in the state.

OLD SAVANNAH

Georgia may be a modern economic powerhouse, but its beginnings were not so auspicious. The last of the original 13

The Georgia Barrier Islands

Once the home of Guale Indians, Spanish conquistadores, and then English colonists, many of the Georgia barrier islands (as well as islands off the coast of South Carolina) are today the residence of a dwindling population descended from slaves brought here to work on rice, indigo, and cotton plantations. So isolated are these isles that the black people here have been able to preserve their melodious language, called Gullah or Geechee—a combination of 18th-century English and West African languages. Equally distinct (and decidedly African-influenced) is Gullah culture, evident in everything from cuisine, music, customs, and handicrafts (handwoven Gullah baskets are nearly indistinguishable from those woven in Sierra Leone, on the West African coast) to the islanders' strong spiritual connection to nature and their ancestors.

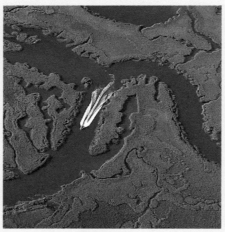

▲ *A speedboat snakes* its solitary way through a channel of Little St. Simons, one of Georgia's "Golden Isles."

▲ *Bull Square, Savannah, 1901.* Founder James Oglethorpe reputedly based his plan for the city on a design he saw for Peking, China.

colonies, Georgia began as a social experiment underwritten by philanthropist and member of Parliament James Edward Oglethorpe, who secured a charter from the Crown in 1732 to establish a refuge in the New World for, among others, residents of England's overcrowded debtor's prisons. Oglethorpe believed that a fresh start could help such men and women rehabilitate themselves, but the results were not what he had hoped for. Mosquitoes, tropical diseases, hostile Indians, and a rebellious population all took their toll, and the colony was turned over to the British government in 1752.

Oglethorpe's experiment may have failed, but the city he founded on the bluffs above the Savannah River endures as a living symbol of Southern charm—and a paragon of civic planning. Savannah's Historic District, a 2½-square-mile grid of cobblestoned streets, stately 18th- and 19th-century homes, and gardenlike squares, is widely considered one of the South's most genteel settings. Warmed by sultry ocean breezes, the city has a decidedly tropical feel—a stark and welcome contrast, no doubt, to the damp British prisons that were the source of a number of the city's first inhabitants. Even Sherman couldn't bear to burn Savannah, as he had Atlanta. When the advancing Union army completed its ruinous "march to the sea" and forced Savannah to surrender in 1864, Sherman spared the torches and instead offered the city to President Lincoln as a Christmas present.

Like Atlanta, Savannah straddles the present and the past, both honoring its colonial heritage and keeping pace with the times. When urban renewal threatened the heart of the old city in the 1950s, the Historic Savannah Foundation intervened; eventually some 1,400 buildings were preserved. A similar effort is now under way in the city's Victorian section, just to the south of the Historic District. Savannah's riverfront, at one time the busiest cotton port in the South, was restored in the 1970s; its old brick warehouses, once fallen into disuse, now contain boutiques, art galleries, restaurants, and shops that cater to Savannah's active tourist trade. The city's flourishing art scene centers on the recently restored City Market, located on the northwestern edge of the Historic District, where local artists display their work in an old-world market setting.

THE GOLDEN ISLES

The Savannah River, which forms the state's irregular border with South Carolina, empties into the Atlantic at Georgia's northernmost intersection with the sea. The rest of the Georgia coastline, a scant 100 miles long, is guarded by a string of barrier islands that Georgians call the "Golden Isles" for the luminous color of their marshlands. Although some islands have been converted to upscale resorts, nearly two-thirds of the land remains in a wild or semiwild state barely touched by time. No causeways connected the islands to the mainland until the 1920s, and most islands are still accessible only by boat. Wild horses, descendants of horses brought here as early as the 18th century, first to work the plantations and later for the enjoyment of vacationers, still roam the beaches and live-oak- and cypress-forested interiors.

Here, too, are the people of the Gullah culture, descendants of 18th-century African slaves.

A PRIMITIVE WILDERNESS

If the topography of Georgia is a long, slow descent to sea level, then in the state's southeastern corner, some 100 miles inland, the distinction between land and water loses meaning altogether. This is the Okefenokee Swamp, a 660-square-mile morass of freshwater marsh, cypress grove, and spongy peat bog that reaches south across

▶ *The Okefenokee Swamp, a huge bog in the southeastern corner of Georgia, rests in a vast indentation that once was part of the ocean floor. Alligators, like those shown in the photo below, are plentiful in the Okefenokee, which is also home to herons, egrets, and many other wading birds.*

the border into neighboring Florida. Incomparably lush, the Okefenokee supports an astounding array of plant and animal life, including some 12,000 alligators, one of the largest concentrations in the nation. Far more scarce is human life. Even native Creek and Seminole Indians, who knew the Okefenokee as "the land of the trembling earth," rarely hazarded into its mysterious interior. Protected as a National Wildlife Refuge, the Okefenokee today offers visitors the chance to sample one of the state's—and the nation's—most bewitching and exotic places.

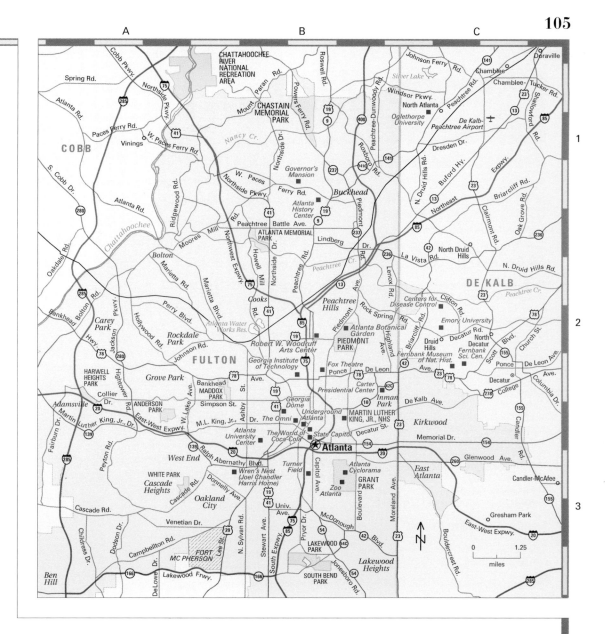

GEORGIA
TIME LINE

1540 Spanish explorer Hernando de Soto leads expedition into Georgia.

1732 Charter from King George II establishes Georgia as 13th colony.

1733 James Edward Oglethorpe, along with British colonists, founds town of Savannah.

1788 Georgia ratifies U.S. Constitution, becoming fourth state.

1793 Eli Whitney invents cotton gin near Savannah.

1838 Georgia's remaining Cherokee are forced to relocate to reservations in the West.

1861 Georgia secedes from the Union; joins Confederacy.

1864 In their "march to the sea," General Sherman's troops ransack the state and burn Atlanta.

1870 Georgia rejoins the Union.

1881 A rebuilt Atlanta holds International Cotton Exposition.

1921 Boll weevils destroy much of the state's cotton crop.

1943 Georgia becomes first state to give 18-year-olds the vote.

1973 Maynard Jackson, Jr., becomes mayor of Atlanta. He is the first black mayor of a major Southern city.

1977 Former governor Jimmy Carter is sworn in as 39th United States president.

1986 Carter Presidential Center opens in Atlanta. A museum and library, it is also a think tank for human rights and environmental issues.

1994 Floods in central and southern Georgia cause 31 deaths and heavy property damage.

A   160°   B

Hawaii

The most isolated region on Earth, Hawaii pricks the surface of the Pacific 2,400 miles off the western coast of North America—it's as remote from California as San Francisco is from Savannah, Georgia. Spawned by the earth's molten core and shaped by the ocean's steady battering, the country's newest state is a work in progress. Although tourism has intruded on Hawaii's past, the islands still nurture the remnants of the most advanced indigenous culture in the United States.

▲ **Closely resembling** the Union Jack of Great Britain, after which it was modeled, Hawaii's flag has eight stripes that represent the main islands of the state. The flag was adopted in 1959.

State bird: Nene (Hawaiian goose)
State flower: Yellow hibiscus
State tree: Kukui (candlenut)
State motto: *Ua mau ke ea o ka aina i ka pono* (The life of the land is perpetuated in righteousness)
State song: "Hawaii Ponoi" ("Our Own Hawaii")
Abbreviation: HI (postal)
Origin of the name: Believed to be from an ancient Polynesian homeland called Hawaiki
Nicknames: Aloha State, Paradise of the Pacific, Pineapple State

AREA AND SIZE
Total area: 6,450 sq. mi.
Rank within U.S.: 47
Extent: 230 mi. north–south; 350 mi. east–west
Highest elevation: Mauna Kea, 13,796 ft. above sea level
Lowest elevation: Sea level along the coast

POPULATION
Total: 1,257,000
Rank within U.S.: 41
Ethnic breakdown: Asian: 60.1%; White: 28.9%; Hispanic: 8.5%; Black: 2.1%; Indian: 0.3%
Population density: 195.9 people per sq. mi.

CLIMATE

Average monthly temperature in Honolulu — 100°F, 80°F, 60°F, 40°F, 20°F, 0°F — J F M A M J J A S O N D

Average monthly precipitation in Honolulu — 10", 8", 6", 4", 2", 0" — J F M A M J J A S O N D

ECONOMY
Service industries: Medical offices, hotels, rental cars, real estate
Manufacturing: Food products, refined petroleum, clothing
Agriculture: Sugarcane, pineapples, flowers, coffee, cattle

▼ **Plumeria blossoms** grow wild and are often used in a traditional necklace of flowers called a lei.

THE BEAUTIFUL WORLD
To its earliest inhabitants, Hawaii was the last stop in a 1,500-year migration from South Asia to Indonesia to Polynesia. Navigating by the sun and stars in double-hulled canoes up to 80 feet long, these island-hopping warriors decided around A.D. 500 that they had found their ancestral home in the sun, Hawaiki. Before long, according to oral tradition, the islands became known affectionately by a more apt name: Ke Ao Nani, or "The Beautiful World."

Some 7 million tourists flock to Hawaii every year in search of this beauty, and they find a land of extremes. Storm clouds pour 450 inches of rain a year on Kauai's Mount Waialeale, known as the wettest place on Earth, while the wizened moonscapes of western Molokai receive less than 10 inches. Silken beaches and calm waters line the leeward shores on each of the eight major islands, while 30-foot waves bombard such surfers' havens as Oahu's north shore.

Hawaii rose from the sea in a violent process that has convulsed the earth's crust for nearly 40 million years. The archipelago's 125 islands are in fact the peaks of huge volcanoes that disgorge molten lava. The Pacific Plate, on which the islands rest, has been inching over a hot spot (now underneath the island of Hawaii) in the earth's mantle that is responsible for the volcanic activity that

▲ **One of three active volcanoes** in Hawaii belches lava, which forms a fiery river down its flank.

formed the islands. It was here that Mount Kilauea, the most active volcano on Earth, swallowed a town in 1990. Today Kilauea—which Mark Twain once said made Vesuvius look like a soup kettle—is creating a new landmass, 20 miles off the coast of the island.

FROM KAPU TO CHRISTIANITY
In January 1778 two ships that would bring more change than any tsunami sailed into Kauai's Waimea Bay. Capt. James Cook, an accomplished British explorer, was on his third voyage to the Pacific when he happened upon the islands. He found a highly developed society with an elaborate caste system. Commoners fell to their knees at the approach of a chief. Women were barred from eating with men. A high priest, or kahuna, presided over human sacrifices. Violating any taboos, or kapu, could result in death. With unintentional but perfect timing, Cook arrived during the annual harvest festival; he was mistaken for a harvest god and all prostrated themselves before him. After heading for Alaskan waters to search for a Northwest Passage to the Atlantic, Cook returned, his ship's mast broken and he himself looking sadly mortal. He was killed by the islanders on the beach during a scuffle over some iron tools.

Before long, new ships arrived with tools and guns. The natives and the Europeans set aside their differences to start a thriving trade. With the help of European weapons, a warrior named Kamehameha unified the islands and ruled as a benevolent despot until his death in 1819. Soon afterward, his dissolute son took the throne. One of Kamehameha's surviving three wives talked the new ruler into dining with her. The taboo was broken—a woman had eaten with a man. With that, 650 years of religious practice crumbled.

▲ **Volcanic cliffs,** lonely beaches, and sea caves are all part of Kauai's Na Pali coast, a remote spot with no land access.

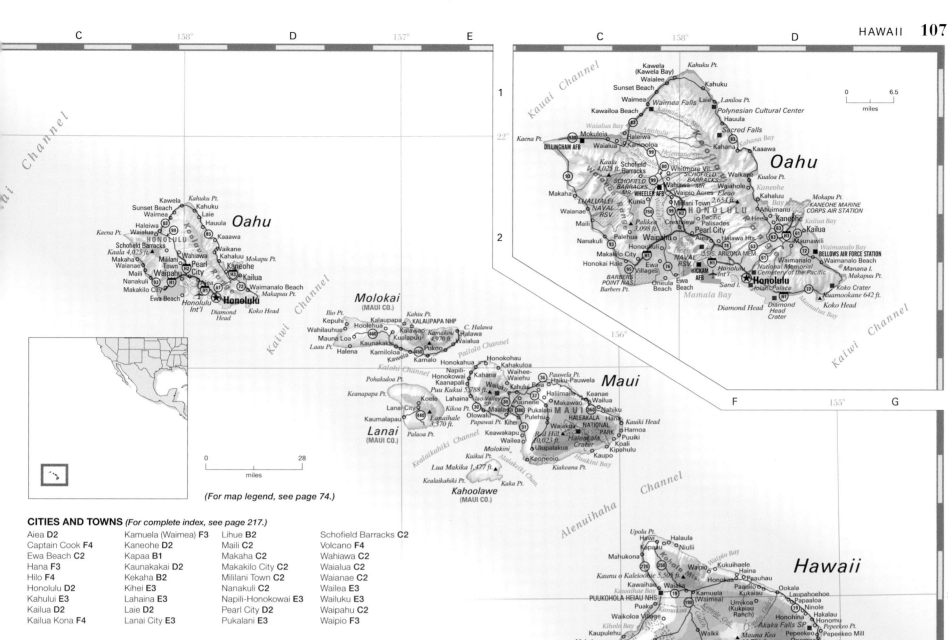

(For map legend, see page 74.)

Into the spiritual void created by the loss of Hawaiian tradition came a volatile mix of high-minded missionaries and hard-drinking whalers from New England. The whalers, who made Hawaii their way station en route to the waters off Japan, produced an instant demand for one commodity—"sin." The ministers, however, were determined to cut off the supply. The first men of the cloth arrived in 1820, striding through the balmy air in long-sleeved woolens and preaching an austerity that somehow caught on. Just before her death in 1823, Queen Keopuolani had herself baptized, and by 1825 no one could dance or ride horseback on Sundays. Liquor, gambling, and prostitution were outlawed. Before long, women were covering themselves in baggy dresses called muumuus, and the hula was banned, silencing the dancers whose chants had preserved island history for generations. To their credit, the missionaries also built the first printing press west of the Mississippi and created a written language for the Hawaiians, and by the mid-1800s they had helped teach 80 percent of the islanders to read. Their sons, however, turned to more worldly pursuits.

PINEAPPLES, TOURISM, AND A NATIVE REVIVAL

In a matter of decades, business-minded Puritans presided over the most productive sugarcane plantations in the world, and their money began to rule Hawaii. Kamehameha III let the genie out of the bottle in 1850 by allowing foreigners to buy land. Many plots went for a case of whiskey, and the new plantations quickly attracted waves of laborers from overseas—first the Chinese, Japanese, and Portuguese, then the Puerto Ricans, Koreans, and Filipinos. By the 1890s less than a quarter of Hawaiian land was owned by native Hawaiians. The island's economy rested in the hands of a dozen or so sugar barons, who chafed at the high duties imposed by the United States on the import of their goods. In January 1893, with the help of the Marines, they toppled Queen Liliuokalani in favor of a republic headed by the future pineapple king, Sanford B. Dole. President William McKinley annexed the islands in 1898, and Hawaii began the 20th century as a U.S. territory.

Hawaii has weathered its upheavals gracefully. When the sugar industry lost ground to cheap foreign labor in the 1930s, tourism revived the economy. Pan Am launched daily air service from San Francisco in 1936. Five years later the Japanese

Air Force decimated the U.S. Pacific fleet at Pearl Harbor, but the tourist industry barely missed a beat, soaring to a $10-billion-a-year business by the 1990s. And while successive waves of immigration could have opened gaping ethnic fault lines, Hawaii simply absorbed each group in turn, evolving into a multiethnic society where one in three marriages is cross-cultural.

Much of Hawaii's historic island character, however, has survived the melting pot and economic development. For example, not far from Waikiki Beach, the site of more than half of Hawaii's hotels, is the privately owned island of Niihau, home to native Hawaiians who raise sheep and cattle without the modern comforts and convenience of electricity, plumbing, or paved roads.

▶ **Iolani Palace,** in Honolulu, is the only royal residence on U.S. soil. It was here that Queen Liliuokalani wrote "Aloha Oe."

HAWAII TIME LINE

C. A.D. 300 Polynesians, probably from the Marquesas, migrate to Hawaiian islands.

1778 British captain James Cook lands on islands and names them Sandwich Islands.

1795 Hawaii is unified under Kamehameha I.

1820 Christian missionaries arrive from New England.

1835 Americans establish the islands' first permanent sugarcane plantation, on Kauai.

1885 Hawaiian pineapple industry begins with plants imported from Jamaica.

1887 King Kalakaua allows U.S. Navy to occupy Pearl Harbor.

1893 Revolution led by Americans ends monarchy.

1894 Republic of Hawaii is established.

1898 U.S. annexes Hawaii.

1941 On December 7 the Japanese attack Pearl Harbor; U.S. enters World War II.

1957 First telephone cable from U.S. mainland to Hawaii begins operating.

1959 Hawaii becomes 50th state.

1982 Hurricane Iwa destroys Kauai and Oahu, causing $300 million in damages.

1990 Kilauea erupts, destroying town of Kalapana, 20 miles east of volcano's crater.

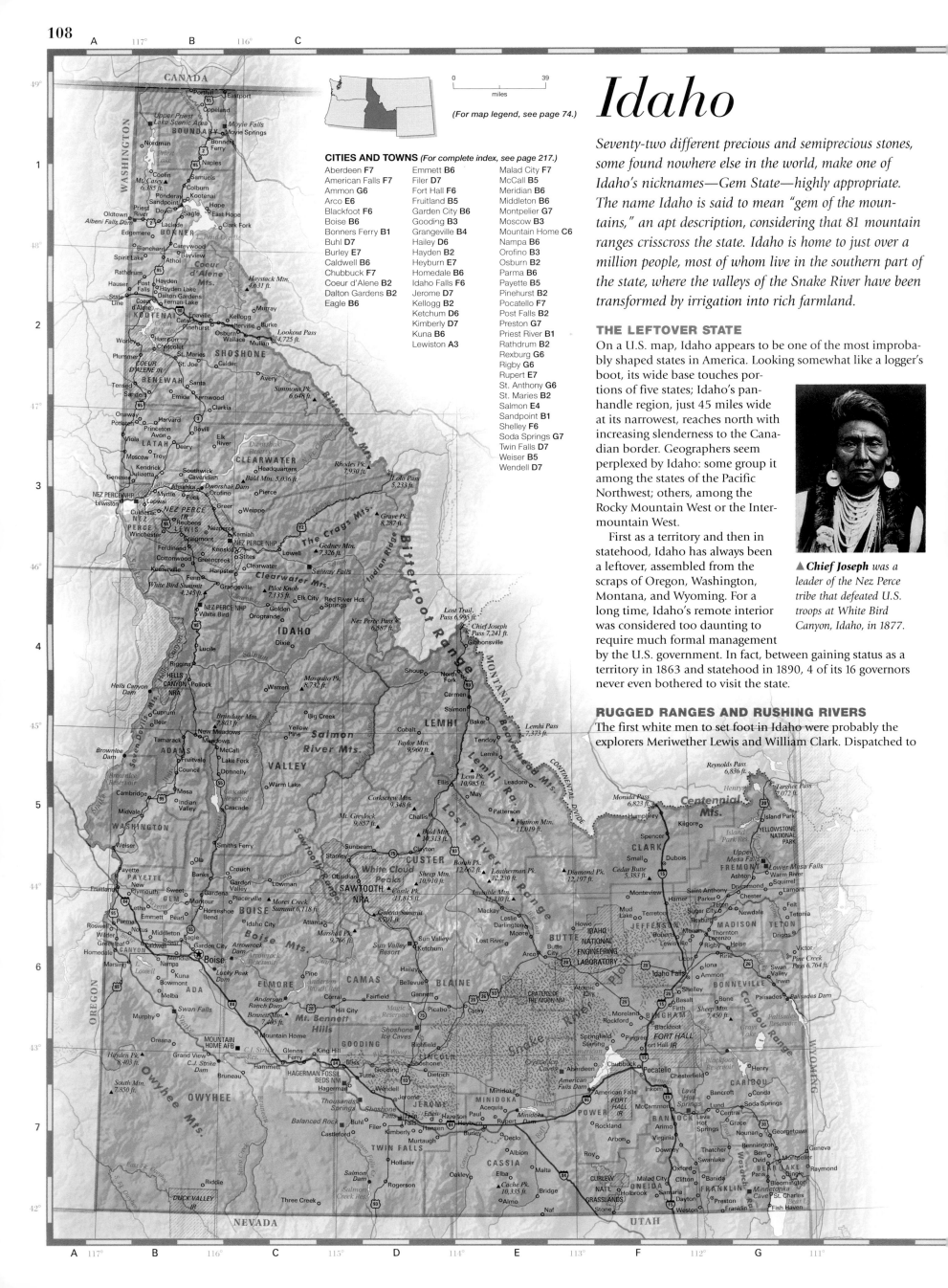

CANADA

(For map legend, see page 74.)

0 ——— 39
miles

Idaho

Seventy-two different precious and semiprecious stones, some found nowhere else in the world, make one of Idaho's nicknames—Gem State—highly appropriate. The name Idaho is said to mean "gem of the mountains," an apt description, considering that 81 mountain ranges crisscross the state. Idaho is home to just over a million people, most of whom live in the southern part of the state, where the valleys of the Snake River have been transformed by irrigation into rich farmland.

THE LEFTOVER STATE

On a U.S. map, Idaho appears to be one of the most improbably shaped states in America. Looking somewhat like a logger's boot, its wide base touches portions of five states; Idaho's panhandle region, just 45 miles wide at its narrowest, reaches north with increasing slenderness to the Canadian border. Geographers seem perplexed by Idaho: some group it among the states of the Pacific Northwest; others, among the Rocky Mountain West or the Intermountain West.

First as a territory and then in statehood, Idaho has always been a leftover, assembled from the scraps of Oregon, Washington, Montana, and Wyoming. For a long time, Idaho's remote interior was considered too daunting to require much formal management

▲ **Chief Joseph** *was a leader of the Nez Perce tribe that defeated U.S. troops at White Bird Canyon, Idaho, in 1877.*

by the U.S. government. In fact, between gaining status as a territory in 1863 and statehood in 1890, 4 of its 16 governors never even bothered to visit the state.

RUGGED RANGES AND RUSHING RIVERS

The first white men to set foot in Idaho were probably the explorers Meriwether Lewis and William Clark. Dispatched to

CITIES AND TOWNS *(For complete index, see page 217.)*

Aberdeen **F7**	Emmett **B6**	Malad City **F7**
American Falls **F7**	Filer **D7**	McCall **B5**
Ammon **G6**	Fort Hall **F6**	Meridian **B6**
Arco **E6**	Fruitland **B5**	Middleton **B6**
Blackfoot **F6**	Garden City **B6**	Montpelier **G7**
Boise **B6**	Gooding **B3**	Moscow **B3**
Bonners Ferry **B1**	Grangeville **B4**	Mountain Home **C6**
Buhl **D7**	Hailey **D6**	Nampa **B6**
Burley **E7**	Hayden **B2**	Orofino **B3**
Caldwell **B6**	Heyburn **E7**	Osburn **B2**
Chubbuck **F7**	Homedale **B6**	Parma **B6**
Coeur d'Alene **B2**	Idaho Falls **F6**	Payette **B5**
Dalton Gardens **B2**	Jerome **D7**	Pinehurst **B2**
Eagle **B6**	Kellogg **B2**	Pocatello **F7**
	Ketchum **D6**	Post Falls **B2**
	Kimberly **D7**	Preston **G7**
	Kuna **B6**	Priest River **B1**
	Lewiston **A3**	Rathdrum **B2**
		Rexburg **G6**
		Rigby **G6**
		Rupert **E7**
		St. Anthony **G6**
		St. Maries **B2**
		Salmon **E4**
		Sandpoint **B1**
		Shelley **F6**
		Soda Springs **G7**
		Twin Falls **D7**
		Weiser **B5**
		Wendell **D7**

▲ **Alpine lakes,** *game reserves, and resorts nestle among the peaks of the Sawtooth Range, which runs 40 miles through south central Idaho.*

▲ **Idaho's flag,** *adopted in 1907, bears the state seal. A woman holding scales and a spear symbolizes justice, equality, and liberty; a miner recalls Idaho's minerals; and an elk, a pine tree, and a sheaf of grain represent wildlife, timber, and agriculture.*

STATE DATA

State bird: Mountain bluebird
State flower: Syringa
State tree: White pine
State motto: *Esto perpetua* (It is perpetual)
State song: "Here We Have Idaho"
Abbreviations: Ida.; ID (postal)
Origin of the name: Unknown, but possibly a word invented to sound Indian. Commonly accepted to mean "gem of the mountains."
Nicknames: Gem State, Gem of the Mountains, Spud State

AREA AND SIZE

Total area: 83,557 sq. mi.
Rank within U.S.: 13
Extent: 483 mi. north–south; 316 mi. east–west
Highest elevation: Borah Peak, 12,662 ft. above sea level
Lowest elevation: Snake River in Nez Perce County, 710 ft. above sea level

POPULATION

Total: 1,347,000
Rank within U.S.: 41
Ethnic breakdown: White: 89.9%; Hispanic: 7.1%; Indian: 1.3%; Asian: 1.1%; Black: 0.4%
Population density: 16.3 people per sq. mi.

CLIMATE

Average monthly temperature in Boise
100°F / 80°F / 60°F / 40°F / 20°F / 0°F
J F M A M J J A S O N D

Average monthly precipitation in Boise
10" / 8" / 6" / 4" / 2" / 0"
J F M A M J J A S O N D

ECONOMY

Service industries: Banks, real estate, grocery stores
Manufacturing: Food processing, chemicals, electrical equipment
Agriculture: Potatoes, wheat, hay, sugar beets, beef cattle, sheep

---

the West by President Thomas Jefferson to inspect the lands added to the United States by the Louisiana Purchase, Lewis and Clark arrived in Idaho in 1805. As they struggled across the Bitterroot Range at Lolo Pass, they were greeted by a band of local Indians, members of the Nez Perce tribe. Although the encounter was friendly—Lewis and Clark stayed with the Nez Perce for nearly a month—Idaho would later be the site of protracted and frequently violent struggles between the white settlers and the indigenous Indian tribes, including the Kutenai, Kalispel, Coeur d'Alene, and Shoshone.

So harsh is the terrain of northern Idaho that it took Lewis and Clark two separate attempts to penetrate the region. Rugged ranges dominate the upper two-thirds of the state, and their names match their intimidating bulk: the Bitterroots, the Sawtooths, the Seven Devils, the Lost River Range. Paved roads are a rarity. Nearly 16,000 miles of rivers and streams lace this wilderness, cutting magnificent gorges as they race westward to the Snake River and, eventually, the sea. The Salmon River, which originates in the Sawtooth Range, is so unpredictable and swift that early settlers nicknamed it the River of No Return.

The Snake River is the grandest of all of Idaho's rivers, and one of the great rivers of the West. Shaped like an upside-down question mark, the Snake loops southwest from its headwaters in Wyoming across the broad plains of Idaho's southern tier, then turns sharply north again to form a portion of the state's western boundary with Oregon—and Hells Canyon, America's deepest gorge. (It's so deep that you could count to 30—slowly—before a rock tossed from its edge would hit bottom, 7,900 feet below.)

FAMOUS POTATOES AND MOON WALKERS

Northern and central Idaho are sparsely populated; 70 percent of the state's residents live within 50 miles of the Snake River, in the southern portion of the state along the fertile valley of the Snake River plain. Located here is the handsome and prosperous capital, Boise (a French word meaning "wooded," which it is), as well as mile after mile of cultivated fields.

Potatoes are Idaho's most important crop. More potatoes are grown in southern Idaho than anywhere else in the nation, and processing plants churn out French fries and potato chips by the billions. But other crops are vital, too—sugar beets,

▲ **Idaho potatoes** *account for one-fourth of all the French fries served in fast-food restaurants.*

alfalfa, even wine grapes. Ironically, much of Idaho's most productive farmland, some 2 million acres, was once sagebrush desert; water diverted from the Snake irrigates the river valley's fertile, lava-enriched soil.

At a distance from the river, mountains and desert take over the land again. Much of the terrain of south central and southeastern Idaho is volcanic in origin, and the violent upheavals of ages past have left behind a tortured landscape. So otherworldly are the lifeless lava flows and blackened cinder cones of Craters of the Moon National Monument that the Apollo astronauts trained here in the 1960s. It is in this part of the state—close to the Utah border—that sheep and cattle ranching compete with potato farming as economic mainstays and a majority of Idaho's Mormon citizens have made their homes.

WESTERN HERITAGE

Because of the state's distinct geophysical characteristics, Idaho may seem like several states cobbled into one: the potato-producing south, the Mormon southeast, and the sparsely populated north. Professing deep connections to their pioneer forebears, as well as economic ties to the neighboring states of Washington and Montana, residents of Idaho's central and panhandle regions maintain a stalwart independence.

Yet such independence of spirit also remains the state's most unifying force. "Idaho is what America was," or so the saying goes. The residents of any region of the state, united by the common bond of a pioneer past and the untamed beauty of the land, are quick to point out that theirs is a special place.

IDAHO TIME LINE

1805 Lewis and Clark travel through Idaho.
1809 Canadians establish first fur-trading post on shore of Lake Pend Oreille.
1834 Fort Hall and Fort Boise are established. They will later be stops on the Oregon Trail.
1860 Franklin, the first permanent settlement, is founded by Mormons. Gold is discovered in Orofino Creek.

1863 Idaho becomes a territory.
1877 Federal soldiers defeat Nez Perce Indians.
1890 Idaho becomes 43rd state.
1907 Defense lawyer Clarence Darrow gets acquittals for two union miners accused of murder.
1927 Completion of U.S. Highway 95 connects northern and southern Idaho.
1955 Arco becomes first town in

the world to be lit completely by atomic power.
1959 Brownlee Dam, the first of three hydroelectric dams on Snake River, is completed.
1972 Shoshone County mine fire kills 91 workers.
1975 New waterway connects Snake and Columbia rivers to Pacific Ocean.
1976 Teton Dam collapses, killing 11 people.

ILLINOIS

▲ *Illinois's flag,* *adopted in 1915, displays a bald eagle holding a shield that represents the original colonies. The rising sun and the laurel symbolize progress.*

STATE DATA
State bird: Cardinal
State flower: Native violet
State tree: White oak
State motto: State sovereignty, national union
State song: "Illinois"
Abbreviations: Ill.; IL (postal)
Origin of the name: From the French version of the Indian word *Illiniwek,* meaning "Superior Men"
Nicknames: Prairie State, Corn State, Land of Lincoln

AREA AND SIZE
Total area: 57,926 sq. mi.
Rank within U.S.: 24
Extent: 378 mi. north–south; 212 mi. east–west
Highest elevation: Charles Mound, 1,235 ft. above sea level
Lowest elevation: 279 ft. above sea level along the Mississippi River in Alexander County

POPULATION
Total: 12,051,000
Rank within U.S.: 6
Ethnic breakdown: White: 71.0%; Black: 15.0%; Hispanic: 10.5%; Asian: 3.3%; Indian: 0.1%
Population density: 215.7 people per sq. mi.

CLIMATE

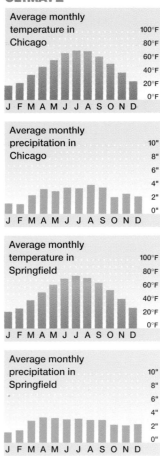

Average monthly temperature in Chicago

Average monthly precipitation in Chicago

Average monthly temperature in Springfield

Average monthly precipitation in Springfield

ECONOMY
Service industries: Real estate, banks, commodities exchanges
Manufacturing: Food processing, machinery, printed materials
Agriculture: Corn, soybeans, hay, wheat, apples, melons, hogs

▲ *Rich topsoil—75 feet thick in some parts of the state—is the key to success for such farms as this one near Forrest, Illinois.*

Illinois

Man-made wonders have put Illinois on the map, but its natural beauties whisper softly to those who listen. The state is home to America's tallest building as well as to the haunting Mississippi Palisades, where a large population of bald eagles spends its winters. Illinois embraces both the sophistication of Chicago, an urban jewel on the great Lake Michigan, and the fertile rolling prairies that feed the world. For years, people have prospered in this state of complex contradictions.

RICHES FOR THE TAKING
An abundance of furs drew the white man to Illinois. The first Europeans to explore the state were Father Jacques Marquette and Louis Jolliet in 1673. Traveling by canoe and portage through the Illinois River valley from Lake Michigan, they marveled at the land: "We have seen nothing like this river for the fertility of the land, its prairies, woods, wild cattle, stag. . . ."

Later, Europeans found mainly a dwindling confederacy of Algonquin tribes who called themselves Illiniwek—"Superior Men." By 1800 most of them had been driven off or killed. What remained was their name, as spelled by the French.

Earlier visitors, too, must have appreciated the bounty they found here. Settlement by Native Americans in Illinois dates from 8000 B.C. By A.D. 900 a thriving city of 20,000 had grown up on the banks of the Mississippi at Cahokia, across the river from present-day St. Louis. Archaeologists have called it the most extensive prehistoric civilization north of Mexico. It was built by a vanished people, and all that is left are their ceremonial mounds.

The first settlers poured in by way of the Ohio River, mainly from Kentucky, Tennessee, and the Carolinas. By 1818 the territory's residents felt ready to petition for statehood, although the area didn't have the required 60,000 inhabitants. At that time, Illinois reached only as far north as the tip of Lake Michigan. To increase the population, state leaders asked Congress to add a narrow strip of land—just 60 miles wide stretching from Lake Michigan to the Mississippi River—to Illinois's northern boundary.

▲ *The Lincoln Home* National Historic Site in Springfield. Lincoln lived here for 17 years.

LAND OF LINCOLN
Immigrants from the South brought their habits with them, including a strong belief in slavery. Until the legislature realized that doing so might stand in the way of statehood, Illinois's proposed new constitution would have legalized the practice. "Long-term indentured servitude," however, was permitted. Nonetheless, hardscrabble farmers like Tom Lincoln and his son, the future president, Abe, who arrived in 1830, tended to regard slaves as economic competitors.

It was in this atmosphere that Abraham Lincoln reached adulthood, working as a riverboat captain, postmaster, clerk, surveyor, and law school student. When Lincoln decided to run for senator in 1858, debates between him and incumbent Stephen Douglas began to change people's minds about slavery. "A house divided against itself cannot stand," Lincoln declared at one of their meetings, paraphrasing the Bible. "I believe this government cannot endure permanently, half slave and half free."

By 1860 an influx of immigrants from New England and New York, their journey made easier by the opening of the Erie Canal, had pushed Illinois increasingly toward the abolitionist cause and helped propel Lincoln into the presidency. Two months after Lincoln left Springfield to take office, the Civil War began. More than 250,000 Illinois men fought for the Union; many of them died.

THE SWAMP THAT BECAME CHICAGO
According to scholars, the Indian word *chicagou,* which became the name Chicago, means "strong-smelling wild onion." Poorly drained and marshy, the swamp where the city evolved was altogether a nasty place, even for a temporary camp. Jean Baptiste Pointe DuSable, a Haitian-born black fur trader, was the first person to see the advantages of settling on Lake Michigan at the mouth of the Chicago River. In his cabin, built in 1779 on Wolf Point, were held the first wedding, first recorded birth, first election, and first court in the city. DuSable became a very wealthy man in Chicago; hordes of others soon sought to do the same.

Nearly 100 years later, Chicago was no longer a lonely outpost but a city crammed with flimsy wooden buildings of all descriptions, hastily erected by ambitious entrepreneurs. So when sparks flew on the night of October 8, 1871—perhaps caused by Mrs. O'Leary's cow kicking over a lantern, perhaps by a meteorite, perhaps by an arsonist—nothing could stop the spread of the flames. Three hundred people were killed,

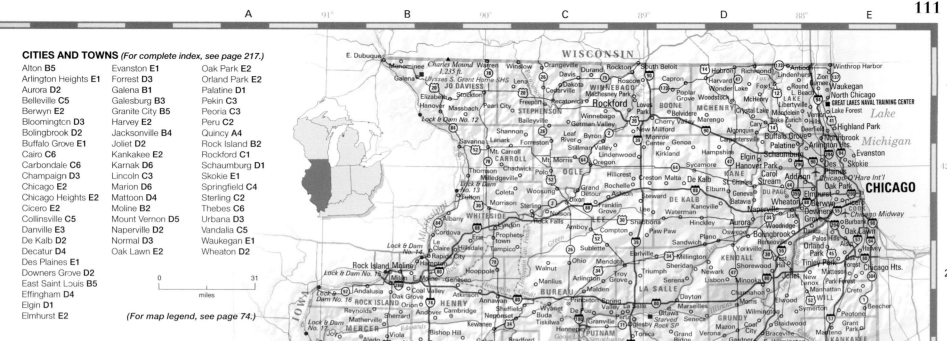

0 —— 31
miles

(For map legend, see page 74.)

and thousands more were left homeless.

It was the city's swift reaction to the fire that said most about its residents. Within days, storekeepers were back in business; within weeks, rebuilding had begun— with brick and stone this time. A real estate agent, W. D. Kerfoot, was the first to build a shanty in the commercial district, and he posted a sign out front: "Everything gone but Wife, Children, and Energy." Within 15 years, another Chicagoan, William Le Baron Jenney, had discovered how steel-skeleton construction made skyscrapers possible. His Home Insurance Building towered an amazing 10 stories.

Chicago's rebirth was celebrated at the 1893 World's Columbian Exposition, a fantasy in classical design—created principally by architect Daniel Burnham— that became the model for government buildings throughout the country for almost a century. At the same time, Burnham also produced a grand plan for the city. Broad boulevards, wooded preserves, numerous parks, and public vistas were all intended to make urban life more tranquil. "Make no little plans," said Burnham. "They have no magic to stir men's blood."

One whose blood was stirred was mail-order magnate A. Montgomery Ward, who declared that the lakeshore should remain "forever open and free." He made sure a law was passed to that effect. Chicago's 29-mile lakefront playground is the result. Sandy beaches, marinas, and seemingly endless bicycle paths and parks framed by an unobstructed skyline and inland sea take on a certain grand style. The only building allowed on the east side of Michigan Avenue by Montgomery Ward's ordinance was the Art Institute, now home to one of the world's finest art collections.

◄ **Uncle Sam** *greets visitors from all nations as they stream into Chicago for the World's Columbian Exposition. More than 27 million people attended the fair, which stretched two miles along Lake Michigan's shore.*

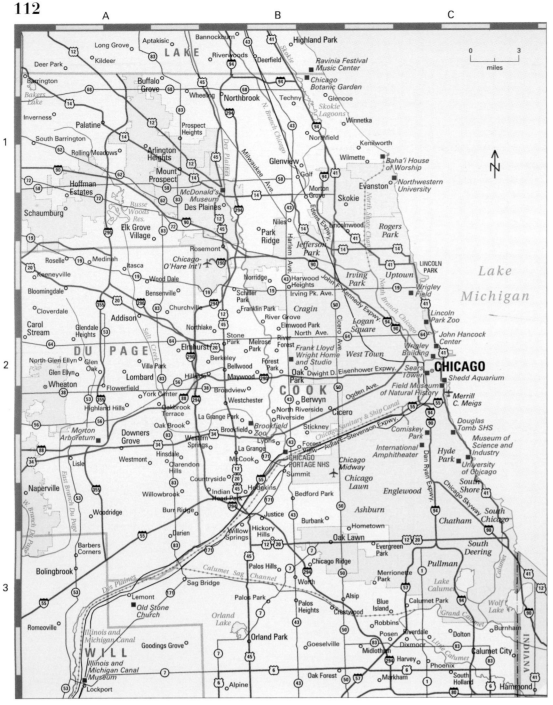

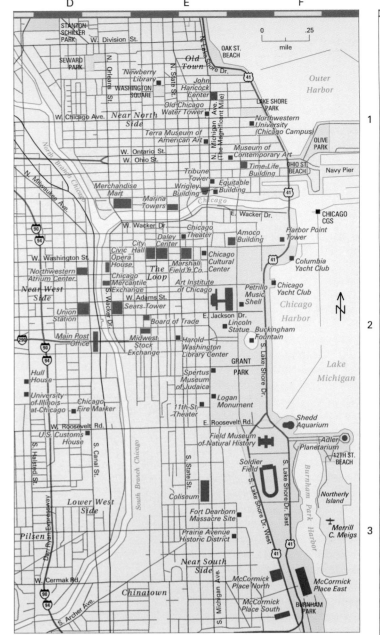

Railroads in 1870
Chicago city limits 1871

Chicago

Illinois Railroads in 1870

The vast expanses of Illinois's flat terrain were ideal for laying railroad track. One company actually laid 100 miles of track without moving even a shovelful of dirt. Chicago, a city built by the railroad, had only one line in 1850. By 1856 the city had 10 lines with almost 3,000 miles of track, which were traveled by 96 trains per day. By 1870 Illinois ranked first in the country in rail mileage.

THE LAND BEYOND CHICAGO

In Illinois 80 percent of the people live in cities; only 20 percent of the state's land is inhabited. Leave any city and you will soon find yourself surrounded by plowed fields dotted with farmhouses. (Almost all of Illinois's 80,000 farms are still family-owned.) During the last ice age, glaciers ground most of Illinois flat, leaving behind some of the best soil in the world when they retreated.

But Illinois is not pancake-flat—hundreds of lazy waterways have carved deep bluffs in the land. And where the glaciers halted, two-thirds of the way down the state, Illinois's rolling hills begin and soon give way to the foothills of the Ozarks. Even farther south, ancient limestone outcroppings grace the awe-inspiring Garden of the Gods and Giant City. Another spectacular formation is the towering Mississippi Palisades in far northwestern Illinois, an area mysteriously untouched by the local glaciers.

At its southern tip, the state levels out once more into the Gulf coastal plain. Early residents noted the resemblance of this area—at the confluence of the Ohio and Mississippi rivers—to the Nile River delta. Ever since, it has been known as Little Egypt, home to such towns as Cairo (KAY-ro), Karnak, and Thebes. Wildlife still abounds in this part of the state, particularly in the Cache River wetlands—called "Illinois's hidden bayou"—and in the nearby Shawnee National Forest.

From north to south, Illinois stretches a length of 378 miles, almost exactly the distance from Portsmouth, New Hampshire, to Portsmouth, Virginia. This great length gives it a range of climates suitable for growing everything from pines to peaches. Temperatures can be extreme in all parts of the state, with hot summers and cold winters being the rule. The record high

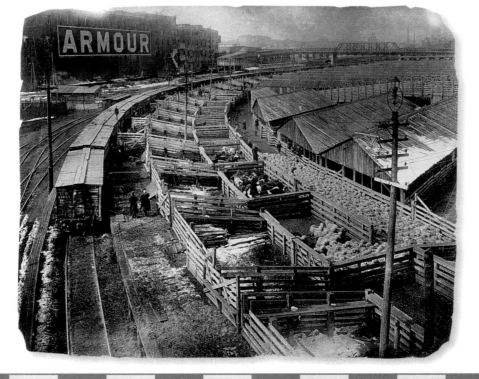

◄ *Livestock await* their fate at a Chicago stockyard in 1907. The yards, which helped make Chicago a major meat-packing center, operated from 1865 to 1971.

temperature is 117°F; the lowest, -35°F. Despite the chill and the breezes that come from Lake Michigan, Chicago is not as windy as its moniker would lead one to believe. The city was so nicknamed for politicians overly fond of the sound of their own voices. And an appropriate name it is: Chicago has been host to 24 national political conventions since 1860, when favorite son Abraham Lincoln was nominated there.

THE STATE THAT WORKS
Cradled by the Mississippi River along its entire western border, with a bustling port on Lake Michigan, Illinois has been a hub of commerce since the Europeans arrived. Early on, railroads linked the East to the West through Chicago. Much of the armament and supplies for the Civil War were manufactured in or distributed from the city; a great deal of the raw material came from farms and mines "downstate." After the war, Chicago soon became the nation's premier grain processor and meat packer.

Because Chicago was a major distribution center, manufacturers established their businesses in the city, bringing with them jobs and a steady influx of new residents. The last mass migration began in the early decades of this century, when tens of thousands of African-Americans came north to escape oppression in the Deep South.

Shipping from the port of Chicago, always heavy, increased dramatically with the completion of the Illinois Waterway System in 1933. Since the opening of the St. Lawrence Seaway in 1959, the waterway has provided a direct shipping link from the North Atlantic to the Gulf of Mexico.

The state has long been a leader in machinery production. Caterpillar Tractor Company, headquartered in Peoria, is America's largest producer of construction equipment. Illinois is a major source of candy, too. Over a third of our nation's supply is made here; perhaps not coincidentally, the state is also the country's largest producer of vending machines.

Smokestack industries are on the wane in Illinois. Service businesses are now the largest producer of income in the state, with real estate, insurance, mail-order, and publishing companies among the major employers. For Chicago, tourism is an industry in itself—the city hosts more trade shows than any other in the country. Among leisure travelers, Chicago is the third most popular destination, after Orlando and Las Vegas.

Corn is Illinois's major crop. Soybeans are grown in each of the state's 102 counties, making it one of the country's leading producers. Vegetables and fruits are grown extensively in the southern part of Illinois, and the area around Chicago is a leading producer of nursery and greenhouse products.

FAMOUS FIRSTS, FAMOUS ILLINOISANS
The people of Illinois have never been shy about basking in the glory of well-known citizens and their accomplishments. It's a "place of unrepressed boosterism," and proud of it. Yet important events have taken place here, such as the invention of "the plow that broke the plains." In the early days, Illinois and other Plains states were prevented from capitalizing on their abundant fertile soil. In many places, settlers trying to till the land for the first time found too often that the gummy soil would break the plow. The problem was solved in

▲ *The Arthur Heurtley House, in Oak Park, was built by Frank Lloyd Wright in 1902. His "Prairie" homes were to be an antidote to the "awful buildings in vogue...all tall and all tight."*

1837 by John Deere, a Vermont blacksmith who had moved to Illinois and invented and manufactured a steel plow, creating one of the enduring success stories in the state.

One of the greatest engineering feats of its day was also inspired by necessity. To prevent future contamination of its water supply by city sewage, Chicago decided to force its river to flow backward. In 1900 a system of locks was put in place, and the river now flows backward. No problem, it seemed, was too daunting for determined Illinoisans.

The atomic age began in 1942 in a small room under the stadium of the University of Chicago, where the first sustained nuclear reaction was observed. Barbed wire was invented in Illinois, too, as were the Pullman sleeping car and the flyswatter. And Ray Kroc flipped his first McDonald's hamburger in Des Plaines; today the company's world headquarters has gobbled up a large section of Oak Brook.

Illinois also inspired Frank Lloyd Wright to create works of art disguised as houses and public buildings. His "Prairie"-style architecture is very much a reflection of the sweeping vistas he encountered in Illinois. Many of the best examples of his work are preserved in Springfield and Oak Park.

That kind of inventiveness is perhaps the key to the spirit of Illinois. Faced with a rich land that couldn't be plowed, somebody invented a better plow. Faced with a river that flowed the wrong way, engineers reversed it. Faced with a land of exuberant vitality, people who come to Illinois learn to appreciate the riches it promises, just around the next bend in the river.

▲ *Chicago, the "City of Big Shoulders," as described by writer Carl Sandburg, is home to some 3 million people and is the third-largest city in the country.*

ILLINOIS
TIME LINE

1673 French explorers Jolliet and Marquette, exploring Mississippi River, reach Illinois.

1699 Across the Mississippi from St. Louis, French priests found Cahokia, Illinois's oldest town.

1763 France cedes Illinois to Great Britain.

1783 Treaty ending Revolutionary War gives Illinois to U.S.

1818 Illinois becomes 21st state.

1832 Black Hawk War, in which Sauk and Fox Indians are driven from state by white settlers, takes place.

1848 Illinois and Michigan Canal opens, linking Great Lakes to Illinois River.

1858 Abraham Lincoln and Stephen Douglas argue abolition of slavery in seven debates.

1860 Abraham Lincoln is elected president.

1871 Great Chicago Fire kills 300 and destroys much of city.

1886 Laborers gather in Chicago's Haymarket Square to protest police intervention in a strike. Eight people are killed in ensuing riot.

1893 Chicago hosts World's Columbian Exposition, which displays America's technological and scientific advances.

1900 Chicago River is forced to flow backward.

1908 Race riots in Springfield leave several blacks dead and lead to the founding of the NAACP.

1933 Century of Progress Exposition, also known as Chicago World's Fair, showcases U.S. industrial achievements.

1968 Demonstrators clash with police during Democratic National Convention in Chicago.

▲ *Indiana's state flag* was adopted in 1917. The flag's torch represents liberty and enlightenment. The largest of the 19 stars stands for Indiana, the 19th state to be admitted to the Union.

STATE DATA
State bird: Cardinal
State flower: Peony
State tree: Tulip poplar
State motto: Crossroads of America
State song: "On the Banks of the Wabash, Far Away"
Abbreviations: Ind.; IN (postal)
Origin of the name: Name given by Congress when it established the territory. Meant to signify "Land of the Indians."
Nickname: Hoosier State

AREA AND SIZE
Total area: 36,519 sq. mi.
Rank within U.S.: 38
Extent: 273 mi. north–south; 177 mi. east–west
Highest elevation: 1,257 ft. above sea level in Wayne County
Lowest elevation: 320 ft. above sea level in Posey County

POPULATION
Total: 6,045,000
Rank within U.S.: 14
Ethnic breakdown: White: 88.3%; Black: 8.2%; Hispanic: 2.3%; Asian: 1.0%; Indian: 0.2%
Population density: 167 people per sq. mi.

CLIMATE

Average monthly temperature in Indianapolis
100°F / 80°F / 60°F / 40°F / 20°F / 0°F
J F M A M J J A S O N D

Average monthly precipitation in Indianapolis
10" / 8" / 6" / 4" / 2" / 0"
J F M A M J J A S O N D

ECONOMY
Service industries: Farm products, groceries, metal products, real estate, medical offices
Manufacturing: Transportation equipment, pharmaceuticals, primary metals
Agriculture: Corn, soybeans, apples, watermelons, tomatoes, popcorn, hogs, eggs

Indiana

Most people know Indiana as the Hoosier State, but few know what a Hoosier is. Some say that an early-19th-century contractor, Samuel Hoosier, preferred workers from the northern bank of the Ohio River to those from the southern bank. Since the northern bank was Indiana, its residents became known as Hoosiers. According to another tradition, the word Hoosier is derived from what Indiana folks called out when they heard a knock on the door: "Who's yere?" No matter the origin of their name, Hoosiers remain fiercely loyal to their state, its subdued but compelling physical beauty, its frontier history, and its culture of inventiveness.

A LAND OF UNEXPECTED CONTRASTS
For many Americans, Indiana conjures up images of rolling farmlands, small towns shaded by large trees, bicycle paths, and two-lane highways. Indiana certainly has all of these, but it is also a state of contrasts.

Consider, for example, the landscape. During the last ice age, a massive glacier scraped the surface of most of the state, leaving behind deep holes and low mounds of debris. The result in northern Indiana was a flat landscape peppered with hundreds of lakes and moraines. In the central part of the state, the glacier left dark, rich soil. Southern Indiana, however, escaped the glacier. The land retained its sheer cliffs, deep valleys, dramatic waterfalls, and forested ravines that are the foothills of the Cumberland Mountains. Underground streams carved out limestone caves, sinkholes, and mineral springs.

The northwestern corner of Indiana is vastly different. The southern edge of Lake Michigan nips off a bit of the state, creating a 41-mile shoreline and long stretches of wide sand beaches. Over the centuries, winds sweeping across the sand gradually built up enormous mounds—the Indiana Dunes—that are justly famous for their substantial height, yellow ocher hue, and delicate dune grasses.

▲ *The Indiana Dunes* National Lakeshore on Lake Michigan is home to massive grass-covered sand dunes.

Yet the same waterfront corner of the state has been home to a massive conglomeration of smokestack industries for more than 100 years. In 1889 the powerful Standard Oil Company elected to build one of the world's largest refineries in the little Indiana town of Whiting. Sixteen years later, in 1905, the U.S. Steel Corporation selected a nearby site for one of the largest mills in the world. To house all the mill workers, the management of U.S. Steel founded a new city, named after the chairman of the board, Judge Elbert H. Gary. The towns of Whiting, Gary, and Hammond transformed Indiana into the steel and oil-refining capital of the United States.

▲ *Cataract Falls Covered Bridge,* in west central Indiana, was built in 1876 and restored in 1995. Cataract Falls, Indiana's largest waterfall, flows beneath it. A ghost is said to visit here every Halloween.

CONFLICTING POPULATIONS
The building of industrial plants in northwestern Indiana brought about the latest in a series of population shifts that started in prehistoric times. Anthropologists are just now learning about the civilization of the Mound Builders—Native Americans who constructed forts, villages, and huge earthen ceremonial mounds. The Mound Builders disappeared hundreds of years ago.

Successor tribes in what is now Indiana began fighting for their land against French trappers and fur traders in the 17th century. The British arrived and drove out the French in 1763, and the Americans forced out the British a few years later, during the Revolutionary War. By 1838 white American settlers had killed or expelled almost all the Indian peoples in Indiana—the Miami, Potawatomi, Piankashaw, Kickapoo, Wea, Delaware, Shawnee, Mahican, and Munsee.

The typical 19th-century Hoosier was a farmer of English, Scottish, Irish, or German ancestry. At the end of the century, however, the massive new mills and refineries recruited workers from other ethnic groups: Poles, Hungarians, Czechs, and Italians. Promise of work also attracted African-Americans from the South, who settled in the northwestern corner of the state after World War II.

CLAIM TO FAME
The Hoosiers have carefully preserved and celebrated their past. Anyone who takes a leisurely drive along the back roads will encounter a dozen historic villages—among them, New Harmony, the site of two 19th-century Utopian communities; Lincoln City (near Evansville), Abraham Lincoln's boyhood home for 14 years; and Newburgh and Madison, 19th-century river towns. The state has also safeguarded a large number of wooden covered bridges—those charming barnlike structures, often painted red, that span creeks and rivers. There are 32 of them in western Indiana's Parke County—the largest concentration anywhere in the world.

Part of Indiana's history includes the many innovations and successful backyard inventions that were created in the state.

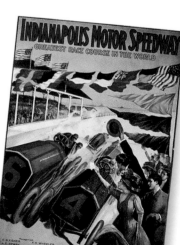

▲ *The Indianapolis Motor Speedway,* the site of the annual Indianapolis 500 race, is advertised in this early poster. The event, which first took place in 1911, is held in late May.

INDIANA TIMELINE

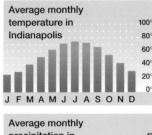

c. 1732 French establish Vincennes, the first permanent European settlement.

1763 After winning the French and Indian War, Great Britain takes control of the Indiana region.

1778 Frontiersman George Rogers Clark leads U.S. troops in a successful campaign to wrest

Vincennes from the British.

1811 Indians are defeated at the Battle of Tippecanoe.

1816 Indiana joins the Union as 19th state.

1905 The city of Gary is founded by the U.S. Steel Corporation.

1911 The first Indianapolis 500 auto race is held on Memorial Day.

1937 Southern Indiana is heavily damaged when the level of the Ohio River reaches record heights.

1963 Studebaker Corporation ends automobile production in South Bend.

1988 Indiana's junior senator, J. Danforth Quayle, is elected vice president.

Residents like to point out that Indiana gave the nation its first theme park, public library, constitutionally mandated system of free public schools, centralized train station (Union Station in Indianapolis), spark-ignition engine, gasoline pump, automobile carburetor, motion picture projector—and the first nighttime baseball game, played on an artificially lighted field.

Indiana is a veritable paradise for aficionados or the merely curious, who can visit the Indiana Basketball Hall of Fame in New Castle, the College Football Hall of Fame in South Bend, the International Circus Hall of Fame in Peru, the International Quilter Hall of Fame in Marion, the Motor Speedway Hall of Fame Museum in Indianapolis, and, in Anderson, the Historic Military Armor Museum, which houses the nation's most extensive collection of light armored vehicles.

BACK TO THE FUTURE

Indiana by no means lives in the past. In fact, preservation of the past is part of the current effort to develop the Hoosier State's tourist industry. After the global economy undermined the preeminent position of American steel and automobiles, Indiana, like many other states, had to create new sources of revenue and jobs. High-tech industries and the service sector have grown in Indiana as they have throughout the United States. This reveals a final—and telling—contrast: in Indiana manufacturing accounts for about 28 percent of the gross state product; the service sector, for about 62 percent; and agriculture, a mere 1 percent. One might think that agriculture is negligible, yet farmlands still cover 70 percent of the state that the Hoosiers call home.

(For map legend, see page 74.)

CITIES AND TOWNS
(For complete index, see page 217.)

Alabaster **C2**	Michigan City **C1**
Anderson **D2**	Mishawaka **C1**
Bloomington **C3**	Muncie **D2**
Carmel **C3**	New Albany **D4**
Columbus **D3**	New Castle **D3**
East Chicago **B1**	Peru **C2**
Elkhart **D1**	Portage **B1**
Evansville **B4**	Richmond **E3**
Fort Wayne **D1**	South Bend **C1**
Gary **B1**	Terre Haute **B3**
Goshen **D1**	Valparaiso **B1**
Greenwood **C3**	Vincennes **B4**
Hammond **B1**	West Lafayette **C2**
Indianapolis **C3**	Whiting **B1**
Jeffersonville **D4**	
Kokomo **C2**	
La Porte **C1**	
Lafayette **C2**	
Lawrence **C3**	
Marion **D2**	
Merrillville **B1**	

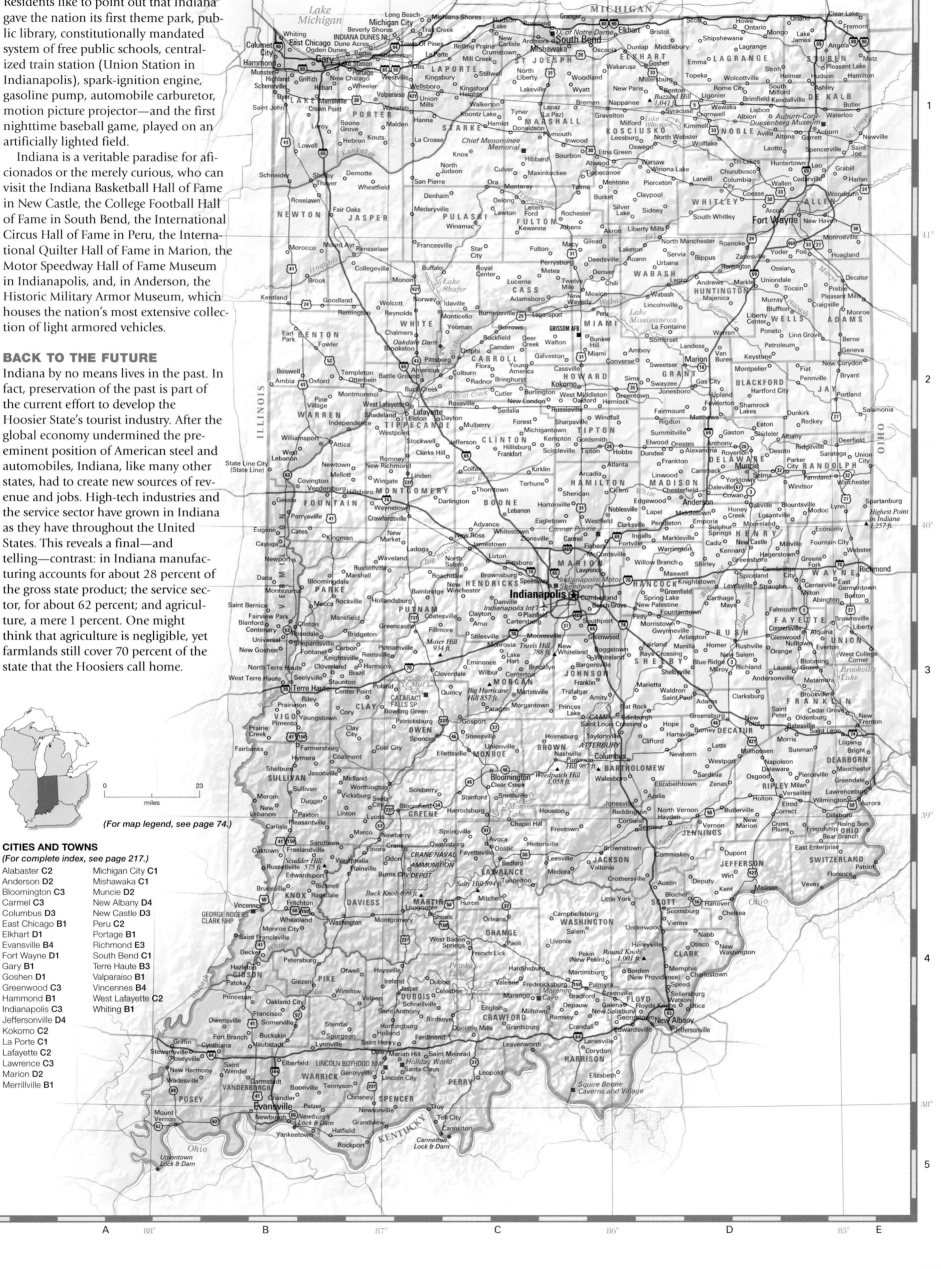

▲ *Adopted in 1921,* Iowa's state flag shows an eagle holding a streamer in its beak. The banner bears the state motto.

STATE DATA

State bird: Eastern goldfinch
State flower: Wild rose
State tree: Oak
State motto: Our liberties we prize and our rights we will maintain
State song: "Song of Iowa"
Abbreviations: Ia.; IA (postal)
Origin of the name: From an Indian word, *ayuhwa,* meaning "beautiful land" or "this is the place"
Nicknames: Hawkeye State, Corn State, Land Where the Tall Corn Grows, Nation's Breadbasket

AREA AND SIZE

Total area: 56,290 sq. mi.
Rank within U.S.: 25
Extent: 214 mi. north–south; 332 mi. east–west
Highest elevation: Ocheyedan Mound, 1,675 ft. above sea level on northern boundary of Osceola County
Lowest elevation: 480 ft. above sea level at the confluence of the Mississippi and Des Moines rivers in Lee County

POPULATION

Total: 2,900,000
Rank within U.S.: 30
Ethnic breakdown: White: 94.4%; Black: 2.1%; Hispanic: 1.9%; Asian: 1.4%; Indian: 0.3%
Population density: 51.7 people per sq. mi.

CLIMATE

Average monthly temperature in Des Moines

Average monthly precipitation in Des Moines

ECONOMY

Service industries: Car dealerships, grocery stores, restaurants, insurance companies
Manufacturing: Meat-packing plants, corn oil, cornstarch, corn sugar, machinery, chemicals
Agriculture: Hogs, beef and dairy cattle, corn, oats, hay

▲ *The skyline of Des Moines,* the largest city in Iowa and the state's main commercial center. *(The Botanical Center is in the foreground.)*

Iowa

A state where the age-old rhythms of planting and harvesting and the civic virtues of small-town life still hold sway, Iowa appears as a green-and-gold patchwork, perfect squares of color unfurling to a far horizon. When Americans speak of the heartland, this is the place many of them are referring to.

FERTILE LANDS

Framed by two of the nation's mightiest rivers—the Missouri to the west and the Mississippi to the east—Iowa is blessed with soil of such fecundity that only giants like California and Texas surpass it in agricultural production. Iowa's bounty results from a succession of glaciers that covered the state in the past 2 million years. As the ice sheets melted, they left behind lopped-off hilltops, filled-in valleys, and land ground to a rich humus. The accumulated deposits of Iowa's glacial period provided the state with a topsoil that is as deep as 600 feet in some areas, a virtual agricultural oil well. Nine-tenths of Iowa's land is in cultivation, with such crops as corn, soybeans, oats, and hay constituting the state's major products.

SMALL-TOWN LIFE

Iowa may be a state of farms, but it is not a state of farmers. In recent decades, advances in agricultural science have made farming much more efficient; nowadays, 9 out of 10 Iowans make their homes in cities and towns. By far the largest of these is Des Moines, the state capital and a leader in the insurance industry. Other good-size cities include Dubuque, a picturesque river town nestled in the bluffs above the Mississippi River; Cedar Rapids, a major corn- and oat-products processing center; Iowa City, home of the University of Iowa; and Sioux City, an old frontier town on the Missouri River, where many of Iowa's hogs spend their final hours on the way to market.

Framed by Dubuque, Iowa City, and Sioux City—and representing Iowa's rural culture—are a multitude of small towns, nearly 1,000 of them. Although they are small, these towns are hard to miss; their names are proudly painted on the sides of gleaming water towers or grain elevators that loom over the surrounding fields and are visible for miles.

In the 1980s Iowa's heartland was put to the test when a worldwide food surplus, low agricultural prices, and high interest rates forced many of the state's farmers into bankruptcy, devastating the rural economy. In recent years, many of Iowa's cities and towns have courted new industries—from fiber optics to telemarketing—to shore up the employment gap, but the fate of many a hamlet still remains in doubt.

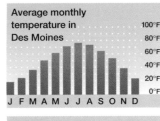

◀ *Effigy Mounds National Monument* is famous for its prehistoric Indian burial mounds, many shaped like birds and bears.

CYCLING ACROSS THE STATE

Every July some 10,000 bicyclists cross the state from west to east in a rolling pageant known as RAGBRAI for the sponsoring *Des Moines Register's* Annual Great Bicycle Ride Across Iowa. Nudged along by tailwinds, RAGBRAI's riders start at the Missouri and finish at the Mississippi. One thing they all agree on: contrary to its reputation, Iowa is definitely not flat.

At least, not all of it is. When out-of-staters think of the Iowa plains, they are thinking of just one region: the Des Moines lobe, a large, mitten-shaped parcel of land reaching from the state's north central border to the city of Des Moines. This is the state's agricultural breadbasket, as productive as any land on earth, and for the most part as level as a tabletop.

On either side, however, the topography is relatively hilly. Most striking of all are the Loess Hills, a wedge-shaped barrier of dunelike formations that runs north and east of Council Bluffs, on the leeward side of the Missouri River valley. These drifts of fine soil pushed into ridges by prevailing westerly winds stand up to 200 feet above the plains and are equaled in only one other place on earth: Kensau Province of northern China. Some of the most beautiful terrain in Iowa is found in the northeastern corner of the state. Since only one glacier crossed the region around Decorah and east to the great bluffs of the Mississippi River, many rugged hills and cliffs remain.

"THE PLOW THAT BROKE THE PRAIRIES"

When pioneers first came to Iowa in the 1830s and settled in the fertile bottomlands along the Mississippi, they discovered that the heavy, root-tangled soil could quickly choke a plow, or even snap it in two. Most of Iowa might have remained untouched were it not for one invention: the sharp-bladed steel plow, courtesy of blacksmith John Deere. Known as the "plow that broke the prairies," Deere's invention opened the door to westward expansion in 1837. In just a few decades, some 30 million acres of prairie had been plowed for agriculture. Today just 10,000 acres of virgin prairie remain.

Like other areas in the Midwest, Iowa attracted many settlers from the agricultural regions of northern and central Europe, hearty, tenacious souls undaunted by the long, snowy winters and the rigors of farm life. German, Scandinavian, Dutch, and Czech place names still dot the map and imbue the state with a distinctly European flavor.

The Woodland and Plains Indians who once roamed Iowa's prairies and lived in its sheltered river valleys are all but gone. There are no reservations in the state; only one community remains, members of the Mesquakie tribe, who live in the Iowa

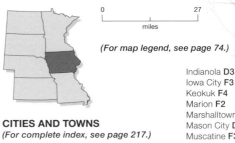

(For map legend, see page 74.)

CITIES AND TOWNS
(For complete index, see page 217.)

Ames **D2**
Ankeny **D3**
Bellevue **G2**
Bettendorf **G3**
Boone **D2**
Burlington **F4**
Carroll **C2**
Cedar Falls **E2**
Cedar Rapids **F2**
Clinton **G3**

Coralville **F3**
Council Bluffs **B3**
Davenport **G3**
Decorah **F1**
Des Moines **D3**
Dubuque **G2**
Dyersville **F2**
Fairfield **F4**
Fort Dodge **C2**
Fort Madison **F4**

Indianola **D3**
Iowa City **F3**
Keokuk **F4**
Marion **F2**
Marshalltown **E2**
Mason City **D1**
Muscatine **F3**
Newton **D3**
Oskaloosa **E3**
Ottumwa **E3**
Sioux City **A2**
Spencer **B1**
Tama **E3**
Urbandale **D3**
Waterloo **E2**
West Des Moines **D3**

River valley near Tama. Still, Iowa's Native American heritage lives on in many place names and in the prehistoric burial mounds that abound in the northeastern corner of the state.

FIELD OF DREAMS

Iowans are quick to admit that their state enjoys a peculiar anonymity—and they are happy to keep it that way. Although modern technology, the growth of agribusiness, and the needs of a diversified economy have brought the state into a deeper connection with the larger world, Iowa remains in many ways a place unto itself, happily removed from the frenzy of modern life.

Nowhere is the spirit of Iowa better captured than on a bumper sticker, seen on cars and pickup trucks across the state, that quotes the movie *Field of Dreams*. In the film (which was shot in the Iowa town of Dyersville), the ghost of a long-dead baseball legend returns to play on a diamond carved out of an Iowa cornfield by a local farmer.

"Is this Heaven?" the ball player asks. "No," the farmer replies. "It's Iowa."

▲ **Farm products** *are a major factor in the economy of Iowa. More corn is grown in Iowa than in any other state—approximately one-fifth of the nation's total harvest. Iowa is also one of the leading producers of soybeans in the United States.*

IOWA
TIME LINE

1673 Explorers Jolliet and Marquette pass through Iowa.

1682 La Salle claims Iowa region for France.

1788 French Canadian Julien Dubuque, the first white settler in Iowa, begins mining lead near what is now Dubuque.

1803 U.S. receives region as part of Louisiana Purchase.

1832 U.S. Army defeats Sauk and Fox Indians, led by Chief Black Hawk.

1833 Permanent settlements—including Bellevue and Burlington—are founded.

1838 Iowa becomes a territory.

1846 Iowa becomes 29th state.

1867 The first railroad to cross Iowa is completed.

1913 New Keokuk Dam on Mississippi River becomes a power supply for Midwestern cities.

1929 Herbert Hoover, an Iowan, becomes 31st president; he is first president born west of the Mississippi.

1936 Farmers form cooperatives in an effort to hold on to their land during the Depression.

1948 Iowa becomes leading producer of corn, oats, hogs, cattle, poultry, and eggs in the country.

1959 Soviet premier Nikita Khrushchev visits an Iowa farm to learn about American agriculture.

1985 U.S. government orders moratorium on farm foreclosures to mitigate the economic hardship faced by many farmers.

▲ **The state flag,** *adopted in 1927, shows the sunflower (the state flower); 34 stars, symbolizing Kansas as the 34th state to enter the Union; and a farmer, representing agriculture.*

STATE DATA
State bird: Western meadowlark
State flower: Sunflower
State tree: Cottonwood
State motto: *Ad astra per aspera* (To the stars through difficulties)
State song: "Home on the Range"
Abbreviations: Kans.; KS (postal)
Origin of the name: From the local Indians, the "Kansa," or "Kaw," meaning "People of the South Wind"
Nicknames: Sunflower State, Jayhawk State, Wheat State

AREA AND SIZE
Total area: 82,264 sq. mi.
Rank within U.S.: 14
Extent: 206 mi. north–south; 408 mi. east–west
Highest elevation: Mount Sunflower, 4,039 ft. above sea level
Lowest elevation: 680 ft. above sea level along the Verdigris River in Montgomery County

POPULATION
Total: 2,668,000
Rank within U.S.: 32
Ethnic breakdown: White: 85.9%; Black: 6.3%; Hispanic: 5.2%; Asian: 1.8%; Indian: 0.9%
Population density: 32.5 people per sq. mi.

CLIMATE

Average monthly temperature in Topeka
100°F 80°F 60°F 40°F 20°F 0°F
J F M A M J J A S O N D

Average monthly precipitation in Topeka
10" 8" 6" 4" 2" 0"
J F M A M J J A S O N D

ECONOMY
Service industries: Car dealerships, grocery stores, law firms, hotels
Manufacturing: Aircraft, missiles, freight trains, automobiles, flour mills, printed materials
Agriculture: Beef cattle, hogs, wheat, corn, grain sorghum, hay

Kansas

For centuries travelers—whether explorers in search of mythical cities, wagoners following the Oregon or Santa Fe trail, or drivers on the asphalt ribbons of interstate highways—have simply passed through Kansas on their way to someplace else. Those who linger, however, discover that Kansas holds a wealth of surprises.

A FRONTIER LEGACY
With its brutal summers and winters, the area that would be Kansas was long left to its native inhabitants—the Wichita, Pawnee, Kansas, and Osage Indians—and vast roaming herds of bison. Then, in 1541, Spanish explorer Francisco Vásquez de Coronado, spurred by tales of a rich city called Quivira, ventured to southwestern Kansas. Finding no gold or silver, he quickly left, leaving little sign that he had ever been there.

Coronado's failure did nothing to quell the fever. In the early 1600s fellow Spaniard Juan de Oñate sent expeditions to Kansas that again proved fruitless. In 1744 the French, who planned to trade fur in the area, built Fort Cavagnial (near today's Leavenworth). Sixty years later Lewis and Clark traveled up the Missouri River along the eastern boundary of Kansas.

The few visitors who did come to the territory found the land inhospitable, a part of the so-called Great American Desert. As displaced Indians from the East were relocated to the territory by the U.S. government, the Indian population grew considerably. Because of this, most white people were convinced that they could not survive there and did not begin moving to the region until 1827, when Col. Henry Leavenworth took charge of the military outpost (soon named Fort Leavenworth) that stood guard over the Santa Fe Trail. This marked the beginning of the end for the Plains Indians in Kansas; as more white settlers arrived, some 50 forts were established, among them, Fort Scott in the southeast, home of the mounted infantrymen of the Dragoons, and Fort Riley in the Flint Hills, longtime headquarters of the U.S. Cavalry. The Indians were forced to move farther west.

A BLOODY PATH TO STATEHOOD
Some of the worst fighting in Kansas history occurred because of the Kansas-Nebraska Act of 1854. According to the law, before Kansas joined the Union, its citizens could determine by popular vote whether it would be a free or a slave state. A

The Crossroads of Kansas

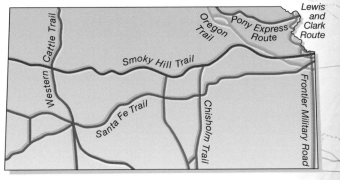

A hotbed of activity in the 1800s, Kansas was crisscrossed with several major trails and routes that were traversed by explorers, gold seekers, cattle drivers, and settlers.

stampede into Kansas Territory to stuff the ballot boxes ensued. Proslavery voters came from Missouri and founded the towns of Leavenworth and Atchison, while abolitionist Northerners established the towns of Lawrence and Topeka. In 1856 Missouri "border ruffians" pillaged the town of Lawrence. In retaliation, the abolitionist guerrilla leader John Brown led an attack at Pottawatomie Creek in which five proslavery men were killed. The murder of five abolitionists near Trading Post on the Marais des Cygnes River followed in 1858. Soon the territory was known as Bleeding Kansas. After seven years of terror, Kansas entered the Union as a free state in 1861. One-fifth of its men, including the first African-American troops—called the First Kansas Colored Infantry—fought in the Union Army during the Civil War.

▲ **Sunflowers,** *although grown around the world, are associated with Kansas, where they are abundant in the summer.*

COWBOYS AND COW TOWNS
When a Kansas newspaper editor looked out of his window one day, he realized that the tiny town of Abilene had become "an island in a sea of cattle." Prosperity had arrived in Kansas

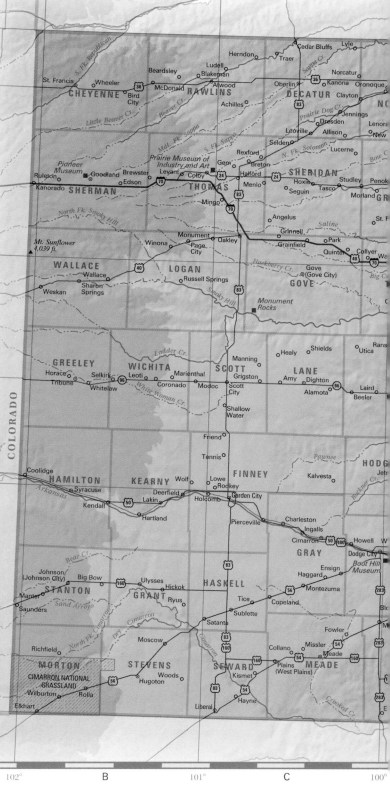

1541 Spanish explorer Coronado comes to Kansas area in search of gold.
1682 La Salle claims Kansas for France.
1762 France cedes Kansas to Spain after the French and Indian War.
1800 Spain gives region back to France.
1803 U.S. obtains most of Kansas as part of Louisiana Purchase.
1821 Santa Fe Trail is established.

1827 Col. Henry Leavenworth establishes Fort Leavenworth as haven for travelers on Santa Fe Trail.
1854 Congress names Kansas a U.S. territory.
1854–59 Fighting between pro- and anti-slavery groups becomes so intense that territory is called Bleeding Kansas.
1860 First railroad reaches Kansas from the East.
1861 Kansas becomes the 34th

state to join the Union.
1867 Abilene becomes first major cow town in Kansas.
1894 Kansas's oil and gas fields begin producing.
1932–39 Dust storms ravage Kansas farms.
1951 Landmark school-desegregation case, *Brown v. Board of Education of Topeka,* is filed.
1986 Kansas citizens approve sale of liquor by the glass; some counties remain dry.

along with the railroads in the 1860s. With depots established at such towns as Abilene, Dodge City, and Wichita, Texas ranchers started moving their cattle along the Chisholm and Western trails into Kansas beginning in 1867. The cowboys—a third of whom were black, Indian, or Latino—brought life to these cities. Dodge City in particular, with its famous lawmen and "wickedest little city in America" reputation, became notorious as a symbol of the American West.

Cow towns were not the only cities peppering the map of Kansas. The arrival of 20,000 African-American "Exodusters," escaping the harsh racial climate of the post-Reconstruction South, resulted in the creation of many all-black towns, including Nicodemus in northwestern Kansas. The state's liberal climate also made it possible for the first woman mayor in the United States (Susanna Salter of Argonia) to be elected in 1887.

WHEAT AND "REAL AMERICA"

Since only 20 inches of rain falls annually on the Great Plains of Kansas, agriculture was not successful there until 1874, when Mennonite immigrants escaping persecution in Russia sowed hardy Turkey Red wheat seeds. The wheat thrived, and Kansas flowered into America's leading wheat-producing state. Despite its strong agricultural base, however, Kansas has evolved into an industrial state, and most of its residents live in urban areas. Kansas is home to 60,000 oil and natural gas wells, and

it leads the nation in helium and small-aircraft production.

In the mid-1980s foreign tourists began to flock to Kansas in search of the "real America," the land of grainfields, open plains, flowing rivers, and cowboys. These tourists found what they were looking for in Kansas, known as Midway, U.S.A., a fitting name for the state that contains the geographic center of the lower 48 states in its Smith County.

▲ **Frost nips the tall grasses** *at the Konza Prairie Research Natural Station, an internationally known 8,600-acre living laboratory in Manhattan, Kansas.*

CITIES AND TOWNS
(For complete index, see page 217.)

(For map legend, see page 74.)

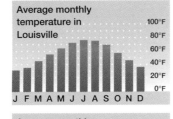

▲ *The state flag, which shows a frontiersman and a statesman embracing, was adopted in 1918. Goldenrod decorates the seal.*

STATE DATA

State bird: Kentucky cardinal
State flower: Goldenrod
State tree: Tulip poplar
State motto: United we stand, divided we fall
State song: "My Old Kentucky Home"
Abbreviations: Ky.; KY (postal)
Origin of the name: From the Iroquoian word *Ken-tah-ten*, meaning "Land of Tomorrow"
Nickname: Bluegrass State

AREA AND SIZE

Total area: 40,395 sq. mi.
Rank within U.S.: 37
Extent: 182 mi. north–south; 417 mi. east–west
Highest elevation: Black Mountain, 4,145 ft. above sea level
Lowest elevation: 257 ft. above sea level along the Mississippi River in Fulton County

POPULATION

Total: 3,995,000
Rank within U.S.: 25
Ethnic breakdown: White: 91.2%; Black: 7.1%; Hispanic: 0.8%; Asian: 0.7%; Indian: 0.2%
Population density: 100.2 people per sq. mi.

CLIMATE

Average monthly temperature in Louisville
100°F 80°F 60°F 40°F 20°F 0°F
J F M A M J J A S O N D

Average monthly precipitation in Louisville
10" 8" 6" 4" 2" 0"
J F M A M J J A S O N D

ECONOMY

Service industries: Automobile dealerships, finance, insurance, real estate
Manufacturing: Transportation equipment, chemicals, machinery, food processing
Mining: Coal, natural gas, petroleum, limestone

▲ *The U.S. Bullion Depository at Fort Knox. Opened in 1937, this treasure-house is constructed of granite, concrete, and steel.*

▲ *The horse-breeding capital of the world, the state of Kentucky is home to more than 350 Thoroughbred-horse farms.*

Kentucky

Renowned for its bluegrass and bourbon, Kentucky is a land of charm and beauty. Nestled between the Appalachian Mountains to the east and the Mississippi River to the west, this state where North meets South boasts precipitous gorges, 1,100 miles of waterways, thunderous waterfalls, and the world's longest cave system known.

EARLY RESIDENTS

Plentiful game and a temperate climate drew members of the Adena tribe to the Kentucky area, perhaps as early as 1100 B.C. The Adena, unlike earlier nomadic tribes, built permanent settlements, erecting stockaded villages and creating huge burial mounds to honor their dead. Recognizing its potential as a hunting ground, later tribes like the Cherokee and Iroquois hunted the rumpled hills, thick forests, and lush valleys in pursuit of buffalo, elk, and deer.

The first white man to set foot in Kentucky was Dr. Thomas Walker, who in 1750 was sent by a Virginia land company seeking to expand its holdings. Almost 20 years later, Daniel Boone led a party of hunters across the Cumberland Gap from North Carolina. Boone was so taken with Kentucky that in 1775 he returned with his family and built a fort called Boonesborough. Soon other white settlers journeyed through the gap to stake out claims.

The state's rich soil proved ideal for growing such row crops as tobacco, corn, wheat, oats, barley, and rye, while the proximity of the Ohio and Mississippi rivers made getting the crops to market easy. As a result, Kentucky's economy boomed. The farmers' newly created wealth helped finance an aristocracy whose legacy can still be seen today in rambling horse farms and antebellum mansions.

FORTUNE'S FALL AND RISE

Kentucky tried to remain neutral throughout the Civil War, even though its residents were sharply divided in their loyalties: approximately 100,000 men joined the Union Army, while 40,000 wore the Confederate gray. Ironically, the Union president, Abraham Lincoln, and the Confederate president, Jefferson Davis, had been born within one year and 100 miles of each other in log cabins in south central Kentucky.

After the war Kentucky became openly sympathetic to the South and suffered when other Southern states could not afford to buy its farm products. Even with an increased interest in horse racing and the development of Burley tobacco during the 1870s and '80s, and rising coal, oil, and timber production in the 1890s, the state's economy continued to lag until the World War II years. During the 1960s, miners began to profit from the state's vast reserves of bitu-

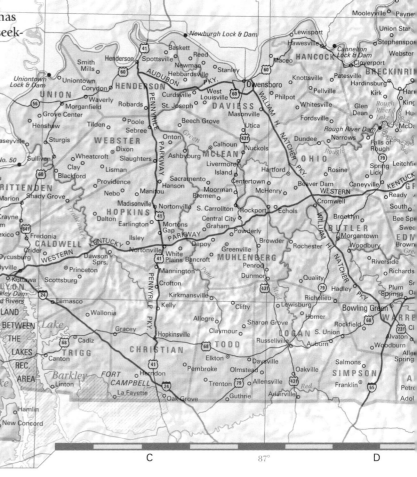

minous coal. Today Kentucky is among the nation's leading producers of the fossil fuel, which accounts for $4 billion of the state's gross product. At present rates of production, Kentucky's reserves are expected to last more than 200 years.

THE RICHES OF COAL

Two-thirds of Kentucky's coal reserves are in the Western Coal Field region of the state, an area of rolling land rich in mineral deposits as well as good farming soil. The best topsoil, however, lies in the extreme southwestern region of the state, in the Jackson Purchase. Acquired from the Chickasaw Indians by President Andrew Jackson in 1818, the Purchase is flat and bounded by a double bend in the Mississippi River. Floodplains, low hills, swamps, and lagoons make up the terrain, and its rich alluvial soil supports sprawling cotton fields and stately homes.

Just east of the Purchase and stretching from Kentucky Lake to the Appalachian Plateau is the Pennyroyal Region, named for the small, aromatic herb that grows wild there. The Pennyroyal's most famous feature is Mammoth Cave, which, as legend has it, was discovered by a hunter chasing a bear. The cavern system stretches some 330 miles and has still not been fully explored.

Part of a chain that extends from Maine to Mississippi, the Appalachian Plateau is a large, triangular-shaped area that includes jagged mountain ridges, forested plateaus, and numerous waterways. It is in Appalachia that the rest of Kentucky's coal reserves can be found. Appalachia was settled by Scotch-Irish pioneers, who brought with them their customs and such skills as weaving and quilting. It was here where bluegrass music—played with the banjo, mandolin, Dobro, guitar, and fiddle and accompanied by a "high, lonesome voice"—was born.

BLUEGRASS AND DERBIES

West of the mountains, in the center of the state, a lovely ritual plays itself out in May, when the famed Kentucky bluegrass blossoms and covers the rolling fields and pastures with a dense blue carpet. The effect is short-lived: the flowers soon die, revealing the green grass underneath.

▲ *Spirits galore! Kentucky produces about 95 percent of the nation's bourbon.*

Limestone bedrock nourishes the grass with lime and calcium and is responsible for the state's alkaline limestone water. Far from being a problem, however, limestone water is considered to be one of the key ingredients in another famous product of bluegrass country: bourbon whiskey. This potent brew of corn mash, mellowed in charred oak casks, was invented in 1789 by the Reverend Elijah Craig. The liquor gets its name from Bourbon County, Kentucky, where another man, Jacob Spears, perfected Rev. Elijah Craig's whiskey-making technique.

Along with the sprouting of the bluegrass, Kentuckians can count on one other thing to occur in the spring: the Kentucky Derby. Held the first Saturday in May at Louisville's Churchill Downs, the 1 1/4-mile race, run by three-year-old horses, is for many people the highlight of the year. For 10 days prior to the race, Louisville is alive with derby fever and a whirlwind of concerts, parties, and fairs. Natives—and visitors—come to sip ice-cold mint juleps out of silver cups, cheer for their favorite horse, and delight in the knowledge that this can happen only in Kentucky.

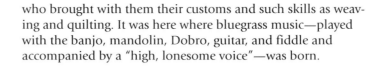

KENTUCKY TIME LINE

1750 Virginia land company scout Thomas Walker explores eastern Kentucky.

1767 Daniel Boone crosses Cumberland Gap into Kentucky.

1774 Harrodsburg is founded as the first permanent white settlement.

1775 Boone establishes Fort Boonesborough in central Kentucky.

1775–83 Pioneers defend themselves against Indians who, aided by the British, attack Colonial settlements during Revolutionary War.

1792 Kentucky joins the Union as 15th state.

1815 First steamboats travel between Louisville and New Orleans, making it easier for Kentucky to export products.

1861 Kentucky, a neutral state, is invaded by both Union and Confederate forces during Civil War.

1875 First Kentucky Derby is held.

1904–09 In Black Patch War, angry farmers smash tobacco monopoly by burning warehouses and fields.

1918 Kentucky begins to construct extensive road system.

1937 U.S. Treasury opens gold depository at Fort Knox.

1944 Kentucky Dam is finished, creating Kentucky Lake.

1969 Tennessee Valley Authority completes its largest steam-generating plant in Muhlenberg County.

1970 Coal mine explosion near Wooton kills 38.

(For map legend, see page 74.)

CITIES AND TOWNS

(For complete index, see page 217.)

Louisiana

A land of lazy bayous and raucous festivals, of bustling waterways and good-natured hospitality, Louisiana often seems a world apart from the surrounding nation. It is a state where foreign languages are native and counties are called parishes, where burned fish is a delicacy and funerals end with brass bands playing ragtime and jazz.

▲ **Louisiana's flag,** adopted in 1912, shows a mother pelican in a nest with her young, symbolizing the state's role as guardian of its people and resources.

MISSISSIPPI MUD

From the earliest years of European contact, Louisiana lured settlers with its promise of easy transportation. Rivers, lakes, and marshes dominate the state, providing some 7,500 miles of navigable waterways. The Mississippi, the longest river in the United States, is Louisiana's main artery. Snaking down the state's eastern border through pine forests and cotton fields, the Mississippi passes the state capital of Baton Rouge, flows by the massive Lake Pontchartrain, and curls around the "Crescent City" of New Orleans, finally spreading into the broad delta that empties into the Gulf of Mexico. The tortuous river claimed its very first European visitor, Hernando de Soto, who succumbed to fever on its banks in 1542. His companions buried his body in the mud, then they sailed downriver to the Gulf of Mexico in makeshift boats. The Mississippi was kinder to Robert Cavelier, Sieur de La Salle, who arrived by canoe at the river's mouth in 1682 after a four-month journey from Lake Michigan. La Salle erected a cross, fired a volley of musket shots, and then claimed the surrounding land for France, naming it after his king, Louis XIV.

CON ARTISTS AND CASKET GIRLS

Louisiana's early settlers wasted no time in establishing the region's reputation for excess. Louis XIV rented out the colony to private developers, who tried to turn the swampy land into a source of massive profits. John Law, a Scottish banker with a penchant for gambling, was granted the Louisiana charter by the French government in 1717 and sold stock in the land, boosting the price with fictitious tales of massive gold mines on the banks of the Mississippi. Investors throughout Europe were ruined when the bubble burst three years later, and Law was forced to flee from France in disgrace.

During his brief stay, Law did manage to populate Louisiana with boatloads of convicts and other undesirables, who, finding themselves on a mostly male frontier, began clamoring for wives. The colony's French governor,

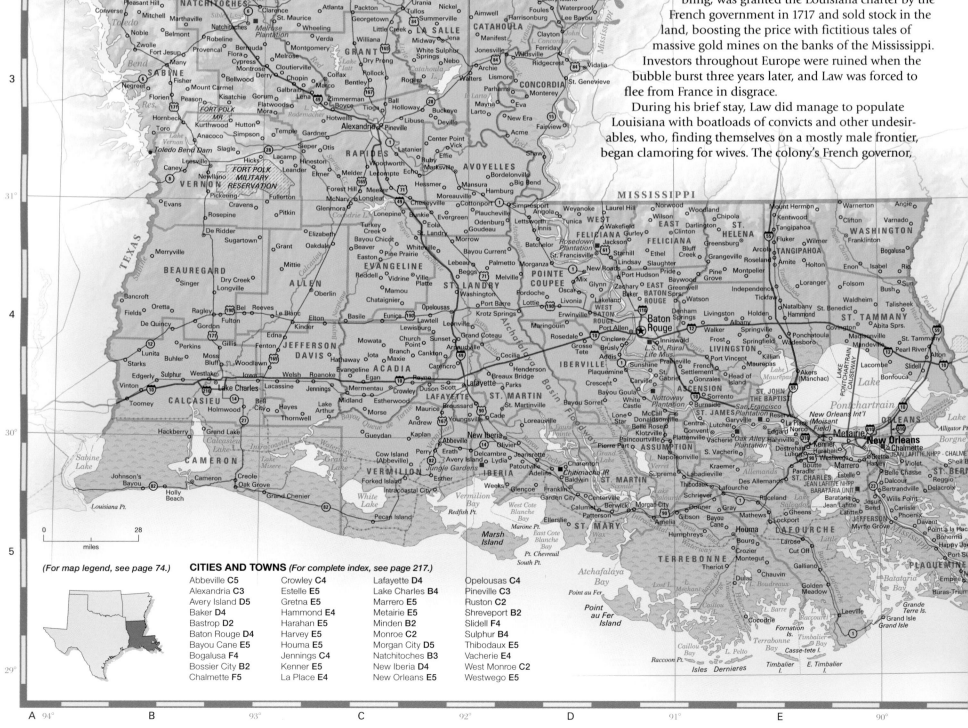

(For map legend, see page 74.)

CITIES AND TOWNS *(For complete index, see page 217.)*

▲ *Miles of marshland* surround the Mississippi at its delta; the waterway branches into bayous here and empties into the Gulf of Mexico.

STATE DATA
State bird: Brown pelican
State flower: Magnolia
State tree: Bald cypress
State motto: Union, justice, and confidence
State song: "Give Me Louisiana"
Abbreviations: La.; LA (postal)
Origin of the name: Named after Louis XIV, king of France
Nickname: Pelican State

AREA AND SIZE
Total area: 48,523 sq. mi.
Rank within U.S.: 31
Extent: 283 mi. north–south; 315 mi. east–west
Highest elevation: Driskill Mountain, 535 ft. above sea level
Lowest elevation: 5 ft. below sea level at New Orleans

POPULATION
Total: 4,425,000
Rank within U.S.: 23
Ethnic breakdown: White: 63.1%; Black: 32.5%; Hispanic: 2.7%; Asian: 1.3%; Indian: 0.4%
Population density: 98 people per sq. mi.

CLIMATE

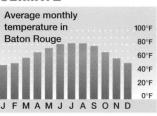

Average monthly temperature in Baton Rouge

Average monthly precipitation in Baton Rouge

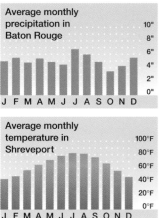

Average monthly temperature in Shreveport

Average monthly precipitation in Shreveport

ECONOMY
Service industries: Finance, insurance, real estate
Manufacturing: Chemicals, petroleum and coal products
Mining: Petroleum, natural gas
Agriculture: Cotton, beef cattle

Jean Baptiste Le Moyne, Sieur de Bienville, who founded New Orleans in 1718, pleaded with authorities in France to rectify the situation. In 1721 a ship carrying women from a house of correction in France landed in Louisiana. They were greeted by dozens of men in pirogues, escorted to shore, and introduced to eager bridegrooms across the colony. Finally, in December 1728, Bienville was able to welcome a respectable group of prospective brides. These young, educated middle-class women earned the nickname "casket girls" because of the shape of the box each had been given in which to carry her trousseau. Before long, they were married to suitable colonists, and Louisiana moved a step away from the unruly frontier.

▲ *Jambalaya,* a famous Creole classic made from green peppers, onions, tomatoes, and meat or seafood, is stirred up.

CULTURAL GUMBO
In the early 1700s Germans, Swiss, and Irish joined French, Spanish, and Africans in settling Louisiana. The first Acadians, ancestors of today's Cajuns, arrived in 1755 after a circuitous journey from Nova Scotia, where they had been ousted by British troops. These French Catholics settled in cottages raised above the "sleeping water" of the bayous; even today, visitors find a distinctive culture marked by a unique Cajun patois and all-night parties called *fais dodos* (literally, "go to sleep"). By 1803, when the United States bought it from Napoleon for a paltry $15 million, Louisiana boasted a lively diversity of lifestyles and livelihoods. The fortunes of the new Louisianans rose as the United States expanded, and the Mississippi River became their lifeline. Nine years later, on January 12, 1812, the river's first steamboat chugged into New Orleans, inaugurating the era immortalized in the novels of Mark Twain. Louisiana's fertile peat was ideal for growing many crops, including sugarcane and cotton, which were shipped north at a staggering rate.

New Orleans, one of the most cosmopolitan cities in the nation at the time, was a major economic and cultural center. Throughout the 18th century France and Spain had passed Louisiana back and forth several times. The French and the Spanish living in the Crescent City dealt with the political confusion adroitly: they intermarried, blending their cultures until they were nearly indistinguishable from one another. New Orleans also boasted a large population of free blacks and mulattoes, many of whom accumulated significant wealth as merchants, barbers, tailors, and shoemakers. Today the "Big Easy," as New Orleans is often called, is still a rich mix of cultures. Nearly a third of Louisianans can trace their ancestry to France. Cajuns who ply the swamps of southwestern Louisiana for fish and fur communicate in a French Creole with touches of English, German, and Spanish. In the backwaters of the Mississippi Delta, Spanish is spoken by the descendants of Canary Islanders, who arrived in the 18th century. At the same time, some blacks in the southern part of the state still speak a dialect flecked with French and West African words.

A "MUSICAL VICE"
The black slaves who shouldered the brunt of Louisiana's agricultural boom added to New Orleans's cultural mix a key ingredient that would eventually yield a unique form of American music. As a way to prevent the slaves from practicing African religion, white authorities staged Sunday dances, during which drummers beat out rhythms for dancing. Genuine voodoo ceremonies, held in secrecy, commanded equal attention. Marie Laveau, queen of the voodoo priestesses, presided over elaborate rituals that might begin with prayers to the Virgin Mary and end with Laveau herself spinning worshipers wildly around the room and dancing while holding a dish of flaming brandy—all to the beat of a drum and a call-and-response chant. These elements of the voodoo ceremony, combined with European musical influences, would eventually become jazz.

▶ *Oak Alley Plantation,* a Greek Revival mansion in Vacherie, is one of the few remaining antebellum plantations along the Mississippi in southeastern Louisiana.

LOUISIANA
TIME LINE

1541 Spaniard Hernando de Soto explores lower Mississippi River area.

1682 La Salle claims Mississippi River valley for France. He names it "Louisiane," after Louis XIV.

1714 France establishes first permanent settlement at present-day Natchitoches.

1718 New Orleans is founded.

1762 France secretly transfers Louisiana to Spain.

1788 Fire almost destroys city of New Orleans.

1800 Spain returns Louisiana to France.

1803 U.S. buys Louisiana for $15 million.

1804 Portion of Louisiana Purchase south of 33°N latitude is organized as the Territory of Orleans.

1812 Orleans Territory is admitted to the Union as Louisiana, the 18th state.
First steamboat to travel the Mississippi arrives in New Orleans from Pittsburgh.

1815 Andrew Jackson defeats British in Battle of New Orleans, ending War of 1812.

1838 First Mardi Gras is held in New Orleans.

1861 Louisiana secedes from the Union; joins Confederacy.

1862 Federal troops capture New Orleans.

1868 Louisiana is readmitted to the Union.

1901 Oil is found near Jennings.

1927 Mississippi River floods a large part of the state.

1935 U.S. senator and former Louisiana governor Huey Long is assassinated by a political enemy.

1960 School integration begins.

1965 Hurricane Betsy kills 61 people and heavily damages southeastern Louisiana.

1984 Louisiana World Exposition opens on Mississippi waterfront site in New Orleans.

▲ **Avery Island,** *a tropical garden and wildlife sanctuary, is home to thousands of graceful birds, including these snowy egrets.*

The Civil War turned life in New Orleans upside down for the blacks. At the same time that the Union victory won freedom for the slaves, it brought hard times for the well-to-do Creoles. When Reconstruction ended, white Louisianans began to draw a clear color line, brutally enforced by the Ku Klux Klan and the White League. As the "downtown" Creoles lost their jobs to whites, they were forced into closer contact with the "uptown" blacks, many of whom made their living as musicians in an infamous little neighborhood called Storyville, named after Alderman Sidney Story, who had turned the district into an enclave of vice. By the turn of the century, cultured Creole musicians suddenly found themselves playing seedy honky-tonks and cabarets.

Jelly Roll Morton got his first job playing piano in a brothel when he was 15. Buddy Bolden—whose improvisation of "hot blues" in the summer of 1894 is often said to have been the

first jazz performance—liked to work in a place called Tin Type Hall, which doubled as a makeshift morgue. When Storyville shut down in 1917, jazz had not exactly become respectable. The following year, the *Times-Picayune* called it a "musical vice." But it was too late. The music had a devout following, and as jobs in Storyville dried up, such native sons as King Oliver and his protégé, Louis Armstrong, moved to cities like Chicago, New York, and Memphis to spread the word.

▶ **Louis "Satchmo" Armstrong** *during a 1936 rehearsal.*

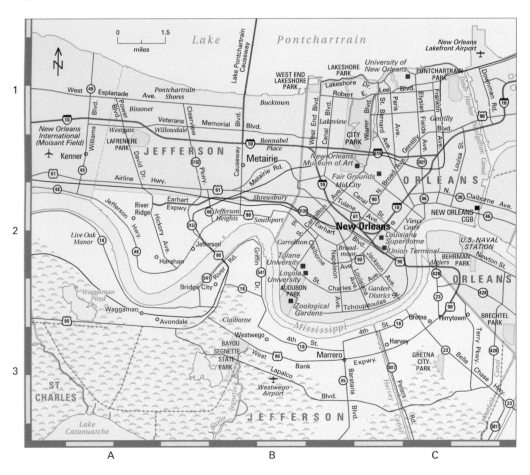

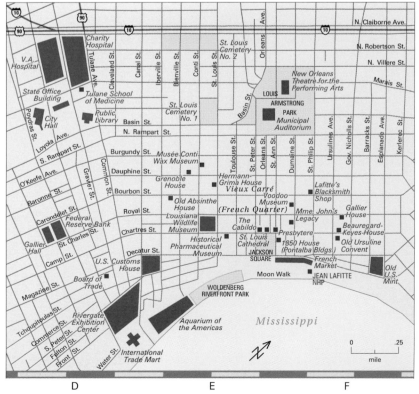

KINGFISH

In 1928, on the eve of the Depression, Louisiana was swept by a kind of tornado that seemed to be equal parts virtue and vice. Its name was Huey Long. A fire-and-brimstone populist, Long won the governorship that year under the slogan "Every man a king, but no one wears a crown." He blasted big business from his stump while accepting generous contributions from the same in the back room. Once in office, he strong-armed Louisiana—crippled by an aging infrastructure and the nation's worst illiteracy rate—into the 20th century. Long paved highways, built bridges and levees, killed the poll tax, gave out free textbooks, and pumped money into the state university. He also ruled with an iron hand and a greedy fist, claiming on one occasion that he played the state legislature "like a deck of cards." When one legislator reminded him that the state had a constitution, Long replied, in the tradition of Louis XIV, "I'm the constitution around here now!" He filled the state payroll with his relatives and brazenly sold state contracts to fatten his political coffers. In Louisiana, however, he was still the "Kingfish."

In 1930 Long was elected to the U.S. Senate, where he launched his Share Our Wealth program. The premise was to give money to the poor and pensions to the aged, cut work hours, and confiscate money from anyone making more than $1 million a year. By 1935 Long claimed the existence of 7.5 million Share Our Wealth supporters, and posed a true third-party threat to President Franklin D. Roosevelt. He never got a chance to put his plan into action, however. In September 1935, under investigation for graft and income tax evasion, he returned to Baton Rouge to meet with his proxies in the state legislature. As he emerged from an all-day Sunday session, a 29-year-old doctor stepped forward and shot the Kingfish. Long died 30 hours later in a Baton Rouge hospital.

NATURAL RESOURCES

Louisiana emerged from the Long years with an economy built around the enormous reserves of oil, salt, and sulfur discovered at the turn of the century. Today the state produces a quarter of all the petrochemicals in the United States and ranks as the third-largest refiner of oil. But water is still the main engine of progress. Every day hundreds of ships and barges bring their cargo through New Orleans and Baton Rouge, two of the five busiest ports in the United States. And Louisiana fishermen land more than a quarter of the seafood pulled out of American waters, including 85 percent of the crayfish.

Louisiana's subtropical wetland environment bears the scars of economic success. One hundred miles of petrochemical plants mar the landscape between New Orleans and Baton Rouge, and they dump approximately 80 pounds of arsenic and 4,800 pounds of lead every day into a stretch of the Mississippi River commonly known as the "cancer corridor." The port at New Orleans is a study in rush-hour traffic, with gigantic industrial ships filled with hazardous chemicals battling barges, ferries, private yachts, and gambling boats for space.

In the meantime, major reforestation projects protect the northern forests from excessive logging. And wildlife refuges shelter the coastal wetlands of the south— home to vast flocks of ibises, egrets, pelicans, cormorants, and geese. The marshes serve as a rest stop for hundreds of thousands of migrating birds. Naturalists say that in January birders can find a quarter of the country's duck population within the state's borders.

But no matter how many mallards or wood ducks make their home in the state, Louisianans must count their passion for revelry as their most valuable natural resource. Every year that passion is devoted to the celebration of Carnival—loosely translated from the Latin as "farewell to flesh"—which brings thousands of tourists and some $500 million to the city of

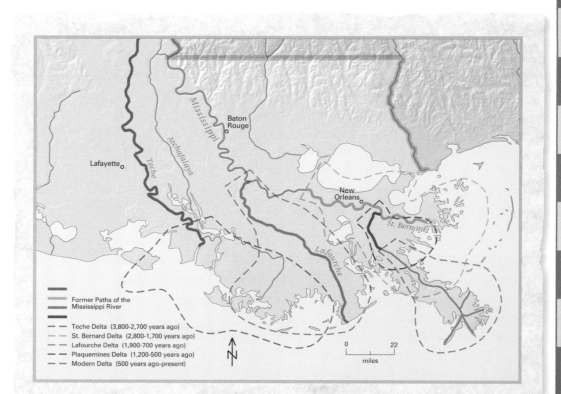

Will New Orleans Remain on the River?

The restless lower Mississippi River has changed its course time and again over thousands of years, breaking through its natural levees (accumulations of earth and rock that raise the river's banks) and altering its route to the Gulf of Mexico. As the Mississippi deposits sediment at its new sea outlets, distributaries (branches) are born, and the deltas shift. If the Mississippi had its way today, it would move west to meet with the Atchafalaya River, changing the main channel and moving the delta to approximately where the Teche Delta used to be. The new course of the river would be almost 200 miles shorter, and Baton Rouge and New Orleans, thriving river towns since their founding, would be left on an abandoned channel. Beginning in the 1950s and continuing to the present, the U.S. Army Corps of Engineers, employing increasingly better technology, has built levees and floodgates to keep the willful Mississippi flowing on its present course.

New Orleans. For 12 days before Lent begins, Mardi Gras revelers live it up, attending some 60 parades and hundreds of dances, masked balls, and private parties. The entire festival is put on by a loosely organized confederation of private clubs called krewes, each of which prepares a float for the main parade and spends thousands of dollars on trinkets to throw to eager onlookers. On Ash Wednesday, turning to the solemn business of cleaning up and observing the rules of Lent is the order of the day. But for almost two weeks out of every year, Louisiana is a world apart, a place where exotic masks stand in for human faces and kissing perfect strangers in the street seems a normal way to greet your fellow man.

▲ **Well-appointed tombs** in a New Orleans cemetery. Settlers buried their dead in these above-ground vaults because the city lies below sea level, and graves could wash away in heavy rains.

◀ **Mardi Gras parade.** Every February, huge crowds flock to the streets of New Orleans to celebrate the "Fat Tuesday" carnival. This world-renowned party features elaborate floats, masked balls, outlandish costumes, and lots of noise!

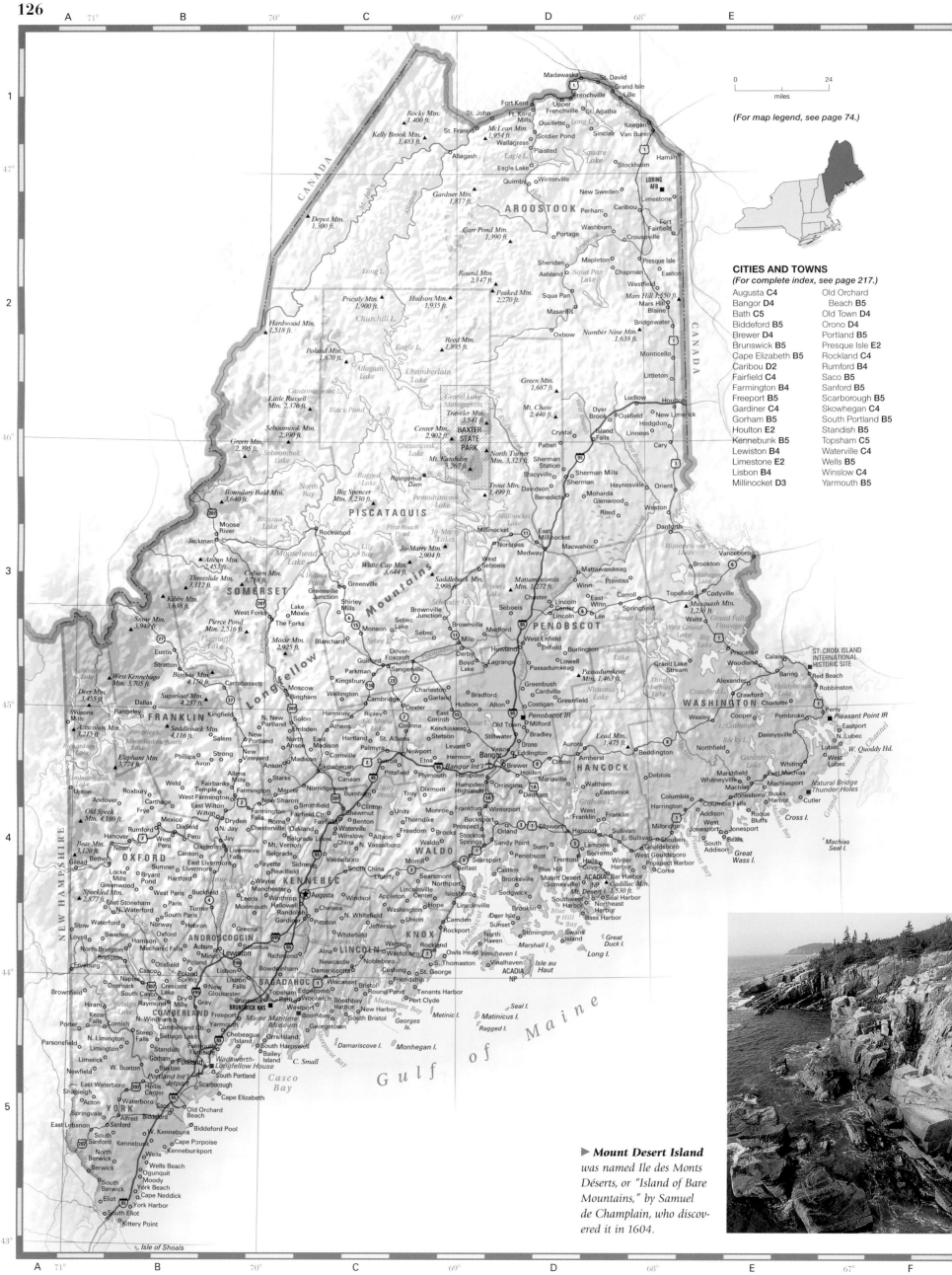

A 71°   B   70°   C   69°   D   68°   E

(For map legend, see page 74.)

CITIES AND TOWNS
(For complete index, see page 217.)

Augusta C4	Old Orchard
Bangor D4	Beach B5
Bath C5	Old Town D4
Biddeford B5	Orono D4
Brewer D4	Portland B5
Brunswick B5	Presque Isle E2
Cape Elizabeth B5	Rockland C4
Caribou D2	Rumford B4
Fairfield C4	Saco B5
Farmington B4	Sanford B5
Freeport B5	Scarborough B5
Gardiner C4	Skowhegan C4
Gorham B5	South Portland B5
Houlton E2	Standish B5
Kennebunk B5	Topsham C5
Lewiston B4	Waterville C4
Limestone E2	Wells B5
Lisbon B4	Winslow C4
Millinocket D3	Yarmouth B5

▶ **Mount Desert Island**
was named Ile des Monts
Déserts, or "Island of Bare
Mountains," by Samuel
de Champlain, who discov-
ered it in 1604.

◀ **Mount Katahdin,** *Maine's highest peak, looms over Abol Pond in Baxter State Park.*

Maine

The first light of dawn in the United States shines on the summit of Cadillac Mountain, at 1,530 feet the highest point on North America's eastern coastline and the pinnacle of Maine's Acadia National Park. The state in which the nation's day begins is a place of primal beauty, famous for its rockbound coast where Atlantic breakers meet granite headlands, pine forests that glint with the silver of rivers, and for loggers and lobstermen who live their lives in the shadow of their own romantic legends.

A REMOTE AND RUGGED LAND

Almost larger in area than all of the other New England states combined, Maine borders only one of them, New Hampshire. Maine's most famous delineating feature is its fantastically convoluted coastline—228 linear miles pleated and gouged into a 3,478-mile littoral that defies both sailors and motorists who wish to navigate it in its entirety.

The state that other New Englanders think of as "down east" (because ships had to sail downwind and easterly to get there), Maine is the least densely populated state east of the Mississippi. Portland, the state's largest city, has found new prosperity with the renovation of its waterfront, and as one of the major trading ports on the Atlantic coast, it plays an important role in Maine's paper and pulp trade. The state's tidily preserved seacoast towns dot mainly the south and central shores; farther north, authentic fishing villages are a bit grittier but no less picturesque.

Beyond central Maine's scattered farms and mill towns sprawls the realm of the northern forest, where the Kennebec, Penobscot, Androscoggin, and St. John rivers gather force from countless tributaries for their rush to the Atlantic. Deep in the Maine woods lies the 201,018-acre preserve of Baxter State Park, in which Mount Katahdin, at 5,268 feet Maine's highest mountain, stands tall. Still farther north is Aroostook County, where Maine's famous potatoes are grown by farmers of predominantly French-Canadian stock.

ROAD TO STATEHOOD

Although the coastline was likely explored by Norsemen 1,000 years ago, the documented history of European settlement in Maine begins in the early 17th century, when British and French explorers—among them the peripatetic Samuel de Champlain—tried to secure beachheads along the shore. The first permanent English settlement was established in 1623, but

Britain's dominion over northernmost New England was not immediately assured. French Canada and its allies among the region's indigenous Algonquin tribes continued to harass English enclaves in Maine until the conclusion of the French and Indian War in 1763.

Within little more than a decade, Maine was at war once again, and throughout the American Revolution, Britain held much of the colony's coastline. During the War of 1812, Maine's coastal communities again fell victim to British naval attacks. But a later revolution would be more peaceful. Since 1691 Maine had been part of Massachusetts, even though the two were separated by New Hampshire. By the end of the War of 1812, however, a growing number of people had become increasingly dissatisfied with being governed by distant Boston. This conflict was quietly resolved in 1820 with Maine's admission to the Union as the 23rd state.

NATURAL RESOURCES

Maine has always earned its living from its two greatest natural resources: the woodlands and the ocean. Although the days of the loggers' heroic river drives are long gone, Maine still extracts more than 1 billion board feet of lumber annually from its 17.5 million acres of forest, and it remains one of the world's largest pulp and paper producers. Along the coast, Maine fishermen and packers are world leaders in the production of canned sardines; they also supply more than half of the country's lobster catch. Shipbuilding, a Maine tradition dating to the days when tall white pines became schooners' masts, lives on at the Bath Iron Works, a major naval contrac-

▲ **Maine lobster traps** *don't sit empty for long. The state's annual catch is about 215 million pounds of fish and shellfish.*

tor. And between the forest and the sea lies a moorlike flatland called the blueberry barrens, where virtually the entire American crop of low-bush blueberries is harvested each year.

Still, the most enduring images of Maine are far removed from stark economics. There is the cry of a loon over a cold northern lake; the clean lines of a canoe as it slices through the waters of the Allagash River; and the bold white shaft of a lighthouse rising above foam and spray on that serpentine rockbound coast.

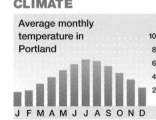

▲ *The Maine state flag,* *adopted in 1909, displays the state seal. On it, a sailor symbolizes commerce and fishing, and a farmer represents agriculture. A pine tree, a moose, and the North Star are also pictured.*

STATE DATA

State bird: Chickadee
State flower: White pine cone and tassel
State tree: White pine
State motto: *Dirigo* (I direct)
State song: "State of Maine Song"
Abbreviations: Me.; ME (postal)
Origin of the name: From the French province Le Maine, or from the word *mainland*
Nickname: Pine Tree State

AREA AND SIZE

Total area: 33,215 sq. mi.
Rank within U.S.: 39
Extent: 303 mi. north–south; 202 mi. east–west
Highest elevation: Mount Katahdin, 5,268 ft. above sea level
Lowest elevation: Sea level along the coast

POPULATION

Total: 1,259,000
Rank within U.S.: 40
Ethnic breakdown: White: 97.7%; Asian: 0.7%; Hispanic: 0.6%; Indian: 0.5%; Black: 0.4%
Population density: 40.7 people per sq. mi.

CLIMATE

Average monthly temperature in Portland
100°F / 80°F / 60°F / 40°F / 20°F / 0°F
J F M A M J J A S O N D

Average monthly precipitation in Portland
10" / 8" / 6" / 4" / 2" / 0"
J F M A M J J A S O N D

ECONOMY

Service industries: Real estate, automobile dealerships, healthcare facilities, hotels, restaurants
Manufacturing: Paper products, transportation equipment, wood products, electrical equipment
Agriculture: Milk, eggs, potatoes
Fishing: Lobsters, soft-shell crabs

MAINE TIMELINE

c. 1000 Norsemen are thought to have landed on Maine coast.
1498 John Cabot is believed to have explored Maine coast.
1604 French establish colony but leave for Nova Scotia after difficult winter.
1607 Popham Colony is founded by English settlers; settlement lasts one winter.
1622 British charter grants Maine territory to John Mason and Ferdinando Gorges.

1641 York becomes first chartered English city in America.
1677 Massachusetts purchases Maine from Gorges's heirs.
1775 In first naval battle of Revolutionary War, Maine colonists capture British schooner.
1788 Maine abolishes slavery.
1820 Maine enters the Union as 23rd state after separating from Massachusetts.
1842 Maine-Canada border dispute is resolved.

1851 First U.S. law forbidding sale of liquor is passed by Maine. Harriet Beecher Stowe writes *Uncle Tom's Cabin* in Brunswick, Maine.
1948 Maine representative Margaret Chase Smith becomes first woman to serve in both houses of Congress.
1980 U.S. government pays $81.5 million to Passamaquoddy and Penobscot Indians for land taken around 1800.

▲ **The state flag,** adopted in 1904, bears the coats of arms of two families who were related to Lord Baltimore: the Calverts (black and gold) and the Crosslands (red and white).

STATE DATA

State bird: Baltimore oriole
State flower: Black-eyed Susan
State tree: White oak
State motto: *Fatti maschii, parole femine* (Manly deeds, womanly words)
State song: "Maryland, My Maryland"
Abbreviations: Md.; MD (postal)
Origin of the name: Named for Queen Henrietta Maria, wife of King Charles I of England, who granted territory to Lord Baltimore
Nicknames: Old Line State, Free State

AREA AND SIZE

Total area: 10,577 sq. mi.
Rank within U.S.: 42
Extent: 124 mi. north–south; 238 mi. east–west
Highest elevation: Backbone Mountain, 3,360 ft. above sea level
Lowest elevation: Sea level along the coast

POPULATION

Total: 5,275,000
Rank within U.S.: 19
Ethnic breakdown: White: 63.9%: Black: 27.7%; Hispanic: 4.1%; Asian: 4.0%; Indian: 0.3%
Population density: 533.9 people per sq. mi.

CLIMATE

Average monthly temperature in Baltimore
100°F / 80°F / 60°F / 40°F / 20°F / 0°F
J F M A M J J A S O N D

Average monthly precipitation in Baltimore
10" / 8" / 6" / 4" / 2" / 0"
J F M A M J J A S O N D

ECONOMY

Service industries: Private health care, support services for business and government, finance, insurance, real estate
Manufacturing: Food processing, search and navigation instruments, electrical equipment, chemicals, printed materials
Agriculture: Broiler chickens, milk, greenhouse and nursery products, soybeans, corn, wheat, tomatoes, apples
Fishing: Clams, crabs, bluefish, catfish, croakers, flounder, mackerel, marlin, sharks, striped bass

▶ **Chesapeake Bay,** the drowned mouth of the Susquehanna River, was explored and charted by John Smith in 1608.

Maryland

Situated on the cusp between North and South just below the Mason-Dixon line, Maryland is a state that is difficult to characterize. While portions of it are distinctly Southern—especially the Eastern Shore, where families mark time in generations and the pace of life is slow—places like Baltimore and Annapolis bustle along at a tempo quick enough to rival that of any Northern city. Even the land is divided—by the Chesapeake Bay—the bountiful heart and soul of the state.

THE GREAT SHELLFISH BAY

Bisecting the eastern portion of the state, Chesapeake Bay is Maryland's most defining natural feature and the source of much of its way of life. Some 190 miles from top to bottom, and covering nearly 3,230 square miles, the Chesapeake—after the Indian word *chesepiook,* meaning "great shellfish bay"—is actually a sunken river valley, or estuary; it is the largest one in the United States and was formed at the close of the last ice age, when rising sea levels inundated the mouth of the Susquehanna River. So twisted are the Chesapeake's margins that, counting all of its bays, inlets, coves, and creeks, it provides tiny Maryland with a shoreline of nearly 4,000 miles, one of the nation's longest.

In terms of European settlement, the Tidewater is Maryland's oldest region; the first to explore the Chesapeake Bay area were the Spanish, who arrived in the 1500s. When they arrived, the region was peopled only by the Algonquin and Susquehannock Indians, who lived off the bay's plentiful stock. Over the course of 500 years, however, human impact, pollution, silting up, agricultural runoff, heavy shipping traffic, and overfishing have taken their toll.

Still, Chesapeake Bay remains one of the East Coast's most bountiful aquatic ecosystems. More seafood—including oysters, clams, fin fish, soft-shell crabs, and nearly 90 million

▲ **Blue crabs** from Chesapeake Bay, whose salinity and shallowness provide an ideal reproductive environment.

pounds of blue crabs—is pulled from its waters each year than from any other body of water its size. Huge flocks of migratory waterfowl, a boon to sportsmen, invade the wetlands each spring and fall.

Since the state's earliest days, the bay has also served as a vital corridor connecting it with the Atlantic Ocean and the rest of the world. Poking its watery finger far inland, Chesapeake Bay cleaves the state nearly in two and gives direct shipping access to Baltimore, Maryland's oldest major port and its largest city. Although joined by a common seagoing heritage, the two sides of the bay are in many ways quite distinct, both topographically and temperamentally. The bay's western side (or Western Shore, as Marylanders call it) is by far the more developed of the two, increasingly a part of the octopuslike urban sprawl connecting Baltimore with Washington, D.C. The Western Shore has always been worldly in outlook. From its sheltered harbors and coves, Colonial merchants and planters shipped the tobacco, lumber, and livestock that made Maryland prosper. Early settlers included a large merchant class, and in the brick-row-house neighborhoods of Baltimore, one still finds Greek, Polish, Italian, and Hispanic enclaves, legacies of Baltimore's 19th-century industrial heritage. Colonial-era towns and cities dot the water's edge, including Annapolis, Maryland's capital and home of the United States Naval Academy.

THE EASTERN SHORE

Across the bay lies the Eastern Shore, carved from a teardrop-shaped landmass named the Delmarva Peninsula after the three states (Delaware, Maryland, and Virginia) that share its land. Although the Eastern Shore is joined to the rest of the

C 77° D 76° E 75°

PENNSYLVANIA

MASON AND DIXON LINE

(For map legend, see page 74.)

state at the Chesapeake's northernmost tip, it has the feel of a remote island—flatter, marshier, and decidedly more rural in character than its twin across the bay. Sprawling fields of wheat, corn, and soybeans push straight to the reeds and cattails of the water's edge; farming and fishing towns with British names (including Oxford and Cambridge) give evidence of the region's original settlers, many of whose descendants still live here. Although the opening of the Chesapeake Bay Bridge in 1952 finally brought the Eastern Shore within easy reach of the rest of the state, residents of the region still pride themselves on their casual indifference to the outside world. Even today, a handful of Eastern shore oystermen dredge the water in graceful wooden sloops known as skipjacks, just as their ancestors did. The Eastern Shore's relative remoteness does not prevent the world from invading once a year, however. On summer weekends, huge traffic jams clog the bay's bridges as thousands of sunseekers flee the confines of sweltering nearby cities for the beaches on the southeastern end of the Delmarva Peninsula. This 120-mile strip of golden sand—Maryland's only open seacoast—has become a world-renowned fishing and beach resort. Tiny Ocean City, a windswept ghost town in winter, bulges with so many summer visitors that at the height of the season it ranks as the state's second most populous city.

BEYOND THE BAY

Away from the water, Maryland's topography runs the gamut. The southernmost reaches of the state are tobacco country, flat and fertile; north and west of the bay, the land rises sharply along a distinct topographical feature known as the Fall Line. Running roughly northeast from the Washington suburbs to the Pennsylvania border, this wall-like formation marks the eastern boundary of the Piedmont Plateau and the state's hilly interior. First settled by Scotch-Irish and German religious minorities (including the Mennonites and the Moravians), many of the Piedmont's small farming towns retain their charming old-world ambience despite their proximity to the densely populated Washington-Baltimore corridor.

Making up one-fifth of the state's total area, the Maryland panhandle is a narrow strip of land between the meandering Potomac River and the state's northern border with Pennsylvania—one of the most famous boundaries in North America. The subject of a long argument between Colonial Maryland and Pennsylvania, the border wasn't defined until the 1760s, when a pair of English surveyors, Charles Mason and Jeremiah Dixon, drew the line that settled the dispute—and inadvertently set the stage for a second, far more difficult struggle. The

northernmost limit of slavery in pre–Civil War America, the Mason-Dixon line represented a profound fissure in the American psyche, and for Maryland was a point of contention. Technically a slave state, Maryland did not secede during the Civil War, and its loyalties were deeply divided, with soldiers fighting for both the Union and the Confederacy.

Culturally and topographically, the mountains of western Maryland have more in common with neighboring West Virginia and south central Pennsylvania than they do with the rest of the state. Dominated by the Blue Ridge and Allegheny mountains, the landscape is austere, softened only by the river valleys that meander between the peaks. Although few people live here, the panhandle has always been well traveled. Many of the region's roads are paved-over Indian footpaths, and the Cumberland Narrows, flanked by rock walls a thousand feet high, served as a gateway to the Appalachians for pioneers en route to the Ohio Valley and beyond. During the Civil War, Confederate and Union forces crisscrossed the panhandle numerous times, and the South used the panhandle as a launching point for an invasion of the

▼ **Wild ponies,** *descendants of 17th-century horses, swim from Assateague to Chincoteague for the annual auction in July.*

▶ *Bloody Lane, in Antietam National Battlefield, was the site of the Civil War's most brutal battle, on September 17, 1862. Casualties numbered 12,410 Union soldiers and 10,700 Confederate soldiers.*

MARYLAND
TIME LINE

1608 British captain John Smith explores Chesapeake Bay.

1631 William Claiborne sets up trading post on Kent Island.

1632 King Charles I grants Maryland charter to Cecilius Calvert, second Lord Baltimore, after the death of his father, George Calvert.

1634 First settlers arrive.

1649 Maryland guarantees religious freedom to all Christians with passage of Act of Religious Toleration.

1767 Surveyors Mason and Dixon set the Delaware-Maryland-Pennsylvania boundaries.

1783 Annapolis becomes nation's temporary capital.

1784 Congress approves Treaty of Paris at Annapolis, ending Revolutionary War.

1788 Maryland becomes seventh state.

1791 Maryland donates land for District of Columbia.

1814 Francis Scott Key writes "The Star-Spangled Banner" during British attack of Fort McHenry.

1828 Construction of the Baltimore and Ohio railroad, the nation's first, begins.

1845 U.S. Naval Academy is founded at Annapolis.

1862 Union troops defeat Confederate troops at Antietam.

1902 Maryland passes country's first workmen's compensation law.

1919–33 Maryland refuses to enforce Prohibition; gains nickname Free State.

1952 Chesapeake Bay Bridge opens to traffic.

1980 Opening of Harborplace complex, signaling renewal of Baltimore's Inner Harbor.

▼ *Maritime marvels in Baltimore's Inner Harbor: the seven-story National Aquarium (far right) and the navy's last all-sail warship, the* Constellation.

A STATE OF TOLERANCE

Maryland's heritage is reflected in the diversity of its people—a mix of religious, racial, and ethnic groups whose ancestors shared a common desire to find a better life. Founded in 1632 by the Calvert family, scions of George Calvert, Lord Baltimore, as a haven for British Catholics, the colony welcomed those of other faiths as well. It formally adopted religious freedom in a landmark piece of legislation, the Act of Religious Toleration, which was passed in 1649. Colonial Maryland's love of liberty was further tested in its gritty resistance to British authority during the Revolutionary War. So renowned for their ferocity were the men of the Maryland First Regiment of the Continental Line that Maryland earned the nickname Old Line State.

In other ways, too, Maryland stands out for its unique role in the founding of the nation and its passionate defense of liberty. Washington, D.C., was built on land donated by the state, and the lyrics to "The Star-Spangled Banner," the country's national anthem, were inspired by the defense of Baltimore Harbor's Fort McHenry during the War of 1812. Although the tobacco fields and fruit and vegetable farms of the Tidewater relied on slavery, pre–Civil War Baltimore had the highest population of free blacks of all the Eastern slave states. In the post–Civil War era, Maryland was one of the first states to adopt universal manhood suffrage. Even the state's motto, *Fatti maschii, parole femine* (Manly deeds, womanly words), suggests the spirit of compromise for which Maryland is known.

BALTIMORE BOOM TIMES

Although large areas of the state remain rural, more and more Marylanders make their homes in the extended metropolis connecting Washington with Baltimore and Wilmington—part of a burgeoning East Coast megalopolis stretching all the way from northern Virginia to Boston. More than three-quarters of the state's population now resides within commuting distance of Baltimore or Washington, D.C. In Baltimore these are boom times. While other old industrial cities on the East Coast have faded, Baltimore launched a major face-lift program in the 1970s. Even so, the city—like the rest of the state—remains in touch with its past. Mixing old with new and Southern charm with Northern grit, and embracing the diversity of its people, Baltimore—and Maryland—stands at the crossroads of America.

North, culminating in the Battle of Antietam, considered by many historians to be the single bloodiest day in the history of American armed conflict.

As in times past, many visitors to Appalachian Maryland come to savor its beautiful mountain terrain, shimmering lakes, and cool summer climate. The region has attracted tourists for nearly 150 years, and today the panhandle offers outdoor diversions to suit every taste, from strenuous backwoods camping and white-water rafting to leisurely strolling along the towpaths of the old Chesapeake and Ohio Canal, one of early America's busiest commercial waterways.

District of Columbia

A PLANNED CITY

The world's first planned capital, Washington was the brain-child of French engineer and architect Maj. Pierre-Charles L'Enfant, who was hired by Congress in 1791 to design a "federal town" at the swampy confluence of the Potomac and Anacostia rivers. With the help of two assistants, Andrew Ellicot and Benjamin Banneker, L'Enfant laid out his city on a precisely measured 10-square-mile grid, on lands ceded to the federal government by neighboring Maryland and Virginia. (In 1846 Virginia's lands were restored and today contain the communities of Arlington and Alexandria, part of the District of Columbia's sprawling suburban ring.)

From the start, L'Enfant's vision was grand—a capital with broad boulevards, beautifully planted circles, mammoth neo-classical edifices, and towering monuments. Following L'Enfant's plan, the cornerstone of the Capitol Building was laid in 1793; seven years later, although the building was only half finished, Congress relocated to the nation's new capital from its temporary quarters in Philadelphia. John Adams moved into the White House at the same time. (George Washington, whose name the city bears, is the only American president who did not live in the White House.)

L'ENFANT'S PLAN

Although two centuries have passed, much of central Washington remains faithful to L'Enfant's original design. Dominating the skyline is the Capitol itself, a massive bulwark of white marble and sandstone capped by an enormous baroque dome. Adjacent to the Capitol are the Supreme Court Building (modeled after an ancient Greek temple) and the Library of Congress, a vast repository equaled only by the Lenin State Library in Moscow. Most of "official" Washington—such as the Justice Department, the FBI, the Treasury Department, and the National Archives—can be found between the Capitol and the Potomac, along two main thoroughfares. Running northwest, Pennsylvania Avenue connects the Capitol with the White House, a little more than a mile away. Set on fire by the British Army during the War of 1812, as was the Capitol itself, the White House was rebuilt. It underwent a major renovation during the 1950s.

A WORLD CAPITAL

Washington is in a unique position among U.S. cities. Not part of any state, its residents are the only Americans with no voting representative in Congress. It wasn't until the 1970s that Washingtonians were able to elect their own mayor and city council. Until then, all local government was overseen by a congressional committee. With almost no heavy industry, Washington is among the cleanest American cities; the government is the largest employer, putting some 370,000 people to work.

In its outlook, Washington is decidedly global. Shifts in the political winds can bring dramatic changes to the tone of the town, while its legions of students and foreign residents enrich it with a diversity of cultures. When L'Enfant set about to design an American capital, he charged himself with designing a city that would be as great as the country it celebrated and a magnet for the world. And so he did.

▶ *The Pavilion of Art and Science in the Thomas Jefferson Building, the oldest Library of Congress building, was built in 1897.*

▲ *The U.S. Capitol contains the House and Senate chambers. Its signature double dome (one inside the other) was completed in 1866.*

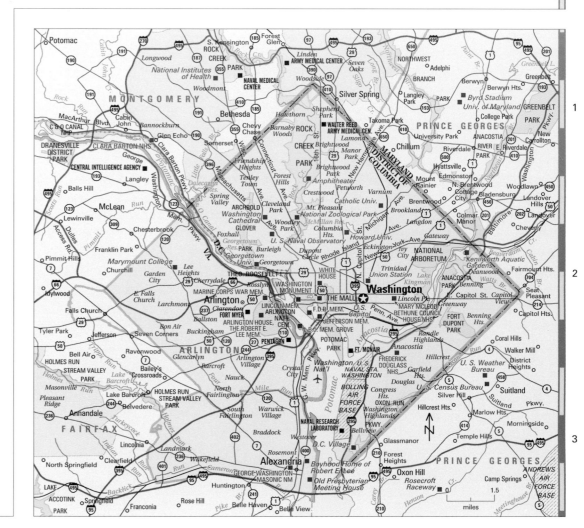

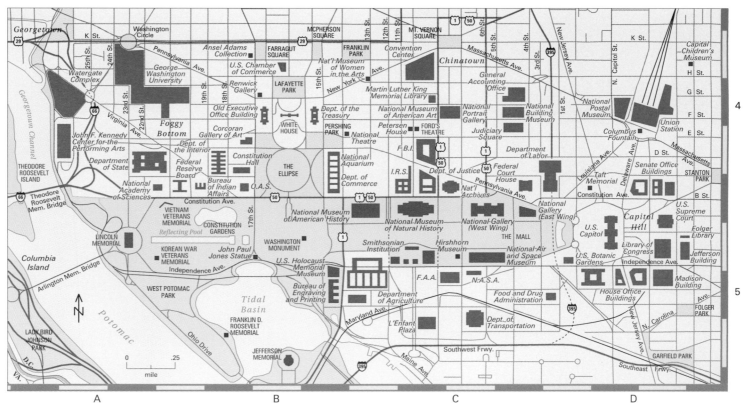

Massachusetts

▲ **Adopted in 1971,** the state flag features an Indian—a state symbol. A star represents Massachusetts as one of the 13 colonies.

STATE DATA
State bird: Chickadee
State flower: Mayflower
State tree: American elm
State motto: *Ense petit placidam sub libertate quietem* (By the sword we seek peace, but peace only under liberty)
State song: "All Hail to Massachusetts"
Abbreviations: Mass.; MA (postal)
Origin of the name: Massachuset Indian for "near the great hill," referring to the Great Blue Hill region
Nickname: Bay State

AREA AND SIZE
Total area: 8,257 sq. mi.
Rank within U.S.: 45
Extent: 113 mi. north–south; 183 mi. east–west
Highest elevation: Mount Greylock, 3,487 ft. above sea level
Lowest elevation: Sea level along the Atlantic coast

POPULATION
Total: 6,199,000
Rank within U.S.: 13
Ethnic breakdown: White: 83.6%; Hispanic: 7.0%; Black: 5.4%; Asian: 3.9%; Indian: 0.2%
Population density: 791 people per sq. mi.

CLIMATE

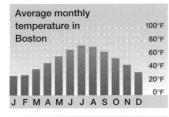

Average monthly temperature in Boston
100°F 80°F 60°F 40°F 20°F 0°F
J F M A M J J A S O N D

Average monthly precipitation in Boston
10" 8" 6" 4" 2" 0"
J F M A M J J A S O N D

Average monthly temperature in Worcester
100°F 80°F 60°F 40°F 20°F 0°F
J F M A M J J A S O N D

Average monthly precipitation in Worcester
10" 8" 6" 4" 2" 0"
J F M A M J J A S O N D

ECONOMY
Service industries: Health-care facilities, schools and universities, banking, insurance, real estate
Manufacturing: Scientific instruments, electrical equipment
Agriculture: Greenhouse and nursery products, cranberries, milk

To the sea-weary Mayflower passengers who sighted present-day Provincetown Harbor in the autumn of 1620, the Massachusetts coast must have seemed particularly harsh and barren; they were, after all, headed for the warm and fertile colony of Virginia. But starting at that uninviting coast, the pioneers who founded Massachusetts created a commonwealth that would serve as a laboratory for bold experiments in politics, education, religion, and the arts.

THE ROCKY SHORES OF THE NEW WORLD

Much of coastal Massachusetts is the creation of the last great ice age. The sands of Cape Cod, as well as the islands of Martha's Vineyard and Nantucket, are largely glacial moraine, the heaped detritus of walls of ice that scoured New England more than 10,000 years ago. To this day, long stretches of the Massachusetts shore remain in a state of flux. The dunes of Cape Cod's Atlantic coast constantly shift and retreat, and the beach has been pushed back hundreds of feet over the past century and a half. Farther north, the elongated barrier formation called Plum Island is transformed according to the whims of wind and ocean currents. But at Rockport and Gloucester on Cape Ann, shoreline outcrops of solid granite challenge the sea to a greater battle.

▲ **Old North Church,** *where the sexton Robert Newman signaled the British route to the patriots.*

West of the seascapes, the Pilgrims found a rolling, wooded countryside that lent itself to the building of small farms and streamside villages. In the state's northeastern corner, the Merrimack River carries New Hampshire's snowmelt past places where it once powered machines that wove cotton and woolen textiles for the world. Farther west lies the broad valley drained by New England's longest river, the Connecticut, which divides eastern from western Massachusetts. Only west of the Connecticut does the state possess anything resembling a mountain—the forested nubs of the Berkshire Hills, which crest near the New York and Vermont borders at 3,487-foot Mount Greylock, the highest point in Massachusetts.

PURITANS' PROGRESS

The story of the first Massachusetts settlements was largely written along the coast. The Pilgrims' Plymouth Colony—which is recalled at today's Plimoth Plantation—occupied much of southeastern Massachusetts until it was united with the Massachusetts Bay Colony later in the 17th century. Massachusetts Bay, which like Plymouth was founded by Puritan dissenters from England's Anglican church, made Boston its capital in 1630.

Farther north along the coast stood Salem, still a small town when witchcraft hysteria and the subsequent executions gripped adjacent Danvers village in the 1690s, and Gloucester, a port intimately associated with cod fishery from the time of

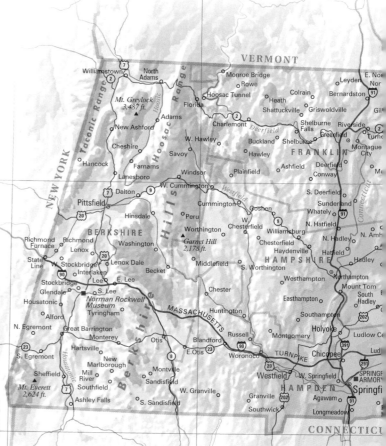

▲ **The Berkshire Hills,** *part of the Appalachians, grace the western edge of Massachusetts and provide spectacular views of fall foliage.*

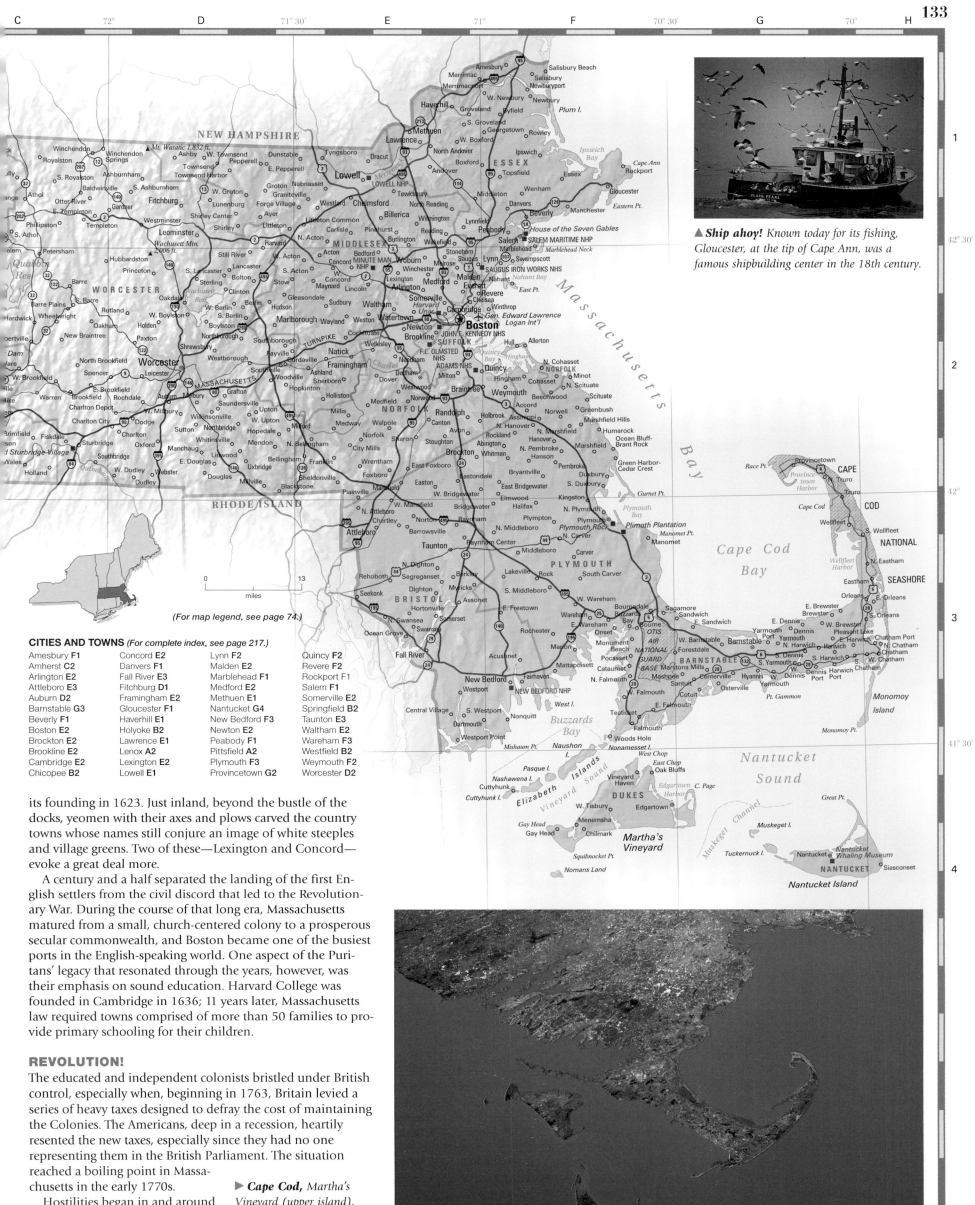

▲ Ship ahoy! *Known today for its fishing, Gloucester, at the tip of Cape Ann, was a famous shipbuilding center in the 18th century.*

(For map legend, see page 74.)

CITIES AND TOWNS *(For complete index, see page 217.)*

its founding in 1623. Just inland, beyond the bustle of the docks, yeomen with their axes and plows carved the country towns whose names still conjure an image of white steeples and village greens. Two of these—Lexington and Concord—evoke a great deal more.

A century and a half separated the landing of the first English settlers from the civil discord that led to the Revolutionary War. During the course of that long era, Massachusetts matured from a small, church-centered colony to a prosperous secular commonwealth, and Boston became one of the busiest ports in the English-speaking world. One aspect of the Puritans' legacy that resonated through the years, however, was their emphasis on sound education. Harvard College was founded in Cambridge in 1636; 11 years later, Massachusetts law required towns comprised of more than 50 families to provide primary schooling for their children.

REVOLUTION!

The educated and independent colonists bristled under British control, especially when, beginning in 1763, Britain levied a series of heavy taxes designed to defray the cost of maintaining the Colonies. The Americans, deep in a recession, heartily resented the new taxes, especially since they had no one representing them in the British Parliament. The situation reached a boiling point in Massachusetts in the early 1770s.

Hostilities began in and around Boston with the Boston Massacre, the Boston Tea Party, and the Revolutionary War battles of Lexing-

▶ Cape Cod, *Martha's Vineyard (upper island), and Nantucket Island (lower island) were fishing and whaling centers in the 1600s.*

▶ **A lone harvester** collects cranberries in a flooded bog in Wareham. There are some 1,400 bogs in Massachusetts, and the state grows almost half of all the cranberries in the United States.

MASSACHUSETTS
TIME LINE

1498 John Cabot explores Massachusetts coast.

1620 Pilgrims land at Plymouth.

1623 First Thanksgiving is celebrated by Pilgrims.

1630 Puritans found Massachusetts Bay Colony at Boston.

1636 Harvard, the first college in the Colonies, is established.

1692 Twenty people are convicted of witchcraft and hanged at Salem Village.

1770 British soldiers kill five colonists during the Boston Massacre.

1773 Boston Tea Party protests British taxation.

1775 Revolutionary War begins at Lexington and Concord.

1788 Massachusetts becomes sixth state to enter the Union.

1796 John Adams of Massachusetts is elected the second U.S. president.

1824 John Quincy Adams is elected sixth U.S. president.

1831 William Lloyd Garrison publishes antislavery newspaper, *The Liberator*, in Boston.

1897 Country's first subway opens in Boston.

1942 Fire at Boston nightclub kills 492 people and spurs better fire laws across country.

1960 Senator John F. Kennedy is elected president.

1974–75 Racial violence breaks out in Boston over busing to integrate schools.

1980s Growth of computer industry boosts state's economy.

ton, Concord, and Bunker Hill, and it was Massachusetts men, such as Samuel Adams, John Hancock, and John Adams, who put their stamp on the political outcome of the war.

Boston's Freedom Trail, a linking of sites in and around the compact city center, highlights many of the shrines to the spirit of liberty that have survived these two and a quarter centuries. Here are the Old North Church, where lanterns were hung to signal to patriots the route the British were taking; Paul Revere's ancient wooden house (the oldest in Boston); the Old South Church, where Samuel Adams exhorted the Tea Party stalwarts; ancient graveyards bearing the remains of patriots

and Tories alike; and the U.S.S. *Constitution*, "Old Ironsides," which was launched during the War of 1812 and is now the oldest commissioned ship in the U.S. Navy.

SHIFTING INDUSTRIES

During the decades immediately following the Revolution, ships sailed from Massachusetts to points all over the globe. Those were the days of the legendary China Trade, dominated by Salem's merchant princes, who imported tea, silk, porcelain, and other luxury goods. Many beautifully preserved mansions built by the seaport's wealthy merchants still stand today.

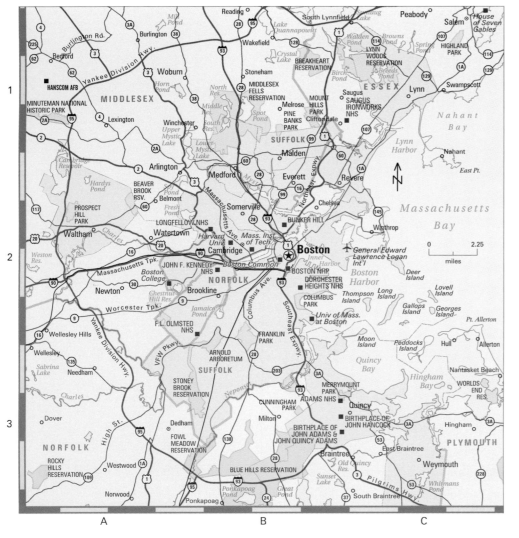

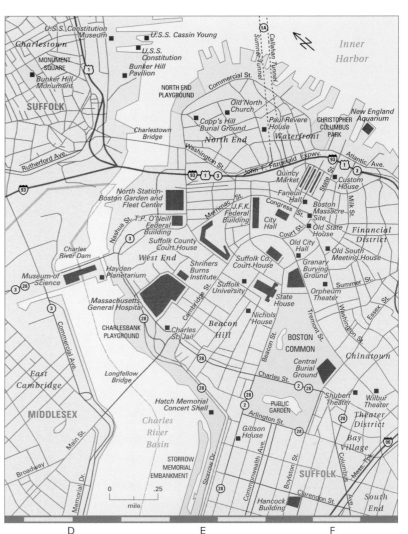

Constructed in the symmetrical Federal style, these splendid homes are a hallmark not only of Salem but of nearby Marblehead, a prosperous seafaring town whose harbor now bristles with the masts of sailing yachts. In New Bedford a whaling museum and the historic district that surrounds it commemorate the epic adventures of the real-life models for Herman Melville's *Moby Dick*.

Much of the profit earned by the sea traders and their Boston financiers was plowed into the great New England experiment of the early 19th century, the Industrial Revolution. Massachusetts entrepreneurs and inventors, millwrights and factory hands, turned the state into a hive of manufacturing: Springfield made small arms for the military; Brockton and Lynn turned out shoes; Amesbury produced carriages and hats; and Lawrence wove countless miles of woolen cloth. But Lowell remains the first of the state's industrial cities. This is where the waters of the Merrimack River were first used to power canalside textile mills. In more recent years, Massachusetts came to depend on high technology as an economic mainstay. Route 128, which girds the Boston suburbs from north to south, became nearly as well known a computer-industry icon as California's Silicon Valley.

FROM THE OCEAN TO THE MOUNTAINS

Fortunately, Massachusetts's ingrained sense of history and cooperative stewardship has resulted in the preservation of thousands of acres of open land, even in the heavily populated Boston area. From the scrub pine forests of Plymouth County to Cape Ann's granite crags and the barrier beaches of the North Shore, it is still possible to see the true lay of the land.

South and east of Boston, the lonely arc of land that the Pilgrims first saw has benefited from a farsighted measure of protection. The Outer Cape, made into the Cape Cod National Seashore by the federal government, is a place of sand, sea, and sky, scented with beach plum and bayberry, where gulls wheel above tidal pools and lighthouse beams pierce the ocean night. Even farther out at sea, the islands of Martha's Vineyard and Nantucket balance upper-crust exclusivity with vistas of open moorland, salt marsh, and towering bluffs.

Worcester, central Massachusetts's main population center and New England's second-largest city after Boston, is a busy educational center. In nearby Auburn, Robert Goddard pioneered rocket science. But central Massachusetts beyond Worcester is mostly a thinly populated forest, much of it farmland that became overgrown with hardwood trees after agriculture peaked and declined in these parts more than a century ago.

Beyond Springfield, the farms and suburbs of the Connecticut River valley yield to the high country and hill towns of the Berkshires. This has been resort territory since the Gilded Age—the grand summer homes of novelist Edith Wharton, sculptor Daniel Chester French, and diplomat Joseph Choate are all open to visitors—but today these gentle mountains are best known for their cultural connections, from the Jacob's Pillow dance and Berkshire Theatre festivals to the Boston Symphony Orchestra's annual festival at Tanglewood in Lenox.

HUB OF THE UNIVERSE

Literature has always been a staple in the state whose capital was once called the "Athens of America." Ralph Waldo Emerson, Nathaniel Hawthorne, Henry David Thoreau, and Louisa May Alcott all lived and worked in Concord, the center of the

▲ *Harvard University* in Cambridge, established in 1636. Two years after it was founded, Harvard opened the doors of its only building—a farmhouse in a cow pasture—to its first freshman class.

great flowering of American literature during the early and middle 19th century. Herman Melville wrote much of *Moby Dick* at Arrowhead, his home in the Berkshires (now restored and open to visitors). The Boston-Harvard orbit included poets Henry Wadsworth Longfellow and James Russell Lowell, historians Francis Parkman and William Prescott, and the doctor-poet-essayist Oliver Wendell Holmes, Sr., who coined the terms *Boston Brahmin* and *Hub of the Universe*—the latter originally referring to the State House on Beacon Hill but later to the city itself.

That Hub, that Athens, is a cultural treasure-house today. The Museum of Fine Arts, Harvard's Fogg and other art museums in nearby Cambridge, and the Isabella Stewart Gardner Museum—a Venetian palazzo built to house its quirky founder and her incomparable collections—are all priceless ornaments of a state that has counted John Singleton Copley, James McNeill Whistler, John Singer Sargent, Winslow Homer, and Edward Hopper among its scions or sometime residents.

Massachusetts's greatest jewel, perhaps, is the city of Boston. At its center, beneath the commercial towers that have shot up over the past few decades, this is still a walkable town with a fine sense of proportion. Within it, Beacon Hill is a tidy enclave bearing the unmistakable Federal stamp of Charles Bulfinch, who designed the brilliant gold-domed State House that stands at its crest. Nearby, the Back Bay, a Charles River marsh filled in during the late 19th century, still presents its straight-as-a-ruler rows of fine Victorian facades. Boston Common is well into its fourth century as just that, the city's common open space. Within its confines pedal-powered swan boats carry passengers around the lagoon in the Public Garden, the nation's oldest urban botanical park. All in all, Massachusetts resonates with the spirit of founding father John Winthrop—a spirit that cherishes tradition, fiercely guards its liberty, and always looks to the future.

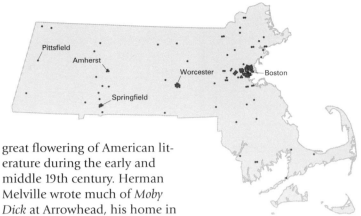

Higher Education in Massachusetts

Of the 257 colleges and universities in New England, 118 are in Massachusetts. The Boston area alone is home to many renowned schools, such as Harvard (1636), the Massachusetts Institute of Technology (1861), the Boston Conservatory (1867), Wellesley (1870), and Harvard's sister school, Radcliffe (1879). The western part of Massachusetts is the address of such schools as Amherst College (1821), the University of Massachusetts (1863), and two well-known women's colleges—Mount Holyoke (1837) and Smith (1871).

▼ *Oak Bluffs* on Martha's Vineyard, a 100-square-mile island, where the population swells from 14,000 to 70,000 in the summer.

▲ **Michigan's flag** shows a bald eagle, an elk, and a moose holding a shield that bears the Latin word Tuebor ("I will defend"). The flag was adopted in 1911.

STATE DATA
State bird: Robin
State flower: Apple blossom
State tree: White pine
State motto: *Si quaeris peninsulam amoenam, circumspice* (If you seek a pleasant peninsula, look about you)
State song (unofficial): "Michigan, My Michigan"
Abbreviations: Mich.; MI (postal)
Origin of the name: From the Chippewa word *michigama*, which means "great lake" or "large lake"
Nickname: Wolverine State

AREA AND SIZE
Total area: 58,216 sq. mi.
Rank within U.S.: 23
Extent: 455 mi. north–south; 400 mi. east–west
Highest elevation: Mount Arvon, 1,979 ft. above sea level
Lowest elevation: 572 ft. above sea level along Lake Erie

POPULATION
Total: 9,679,000
Rank within U.S.: 8
Ethnic breakdown: White: 80.5%; Black: 14.6%; Hispanic: 2.7%; Asian: 1.6%; Indian: 0.6%
Population density: 170.4 people per sq. mi.

CLIMATE

Average monthly temperature in Lansing
100°F / 80°F / 60°F / 40°F / 20°F / 0°F
J F M A M J J A S O N D

Average monthly precipitation in Lansing
10" / 8" / 6" / 4" / 2" / 0"
J F M A M J J A S O N D

Average monthly temperature in Sault Ste. Marie
100°F / 80°F / 60°F / 40°F / 20°F / 0°F
J F M A M J J A S O N D

Average monthly precipitation in Sault Ste. Marie
10" / 8" / 6" / 4" / 2" / 0"
J F M A M J J A S O N D

ECONOMY
Service industries: Banking, insurance, real estate, health care
Manufacturing: Transportation equipment, machinery
Agriculture: Corn, wheat, cherries
Mining: Natural gas, iron ore

▲ **Sleeping Bear Dunes National Seashore** stretches 35 miles along Lake Michigan's eastern coastline. Its striking landscape features steep, sandy slopes, rugged bluffs, and dense beech and maple forests. At right, tenacious visitors climb up and over the dunes.

Michigan

Four of the five Great Lakes—Michigan, Superior, Huron, and Erie—lap at the shores of Michigan; in fact, no point in the state is more than 85 miles from one lake or another. Separated by the 4½-mile-wide Straits of Mackinac, the state's two peninsulas are as distinct in character as the lakes that frame them. Poking eastward from Wisconsin, the Upper Peninsula is the more rugged of the two, a sparsely populated wilderness with long, snowbound winters and rocky terrain. The Lower Peninsula contains some of the Midwest's largest industrial centers, including Detroit, one of America's 10 most populous cities and home of the automobile industry.

LEGACY OF THE GLACIERS
Michigan was created some 15,000 years ago, when glaciers bulldozed their way across the upper Midwest, scooping out the lakes and then filling them in with meltwater. Long before Europeans appeared, the area was inhabited by Native Americans. Sustained by the abundant wildlife in the region's forests, Michigan's Algonquin Indian tribes—the Ottawa, the Chippewa, and the Potawatomi—built a thriving culture.

The first Europeans to arrive in Michigan and the upper Great Lakes came in the early 1600s. Étienne Brulé explored the Upper Peninsula in 1620, and French Jesuit missionary Jacques Marquette established the first permanent white settlement at Sault Ste. Marie in 1668. The vast majority of the early arrivals came in search of furs. Forging close trading ties with Michigan's Indians, French trappers transformed the region into a vital arm of the burgeoning French fur empire centered in Montreal. No significant attempts were made to establish more permanent settlements, however, until 1701, when Antoine de la Mothe Cadillac secured the support of French king Louis XIV to

found La Ville d'Etroit ("Village of the Strait") at the strategic narrows connecting Lakes Huron and Erie. Cadillac's town—Detroit—soon became a thriving commercial outpost and Michigan's largest city, a distinction it has retained for nearly 300 years.

EARLY CONFLICTS
The history of Michigan is a tale of shifting allegiances. Although French names still dot the map, French domination was brief, ending in 1763, when a British victory in the French and Indian War forced the French to cede Michigan, along with the rest of Canada and the Great Lakes, to their rivals in the New World. The transfer of power was anything but peaceful. Still loyal to their French trading partners, Michigan's Indians waged a fierce battle to push their new landlords out, attacking Great Lakes outposts all the way to western New York before the British could quell them.

During the American Revolution the tables were turned; this time the British, using their bases in Michigan to stage raids across the border in Ohio and in western Pennsylvania, encouraged Indian attacks on the American settlers. Although recognized as part of the United States at the end of the war, Michigan remained under British rule until 1796. The renewal of Anglo-American conflict in 1812 found the territory wide open to attack. Supported by the Indians, British forces took control of the area from Mackinac Island to Detroit. It was not until a year later that American naval victories on Lake Erie and the Thames River in Canada restored Michigan to the United States.

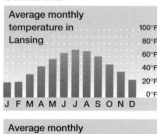

▲ **The Soo Locks,** which link Lake Superior with Lake Huron, serve approximately 5,000 ships a year.

Once the territory was back in American hands, settlement progressed rapidly. Steamships reached the upper Great Lakes in 1818, and the opening of New York's Erie Canal in 1825 quickened the pace of westward migration. Many of the territory's settlers were New Englanders, and today towns along the southern tier of the Lower Peninsula retain a decidedly Yankee appearance, with white clapboard houses and green town squares. Meanwhile, the logging of Michigan's virgin white pine, as well as the discovery of copper and iron ore in the Upper Peninsula, fueled boom times in the north.

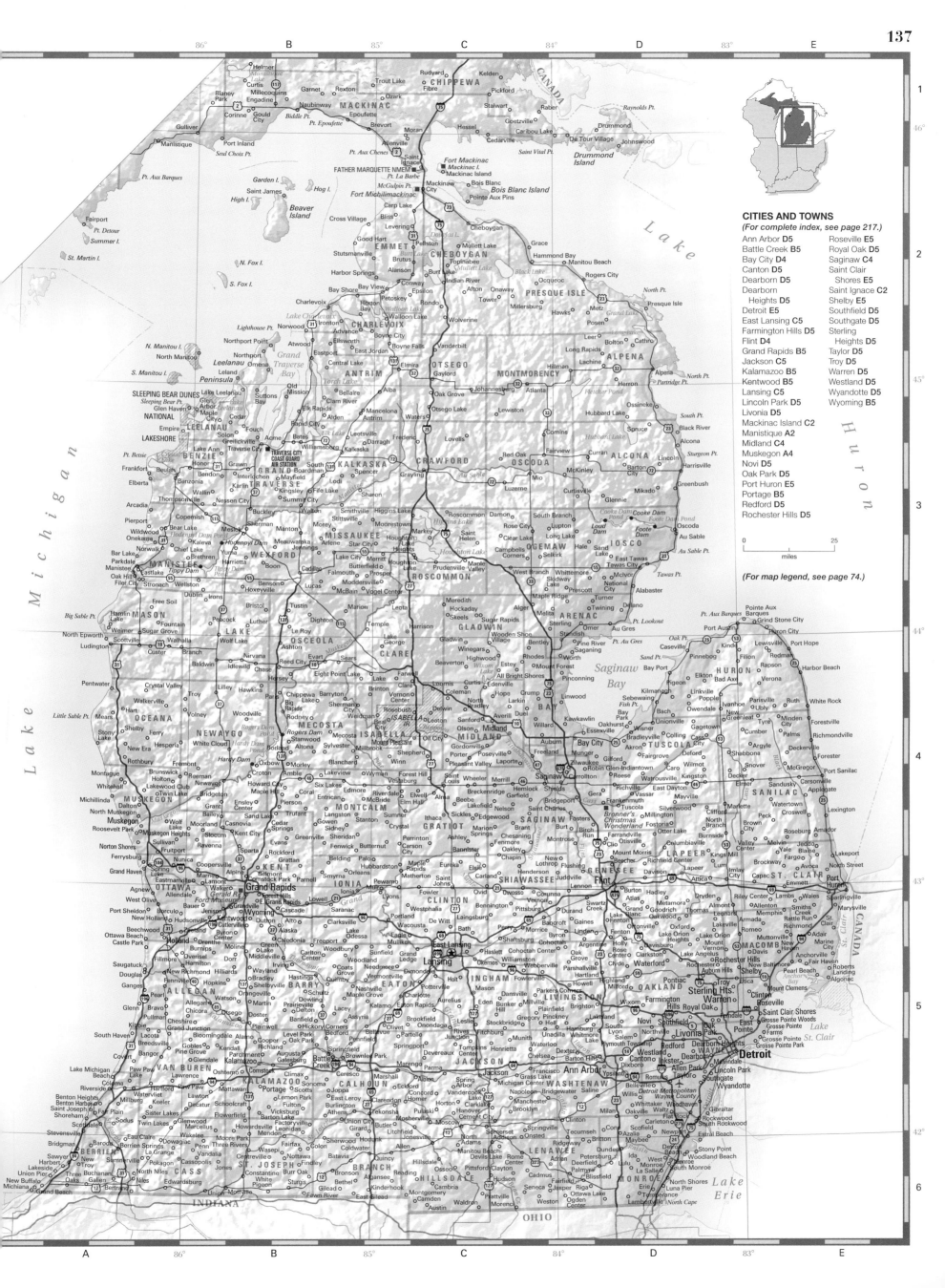

(For map legend, see page 74.)

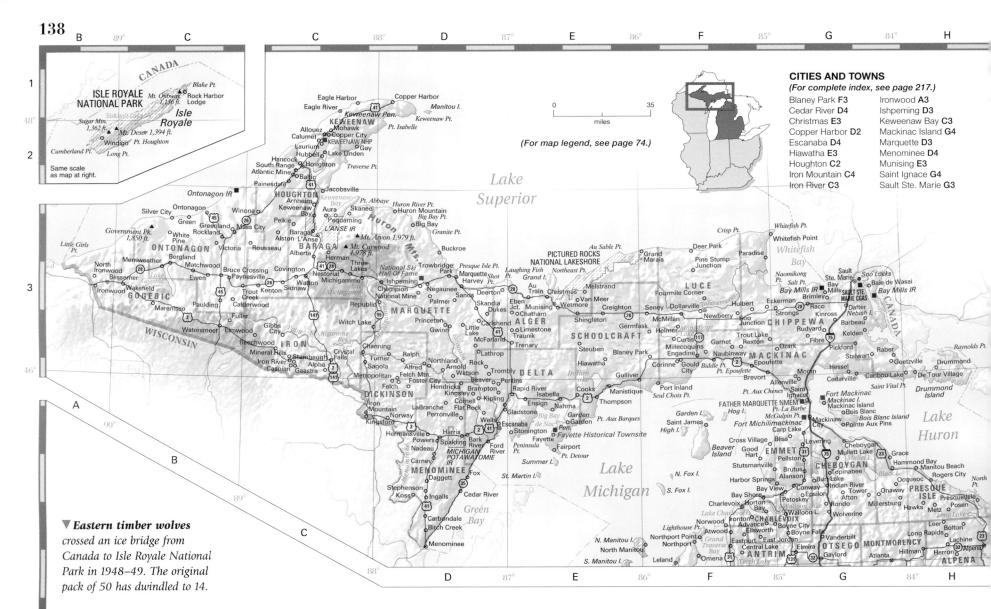

ISLE ROYALE NATIONAL PARK

CANADA

Mt. Ojibway 1,136 ft. • Blake Pt.
Rock Harbor Lodge
Isle Royale
Sugar Mtn. 1,362 ft. • *Mt. Desor 1,394 ft.*
Siskiwit Lake
Windigo • Pt. Houghton
Cumberland Pt. • Long Pt.

Same scale as map at right.

CITIES AND TOWNS
(For complete index, see page 217.)

Blaney Park **F3**
Cedar River **D4**
Christmas **E3**
Copper Harbor **D2**
Escanaba **D4**
Hiawatha **E3**
Houghton **C2**
Iron Mountain **C4**
Iron River **C3**

Ironwood **A3**
Ishpeming **D3**
Keweenaw Bay **C3**
Mackinac Island **G4**
Marquette **D3**
Menominee **D4**
Munising **E3**
Saint Ignace **G4**
Sault Ste. Marie **G3**

Lake Superior

Lake Huron

Lake Michigan

Green Bay

0   35
miles

(For map legend, see page 74.)

WISCONSIN

GOGEBIC   ONTONAGON   BARAGA   MARQUETTE   ALGER   SCHOOLCRAFT   LUCE   CHIPPEWA   MACKINAC

IRON   DICKINSON   DELTA   MENOMINEE   EMMET   CHEBOYGAN   PRESQUE ISLE

OTSEGO   MONTMORENCY   ALPENA   ANTRIM   CHARLEVOIX

▼ *Eastern timber wolves crossed an ice bridge from Canada to Isle Royale National Park in 1948–49. The original pack of 50 has dwindled to 14.*

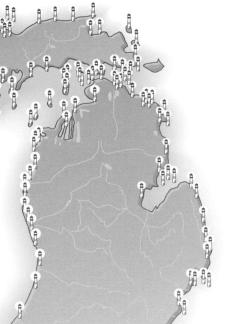

THE TOLEDO STRIP

Yet to be resolved was the issue of Michigan's borders; by 1834, the Michigan Territory comprised lands as far west as the Missouri River. Michigan's bid for statehood was complicated by a dispute with neighboring Ohio over its southern border, a patch of ground known as the Toledo Strip. Statehood for Michigan was further impeded by U.S. senators from Southern states, who were loath to upset the balance between slave states and free states. It took a federally engineered compromise to finally settle Michigan's borders and statehood status: Arkansas would be admitted as a slave state, Michigan as a free state; Ohio would retain the Toledo Strip, while, as compensation, Michigan would receive land, now known as the Upper Peninsula, shorn from the newly formed Wisconsin Territory. Michigan finally joined the Union on January 26, 1837, becoming the 26th state.

THE LOWER PENINSULA

The fur traders who first explored Michigan came by water, paddling their canoes south from the St. Lawrence River into Lake Huron. The route they followed would later be the source of the state's prosperity: although it is far inland, Michigan sits at the terminus of a vast intercoastal waterway that connects the industrial and natural resources of the middle American continent with the ocean—and the world.

The countryside the explorers found was, in many ways, not very different from the way it appears today. After decades of overlogging, nearly half of Michigan is once again covered by dense forest, thanks to managed reforestation programs. And the state's population remains heavily concentrated in the bottom half of the Lower Peninsula, south of an imaginary line running from Bay City to Muskegon. Although the region is less heavily dependent on agriculture than it was in the past, farms still fill in the wide-open spaces between towns, producing such traditional crops as corn and wheat, as well as beans, cucumbers, geraniums, Easter lilies, and bedding plants. Early settlers on the eastern shore of Lake Michigan discovered that the moderating effects of the lake's microclimate made the region ideal for growing fruit, and these days Michigan's orchards produce 80 percent of the nation's supply of red sour cherries, along with a high percentage of its apples, peaches, and blueberries.

Michigan's Many Lighthouses

Michigan's 116 lighthouses were built to mark harbors and to warn of danger zones on the Great Lakes. The first, the Fort Gratiot Light, was erected in Port Huron in 1825. Early beacons used wicks that were originally fueled by whale oil, then kerosene and acetylene. Later lamps were electric with metal reflectors and a Fresnel lens. Keepers, who lived in the lighthouses, lit and maintained the lights. Today all of Michigan's working lighthouses are automated.

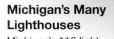

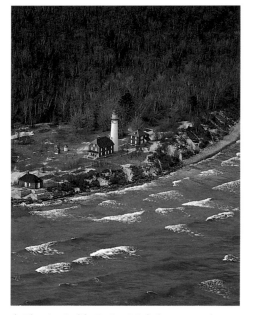

▲ *The Au Sable Point Lighthouse* on the Pictured Rocks National Lakeshore of Lake Superior has been in operation since 1874.

MOTOR CITY

Thanks to logging, mining, and the railroads, Detroit was already an industrial powerhouse by the time Henry Ford rolled out his first Model T in 1908. But the age of the automobile brought widespread and permanent changes to Michigan and the nation. While the rest of the country only drove cars, Michigan also made them—and for many years it made nearly all of them. More important even than the cars themselves was Ford's practical assembly-line technique, a revolution in manufacturing that had

The Grand Hotel on Mackinac Island offers views of Lake Huron and the Mackinac Bridge and showcases the longest veranda in the world.

ramifications for virtually every other industry. By 1925, Detroit's Big Three—Ford, Chrysler, and General Motors—had established themselves as the triumvirate of American automobile makers. To the state's already large working-class populations of Poles, Hungarians, Czechs, and Germans were added, in the huge plants around Detroit, vast numbers of African-Americans fleeing the Deep South in search of economic opportunity.

Henry Ford gave America the passenger car, but to Michigan he gave an industrial culture. Many towns and cities in the state have at least one factory, and working-class roots run deep, as does a long tradition of organized labor. Other major manufacturers in Michigan include Dow Chemical in Midland, Upjohn in Kalamazoo, and Kellogg, headquartered in Battle Creek, the self-proclaimed "cereal bowl of America."

THE RAVISHING NORTH

Far from the industrial anthills of southern Michigan, the Upper Peninsula (or the U.P., as Michiganders call it) is an altogether different world. Although it makes up a quarter of the state's total area, the U.P. is home to just 3 percent of its people, many of whom are descendants of the Scottish and Welsh miners and Finnish loggers who came here in the 19th century. The snowy, frigid winters of the Upper Peninsula are not for the faint of heart, but Michigan's northernmost tier more than makes up for such hardship with its dramatic scenery. Embraced by Lakes Huron and Michigan to the south and cold, stern Lake Superior to the north, the ore-rich hills of the U.P. are densely forested and laced with crystalline streams and nearly 150 waterfalls. Striking rock formations can be found on the north coast at Pictured Rocks National Lakeshore, a 50-mile strip where the lake meets the land in a playful arrangement of arches, caves, and multicolored cliffs. Popularized as the "shores of Gitche Gumee" in Longfellow's poem *The Song of Hiawatha*, the U.P. is a realm of Indian legends, tales of sunken ships swallowed whole by the lakes' rages, and mist-shrouded forests made hauntingly beautiful by the mournful cries of the eastern timber wolf.

MICHIGAN'S ISLANDS

Perhaps the most enchanting of all of Michigan's remote places are the islands of the Beaver Archipelago, which arcs

over the tip of the Lower Peninsula. Most of the islands are sparsely inhabited, if not altogether deserted. But two—Beaver Island, in upper Lake Michigan, and Mackinac (pronounced "Mackinaw") Island, overlooking the narrow strait that separates Michigan's peninsulas—are popular tourist resorts. The site of an 18th-century British fort, Mackinac Island later became one of the 19th century's most exclusive summertime colonies. From the island, you can see the Mackinac Bridge—a five-mile-long suspension bridge that connects the Upper and Lower peninsulas; but Mackinac itself remains resistant to modern technology: to preserve its Gilded Age character, cars are not allowed on the island.

Just 14 miles from the shores of Ontario, 45-mile-long Isle Royale is the largest island in Lake Superior and the only island national park in the country. Some 400 smaller islands surround it, guarding an interior of craggy ridges fringed by maple forest and cedar swamp and a home to large herds of moose. Protected by law, this distant wilderness outpost ensures that a portion of Michigan will always remain as it was before the trappers came—lake-linked, leafy, and lovely.

▶ *The annual Detroit-Windsor International Freedom Festival,* the world's largest trans-border celebration, commemorates Canada Day (July 1) and U.S. Independence Day (July 4).

▲ *Workers at the Ford factory* in Dearborn in 1928. Eighty-five percent of all the motor vehicles produced in the United States are still made by Michigan-based companies.

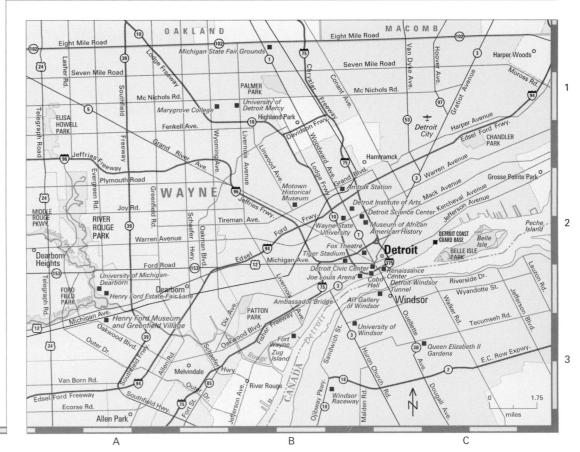

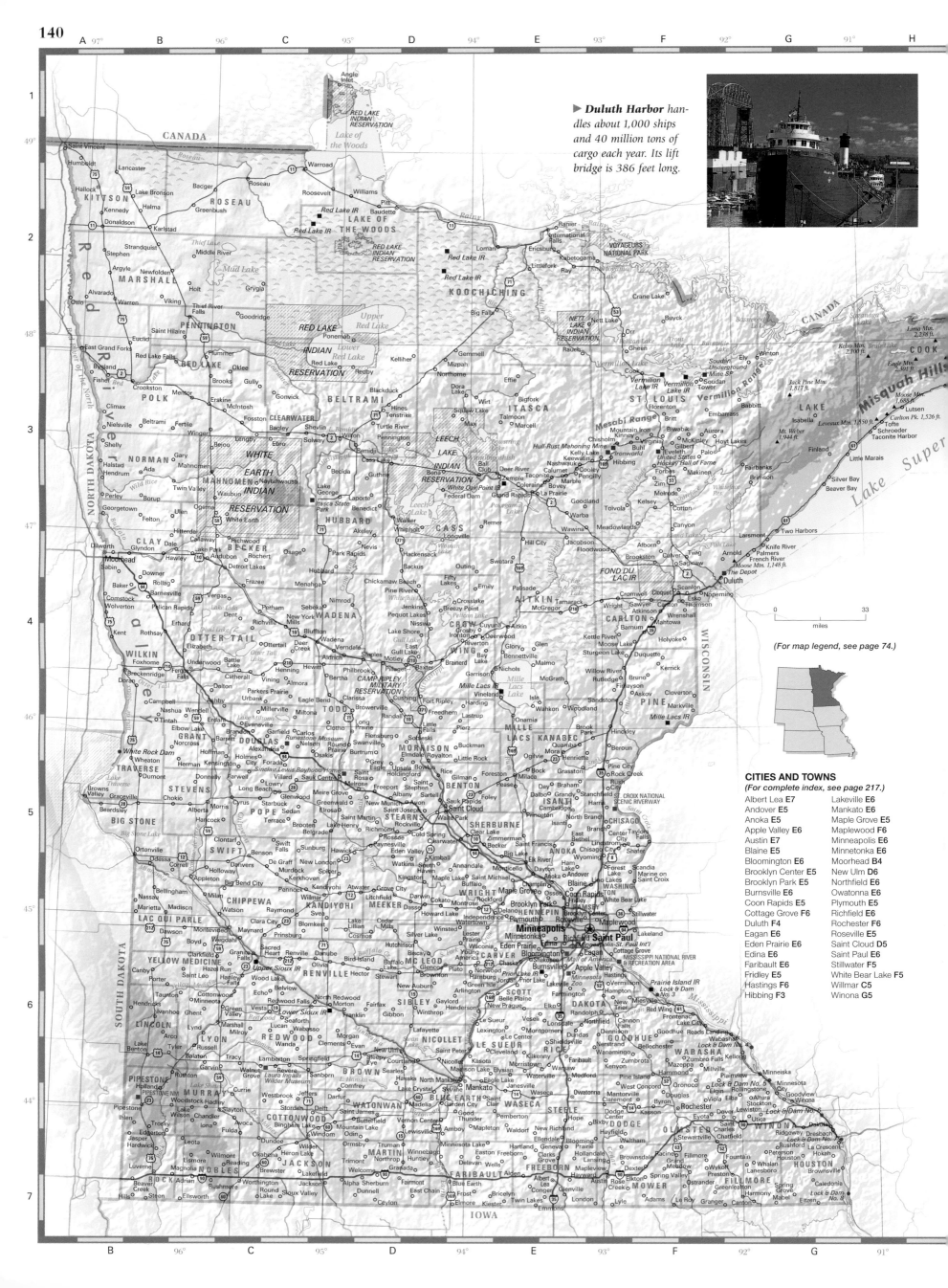

▶ *Duluth Harbor* handles about 1,000 ships and 40 million tons of cargo each year. Its lift bridge is 386 feet long.

(For map legend, see page 74.)

CITIES AND TOWNS
(For complete index, see page 217.)

Albert Lea E7	Lakeville E6
Andover E5	Mankato E6
Anoka E5	Maple Grove E5
Apple Valley E6	Maplewood F6
Austin E7	Minneapolis E6
Blaine E5	Minnetonka E6
Bloomington E6	Moorhead B4
Brooklyn Center E5	New Ulm D6
Brooklyn Park E5	Northfield E6
Burnsville E6	Owatonna E6
Coon Rapids E5	Plymouth E5
Cottage Grove F6	Richfield E6
Duluth F4	Rochester F6
Eagan E6	Roseville E5
Eden Prairie E6	Saint Cloud D5
Edina E6	Saint Paul E6
Faribault E6	Stillwater F5
Fridley E5	White Bear Lake F5
Hastings F6	Willmar C5
Hibbing F3	Winona G5

Minnesota

Long the most remote northern outpost of the American frontier, Minnesota has matured into a state whose economy makes excellent use of its natural resources, technological savvy, and cultural riches. An ever-increasing number of visitors are attracted to Minnesota's stunning scenery, friendly cities, and diverse attractions.

A SUCCESSION OF SETTLERS

For centuries the Dakota Indians were the sole occupants of Minnesota. Their first competitors for the land were the Ojibwa Indians, who had been displaced by whites from regions farther east. Then, in 1679, a French fur trader, Daniel Greysolon, Sieur Duluth (for whom the city of Duluth is named), claimed the territory in the name of the French king Louis XIV. He was probably the first white man to set foot in Minnesota. Following on Greysolon's heels in 1680 was a Belgian missionary, Father Louis Hennepin. He was exploring the upper Mississippi River, when some Dakota Indians captured him and took him to an area near what is now Minneapolis. Hennepin was the first white man to see (and name) the Falls of Saint Anthony, a 50-foot waterfall on the Mississippi River.

With the founding in 1819 of Fort Snelling, a military post at the confluence of the Mississippi and Minnesota rivers, the United States took control of Minnesota, the western portion of which it had gained in the Louisiana Purchase of 1803. Treaties with the Dakota and Ojibwa Indians over the next several years opened the area to settlers.

LAND OF LAKES

Minnesota's major attraction has always been its natural resources. The northern half of the state, which was formed by the advancing and retreating of a series of glaciers, is rich with lumber, iron ore, fish, and fur-bearing animals. It also contains most of Minnesota's more than 10,000 lakes, including Lake Itasca, the source of the Mississippi River.

In the Red River valley, in the northwestern part of the state at the edge of a prehistoric inland sea called Lake Agassiz, early farmers discovered that the soil—laced with rich topsoil called

▲ *Capital City Lights, a festival that runs from November through February, features 227,000 twinkling lights in Saint Paul's Rice Park.*

drift—was ideal for the cultivation of sugar beets, spring wheat, and potatoes. To the south, the glaciers had planed the land into fertile swaths well suited to the growing of corn and oats and the feeding of beef cattle and dairy cows.

INTO THE 20TH CENTURY

The settlement of Minnesota did not come without cost. Angered by the U.S. government's failure to live up to its promises, the Dakota Indians declared war on the United States in 1862, and the ensuing conflict was bloody. When the smoke had cleared, more than 500 settlers were dead, and most of the remaining Dakota were banished from the state.

By the end of the 19th century, settlers had claimed the best of the land. Saint Paul, a Mississippi River town, which was originally known as Pig's Eye Landing, grew into the state's center of finance, transportation, and government. Upriver, the lumber- and flour-milling village of Saint Anthony evolved into Minneapolis, a locus of trade and retailing. Duluth, situated at the western edge of Lake Superior—an amazing 2,400 miles inland from the Atlantic Ocean—became the busiest freshwater port in the United States.

Minnesota is a state of wild yet quiet charms. Some people travel to Alexandria to marvel at the intriguing Kensington Rune Stone, on which a 14th-century visit to Minnesota by the Vikings is said to be recorded; others venture to Cottonwood County to see the Jeffers petroglyphs—figures and designs carved into red quartzite by humans some 5,000 years ago. The Saint Paul Winter Carnival, the Minnesota State Fair, and the Guthrie Theater are just a few of the state's other attractions. Unlike Father Hennepin more than 300 years ago, today's visitors to the land of 10,000 lakes do not have to be forced to stay—Minnesota is hard to resist.

▲ *Bloomington's Mall of America has some 500 shops, 60 restaurants, and—for the hearty—nightclubs.*

▲ *The state flag, adopted in 1957, displays a version of the state seal. The seal shows an Indian, a man plowing, and a tree stump.*

STATE DATA

State bird: Common loon
State flower: Pink-and-white lady's slipper
State tree: Norway pine
State motto: *L'Etoile du nord* (The star of the north)
State song: "Hail! Minnesota"
Abbreviations: Minn.; MN (postal)
Origin of the name: From the Dakota Sioux language, meaning "sky-tinted water," which refers to the Minnesota River
Nicknames: North Star State, Gopher State, Land of 10,000 Lakes, Bread and Butter State, Land of Sky-Blue Waters

AREA AND SIZE

Total area: 84,068 sq. mi.
Rank within U.S.: 12
Extent: 407 mi. north–south; 360 mi. east–west
Highest elevation: Eagle Mountain, 2,301 ft. above sea level
Lowest elevation: 602 ft. above sea level along Lake Superior

POPULATION

Total: 4,830,000
Rank within U.S.: 20
Ethnic breakdown: White: 90.8%; Black: 3.1%; Asian: 2.8%; Hispanic: 2.0%; Indian: 1.3%
Population density: 60.9 people per sq. mi.

CLIMATE

Average monthly temperature in Minneapolis-Saint Paul
100°F 80°F 60°F 40°F 20°F 0°F
J F M A M J J A S O N D

Average monthly precipitation in Minneapolis-Saint Paul
10" 8" 6" 4" 2" 0"
J F M A M J J A S O N D

ECONOMY

Service industries: Finance, insurance, real estate
Manufacturing: Machinery, food products, printed materials
Agriculture: Milk, corn, soybeans, beef cattle, hogs
Mining: Iron ore

▲ *Moose Lake in the Boundary Waters Canoe Area Wilderness, a 3-million-acre sportsman's paradise and home to bears, elk, and deer.*

MINNESOTA TIMELINE

1679 Daniel Greysolon, Sieur Duluth, explores region near present-day Duluth.
1680 Louis Hennepin discovers Falls of Saint Anthony, where Minneapolis is now located.
1783 U.S. acquires eastern Minnesota from Great Britain as part of Treaty of Paris.
1803 Western Minnesota acquired as part of Louisiana Purchase.
1832 Henry Rowe Schoolcraft discovers the source of the Mis-

sissippi River at Lake Itasca.
1837 Land between Saint Croix and Mississippi rivers ceded by Sioux and Chippewa.
1849 Minnesota becomes a U.S. territory.
1851 Most of southern Minnesota ceded by Sioux Indians.
1858 Minnesota joins the Union as 32nd state.
1862 Thirty-nine Sioux are executed after Sioux rebellion.
1884 Iron ore is first shipped from

the Vermilion Range.
1889 Mayo Clinic is founded in Rochester.
1890 Huge iron-ore deposits are discovered in Mesabi Range.
1944 Democratic-Farmer-Labor Party is formed.
1959 Opening of Saint Lawrence Seaway makes Duluth westernmost Atlantic port.
1976 Minnesotan Walter Mondale is elected vice president under Jimmy Carter.

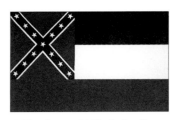

▲ *The bars of Mississippi's state flag,* adopted in 1894, are red, white, and blue—the national colors. The Confederate flag is displayed in the upper-left corner.

STATE DATA

State bird: Mockingbird
State flower: Magnolia
State tree: Magnolia
State motto: *Virtute et armis* (By valor and arms)
State song: "Go, Mississippi!"
Abbreviations: Miss.; MS (postal)
Origin of the name: From the Choctaw for "Father of Waters," referring to the Mississippi River, after which the state is named
Nickname: Magnolia State

AREA AND SIZE

Total area: 47,716 sq. mi.
Rank within U.S.: 32
Extent: 331 mi. north–south; 208 mi. east–west
Highest elevation: Woodall Mountain, 806 ft. above sea level
Lowest elevation: Sea level along the coast

POPULATION

Total: 2,816,000
Rank within U.S.: 31
Ethnic breakdown: White: 62.3%; Black: 35.9%; Asian: 0.7%; Hispanic: 0.7%; Indian: 0.3%
Population density: 59.5 people per sq. mi.

CLIMATE

Average monthly temperature in Jackson
100°F
80°F
60°F
40°F
20°F
0°F
J F M A M J J A S O N D

Average monthly precipitation in Jackson
10"
8"
6"
4"
2"
0"
J F M A M J J A S O N D

ECONOMY

Service industries: Automobile dealerships, restaurants, finance, insurance, real estate
Manufacturing: Food processing, transportation equipment, electrical equipment, wood products
Agriculture: Broiler chickens, beef and dairy cattle, cotton, soybeans, corn, grain sorghum, hay for livestock feed

▲ *Catfish farmers* (above) wade waist-high to harvest fish from a pond much like the ones in the delta town of Greenville (left). Annual sales of catfish rose from 192 million pounds in 1986 to 472 million pounds in 1996, greatly bolstering Mississippi's economy.

Mississippi

Like the river that shares its name, Mississippi takes its time. Slow to change, deeply traditional, and haunted by a rich and tragic history, Mississippi is in many ways the most quintessentially Southern of all the Southern states—a lush land of backwoods shanties and palatial plantations, of Old Man River and the Delta blues.

ON THE COASTAL PLAINS

Although Mississippi is low-lying, the state's topography is far from uniform. Instead, it features a mix of hills and prairies, forests and farmland. South and west of the Tennessee River Hills (the southernmost tier of the Appalachian Mountains, which cut across the state's northeastern corner) lies the Black Prairie, so named for the rich, dark soil that supports its abundant cotton and soybean crops. To the west, the Black Prairie is bordered by the Ponotoc Ridge and the North Central Hills.

A large part of southern Mississippi is covered by the Piney Woods, a hilly region that is the source of the bulk of Mississippi's wood products, a major industry in the state. Nearer the coast, the topography flattens again; this is the area known as the Coastal Meadows, a strip of sandy soil that divides the interior from the Gulf and the waterfronts of semitropical seaport towns like Biloxi, Gulfport, and Pascagoula.

OLD MAN RIVER

By far the state's most distinctive region can be found along its western border, where the Mississippi River casts its languid spell over the land. The delta region of Mississippi

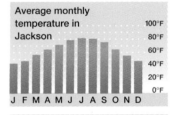

▲ *Stanton Hall* was built in Natchez in 1857. The home dates to an era when the city had more millionaires than any other place in America except New York.

is an ancient alluvial floodplain, left over from the last ice age, when the river was much wider. In those days, polar ice extended as far south as the middle of Missouri and Ohio; when the climate began to warm up and melt the ice, about 12,000 years ago, the Mississippi River served as the continent's drainpipe, carrying tons of sediment to the Gulf. By the time the current slowed, it had left behind great beds of silt and other nutrient-rich soil—and some of the South's most productive land.

Flat, treeless, and fertile, the elliptical delta extends roughly 160 miles south from the Tennessee border—or, as Nobel laureate and Mississippi native son William Faulkner wrote, "from the lobby of the Peabody Hotel in Memphis to Catfish Row in Vicksburg." At its widest, near Greenwood, it fills in the flat basin between the Mississippi and Yazoo rivers. Vulnerable to flooding, many a river town has been washed away. The Great Flood of 1927 left much of the delta under water; today, a network of dikes and levees controls the flow.

Although soybeans bring in more dollars to Mississippi these days, delta culture will always be cotton culture, as unhurried as the muddy river itself. Delta roots run deep. Many families can trace their ancestry back to the days of slaves and slave owners, and the landscape is littered with pointed reminders of the region's complex past. While white-columned mansions bespeak the near mythic luxuries of plantation life, lean-to shacks and sharecropper ghost towns testify to slavery's brutal legacy and the poverty that still exists. Most hauntingly, the strains of the delta blues—a melancholy music derived from slave spirituals and work songs—evoke the history and spirit of this unique place.

FROM SETTLEMENT TO CIVIL RIGHTS

Mississippi was discovered early, but it was settled late. The first European to set foot in the region was the Spanish conquistador Hernando de Soto, in 1540. Rather than the gold he hoped to find, he discovered the Mississippi River in 1541, stumbling upon it at a point just north of present-day Clarksdale. In 1699 the French established a permanent European presence in the region, building a fort near Biloxi, but the state's dense woods, snake-infested swamps, and large indigenous Indian population discouraged any significant white encroachment until the early 19th century.

The French cession of all territory east of the Mississippi River at the end of the French and Indian War opened the door to settlement, and the Mississippi Territory was established in 1798. From the start, Mississippi was a stratified society of

MISSISSIPPI TIMELINE

1540 Hernando de Soto of Spain explores Mississippi region.
1699 French establish settlement at Old Biloxi (Ocean Springs).
1763 England gains Mississippi in French and Indian War.
1775 Mississippi remains loyal to British crown in Revolution.
1817 Mississippi joins the Union as 20th state.
1858 Initiation of efforts to convert delta swamps to farmland.

1861 Mississippi secedes from the Union; joins Confederacy.
1870 Mississippi rejoins the Union.
1874 Seventy blacks are killed in Vicksburg race riot.
1927 Mississippi River floods, leaving 100,000 homeless.
1939 Petroleum is discovered at Tinsley and Vaughan.
1962 James Meredith becomes the first black to enroll at the

University of Mississippi.
1964 Three civil rights workers are killed near Philadelphia, Mississippi.
First nuclear-test explosion east of Mississippi River is set off in Baxtonville.
1969 Federal courts order desegregation of public schools. Charles Evers is elected first black mayor (Fayette) in Mississippi since Reconstruction.

haves and have-nots, and two inventions widened the gap profoundly: the cotton gin and, to a lesser extent, the steamboat. Able to process their harvest more efficiently and get it quickly to market, white planters prospered while much of the rest of Mississippi society was left far behind. By the 1840s, more than half of Mississippi's population was enslaved.

The Civil War brought wrenching changes to the state. The focus of Union campaigns in the West, Mississippi saw violent fighting, including the sieges of Vicksburg, Corinth, and Jackson. Federal troops crossed the state repeatedly, destroying much that lay in their path. By the cessation of hostilities, the state lay in ruins.

Following the Civil War, tenant farmers, or sharecroppers, replaced the slaves; but change came slowly, particularly in the area of civil rights. As a group, white Mississippians remained fiercely protective of a segregated social order. Many of the civil rights movement's most violent battles for equality were waged on Mississippi soil.

HOME AND HISTORY

In recent decades life in Mississippi has seen a shift, both economically and socially. The rigid racial boundaries that kept the state bitterly divided for so long are gone. A diversified economy has brought new opportunities to many Mississippians, who now find work in a variety of industries, from the manufacture of upholstered furniture to wood-products processing and space technology.

What has not changed—and doubtless never will—is Mississippi's deeply felt sense of home and history. Nearly 90 percent of Mississippians were born in the state, a statistic that testifies to its powerful hold on the people—and the imagination. Indeed, few states can boast such a pantheon of creative spirits to call its own: writers like Tennessee Williams, Eudora Welty, Richard Wright, and William Faulkner and musicians like Muddy Waters, B. B. King, and the king of rock and roll, Elvis Presley, a trucker's son born in a shotgun shack in Tupelo. Immortalized in story and song, blessed with abundant natural beauty, and always doggedly itself, Mississippi remains a unique and fascinating corner of America.

The Natchez Trace

The early settlers used flatboats to transport their products down the Mississippi River, then sold their boats for lumber and walked back home. Their arduous journey helped carve a clear path—the Natchez Trace—about 450 miles long. Today a parkway closely follows the early trace.

(For map legend, see page 74.)

CITIES AND TOWNS
(For complete index, see page 217.)

Baxterville C4	Columbia C4	Gulfport C5	Pascagoula D5
Biloxi D5	Corinth D1	Hattiesburg C4	Pearl B3
Brandon C2	Fayette A4	Indianola B2	Philadelphia C3
Clarksdale B1	Greenville A2	Jackson B2	Picayune C5
Cleveland B2	Greenwood B2	Laurel C4	Ridgeland B3
Clinton B3	Grenada C2	Long Beach C5	Southaven C1
		McComb B4	Starkville D2
		Meridian D3	Tinsley B3
		Moss Point D5	Tupelo D1
		Natchez A4	Vaughan B3
		Ocean Springs D5	Vicksburg B3
		Orange Grove C5	Yazoo City B3

▲ **The state flag,** *adopted in 1913, is red, white, and blue to symbolize loyalty to the Union. The coat of arms in the center is circled by 24 stars, showing Missouri's status as the 24th state.*

STATE DATA
State bird: Bluebird
State flower: Hawthorn
State tree: Flowering dogwood
State motto: *Salus populi suprema lex esto* (The welfare of the people shall be the supreme law)
State song: "Missouri Waltz"
Abbreviations: Mo.; MO (postal)
Origin of the name: Named after the Missouri Indians. *Missouri* means "town of the large canoes."
Nicknames: Show Me State; Bullion State, Cave State, Lead State, Mother of the West, Ozark State

AREA AND SIZE
Total area: 69,686 sq. mi.
Rank within U.S.: 19
Extent: 319 mi. north–south; 365 mi. east–west
Highest elevation: Taum Sauk Mountain, 1,772 ft. above sea level
Lowest elevation: 230 ft. above sea level, along the St. Francis River near Cardwell

POPULATION
Total: 5,540,000
Rank within U.S.: 17
Ethnic breakdown: White: 85.6%; Black: 11.2%; Hispanic: 1.6%; Asian: 1.1%; Indian: 0.4%
Population density: 80.2 people per sq. mi.

CLIMATE

Average monthly temperature in St. Louis
100°F 80°F 60°F 40°F 20°F 0°F
J F M A M J J A S O N D

Average monthly precipitation in St. Louis
10" 8" 6" 4" 2" 0"
J F M A M J J A S O N D

ECONOMY
Service industries: Community, business, and personal services; tourism; data-processing services
Manufacturing: Transportation equipment, chemicals, food processing, beer brewing
Agriculture: Beef cattle, hogs, turkeys, soybeans, corn, cotton, hay, apples, peaches, grapes

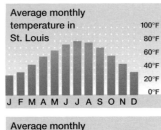

▲ **The Gateway Arch** *in Saint Louis, the highest freestanding arch ever built, symbolizes Missouri's early role as the gateway to the West.*

Missouri

Once known as the "Mother of the West," Missouri was the place from which homesteaders and gold rushers set off to seek their fortunes along the Oregon and Santa Fe trails. Many of those who came, however, settled here instead, enticed by the state's bountiful waters, abundant resources, and unexpected natural splendor.

LAND OF FLOWING WATERS
For thousands of years Missouri has lured visitors by means of its major waterways—the Missouri and Mississippi rivers. The first people to settle in the area, possibly as early as 20,000 years ago, were the mound builders. By the time the first Europeans—Father Jacques Marquette and Louis Jolliet—arrived in 1673, the Mound Builders were long gone, replaced by Missouri, Fox, Shawnee, and Osage Indians.

Indian tales shared with the European visitors told of gold, silver, and furs for the taking. These stories soon drew many fortune seekers, and although only lead and salt were found, these substances were worth their weight in gold in the 18th century. In 1735 miners and trappers established the first permanent European settlement, Ste. Genevieve on the Mississippi River.

By the early 1800s opportunity seekers were arriving in droves. Although the new settlers were mainly Northerners, the territory's leadership was dominated by slaveholders, whose cotton plantations thrived along the Missouri River. In 1818 the state petitioned for admission to the Union as a slave state, spurring the first clash between North and South that would lead to the Civil War. The conflict was defused, for a time, by the Missouri Compromise of 1820, which allowed for the practice of slavery.

Thomas Jefferson described the pro- and anti-slavery furor as "a fireball in the night." When the explosion finally came with the start of the Civil War, Missouri sent 110,000 sons to fight for the North and 30,000 to fight for the South; it is the only state in which Confederate and Union dead are buried side by side.

The end of the war did not mark the end of violence, as many former Confederate soldiers turned to lives of crime. Missouri was at the mercy of these outlaws, who held up stagecoaches, banks, and trains. In

Missouri's Floodplain
Low-lying land and overflowing waters from the Mississippi, Missouri, and Ohio rivers combine to create the floodplains of southeastern Missouri, part of the Mississippi Alluvial Plain.

1881 Gov. Thomas Crittenden put a $5,000 bounty on the heads of the notorious outlaws Jesse and Frank James. For 15 years Jesse and his older brother had been pulling off heists and eluding justice, becoming Wild West legends. Ironically, Jesse did not go out in a blaze of glory during a holdup. A year after the bounty was announced, Jesse was adjusting a picture on his parlor wall when he was shot in the head by Robert Ford, a member of his own gang, who wanted to collect the reward money.

GATEWAY TO WEALTH
Lying at the center of the continental United States, Missouri became the last outpost of civilization for those seeking their fortunes in the West. Kansas City, St. Louis, and many smaller towns grew rich by meeting the travelers' needs, which included everything from covered wagons and corncob pipes to mail service. The first Pony Express rider left St. Joseph, Missouri, on April 3, 1860, for San Francisco, California; this innovative relay mail service became indelibly stamped on the American psyche as a major chapter in the story of the Wild West.

Missourians have retained their knack for capitalizing on dreams of the unconquered frontier. Both the Mercury and the Gemini program space capsules were built here. Tourism is the state's second-largest industry. And although farming contributes very little, comparatively, to Missouri's wealth, you wouldn't know it to drive through most of the landscape. The northern glacial plains, western Osage plains, and table-flat Bootheel region in the far southeast corner are almost entirely given over to agriculture. Purebred livestock, soybeans, corn, hay, and cotton are the most common crops.

Increasing numbers of travelers are attracted to Missouri's bustling cities and quiet Ozark Mountain retreats. Kansas City and St. Louis, locked in a rivalry, compete to offer the best ribs, tunes, and riverside delights. Kansas City is somewhat larger,

▲ **The Bird Baths** *in Elephant Rocks State Park in Missouri's Ozarks. Dumbo, the largest of the boulders at the back, weighs 680 tons and is about 1.2 billion years old.*

but St. Louis has the Gateway Arch, a 630-foot-high stainless steel monument to the pioneers who passed this way.

In the Ozarks, which embrace most of the southern half of Missouri, deep ravines make these ancient hills unsuitable for little more than peaceful contemplation. But happily for vacationers, many of the region's 10,000 springs have been dammed for flood control, creating a water-recreation mecca. The Lake of the Ozarks, which attracts more than 3.2 million visitors a year, has a longer shoreline than the entire state of California. Traditional bluegrass music and native mountain crafts pique the interest of other visitors. And, of course, there's always Branson. With its country music/comedy show center that started out 30 years ago with two homegrown acts—Presley's Jubilee and the Baldknobbers Jamboree Show—Branson is one of America's top tourist attractions.

THE POWER OF NATURE

The most powerful earthquake in this nation's recorded history, measuring an estimated 8 on the Richter scale, occurred in New Madrid (pronounced MAD-rid), Missouri, in 1811–12. Amazingly, the tremors and aftershocks lasted for nearly two years. It was almost certainly more powerful than the San Francisco quake of 1906, but only a few hearty pioneers were around to be affected in the New Madrid region.

Missourians are repeatedly made aware that nature can be unpredictable. Floods are a way of life in a place laced with more rivers, springs, and streams than any other state. But even its massive flood-control systems are no match for the Mississippi River when it changes course. The flood of 1993, which caused hundreds of miles of dikes to burst, proved to Missourians once again that nature can never be completely controlled.

Exploring Missouri will reveal natural wonders around every bend of the road. In fact, some parts of the state are so unusual that they are almost unbelievable. For instance, there's room for 300 cars in one of the towering chambers in the Ozarks' Meramec Caverns—just the kind of Missouri superlative that must have helped inspire the state's famous slogan: "I'm from Missouri. You'll have to show me."

▲ *Country Tonite is one of the more than three dozen theaters in Branson that offer shows morning, noon, and night. The area draws about 5 million visitors each year.*

CITIES AND TOWNS
(For complete index, see page 217.)

Affton **F3**	Hannibal **E2**
Arnold **F3**	Independence **B2**
Belton **B3**	Jefferson City **D3**
Blue Springs **B2**	Joplin **B4**
Branson **C5**	Kansas City **B2**
Cape	Liberty **B2**
Girardeau **G4**	Melhville **F3**
Chesterfield **F3**	New Madrid **G5**
Columbia **D3**	O'Fallon **F3**
Festus **F3**	Raytown **B3**
Florissant **F3**	St. Charles **F3**
Gladstone **B2**	Ste. Genevieve **F4**
Grandview **B3**	St. Joseph **B2**
	St. Louis **F3**
	St. Peters **F3**
	Sedalia **C3**
	Sikeston **G5**
	Spanish Lake **F3**
	Springfield **C4**
	University City **F3**
	Webster
	Groves **F3**

MISSOURI
TIME LINE

1673 Marquette and Jolliet explore mouth of Missouri River.

1682 Robert Cavelier, sieur de La Salle, claims area for France.

c. 1735 Ste. Genevieve is first permanent white settlement.

1803 U.S. gains Missouri as part of Louisiana Purchase.

1804 Lewis and Clark leave St. Louis to travel westward.

1811–12 Three massive earthquakes rock part of Missouri.

1812 Missouri is made a territory.

1815 Indian raids on Missouri settlements end with treaty.

1821 Missouri becomes slave state under Missouri Compromise of 1820.

1837 With Platte Purchase, the state gains six counties.

1857 Dred Scott decision in Missouri escalates slavery crisis.

1860 Pony express service begins in St. Joseph.

1882 Jesse James is killed by Robert Ford at St. Joseph.

1890 First modern skyscraper is designed in St. Louis.

1904 Louisiana Purchase Exposition opens in St. Louis.

1927 Charles Lindbergh of St. Louis makes first solo flight across Atlantic.

1931 Bagnell Dam is built, forming the Lake of the Ozarks.

1945 Harry S. Truman of Independence becomes president.

1965 Gateway Arch is completed in St. Louis.

1983 Dioxin contaminates Times Beach; residents move out.

1988 Severe drought causes major river transport problems.

(For map legend, see page 74.)

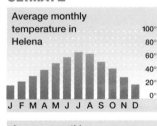

MONTANA

▲ **The state flag,** adopted in 1905, bears the state seal. Mountains and the Great Falls of the Missouri River symbolize Montana's terrain. The pick and shovel and the plow represent mining and agriculture.

STATE DATA

State bird: Western meadowlark
State flower: Bitterroot
State tree: Ponderosa pine
State motto: *Oro y plata* (Gold and silver)
State song: "Montana"
Abbreviations: Mont.; MT (postal)
Origin of the name: From the Spanish word meaning "mountainous"
Nicknames: Treasure State, Big Sky Country, Mountain State

AREA AND SIZE

Total area: 147,138 sq. mi.
Rank within U.S.: 4
Extent: 321 mi. north–south; 559 mi. east–west
Highest elevation: Granite Peak, 12,799 ft. above sea level
Lowest elevation: 1,800 ft. above sea level along the Kootenai River in Lincoln County

POPULATION

Total: 950,000
Rank within U.S.: 44
Ethnic breakdown: White: 90.6%; Indian: 6.2%; Hispanic: 2.1%; Asian: 0.7%; Black: 0.3%
Population density: 6.5 people per sq. mi.

CLIMATE

Average monthly temperature in Helena

100°F
80°F
60°F
40°F
20°F
0°F

J F M A M J J A S O N D

Average monthly precipitation in Helena

10"
8"
6"
4"
2"
0"

J F M A M J J A S O N D

ECONOMY

Service industries: Health care, real estate, education, trade, tourism
Agriculture: Beef cattle, wheat, barley, hay, black cherries, beets
Mining: Coal, petroleum, gold, silver, copper, lead, talc, vermiculite
Manufacturing: Lumber and wood products, food processing

Montana

The seemingly endless dry plains and forbidding glacial mountains that stretch 550 miles across the state still bear the mark of the frontier days. Yet Montanans have turned their greatest challenge—the land—into their greatest asset, pumping out billions of dollars in precious minerals and putting more land under the hoe than any other state except Texas. Despite this development, long stretches of roadless prairie and icy peaks untouched by humans remain—Montana's most memorable monuments.

BIG SKY COUNTRY

Stark, rugged, and beautiful, Montana is a remote wilderness. Solemn badlands press against the eastern border of the state, where wind and water have eaten away at the land, leaving a moonscape of shallow gullies and stone columns. In the east, farmers and ranchers share the northern reaches of the Great Plains, a vast rolling sea of amber wheat fields and brittle prairie grasses, domed, according to American writer Wallace Stegner, by "the biggest sky anywhere." As the prairie rolls west, a few isolated mountain ranges break the horizon, foreshadowing the massive sheets of bare rock that form the Front Range of the Rockies.

Some 40 mountain ranges crowd the western third of Montana, with peaks reaching almost 13,000 feet high. To the north, straddling the Continental Divide, Glacier National Park shelters mountains so steep and icy that no one has climbed them. Those who scale the more hospitable peaks experience dramatic climatic changes as they ascend. From the valleys up, the mountain landscape evolves from grassland to deciduous forest, coniferous forest, alpine tundra, and finally glacial ice.

▲ **Rugged, sky-high peaks** form part of the Continental Divide in Glacier National Park.

A WILD BUT PROFITABLE LAND

Meriwether Lewis and William Clark traveled up the Missouri River and into this unpredictable land in the summer of 1805, during their journey to the Pacific Ocean. In the great northern plains, they found a confluence of Indian cultures, where the Crow, Cheyenne, Blackfeet, Assiniboin, Flatheads, and Kutenai all hunted vast herds of buffalo. Guided by a French-Canadian interpreter and his Shoshone wife, Sacagawea (also called Sakakawea), the explorers crossed the Continental Divide, reached the Pacific, and then returned to report that the area was "richer in beaver and otter than any country on earth." Their optimism helped lure British, Canadian, and American

fur traders, and served up the watchword for the settlement of the Rocky Mountain West: *exploitation.* Until the late 19th century, most people arrived in Montana to get rich quick: there were pelts to sell back east, precious minerals to wrest from the cliffs, and fields of grass on which to fatten their cattle.

Teeming with mountain men, gold hunters, and cowboys, Montana became a hotbed of frontier barbarism. Prospectors arrived on the heels of a gold strike in 1862, launching the raucous boomtowns of Helena, Virginia City, and Bannack. Corrupt sheriffs presided over the cities, while bandits, known as road agents, prowled the countryside to prey on traveling miners. The miners fought back, and in one confrontation early in 1864, they hanged an outlaw sheriff named Henry Plummer and 20 other renegades. Montana ranchers had similar methods. Their own vigilantes killed 35 supposed cattle thieves in 1884. It just so happened that many of the unfortunate men were legitimate small ranchers competing for land coveted by the big cattle companies.

A LOST WAY OF LIFE

But the true losers were the Indians, whose hunting grounds were swallowed up by miners and cattle. In June 1876 the warriors of the northern plains fought their last great battle at Montana's Little Bighorn River, annihilating 210 men under Lt. Col. George Custer's command, including Custer himself. Divided by tribal loyalties and differing stances on their grim future, however, the tribes split up and were assigned to reservations. The following year, Chief Joseph led 900 Nez Perce in

MONTANA TIMELINE

1743 France's La Vérendrye brothers reach the "Shining Mountains" of Montana.

1803 U.S. buys eastern Montana as part of Louisiana Purchase.

1805–06 Lewis and Clark explore region while traveling to and from Pacific Ocean.

1807 Manuel Lisa builds fur-trading post at mouth of Yellowstone and Bighorn rivers.

1846 U.S. gains northwestern Montana in treaty with England.

1862 Thousands of prospectors flock to Grasshopper Creek when gold is discovered.

1864 Montana becomes a territory.

1876 Sioux and Cheyenne Indians defeat Custer's troops in Battle of Little Bighorn.

1877 Chief Joseph and the Nez Perce Indians surrender to federal troops.

1880 Railway line enters Montana.

1889 Montana becomes 41st state.

1940 Fort Peck Dam, nation's largest earth-filled hydraulic dam, is completed.

1951 Production from oil wells begins in eastern Montana.

1975 Libby Dam, which created 90-mile-long Lake Koocanusa, begins operation.

1983 The once-lucrative Anaconda Copper Company closes after a century of production.

a flight through Montana toward Canada. Just three days from the Canadian border, he surrendered to the U.S. Cavalry.

With Chief Joseph's surrender, the frontier began to wither. By 1887 the northern bison herd, having been hunted down or lost in the blizzard of that year, had been reduced to a few stragglers, and barbed wire fenced in the open range. Huge copper and silver deposits discovered in Butte launched another mineral boom, tripling Montana's population between 1880 and 1890.

EXPLOITATION VERSUS APPRECIATION

If the frontier mentality can be divided into two impulses—the desire to exploit the wilderness on the one hand and to appreciate it on the other—then Montana is a state divided. Open-pit mining has made Butte into a Superfund site, targeted for toxic-waste cleanup. The search for oil and gas is carving huge chunks out of the Front Range, while coal mines mar the prairies between the Bighorn and the Powder rivers. All of this activity has sparked an angry response from other Montanans, who also battle with mining interests over scarce water reserves. They were joined by environmentalists in the early 1970s and engineered the passage of some of the

nation's strictest conservation laws, clamping down on water use, reclaiming old mined land, and cleaning up air pollution.

In the end, it may be tourism that provides the biggest counterweight to rampant development. Montana's pristine wilderness draws some 8 million visitors to the state every year. Many dude ranches trace their histories back to the 1920s, when drought-ridden ranches saved themselves by moonlighting as vacation spots. For many American city dwellers, these ranches are the gateway to the old frontier world.

(For map legend, see page 74.)

CITIES AND TOWNS

(For complete index, see page 217.)

◄ *American buffalo graze peacefully at the National Bison Range—an 18,541-acre refuge that opened in 1909 in Moiese.*

Nebraska

▲ **Nebraska's flag,** adopted in 1925, bears the state seal. The seal displays a smith with a hammer and anvil; a settler's cabin, wheat, and corn; and a steamboat on the Missouri River and a train. These symbolize the mechanical arts, agriculture, and transportation. In the background are the Rocky Mountains.

STATE DATA

State bird: Western meadowlark
State flower: Goldenrod
State tree: Cottonwood
State motto: Equality before the law
State song: "Beautiful Nebraska"
Abbreviations: Nebr. or Neb.; NE (postal)
Origin of the name: From the Oto Indian word *nebrathka* ("flat water"), referring to the Platte River
Nicknames: Cornhusker State, The Tree Planter State, Beef State, Antelope State, Bug-Eating State

AREA AND SIZE

Total area: 77,227 sq. mi.
Rank within U.S.: 15
Extent: 206 mi. north–south; 462 mi. east–west
Highest elevation: 5,426 ft. above sea level in southwestern Kimball County
Lowest elevation: 840 ft. above sea level in Richardson County

POPULATION

Total: 1,705,000
Rank within U.S.: 38
Ethnic breakdown: White: 90.3%; Black: 4.1%; Hispanic: 3.6%; Asian: 1.2%; Indian: 0.8%
Population density: 22.3 people per sq. mi.

CLIMATE

Average monthly temperature in Lincoln
100°F / 80°F / 60°F / 40°F / 20°F / 0°F
J F M A M J J A S O N D

Average monthly precipitation in Lincoln
10" / 8" / 6" / 4" / 2" / 0"
J F M A M J J A S O N D

ECONOMY

Service industries: Insurance, real estate, telemarketing, engineering
Manufacturing: Food processing, machinery, scientific and medical instruments
Agriculture: Corn, soybeans, beef cattle, hogs

▶ **Fossilized remains** of ancient animals have been found in 90 of Nebraska's 93 counties. These 10-million-year-old rhinoceros fossils were uncovered in 1981.

Straddling the invisible border between the Midwest's farmlands and the Great Plains, Nebraska runs west from the Missouri River in a wide expanse of fields and grasslands. Initially believed to have a climate too hostile for cultivation, today America's "Cornhusker State" feeds millions while proudly touting its pioneer heritage.

FARMS AND RANCH LANDS

At first glance, Nebraska may appear to be one giant agricultural machine stretching from border to border. But a closer look reveals subtle differences in the landscape, climate, and topography. The eastern part of the state, where about two-thirds of Nebraskans live, is virtually indistinguishable from neighboring Iowa and Missouri—flat, fertile, and nearly 100 percent cultivated. Some 95 percent of the land is used for farming or ranching, more than in any other state. Here, adequate moisture nourishes huge crops of wheat, oats, and the state's number one crop, corn.

Somewhere in the middle of Nebraska, though, a change occurs. The average annual rainfall dips below 20 inches—considered the minimum for large-scale farming without extensive irrigation—and the landscape opens to breathtaking vistas. With every passing mile, walls of tall corn and billowing wheat fields yield to semiarid grasslands and the pale hills of the western plains. The change is cultural, too. Farmers' caps are replaced by Stetsons, combines by cattle. There is no doubt that, in both fact and attitude, somewhere in Nebraska the West begins.

"A MILE WIDE AND AN INCH DEEP"

Nebraska takes its name from the Oto Indian word *nebrathka*, meaning "flat water," the name these early residents gave to the slow, wide river that runs across the state. And flat it was: before it was dammed and regulated for agricultural purposes, the Platte, as French fur traders aptly redubbed it, was said to be "a mile wide and an inch deep." Early settlers joked that the Platte's chocolate-pudding muddiness was due to the fact that it flowed upside down.

The Plains Indians handily navigated the Platte in shallow boats, but the first white explorers in the area found it useless as a navigable waterway. What the Platte floodplain region offered instead was the shade of cottonwood trees—a rare luxury on the open plain—and a ready source of water. By the 1840s, however, the Platte had become a natural highway through the region, used by pioneers, prospectors, and Pony Express riders as they traveled the Oregon and Mormon trails to destinations in California, Oregon, and Utah. In all, some 350,000 people traversed the Platte River valley between 1840 and 1866. In many spots along the river, deep ruts remain, carved by the wheels of thousands of covered wagons.

THE GREAT AMERICAN DESERT

Early travelers knew the Great Plains by a different name: the "Great American Desert." Discouraged by tales of hostile Indians, crop-devouring grasshoppers, deadly tornadoes, and torrential floods, few people were tempted to linger in the area. It wasn't until 1862, when the Homestead Act was passed, that Nebraska's bad reputation was dispelled. Tempted by cheap land, settlers from Eastern states began to pour in, their numbers swelled by immigrants from Eastern and Northern Europe. The life they found was harsh, but worth the struggle. By 1890 virtually all of Nebraska had been carved into homesteads despite fierce resistance by the Pawnee, Sioux, and Cheyenne tribes.

▲ **Nebraska's cornfields** make up approximately a third of the state's cultivated acreage.

CITY LIFE

When Nebraskans speak of "the cities," they mean just two places: Omaha and Lincoln, both located in eastern Nebraska near the Iowa border. Originally a jumping-off point for steamboat traffic down the Missouri River, Omaha remains a center of transportation, as well as a regional leader in meat packing, finance, insurance, and food processing. Only 60 miles southwest, the capital city of Lincoln is strikingly different. Just a third of Omaha's size,

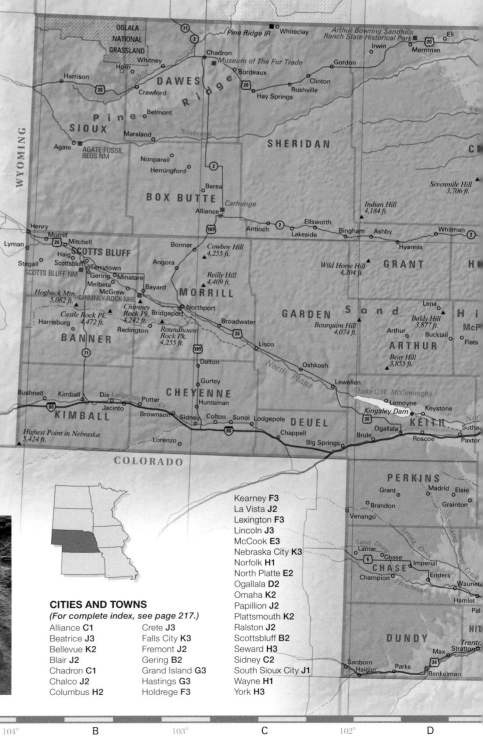

CITIES AND TOWNS
(For complete index, see page 217.)

Alliance **C1**	Crete **J3**	Kearney **F3**
Beatrice **J3**	Falls City **K3**	La Vista **J2**
Bellevue **K2**	Fremont **J2**	Lexington **F3**
Blair **J2**	Gering **B2**	Lincoln **J3**
Chadron **C1**	Grand Island **G3**	McCook **E3**
Chalco **J2**	Hastings **G3**	Nebraska City **K3**
Columbus **H2**	Holdrege **F3**	Norfolk **H1**
		North Platte **E2**
		Ogallala **D2**
		Omaha **K2**
		Papillion **J2**
		Plattsmouth **K2**
		Ralston **J2**
		Scottsbluff **B2**
		Seward **H3**
		Sidney **C2**
		South Sioux City **J1**
		Wayne **H1**
		York **H3**

A 104°   B 103°   C 102°   D

Lincoln was founded in 1867, when it stood at the very edge of the Western frontier, and became the new state's capital. Although its population—about 200,000—makes it a giant by Nebraskan standards, Lincoln retains the unassuming feel of a small town, wrapped by corn and wheat fields that push right up to the city's edges.

Like that of most Western states, Nebraska's population has become increasingly urban. About half of all Nebraskans live within striking distance of Omaha or Lincoln. But in most ways, Nebraska remains a rural state, its economy and way of life deeply connected to the soil. Away from the cities, the population quickly thins. One-third of Nebraska's counties have fewer than 5,000 inhabitants. In the state's westernmost Panhandle region, towns are few and far between, and separated by vast stretches of grassland.

THE SAND HILLS

Austere though they may be, the state's open spaces possess a hypnotic loveliness that is treasured by Nebraskans. Most prized of all is the Sand Hills region, a 20,000-square-mile zone of unearthly emptiness blanketing the north central portion of the state. The largest area of dunes in North America—greater in size than Connecticut, Massachusetts, and Rhode Island combined—the Sand Hills date back just a few thou-

sand years, when prevailing westerly winds blew the powdery soil of dry river bottoms into drifts. Prairie grasses then took root, fixing the undulating shapes in place. Although the western region of the Sand Hills has valleys that contain meadows and shallow lakes, the area is too dry for cultivation and is today the domain of grazing cattle—and a haunting place to savor the wild, barren beauty of the Great Plains.

▲ **Chimney Rock,** *visible from 30 miles away, was the most famous landmark for pioneers traveling west through Nebraska on the Oregon Trail. It rises 470 feet above the North Platte Valley.*

(For map legend, see page 74.)

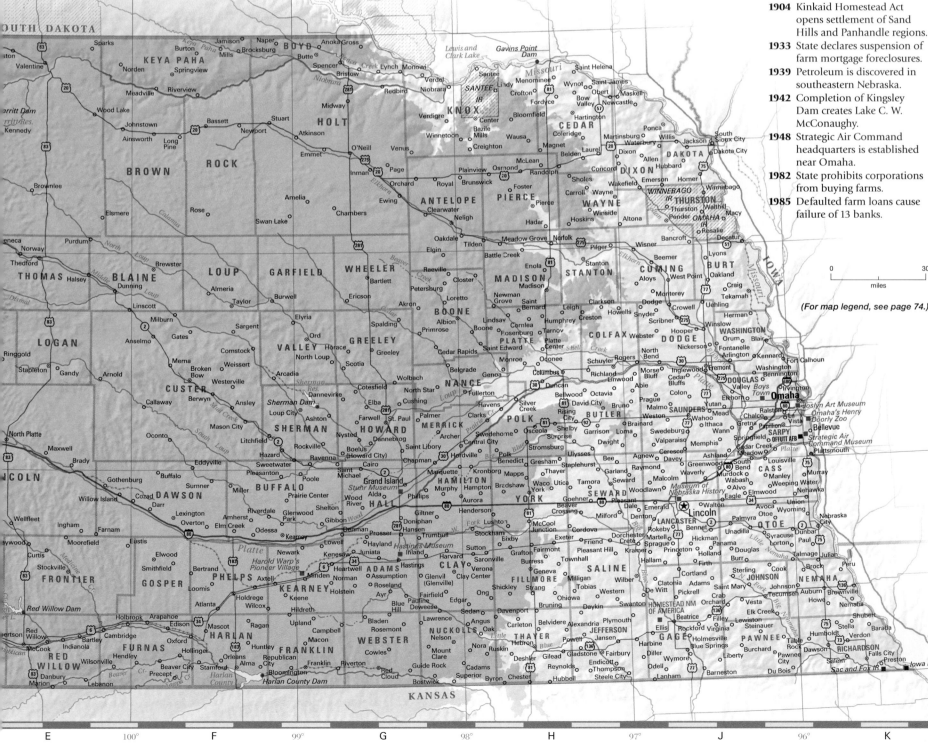

Nevada

From silver mines to neon signs, from desert scenes to slot machines, Nevada is a place of superlatives. Here in the nation's seventh-largest state, few people live outside the two biggest cities, all rivers flow inland, and the loneliest highway in the country stretches for 300 miles. Nevada boasts America's lowest average rainfall, the most mountain ranges, the greatest collection of hotel rooms in any one city, more ghost towns than anywhere else, and the biggest herd of wild mustangs.

▲ *Nevada's flag,* adopted in 1929, displays a silver star. Above the star, the words "Battle Born" allude to the state's admission during the Civil War.

STATE DATA
State bird: Mountain bluebird
State flower: Sagebrush
State trees: Single-leaf piñon and bristlecone pine
State motto: All for our country
State song: "Home Means Nevada"
Abbreviations: Nev.; NV (postal)
Origin of the name: From the Spanish word meaning "snow-clad"
Nicknames: Sagebrush State, Silver State, Battle Born State

AREA AND SIZE
Total area: 110,540 sq. mi.
Rank within U.S.: 7
Extent: 478 mi. north–south; 318 mi. east–west
Highest elevation: Boundary Peak, 13,140 ft. above sea level
Lowest elevation: 470 ft. above sea level along the Colorado River in Clark County

POPULATION
Total: 1,871,000
Rank within U.S.: 35
Ethnic breakdown: White: 73.0%; Hispanic: 14.8%; Black: 6.8%; Asian: 4.1%; Indian: 1.3%
Population density: 17 people per sq. mi.

CLIMATE

Average monthly temperature in Las Vegas	
	100°F
	80°F
	60°F
	40°F
	20°F
	0°F
J F M A M J J A S O N D	

Average monthly precipitation in Las Vegas	
	10"
	8"
	6"
	4"
	2"
	0"
J F M A M J J A S O N D	

ECONOMY
Service industries: Tourism, gambling, recreation
Mining: Gold, silver, diatomite, petroleum
Manufacturing: Printed materials, computers and electronic components, concrete, food products
Agriculture: Beef cattle, hay

SILVER STATE

Although it is Spanish for "snow-clad," Nevada's name conjures images of glittering gambling casinos and arid deserts. Yet the moniker is well deserved. Nevada is filled with mountaintops, many of them cloaked in white in wintertime. There are 150 mountain ranges in the state, with 31 peaks soaring above the 11,000-foot level. Nevada's alpine topography is just one of the many surprises in this Great Basin state.

Humans have been calling Nevada home since at least 12,000 years ago, when the first Paleo-Indian hunters followed

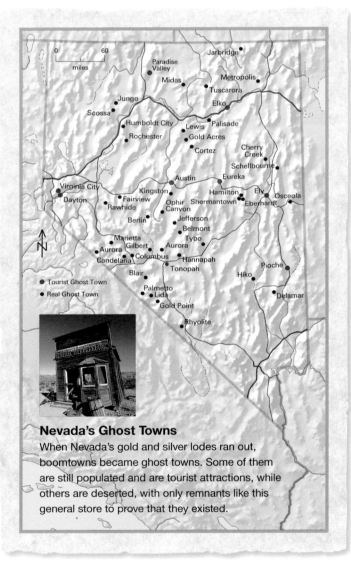

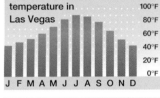

Nevada's Ghost Towns
When Nevada's gold and silver lodes ran out, boomtowns became ghost towns. Some of them are still populated and are tourist attractions, while others are deserted, with only remnants like this general store to prove that they existed.

▲ *Lake Tahoe,* lying on the border between California and Nevada, is distinguished by its great beauty and depth (more than 1,600 feet).

mammoths here. Among the later groups to live within its borders were the Mohave, Paiute, Shoshone, and Washo Indians.

Probably because of the harsh climate and terrain, Nevada was the last of the Lower 48 states to be explored by Europeans. It wasn't until 1776 that Franciscan priests came seeking a southern route to connect the Spanish settlements in New Mexico with those in California. They were followed 50 years later by Canadian trader Peter Skene Ogden, who traveled over the northern boundary of the state and in 1828 discovered the Humboldt River. Additional trails were blazed across the central and southern part of Nevada around the same time by American explorer and fur trader Jedediah Smith and American fur trapper Joseph Walker. The trails were heavily used by pioneers making their way to the gold mines in California. The first permanent settlement in Nevada was Mormon Station (known today as Genoa), located in the Carson Valley.

It took the discovery in 1859 of an enormous deposit of silver called the Comstock Lode to bring a population of any measure to Nevada. Virginia City and other boomtowns sprouted up overnight as tens of thousands of prospectors flocked to the state in hopes of striking it rich. The silver mines played out in the 1870s, leaving hundreds of once bustling towns abandoned in the dust.

GOLD AND GAMBLING
After the turn of the century, mining picked up again with a major gold strike at Goldfield. Nevada now produces 60 percent of the country's and 10 percent of the world's gold supply. Despite these earthly riches, the state's real wealth comes from a 1931 decision to legalize gambling. Since then the state has undergone tremendous growth. Witness the impact on a settlement for railroad workers located 300 miles east of Los Angeles. That once dusty outpost known as Las Vegas has become the acknowledged "fantasy vacation destination" capital of the world. It has more hotel rooms and casinos than anyplace else on earth. The mind-boggling collection of themed resorts that line the famed Las Vegas Strip attracts millions of tourists each year. Among the mega-resorts are re-creations of New York City, Paris, Luxor, and Monte Carlo.

Building and servicing this entertainment mecca has helped turn Las Vegas into one of the fastest-growing cities in the country. Between 1980 and 1995, the population surged more than 350 percent. In the early part of the 1990s, more than 322 people joined the city's population every single day.

NATURAL NEVADA
Not all of Nevada is a neon oasis. Despite being the driest of all the 50 states, it is among the top 10 in terms of natural diversity—that is, the number of different types of habitat and types of wildlife species. The state lists 370 species of birds, 129 of mammals, 64 of reptiles and amphibians, and 46 of fish.

A portion of the Mojave Desert creeps over the border into southern Nevada. Here the climate is hot and dry, with little vegetation other than creosote bushes, Joshua trees, and yuccas. Still, not all is stark and severe. Just north of the Mojave, the colorful sandstone escarpments and canyons of Red Rock

NEVADA TIME LINE

1776 Spanish missionaries enter southern Nevada.
1826–27 Fur trader Jedediah Smith crosses Nevada.
1828 Peter Skene Ogden discovers Humboldt River in northern Nevada.
1843–46 John Frémont and Kit Carson explore Great Basin and Sierra Nevada.
1848 United States gains Nevada after Mexican War.
1849 Mormon Station (later called

Genoa) becomes Nevada's first white settlement.
1859 Gold and silver are found at Comstock Lode; prospectors settle Virginia City.
1861 Nevada Territory is founded.
1864 Nevada joins the Union as 36th state.
1873 Federal government limits use of silver in coins; mining industry begins to wane.
1880 As gold and silver mines peter out, Nevada's popula-

tion begins a 10-year decline.
1900 Nevada's mining industry is revived when silver, gold, and copper are discovered in several locations.
1909 State makes gambling illegal.
1931 State legalizes gambling and reduces residency requirement for divorce to six weeks.
1980 Antipollution laws are passed to protect Lake Tahoe.
1986 Great Basin National Park, first in state, is established.

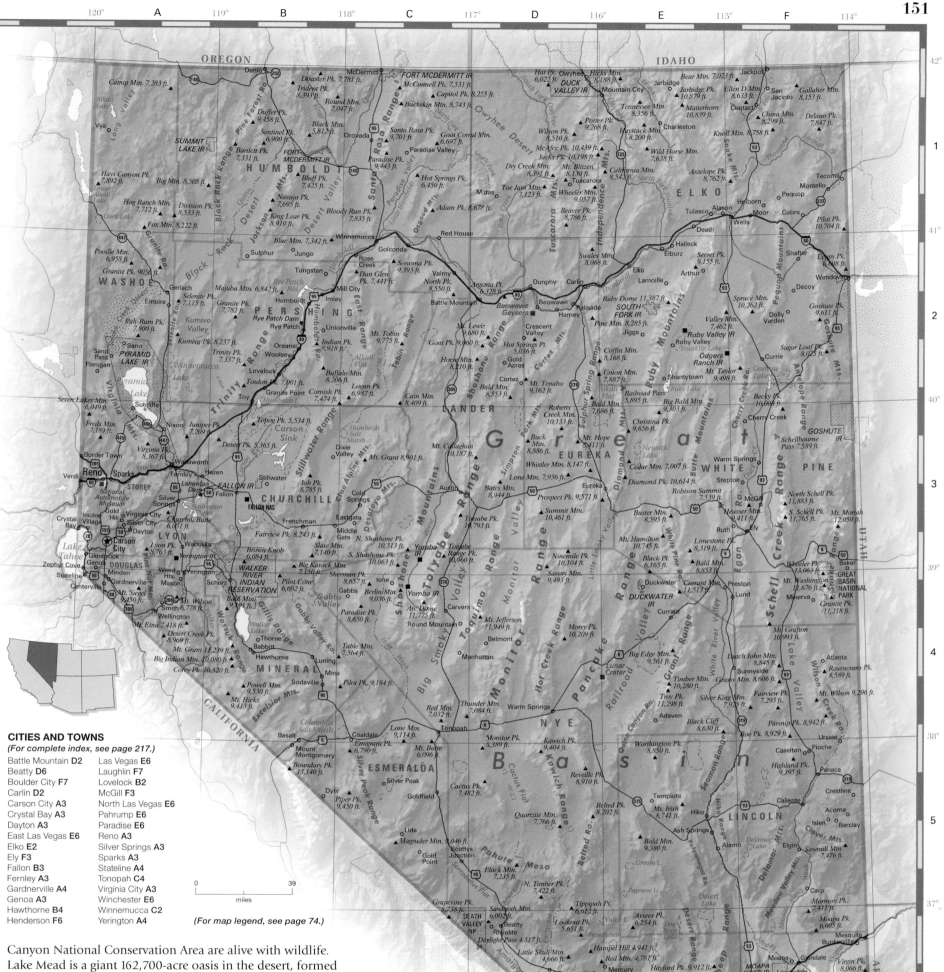

0   39

miles

(For map legend, see page 74.)

▲ *The New York-New York Hotel & Casino is one of several Las Vegas resorts that showcase another city's landmarks.*

Canyon National Conservation Area are alive with wildlife. Lake Mead is a giant 162,700-acre oasis in the desert, formed when the Hoover Dam was built to control the mighty Colorado River in 1936.

The Great Basin, the desert that stretches from the base of the Rocky Mountains to the Sierra Nevada, makes up the northern three-quarters of the state. Wetter and cooler than southern Nevada, the region is covered with a series of depressions and ranges that, when viewed from above, resemble the folds of an accordion. On the far eastern reaches of the basin, along the Nevada-Utah border, is a land of glacier-shrouded mountains, labyrinthine caverns, and bristlecone pine trees that are between 2,000 and 3,000 years old.

Pyramid Lake, a turquoise body of water dominated by a sphinxlike rock formation, lies in the northwestern corner of Nevada. The lake is rich in bird life and is home to a large flock of nesting Canadian geese. Just northeast of the lake is the Black Rock Desert, an ancient lake bed that dates back to the Pleistocene epoch, when this part of the state was under an ancient inland sea. The salt pan supports no vegetation and offers an endless horizon. It is as eerie as it is beautiful.

New Hampshire

STATE DATA

State bird: Purple finch
State flower: Purple lilac
State tree: White birch
State motto: Live free or die
State song: "Old New Hampshire"
Abbreviations: N.H.; NH (postal)
Origin of the name: Named by Capt. John Mason for the county of Hampshire in England
Nicknames: Granite State, Mother of Rivers, Switzerland of America, White Mountain State

AREA AND SIZE

Total area: 9,304 sq. mi.
Rank within U.S.: 44
Extent: 180 mi. north–south; 93 mi. east–west
Highest elevation: Mount Washington, 6,288 ft. above sea level
Lowest elevation: Sea level along the Atlantic Coast

POPULATION

Total: 1,224,000
Rank within U.S.: 42
Ethnic breakdown: White: 96.7%; Hispanic: 1.4%; Asian: 1.1%; Black: 0.6%; Indian: 0.2%
Population density: 135.5 people per sq. mi.

CLIMATE

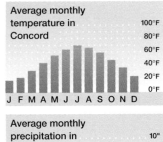

Average monthly temperature in Concord

100°F
80°F
60°F
40°F
20°F
0°F

J F M A M J J A S O N D

Average monthly precipitation in Concord

10"
8"
6"
4"
2"
0"

J F M A M J J A S O N D

ECONOMY

Service industries: Education, health care, real estate, tourism
Manufacturing: Machinery, scientific instruments, electrical equipment
Agriculture: Dairy products, eggs, hay, apples, potatoes, sweet corn, maple syrup, beef cattle, hogs
Mining: Sand and gravel, granite

Renowned as the "Granite State" as much for its uncompromising Yankee spirit as for its rugged stone foundations, New Hampshire is proud of its superlatives. Within its borders are the highest mountain in the northeastern United States, Mount Washington, and the remote headwaters of the Connecticut, New England's longest river. New Hampshire also cherishes its political role as the site of the nation's first presidential primary every four years.

WATERPOWER

Of all the maritime New England states, New Hampshire has the shortest seacoast—13 miles tightly wedged between Maine and Massachusetts. Just behind the coast lies a broad, lakelike tidal estuary called Great Bay, beyond which suburbs sprawl across onetime rolling farmland. This south central portion of New Hampshire is drained by the longest river in the state, the Merrimack, the source of the waterpower that at one time turned the mill wheels of Manchester and Nashua, its leading industrial cities.

Southwestern New Hampshire is dominated by the lone massif of Monadnock, whose name has come to signify any isolated peak that is not connected to a surrounding mountain range. The state's western border with Vermont, from Massachusetts almost all the way to Quebec, is the Connecticut River. In its valley nestle dozens of white-steepled colonial towns; the most famous, Hanover, is home to the Ivy League college of Dartmouth.

Central New Hampshire's most distinctive feature is its skein of glacially gouged lakes. Lake Winnipesaukee, the largest, is an island-studded mecca for vacationers, and its waters are plied by the venerable excursion vessel *Mount Washington;* farther northwest, the deeply indented shoreline of Squam Lake conceals the quietly dignified summer retreats that were made famous in the film *On Golden Pond.*

▲ **The Stark Covered Bridge**—one of 50 in the state—leads over the Ammonoosuc River to the Union Church.

A TOWERING WILDERNESS

The White Mountains, whose highest peaks are in the Presidential Range, dominate the New Hampshire landscape north of the lakes. A substantial portion of this lofty domain lies within the 800,000-acre White Mountain National Forest, much of which is federally protected wilderness. Penetrated by roads and settlement along the three great north–south passes—Pinkham, Crawford, and Franconia Notch—the White Mountains are capped by 6,288-foot Mount Washington, famous for some of the world's fiercest weather. The world's second-highest recorded wind speed—an astounding 231 miles per hour—was documented on the mountain's summit on April 12, 1934.

Farther west, in Franconia Notch, another New Hampshire icon watches over the great white hills—the Old Man of the Mountains, a granite "Profile" that projects from the side of Cannon Mountain. According to a remark often attributed to New Hampshire native Daniel Webster, the Old Man is a sign hung out to signify that here "in the mountains of New Hampshire . . . God makes men."

The northernmost tip of New Hampshire is a forest redoubt where the moose and the loon prevail. Although the days of the great log drives on the Androscoggin and Dead Diamond rivers near Dixville Notch are long gone, logging and the paper industry are still a major force in the north-country economy.

EARLY COMMERCIAL SUCCESS

The ancestral lands of the Abenaki and Pennacook Indian confederations were colonized by the English beginning in 1623, when a small party of settlers established a fishing and trading center on the coast just south of present-day Portsmouth. Penetration of the interior was gradual and slow; throughout the colonial period, New Hampshire's political, social, and commercial life revolved around the bustling shipbuilding and mercantile capital of Portsmouth.

Eighteenth- and early-19th-century Portsmouth was a center of wealth and refinement, virtually on a par with Boston. Ample evidence of this early prosperity survives in its handsomely restored mansions, such as the 1763 Moffatt-Ladd and 1784 Governor John Langdon houses. In the heart of Portsmouth, the 10-acre, 40-building Strawbery Banke restoration celebrates the city's rich history as well as its present-day commitment to historic preservation.

During the first half of the 19th century, the economic center of New Hampshire shifted away from the seacoast toward the inland Merrimack Valley towns of Concord and Manchester. Concord had become the state capital at the beginning of the century; today its gold-domed granite State House is the oldest (1819) capitol building in which a state legislature still meets in its original chambers. Granite was an early Concord staple, but the most storied of the city's businesses was the Concord Coach, the quintessential stagecoach that rumbled over highways and byways a century and a half ago.

It was Manchester, though, that was destined for industrial greatness. Named after the British textile city, Manchester became the center of waterpowered spinning and weaving after a group of Boston capitalists made a substantial investment during the 1850s. By the beginning of the 20th century, the enormous riverside complex known as the Amoskeag Mills was the world's largest producer of cotton cloth and employed some 17,000 workers on 700,000 spindles and 23,000 looms. By the 1930s, however, the company had closed, a victim of the American textile industry's move to the Southern states. Today the old mills house a variety of smaller firms, many of them part of the boom in high-technology and service industries that now drives southern New Hampshire's economy.

NEW HAMPSHIRE TIMELINE

1603 Martin Pring is sent by British merchants to explore mouth of Piscataqua River.

1614 Capt. John Smith lands at Isles of Shoals, off New Hampshire coast.

1623 Permanent settlements are established at present-day Dover, Rye, and Portsmouth.

1641 New Hampshire becomes part of Massachusetts.

1679 New Hampshire becomes a separate royal province.

1769 Dartmouth College is established at Hanover.

1776 New Hampshire is first colony to declare independence from England.

1788 New Hampshire becomes ninth state after ratifying U.S. Constitution.

1849 The nation's first state general library law is enacted.

1853 Franklin Pierce of Hillsboro becomes 14th U.S. president.

1944 Representatives of 44 nations

come to Bretton Woods to participate in International Monetary Conference.

1961 Alan B. Shepard, Jr., from East Derry, becomes first American to travel in space.

1964 New Hampshire holds the first legal U.S. lottery since the 1890s.

1986 Christa McAuliffe, a Concord schoolteacher and a *Challenger* crew member, is killed in space shuttle explosion.

◀ *Mount Franklin and Mount Eisenhower*—part of the White Mountains's Presidential Range—dwarf a forest of pine trees in the valley below.

(For map legend, see page 74.)

0 ——— 16
miles

CITIES AND TOWNS
(For complete index, see page 217.)

Bedford **C6**
Berlin **D3**
Bretton Woods **D3**
Claremont **B5**
Concord **C5**
Conway **D4**
Derry **D6**
Dixville Notch **D2**
Dover **E5**
Durham **E5**
East Derry **D6**
Exeter **E6**
Franklin **C5**
Goffstown **C5**
Hampton **E6**
Hanover **B4**
Hillsboro **5C**
Hooksett **D5**
Hudson **D6**
Keene **B6**
Laconia **D4**
Lebanon **B4**
Littleton **C3**
Londonderry **D6**
Manchester **D6**
Merrimack **D6**
Milford **C6**
Nashua **D6**
Pelham **D6**
Plymouth **C4**
Portsmouth **E5**
Rochester **E5**
Rye **E5**
Salem **D6**
Somersworth **E5**
Wolfeboro **D4**

FRESH AIR AND MOUNTAIN RESORTS

Northern New Hampshire is largely the creation of another 19th-century revolution, the development of mass tourism and mountain recreation. Once neglected, if not shunned altogether by Indians and white settlers alike (the Pennacook avoided the summit of Mount Washington because they believed it was inhabited by ghosts), the high peaks of the Presidential Range began to draw Victorian-era vacationers newly interested in fresh air, healthful exercise, and luxury resorts. Stagecoaches and, later, the railroad brought travelers to rambling wooden hotels, beginning with a succession of inns in Crawford Notch and culminating in the stately Mount Washington Hotel, built in 1902 and today a restored grande dame of the mountains.

A different kind of mountain hospitality was pioneered by the Appalachian Mountain Club, an organization based in Boston and Pinkham Notch, which in 1888 began constructing the first of its string of eight huts in the Presidential Range. Located between three and six miles apart, the huts offer meals and lodging to hikers who take up the challenge of a rigorous network of trails across the starkly beautiful rooftop of New England.

But there are other agendas in the mountains of New Hampshire. In a meeting room at the Balsams, a 15,000-acre resort near the Canadian border, the citizens of Dixville Notch open their polls at midnight on primary and presidential election days. That way, their votes are counted earliest, and New Hampshire's voice is the first heard in the nation. It's another show of individualism in a state whose license plates read "Live Free or Die."

▲ *Grassroots democracy* in action at a New Hampshire town meeting.

▲ **The state flag,** adopted in 1896, displays a variation of the state seal. In the center of the shield are three plows, symbolizing agriculture; Ceres, the goddess of agriculture, and Liberty stand on either side. A sovereign's helmet represents New Jersey's sovereignty. A horse's head stands for agriculture and the animal's speed, strength, and usefulness.

STATE DATA
State bird: Eastern goldfinch
State flower: Purple violet
State tree: Red oak
State motto: Liberty and prosperity
State song: No official state song
Abbreviations: N.J.; NJ (postal)
Origin of the name: For the island of Jersey in the English Channel.
Nickname: Garden State

AREA AND SIZE
Total area: 7,836 sq. mi.
Rank within U.S.: 46
Extent: 167 mi. north–south; 88 mi. east–west
Highest elevation: High Point, 1,803 ft. above sea level
Lowest elevation: Sea level along the Atlantic Ocean

POPULATION
Total: 8,178,000
Rank within U.S.: 9
Ethnic breakdown: White: 68.0%; Black: 13.5%; Hispanic: 12.8%; Asian: 5.6%; Indian: 0.2%
Population density: 1,086 people per sq. mi.

CLIMATE

Average monthly temperature in Atlantic City

J F M A M J J A S O N D — 0°F to 100°F

Average monthly precipitation in Atlantic City

J F M A M J J A S O N D — 0" to 10"

ECONOMY
Service industries: Real estate, life insurance, hotels and casinos, research laboratories
Manufacturing: Pharmaceuticals, food processing, printed materials
Agriculture: Greenhouse flowers, milk, tomatoes, peaches, corn

▲ **At Island Beach State Park,** a 10-mile-long natural barrier peninsula, autumn goldenrod and dune grass add color to the sandy expanses.

New Jersey

Hinged to the mainland along its northern border with New York, the most densely populated of the 50 states is actually a large peninsula. The Garden State incorporates not only an urban corridor but also long stretches of rolling farmland, magnificent sandy beaches, and, surprisingly, even near wilderness.

SANCTUARY IN THE INDUSTRIAL NORTH

"What exit are you from?" This question is jokingly asked of most residents of New Jersey at least once. It's not an unreasonable query, considering that 89 out of 100 New Jerseyans live in urban areas and that many cities—such as Newark, Elizabeth, Camden, and the state capital, Trenton—are clustered near the New Jersey Turnpike, a 143-mile toll road connecting New York City to Philadelphia and Delaware. Urbanization is so complete along this corridor that only the road signs reveal where one city leaves off and the next begins.

When outsiders think of the Garden State, they associate it with the industrial Northeast—a region bound tightly to New York City by one of the world's most elaborate systems of bridges and tunnels. Belching oil refineries, rail yards, and factories are all part of the landscape here, but so are the Hackensack Meadowlands—wetlands of more than 8,000 acres that stretch from Hackensack to Harrison. After some 200 years of being drained, dammed, and polluted, with the help of environmental controls, including the 1970 Clean Water Act, the closing of all but one landfill, and better sewage treatment, the marshes are returning to life and supporting killifish, grass shrimp, and 17 endangered or threatened species.

FROM MOUNTAINS TO SEASHORES

West of the industrial belt, urban sprawl gives way to bedroom communities that once were dairy farms. But not all of northern New Jersey has been developed; still pristine are the shire-like horse country near the university town of Princeton and the all-but-impenetrable Great Swamp just south of Morristown. Some of the most compelling wilderness is in the northwestern corner of the state in the Delaware Water Gap, a deep fissure in the Kittatinny Mountains through which the Delaware River runs on its way south toward Philadelphia and, eventually, the Delaware Bay. Within the boundaries of the 35-mile-long Kittatinny range (part of the Appalachian Mountain range that stretches from Quebec to Alabama) lie fragrant forests and hundreds of lakes and ponds.

On the opposite side of the state lies a long strip of Atlantic shoreline. Boasting some of the finest white-sand beaches on the Eastern seaboard, New Jersey's coast also has nearly 130 miles of mainland and barrier islands, reaching from Sandy Hook in the north to Cape May at the state's southernmost point. Both natives and out-of-staters have pilgrimaged for decades to beaches at Long Branch, Seaside Heights, and Atlantic City, the last, home to glittering casinos and resorts. With its miles of gaudy motels, Wildwood contrasts sharply with the Victorian charm of Cape May, but both are popular summer havens. However crowded it becomes in the summer months, the Jersey Shore is nevertheless protected in many places. One such area is the pristine shorebird haven of Brigantine National Wildlife Refuge.

▲ **Jersey tomatoes,** famous for their sweet, delicate flavor and tender skin, are one of the state's top agricultural commodities.

SETTLEMENT AND REVOLUTION

The ancestral home of the Leni-Lenape Indians, North Jersey was part of the 17th-century Dutch settlement of New Netherland, which was centered around Manhattan. Far to the south, at about the same time, the Swedish had established outposts along the Delaware River; their land was peacefully annexed by the Dutch, however, who in turn were ousted in 1664 by a British naval force that seized what would henceforth be called New Jersey (after the island of Jersey in the English Channel).

By the 1770s the British Crown had outlived its welcome in America, and New Jersey sued for liberty along with the other rebellious colonies. The state earned the nickname Cockpit of

NEW JERSEY TIMELINE

1524 Giovanni da Verrazano explores New Jersey coast.
1609 Henry Hudson sails up Hudson River.
1660 The Dutch found first permanent white settlement in New Jersey at Bergen.
1664 England acquires New Jersey from the Netherlands.
1758 First Indian reservation in America is founded in Burlington County.

1776 George Washington and American soldiers defeat British forces at Trenton.
1787 New Jersey is third state to ratify the U.S. Constitution.
1804 Legislation declares that all persons born in the state after July 4, 1804, are free.
1825 John Stevens builds first successful steam-powered locomotive in the country.
1838 Samuel Morse demonstrates

his electric telegraph.
1858 First dinosaur skeleton uncovered in North America is found in Haddonfield.
1879 Thomas Edison develops the incandescent electric lamp.
1912 New Jersey governor Woodrow Wilson is elected president.
1978 Atlantic City casinos open.
1994 Christine Whitman becomes state's first woman governor.

the Revolution when its citizens likened the many battles fought there to cockfights. It was from New Jersey that Gen. George Washington executed a brilliant strategic retreat into Pennsylvania in 1776, then recrossed the Delaware to surprise the Hessians at Trenton that Christmas.

GATEWAY TO INDUSTRY

New Jersey's emergence as an industrial powerhouse dates to just after the Revolutionary War, when Alexander Hamilton founded the Society for Establishing Useful Manufactures in Paterson. Hamilton had recognized the waterpower potential of the Great Falls of the Passaic River and decided that America's first industrial city should be built there. Manufacturing, especially of textiles, flourished in the area. By the 20th century New Jersey was an industrial force in the nation (some 90 of the largest industrial firms are still represented in the state), as well as a center of research and development: it was in West Orange, for instance, that Thomas Edison built laboratories and workshops that amounted to a virtual invention factory.

FARMLAND TO PINELANDS

The nickname Garden State describes New Jersey more accurately than many people might think. Blessed with fertile soil in the southern part of the state, New Jersey's rolling farmland produces a bountiful harvest. It is the plump red icon of the Garden State, the Jersey tomato, however, that has brought the state fame. Since the 18th century much of the fresh produce eaten by people in New York City and Philadelphia has come from New Jersey, prompting one of Philadelphia's former leading citizens, Benjamin Franklin, to liken the state to "a cider barrel tapped at both ends."

In the middle of southern New Jersey sprawls perhaps the state's greatest treasure and resource, the 1.1-million-acre Pine Barrens. Protected by federal law, this sparsely populated area of pine and oak forests, cedar swamps, and marshes teems with wildlife. Once the focus of bustling iron and glass industries, the Pine Barrens now supports vast cranberry bogs and blueberry fields and—ironically for the most urbanized state in the nation—a reservoir estimated to contain more than 17 trillion gallons of some of the purest water in the world.

▲ **The Pine Barrens's** *vast forests and swamps are off-limits to development because of the huge freshwater aquifer beneath the soil.*

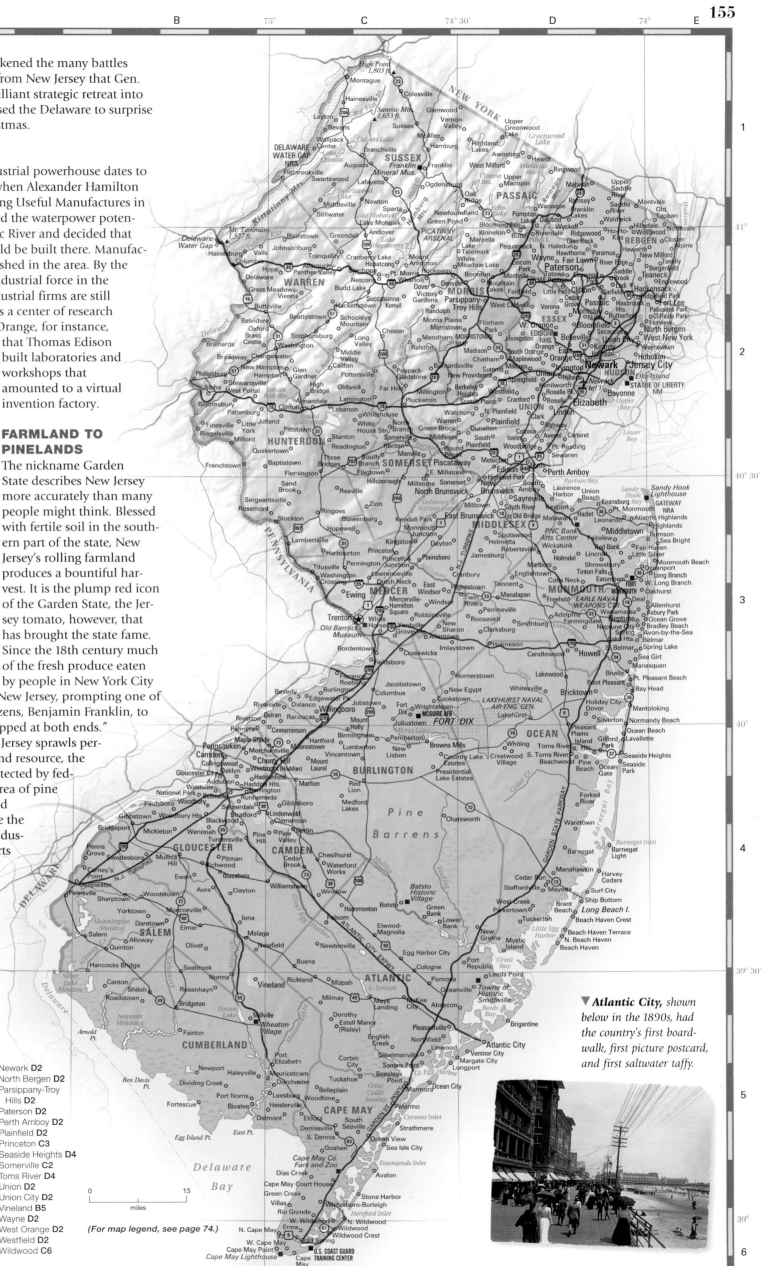

▼ **Atlantic City,** *shown below in the 1890s, had the country's first boardwalk, first picture postcard, and first saltwater taffy.*

(For map legend, see page 74.)

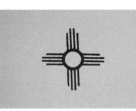

▲ *The state flag,* adopted in 1925, displays the sun symbol of the Zia Pueblo Indians. Red and gold were the colors of Queen Isabella of Spain, who sent conquistadores to the New World.

STATE DATA

State bird: Roadrunner
State flower: Yucca
State tree: Piñon
State motto: *Crescit eundo* (It grows as it goes)
State song: "O, Fair New Mexico"
Abbreviations: N. Mex. or N.M.; NM (postal)
Origin of the name: Named by the first Spanish settlers, who had traveled from Mexico
Nicknames: Land of Enchantment, Sunshine State, Cactus State

AREA AND SIZE

Total area: 121,666 sq. mi.
Rank within U.S.: 5
Extent: 389 mi. north–south; 352 mi. east–west
Highest elevation: Wheeler Peak, 13,161 ft. above sea level
Lowest elevation: 2,817 ft. above sea level at Red Bluff Reservoir in Eddy County

POPULATION

Total: 1,860,000
Rank within U.S.: 36
Ethnic breakdown: White: 49.0%; Hispanic: 39.6%; Indian: 8.4%; Black: 1.8%; Asian: 1.2%
Population density: 15.3 people per sq. mi.

CLIMATE

Average monthly temperature in Albuquerque

	100°F
	80°F
	60°F
	40°F
	20°F
	0°F

J F M A M J J A S O N D

Average monthly precipitation in Albuquerque

	10"
	8"
	6"
	4"
	2"
	0"

J F M A M J J A S O N D

ECONOMY

Service industries: Government research laboratories, military bases, medical offices, ski resorts
Manufacturing: Electrical equipment, scientific instruments
Mining: Natural gas, petroleum, copper, coal, molybdenum, potash
Agriculture: Beef cattle, hay, chili peppers, pecans

◀ *Pueblo Bonito is the largest excavated ruin of Chaco Canyon, the center of Anasazi culture between* A.D. *900 and 1200. A long period of drought in the late 13th century probably drove the Anasazi from the area.*

New Mexico

Mountains clad with fragrant piñon and juniper forests; sagebrush deserts spangled with wildflowers; adobe houses in warm earthen tones; the western plains unfurling in a timeless sweep beneath a sky of crystalline blue—so many artists have tried to capture the beauteous essence of this quintessentially Southwestern state.

THE SPELL OF THE SOUTHWEST

Anyone who has ever seen a painting by the artist Georgia O'Keeffe knows how mesmerizing the light and color of New Mexico can be. O'Keeffe first visited the state in 1930 and was immediately struck by the vivid hues and dramatic shapes of the land. Her colorful canvases—especially her dramatic desert landscapes and bold still lifes of bones and wildflowers—have become synonymous with the dazzling beauty of New Mexico. But O'Keeffe was not alone. The great photographers Ansel Adams, Edward Weston, and Henri Cartier-Bresson all worked here, too. Today New Mexico boasts the nation's highest proportion of artists in residence.

EARLY PEOPLES

New Mexico's artistic heritage dates back nearly 1,000 years to the Anasazi, master potters and weavers who were the ancestors of the Pueblo Indians. By the time the Spanish arrived in the 1500s, some 30,000 Native Americans lived in northern New Mexico, making their homes in distinctive groups of apartmentlike structures called pueblos, which is Spanish for "towns." Other non-Pueblo peoples, including the

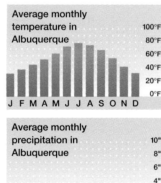

▲ *Native American artistry from New Mexico. A Navajo serape, woven around 1885, forms a backdrop for a Hopi pin (left) and a painted earthenware jar (right), made at the Acoma Pueblo around 1940.*

Navajo and Apache, also roamed the region.

The beginning of Spanish settlement in 1598 ushered in a 300-year period during which New Mexico was a colony—first of Spain and later of Mexico. Well before the Pilgrims set sail for New England, Spanish settlers were traveling north along the Rio Grande into New Mexico's north central region, establishing missions and ranches along the way. In 1610 they founded the town of Santa Fe—the oldest capital city in the United States and the second-oldest permanent settlement (after St. Augustine, Florida). New Mexico existed as a distant outpost, isolated from the rest of Spain's holdings in the New World.

LITTLE TEXAS

Americans started to arrive in the early 19th century, following the Santa Fe Trail, a thriving trade route that began in Missouri; they later traveled by rail on the Atchison, Topeka, and Santa Fe line. Others came north and west from Texas, settling in the eastern third of the state, where the Great Plains reign and winds sweep across flatlands rich with wheat, cotton, cattle, and oil. So close is the resemblance of eastern New Mexico to its neighbor that it is sometimes called Little Texas.

In modern times, another group of newcomers left its mark on the state. Their purpose was grave: to win a world war. Arriving in secret in 1943, the men and women of the Manhattan Project were whisked away to a boarding school near Santa Fe, in the town of Los Alamos, where a classified government laboratory had been set up to build the first atomic bomb.

THE UNTAMED DESERT

To the northwest, the rugged Four Corners region (so named for its four-way meeting point of state borders, the only place in the United States where this juxtaposition occurs) is home to many of the state's Navajo Indians; their reservation, which extends well across the border into neighboring Utah and Arizona, is America's largest.

Largely unsettled and untamed, the southernmost deserts are a barren sprawl of wrinkled mountains, ancient lava flows, and arid basins, bisected by the muddy, slow-flowing Rio Grande. Situated in this mostly uninhabited area, the desert town of Alamogordo was chosen as the site for the first atomic bomb test in 1945.

CARLSBAD CAVERNS

Although beauty abounds in the open, even more abides underground in the Carlsbad Caverns. Located near the Texas border, this three-mile-long realm of subterranean chambers is one of the largest cave systems in the world. Glistening limestone icicles bedeck its massive vaults, home to nearly half a million bats. The Big Room, aptly named indeed, is large enough to hold 14 football fields; overhead, its ceiling arcs 256 feet above the dank floor, high enough to house a 22-story building. It is a humbling sight—and one that reminds visitors of all of New Mexico's many enchantments.

NEW MEXICO TIMELINE

1540 Francisco Vásquez de Coronado explores New Mexico.
1598 Spaniards settle San Juan.
1680 Pueblo Indians force Spanish settlers to flee to Mexico.
1692–96 New Mexico is reconquered by Spaniards.
1821 Mexico wins independence from Spain; New Mexico becomes part of Mexico. William Becknell blazes

Santa Fe Trail from Missouri.
1848 Mexico cedes New Mexico to U.S. after Mexican War.
1886 Warfare between the Apache and white settlers ends with surrender of Geronimo.
1912 New Mexico joins the Union as 47th state.
1916 Mexican outlaw Pancho Villa raids town of Columbus.
1924 Gila National Forest becomes

the first U.S. wilderness area.
1945 First atomic bomb is tested at Trinity Site near Alamogordo.
1950 Uranium ore is discovered in northwestern New Mexico.
1970 Taos Pueblo Indians gain title to 48,000 acres in Carson National Forest.
1986 Gov. Toney Anaya declares New Mexico a sanctuary for Central American refugees.

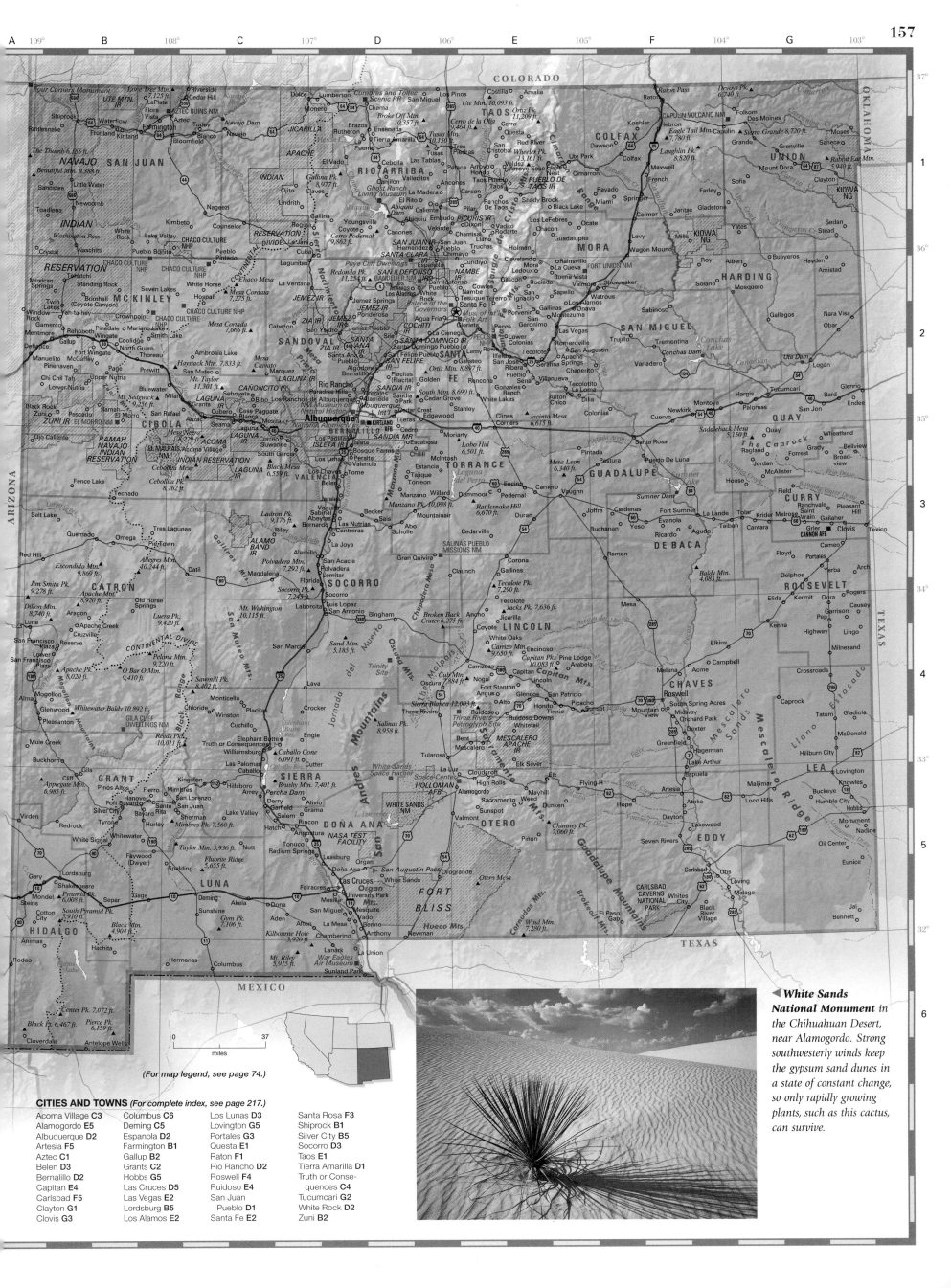

◀ **White Sands National Monument** in the Chihuahuan Desert, near Alamogordo. Strong southwesterly winds keep the gypsum sand dunes in a state of constant change, so only rapidly growing plants, such as this cactus, can survive.

miles

(For map legend, see page 74.)

CITIES AND TOWNS *(For complete index, see page 217.)*

New York

▲ **The state flag,** adopted in 1909, displays the state coat of arms. The shield depicts mountains, ships, and a rising sun. Above it, a bald eagle sits on a globe. The two figures on either side represent liberty and justice.

STATE DATA
State bird: Bluebird
State flower: Rose
State tree: Sugar maple
State motto: *Excelsior* (Ever upward)
State song: "I Love New York"
Abbreviations: N.Y.; NY (postal)
Origin of the name: Named for the duke of York after the British took the area from the Dutch
Nickname: Empire State

AREA AND SIZE
Total area: 49,576 sq. mi.
Rank within U.S.: 30
Extent: 310 mi. north–south; 409 mi. east–west
Highest elevation: Mount Marcy, 5,344 ft. above sea level
Lowest elevation: Sea level along the Atlantic Ocean

POPULATION
Total: 18,146,000
Rank within U.S.: 3
Ethnic breakdown: White: 64.1%; Hispanic: 15.5%; Black: 14.7%; Asian: 5.4%; Indian: 0.3%
Population density: 379.4 people per sq. mi.

CLIMATE

Average monthly temperature in Albany

Average monthly precipitation in Albany

Average monthly temperature in New York City

Average monthly precipitation in New York City

ECONOMY
Service industries: Banking, securities, real estate; medical offices, law firms, advertising agencies, entertainment companies
Manufacturing: Printed materials, scientific instruments, machinery
Agriculture: Milk, beef cattle, cabbages, potatoes, apples, grapes

---

Linking New England with the Midwest and the Great Lakes with the sea, the "Empire State" dazzles with its endless variety. New York is best known for its great metropolis—the frenetic vertical circus of steel and glass and hurrying humanity that New Yorkers know simply as "the city." But Manhattan and its adjacent boroughs represent only a tiny fraction of the state, most of which is rural. Upstate lie great tracts of undeveloped land— including Adirondack Park, which crowns the state with 6 million acres of mountain wilderness—as well as enough rivers, lakes, pastures, beaches, and farmlands to soothe the most city-weary soul.

AN AMAZING DIVERSITY
Although it ranks just 30th among the 50 states in area, New York is immense by Northeastern standards, covering an area about the size of Maine, New Hampshire, and Vermont combined. No fewer than eight distinct regions are contained within the state's borders. The Atlantic Coastal Plain includes Staten Island and Long Island, while the New England Upland connects Manhattan with the Taconic Mountains and the Hudson River Highlands to the north. Arcing through the central portion of the state from Albany west to Buffalo is the Hudson-Mohawk River Lowland. The Adirondack Plateau contains 46 distinct peaks, including Mount Marcy, at 5,344 feet New York's loftiest. The Tug Hill Plateau is an upland tucked between the Adirondacks and the eastern shore of Lake Ontario; more snow falls here each year (about 225 inches) than anywhere else east of the Rockies. The St. Lawrence-Lake Champlain Lowland traces New York's borders with Vermont and Canada. The Erie-Ontario Plain abuts most of New York's

▲ **Autumn foliage** surrounds Roaring Brook Falls in Adirondack Park. It is the country's largest state park, roughly the size of Vermont.

275 miles of Great Lake frontage. New York's largest region, the Appalachian Plateau, extends north through the central portion of the state and includes both the Finger Lakes and the Catskill Mountains.

No less varied are New York's inhabitants. Some 18 million people call the Empire State their home, and among them one finds virtually every ethnic group, language, and lifestyle. Such variety is nothing new; in 1644 the Dutch governor estimated that as many as 18 different languages were spoken in the colony.

▲ **The Chautauqua Institution** in western New York was founded in 1874 to offer intellectual and spiritual stimulation to summer guests.

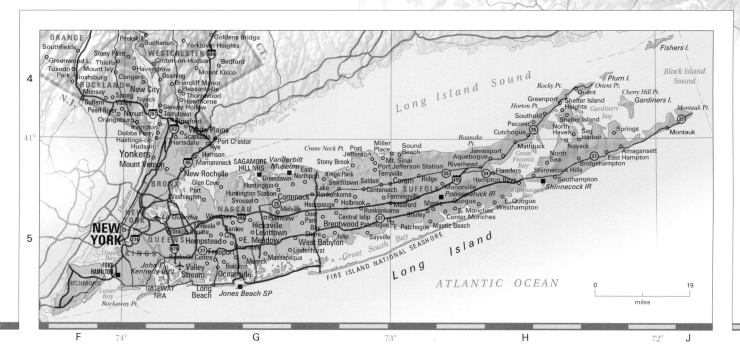

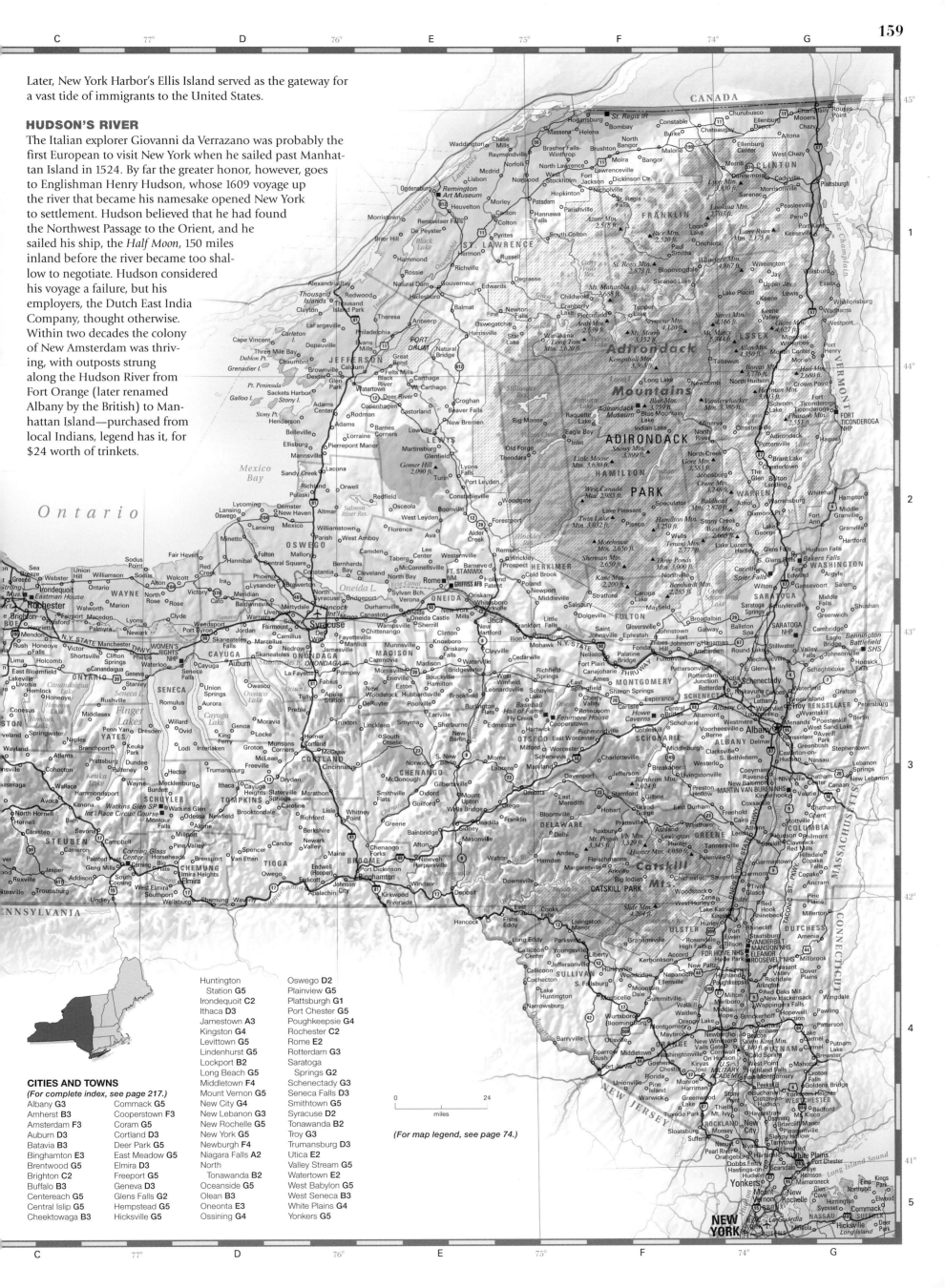

Later, New York Harbor's Ellis Island served as the gateway for a vast tide of immigrants to the United States.

HUDSON'S RIVER

The Italian explorer Giovanni da Verrazano was probably the first European to visit New York when he sailed past Manhattan Island in 1524. By far the greater honor, however, goes to Englishman Henry Hudson, whose 1609 voyage up the river that became his namesake opened New York to settlement. Hudson believed that he had found the Northwest Passage to the Orient, and he sailed his ship, the *Half Moon*, 150 miles inland before the river became too shallow to negotiate. Hudson considered his voyage a failure, but his employers, the Dutch East India Company, thought otherwise. Within two decades the colony of New Amsterdam was thriving, with outposts strung along the Hudson River from Fort Orange (later renamed Albany by the British) to Manhattan Island—purchased from local Indians, legend has it, for $24 worth of trinkets.

CITIES AND TOWNS

(For complete index, see page 217.)

0   24
miles

(For map legend, see page 74.)

▶ *The skyscrapers of Manhattan, the central borough of New York City, as seen from the waters off the island's southern shore.*

NEW YORK
TIMELINE

1524 Giovanni da Verrazano sails into New York Bay.
1609 Henry Hudson travels up the Hudson River.
Samuel de Champlain explores Lake Champlain.
1624 Dutch establish New Netherland colony at Albany.
1625 Dutch found New Amsterdam, now New York City.
1626 Dutch buy Manhattan Island from Manhattan Indians.
1664 British capture New Amsterdam and rename it New York City.
1735 In major victory for freedom of the press, John P. Zenger is cleared of libel charges.
1765 New York City hosts congress to fight Stamp Act.
1787 First formally organized U.S. Shaker community is established in New Lebanon.
1788 New York ratifies U.S. Constitution; becomes 11th state.
1789 In New York City, George Washington is inaugurated as first U.S. president.
1825 Erie Canal opens.
1830 Church of Latter-day Saints is founded at Fayette.
1848 First women's rights convention is held at Seneca Falls.
1863 During Civil War, antidraft riots cause 1,000 casualties.
1886 Statue of Liberty is dedicated in New York Harbor.
1901 President William McKinley is assassinated in Buffalo.
1911 Triangle Shirtwaist factory fire kills 145 in New York City and leads to reforms.
1929 New York stock market crashes.
1939 World's Fair opens in Queens, New York City.
1946 New York City is chosen as site for U.N. headquarters.
1959 St. Lawrence Seaway opens.
1964 Second New York World's Fair opens.
1987 New York Stock Exchange experiences a record drop in the Dow-Jones average.

Perhaps no other river has played a greater role in the history of the Americas than has the Hudson. Algonquin and Iroquois Indians used it to travel around the state, and settlers closely followed the river's northward course, spreading out into its fertile valleys. During the Revolutionary War the Hudson served as a natural barrier, separating the free colonies of New England from British-held New York City. With control of the Hudson, and the military installation situated on the river at West Point, Americans were able to throttle British supply lines while keeping their own ships moving.

With the opening of the 363-mile-long Erie Canal in 1825, the Hudson assumed yet another role. Linking the Atlantic with the Great Lakes—and thence the Ohio and Mississippi rivers—the Hudson-Mohawk-Erie waterway served as the gateway to the west for thousands of pioneer families. As the state's lumber, manufacturing, and railroad interests all prospered, New York City rapidly grew to become the nation's leader in banking, commerce, and culture.

▲ *Above, an early poster advertising Kodak. At right is a Kodak Vest Pocket camera, popular in the 1920s.*

The Hudson also has an aesthetic appeal. Embraced by towering granite cliffs and the stony bulk of Storm King Mountain, the Hudson Highlands region, about 50 miles north of Manhattan, resembles a Norwegian fjord. Countless writers and artists have drawn inspiration for their work here.

THE BIG APPLE
Even in the early 19th century, New York City's special status seemed assured. "No one thinks of the place as belonging to a particular state, but to the United States," observed writer James Fenimore Cooper. Two hundred years later, the city belongs not only to the nation but also to the world. Hundreds of America's largest companies are based here, and each day millions of workers disappear into New York's skyscrapers. On Wall Street, a financial center since colonial times, the net worth of American business is redetermined each day on the New York and American Stock Exchanges, while uptown, New York's fashion, publishing, and entertainment industries buzz with the latest on what to wear, read, and watch on television. Some 30 million tourists visit New York City from all corners of the globe each year to soak in the feverish pace that is the essence of life in America's greatest city.

INDUSTRIAL MUSCLE
New York City is by no means New York's only major population center. Although tiny by comparison, the thriving upstate cities of Albany, Buffalo, and Rochester boast about a million inhabitants each. Albany, the state capital, employs thousands in government jobs, while Rochester is home to Eastman Kodak, which specializes in optical, photographic, medical, scientific, and business imaging equipment and products. Corning, near the state's southern border with Pennsylvania, is world renowned for its glassworks. In Buffalo huge steel mills, chemical plants, and grain elevators along Lake Erie's shores bespeak the city's heritage as a shipping and manufacturing giant; hard hit by the decline of domestic steel and automobile manufacturing in the 1970s and 1980s, Buffalo has since worked to diversify and rebuild its economy.

FROM THE HAMPTONS TO THE BORSCHT BELT
Twenty-three miles wide and 118 miles long, the sandy finger of Long Island pokes east from Manhattan. Although the western portion of the island is densely populated, much of it is surprisingly rural. Every summer huge crowds seek

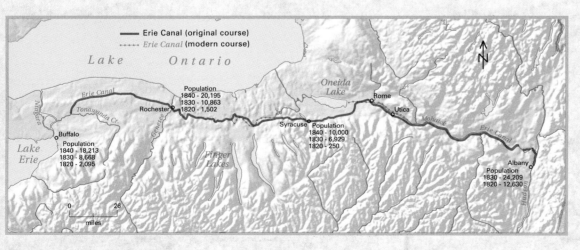

The Erie Canal—Passageway to the West
Begun on July 4, 1817, the Erie Canal was derided by critics as the "Big Ditch." Nevertheless, laborers spent the next several years using shovels, blasting powder, stump-pulling machines, and mules to dig the waterway.

The canal—which rose 688 feet through 83 locks over 363 miles between Albany and Buffalo—was an instant success when it opened in 1825. Travel time and shipping costs to the Midwest dropped, New York Harbor boomed, and cities sprang up along the canal's route.

out the beaches along the island's windswept southern shore. The Catskill Mountains, another vacation option, have been a popular resort area since the 19th century. In their prime, many of these summer retreats were known for their Jewish clientele, earning the region the nickname The Borscht Belt. Those days have mostly passed, but the Catskills remain as beautiful as ever. Tucked between the Hudson Valley and the Delaware River basin, the Catskills' soft peaks—about 4,000 feet at their highest—contain pure, cold streams that offer some of the best trout fishing in the East.

ADIRONDACK PARK

Much of New York State is forested, and a large portion of it always will be. Adirondack Park comprises some 6 million mountainous acres, or nearly a third of the entire state—making it America's largest wilderness area east of the Mississippi. The original 2.8-million-acre forest preserve was mapped off in 1885. Seven years later the park was founded and declared "forever wild" with the addition of thousands of acres of surrounding land; today about half the land is privately owned, but fierce winters, blackflies in summer, and inaccessible terrain all keep development at bay.

▲ *The Baseball Hall of Fame* in Cooperstown showcases the history of baseball in photographs and memorabilia.

Separate from the Appalachian Highlands, the Adirondacks actually have more in common, geologically speaking, with the Green Mountains, across Lake Champlain in Vermont. Mount Marcy is the highest peak, but more than 40 others rise above 4,000 feet, all built upon a platform of ancient stone that is considered some of the oldest exposed bedrock in North America. Mountain lakes (about 2,800 of them) lie cradled between the peaks, and 30,000 miles of rivers and streams gurgle through the Adirondacks' deep pine forests, which are filled with wildlife, including loons, moose, and a substantial population of black bears.

WINERIES AND WATERFALLS

Splayed like an outstretched hand across the west central portion of the state, New York's Finger Lakes are unmistakable on any map. Part of the Allegheny Highlands of the Appalachians, these slender waterways—deep, cold, and glacier dug—represent the heart of New York State's wine-making district. Dozens of waterfalls drain into the lakes; at 215 feet, Taughannock Falls, on Cayuga Lake's western shore near Trumansburg, is the state's highest, but the waterfall is not as popular as Niagara. Straddling the U.S.-Canadian border at the far western edge of

the state, Niagara Falls stands 167 feet high (on the American side) and nearly two-thirds of a mile across; 40 million gallons of water pour over its edge each minute, filling the air with thunder and sparkling mist. Niagara is an awesome spectacle—a fitting display of nature's power in a place that proudly calls itself the Empire State.

▲ *A Long Island vineyard.* The state's newest wine-making region began production in the late 1970s.

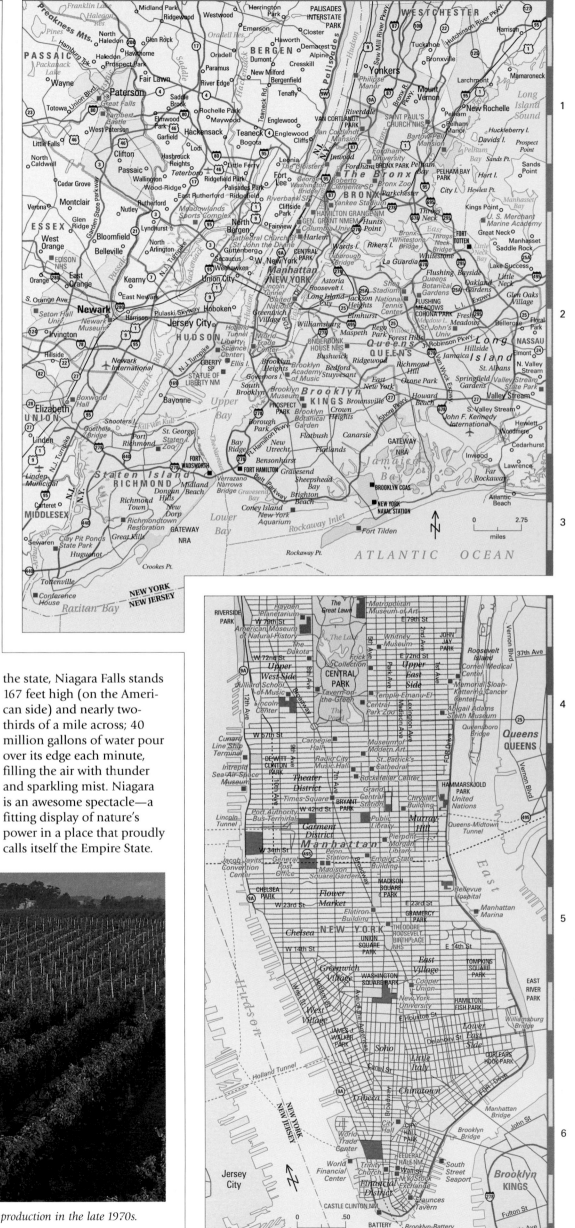

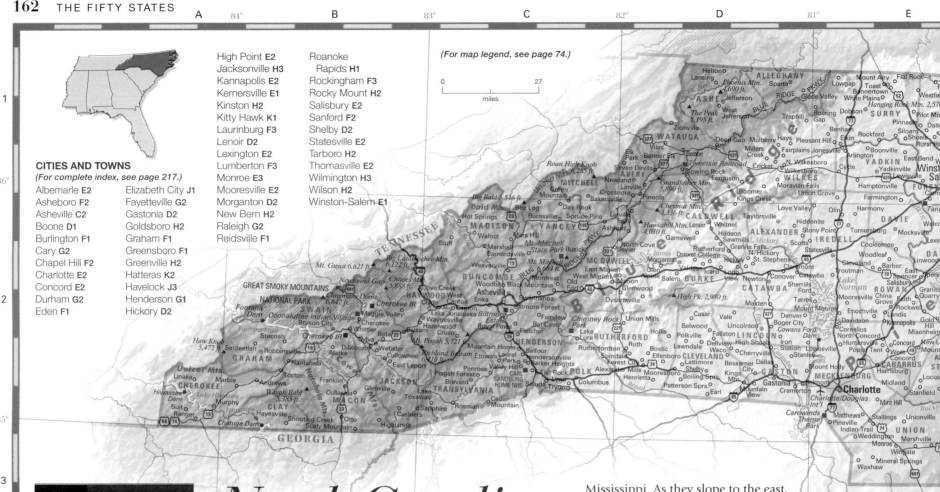

A 84° B 83° C 82° D 81° E

1

36°

2

35°

3

(For map legend, see page 74.)

0   27
miles

CITIES AND TOWNS

(For complete index, see page 217.)

High Point **E2**
Jacksonville **H3**
Kannapolis **E2**
Kernersville **E1**
Kinston **H2**
Kitty Hawk **K1**
Laurinburg **F3**
Lenoir **E2**
Lexington **E2**
Lumberton **F3**
Monroe **E3**
Mooresville **E2**
Morganton **D2**
New Bern **H2**
Raleigh **G2**
Reidsville **F1**

Roanoke
  Rapids **H1**
Rockingham **F3**
Rocky Mount **H2**
Salisbury **E2**
Sanford **F2**
Shelby **D2**
Statesville **E2**
Tarboro **H2**
Thomasville **E2**
Wilmington **H3**
Wilson **H2**
Winston-Salem **E1**

Albemarle **E2**	Elizabeth City **J1**
Asheboro **F2**	Fayetteville **G2**
Asheville **C2**	Gastonia **D2**
Boone **D1**	Goldsboro **H2**
Burlington **F1**	Graham **F1**
Cary **G2**	Greensboro **F1**
Chapel Hill **F2**	Greenville **H2**
Charlotte **E2**	Hatteras **K2**
Concord **E2**	Havelock **J3**
Durham **G2**	Henderson **G1**
Eden **F1**	Hickory **D2**

North Carolina

Guarded by shoals to the east and mountains to the west, North Carolina was not easy to colonize. Roanoke Island hosted the first and second English settlements in the New World, but the latter disappeared three years after its founding. As a result, North Carolina became one of the few states on the Eastern seaboard that was settled by inland routes. Today it has the highest manufacturing output in the South and is known for its textiles, tobacco, and furniture.

PARADISE DISCOVERED

In the summer of 1584, Capt. Arthur Barlowe returned from a voyage to the New World to report to his patron, Sir Walter Raleigh, that he had found a land ranking among "the most plentiful, fruitful and wholesome of all the world." Raleigh named the region "Virginia," after the virgin queen, but the land would eventually have its own identity as North Carolina.

It took quite some time for Barlowe's paradise to live up to its promise of plenty, but its beauty has always been evident. The climate vaults from subtropical to subarctic, embracing snowy egrets and black bears, palm trees and spruces, azaleas and the voracious Venus's-flytrap—found only in the wet coastal plains of North and South Carolina. The state is bounded by two southern Appalachian ranges—the Blue Ridge and the Great Smoky mountains—that are home to the highest peaks east of the

Mississippi. As they slope to the east, the mountains dissolve into a broad piedmont of rolling hills, nurtured by large lakes and meandering rivers that wind past the state's industrial core and its six largest cities. They then plunge into a shower of dramatic waterfalls over the Fall Line and flow gently into the waters of Pamlico and Albemarle sounds. The 320-mile coast is part of the coastal plain, which reaches inland to encompass forested dunes, swamps, and tobacco farms. Standing guard on the horizon are the Outer Banks, an ever-shifting line of sandy barrier islands.

THE LOST COLONY

A year after Barlowe returned from this "wholesome" land, Raleigh decided to see just how plentiful it was and sent 108 colonists to Roanoke Island. They left after scuffles with Indians, only to be replaced in 1587 by another boatload of fortune seekers, who promptly vanished, along with Virginia Dare, the first English child born in America. When their governor, John White, returned with supplies in 1590, he found just a single message—the word *Croatoan*, carved into a tree.

▲ **The state flag,** *adopted in 1885, shows two dates. On May 20, 1775, Mecklenburg County declared independence from Britain. On April 12, 1776, North Carolina voted for independence from Britain at the Constitutional Congress.*

STATE DATA

State bird: Cardinal
State flower: Dogwood
State tree: Pine
State motto: *Esse quam videri* (To be, rather than to seem)
State song: "The Old North State"
Abbreviations: N.C.; NC (postal)
Origin of the name: From the Latin Carolus, meaning Charles, in honor of King Charles I
Nicknames: Tar Heel State, Old North State, Turpentine State

AREA AND SIZE

Total area: 52,586 sq. mi.
Rank within U.S.: 28
Extent: 188 mi. north–south; 499 mi. east–west
Highest elevation: Mount Mitchell, 6,684 ft. above sea level
Lowest elevation: Sea level along the Atlantic Ocean

▶ *The 250-room Biltmore Estate is the largest private home in the country. It was built in Asheville for George Vanderbilt.*

NORTH CAROLINA TIMELINE

1524 Giovanni da Verrazano explores coastal region.

1585 First English colony in America is built on Roanoke Island.

1587 The English settle Roanoke Island a second time. Virginia Dare is first English baby to be born in America.

c.1650 Settlers come to Albemarle area from Virginia.

1712 Separate governors are appointed for North and South Carolina.

1713 Settlers defeat Tuscarora tribe.

1729 North Carolina comes under royal jurisdiction.

1776 North Carolina is first colony to resolve to vote for independence at the Continental Congress.

1789 North Carolina joins the Union as 12th state.

1861 North Carolina secedes from the Union.

1868 North Carolina is readmitted to the Union.

1903 The Wright brothers successfully fly a powered airplane at

Kitty Hawk.

1945 Fontana Dam, largest in the Tennessee Valley Authority, begins operation.

1960 Four black students remain seated at a segregated lunch counter in Greensboro, leading to statewide sit-in demonstrations.

1978 Tobacco sales in state surpass $1 million for first time.

1996 Hurricane Fran kills 31 people and causes billions of dollars in damage to coast.

When White saw that his chests had been dug up and his belongings ruined by the rain, he decided he had solved the mystery: "This could be no other but the deed of the savages our enemies." Contemporary historians believe, however, that the settlers may have been assimilated into the culture of the Indians from the village of Croatoan.

SLOW BUT STEADY PROGRESS

For the next two centuries, North Carolina developed slowly, as English settlers battled against Indians, pirates, the vagaries of the terrain, and the royal government. In 1776 North Carolina became the first colony at the Continental Congress to vote for independence from England. But even this giant step forward inspired no progress. By the early 1800s the state was still lacking in vital seaports and interstate transportation and had little commerce or industry.

By 1835, however, the tide had begun to turn. Armed with a new state constitution, North Carolina hit its stride: public schools, roads, and railroads were built, and agriculture and manufacturing began to prosper.

Then came the Civil War. North Carolina eventually threw itself behind the Confederate cause, contributing more troops than any other state and suffering a quarter of the casualties. The period after Reconstruction found North Carolina making

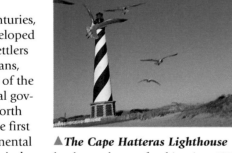

▲ *The Cape Hatteras Lighthouse* *has been a beacon for ships since 1870.*

tremendous progress. The Piedmont started buzzing with hydroelectric power, and the revived state piggybacked the tobacco empire of James Buchanan Duke into the 20th century. Some 350,000 freed slaves were left behind, however, disenfranchised by poll taxes and grandfather clauses, relegated to inferior schools, and saddled with no-win sharecropping contracts. Three generations later, their struggle for freedom had one of its most symbolic moments, in a Greensboro Woolworth store on February 1, 1960. That afternoon, four black students from North Carolina Agricultural and Technical State University (A&T) sat down at the store's segregated lunch counter. After the waitress refused to serve them, they continued to sit, and the next day they came back with more people. In a matter of days, the protesters numbered 400 strong. Within two weeks sympathetic sit-ins were launched across the South. Less than six months later, Woolworth opened its lunch counters to everyone.

A PROMISING FUTURE

North Carolina became integrated with greater ease than most Southern states did, and its black population has shared in the fruits of the economic boom. Factories powered by the Piedmont's gushing rivers produce more textiles than those of any other state. North Carolina's pines and hardwoods supply the largest furniture industry in the country. In summer vast warehouses vibrate with the voices of tobacco auctioneers portioning out the "brown gold" to factories that produce more tobacco products than all other states combined.

Vacationers, too, have fallen under the spell. Tourism has grown sharply in the past 50 years in the Outer Banks and in the mountains, especially on the state's signature attraction—the Blue Ridge Parkway, the nation's longest parkway, which ends at the nation's busiest national park: the Great Smoky Mountains National Park. Between the misty scenery and the average elevation of some 4,000 feet, a drive on the parkway feels like a bit of heaven on earth. And, as those in North Carolina know, nothing could be finer.

POPULATION

Total: 7,777,000
Rank within U.S.: 11
Ethnic breakdown: White: 73.9%; Black: 22.2%; Hispanic: 1.6%; Asian: 1.2%; Indian: 1.2%
Population density: 158.5 people per sq. mi.

CLIMATE

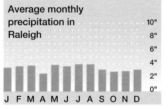

Average monthly temperature in Raleigh

Average monthly precipitation in Raleigh

ECONOMY

Service industries: Automobile dealerships, real estate, banking
Manufacturing: Tobacco products, chemicals, textiles, machinery
Agriculture: Broiler chickens, hogs, turkeys, tobacco, corn, soybeans

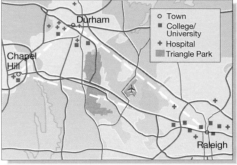

North Carolina's Research Triangle

The cities of Raleigh, Durham, and Chapel Hill, each with its own renowned university, serve as the anchors of the 3,000-square-mile Research Triangle. The area has attracted hundreds of high-tech businesses and organizations devoted to innovation in everything from electronics and biotechnology to environmental and health issues.

North Dakota

STATE DATA
State bird: Western meadowlark
State flower: Wild prairie rose
State tree: American elm
State motto: Liberty and union, now
and forever, one and inseparable
State song: "North Dakota Hymn"
Abbreviations: N.D.; ND
Origin of the name: From the Sioux
word *dakota* or *lakota*, meaning
"allies" or "friends"
Nicknames: Peace Garden State,
Flickertail State, Sioux State

AREA AND SIZE
Total area: 70,665 sq. mi.
Rank within U.S.: 17
Extent: 212 mi. north–south; 360 mi.
east–west
Highest elevation: White Butte,
3,506 ft. above sea level
Lowest elevation: 750 ft. above sea
level in Pembina County

Among the most isolated regions of our country, North Dakota occupies the geographic center of North America. Although it is far from oceans, large cities, and cultural and manufacturing centers, the state has throughout its history been the setting of extraordinary dramas of nature and human perseverance.

THE PASSION OF A PRESIDENT
Years before he became president, Theodore Roosevelt developed a deep love of North Dakota—of its windswept winters and dry summers, its seemingly limitless grazing land, and its surreal and colorful terrain carved by millions of years of meandering and flooding of the Little Missouri River.

Although he never returned to live in the area after his political career took off in the latter half of the 1890s, Roosevelt's several years in residence there shaped his life. His North Dakota was the state's southwestern corner, where a hauntingly beautiful national park now bears his name and includes his Elkhorn Ranch. Here visitors can come face to face with herds of bison

and antelope and contemplate the Badlands—a region 190 miles long and 20 miles wide, where wind and water have conspired to reveal the earth's stratified history of floods and volcanic turmoil, as well as the birth and death of prehistoric beasts and forests.

A FERTILE VALLEY
At North Dakota's eastern edge, there is an entirely different world. The Red River Valley, the fertile bed of a prehistoric inland sea called Lake Agassiz, straddles the border with Minnesota. Although the valley encompasses just 10 percent of North Dakota's area, 40 percent of the state's population lives there. While Roosevelt ranched in the Badlands, agricultural entrepreneurs transformed the valley into an example of how bumper crops and wealth could result from efficient, one-crop farming. Because these large "bonanza" farms grew only wheat, their success was dependent upon a robust wheat market. When the market crashed in the 1930s, so did the farms, and the tracts were parceled up and sold.

Between the Red River Valley and the Badlands of the Missouri Plateau lies North Dakota's largest region, the Central Plateau. This area includes several of the state's most popular attractions: Lake Sakakawea (named after Meriwether Lewis's and William Clark's Shoshone Indian guide), the country's second-largest man-made lake; the International Peace Garden, which pays

▲ **A step back into the past.** *The Bagg farm, in Mooreton, is the last remnant of North Dakota's "bonanza" era.*

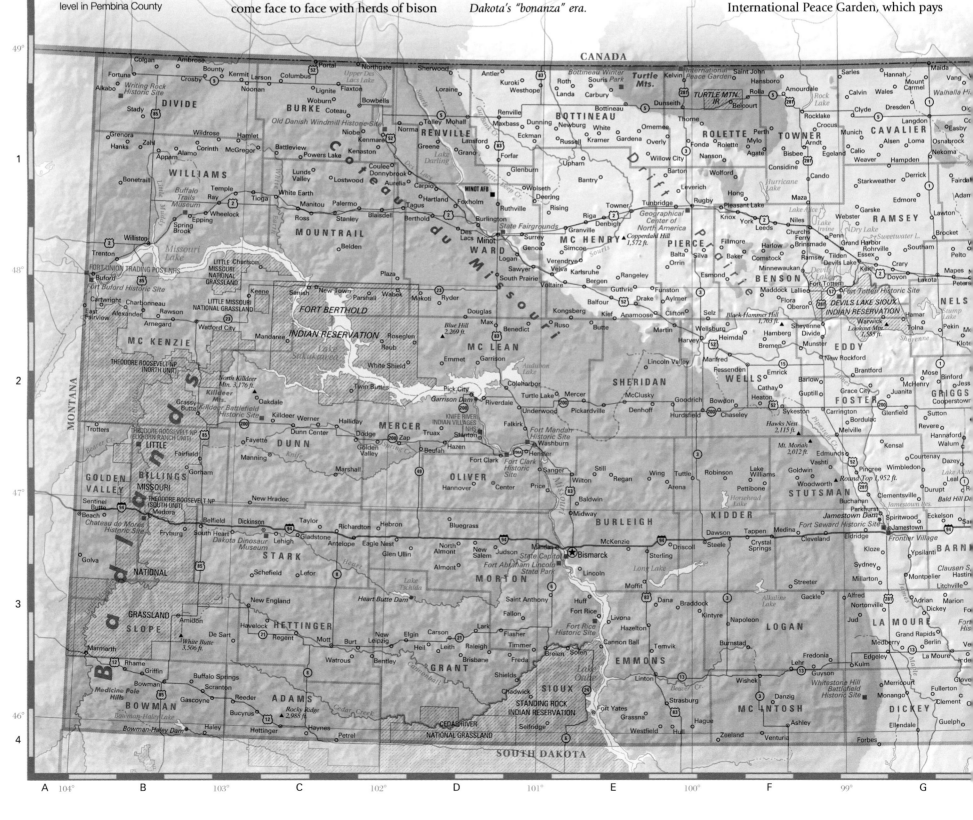

tribute to the long history of uninterrupted peace between the United States and Canada; and Fort Abraham Lincoln State Park, just southwest of Bismarck, which served as Lt. Col. George A. Custer's base before he embarked upon his doomed 1876 expedition to confront Dakota warriors at Little Big Horn.

FRONTIER HISTORY

Drawing its name from the Sioux Indian word *dakota,* meaning "friend" or "ally," North Dakota has been inhabited almost exclusively by Indians for most of the past 9,000 years. Around 1300 the Mandan established farming communities along the Missouri River. The Hidatsa and Arikara tribes joined them in the mid-17th century. After the encroachment of whites and other tribes upon their land to the east, the Sioux (sometimes called the Dakota) also began to enter the area in the 17th century.

A French-Canadian fur trader named Pierre Gaultier de Varennes, sieur de La Vérendrye, was perhaps the first European to visit the region in 1738. Although the United States acquired part of North Dakota with the Louisiana Purchase of 1803, and Lewis and Clark built Fort Mandan and wintered there during 1804–05, it was a British subject, the earl of Selkirk, who established North Dakota's first permanent settlement at Pembina in 1812, when he sponsored several Scottish and Irish farming families. Six years later a treaty with Great Britain granted the United States the remainder of North Dakota, and over the next 71 years the sparsely populated land was shifted in and out of the jurisdiction of nine different U.S. territories.

By the time North Dakota entered the Union in 1889 (on the same day as South Dakota), the Sioux Indians had lost their war against the United States, and most of the survivors lived on reservations. The earlier settlers had moved on, but new immigrants from Germany, Norway, and other northern European countries arrived. For the next 25 years, the population boomed.

▲ **Theodore Roosevelt National Park.** *As Roosevelt said, its Badlands are "so fantastically broken in form and so bizarre in color as to seem hardly properly to belong to this earth."*

MAINTAINING A RURAL HERITAGE

North Dakota has seen its fortunes rise and fall throughout the 20th century: drought and Depression in the 1920s and 1930s, the discovery of oil in the late 1940s, and the growth of the lignite coal industry in the 1950s. The state has always, however, remained predominantly rural, and farms still cover 90 percent of the land. No city has more than 100,000 people, and North Dakota's population is the same as it was in 1920. Bismarck, the state capital, typifies what little there is of urban North Dakota: a modest plains city well aware of its rough-edged history. Fargo, North Dakota's largest metropolis, is home to North Dakota State University and Bonanzaville—a historic village of 40 buildings preserved from pioneer times.

But to focus on its cities is to miss the point of North Dakota. In this most rural of the 50 states, the charm lies not along streets but at the edge of fields of durum wheat, in the rolling land of the Turtle Mountains, in the beauty and grit of the Badlands, and in the steady wind of wide-open spaces.

▲ **The Red River Valley,** *along the border with Minnesota, is renowned for its sugar beet production and its tremendous sunflower yield (bigger than that of all of Kansas).*

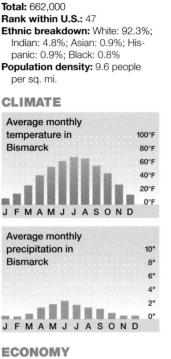

POPULATION

Total: 662,000
Rank within U.S.: 47
Ethnic breakdown: White: 92.3%; Indian: 4.8%; Asian: 0.9%; Hispanic: 0.9%; Black: 0.8%
Population density: 9.6 people per sq. mi.

CLIMATE

Average monthly temperature in Bismarck

100°F 80°F 60°F 40°F 20°F 0°F
J F M A M J J A S O N D

Average monthly precipitation in Bismarck

10" 8" 6" 4" 2" 0"
J F M A M J J A S O N D

ECONOMY

Service industries: Real estate, banking, insurance, repair shops
Agriculture: Wheat, barley, sunflower seeds, hay, flaxseed, milk, sugar beets, honey, beef cattle
Manufacturing: Machinery, food processing
Mining: Petroleum, coal, natural gas, sand, gravel

NORTH DAKOTA
TIME LINE

1682 Robert Cavelier, sieur de La Salle, claims area for France.
1738 Pierre La Vérendrye explores central North Dakota.
1803 U.S. acquires southwestern North Dakota as part of Louisiana Purchase.
1804 Lewis and Clark build Fort Mandan on Missouri River while crossing the area.
1812 Scottish and Irish colonists build settlement at Pembina.
1818 Through an agreement with Britain, U.S. gains remaining part of North Dakota.
1837 Smallpox epidemic devastates Mandan people.
1861 Dakota Territory is created.
1863 Homestead Act opens land to settlers.
1868 Last of Dakota people are confined to reservations.
1870 Arikara, Hidatsa, and Mandan peoples are sent to Fort Berthold Reservation.
1871 Northern Pacific Railroad reaches Fargo.
1876 Oliver Dalrymple builds the first "bonanza" farm in Casselton.
1883 Bismarck becomes capital of territory.
1889 North Dakota joins the Union as 39th state.
1915 Nonpartisan League is founded to fight for state control over wheat trade monopolies.
1929 Seven-year drought begins.
1932 International Peace Garden is dedicated.
1951 Oil is discovered near Tioga.
1956 Garrison Dam on Missouri River begins to produce electric power.
1968 Garrison Diversion Project is begun to increase state's water supply.
1988 Drought kills much of North Dakota's wheat crop.

(For map legend, see page 74.)

CITIES AND TOWNS
(For complete index, see page 217.)

Belcourt **F1**
Beulah **D2**
Bismarck **E3**
Bottineau **E1**
Bowman **B3**
Carrington **F2**
Casselton **H3**
Devils Lake **G1**
Dickinson **C3**
Ellendale **G3**
Fargo **J3**
Grafton **H1**
Grand Forks **H2**
Harvey **F2**
Hazen **D2**
Jamestown **G3**
Langdon **G1**
Lisbon **H3**
Mandan **E3**
Mayville **H2**
Minot **D1**
Mooreton **J3**
Oakes **G3**
Pembina **H1**
Rugby **F1**
Tioga **C1**
Valley City **G3**
Wahpeton **J3**
West Fargo **J3**
Williston **B1**

0   30
miles

▲ **The state flag,** *adopted in 1902, is a two-pointed pennant. The 17 stars represent Ohio as the 17th state. The red and white circle stands for the letter O (for Ohio) and the buckeye nut.*

STATE DATA
State bird: Cardinal
State flower: Scarlet carnation
State tree: Buckeye
State motto: With God, all things are possible
State song: "Beautiful Ohio"
Abbreviation: OH (postal)
Origin of the name: From the Iroquoian word meaning "great river"
Nicknames: Buckeye State, Gateway State, Heartland of the Nation, Mother of Presidents

AREA AND SIZE
Total area: 41,222 sq. mi.
Rank within U.S.: 35
Extent: 245 mi. north–south; 227 mi. east–west
Highest elevation: Campbell Hill in Logan County, 1,549 ft. above sea level
Lowest elevation: 433 ft. above sea level along the Ohio River in Hamilton County

POPULATION
Total: 11,319,000
Rank within U.S.: 7
Ethnic breakdown: White: 85.4%; Black: 11.5%; Hispanic: 1.6%; Asian: 1.2%; Indian: 0.2%
Population density: 276 people per sq. mi.

CLIMATE

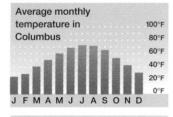

Average monthly temperature in Columbus

Average monthly precipitation in Columbus

ECONOMY
Service industries: Department stores, food stores, restaurants, banks
Manufacturing: Transportation equipment, machinery, fabricated metal products, chemicals
Agriculture: Corn, soybeans, milk
Mining: Coal, natural gas, sandstone

The Hopewell and Adena Mounds
Built between 700 B.C. and A.D. 600 by Hopewell and Adena Indians throughout southern Ohio, earthworks and mounds were used primarily as burial sites, for ceremonial purposes, or, as with the Serpent Mound (left), as sacred effigies.

Ohio

The linchpin in commerce between the Northeast and the Midwest, Ohio combines the character and pace of America's agricultural heartland with an ample measure of industrial muscle. Sprawling between the Great Lakes and the Ohio River, the state's broad expanses provided an early relief valve for pent-up populations living along the East Coast; today the state's rolling farms and serene small towns with tree-lined streets remain a quintessential part of America's identity.

A PRIMEVAL LAND
Ohio is defined by its waterways. The Ohio River, which winds along a tortuous but navigable route from western Pennsylvania to Ohio's southeastern boundary with Kentucky and Indiana, forms the state's entire southern border. In the north, Ohio has more than 230 miles of frontage on Lake Erie, part of an international waterway that provides access from the Atlantic Ocean far into the North American interior.

Covered by glaciers during the last ice age, northern Ohio is mostly flat country. The south, especially the southeast, is a region of hills rising toward the highlands of Kentucky and West Virginia. Before the arrival of white settlers, the state was 95 percent forested. Now, with its woodlands substantially cleared to create farmland and town sites, much of Ohio suggests the open vistas of the prairie states; in the south central counties of the state, however, forests still cover considerable acreage.

Ohio's history of settlement is among the oldest documented in

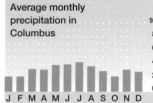

▲ **Soybeans** *are Ohio's second-leading agricultural product and are grown mainly in the western part of the state.*

North America. Dating back some 3,000 years, the Adena and Hopewell cultures left behind a number of ceremonial mounds, such as the 900-foot-round Miamisburg Mound and the more than 1,000-year-old Great Serpent Mound, near Peebles. By the time the first Europeans arrived, these early natives had been supplanted by Algonquin and Iroquoian tribes.

A MIGRATION WEST
European exploration of what is now Ohio may date to a visit by French explorer Robert Cavelier, sieur de La Salle, to the Ohio River valley in 1670. La Salle claimed the region for France, although, like most of the fur-rich North American interior, it was a bone of contention between France and Great Britain for almost a century. Ohio finally passed into British hands with the conclusion of the French and Indian War in 1763. After the Revolutionary War, Ohio was turned over to the Americans and became part of the Northwest Territory.

Because the Ohio River drains into the Mississippi, Ohio commerce had a Southern orientation. Starting in 1788, this was balanced by an influx of New Englanders into the northern Ohio region known as the Western Reserve, so named because it had been "reserved" in colonial times for Connecticut's eventual expansion. Connecticut sold its holdings in 1795. It was at this time that the local Indians, after being defeated by Gen. Anthony Wayne at Fallen Timbers (near present-day Toledo), ceded some two-thirds of Ohio territory. The following year Connecticut's Gen. Moses Cleaveland surveyed the future site of the city that would—with a slight change in spelling—bear his name. Less than a decade later, in 1803, Ohio became a state.

INDUSTRIAL GROWTH
Although early-19th-century migrations to the Midwest gave towns in northeastern Ohio a decidedly New England appearance, improved transportation facilities—the Erie Canal, navigation along Lake Erie, and by midcentury a belt of steel rails—did even more to further bind the state to Eastern markets and no doubt ensured Ohio's Union sympathies during the Civil War. At the war's end, Ohioans stood poised for an era of industrial and commercial development.

Ohio's industrial growth benefited from its supplies of coal, rock salt, clay, and limestone; from the ease with which goods could be shipped via the Great Lakes; and from the railroad companies' natural inclination to use the state's level ground for its routes linking New York and Chicago. But Ohio received a tremendous boost when a young entrepreneur from Cleveland named John Davison Rockefeller founded the Standard Oil Company in 1870. In that same year Benjamin F. Goodrich

OHIO TIMELINE

c. 1670 Robert Cavelier, sieur de La Salle, may have crossed into Ohio.

1747 Ohio Company is formed to colonize Ohio River valley.

1787 Northwest Territory, which includes Ohio, is established.

1803 Ohio becomes 17th state.

1813 Commodore Oliver H. Perry defeats British in Battle of Lake Erie.

1832 Ohio and Erie Canal opens.

1833 Oberlin, the country's first coeducational college, opens.

1869 Ulysses S. Grant is first U.S. president born in Ohio. Cincinnati Red Stockings become world's first professional baseball team.

1870 John D. Rockefeller founds Standard Oil Company in Cleveland. B. F. Goodrich begins making rubber goods in Akron.

1903 Wright brothers build functional aircraft at Dayton.

1913–14 Floods kill more than 350 people, prompting Conservancy Act for flood control.

1959 St. Lawrence Seaway links Lake Erie to Atlantic Ocean.

1970 At Kent State University, four students are killed by National Guardsmen during campus protest against the Vietnam War.

began manufacturing rubber products in Akron, marking the start of that city's reign as the tire capital of the world.

RENEWED VIGOR

While considerable media attention was devoted to the Rust Belt syndrome of industrial decline in Ohio and other upper Midwestern states during the 1970s and 1980s, Ohio has retained much of its industrial vigor, along with a commitment to revitalizing areas hardest hit by the environmental toll of manufacturing's good years and the civic toll of its decline. After being declared virtually "dead" in the late 1960s, Lake Erie is well on its way to recovery, and the city of Cleveland has rebuilt its downtown around such popular attractions as the new Rock and Roll Hall of Fame and Museum.

But for all urban Ohio's ups and downs, the state's image is most fixed in the American imagination in terms of its vast farmlands and the small cities that dot this splendidly cultivated landscape. This is the environment that produced seven American presidents, inventor Thomas Edison, pioneer of flight Orville Wright, John Glenn, and the quintessential image of front-porch Americana.

0 ————— 24
miles

(For map legend, see page 74.)

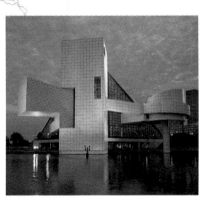

◀ *The Rock and Roll Hall of Fame,* which opened in 1995, was designed by I. M. Pei.

CITIES AND TOWNS
(For complete index, see page 217.)

Akron **D1**	Lakewood **D1**
Austintown **E1**	Lancaster **C3**
Beavercreek **A3**	Lima **A2**
Boardman **E1**	Lorain **C1**
Bowling Green **B1**	MaMassillon **D2**
Canton **D2**	Mansfield **C2**
Chillicothe **C3**	Mentor **D1**
Cincinnati **A3**	Miamisburg **A3**
Cleveland **D1**	Middletown **A3**
Cleveland	Newark **C2**
Heights **D1**	North Olmsted **D1**
Columbus **C3**	Parma **D1**
Cuyahoga Falls **D1**	Peebles **B4**
Dayton **A3**	Sandusky **C1**
Elyria **C1**	Springfield **B3**
Euclid **D1**	Strongsville **D1**
Fairborn **A3**	Toledo **B1**
Fairfield **A3**	Warren **E1**
Findlay **B1**	Westerville **C2**
Hamilton **A3**	Wooster **D2**
Kent **D1**	Xenia **B3**
Kettering **A3**	Youngstown **E1**

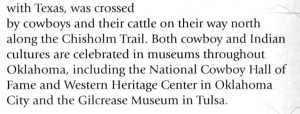

OKLAHOMA

▲ *Oklahoma's flag* shows an Osage warrior's shield adorned with eagle feathers. A peace pipe and an olive branch—both symbols of peace—cross the shield. The flag was adopted in 1925.

STATE DATA
State bird: Scissor-tailed flycatcher
State flower: Mistletoe
State tree: Redbud
State motto: *Labor omnia vincit* (Labor conquers all things)
State song: "Oklahoma!"
Abbreviations: Okla.; OK (postal)
Origin of the name: From the Choctaw words *okla humma*, meaning "red people"
Nicknames: Sooner State, Boomer State

AREA AND SIZE
Total area: 69,919 sq. mi.
Rank within U.S.: 18
Extent: 231 mi. north–south; 478 mi. east–west
Highest elevation: Black Mesa, 4,973 ft. above sea level
Lowest elevation: 287 ft. above sea level along the Little River in McCurtain County

POPULATION
Total: 3,373,000
Rank within U.S.: 28
Ethnic breakdown: White: 78.7%; Black: 8.2%; Indian: 8.1%; Hispanic: 3.7%; Asian: 1.4%
Population density: 48.9 people per sq. mi.

CLIMATE
Average monthly temperature in Oklahoma City
100°F
80°F
60°F
40°F
20°F
0°F
J F M A M J J A S O N D

Average monthly precipitation in Oklahoma City
10"
8"
6"
4"
2"
0"
J F M A M J J A S O N D

ECONOMY
Service industries: Wholesale and retail trade; community, business, and personal services; finance
Manufacturing: Machinery, transportation equipment
Mining: Natural gas, petroleum, iodine, coal, crushed stone
Agriculture: Beef cattle, wheat, hay

Oklahoma

A 20th-century state with an ancient history, Oklahoma is an all-American combination of rolling prairies, high plains, stark buttes, and lush river valleys. For centuries the state was home only to Native Americans; then waves of pioneers transformed it into a land of farms and ranches, as well as a major source of energy.

FROM BLACK MESA TO RED RIVER
Spanish explorer Francisco Vásquez de Coronado was bitterly disappointed when he arrived in northern Oklahoma in 1541; instead of the city of gold that had been rumored to exist there, he found Plains Apache Indians roaming the prairies, hunting "humpbacked cows" (buffalo).

A land of prairies may have been the only impression Coronado was left with, and this is how the Sooner State is often described. The description, however, is only partially correct, for within the boundaries of Oklahoma a world of extremes exists. From the towering Black Mesa in the northwestern Panhandle the land drops a few thousand feet and joins the prairies of the central lowlands. Mountains dominate a substantial part of the landscape, from the Arbuckle Mountains in south central Oklahoma to the Wichitas in the southwest and the Ouachitas in the southeast —a region of towering pines and mountain lakes. Reaching across the Texas border, the coastal plain creeps into the sandy Red River region. The Red River, which forms the border with Texas, was crossed by cowboys and their cattle on their way north along the Chisholm Trail. Both cowboy and Indian cultures are celebrated in museums throughout Oklahoma, including the National Cowboy Hall of Fame and Western Heritage Center in Oklahoma City and the Gilcrease Museum in Tulsa.

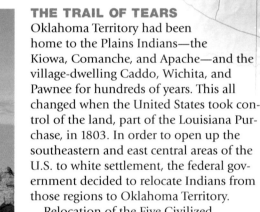
▲ *Oklahoma City's* neoclassical capitol stands in sharp contrast to the working oil rig on the capitol grounds.

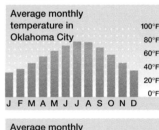

▲ *A sandstone formation* stands watch over the juniper-dotted plains of Cimmaron County, once the hunting ground of the Apache, Comanche, Cheyenne, Arapaho, and Kiowa tribes.

THE TRAIL OF TEARS
Oklahoma Territory had been home to the Plains Indians—the Kiowa, Comanche, and Apache—and the village-dwelling Caddo, Wichita, and Pawnee for hundreds of years. This all changed when the United States took control of the land, part of the Louisiana Purchase, in 1803. In order to open up the southeastern and east central areas of the U.S. to white settlement, the federal government decided to relocate Indians from those regions to Oklahoma Territory.

Relocation of the Five Civilized Tribes—the Cherokee, Chickasaw, Choctaw, Creek, and Seminole—began in the 1820s. By 1830 all Indians who lived east of the Mississippi River had been ordered to move into the designated territory. The forced migrations were heartbreaking enough, but one in particular has remained infamous. A Cherokee migration, later to be known as the Trail of Tears, was carried out during the winter of 1838–39. It claimed the lives of some 4,000 Cherokee Indians who died of hunger and disease.

LAND FREE FOR THE TAKING
As Indians were pushed onto ever-shrinking parcels of land, white settlers waited to participate in government-supervised land rushes. On the morning of April 22, 1889, thousands of hopeful homesteaders stood just outside the boundaries of the unassigned territories. At noon a signal was given, and they surged across the borders to claim the coveted 160-acre homestead parcels. By nightfall the lucky ones were setting up temporary camps. Oklahoma City, previously just a train depot, became a community of 10,000 people by the end of the day.

The land rush did not occur without incident. There were some dishonest and unscrupulous individuals who had sneaked over the borders early and hidden themselves, jump-

OKLAHOMA TIME LINE

1803 U.S. buys Oklahoma as part of Louisiana Purchase.

1820–42 The Five Civilized Tribes—Cherokee, Chickasaw, Choctaw, Creek, and Seminole—are forced to relocate to Oklahoma.

1834 U.S. government proclaims Oklahoma Indian Territory.

1866 The Five Civilized Tribes are forced to cede part of Oklahoma.

1872 Railroad crosses Oklahoma.

First commercial coal is mined near McAlester.

1889 Oklahoma's first producing oil well opens at Chelsea. Land is made available to white homesteaders.

1890 Oklahoma Territory is established, including panhandle.

1893 Indian nations are divided; land is allocated to individual Indians and white settlers.

1907 Oklahoma joins the Union as 46th state.

1930's Depression and drought ruin Oklahoma's farmers.

1959 Statewide prohibition of liquor sales is repealed.

1971 Arkansas-Verdigris waterway connects Muskogee and Tulsa to the Mississippi River.

1987 Twenty-nine banks fail.

1990 Oklahoma is first state to limit state legislators' terms.

1995 Terrorist bomb blows up federal building in Oklahoma City and kills 168 people.

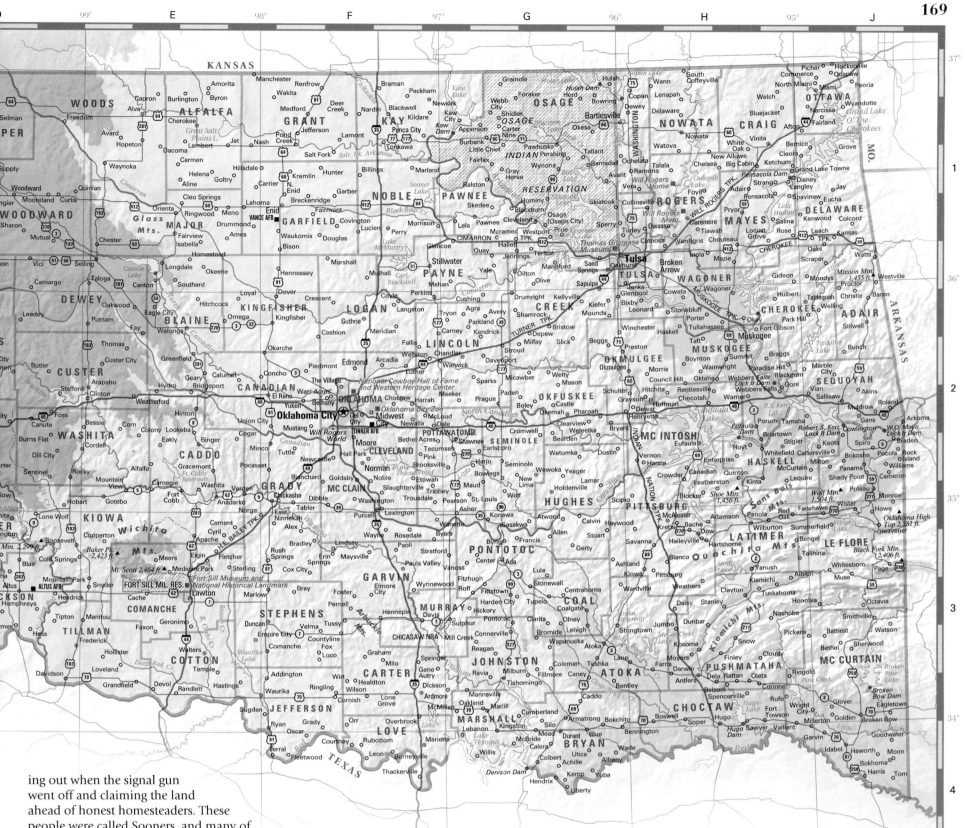

ing out when the signal gun went off and claiming the land ahead of honest homesteaders. These people were called Sooners, and many of them eventually lost their ill-gotten land.

BOOM AND BUST

Not even the land rush rivaled the oil boom and the Dust Bowl in importance and drama. In 1897 the first profitable well spouted oil near Bartlesville, and by 1904 Oklahoma had become a major petroleum producer. Oklahoma City was booming. Surrounded by oil fields, Tulsa, formerly a cow town, became known as the oil capital of the world. The good times did not last long, however. In the 1930s the nation suffered a deep economic depression. Oil production slowed, and hundreds of thousands of oil workers lost their jobs.

But the worst was yet to come. Few people realized that the broad grasslands of Oklahoma should never have been plowed, and no soil-conservation measures had been taken. When drought and unusually hot summers dried the land, winds finished the job by stripping away the topsoil. Thousands of Oklahomans fled the Dust Bowl to try their luck elsewhere.

▲ *A tent city*, complete with land attorneys to settle claim disputes, bustles with activity in Guthrie, Indian Territory, 1889.

In the seven years that followed, soil-conservation practices helped restore many of the farms damaged during the 1930s drought. The land was brought back to health by environmental action. More than 200 artificial lakes have been created from rivers and larger streams for the purpose of flood control, irrigation, hydroelectric power, recreation, and municipal water supplies. The landlocked state also has a lifeline to the sea. From Catoosa, a port near Tulsa, the Arkansas-Verdigris Navigation System rivals the St. Lawrence Seaway in shipping potential and is a commercial route to the Gulf of Mexico for oil- and wheat-laden barges.

Modern success, however, has not been without tragedy. On April 19, 1995, the nation was focused upon Oklahoma City, when a truck-bomb explosion destroyed part of the Alfred P. Murrah Federal Building. The deadliest terrorist incident ever to occur in the United States, it left 168 people dead and more than 500 injured. Through this horrible event Oklahomans have demonstrated the unique qualities and strengths of their Indian and pioneer heritage.

(For map legend, see page 74.)

CITIES AND TOWNS
(For complete index, see page 217.)

Ada G3	Elk City D2
Altus D3	Enid F1
Ardmore F3	Guthrie F2
Bartlesville H1	Guymon B1
Bethany F2	Lawton E3
Bixby H2	McAlester H3
Broken Arrow H1	Miami J1
Catoosa H2	Midwest City F2
Chelsea H2	Moore F2
Chickasha F2	Muskogee H2
Choctaw F2	Mustang F2
Claremore H1	Norman F2
Clinton E2	Oklahoma City F2
Cushing G2	Okmulgee H2
Del City F2	Ponca City F1
Duncan F3	Shawnee G2
Durant G4	Stillwater F1
Edmond F2	Tulsa H1
El Reno F2	Yukon F2

Oregon

Fertile valleys, abundant forests, and the promise of free land were such irresistible lures that more than 350,000 immigrants and their families endured the hardships of the 2,000-mile Oregon Trail to settle this area. Although more than a century has passed, the attraction remains strong. Oregon's population now tops 3 million, and millions more visit each year to enjoy a bounty of natural wonders that rightfully earns the state the reputation as the nation's Pacific wonderland.

A COLORFUL HISTORY

Chinook, Paiute, Modoc, and Nez Perce were among the some 125 different tribes of Native Americans who were living in Oregon when the first Europeans stepped ashore in the 1700s. The land provided these early inhabitants with everything they needed. Deep forests yielded wood for shel-

ter. Rivers ran thick with salmon and trout. Game was plentiful, and edible plants grew in wild profusion.

Although Spanish explorers sailed off its coast as early as the 16th century, Oregon was literally put on the map in 1778, when Capt. James Cook charted a portion of the coastline during his search for the fabled "great river of the West." British fur traders soon followed. In 1792 Robert Gray, an American trader, became the first to sail into the river the state is named after, the mighty Ouragan. Gray renamed the waterway in honor of his ship, the *Columbia Rediviva.*

Interest in the new lands of the Louisiana Purchase led President Thomas Jefferson to send an expedition, in 1804, to explore and map the territory all the way to the Pacific Ocean. The expedition's leaders, Meriwether Lewis and William Clark, described a land abundant with natural resources. Soon other adventurers were heading overland to Oregon. Tales of an enormous beaver population led fur trader John Jacob Astor to send merchants there, where they founded the first American outpost in 1811 and named it Astoria.

The real push to settle Oregon came with the blazing of the Oregon Trail in the late 1830s and 1840s. Stretching from Independence, Missouri, to Oregon City, the trail was followed by pioneers in oxen-pulled wagons bound for what was then touted as "the Garden of Eden." Theirs was a difficult journey—one in 17 people died

▲ **Portland,** *the state's commercial center, is renowned for its natural beauty. Mount Hood, Oregon's highest peak, stands in the background.*

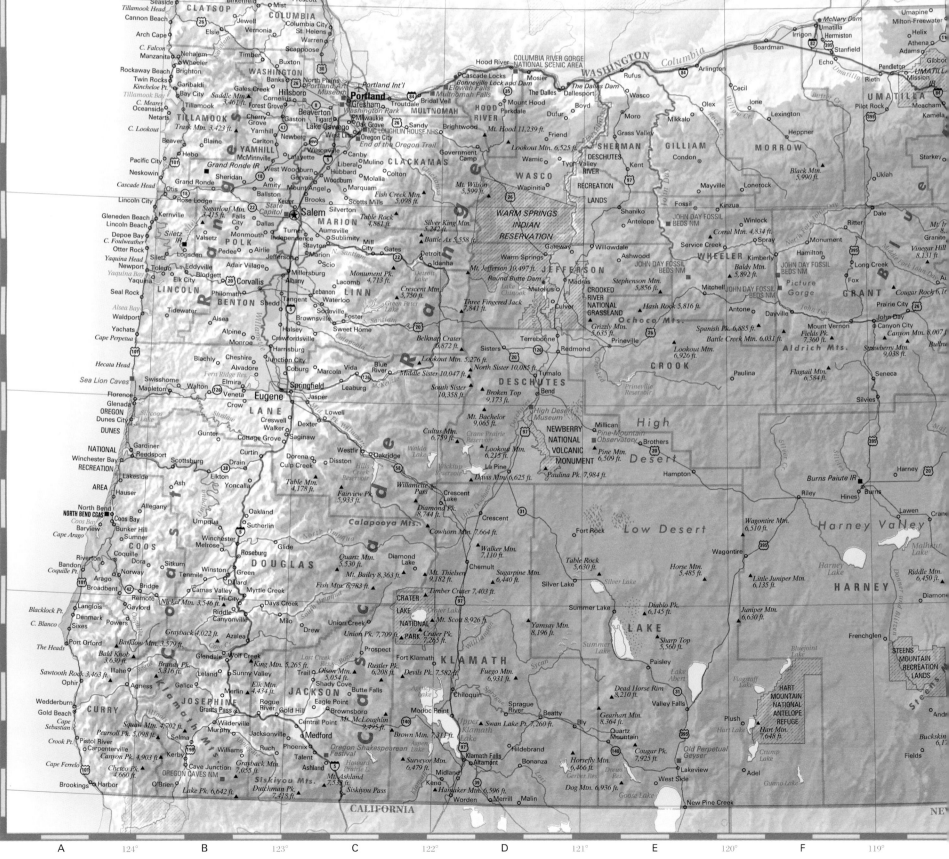

en route—but the goal lived up to its promise. Settlers found a land whose fertile soil and temperate climate proved ideal for farming. To this day agriculture remains important, contributing about $6 billion annually to the state's economy.

THE PROMISED LAND

From its snowcapped volcanic peaks to its temperate rain forests, Oregon's topography—divided into six main regions—is spectacularly diverse. The rugged coastline, part of what is called the Coast Ranges, extends 296 miles from the mouth of the Columbia River to the California border. Indented by a few bays and harbors, Oregon's coast is heavily forested by coniferous trees, as is nearly half of the state's total land area of 98,386 square miles. The trees flourish because of the region's moist climate; the average annual rainfall here is 80 inches, although as much as 130 inches is not uncommon in some areas. The abundance of forests—of primarily Douglas fir, Sitka spruce, hemlock, and ponderosa pine trees—makes the processing of wood products one of the state's main industries.

To the east of the Coast Ranges lies the Willamette Valley, a fertile lowland that was the focus of early settlement; today it is home to the majority of the state's population. The valley was carved by the Willamette River, which flows northward into the Columbia River at Portland. With 471,325 residents, Portland is Oregon's largest city. It is also one of the country's most beautiful. Built at the confluence of two major rivers, the "City of Roses" boasts a compact downtown with skyscrapers standing side by side with historical buildings and the nation's largest municipal forested park. A snowcapped volcanic peak 50 miles to the east serves as a backdrop; the mountain, 11,239-foot-high Mount Hood, is part of the Cascade Range, a chain that runs the length of the state like a volcanic spine. The lakes, rivers, and hiking trails in this heavily forested range serve as a popular playground for outdoors enthusiasts.

Two-thirds of the state lies east of the Cascades. The north-

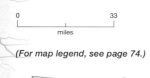

(For map legend, see page 74.)

CITIES AND TOWNS

ern part includes the Columbia Plateau, a land of gently rolling hills and dry uplands. The plateau is divided by its namesake river, which has cut a deep, wide gorge. Dozens of waterfalls tumble into the Columbia River gorge, including the spectacular two-level, 620-foot Multnomah Falls.

The Blue, Wallowa, and Umatilla mountains occupy the northeastern corner of the state. The Wallowa Valley at one time served as a temporary home for a band of the Nez Perce and their charismatic leader, Chief Joseph.

The southeastern corner of Oregon is part of the Great Basin. Compared with the western part of the state, rain seldom falls here, yet when it does, lakes and wetlands are quick to form. Lakes Harney and Malheur attract flocks of migrating waterfowl and other birds. The Malheur National Wildlife Refuge is famous among bird-watchers, and on a single spring day during migration, it's possible to see more than 100 different species, including golden eagles, bobolinks, and loons. That so many birds can be found in what at first appears to be a barren desert is just one of the many surprises that Oregon holds in store.

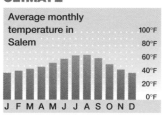

▶ *Salmon swim* up ladders, or water-filled terraces, at the Bonneville Dam. The fish are on their way up the Columbia River, home of the legendary salmon runs.

▲ *Yellow bee plants bloom on the Painted Hills of the John Day Fossil Beds National Monument in north central Oregon. Layers of volcanic ash created the ribbons of varicolored soil.*

▲ **The state flag,** adopted in 1925, displays the state seal. On it are 33 stars, showing that Oregon was the 33rd state. An ox-drawn wagon represents pioneer settlers; grain, a miner's pick, a plow, and timber symbolize Oregon's resources and industries.

STATE DATA
State bird: Western meadowlark
State flower: Oregon grape
State tree: Douglas fir
State motto: *Alis volat propriis* (She flies with her own wings)
State song: "Oregon, My Oregon"
Abbreviations: Oreg. or Ore.; OR (postal)
Origin of the name: Possibly from *Ouragan* (Hurricane), an early French name for the Columbia River
Nickname: Beaver State

AREA AND SIZE
Total area: 98,386 sq. mi.
Rank within U.S.: 10
Extent: 294 mi. north–south; 401 mi. east–west
Highest elevation: Mount Hood, 11,239 ft. above sea level
Lowest elevation: Sea level

POPULATION
Total: 3,397,000
Rank within U.S.: 27
Ethnic breakdown: White: 88.0%; Hispanic: 5.7%; Asian: 3.2%; Black: 1.7%; Indian: 1.3%
Population density: 35.3 people per sq. mi.

CLIMATE

Average monthly temperature in Salem
100°F
80°F
60°F
40°F
20°F
0°F
J F M A M J J A S O N D

Average monthly precipitation in Salem
10"
8"
6"
4"
2"
0"
J F M A M J J A S O N D

ECONOMY
Service industries: Real estate, banking, medical offices, resorts
Manufacturing: Wood processing, electrical equipment
Agriculture: Timber, potatoes, milk, berries, cherries, wheat, beef cattle

OREGON TIME LINE

1792 Capt. Robert Gray explores Columbia River.

1805 Lewis and Clark reach mouth of Columbia River.

1811 John Jacob Astor founds fur-trading post at Astoria.

1818 Britain and U.S. agree to occupy Oregon area jointly.

1819 Treaty between U.S. and Spain sets Oregon's current southern border.

1843 About 900 people migrate to Oregon via Oregon Trail.

1848 Oregon Territory is created.

1853 Washington Territory is separated from Oregon Territory.

1859 Oregon joins the Union as 33rd state.

1868 Oregon's first salmon-canning plant is established at Westport.

1883 Northern Pacific Railway connects Portland to the East.

1933 Tillamook Burn forest fire destroys 300,000 acres.

1937 Bonneville Dam hydroelectric project on Columbia River is completed.

1961 Maurine Neuberger becomes Oregon's first woman senator.

1964 Heavy flooding damages western Oregon.

1966 Astoria Bridge links Oregon with Washington.

1971 Oregon becomes first state to ban nonreturnable bottles and cans.

1977 Oregon establishes statewide ban on aerosol sprays.

1991 Barbara Roberts becomes Oregon's first woman governor.

Pennsylvania

▲ **The state flag,** adopted in 1907, displays the state seal held by two horses. On the seal is a shield picturing a plow, a sailing ship, and wheat, surrounded by a stalk of corn and an olive branch. An eagle sits on top.

STATE DATA

State bird: Ruffed grouse
State flower: Mountain laurel
State tree: Hemlock
State motto: Virtue, liberty, and independence
State song: "Pennsylvania"
Abbreviations: Pa., Penn., or Penna.; PA (postal)
Origin of the name: Latin for "Penn's Woods," after the father of the colony's founder, William Penn
Nicknames: Keystone State, Quaker State

AREA AND SIZE

Total area: 46,068 sq. mi.
Rank within U.S.: 33
Extent: 175 mi. north–south; 306 mi. east–west
Highest elevation: Mount Davis, 3,213 ft. above sea level
Lowest elevation: Sea level along the Delaware River

POPULATION

Total: 12,202,000
Rank within U.S.: 5
Ethnic breakdown: White: 85.7%; Black: 9.7%; Hispanic: 2.7%; Asian: 1.7%; Indian: 0.1%
Population density: 271 people per sq. mi.

CLIMATE

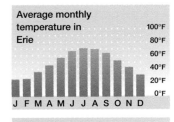

Average monthly temperature in Erie
J F M A M J J A S O N D
100°F 80°F 60°F 40°F 20°F 0°F

Average monthly precipitation in Erie
J F M A M J J A S O N D
10" 8" 6" 4" 2" 0"

Average monthly temperature in Philadelphia
J F M A M J J A S O N D
100°F 80°F 60°F 40°F 20°F 0°F

Average monthly precipitation in Philadelphia
J F M A M J J A S O N D
10" 8" 6" 4" 2" 0"

ECONOMY

Service industries: Community, business, and personal services
Manufacturing: Food processing, pharmaceuticals, machinery
Agriculture: Milk, mushrooms, eggs

Since its founding as a "holy experiment" in religious tolerance, many important words and ideas have come out of Pennsylvania. The Articles of Confederation, the Declaration of Independence, and the U.S. Constitution were all written here. Later, when the nation's mettle was tested during the Civil War, America once again found its voice in the state. It was on the battlefield at Gettysburg that Abraham Lincoln's short but eloquent speech captured all the pain and purpose of the struggle. Called the Keystone State for its central location among the original Thirteen Colonies, Pennsylvania stands center stage in the drama of American history as well.

WILLIAM PENN'S FREE COLONY

In 1681 the British king Charles II granted Quaker leader William Penn a charter to a tract of land in the New World that included

▲ **Hershey kisses** being produced by a factory worker in 1937. The company's founder, Milton S. Hershey, had two candy shops fail before he became a confectionary success.

0   20
miles

(For map legend, see page 74.)

CITIES AND TOWNS
(For complete index, see page 217.)

everything between latitudes 39 and 42 degrees north and longitude 5 degrees west of the Delaware River. Penn gave the territory his family surname, coupled with the Latin word *sylvania*, which means "woods." Concentrating his energies in the eastern part of Pennsylvania, Penn established Philadelphia, his "city of brotherly love," at the confluence of the Delaware and Schuylkill rivers. Blessed with a strategically central location in the colonies, Philadelphia quickly became a cultural, political, and economic hub of Britain's New World holdings and the preeminent city of 18th-century America; originally laid out on an orderly grid, it stood as a model of urban planning as well, a template for cities from Washington, D.C., to Phoenix, Arizona.

Penn's greatest innovation, though, lay in his idealistic vision of a "free colony for all mankind," where freedom of worship and conscience, just taxation, economic opportunity, and voting rights were all sanctified by law. He set forth these principles in his "Great Law of Pennsylvania," which was later rewritten and strengthened in the Charter of Privileges of 1701. With one of the colonies' soundest and most welcoming systems of government, Pennsylvania proved to be a magnet for immigrants from many lands. Penn's Quaker brethren from England and Wales were soon joined by French, Swedish, and German settlers (the so-called Pennsylvania Dutch, a mispronunciation of the word *Deutsch*, meaning "German"), who fanned out from Philadelphia to till the fertile soil of the state's southeastern corner.

THE PLAIN PEOPLE

Among the most distinctive of Pennsylvania's early arrivals were members of several Protestant sects, including the Amish, Mennonites, Moravians, and Dunkers. Some were known as the Plain People for their simple way of life and their austere wardrobes of black and brown. Today the Amish of Lancaster County, about 100 miles west of Philadelphia, still live much as they always have, eschewing modern technology for old-fashioned folkways, religious devotion, and a life close to the earth. Along the country lanes of Amish country, electric lines and telephone poles are scarce, and pickup trucks and tourist buses share the road with horse-drawn buggies, which run past fields where farmers still use teams of mules and horses to pull their plows.

▲ *Amish men* hold a "frolic" (work party) to raise a new barn for a neighbor. Traditionally, the barn should be finished within a single day.

▲ *Farmland in Lancaster County* spreads across southeastern Pennsylvania's Piedmont region. Preservation programs begun in 1989 have saved more than 86,000 acres of farmland from development.

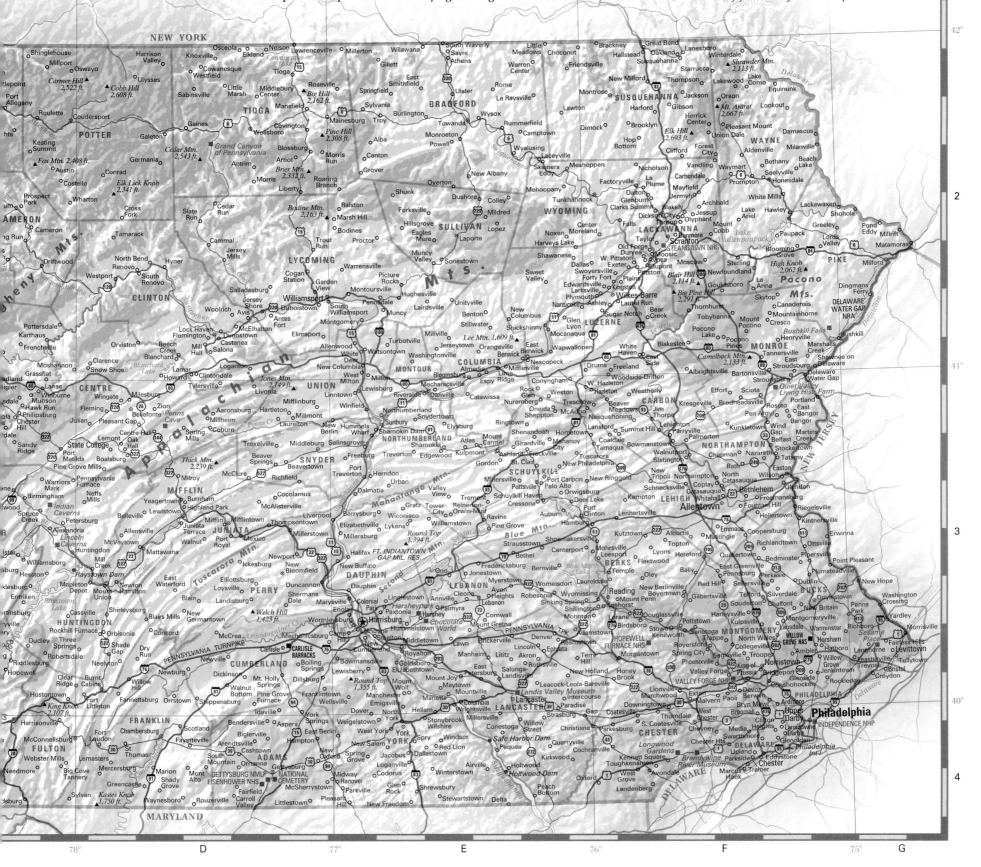

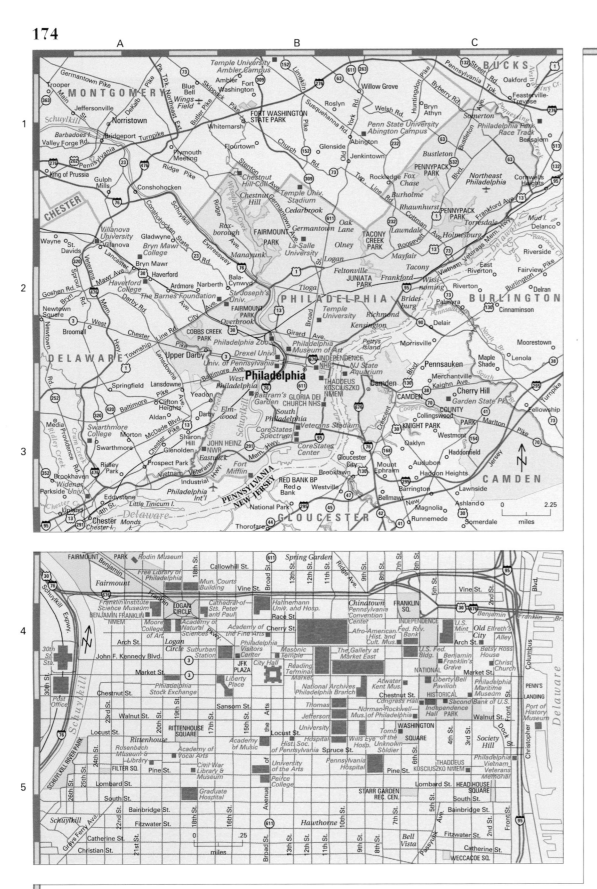

(where his troops were so badly beaten by the British in the fall of 1777). The heaviest concentration of Revolutionary historical sites is in Philadelphia itself, and these center on Independence Hall. Within sight of skyscraping hotels and office towers, this simple but majestic building houses the chamber in which in July 1776 the Founding Fathers put pen to paper and pledged their lives and fortunes to declare America a sovereign nation. A few blocks away, the Betsy Ross House memorializes the life of America's most patriotic seamstress; just to the north, the Liberty Bell, on display in a modern pavilion (and still cracked), continues to draw camera-clicking crowds.

GHOSTS OF GETTYSBURG

Nearly a century after Pennsylvania fulfilled its role as the birthplace of the Union, in the summer of 1863, the state was the site of one of the Civil War's most harrowing ordeals—the bloody three-day battle at Gettysburg. In this picturesque south central farming town, federal troops clashed with a seasoned invasion force under the command of Confederate general Robert E. Lee. Until that time, the South seemed to be winning the war, or at least holding its own; when the smoke had cleared over Cemetery Ridge, some 7,000 men lay dead and more than 44,000 were wounded or missing. Lee's hopes of a Southern stronghold on Union soil had

▲ *Union and Confederate dead lay side by side on the Gettysburg battlefield. The fierce, three-day battle was the last Confederate attack on Northern soil.*

been dashed. The war ground on for two more years, but at Gettysburg the corner was turned toward Union victory.

Today Gettysburg National Military Park draws thousands of curious visitors each year from both sides of the Mason-Dixon line. Part cemetery, part historic site, part parkland, this verdant patch of ground is, above all, a place of quiet contemplation—quiet enough, some say, to hear the ghostly echo of spattering gunfire from the trees, the moans of the wounded, the clear, purposeful voice of a war-weary president, uttering the immortal words of his dedication that would begin to bind the nation's wounds. Haunted and haunting, the green hills of Gettysburg—like much of Pennsylvania—remain a realm where past and present join together, and the very idea of America seems as potently real as the place itself.

KEYSTONE STATE INDUSTRY

Fueled by a tide of hardworking immigrants—Italians, Germans, Poles, Swedes, and, later, African-Americans—Philadelphia grew to become one of 19th-century America's economic powerhouses, with factories that produced everything from sausages to shoes to ships. (Philadelphia's shipyards remain some of the nation's largest and busiest.) Although the decline of domestic manufacturing in recent decades has brought hard times to some portions of the city, a diversified economy continues to bring wealth to the city's ever-widening suburban ring, home to more than one-third of all Pennsylvanians.

The greatest source of Philadelphia's prosperity has always been the Delaware River, a vital waterway since colonial times. Boasting more commercial traffic than any other American river except the Mississippi, the Delaware flows south to form the state's eastern border with New York and New Jersey. Although the lower shores of the river are crowded by commerce, some of the state's most scenic vistas can be found upriver, where the Delaware cuts a winding gorge through the Kittatinny mountain range on the border. This region, known as the Delaware Water Gap, was a popular resort area in the late 19th century; today the hiking trails and riverside campsites of the Delaware Water Gap National Recreation Area bring cooling relief to sweltering city dwellers.

Some 300 miles across the state, Pennsylvania's second major river system and second-largest city meet to form one of America's great industrial giants: the "steel city" of Pittsburgh,

▲ *Independence Hall (formerly called the State House) is well guarded by Gen. George Washington—a fitting sentinel for the birthplace of the Declaration of Independence and the U.S. Constitution.*

REVOLUTIONARY BYWAYS

Pennsylvania's history is a litany of firsts—including America's first stone-paved toll road, or turnpike. Connecting Philadelphia with Lancaster, it opened for business in 1794. The name turnpike is descriptive: a toll taker would collect the fare, then turn a pike, or gate, to let travelers pass. Almost 150 years later, in 1940, the Pennsylvania Turnpike became the nation's first limited-access highway, tracing the route of the original toll road for part of its journey across the state.

Just west of Philadelphia, an exit off the Pennsylvania Turnpike bears a name familiar to every student of American history: Valley Forge. After the Battle of Germantown, General Washington's Continental Army quartered here during the brutal winter of 1777–78. Nearly one-fourth of the undersupplied troops (2,500 out of 10,000 men) perished from exposure, malnutrition, or disease before spring arrived. Valley Forge National Historical Park is now a popular getaway for Philadelphians, who bicycle and in-line-skate along the pathways where America's resolve was once so deeply tested.

An abundance of other Revolutionary War sites dots the map of southeastern Pennsylvania, from Washington Crossing (where Washington launched his surprise Christmas-night raid on the British and Hessian garrison across the Delaware River in Trenton, New Jersey) to the Brandywine Battlefield

◄ *A system of bridges* and highways spans the Monongahela River—one of three waterways that form "The Golden Triangle"—transporting travelers to Three Rivers Stadium and to Pittsburgh beyond.

PENNSYLVANIA
TIME LINE

1609 Henry Hudson explores Delaware Bay.

1643 Swedes establish settlement on Tinicum Island in Delaware River.

1655 The Dutch conquer the Swedish colony.

1664 English troops take over Dutch territory.

1681 King Charles II grants Pennsylvania to William Penn, who establishes colony as "holy experiment."

1744 Benjamin Franklin founds American Philosophical Society in Philadelphia.

1754 The French and Indian War begins in western Pennsylvania.

1776 Declaration of Independence is adopted in Philadelphia.

1780 State passes first abolition law, providing for the gradual emancipation of slaves.

1787 Constitutional Convention meets in Philadelphia. Pennsylvania becomes second state to ratify Constitution.

1790–1800 Philadelphia is capital of the United States.

1792 Shoemakers in Philadelphia establish first labor union in the country.

1794 Federal troops squelch a tax protest called the Whiskey Rebellion.

1856 First Republican National Convention is held in Philadelphia.

1859 Titusville is site of nation's first commercial oil well.

1863 Civil War Battle of Gettysburg is important victory for Union forces.

1886 The American Federation of Labor is founded in Pittsburgh.

1889 Johnstown flood kills more than 2,000 people.

1920 KDKA radio station in Pittsburgh becomes first in world to broadcast daily.

1940 First section of Pennsylvania Turnpike opens. It is the country's first multilane highway.

1972 Tropical storm Agnes kills more than 50 people.

1979 Accident occurs at Three Mile Island nuclear power plant near Harrisburg.

1982 Steel plants begin to close because of growing foreign competition and decreasing domestic demand.

1985 Series of tornadoes in Pennsylvania kills 65 people and causes approximately $375 million in damages.

rising at the point where the Monongahela and Allegheny rivers run together to form the Ohio River. Situated on one of early America's most important trade routes to the West, with easy access to iron ore shipped on the Great Lakes, and surrounded by hills containing some of the world's richest deposits of soft coal, Pittsburgh was fated to make steel. By 1870 it was producing two-thirds of the nation's steel, blotting out the sun with soot and making fortunes for such industry magnates as Andrew Carnegie, Henry Clay Frick, and J. P. Morgan. It took a little more than a century for steel to be eclipsed, a victim of foreign competition. All of the old steel mills built along Pittsburgh's riverfronts now stand empty, memorials to the past; others have been torn down to make way for the city's downtown of gleaming skyscrapers and high-tech office parks.

The metropolitan populations of Pittsburgh and Philadelphia together account for slightly more than half of Pennsylvania's inhabitants. Most of the rest live in midsize cities like Allentown and Bethlehem (near the headquarters of Bethlehem Steel at Steelton, a four-mile industrial megalith stretched along the banks of the Lehigh River), Scranton (in the heart of northeastern Pennsylvania's coal-mining country), Wilkes-Barre (pronounced "Wilkes-berry"), Erie (Pennsylvania's back door to the Great Lakes), Harrisburg (the state capital), and Williamsport (the birthplace of Little League baseball as well as the site of its annual World Series).

A MOUNTAINOUS BARRICADE

Away from the cities, much of Pennsylvania is sparsely populated, and a look at a topographical map tells the entire story. Ribbed by mountains, nearly all of the state lies in the Appalachian Highlands, a patchwork of rocky ridges, high plateaus, and narrow valleys with some of the roughest terrain found in eastern America.

The Appalachian Mountains of Pennsylvania (and their largest subrange, the Alleghenies) curve roughly southwest to northeast across the state, forming an unbroken, rocky barricade that cleaves the state in two. Although not especially

high (Mount Davis, near the Maryland border, is the state's highest peak at just 3,213 feet), what they lack in elevation they make up for in sheer volume and visual drama. Early travelers dubbed them "the endless mountains," and with no east–west waterway on which to blaze a trail across the state, many pioneers turned back, rather than face a grueling journey across the mountain range. Thus, much of the state was barely settled, and to this day more than half of Pennsylvania's land remains covered with forests. Pennsylvania's wilderness areas are unmatched in the Northeast; more publicly owned parks and forestlands are found here than in all the other Northeastern states put together.

The greatest of Pennsylvania's wilderness areas lies north and west of the state's mountainous core, atop the Allegheny Plateau. Blanketing the north central portion of the state, the Allegheny National Forest comprises nearly a half-million acres, while dozens of state parks fill in the gaps. Logging and coal mining still go on here—95 million tons of coal are dug from Pennsylvania soil each year—but most of the state's north central region is pure backcountry, laced with deep rivers, hundreds of miles of hiking trails, and scenic routes that twist and turn up and down the hollows. Snaking south through the mountain forests of Tioga County, the "Grand Canyon of Pennsylvania," or Pine Creek Gorge, is 50 miles long, 1,000 feet deep, and one of the state's most breathtaking sights. Although 19th-century loggers stripped the canyon walls of their white pine and hemlock, over time a second-growth forest of oak, maple, birch, cherry, and aspen began to cover the canyon. The new trees, unlike the evergreens before them, drape Pine Creek Gorge in brilliant colors during autumn. The new growth stands as a testament to rebirth and a confirmation that Pennsylvania is truly the land of beautiful woods.

◄ *The Delaware River* wends its way along the border between Pennsylvania and New Jersey. The Appalachian Trail crosses the Delaware River at the Delaware Water Gap, an ancient three-mile-long gorge that is part of a 70,000-acre recreation area.

▲ **The state flag,** *adopted in 1897, has 13 stars that stand for the 13 original colonies. The state motto, Hope, is displayed on a ribbon below an anchor, which symbolizes hope.*

STATE DATA
State bird: Rhode Island red hen
State flower: Violet
State tree: Red maple
State motto: Hope
State song: "Rhode Island"
Abbreviations: R.I.; RI (postal)
Origin of the name: From the Greek island of Rhodes
Nicknames: Little Rhody, Ocean State, America's First Resort

AREA AND SIZE
Total area: 1,214 sq. mi.
Rank within U.S.: 50
Extent: 48 mi. north–south; 37 mi. east–west
Highest elevation: Jerimoth Hill, 812 ft. above sea level
Lowest elevation: Sea level along the Atlantic coast

POPULATION
Total: 998,000
Rank within U.S.: 43
Ethnic breakdown: White: 85.3%; Hispanic: 7.6%; Black: 4.0%; Asian: 2.6%; Indian: 0.4%
Population density: 948.7 people per sq. mi.

CLIMATE

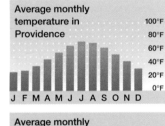

Average monthly temperature in Providence
100°F
80°F
60°F
40°F
20°F
0°F
J F M A M J J A S O N D

Average monthly precipitation in Providence
10"
8"
6"
4"
2"
0"
J F M A M J J A S O N D

ECONOMY
Service industries: Real estate, banking, insurance, computer-programming, law
Manufacturing: Jewelry and silver-ware, fabricated metal products, scientific instruments
Agriculture: Greenhouse and nurs-ery products, milk, potatoes, hay, apples, chickens, eggs, turkeys
Fishing industry: Lobsters, angler-fish, clams, cod, flounder, squid

▲ **South East Lighthouse,** *built in 1873, stands in solitude on the 200-foot-high Mohegan Bluffs on Block Island.*

Rhode Island

Measuring 37 miles wide by 48 miles long, Rhode Island has an image of diversity despite its modest size: it wears at once the demeanor of colonial New England, the gloss of gilded-age Newport, and the blue collar of Providence, Woonsocket, and Pawtucket, three of the oldest proving grounds of the American Industrial Revolution.

DISSIDENT BEGINNINGS
A safe haven for religious outcasts, Providence, Rhode Island's oldest city, was founded in 1636 by an exile from colonial Massachusetts, Roger Williams. This religious dissenter, at odds with the older colony's hard-line Puritan theocracy, held two beliefs that were unorthodox for their time and place: church membership ought not to be a requirement for participation in civic life, and New England lands belonged to their native inhabitants and could not rightfully be granted to settlers by the king. Banished from the Massachusetts Bay Colony, Williams founded settlements at the head of Narragansett Bay. They were initially called the Providence Plantations, and the land had been purchased from the Narragansett Indians.

Following in Williams's footsteps, other Massachusetts dissi-dents bought land from the Indians and founded two settle-ments on an island in the bay. In 1647 these communities were united under a parliamentary patent, and in 1663 King Charles granted the settlements a royal charter. Ironically, the develop-ment of the colony, which was founded on principles liberal with regard to the Native Americans, was interrupted when southern New England became the theater of King Philip's War in 1675–76. Metacomet, a Wampanoag chief who was deri-sively nicknamed King Philip by the British (he had been given

the Christian name Philip by his father), joined with the Nar-ragansett Indians to fight English settlers in the last of New England's Indian wars. The Indians' hold was broken in the Great Swamp Fight, which took place near Kingston in 1675.

WEALTH AND INDEPENDENCE
Because Rhode Island's merchants owned large shipping fleets, during the colonial period its economy was built primarily on trade—particularly the notorious "triangular trade." Ships car-rying cargo, such as rum and iron, would sail from Newport, Rhode Island, to the Gold Coast of Africa, where the goods would be traded for African slaves. The slaves, along with spices and gold dust, would sail on the infamous "Middle Pas-sage" to the West Indies, where they would be sold for molasses, sugar, salt, rice, wine, and British bills of exchange. The boats would then return to Newport.

The restrictions and tariffs levied by England drove the colonies to the breaking point. Rhode Island was the first American colony to declare independence from Great Britain. On May 4, 1776—exactly two months before the Continental Congress in Philadelphia issued the Declaration of Indepen-dence—the Rhode Island General Assembly voted to sever its ties with England. Despite its initial desire for independence, however, the colony was the last one to ratify the U.S. Consti-tution because, regarding taxation, its merchants feared the taxation authority of a strong federal government as much as they had feared the British monarchy; these Rhode Island tradesmen wanted to enjoy their freedom and their wealth.

Rhode Island's 18th-century merchant princes settled in Providence and Newport, and many of their Georgian and Fed-eral mansions have been preserved. Perhaps the finest is the 1786 John Brown House, located in Providence. Once pro-claimed by an eminent visitor named John Quincy Adams as the "most magnificent and elegant private mansion" in North America, the house is filled with period silver, furniture, and original woodwork. John Brown was one of the four wealthy Brown brothers, the family whose endowments created Provi-dence's Ivy League Brown University. At one time the owner of slaving vessels, John Brown turned against the slave trade in later life—perhaps at the urging of his abolitionist brother Moses.

"Little Rhody"
At only 1,214 square miles, Rhode Island is just a little more than half the size of the next largest state, Delaware. It would take 200 Rhode Islands to equal the size of Texas, and 500 Rhode Islands to cover Alaska.

Rhode Island

RHODE ISLAND TIMELINE

1524 Giovanni da Verrazano explores Narragansett Bay.
1614 Dutch mariner Adriaen Block reaches Block Island.
1636 Roger Williams founds Provi-dence, the first permanent settlement.
1663 Rhode Island is granted a royal charter.
1675 Settlers defeat Narragansett Indians in Great Swamp Fight during King Philip's War.
1772 Colonists burn the *Gaspée*, a

British revenue cutter, to protest trade restrictions.
1774 Rhode Island prohibits importation of slaves.
1776 Rhode Island is first colony to declare independence.
1790 Rhode Island joins the Union as 13th state. Samuel Slater builds nation's first water-powered spinning machines in Pawtucket.
1842 Dorr's Rebellion leads to state constitutional reforms.

1938 Severe hurricane and tidal wave kill more than 250 peo-ple and cause about $100 million in property damage.
1969 Newport Bridge is built across Narragansett Bay, linking Jamestown and Newport.
1971 State income tax is imposed.
1976 Tall ships arrive in Newport for the nation's Bicentennial.
1980 Referendum pledging $87 million to protect Narra-gansett Bay is passed.

Among the artifacts of Newport's colonial era stands a reminder of Rhode Island's long tradition of religious tolerance, Touro Synagogue. Built in 1763 by Sephardic Jews from Spain and Portugal, it is the oldest Jewish house of worship in North America. In 1790, in a letter to the congregation that continues to be read each year, President George Washington underscored the nation's commitment to religious liberty.

NEW ENGLAND INDUSTRY

Tucked against the Blackstone River in the city of Pawtucket, just north of Providence, a cluster of old mill buildings marks the site where the former colonies declared independence of a different sort. Here a machinist named Samuel Slater, an expert on cotton mills in his native England who had come to America in 1789, built the first water-powered spinning machines. His 1793 cotton mill still stands—and all of the countless miles of machine-made fabric this nation has since produced can be traced to this simple wooden structure.

Manufacturing became the leading source of wealth in Rhode Island in the 19th century. Part of the state's legacy of smokestacks and power looms is represented in the sizable French-Canadian population of such cities as Pawtucket and Woonsocket. As they did in most major New England manufacturing centers, Quebecois moved from Canada to take factory jobs, filling the working-class neighborhoods near the factories. To this day there are a number of French-speaking neighborhoods in Rhode Island.

Although electronics and service-based industries have supplanted much of the old textile trade, Rhode Island continues to be a major producer of jewelry and silverware. Agriculture in this densely populated state is minimal—despite the long-standing fame of a breed of chicken called the Rhode Island red.

▲ **Fine silver work,** such as these 1878 pieces from the Gorham Manufacturing Company, won Rhode Island world renown.

HIGH SOCIETY

The Rhode Island of a century ago was for most of its inhabitants a place where the days were framed by the sound of factory whistles. Still, any mention of that era in the state's history conjures images of extravagant displays of concentrated wealth. The reputation of Newport as a resort town grew throughout the 18th and 19th centuries. By the 1890s, people with vast fortunes were creating a style of summer rustication that would have boggled the mind of a Venetian doge.

These sumptuous mansions stand along Newport's Bellevue Avenue and Ochre Point, and each one is more opulent than the last: the Italian Renaissance grandeur of the Breakers and the magnificent Marble House, both designed by Richard Morris Hunt for two Vanderbilt brothers; William Wetmore's lavish Victorian Château-sur-Mer; and Rosecliff, a confection designed by Stanford White to mimic the Grand Trianon at Versailles. Some of the "cottages," as their social-register owners coyly called them, are open to the public. Newport's famous Cliff Walk, which skirts the town's rocky Rhode Island Sound shoreline, offers an intriguing "back-door" look at many of the mansions, along with outstanding ocean views.

A TRUE OCEAN STATE

Rhode Island is so thoroughly identified with its seacoast, its islands, and the jagged intrusion of Narragansett Bay, even natives sometimes overlook the fact that the state's western two-thirds—its inland portion—is part of what geologists call the New England Upland. However, this term is deceptive: no part of the wooded, lake-pocked interior rises much more than 800 feet above sea level.

Yet it is the ocean and Narragansett Bay that give color and character to this little state. Newport has hosted the America's Cup race and is considered a world-class yachting capital; the famous lobster fleet still works out of Galilee and Point Judith; and the beaches that range from Narragansett west to the staid

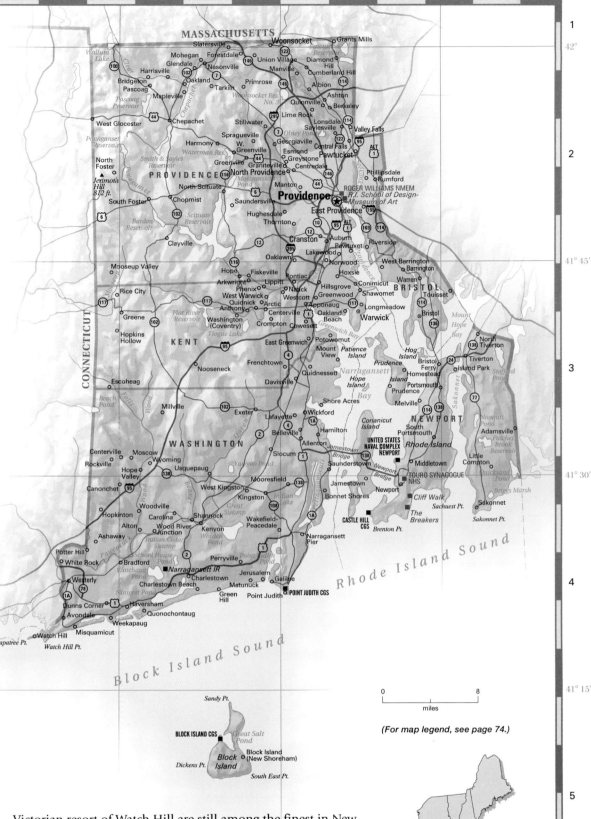

Victorian resort of Watch Hill are still among the finest in New England. Some 12 miles out to sea, southward toward the tip of New York's Long Island, Block Island stands as a salt-sprayed sandy hummock of land with a centuries-old maritime tradition. Even in busy Providence, it's impossible to walk along Benefit Street's rows of colonial homes without remembering that this was a seaport, first and foremost, in the Ocean State—a place where salt water is as important as dry land.

(For map legend, see page 74.)

◄ **"The Breakers,"** considered the most magnificent Newport mansion. Tycoon Cornelius Vanderbilt spent $5 million to build this 70-room "cottage" in 1895.

▲ *The state flag* *displays a pal-*
metto, the state tree, and a cres-
cent, which is the emblem that
South Carolina's Revolutionary
War soldiers wore on their caps.
The flag was adopted in 1861.

▶ *The section of Charleston*
near the Battery contains some
of the city's grandest 18th- and
19th-century homes. In 1931
Charleston passed the nation's
first historic-zoning ordinance in
order to preserve them.

STATE DATA
State bird: Carolina wren
State flower: Yellow jessamine
State tree: Palmetto
State mottoes: *Dum spiro spero*
(While I breathe, I hope); *Animis*
opibusque parati (Prepared in mind
and resources)
State song: "Carolina"
Abbreviations: S.C.; SC (postal)
Origin of the name: Named for King
Charles I of England
Nickname: Palmetto State

AREA AND SIZE
Total area: 31,055 sq. mi.
Rank within U.S.: 40
Extent: 218 mi. north–south;
275 mi. east–west
Highest elevation: Sassafras Moun-
tain, 3,560 ft. above sea level
Lowest elevation: Sea level along
the coast

POPULATION
Total: 3,858,000
Rank within U.S.: 26
Ethnic breakdown: White: 68.0%;
Black: 29.9%; Hispanic: 1.1%;
Asian: 0.8%; Indian: 0.2%
Population density: 127.4 people
per sq. mi.

CLIMATE

Average monthly
temperature in
Columbia
100°F
80°F
60°F
40°F
20°F
0°F
J F M A M J J A S O N D

Average monthly
precipitation in
Columbia
10"
8"
6"
4"
2"
0"
J F M A M J J A S O N D

ECONOMY
Service industries: Tourism, wholesale and retail trade, medical facilities, real estate
Manufacturing: Dyes, fibers, textiles, pharmaceuticals, soaps,
machinery, paper
Agriculture: Tobacco, soybeans,
cotton, vegetables, fruits, beef cattle, hogs, broiler chickens, eggs

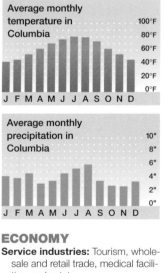

▶ *Table Rock Mountain,* in the
Blue Ridge range in northeastern
South Carolina, stands veiled in
mist, while Caesar's Head looms
in the foreground.

South Carolina

Although it is the smallest of the Southern states, South
Carolina has nevertheless done more than its share to
create both the reality and the enduring myth of the
Deep South. A center of plantation aristocracy, the state
was the first to secede from the Union when hostilities
came to a head. Despite this position, the Palmetto State
later accepted civil rights legislation with relative dignity
and peace. South Carolina also led the old Confederacy
in turning away from a near-total dependence on agri-
culture—yet its greatest modern treasure, the strikingly
handsome city of Charleston, remains a testament to an
older, agrarian wealth.

A PLANTER'S SOCIETY
The territory that was to become South Carolina, the ancestral
home of the Cherokee, Yamasee, and a host of other Native
American tribes, was first visited by Europeans when a Spanish
expedition explored the coastline in 1521. Both the Spanish

and the French made a few
attempts at settlement, but it
was not until 1663—when
Britain's King Charles II
granted the lands between
Florida and Virginia to eight
"lords proprietors"—that
Europeans began to colo-
nize the area in earnest.

The first English settlers of
the granted land, named
"Carolina" after the Latin
form of Charles, included
many planters from Barba-
dos. They landed near present-day Charleston, on the
Ashley River, and by the
beginning of the 18th century had begun to create an
economy based upon the
cultivation of tobacco,
indigo, and, eventually, the
crop that would prove to be
the mainstay of the low country's economy and diet: rice.

The cultivation of rice was especially labor-intensive, since it
involved controlled flooding of rich bottomlands by means of
dikes and canals. The labor on South Carolina plantations was
provided by African slaves. By the 1730s blacks accounted for
about two-thirds of South Carolina's population.

The colony's ethnic makeup grew slightly more varied at the
end of the 17th century, when Scots arrived and French
Huguenot refugees established plantations. Also within 50
years the up-country saw an influx of Scotch-Irish, Welsh,
Swiss, and German immigrants (many of them from the northern Appalachians) that presaged not merely greater ethnic
diversity but a socioeconomic order vastly different from and
often at odds with that of the low-country plantation aristocracy. After all, a hardscrabble Blue Ridge farm was a far cry
from a low-country plantation. In 1786 tension between the
two regions led to the compromise choice of inland Columbia
as capital, replacing the planters' hub of Charleston.

A MORE VARIED ECONOMY
South Carolina agriculture was transformed by the introduction in 1793 of the cotton gin, which so streamlined the processing of cotton that in the early 1800s the crop joined rice
and tobacco as an economic mainstay. The state's massive
dependence on slavery for labor ensured its continuing ani-
mosity to the new Republican Party; in 1860, shortly before
Abraham Lincoln took office, South Carolina was the first state
to secede from the Union.

The Civil War began with a Confederate attack on Fort
Sumter in Charleston Harbor, and it ended with the devastation of the plantation economy. Cotton eventually recovered,
at least until the boll weevil infestation of the early 1920s; rice
cultivation, its water-regulating infrastructure destroyed by
Union troops, was seriously diminished.

The years after the Civil War saw the rise of a new force in
South Carolina's economy—manufacturing, especially of textiles. The state's first large cotton-cloth factory had been established at Graniteville in 1846; it was around 1880 that the
industry burgeoned as New England textile firms began to take
advantage of the Piedmont's waterpower and the region's
cheap labor. Manufacturing is still a major part of South Carolina's economic picture, although it's now behind the service
sector. The interspersal of manufacturing jobs throughout
South Carolina has helped to erase the rich low country/poor
mountain farms division around which South Carolina's political factions squared off a century ago. Agriculture, too, is more
diverse today: the state produces beef and dairy cattle, poultry,
hogs, soybeans, peanuts, truck vegetables, and—despite the
state nickname of neighboring Georgia—more peaches than
any other state east of the Mississippi River.

FROM BLUE RIDGE FARMS TO SEA ISLES
Despite its small size, South Carolina is divided into well-
defined geographical regions—and those regions, in turn, have
put their stamp on distinct cultures and economic realities. The

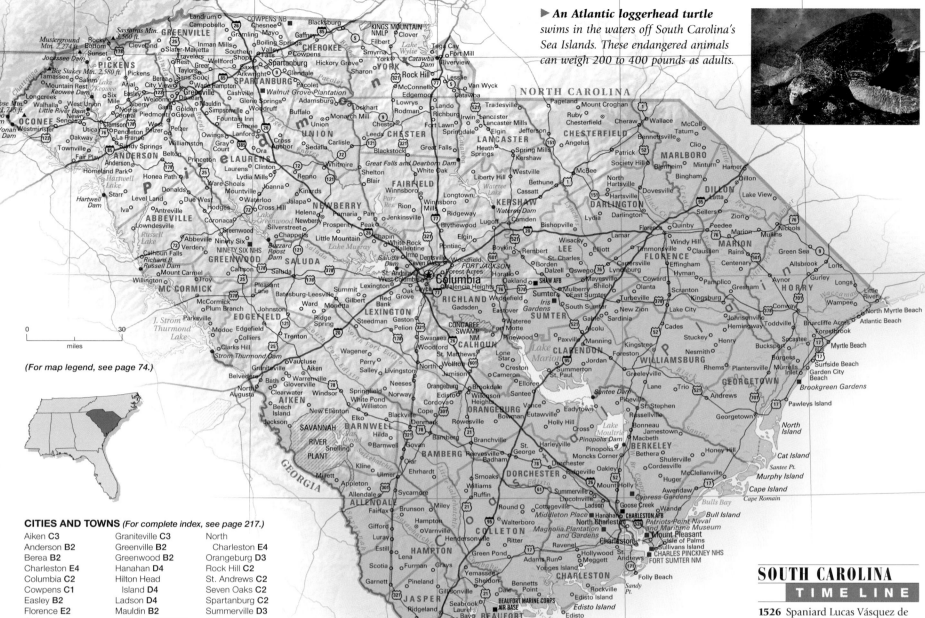

▶ **An Atlantic loggerhead turtle** swims in the waters off South Carolina's Sea Islands. These endangered animals can weigh 200 to 400 pounds as adults.

(For map legend, see page 74.)

far northwestern portion of the state lies within the Blue Ridge Mountains; its small-farm culture is similar to that of the mountain counties in adjacent Southern states. The west central portion of South Carolina is part of the Piedmont Plateau, a region once largely planted with cotton but later known primarily for its textile mills, which are situated here because of the abundant power provided by rivers rushing from the Appalachians to the sea. And along a wide belt extending from southwest to northeast extends the coastal plain, the fertile low country.

Lying off the coast of South Carolina are a string of islands with a history of their own. Among the first territories the early colonists cultivated, the Sea Islands are low-lying barrier formations situated between the Atlantic Ocean and the estuaries just north of the Georgia coast. Largely abandoned after the Civil War, the islands were left to freed slaves and their descendants, in whose diminishing communities the nearly impenetrable language known as Gullah still survives. In recent years the Sea Islands have become prime resort property—Hilton Head is the best-known example—but some undeveloped portions manage to survive, most notably in the Savannah National Wildlife Refuge and the state parks on Hunting and Edisto islands. This is where, at the right time of day when no one is around, South Carolina still looks like virgin land.

PROGRESS AND PRESERVATION

The legacy of slavery and the systematic dismantling of federal Reconstruction laws made the road to equality for blacks a rocky one. But South Carolina rose to the occasion better than many other Southern states. When faced with the new federal civil rights laws and court decisions in the 1950s and 1960s that desegregated schools and gave blacks the right to vote, South Carolina's leadership made it very clear that it would tolerate no violence. The policy appeared to succeed—Harvey Gannt, the first black to attend all-white Clemson College, walked through the doors in 1963 to a peaceful reception.

With all of its progress, South Carolina still husbands its antebellum past, especially along the coast. Not far from Charleston stands Drayton Hall, a masterpiece of early-18th-century Georgian architecture that was the only Ashley River plantation house to survive the Civil War in good condition. Nearby, the gardens of Middleton Place resemble an American Versailles. Along the Santee River, Hampton and Hopsewee plantations are grandly preserved colonial-era country seats. In the meantime, Charleston—particularly the neighborhoods nearest the seafront park called the Battery—is a vast museum of antebellum architecture. (The Charleston Museum, founded in 1773, is the nation's oldest.) And in the harbor, Fort Sumter itself stands like a healed but still-gnarled old wound and a testament to fortitude.

◀ **Middleton Place,** on the banks of the Ashley River, has the oldest formal landscaped gardens in the United States. This plantation, which took 10 years to build, is one of several in the Charleston area that survive from the 18th century.

SOUTH CAROLINA
TIME LINE

1526 Spaniard Lucas Vásquez de Ayllón founds settlement.

1562 French Huguenots settle near Parris Island.

1663 King Charles II of England gives charter for Carolina to eight lords proprietors.

1670 English planters settle at Albemarle Point near present-day Charleston.

1712 Separate governors are appointed for North and South Carolina.

1780–81 American forces defeat loyalist troops at Kings Mountain and Cowpens.

1788 South Carolina joins the Union as eighth state.

1822 Slave uprising is suppressed.

1832 State legislature nullifies a federal tariff, leading to crisis over states' rights.

1860 South Carolina is first state to secede from the Union.

1861 Confederate attack on Fort Sumter begins Civil War.

1865 Union troops led by General Sherman burn Columbia.

1868 South Carolina is readmitted to the Union.

1886 Earthquake kills 92 people in Charleston.

1895 Rewriting of state constitution effectively disenfranchises most blacks.

1921 Boll weevils destroy large portion of cotton crop.

1948 District court ruling strikes down "white primary" law.

1953 Savannah River Plant begins to make nuclear materials.

1963 Integration of South Carolina's public schools begins.

1989 Hurricane Hugo devastates coast, killing 13 people.

A 104° B

South Dakota

The wind and the open sky rule in South Dakota, where the rolling prairie and the pine-clad Black Hills are haunted by the ghosts of the Old West—the rumble of long-vanished herds of bison, Sioux leaders like Sitting Bull and Crazy Horse, and such soldiers as George A. Custer. While Sioux Falls and Rapid City hum with the typical urban activities, echoes of the frontier live on in the state's cattle ranches and farms and in the colorful spectacle of tribal powwows.

▲ **The state flag,** adopted in 1963, shows the state seal, surrounded by golden rays. The farmer, corn, cattle, smelting furnace, and boat represent agriculture, dairying, ranching, mining, transportation, and commerce.

STATE DATA

State bird: Ring-necked pheasant
State flower: Pasqueflower
State tree: Black Hills spruce
State motto: Under God, the people rule
State song: "Hail, South Dakota"
Abbreviations: S. Dak. or S.D.; SD (postal)
Origin of the name: From the Sioux word *dakota* or *lakota,* meaning "allies" or "friends"
Nicknames: Coyote State, Mount Rushmore State

AREA AND SIZE

Total area: 77,047 sq. mi.
Rank within U.S.: 16
Extent: 237 mi. north–south; 383 miles east–west
Highest elevation: Harney Peak, 7,242 ft. above sea level
Lowest elevation: Big Stone Lake, 962 ft. above sea level

POPULATION

Total: 777,000
Rank within U.S.: 45
Ethnic breakdown: White: 89.8%; Indian: 7.7%; Hispanic: 1.0%; Asian: 0.6%; Black: 0.6%
Population density: 10.2 people per sq. mi.

CLIMATE

Average monthly temperature in Sioux Falls
100°F
80°F
60°F
40°F
20°F
0°F
J F M A M J J A S O N D

Average monthly precipitation in Sioux Falls
10"
8"
6"
4"
2"
0"
J F M A M J J A S O N D

ECONOMY

Service industries: Banking, real estate, restaurants, law firms
Agriculture: Beef cattle, hogs, sheep, wheat, corn, sunflowers
Manufacturing: Meat processing, computers, farm equipment

FARMLANDS AND BADLANDS

A rectangular block in the jigsaw puzzle of the northern Plains states, South Dakota is split down the middle by the Missouri River, which divides it in both geography and spirit. The gently rolling east was dubbed the Coteau des Prairies (Prairie Hills) by French explorers in the 18th century. Now it is farmland, blessed with rich soil that grows bumper crops of corn, flax, and oats. Two-thirds of South Dakota's 777,000 residents live in this easternmost slice, in cities like Sioux Falls and on prosperous farms that maintain the state's vital link to the land.

To the west of the Missouri River, the land rises and writhes, a place of stark, flat-topped buttes, weird badlands, and twist-

▲ **The otherworldly landscape** of Badlands National Park. The park encompasses about 13 percent of the Big Badlands, a 6,000-square-mile area of South Dakota and Nebraska.

CITIES AND TOWNS
(For complete index, see page 217.)

Aberdeen **G1**	Milbank **J1**
Belle Fourche **B2**	Mitchell **G3**
Beresford **J3**	Mobridge **E1**
Box Elder **B2**	Pierre **E2**
Brandon **J3**	Pine Ridge **C3**
Brookings **J2**	Rapid City **B2**
Canton **J3**	Redfield **G2**
Chamberlain **F3**	Sioux Falls **J3**
Deadwood **B2**	Sisseton **H1**
Dell Rapids **J3**	Spearfish **B2**
Flandreau **J2**	Sturgis **B2**
Fort Pierre **E2**	Vermillion **J4**
Hot Springs **B3**	Watertown **H2**
Huron **G2**	Webster **H1**
Lead **B2**	Winner **F3**
Madison **H2**	Yankton **H4**

0   31
miles

(For map legend, see page 74.)

ing coulees, or canyons. The short-grass prairie, which once supported huge herds of bison, now provides grazing for millions of cattle. Ranches, sprawling operations that still depend on the self-reliance and ingenuity of cowboys to keep them running, cover all but a small fraction of western South Dakota.

NATIVE INHABITANTS, EARLY EXPLORERS

People have lived in South Dakota for some 10,000 years. The first residents were Ice Age hunters, but when temperatures warmed up, South Dakota became home to the Arikara, a farming culture that lived along the Missouri River, who built villages of elaborate earthen lodges. The Cheyenne, a hunting nation, lived to the west. South Dakota is indelibly linked, however, with the Sioux, who emigrated from Minnesota in the 1700s.

The Sioux (or Dakota) reached South Dakota in time for the great blossoming of Plains Indian culture, brought on by the introduction of horses to the New World by the Spanish in the 16th century. The animals gave the tribes the ability to hunt widely for bison, creating a highly mobile lifestyle that revolved around the massive herds. In the 1740s, Lewis-Joseph and François La Vérendrye were the first Europeans to penetrate the Missouri River valley as they sought a route to the Pacific. Meriwether Lewis and William Clark were the first Americans to pass through the region in 1804 when they explored the nation's newly purchased Louisiana Territory.

A BLOODY STRUGGLE FOR LAND

South Dakota's vivid history is a pairing of violence and peace, encroachment and defense. Settlers began moving into the farmland of the eastern prairies in the 1850s; their trespassing brought a bloody response from the Sioux. By treaty, their hunting lands in the west—especially the sacred Paha Sapa, the Black Hills—were off-limits to whites, but in 1874 Lt. Col. George Armstrong Custer led an expedition to the isolated mountain range. His discovery of gold there set off a stampede of prospectors, and lawless boomtowns like Deadwood and Lead torpedoed into existence. The Homestake Mine at Lead, which opened in 1876, is still in operation and has given up millions of tons of gold ore already, with millions more to go.

The Sioux and Northern Cheyenne responded to this invasion with one last uprising, led by Sitting Bull, Crazy Horse, and others. For a time the resistance was successful, ending

SOUTH DAKOTA TIMELINE

1743 La Vérendrye brothers are the first whites to enter South Dakota region.

1803 U.S. gains South Dakota from France in Louisiana Purchase.

1861 Dakota becomes a territory.

1868 Fort Laramie Treaty founds Great Sioux Reservation.

1874 In violation of Laramie Treaty, Lt. Col. George Custer enters the Black Hills and finds gold.

1877 Sioux are forced to surrender the Black Hills.

1878 "Great Dakota Boom" land rush begins.

1889 South Dakota joins the Union as 40th state.

1890 U.S. troops kill about 200 Sioux at Wounded Knee Creek, ending Indian wars.

1927 Work begins on Mount Rushmore National Memorial.

1930s Drought hits South Dakota.

1960 Ben Reifel is the state's first American Indian to be elected to Congress.

1963 Missiles are placed at several

sites in South Dakota.

1972 Floods in Rapid City area cause more than 200 deaths.

1973 Armed American Indians occupy village of Wounded Knee for 71 days.

1980 Supreme Court orders U.S. government to pay Sioux tribes $105 million for 1877 forced surrender of Black Hills. They refuse the money, seeking return of land.

1991–94 Government removes all missiles from South Dakota.

with Custer's defeat at the Little Bighorn in Montana in 1876, but eventually the Sioux were forced onto reservations. The final, tragic chapter of these wars took place in 1890 in South Dakota, along a creek called Wounded Knee. Fighting broke out as troops tried to disarm a band of Sioux, and soldiers opened fire with artillery, leaving at least 150 men, women, and children dead in the snow.

CARVED IN STONE

With forested peaks that rise abruptly from the plains, the Black Hills are the western anchor of South Dakota. The state's most enduring symbol is found here—Mount Rushmore, with its monumental busts of Presidents George Washington, Thomas Jefferson, Theodore Roosevelt, and Abraham Lincoln. Each granite head is 60 feet high. Nearly half a million tons of rock were removed in the 14 years that workers labored on this project, which began in 1927.

It is only fitting that the sacred hills of the Sioux also hold a monument to one of their greatest leaders. Not far from Mount Rushmore, the world's largest sculpture is emerging from the mountains—a 563-foot-tall carving of the mounted warrior Crazy Horse, arm pointing to the horizon. So massive that all four Rushmore heads could fit into Crazy Horse's, with room to spare, the project was the one-man dream of sculptor Korczak Ziolkowski, an assistant to Mount Rushmore's creator, Gutzon Borglum. Although Ziolkowski died in 1982, the privately funded carving is nearing completion—a stunning memorial to the native people who fought bravely for their land.

Yet not even the best sculptors can match the work of millions of years of wind, rain, and ice, which created the spectacular Badlands in south central South Dakota. Here the land is a fantastic maze of canyons and gullies, where the yellows, browns, and reds of the soil provide the only color. Yet Badlands National Park, which protects part of this fragile environment, is rich in wildlife. Herds of bison, bighorn sheep, mule deer, and pronghorn live here, beneath the wheeling wings of golden eagles and prairie falcons—living links to South Dakota's natural past.

▼ *A September snowfall laces the fall foliage at Spearfish Creek Canyon in the Black Hills National Forest.*

◄ *Sitting Bull (above left, in 1884), an esteemed medicine man and leader of the Hunkpapa Sioux, was instrumental in the Indian resistance that led to the Battle of Little Bighorn in 1876. At left is a painting of the battle by Lakota Sioux artist Amos Bad Heart Bull, whose father and uncle took part in the struggle.*

STATE DATA
State bird: Mockingbird
State flower: Iris
State tree: Tulip poplar
State motto: Agriculture and commerce
State songs: "My Homeland, Tennessee," "When It's Iris Time in Tennessee," "My Tennessee," "The Tennessee Waltz," "Rocky Top"
Abbreviations: Tenn.; TN (postal)
Origin of the name: From the old Yuchi Indian word *tana-see,* which means "the meeting place"
Nickname: The Volunteer State

AREA AND SIZE
Total area: 42,244 sq. mi.
Rank within U.S.: 34
Extent: 116 mi. north–south; 482 mi. east–west
Highest elevation: Clingmans Dome, 6,643 ft. above sea level
Lowest elevation: 182 ft. above sea level in Shelby County

POPULATION
Total: 5,657,000
Rank within U.S.: 16
Ethnic breakdown: White: 81.4%; Black: 16.4%; Asian: 1.0%; Hispanic: 1.0%; Indian: 0.2%
Population density: 136.8 people per sq. mi.

CLIMATE

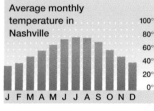

Average monthly temperature in Nashville
100°F 80°F 60°F 40°F 20°F 0°F
J F M A M J J A S O N D

Average monthly precipitation in Nashville
10" 8" 6" 4" 2" 0"
J F M A M J J A S O N D

ECONOMY
Service industries: Restaurants, business services
Manufacturing: Heating and refrigeration equipment, automobile parts
Agriculture: Beef cattle, milk, cotton

▲ **Cades Cove,** *a frontier farming community in Great Smoky Mountains National Park. Before the first European farmers settled here in 1818, Cades Cove was part of the Cherokee nation.*

Tennessee

Long and lanky as a split-rail fence, Tennessee is nestled between the misty Appalachian hollows to the east, where the wolves once again roam, and the Mississippi River to the west, where paddle wheelers still churn the muddy water and the poignant sound of Memphis blues drifts out of smoky Beale Street clubs.

THREE STATES IN ONE
Residents often refer to the "three states of Tennessee" because the eastern, middle, and western parts of the state have such strikingly different characteristics. The Appalachian highlands in the east are a majestic confusion of forested mountains and sheltered valleys known as coves. It was here that for more than two centuries descendants of English, Scottish, and Irish settlers maintained their distinctive, self-reliant way of life. The mountains wring moisture from the clouds that gather among them, and the rain that falls creates powerful rivers, such as the Ocoee, Pigeon, and Nolichucky.

The valleys of the state's mid-section are home to quiet farms, bluegrass, the famous Tennessee walking horses, and "Music City USA," as Nashville is often called. Elsewhere, middle Tennessee moves to older rhythms. Northwest of Knoxville, the Big South Fork of the Cumberland River was once condemned to be dammed for hydroelectric power; instead, in 1974 Congress created a 106,000-acre national river and recreation area.

West Tennessee looks not to the mountains but to the Mississippi River for its heritage. This is a land of farm fields, where the cotton business was the lifeblood of Memphis. Today visitors come to hear Memphis blues or to visit Graceland, the brash Southern mansion and grave site of rock and roll king Elvis Presley. Davy Crockett, who hunted through the forests of western Tennessee in his youth, called this country "The Shakes" for the greatest earthquakes in U.S. history, which struck in 1811–12 and caused a large part of western Tennessee to sag like a punctured balloon. The Mississippi flowed backward and filled this vast depression, creating 14,500-acre Reelfoot Lake, today a paradise for anglers, hunters, and birders.

EARLY CITIZENS
Tennessee was Indian land first; the name comes from the old Yuchi word *tana-see,* which means "the meeting place." The first Europeans to lay eyes on the state were Spaniards under the command of the conquistador Hernando de Soto; the group searched fruitlessly here for gold in 1540. It wasn't until 1769, when William Bean of Virginia built a cabin on the banks of the Watauga River, that there were any permanent settlers. Other pioneers soon followed, traveling down the valleys of the northeast or along the broad Cumberland River from Kentucky. Although Tennessee was originally part of North

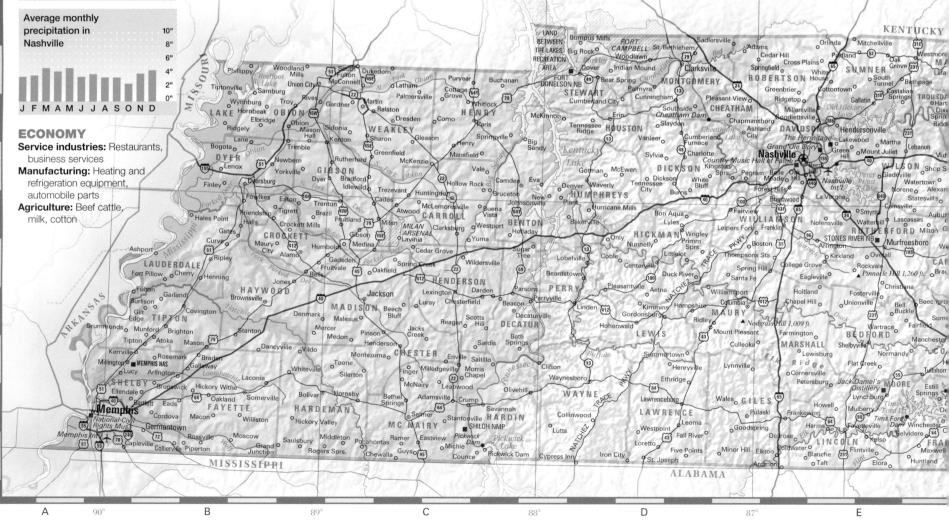

Carolina, residents in the eastern section split off in 1784 to create the state of Franklin; the political entity lasted just four years before being reabsorbed into North Carolina. Finally, in 1796, Tennessee was admitted to the Union as the 16th state.

The eastern mountains were the heartland of the Cherokee nation. By the early 19th century, the Cherokee lived in farming communities and were governed by their own written legal code; most Cherokee were literate, and the tribe even published a newspaper, written in the newly invented Cherokee alphabet. The discovery of gold in Cherokee land to the south spurred President Andrew Jackson (himself a Tennessee native) to evict the tribe in 1838–39, forcing them into Oklahoma. The bitter march west, during which more than 4,000 Cherokee died, would later be known as the Trail of Tears.

DIVIDED LOYALTIES

By the time of the Civil War, Tennessee was a microcosm of the nation—a state divided against itself. The eastern highlanders were staunchly pro-Union, while the middle and especially the western population leaned strongly toward the Confederacy. Tennessee was the site of more than 400 battles and engagements—more than any other state except Virginia.

One of the first Union victories came in 1862 at Fort Donelson on the Cumberland River, but the bloodiest by far was the Battle of Shiloh, which began on April 6, 1862, near a church of the same name, not far from the Tennessee River. For two days, 100,000 Rebel and Union troops turned quiet orchards and woodlands into a nightmare of artillery and musket fire that left more than 3,400 dead—more men than were killed in all the battles of America's previous three wars combined.

A PROMISING FUTURE

Tennessee shares Great Smoky Mountains National Park with North Carolina. Here the Blue Ridge rears skyward—mountains capped with spruce and fir. At lower elevations, hardwood forests explode with wildflowers in spring, and endangered red wolves once again make the hills echo with their howls, thanks to conservationists who returned them to the wild in 1991. At Cades Cove, the cabins, barns, and churches of a 19th-century village have been preserved—weathered relics of another era. But if Cades Cove is a glimpse of Tennessee's past, Oak Ridge is part of its future. Founded as a secret atomic facility during World War II, it zoomed from a population of zero to more than 70,000 in just four years. Today Oak Ridge's research labs are exploring the potential for peaceful energy, taking Tennessee into the next century.

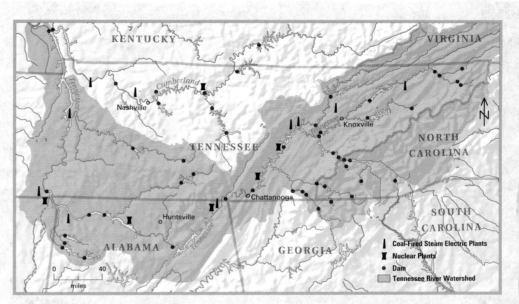

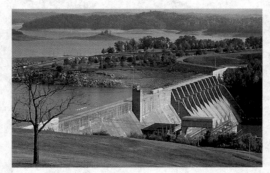

The Tennessee Valley Authority

Part of Franklin D. Roosevelt's New Deal, the Tennessee Valley Authority (TVA) put thousands of the unemployed to work on the Tennessee River and its tributaries. The TVA built most of the 39 dams that work as one system to produce electricity, control flooding, and improve navigability.

◀ **Norris Dam,** built on the Clinch River in 1936, was the first TVA dam to be completed.

TENNESSEE ▏TIME LINE

1540 Explorer Hernando de Soto enters Tennessee area.

1682 Robert Cavelier, sieur de La Salle, claims land, including Tennessee, for France.

1763 Britain gains land east of Mississippi River from France.

1784 State of Franklin is formed in East Tennessee. It lasts only four years.

1796 Tennessee joins the Union as 16th state.

1818 Chickasaw tribe sells West Tennessee to United States.

1838 The Cherokee are pushed out of Tennessee into Oklahoma.

1861 Tennessee is last state to secede from the Union.

1866 Tennessee is first state to be readmitted to the Union.

1925 In Dayton, public school teacher John Scopes is convicted of teaching evolution.

1933 Congress authorizes Tennessee Valley Authority.

1942 Manhattan Project, to create an atomic bomb, is established at Oak Ridge.

1962 In historic Tennessee case, U.S. Supreme Court rules that federal courts can challenge legislative apportionment.

1964 Tennessee Space Institute is founded at Tullahoma.

1968 Martin Luther King, Jr., is assassinated in Memphis.

1985 Tennessee-Tombigbee Waterway connects Tennessee River to Gulf of Mexico.

CITIES AND TOWNS *(For complete index, see page 217.)*

(For map legend, see page 74.)

▲ **Minnie Pearl** in a 1955 televised performance of Nashville's Grand Ole Opry. The Opry's live radio shows have been airing since 1925.

Texas

STATE DATA
State bird: Mockingbird
State flower: Bluebonnet
State tree: Pecan
State motto: Friendship
State song: "Texas, Our Texas"
Abbreviations: Tex.; TX (postal)
Origin of the name: From the Caddo Indian word *tejas*, which means "friends" or "allies"
Nickname: Lone Star State

AREA AND SIZE
Total area: 267,339 sq. mi.
Rank within U.S.: 2
Extent: 737 mi. north–south; 774 mi. east–west
Highest elevation: Guadalupe Peak, 8,749 ft. above sea level
Lowest elevation: Sea level, along the Gulf of Mexico

POPULATION
Total: 20,119,000
Rank within U.S.: 2
Ethnic breakdown: White: 56.0%; Hispanic: 29.2%; Black: 12.0%; Asian: 2.5%; Indian: 0.3%
Population density: 76.5 people per sq. mi.

CLIMATE

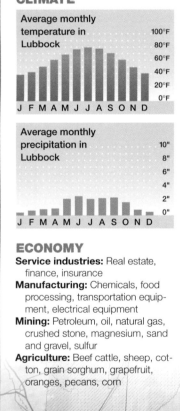

Average monthly temperature in Lubbock

Average monthly precipitation in Lubbock

ECONOMY
Service industries: Real estate, finance, insurance
Manufacturing: Chemicals, food processing, transportation equipment, electrical equipment
Mining: Petroleum, oil, natural gas, crushed stone, magnesium, sand and gravel, sulfur
Agriculture: Beef cattle, sheep, cotton, grain sorghum, grapefruit, oranges, pecans, corn

With two time zones, four major geographic regions, 19 million people, and 15 million cattle contained within its ample borders, Texas lives up to its reputation as a place where all things are bigger. Second only to Alaska in size, Texas takes up a twelfth of the contiguous United States. Travelers can drive some 850 miles north to south or east to west without leaving the state; while doing so, they'll find a surprisingly urbane place, with a vibrant Hispanic influence, a diversified economy, and major aerospace and biotech centers. Still, it's the remnants of the old cattle frontier that really set Texas apart—the rolling prairies dotted with longhorns and oil rigs.

A BEAUTIFUL, UNYIELDING LAND

Texas's sprawling landscape can be as unyielding as its early settlers, who had to cling to the fertile eastern Blackland Prairie or try to coax their subsistence out of vast dry plains and cactus desert in the west. The state rises in a series of broad steps, from the welcoming Gulf coastal plain of the southeast to the parched, treeless high plain of the northwest. Along the Louisiana border the mysterious Big Thicket National Preserve, 84,550 acres of oak, pine, and cypress forest, houses a tangle of nearly impenetrable stands of trees.

To the south, the forest yields to the Gulf Coast, a marshy 624-mile crescent of beaches, oil refineries, and offshore rigs dominated by Houston, the fourth-largest city in the United States, as well as the port cities of Corpus Christi and Galveston. Lush fields of cotton, alfalfa, rice, and sweet potatoes grow between the shore and the Balcones Escarpment, a line of

cliffs that separates the fertile east from the arid west. The craggy, juniper-cloaked Hill Country, famous for its German heritage that dates to 1845, fills the south central part of the state, then ripples west of the escarpment before settling into the high plains that have come to symbolize the Texas frontier. To the southwest lies the rugged southern tip of the Rocky Mountains and the wild beauty of the Rio Grande's Big Bend country.

The most inhospitable land in all of Texas, the Llano Estacado, or staked plains, stretches across the panhandle in the north. Indians rarely ventured onto these barren plains, and the explorers of an early Spanish expedition had to lay stakes along their path to make sure they could find their way back. Beaten by sandstorms, flash floods, and bitter "blue northers" that blow in from the Rockies even to this day, the Llano Estacado offers precious little sustenance to any but the sheep and cattle that graze its brittle grass.

▲ **Texas bluebonnets** (Lupinus texensis) bloom in early spring, gracing the southern and central portions of the Lone Star State with their delicate beauty. The flowers are so named because their petals resemble a woman's bonnet.

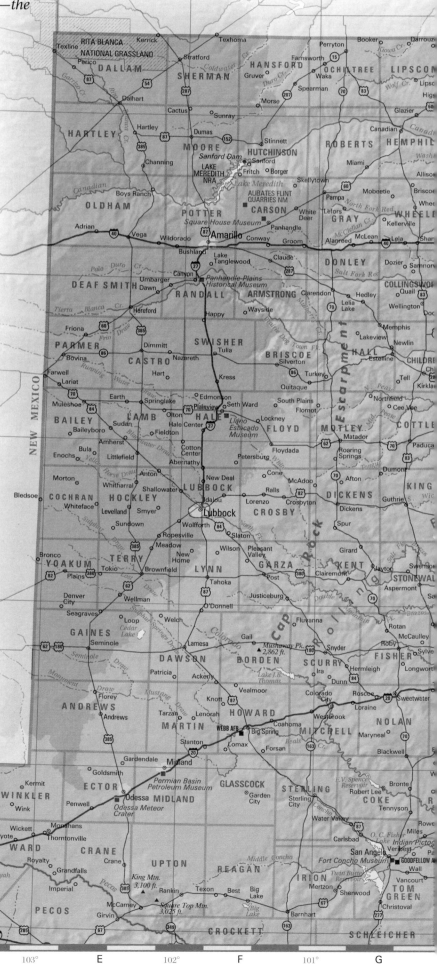

SPANISH SETTLEMENT

The first white men in this forbidding land arrived exhausted, emaciated, and hopeless, washing ashore on Galveston Island sometime in 1528 after being shipwrecked off the Texas Gulf Coast. On Galveston, all but four succumbed to starvation or Indian attack. Only the expedition's leader, Alvar Núñez Cabeza de Vaca, a Moor named Estéban, and two others survived. Trudging half-naked for eight years across the Southwest, they worked as bearers for various Indian tribes and used their knowledge of Western medicine and astronomy to work as shamans. By the time they finally reached Mexico, they had attracted thousands of worshipers, each hoping to benefit from the mystical powers of the "children of the sun."

For the next two centuries after Cabeza de Vaca's adventure, most white visitors came to Texas with the same plan: to find gold and then to pass through unharmed. When Spanish priests began to follow the fortune-hunting soldiers into the coastal plains in the late 17th century, they found the Caddo Indians less than willing to

trade their rugged existence for a pastoral life of worship. After a few conspicuous failures, the Spanish finally managed to establish stable missions: in 1716 at Nacogdoches, in 1718 at San Antonio, and in 1749 at Goliad. These remained the only permanent settlements in Texas for a century, until a Missouri banker's son and 300 ragged Anglos arrived on the banks of the Brazos River and made a settlement with that most American of names: Washington.

THE REPUBLIC OF TEXAS

When Stephen F. Austin and company arrived in Texas in 1821, there were few signs of the troubles to come. They were there at the invitation of the Mexican government, which had just won independence from Spain and wanted to wrest the territory from the wilderness. Pleased with Austin's industrious group, Mexico granted huge tracts of land to American entrepreneurs, and settlers poured in from the American South, bringing with them thousands of black slaves. Before long, the

▲ *Mission San José y San Miguel de Aguayo,* *an impressive stone-walled compound, was completed in 1782. Situated on the banks of the San Antonio River, San José was known as the Queen of the Missions.*

◄ *The Texas horned lizard's ferocious appearance belies its gentle nature; it spends most of its day sunbathing and eating.*

(For map legend, see page 74.)

TEXAS

TIME LINE

1519 Alonso Alvarez de Piñeda of Spain maps Texas coast.

1528 Cabeza de Vaca and party explore interior of Texas.

1682 Spanish Franciscans build two missions at Ysleta near El Paso.

1718 Spaniards found San Antonio de Valero mission.

1821 Mexico wins independence from Spain; Texas becomes part of Mexico. Anglo-Americans settle Texas.

1835 Texas Revolution begins.

1836 Americans lose Battle of the Alamo. They later win Battle of San Jacinto and form Republic of Texas.

1845 Texas joins the Union as 28th state.

1861 Texas joins the Confederacy.

1865 One month after war's end, last battle of Civil War is fought at Palmito Hill near Port Isabel.

1867 First major cattle drive heads from Texas to Kansas.

1900 Hurricane in Galveston kills 6,000 people.

1901 Discovery of Spindletop oil field launches modern petroleum industry.

1947 Ship explosion at Texas City refinery dock causes 500 deaths and 4,000 injuries.

1963 President John F. Kennedy is assassinated in Dallas. Vice President Lyndon B. Johnson, a former Texas senator, becomes president.

1964 Manned Spacecraft Center at Houston becomes headquarters for U.S. astronauts.

1970 Hurricane devastates Corpus Christi area.

1980s Drop in oil prices causes recession in Texas.

strong-willed pioneers began to clash with an increasingly authoritarian government in Mexico. The Anglos wanted to maintain American law, slavery, Protestantism, and local autonomy, all of which placed them in direct conflict with the Mexican constitution. In 1828 a draftsman named Jose Maria Sanchez passed through one of Austin's settlements and subsequently reported that Mexico's newest colonists were dangerous. His prediction: "The spark that will start the conflagration that will deprive us of Texas will start from this colony."

Two years later, with Anglos outnumbering Tejanos three to one, Mexico provided fuel for the fire by cutting off immigration from the United States. Troops were sent to garrison the border, occupy seaports, and collect taxes on imported goods. In two years the occupation was over, but the Americans felt they could no longer trust their livelihood and their way of life to the Mexicans. Austin traveled to Mexico City to petition the government for greater autonomy and was thrown in jail by Antonio López de Santa Anna, who declared himself dictator, suspended the Mexican constitution, and banned slavery in all the Mexican territories. The Texans promptly formed

their own legislature and started selling land, inviting a new incursion by Mexican troops.

Idealists and mercenaries alike poured into Texas from the Southern states, relishing the prospect of a good fight. But the Texans couldn't decide whether they were fighting to restore the Mexican republic or to form one of their own. Santa Anna helped to resolve the argument, appearing at the gates of San Antonio in February 1836 with an army that may have numbered up to 5,000 men. While Col. William B. Travis of South Carolina hid his outnumbered force behind the walls of an old mission called the Alamo, a convention in Washington-on-the-Brazos declared its independence from Mexico. Texas legend has it that Travis valiantly swore "victory or death" from the start, although Mexican accounts of the battle insist his resolve strengthened only after a request for surrender was denied. On March 6, after a 12-day siege, the Mexican army stormed the mission and overwhelmed the Texans in hand-to-hand combat. At the end of the day, 187 defenders of the Alamo lay dead, including frontier icons James Bowie and Davy Crockett. Santa Anna, who called himself the "Napoleon of the West," mutilated, stripped, and burned many of the bodies, handing the Texans their rallying cry for the rest of

▲ *San Antonio de Valero,* built in 1718, is the oldest of the five missions in San Antonio. Popularly known as the Alamo, it was the site of the famous 1836 siege and is considered the "cradle of Texas liberty."

the war "Remember the Alamo!" Inspired by the memory, a ragtag force under Gen. Sam Houston cornered the Mexican army at San Jacinto and forced its surrender. Santa Anna traded Texas's independence for his own release.

WAR AND DESTINY

As an independent republic, Texas became a bone of contention in the slavery-dominated politics of antebellum Washington. Pro-Unionist Sam Houston, the republic's first president, wanted statehood. But so did many Southerners, who coveted the prospect of welcoming a vast area of slave territory into the Union. Finally, in 1845, Texas was annexed as a slave state.

Peace became the great casualty of the day when President James K. Polk sent troops into a disputed region near the Mexican border. Similar to almost every other political act in those turbulent times, the Mexican War split the country down the

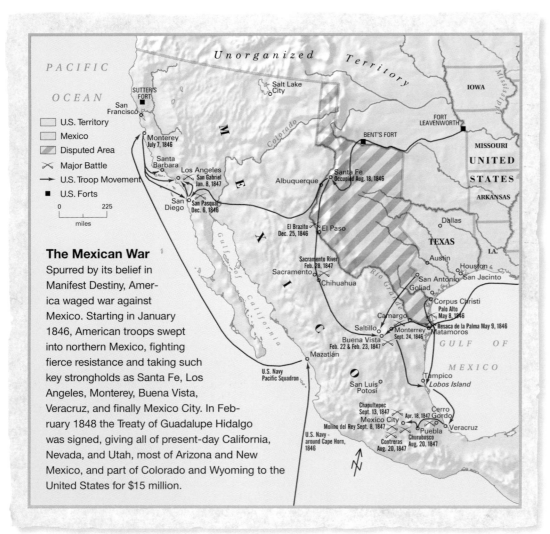

The Mexican War

Spurred by its belief in Manifest Destiny, America waged war against Mexico. Starting in January 1846, American troops swept into northern Mexico, fighting fierce resistance and taking such key strongholds as Santa Fe, Los Angeles, Monterey, Buena Vista, Veracruz, and finally Mexico City. In February 1848 the Treaty of Guadalupe Hidalgo was signed, giving all of present-day California, Nevada, and Utah, most of Arizona and New Mexico, and part of Colorado and Wyoming to the United States for $15 million.

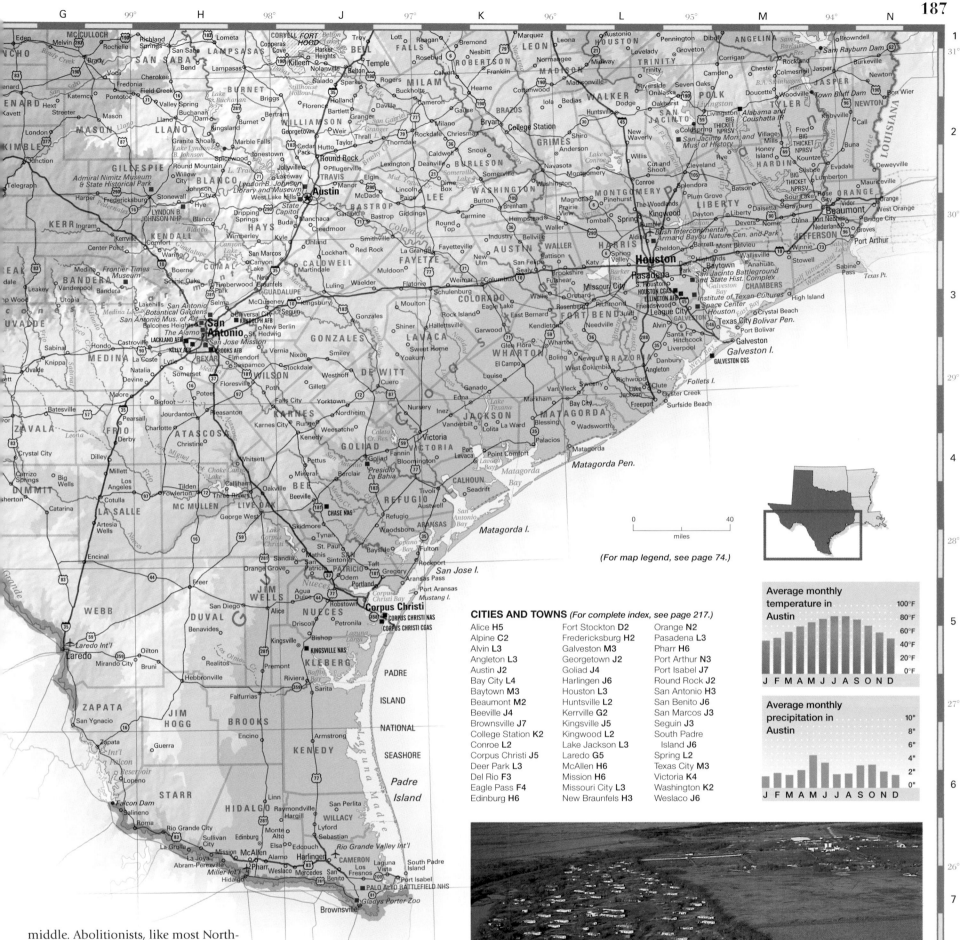

0   40
miles

(For map legend, see page 74.)

CITIES AND TOWNS (For complete index, see page 217.)

Alice **H5**	Fort Stockton **D2**	Orange **N2**
Alpine **C2**	Fredericksburg **H2**	Pasadena **L3**
Alvin **L3**	Galveston **M3**	Pharr **H6**
Angleton **L3**	Georgetown **J2**	Port Arthur **N3**
Austin **J2**	Goliad **J4**	Port Isabel **J7**
Bay City **L4**	Harlingen **J6**	Round Rock **J2**
Baytown **M3**	Houston **L3**	San Antonio **H3**
Beaumont **M2**	Huntsville **L2**	San Benito **J6**
Beeville **J4**	Kerrville **G2**	San Marcos **J3**
Brownsville **J7**	Kingsville **J5**	Seguin **J3**
College Station **K2**	Kingwood **L2**	South Padre
Conroe **L2**	Lake Jackson **L3**	Island **J6**
Corpus Christi **J5**	Laredo **G5**	Spring **L2**
Deer Park **L3**	McAllen **H6**	Texas City **M3**
Del Rio **F3**	Mission **H6**	Victoria **K4**
Eagle Pass **F4**	Missouri City **L3**	Washington **K2**
Edinburg **H6**	New Braunfels **H3**	Weslaco **J6**

Average monthly temperature in Austin

Average monthly precipitation in Austin

middle. Abolitionists, like most Northerners, felt it was a war to extend slavery.
Three years later, when the fight was over, the United
States had grown by a third, adding most of the present-day
Southwest to its empire. After the Civil War, towns like Dallas,
which originally had been a French trading post in the 1700s,
grew as Southerners moved to the area. There was nothing particularly attractive about Dallas;
its river, the Trinity, was unnaviga-
ble, and it wasn't near a railroad.
What Dallas and its surrounding
area did have, however, was rich,
black soil, perfect for planting
cotton. By the time the first train

▶ *Cowboy boots have been associated
with Texas since 1878, when a cowboy
and a boot maker invented them in the
town of Spanish Fort. Although they
were designed for range work, most people wear cowboy boots today for fashion.*

▲ *The King Ranch headquarters spreads out near the banks of the Santa Gertrudis
Creek on the Gulf coastal plain. The 825,000-acre ranch, founded in 1853 by steamboat
captain Richard King, is larger than the state of Rhode Island. Still in operation, the King
Ranch breeds cattle and horses and grows the most cotton in Texas.*

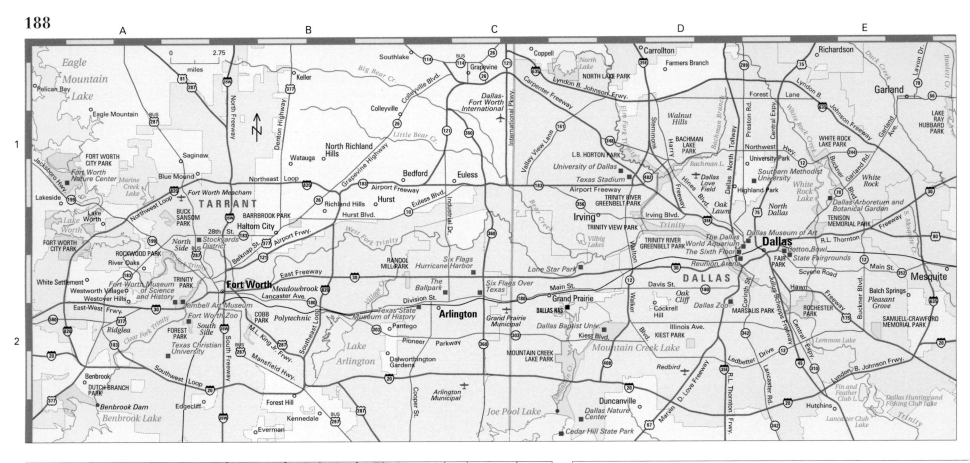

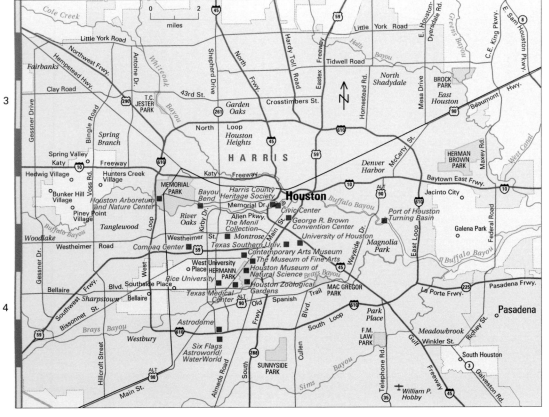

*◀ **Downtown Houston** stands proud as the largest city in Texas. The headquarters for many major petroleum firms, it is also an important grain depot and port as well as the main base of operations for the National Aeronautics and Space Administration.*

finally arrived in 1872, cotton growers were ready with large crops. In no time, farmers were shipping cotton all over the country. Dallas, which would never be the locus of the great Texas oil boom that occurred just at the start of the 20th century, did, however, become a banking city, innovating new ways to finance oil-drilling projects.

COWBOYS AND CATTLE TRAILS

When settling Texas, pioneers had two major obstacles to overcome: the daunting distance between their home state and everything else, and the expanse of arid wasteland in the west. Taking a cue from Mexican ranchers, the pioneers put the vast unwatered acres of brittle grass to use by feeding it to cattle. But in the 1860s local consumers were still few and far between. The Texas cattle herd—some 3 million to 4 million strong—had supplied the Confederate army with beef, but with the army disbanded and the South in disarray, the ranchers needed a new market. In 1867 they found it. Joseph McCoy, an Illinois beef salesman, chose the sleepy little town of Abilene, Kansas, as the location for a cattle-shipping business. McCoy built stock-holding pens, stables, and a world-class hotel, then got Texas ranchers to run their cattle 1,000 miles up the Chisholm Trail. There the scrawny longhorns were weighed 20 at a time on 10-ton scales and chased into boxcars for their terminal voyage east, where they sold for 10 times their value in Texas.

The long cattle drives produced massive profits for ranchers, jobs for 20,000 to 50,000 cowboys, and a powerful mythology that even today accounts for America's image in distant corners of the world. In countless dime novels and B-movies, Texas and the West—and, by extension, America—were wide-open lands where rugged white men in chaps roamed freely, defending civilization from the savage, then rode off into the sunset. The reality, however, was a lot less romantic. Texas cowboys, many of whom were Mexican or black, worked 18-hour days helping plodding herds of cattle across rivers and pulling stragglers out of mud holes. A bolt of lightning, a gunshot, even a rabbit could touch off a thundering stampede, forcing an entire crew to give chase in the middle of the night. The cowboys' encounters with Indians rarely went beyond the occasional brush with

*▲ **An offshore drilling rig** in the Gulf of Mexico off the Texas coast. Today the state has less than a tenth of the rigs that it had in the early 1980s. Texas still produces more natural gas than any other state, but its oil economy is currently half the size that it was in 1982.*

Comanche rustlers or mundane negotiations with Cherokee envoys, who charged 10 cents for each head of cattle that crossed their land. Ultimately, in just under 20 years, thanks in part to a resourceful Illinois farmer named Joseph Glidden, the era of the open range was over. In 1873 Glidden invented barbed wire to keep dogs out of his wife's garden, and by the early 1880s, farmers were wrapping it around the best pasture-land and watering holes in the West.

◀ *The Rio Grande twists and turns through a variety of landscapes in Big Bend National Park in southwestern Texas. Bathed in sunlight from behind the Sierra del Carmen, prickly pear cacti cover the desert surrounding the river (left). In Big Bend, the Rio Grande flows through three canyons—the Santa Elena, the Mariscal, and the Boquillas. Although the gorge waters are often placid (above), because of damming, stretches of the river contain wild and exhilarating whitewater rapids.*

BLACK GOLD

In January 1901 a rumbling deeper than anything ever attributed to a cattle stampede spread through tiny Beaumont, in the northeast corner of Texas. It was the sound of the 20th century rolling through. Spindletop, the greatest gusher to date, had come in, spurting oil 200 feet up in the air and then down onto every tree, bush, and person within acres. The well ran for nine days, launching Texas into the new, oil-powered world. Spindletop and the great East Texas oil fields of the 1930s turned the cattle state into America's greatest oil producer, keeping countless lucky ranchers in business and earning fortunes for a new breed of frontier businessmen.

Cities changed, too; Houston, a center of commerce, a railroad hub, and an important shipping port since the mid-19th century, grew in population as people from other parts of the United States sought their fortune there. World War II brought chemical and defense industries to Houston, and after the war natural gas and a building boom contributed greatly to the economy. Between 1950 and 1970 the population doubled, and it seemed like the economy in Houston, and all of East Texas, had nowhere to go but up.

In the early 1980s, however, the bottom dropped out of the Texas oil market. Many existing oil fields had been tapped out by the early 1970s, and offshore drilling was more expensive. In addition, Mexico discovered its second vast reserve of oil in 1976. (The first had petered out long ago.) The resulting glut sent prices plummeting and plunged parts of Texas into a full-fledged depression. But with new strength in biotech industries, chemicals, electronics, and aircraft production, the state's economy has once again rebounded. It is hoped, furthermore, that the 1994 North American Free Trade Agreement (NAFTA) will help Texas become the gateway to untapped Mexican markets.

A NEW FUTURE

It's probably fitting that Texas's future depends so heavily on its neighbor to the south. After all, Texans owe their unique character to their frontier heritage—most visible in the countless state fairs, rodeos, and quarter-horse shows that enliven the smallest of towns—and their relationship with Mexico. More than a quarter of the people in Texas are Tejanos, tracing their ancestry back to Mexico and other countries of Latin America. The flavor of Mexico can be found in everything, from the tongue-searing chilis in Tex-Mex cooking to the adobe architecture of the suburbs. Many cities are virtually bilingual, including San Antonio, where the Alamo stands not just as a monument to such men as Stephen Austin, Jim Bowie, and Davy Crockett but also as a memorial to the Tejanos who fought and died at the Alamo right alongside them. As more and more Tejanos move into positions of economic and political power, a new mythology will no doubt surface, and in it Texas will find the key to its future.

▲ *Cotton is the number one field crop in Texas. The entire plant is of value, not just the soft cotton lint (fibers). Cottonseeds are used for oil and as a base for certain foods, while the linters (seed fuzz) are used to make paper, cushioning, and plastics.*

◀ *The Ottine Swamp in Palmetto State Park east of San Antonio was once believed to have healing powers because of its sulfurous waters. Dwarf palmettos cover the 178-acre park, home to armadillos, opossums, and 240 species of birds.*

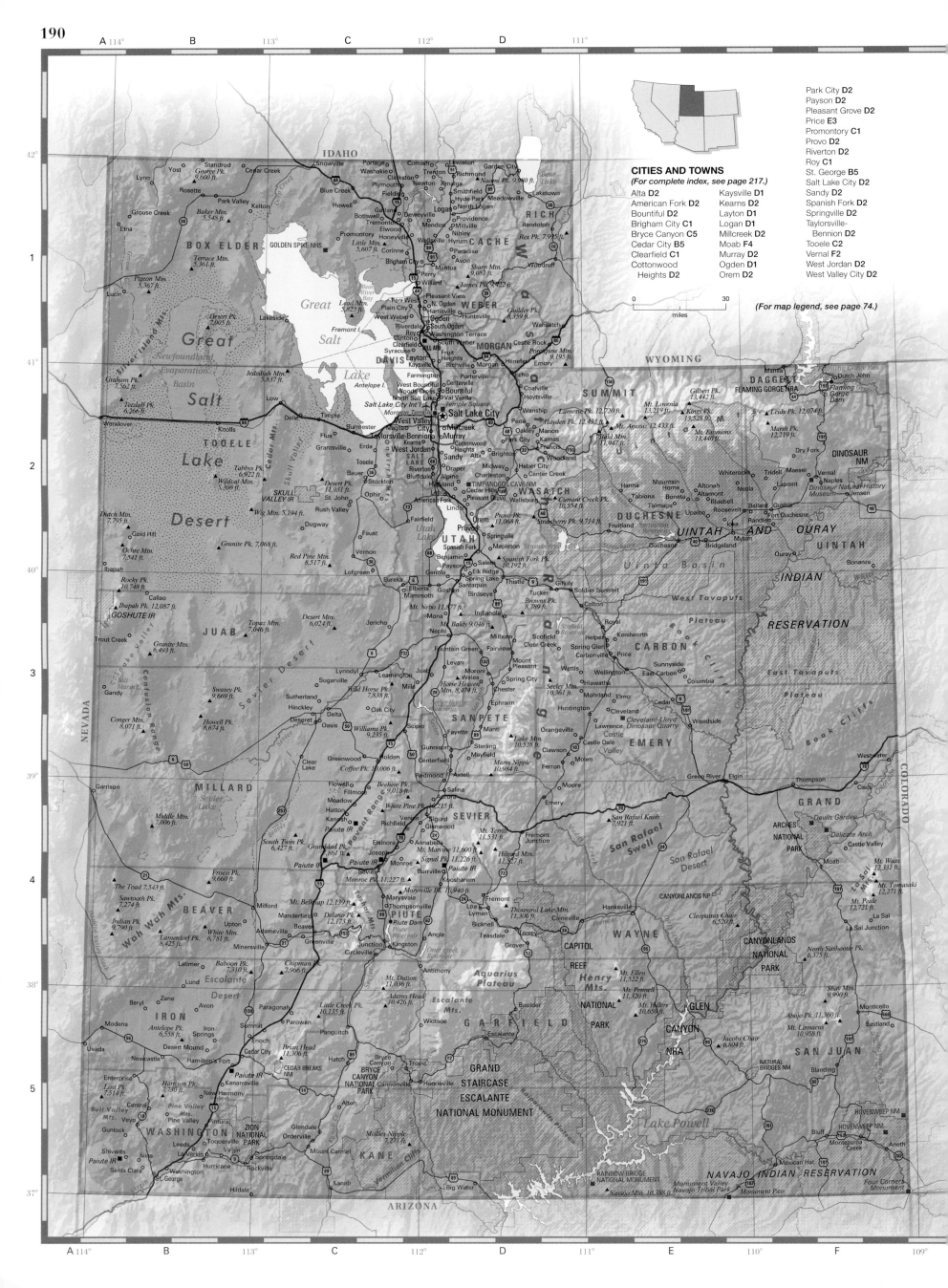

A 114° B 113° C 112° D 111°

0   30
miles

(For map legend, see page 74.)

A 114° B 113° C 112° D 111° E 110° F 109°

▲ *Salt Lake City rests in a fertile valley, with the Great Salt Lake Desert to the west and mountains from the Wasatch Range (shown in the background) to the east.*

Utah

Carved from the desert by Mormon pioneers, Utah began like America itself, as a haven from religious persecution. Salt Lake City—encircled by mountains, a desert, a vast arid plateau, and a giant salt lake—was to be the capital of a great promised land in the wilderness. But the early Mormon vision of a self-sustaining, communal theocracy died with the coming of the railroad, giving way to a modern Utah that boasts a flourishing economy, lavish ski resorts, and a world-renowned choir.

A LAND OF PROMISE

In the 1840s Brigham Young scoured surveys of the unsettled West in order to identify a place where his people might relocate. The tightly knit Mormon community—which proselytized aggressively, held property communally, and practiced polygamy—seemed to invite persecution wherever it went, and its home at that time in Nauvoo, Illinois, was no exception. A friend suggested that the Mormon leader consider California. But a palm-studded paradise wasn't what Young had in mind. "If there is a place on earth that nobody else wants," he told his friend, "that's the place I am hunting for."

He found his Promised Land in Utah, a magnificent, empty land. To the southeast lay the Colorado Plateau, where wind and water had carved endless miles of arid sandstone into a moonscape of arches, pinnacles, mesas, and gorges. In the northeast, two towering spurs of the Rockies, the Uintas and the Wasatch, soared to snow-capped peaks 13,000 feet high. In the northwest was the Great Salt Lake Desert. Nestled between the mountains and the desert was an oasis on the shores of an enormous salt lake.

On July 24, 1847, Brigham Young's wagon train arrived in northwestern Utah. Sick with mountain fever, Young lifted himself from his cot and, according to Mormon lore, said simply, "This is the place."

▲ *Bryce Canyon National Park's 14 natural amphitheaters are abrim with shimmering stone formations.*

THE EFFECTS OF PROGRESS

The early Mormons carved Salt Lake City out of the cracked earth with a fervent sense of mission. Within a month they had dammed a stream to provide water for more than 100 planted acres, thereby setting up the first modern irrigation system in North America. By the end of the year, 4,000 settlers had arrived, and the desert had been transformed into a self-sufficient beehive of industry. In the next 40 years, 80,000 more people descended on Utah. The truly eager arrived by handcart, hauling their belongings hundreds of miles to the Promised Land on foot. For the early Mormons, it meant a kingdom of God in the wilderness.

But the Mormons' fate, in the end, had more to do with politics than religion. The U.S. government incorporated the Utah Territory in 1850. Federal troops arrived in 1857 and again in 1862; the second batch was commanded by Col. Patrick Edward Connor, who urged his soldiers to mine the mountainside for precious metals. Before long, silver was discovered in nearby Park City and copper in the Oquirrh Mountains. Then, in 1869, the final golden spike was driven into the first transcontinental railroad at Promontory. The Mormons suddenly found themselves part of a hungry national economy that brought with it manufactured goods, non-Mormon settlers, and the meddling interference of federal authorities. In 1896 Utah became a state; it was still primarily Mormon, but it was no longer the peaceable kingdom.

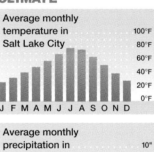

▲ *When Leland Sanford swung the mallet to drive the golden spike that would complete America's first transcontinental railroad, he missed.*

A MODERN MECCA

Even today, however, Utah bears the stamp of its founders' vision. Salt Lake City is a monument to early urban planning, its streets built wide enough to turn a team of oxen. The cavernous dome of the Mormon Tabernacle, home of the world-renowned choir, is held together largely by wooden pins and rawhide, since metal nails were scarce when it was built. And the work ethic that the settlers brought with them has built one of the country's most successful economies.

Tourism, which draws $2 billion a year to the state, is responsible for much of the growth. Every winter millions of people flock to Park City, Snowbird, Alta, and other resorts. Others come to visit the many national parks, national monuments, and national forests that offer some of the most spectacular wilderness in the world. One of the five national parks in the state, Capitol Reef National Park derives its name from a white sandstone outcropping that looks eerily like the Capitol dome in Washington, D.C., and the mountains that resembled coral reef to early pioneers. Perhaps the most famous natural attractions are found in Monument Valley Navajo Tribal Park, which straddles the Utah and Arizona border. Its giant red sandstone crags have served as the quintessential lonesome and windswept backdrop for a number of Western movies, including the classic *Stagecoach*.

In recent decades many visitors have been deciding to stay. Since 1970 Utah's growth rate has outpaced the nation's by three to one. The place that nobody else wanted has become one of America's most favored places to live.

▲ *The state flag, adopted in 1913, displays the state seal. The seal shows a beehive, symbolizing industriousness, on a shield. A bald eagle sits on the top of the shield. The date 1896 is the year the shield was adopted; 1847, the year the Mormons first settled Utah.*

STATE DATA

State bird: Seagull
State flower: Sego lily
State tree: Blue spruce
State motto: Industry
State song: "Utah, We Love Thee"
Abbreviation: UT (postal)
Origin of the name: After the Ute tribe, meaning "people of the mountains"
Nickname: Beehive State

AREA AND SIZE

Total area: 84,916 sq. mi.
Rank within U.S.: 11
Extent: 342 mi. north–south; 276 mi. east–west
Highest elevation: Kings Peak, 13,528 ft. above sea level
Lowest elevation: Beaverdam Creek in Washington County, 2,000 ft. above sea level

POPULATION

Total: 2,207,000
Rank within U.S.: 34
Ethnic breakdown: White: 88.9%; Hispanic: 6.3%; Asian: 2.6%; Indian: 1.5%; Black: 0.8%
Population density: 26.8 people per sq. mi.

CLIMATE

Average monthly temperature in Salt Lake City

100°F
80°F
60°F
40°F
20°F
0°F

J F M A M J J A S O N D

Average monthly precipitation in Salt Lake City

10"
8"
6"
4"
2"
0"

J F M A M J J A S O N D

ECONOMY

Service industries: Hotels and ski resorts, real estate, banking
Manufacturing: Transportation equipment, steel, aluminum
Mining: Petroleum, copper, coal, natural gas, gilsonite, uranium
Agriculture: Milk, beef cattle, turkeys, sheep, hay

UTAH TIMELINE

700 Anasazi people begin building pueblos.
1600 Shoshonean cultures dominate region.
1776 Silvestre Vélez de Escalante and Francisco Atanasio Dominguez explore Utah.
1847 Brigham Young brings Mormons to Great Salt Lake area.
1849 Mormons found the state of Deseret.
1850 Utah is made a U.S. territory.

1857 Federal troops try unsuccessfully to revoke Brigham Young's governorship. Mormons, aided by Paiute Indians, massacre immigrants from Arkansas and Missouri.
1861 Telegraph lines joining at Salt Lake City provide first transcontinental telegraph service.
1869 First transcontinental railroad is completed at Promontory.
1890 Mormons give up polygamy.

1896 Utah joins the Union as the 45th state.
1913 Strawberry River project provides power and irrigation.
1952 Rich uranium deposits are discovered near Moab.
1964 Flaming Gorge Dam begins generating electrical power.
1967 The Central Utah Project begins to supply water to growing areas.
1985 Great Salt Lake floods region.

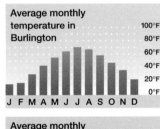

▲ *The state flag,* adopted in 1923, displays the Vermont coat of arms. It shows a pine tree, a cow, three sheaves of grain, and mountains in the background.

STATE DATA

State bird: Hermit thrush
State flower: Red clover
State tree: Sugar maple
State motto: Freedom and unity
State song: "Hail, Vermont!"
Abbreviations: Vt.; VT (postal)
Origin of the name: From the French words *vert* and *mont,* which mean "green mountain"
Nickname: Green Mountain State

AREA AND SIZE

Total area: 9,609 sq. mi.
Rank within U.S.: 43
Extent: 158 mi. north–south; 97 mi. east–west
Highest elevation: Mount Mansfield, 4,393 ft. above sea level
Lowest elevation: Lake Champlain in Franklin County, 95 ft. above sea level

POPULATION

Total: 617,000
Rank within U.S.: 49
Ethnic breakdown: White: 97.2%; Asian: 1.0%; Hispanic: 1.0%; Black: 0.3%; Indian: 0.3%
Population density: 66.5 people per sq. mi.

CLIMATE

Average monthly temperature in Burlington
100°F
80°F
60°F
40°F
20°F
0°F
J F M A M J J A S O N D

Average monthly precipitation in Burlington
10"
8"
6"
4"
2"
0"
J F M A M J J A S O N D

ECONOMY

Service industries: Community, business, and personal services; real estate; finance; insurance
Manufacturing: Semiconductors and other electronic components, printed materials, dairy products
Agriculture: Milk, maple syrup
Mining: Granite, marble, slate

Vermont

Of all the 50 states, perhaps Vermont summons the clearest set of images: an Arcadian pasture dotted with cows, a white-steepled church, the fiery hues of autumnal foliage, skiers carving wide arcs on a snowy mountainside. These are not hazy flashbacks in some bucolic dream but real elements of Vermont's character.

A RURAL LANDSCAPE

Although Vermont is close to the great metropolitan corridor of the eastern seaboard, geography has had its say in the stubborn survival of the state's rural character. Vermont is the only New England state without a seacoast; consequently, it never experienced the urban concentration that accompanies maritime trade. Much of its terrain is locked within the wooded fastness of the Green Mountains, which run along the entire length of Vermont and defy all but the most hardscrabble attempts at cultivation.

But history, too, has nudged Vermont along its quirky path. The area was first explored by the French navigator Samuel de Champlain, who in 1609 ventured south from Quebec into the 125-mile-long lake that now bears his name and that today forms much of Vermont's border with New York State. The French presence never really extended beyond a series of 17th- and early-18th-century forts on Lake Champlain, but because of the threat posed by the French and their Indian allies, English settlement in what is now Vermont was almost nonexistent prior to the end of the French and Indian War in 1763.

INDEPENDENT SENSIBILITIES

In the years leading up to the American Revolution, Vermont's fledgling towns were known collectively as the "New Hampshire Grants," since most had been chartered by the neighboring state's colonial governor. Still, Vermont was really a political no-man's-land. New Hampshire claimed the territory extending nearly all the way west to the Hudson River, while New York declared sovereignty over all lands west of the Connecticut River—a distinct overlap that neatly defined Vermont. New York's refusal to recognize Vermont land titles granted by New Hampshire, and many Vermonters' refusal to accept New York's land claims, led to the organization of the Green Mountain Boys, a backwoods militia led by Ethan Allen that constantly harassed "Yorker" surveyors and court officers.

When the Revolution began, Ethan Allen and his men turned their attention toward fighting for independence, capturing Fort Ticonderoga on Lake Champlain in New York. The most important Revolutionary War battle associated with Vermont, however, was the 1777 Battle of Bennington—the Vermont town that was the target of British troops. This engagement was a sharp setback for the British in the days preceding their decisive defeat at Saratoga.

Beginning in 1777, Vermont functioned as an independent republic under its own constitution, electing its own officials and even minting its own coins. Fourteen years later, it joined the Union as the 14th state. New York, still aggrieved over its perceived territorial loss, was paid $30,000 in compensation.

GREEN MOUNTAIN STATE INDUSTRY

There is a good reason that a statue of Ceres, the Roman goddess of agriculture, stands atop the Vermont State House in Montpelier. The closing years of the 18th century and the first half of the 19th century were the golden age of farming in Vermont. By 1840 roughly three-quarters of the land was cleared, and small-scale farming had become the backbone of the state's economy. Since no large industrial enterprise gained a foothold in this era, as the giant textile mills had in neighboring New Hampshire, no single urban area came to dominate the state. To this day, Vermont has only one large city: Burlington. Built on a hill that overlooks Lake Champlain, Burlington is home to a symphony orchestra, three colleges, and the University of Vermont.

In the years following the Civil War, Vermont began to change. Many of the state's veterans headed west, and hill farms went fallow. (Even now, it is not uncommon to find 150-year-old cellar holes and tumbling stone walls deep in the woods that were once wide-open pastures.) Agriculture was consolidated in the

◀ *Winter in East Orange,* in central Vermont. This remote village typifies the serenity and simplicity of rural life; the church (at left) was restored in 1990, in honor of the village's centennial. Almost three-quarters of Vermont's residents live in small towns or on farms.

▲ *Lake Champlain,* the largest lake in New England, is a favorite spot for boating, fishing, and other leisure-time activities. The lake serves as the focal point of Burlington, the state's "Queen City."

more fertile valleys, where today most of Vermont's roughly 1,900 working dairy farms are found.

The latter half of the 19th century also saw the rise of the mining industry in Vermont, centering in quarries that extracted marble near Rutland and granite in Barre. (Barre is still one of the granite capitals of the world.) At the same time, Vermont developed—and still maintains—a substantial logging industry, both in the remote private lands of the sparsely populated "Northeast Kingdom" and within more than 260,000 acres of the Green Mountain National Forest.

Manufacturing was once concentrated in the southern Connecticut River valley, where Springfield hummed with machine shops, which are now mostly closed. Today the state's leading private employer is IBM near Burlington. And, of course, there's ice cream: Ben & Jerry's, whose Waterbury plant is one of the state's most popular attractions, is firmly founded on Vermont butterfat. In the meantime, Vermont remains the nation's leading producer of pure maple syrup, boiled down from sap gathered early each spring.

YEAR-ROUND FUN AND BEAUTY

Tourism has had a tremendous influence on late-20th-century Vermont. The ski industry got its start in the 1930s, when enthusiasts built the state's first mechanical tow near Woodstock, and Civilian Conservation Corps crews began cutting trails on Mount Mansfield, Vermont's highest peak, in Stowe. Today dozens of major resorts offer some of the East's finest skiing and bolster the state economy's hospitality sector. Throughout the year, however, tourists fan out across the byways of Vermont, whether to gaze at the incomparably colorful fall foliage, to enjoy summer along Lake Champlain, or to seek out such attractions as the Shelburne Museum, with its collection of American folk art and artifacts. Perhaps Vermont's greatest attraction, though, is the land itself, a pleasingly varied mix of mountain wilderness and rolling farmscapes. Aware of the pricelessness of this prime resource, Vermonters in recent years have worked to save some 20,000 acres per year from development.

Many of the tourists never leave. Natives and newcomers are now roughly of equal number in Vermont, and the outsiders have shown considerable cultural and political strength. There is friction—not all of the state fits the calendar-photo image—but people do have a chance to air their grievances at the annual town meeting, where every voter is his or her own representative. The town meeting is still the bedrock expression of democracy in all but the largest municipalities in Vermont. Prior to 1965 each town, regardless of its population, sent one representative to the legislature's lower house—a practice that vastly favored small towns at the expense of cities. Proportional representation has since been adopted, but local prerogatives are still jealously guarded. There is something about Vermont that seems to foster a deep spirit of independent yeomanry for natives and even for those whose own ancestors lived very far from that long-ago Republic of Vermont.

▲ **Rock of Ages,** in Barre, is one of the world's largest sources of granite. The blue-gray and white stone that is quarried here is almost flawless in texture.

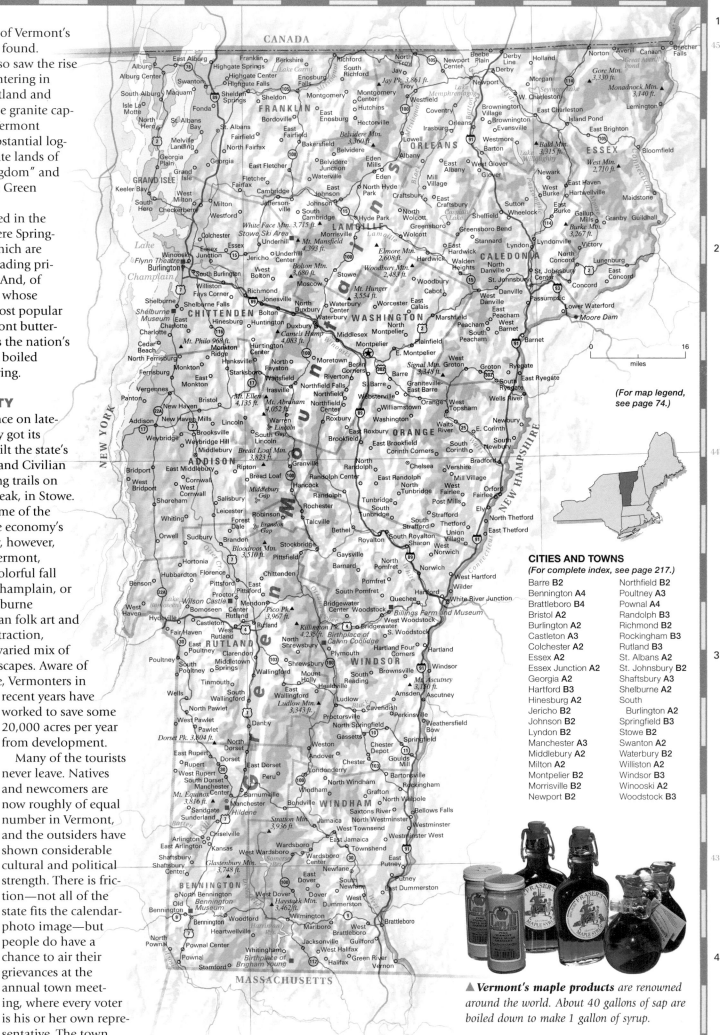

(For map legend, see page 74.)

CITIES AND TOWNS
(For complete index, see page 217.)

▲ **Vermont's maple products** are renowned around the world. About 40 gallons of sap are boiled down to make 1 gallon of syrup.

VERMONT TIME LINE

1609 Samuel de Champlain claims Vermont region for France.

1724 Fort Dummer becomes first permanent white settlement.

1764 New York gains jurisdiction over Vermont.

1770 Ethan Allen and the Green Mountain Boys drive New York settlers from Vermont.

1775 Green Mountain Boys help capture Fort Ticonderoga from British.

1777 Vermont declares independence from Britain and prohibits slavery.

1791 Vermont becomes 14th state.

1823 Champlain Canal links Vermont to New York City.

1850 Vermont nullifies U.S. Fugitive Slave Law.

1864 Confederate soldiers attack St. Albans.

1881 Chester A. Arthur of Vermont becomes U.S. president.

1923 Calvin Coolidge, another Vermonter, becomes president.

1927 Floods kill 60 people and cause extensive damage.

1934 First ski tow in the U.S. is built in Woodstock.

1940 First chairlift begins operation on Mount Mansfield.

1970 Environmental Control Act limits major development.

1985 Madeleine M. Kunin becomes state's first woman governor.

▲ **The state flag,** *adopted in 1931, displays the state seal. On the seal Virtue is clad in the clothes of an Amazon. Holding a spear and a sheathed sword, she triumphs over Tyranny, whose crown lies nearby and who holds a broken chain in his hand.*

STATE DATA

State bird: Cardinal
State flower: Dogwood flower
State tree: Flowering dogwood
State motto: *Sic semper tyrannis* (This always to tyrants)
State song (emeritus): "Carry Me Back to Old Virginia"
Abbreviations: Va.; VA (postal)
Origin of the name: Named for Queen Elizabeth I, "Virgin Queen" of England, by Sir Walter Raleigh
Nicknames: Old Dominion, Cavalier State, Mother of Presidents, Mother of States, Mother of Statesmen

AREA AND SIZE

Total area: 40,817 sq. mi.
Rank within U.S.: 36
Extent: 201 mi. north–south; 462 mi. east–west
Highest elevation: Mount Rogers, 5,729 ft. above sea level
Lowest elevation: Sea level

POPULATION

Total: 6,997,000
Rank within U.S.: 12
Ethnic breakdown: White: 72.3%; Black: 19.9%; Hispanic: 3.8%; Asian: 3.7%; Indian: 0.2%
Population density: 175.6 people per sq. mi.

CLIMATE

Average monthly temperature in Richmond

Average monthly precipitation in Richmond

ECONOMY

Service industries: Community, business, and personal services; finance, insurance, real estate
Manufacturing: Textiles, cigarettes, transportation equipment
Agriculture: Beef cattle, broiler chickens, milk, tobacco, corn, apples, peanuts, potatoes, tomatoes
Mining: Coal, limestone, granite

▲ **The gently rolling Shenandoah Valley,** *site of Shenandoah National Park, is one of Virginia's most-visited scenic attractions.*

Virginia

From the westernmost reaches of the Appalachian Plateau to the eastern Atlantic shores of the Delmarva Peninsula, Virginia abounds with natural splendor. Mountainous terrain characterizes the western part of the state, where the Shenandoah Valley, a broad, 150-mile-long upland is nestled between the Allegheny and Blue Ridge mountains. Tobacco thrives in the Piedmont and Tidewater regions to the east, bounded by historic Chesapeake Bay. Strategically located on the southern end of the bay, Virginia's massive Hampton Roads Harbor has been one of America's most vital shipping and military ports from colonial times to the present.

AMERICA'S FIRST COLONY

Concerned about Spanish and French progress in settling the New World, England's King James I decided to secure a foothold by establishing a trading post on the Chesapeake Bay. In 1607 three ships carrying 104 men and boys landed at a site

they called Jamestown, a 1,500-acre island that Capt. John Smith, the head of the colony, considered to be "a verie fit place for the erecting of a great cittie." These first settlers were not yeoman farmers intent on cultivating the wilderness but, rather, adventurers and entrepreneurs in search of gold, silver, and other valuables. Nor were they the first Englishmen to attempt to settle in what would be known as Virginia. Two earlier attempts had been made at a place called Roanoke, in 1584 and again in 1587. The first group returned home after a year; the second group mysteriously vanished.

The early history of the colony was fraught with hardship. Ill-equipped for life in the New World, the settlers succumbed in considerable numbers to starvation, disease, and Indian attack during the first winter. In the hope of securing supplies for the winter, Captain Smith led a trading mission to the camp of Chief Powhatan, who ruled several tribes in the Chesapeake Bay area. Smith quickly won the favor of the chief's teenage daughter, Princess Pocahontas, whose gifts of food helped sustain the colony during the winter of 1608. After Smith returned to England, Pocahontas married an Englishman named John Rolfe, who had raised Jamestown's first tobacco crop for export. Failing to find gold or silver, the colonists followed suit, and tobacco farming was on its way to becoming one of Virginia's most profitable enterprises.

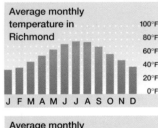

(For map legend, see page 74.)

CITIES AND TOWNS *(For complete index, see page 217.)*

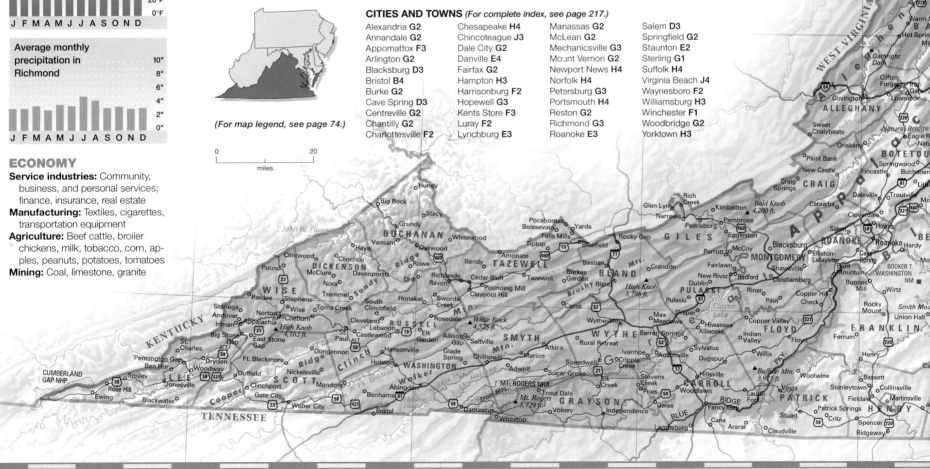

AT A CROSSROADS

Virginia was settled from two directions—first from the sea and, beginning in the 1730s, by way of the Great Wagon Road. This followed an ancient Indian trail called the Great Warrior Road, which ran west from Philadelphia and descended into the Shenandoah Valley. The most famous section of the road, the Wilderness Road—a path blazed by the pioneer Daniel Boone—led southwest from the valley into Tennessee and Kentucky, crossing the Allegheny Mountains at the Cumberland Gap. By the late 1700s more than 100,000 settlers—many of them Scotch-Irish and Germans—had traveled this route to the West. Part of the Appalachians, the Allegheny Mountains, presented a formidable barrier to this westward migration but provided a highway for a different sort of migration later on. Runaway slaves fled west from the tobacco country to reach these mountains, which offered escape routes to freedom in Pennsylvania and Ohio.

BROWN GOLD

Despite its promising future, tobacco farming did not have a favorable launching. King James I was firmly opposed to tobacco and smoking, a vice he called "the horrible Stygian smoke of the pit that is bottomless." Nonetheless, tobacco ensured the survival of the early English settlement and eventually determined the shape of Virginia's economy and society. England's

◀ *Tobacco*—seen in this photo as it hangs out to dry—was the economic mainstay of the fledgling colony of Virginia. It is still the state's most lucrative crop.

appetite for smoking was insatiable: in just two years, from 1616 to 1618, Virginia's shipments to England increased by 2,000 percent. In the Tidewater region, where four great rivers drain into the Chesapeake, the shores of the Potomac, Rappahannock, York, and James were dotted with plantations—virtual self-contained villages in which small families of whites were supported by scores or even hundreds of African slaves who raised the labor-intensive tobacco crop. (The first slaves were brought to Virginia aboard a Dutch ship in 1619.) Each plantation had its own river landing, where ships docked to collect tobacco and receive other goods for export to England.

The tobacco weed created great wealth and promoted the growth of a genteel aristocracy. By the early 1700s landholdings began to be consolidated in fewer hands. Farmers with small tracts of land had little opportunity to acquire the large acreages

VIRGINIA
TIME LINE

1607 Jamestown becomes first permanent English settlement in America.

1612 John Rolfe introduces tobacco growing and exporting to colony.

1619 House of Burgesses, America's first representative assembly, convenes. Dutch traders sell Africans as indentured servants.

1624 Virginia is designated a royal colony.

1693 College of William and Mary is founded.

1765 Patrick Henry spurs passage of Stamp Act Resolves.

1774 Virginia convention calls for first Continental Congress.

1776 Virginia convention declares Virginia independent.

1781 Lord Cornwallis of Britain surrenders at Yorktown, ending Revolutionary War.

1788 Virginia becomes 10th state.

1789 George Washington of Virginia is sworn in as first U.S. president.

1792 Kentucky is created from three Virginia counties.

1819 Thomas Jefferson founds University of Virginia.

1831 Nat Turner's revolt leads to stricter controls over slaves.

1861 Virginia secedes from the Union. Richmond becomes Confederate capital.

1863 West Virginia becomes separate state.

1865 Lee surrenders at Appomattox, ending Civil War.

1870 Virginia rejoins the Union.

1902 New poll tax and literacy test disenfranchise blacks.

1959 First public school integration in Virginia takes place.

1964 Chesapeake Bay Bridge-Tunnel is completed.

1989 L. Douglas Wilder becomes first elected black governor in U.S. history.

▲ **Monticello,** *designed and built by Thomas Jefferson between 1768 and 1809 to serve as his permanent home, is furnished with many of his inventions. Parts of the mansion and its gardens are now open to the public.*

▲ **The Appomattox Court House** *marks the spot where Robert E. Lee surrendered to Ulysses S. Grant on April 9, 1865, effectively ending the Civil War. The restored area is now a national historical park.*

▼ **The Pentagon,** *in Arlington, is the headquarters of the U.S. Department of Defense. One of the largest office buildings in the world, it covers 29 acres of land. Its more than 20,000 employees are comprised of civilians, officers, and enlisted personnel.*

▲ **The James River** *has sustained the Jamestown settlers, many colonial plantations, and Richmond, the current state capital.*

needed to prosper and either resigned themselves to a marginal existence or left Virginia for more open lands to the west.

WARTIMES
Virginia played a significant role in both the American Revolution and the Civil War. Many of the wars' most important political and military leaders, including George Washington, Thomas Jefferson, George Mason (author of the Bill of Rights), Patrick Henry, Jeb Stuart, Stonewall Jackson, Jubal Early, and the five Lee brothers (including Robert E. Lee and his half brothers, Francis and Richard Henry Lee, the only brothers to sign the Declaration of Independence) were Virginians. During the Revolution, Virginia saw numerous raids, skirmishes, and small battles, while the Marquis de Lafayette did his best to protect the colony from British raiders under Lord Cornwallis and the turncoat Benedict Arnold. In 1781 the British raided Monticello, the mountaintop home of Thomas Jefferson, who just barely escaped capture. The last Revolutionary War battle took place at Yorktown, where George Washington's army, in cooperation with a French fleet, trapped Cornwallis and forced his surrender, a defeat that ensured independence for the Americans.

The Civil War exacted an even heavier toll on Virginia. The bloody meeting ground of North and South, Virginia saw 26 major battles and over 400 other engagements—more men fought in Virginia, and more lost their lives here, than in any other state. The fighting was so intense that towns were frequently tossed back and forth between the Confederacy and the Union. The town of Winchester, for example, changed hands 72 times during the course of the war. Bull Run, the first major battle, took place in Virginia, and the war came to its end here on the surrender of Robert E. Lee's army to Ulysses S. Grant at Appomattox Court House.

HAMPTON ROADS
One of the most important ports in America since colonial times, Hampton Roads was a focal point in both wars. A year-round port with a depth of about 40 feet,

Hampton Roads has approximately 50 miles of shoreline. Located at a central point on the eastern seaboard, the massive harbor overlooks four cities—Hampton, Norfolk, Newport News, and Portsmouth—and a network of highways and rail lines that link it to the hinterland. Norfolk, the most cosmopolitan of the Hampton Roads cities and home to the largest naval base in the world, began as a port for trade with England and the West Indies. The city was burned by the British in 1776. During the Civil War the Union navy imposed a blockade in the harbor, which led to the world's first confrontation of ironclads—the *Monitor* and the *Merrimack*—in 1862. Later, during World War I, the Hampton Roads shipyards constructed more naval tonnage than did the rest of the country's yards combined. And during World War II, more than 400 ships came from Newport News. The shipyards and the military bases surrounding Hampton Roads have long lured workers from Virginia's rural regions and made this the state's most populous region.

ENCHANTING BEAUTY
The wealth and sophistication of Virginia's aristocracy are vividly expressed in the architecture that is preserved in hundreds of distinguished old homes, many of them open to the public. Examples of various architectural styles, derived from

▲ **The Norfolk Naval Base,** *whose 15 piers serve as home port for more than 150 ships, includes the headquarters of the NATO Allied Command Atlantic, the Atlantic Fleet, and the Fifth Naval District.*

▲ *The Governor's Palace in Williamsburg, with its formal gardens, was once the residence of Governors Patrick Henry and Thomas Jefferson. The reconstructed mansion is in the restored historic area of the city, which was Virginia's capital from 1699 to 1780.*

18th-century European design, include George Washington's mansion, Mount Vernon, and a trio of presidential homes near Charlottesville: Thomas Jefferson's Monticello, James Monroe's Ash Lawn, and James Madison's Montpelier. Another cluster of fine mansions lies along the James River; here three great colonial homes—Shirley, Berkeley, and Westover—delight visitors with their history and splendor.

The grandeur of these homes notwithstanding, Virginia's crowning glory is its natural beauty and resources. The Chesapeake Bay, the life force of coastal Virginia, has for centuries been a rich source of seafood. Although pollution has drastically reduced the fish and shellfish populations since the 1950s, conservation efforts in recent years have slowly brought the bay back to life. Chincoteague Island and National Wildlife Refuge, just south of the Maryland border on the Delmarva Peninsula, is home to a herd of wild ponies fabled to have swum ashore from a shipwrecked Spanish galleon. The ponies spend most of their time on nearby Assateague Island off the coast of Maryland. Once a year during July, however, the foals are taken across the inlet to be sold at auction. The Great Dismal Swamp, which spreads over the border into North Carolina, is a 107,000-acre wetland sanctuary for more than 200 species of birds, including the great blue heron and the barred owl; a variety of mammals, including minks, otters, bats, black bears, and bobcats; such reptiles as yellow-bellied turtles and canebrake rattlers; and diverse plant life that includes orchids, papaws, and devil's-walking-sticks.

Perhaps one of the most beautiful areas in Virginia is the Shenandoah Valley. A broad upland that is 150 miles long, the Shenandoah is part of a series of valleys, collectively known as the Valley of Virginia, that stretches from the Potomac River to Tennessee. Orchards, pastures, fields, and vineyards blanket the valley, and the best way to view it is from the Skyline Drive, the majestic highway that weaves along the rugged mountain passes and 4,000-foot peaks of the Blue Ridge. Spectacular both above ground and below, the Shenandoah sits atop limestone that is riddled with caves, including the 64-acre Luray Caverns, the largest in the East. "How full of breadth the scenery"—Walt Whitman's words could not ring more true.

▶ *Virginia Beach, a popular resort city with miles of Atlantic beaches, has been growing rapidly in recent years. At the city's northern end is Cape Henry, where the Jamestown settlers first landed in 1607.*

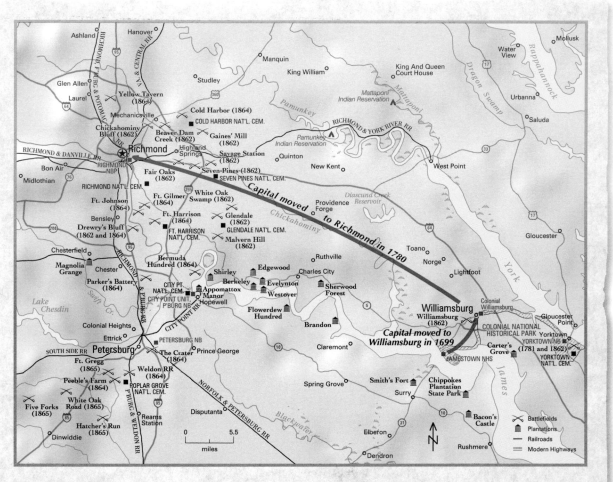

The Three Capitals of Virginia

Early Virginians regarded Jamestown, the first capital of the colony, as a mistake. Ordered to establish a town, in 1607 the first colonists sailed from the Chesapeake Bay up the James River until they arrived at a spot that could be easily defended and had water deep enough to accommodate ships. The site was not ideal, however, as it lay in the middle of a disease-harboring swamp.

In 1699 Gov. Francis Nicholson established Williamsburg as the colonial capital, laying out an elegant town of brick buildings. The College of William and Mary (founded in 1693) was located there, and Nicholson thought that the conjunction of capital and college would enhance both. Williamsburg, although more pleasant than James-town, was never a heavily populated settlement; rather, it was a place to which planters went to do business.

During the Revolutionary War, the capital was moved from Williamsburg to the small settlement of Richmond. The town's location on the fall line of the James River had led to its establishment as a trading post in 1737. When the war was over, Richmond prospered as a shipping point; such commodities as tobacco were sent from the state's interior to the city by canal and later by railroad.

At the start of the Civil War, Richmond was chosen as the Confederate capital because it was a crucial hub. The fall of Richmond to Ulysses S. Grant in March 1865 sealed the Confederacy's fate. After the war Richmond was revived as a shipping and manufacturing center.

▲ **The state flag,** adopted in 1923, displays the state seal. It shows a picture of George Washington, for whom the state was named; the green background represents Washington's forests.

STATE DATA
State bird: Willow goldfinch
State flower: Coast rhododendron
State tree: Western hemlock
State motto: *Alki* (an Indian word meaning "by and by")
State song: "Washington, My Home"
Abbreviations: Wash.; WA (postal)
Origin of the name: Named after George Washington
Nickname: Evergreen State

AREA AND SIZE
Total area: 68,192 sq. mi.
Rank within U.S.: 20
Extent: 239 mi. north–south; 370 mi. east–west
Highest elevation: Mount Rainier, 14,410 ft. above sea level
Lowest elevation: Sea level along the coast

Washington

Wet and wild, Washington is a rain-splashed, evergreen wonderland. Temperate rain forests, fjordlike bays, and idyllic islands hug the state's shoreline; volcanic mountains run down its spine; prairies and farmland blanket its eastern reach. Set amid this splendor are colorful coastal towns and a bustling metropolis. With one foot planted in the past and the other striding into the future, Washington is a rich mix of Native American tradition, pioneer spirit, and Western independence.

EXPLORATION
Named for the country's first president and nicknamed the Evergreen State for the thick stands of evergreens that cover approximately half of its 68,192 square miles, Washington occupies the northwestern corner of the continental United States. It was originally part of the vast Oregon Territory until it was admitted to the Union in 1889 as the 42nd state.

Artifacts discovered at the Marmes Rock Shelter in eastern Washington indicate that humans inhabited the region at least 10,000 years ago. By the time Europeans arrived, many different groups of Native Americans called the area home: the Cayuse, Colville, Nez Perce, Spokane, and Yakima tribes lived in the plains and valleys east of the Cascade Mountains; and the Chinook, Clallam, Clatsop, Nisqualli, and Puyallup tribes dwelled along the coast.

When the English explorer Sir Francis Drake sailed along the western coast of North America in 1579 in his ship the *Golden Hind,* his voyage sparked a competition between Britain and Spain for control of the area. Although the Spanish were eager to best their English rivals, no serious trips were made to the West Coast until 1774, when Juan Perez, on his way back to Mexico from Canadian waters, spotted a gleaming peak in a mountain range. He named the peak El Cerro Nevada de Santa Rosalia ("The Snowy

▶ **Harbor seals** *are the most plentiful species of marine mammal living in the Strait of Juan de Fuca off Washington's coast.*

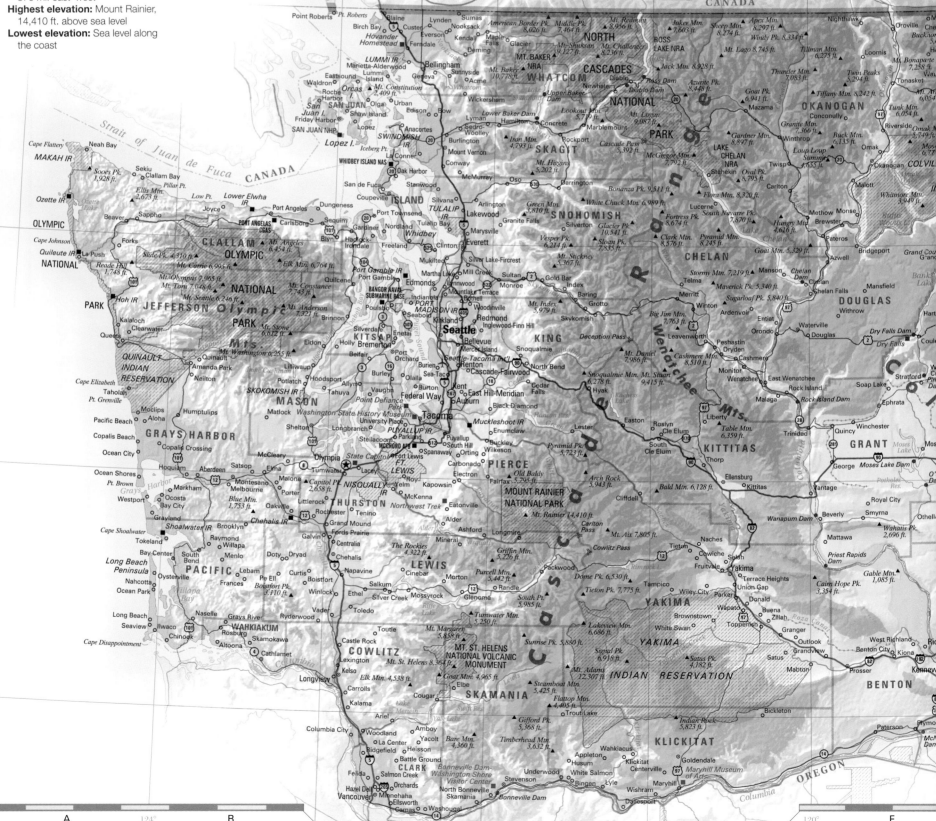

▶ *The Palouse Hills,* a fertile region in southeastern Washington, produces much of the wheat grown in the state.

Hill of St. Rosalia"). The mountain would later be renamed Olympus.

On Perez's heels came fellow Spaniards Bruno Heceta and Juan Francisco de la Bodega y Quadra, who charted the coastline on a trip north from California in 1775. They landed north of the Columbia River and claimed the entire area for Spain. Not to be outdone, English explorer Capt. James Cook traveled to the Pacific Northwest in 1778 with instructions to find a waterway that linked the Pacific Ocean to the Atlantic. Because heavy storms made it impossible for him to approach the rocky coast, Cook never set foot on land, nor did he find a Northwest Passage. He did find sea otters, however, whose pelts proved to be so valuable that British and American fur trappers and traders flocked to the region in great numbers.

In 1792 British naval officer George Vancouver, who had served on two of Cook's voyages, sailed into Puget Sound while making his own attempt to find the elusive Northwest Passage. The same year, American explorer Robert Gray sailed into the mouth of the Columbia River. His discovery brought the Americans into competition for control over the Pacific Northwest and established America's foothold in the region.

PIONEER PAST

Spain eventually relinquished all claims to the Pacific Northwest, leaving England and America to scramble for ownership of the vast territory. The English developed a thriving fur trade by establishing outposts along the coast and the rivers. To strengthen America's earlier claim, in 1804 Thomas Jefferson sent explorers Meriwether Lewis and William Clark to blaze a trail from the East. They reached Washington in 1805.

Despite increasing opposition from various Indian tribes, the federal government declared the area between the Columbia River and the 49th parallel Washington Territory in 1853. Pioneers began trickling in, many arriving on the Oregon Trail. Although Gov. Isaac Stevens negotiated treaties with the Indians in 1855, claiming most of their land for the U.S. government, the population did not grow until the building of the first railroad, in 1883. Vast quantities of the territory's timber, coal, apples, and wheat could now be shipped by rail to Western and Midwestern states, and the economy boomed. When gold was discovered in Alaska and the Yukon Territory in 1896, Seattle served as a boomtown for the Klondike gold rush.

TIMBER AND TECHNOLOGY

Since the earliest sawmills began operating in 1825, the timber industry in particular has played an important role in Washington's economy. Today Washington has 18 million acres of commercial forestland.

More than a third of the state is devoted to farmland, and Washington is the nation's leading producer of apples, pears, and hops; only Idaho grows more potatoes. The state is also

POPULATION
Total: 5,858,000
Rank within U.S.: 15
Ethnic breakdown: White: 83.3%; Hispanic: 6.1%; Asian: 5.8%; Black: 3.1%; Indian: 1.6%
Population density: 87.9 people per sq. mi.

CLIMATE

Average monthly temperature in Seattle
100°F / 80°F / 60°F / 40°F / 20°F / 0°F
J F M A M J J A S O N D

Average monthly precipitation in Seattle
10" / 8" / 6" / 4" / 2" / 0"
J F M A M J J A S O N D

Average monthly temperature in Spokane
100°F / 80°F / 60°F / 40°F / 20°F / 0°F
J F M A M J J A S O N D

Average monthly precipitation in Spokane
10" / 8" / 6" / 4" / 2" / 0"
J F M A M J J A S O N D

ECONOMY
Service industries: Community, business, and personal services; finance; insurance; real estate
Manufacturing: Aircraft, ships
Agriculture: Timber, apples, milk, wheat, pears, hops, beef cattle

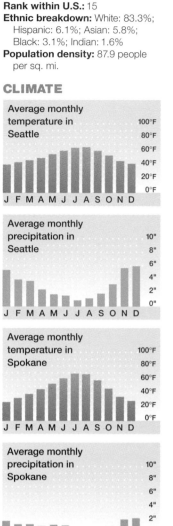

◀ *Totem poles,* such as this one on the northern coast of Washington, were carved by Pacific Northwest Indians to portray family and clan emblems and legends.

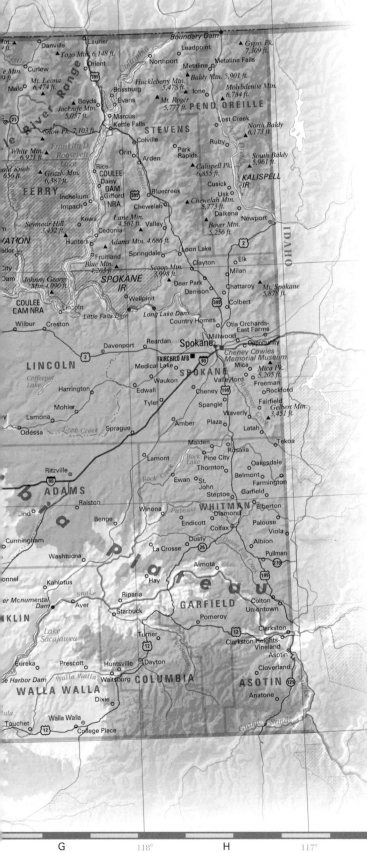

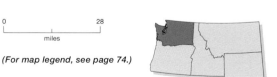

0 _____ 28
miles

(For map legend, see page 74.)

CITIES AND TOWNS *(For complete index, see page 217.)*

Aberdeen **B3**	Ellensburg **E2**	Marysville **C1**	Redmond **C2**
Anacortes **C1**	Ephrata **F2**	Mercer Island **C2**	Renton **C2**
Auburn **C2**	Everett **C2**	Moses Lake **F2**	Richland **F3**
Bellevue **C2**	Federal Way **C2**	Mount Vernon **C1**	Sea-Tac **C2**
Bellingham **C1**	Hoquiam **B3**	Oak Harbor **C1**	Seattle **C2**
Bremerton **C2**	Kelso **C3**	Olympia **C2**	Spanaway **C2**
Burien **C2**	Kennewick **F3**	Omak **F1**	Spokane **H2**
Centralia **C3**	Kent **C2**	Parkland **C2**	Tacoma **C2**
Colville **H1**	Kirkland **C2**	Pasco **F3**	Tumwater **C2**
Coolee Dam **G2**	Lacey **C2**	Port Angeles **B1**	Vancouver **C4**
East Hill-	Lakewood **C1**	Port Townsend **C1**	Walla Walla **G3**
Meridian **C2**	Longview **C3**	Pullman **H3**	Wenatchee **E2**
Edmonds **C2**	Lynnwood **C2**	Puyallup **C2**	Yakima **E3**

G 118° H 117°

▲ *Dense forests* of firs, hemlocks, pines, spruces, cedars, and other trees have made Washington a major lumber producer since the early 19th century. Timber creates more wealth for the state than any other agricultural product, and is its third-largest industry overall.

one of the world's top producers of iris, tulip, and daffodil bulbs. Commercial fishing ranks high in the economy, with an annual catch valued at about $105 million.

Washington's long and illustrious maritime tradition came into play during World War I, as the state's shipyards at Bremerton, Seattle, and Tacoma went into full production to help the war effort. To this day Washington is one of the nation's leading shipbuilders.

During World War II, the state added the manufacture of military aircraft to its list of leading industries. The first American commercial jet was produced in Washington, and today the Seattle area–based Boeing Company is the largest aircraft manufacturer in the United States. The expansion of the aerospace industry was largely responsible for Washington's huge increase in population and its economic expansion throughout the 1960s.

Abundant hydroelectric power can be credited for much of the state's manufacturing success. Located on the Columbia River near the center of Washington, the Grand Coulee—the largest concrete dam in the world—rises 550 feet above bedrock and measures four-fifths of a mile wide. The gigantic plug backs up the Columbia River into a lake 151 miles long. Cheap electricity helps power the state's aluminum smelting and refining industry (the nation's largest), which, in turn, provides the raw materials for aircraft and other manufactured goods.

The dawning of the age of personal computers has fostered Washington's latest economic boom. The world's leading computer software company, Microsoft, is based in Redmond. Other high-tech companies are also located in the greater Seattle area. In addition, the region has become an important base for the telecommunications and biotechnology industries.

THE EMERALD CITY

Washington's largest city, Seattle, is the heart of this rich and varied land. More than half of the state's 5.4 million residents live within 50 miles of the center of the city. Nicknamed the Emerald City as much for its abundant greenery as for its Oz-like allure, Seattle is a glittering urban landscape of sleek skyscrapers and leafy parks. One of the most eye-catching points on the city's dramatic skyline is the Space Needle, a futuristic tower topped by a revolving restaurant, built for the 1962 Century 21 Exposition.

Named for a respected Duwamish Indian chief who befriended the region's early white settlers, Seattle has grown from its humble beginnings as a lumber port into an economic powerhouse and America's gateway to Asia. The city's open-air markets, coffeehouses, trendy clubs, chic boutiques, gourmet restaurants, and diverse museums have also made it a popular destination for tourists.

NATURAL DIVERSITY

A paradise for people who love the outdoors, Washington has something for everyone—beaches, forests, mountains, meadows, rivers, lakes, canyons, even lava flows. In the far northwest, the Olympic Mountains tower above the Strait of Juan de Fuca to the north and the Pacific Ocean to the west. Washington's youngest mountain range, this rugged collection of peaks rises as high as 7,965 feet and was formed when two pieces of the earth's crust collided. Most of the region is part of Olympic National Park, which features 63 miles of pristine coastline and nearly 900,000 acres of wilderness, includ-

WASHINGTON
T I M E L I N E

1775 Bruno Heceta and Juan Francisco de la Bodega y Quadra of Spain land on Washington's coast.

1792 Robert Gray, an American, discovers Columbia River. George Vancouver of England surveys Puget Sound.

1805 Lewis and Clark follow Snake and Columbia rivers to Pacific Ocean.

1810 British-Canadian fur company establishes post near Spokane.

1818 U.S. and Great Britain agree to jointly occupy Oregon region, including Washington.

1825 Hudson's Bay Company establishes Fort Vancouver.

1846 Canada-Washington boundary is set at 49th parallel.

1853 Washington Territory is organized.

1855 Indian wars begin.

1883 Northern Pacific Railroad reaches Spokane.

1889 Washington joins the Union as 42nd state.

1909 Alaska-Yukon-Pacific Exposition is held in Seattle.

1917 Lake Washington Ship Canal opens.

1937 Bonneville Dam, on the Columbia River, is completed.

1942 Grand Coulee Dam opens.

1962 Seattle hosts a world's fair, the Century 21 Exposition.

1964 U.S. and Canada approve final form of Columbia River Treaty of 1961.

1974 Expo '74, a world's fair, is held in Spokane.

1980 Eruption of Mount Saint Helens kills 57 people and many animals.

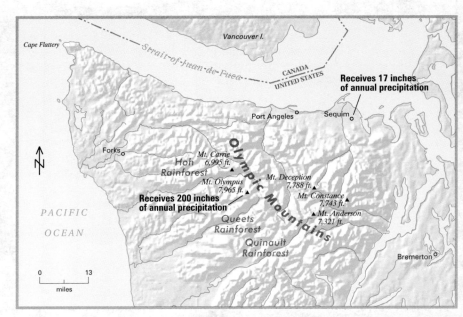

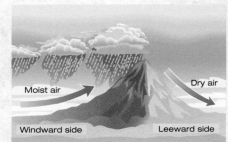

The Rain Shadow Effect

The Olympic peninsula features a variety of climates. Rain forests in Olympic National Park flourish because of the moisture released from Pacific air that cools as it travels up the windward side of the Olympic Mountains. Western slopes receive generous rainfall—Mount Olympus gets approximately 200 inches of rain per year.

But just as a mountain can cast a shadow, blocking out the light of the sun, it can also cast a rain shadow. After the moist air has released its precipitation on the windward side of the mountain and passed over the top, it descends and becomes warm. Since at this point the air has lost most of its moisture, it cannot produce rain. What's more, the dry air blows over the leeward land, parching it. Sequim, a town less than 30 miles from Mount Olympus in the northeastern section of the Olympic peninsula, is a victim of the so-called rain shadow effect—it receives a mere 17 inches of rain annually.

◀ *Giant Sitka spruce,* western hemlock, and big-leaf maple trees dominate the temperate rain forests in Olympic National Park.

sound and its adjacent waters are dotted with some 300 forested islands that stretch from the mainland to Vancouver Island. The isles, linked by a ferry system, are actually the summits of a sunken mountain range.

Washington's backbone is the Cascade Range, which extends from the Canadian border to the Columbia River. The mountains serve as the climatic dividing line between the state's temperate western side and its arid east. The crown jewel in this stretch of peaks is 14,410-foot-high Mount Rainier, a white-topped beauty that serves as a stunning backdrop to downtown Seattle and as the centerpiece of a popular national park.

The Cascade Range's scenic splendor and proximity to a metropolis of 2.5 million people belies its true potential for violence. The range is comprised of volcanoes, and, as was revealed on May 18, 1980, not all of the peaks are dormant. On that morning, Mount Saint Helens erupted, blowing 1,300 feet off its top in southern Washington, knocking down more than 150,000 acres of trees, and killing 57 people and countless deer, elk, goats, and other animals in the process.

East of the Cascades, the Columbia Plateau covers much of the state. A great basin, it was formed thousands of years ago by molten lava that poured out of cracks in the earth's surface. Water, wind, and time have etched deep canyons in the plateau, creating a series of coulees and scablands. Large portions of the plateau's river valleys have filled with fertile soil, which irrigation has helped turn into productive cropland.

Located in northeastern Washington, where branches of the Rocky Mountains cut across the state's borders, the peaks of the Kettle River Range are much older than the Cascades to the west; they are also shorter, rising no more than 7,300 feet. With only one person to every 10 square miles, the region is the least populated in the state. It is, however, a haven for grizzly bears and mountain caribou, two of the state's most endangered species and reminders of the Evergreen State's early days—wild, remote, and beautiful.

▲ **The 1980 eruption** of Mount Saint Helens in southwestern Washington blew off the peak's north face, created floods and mud slides, and covered land hundreds of miles downwind in ash. Today the area is protected as a national volcanic monument to ensure the renewal process.

▲ **"The mountain is out,"** as Seattleites say. That mountain is Rainier, gleaming on a rare sunny day over the skyline of Seattle and boats docked in Lake Union.

ing temperate rain forests and plentiful wildlife, such as Roosevelt elk, bald eagles, mountain sheep, and black bears.

The Coast Range parallels the Pacific coastline in the southwestern corner of Washington. These mountains are lower than the Olympics to the north and the Cascades to the east. The 175-mile coastline is indented by large bays, including Willapa Bay, a tidewater area of mudflats, eelgrass, and estuaries. It teems with migratory birds that are winging their way up and down the Pacific flyway.

Wedged between the Olympic Mountains to the west and the Cascades to the east is the Puget Sound Lowland, a region marked by mild temperatures and plentiful rain, averaging about 36 inches a year. Puget Sound is an 80-mile-long flooded valley that was carved by glaciers and now serves as a long arm of the Pacific Ocean, reaching deep into the state. Its eastern shore lined by the greater Seattle-Tacoma area, the

▼ **An apple orchard** in bloom in central Washington, with the Cascade mountains in the background. A wide variety of apples are grown throughout the state.

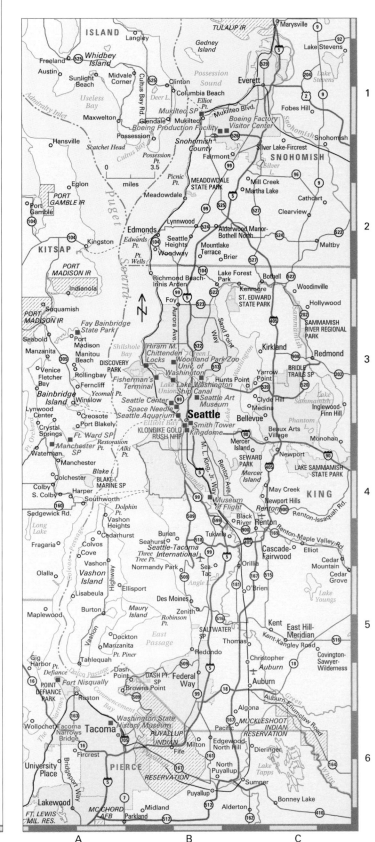

▲ **The state flag**, *adopted in 1929, displays the state seal. A miner and a farmer flank a rock showing the date of West Virginia's statehood. A pair of rifles represents the readiness to fight for freedom.*

STATE DATA
State bird: Cardinal
State flower: Rhododendron
State tree: Sugar maple
State motto: *Montani semper liberi* (Mountaineers are always free)
State songs: "West Virginia, My Home Sweet Home," "The West Virginia Hills," and "This Is My West Virginia"
Abbreviations: W. Va.; WV (postal)
Origin of the name: *West* was added to Virginia when the region would not secede from the Union during the Civil War
Nickname: Mountain State

AREA AND SIZE
Total area: 24,181 sq. mi.
Rank within U.S.: 41
Extent: 237 mi. north–south; 265 mi. east–west
Highest elevation: Spruce Knob, 4,861 ft. above sea level
Lowest elevation: 240 ft. above sea level along the Potomac River in Jefferson County

POPULATION
Total: 1,841,000
Rank within U.S.: 37
Ethnic breakdown: White: 95.5%; Black: 3.2%; Asian: 0.6%; Hispanic: 0.6%; Indian: 0.1%
Population density: 76.4 people per sq. mi.

CLIMATE

Average monthly temperature in Charleston	
	100°F
	80°F
	60°F
	40°F
	20°F
	0°F
J F M A M J J A S O N D	

Average monthly precipitation in Charleston	
	10"
	8"
	6"
	4"
	2"
	0"
J F M A M J J A S O N D	

ECONOMY
Service industries: Transportation, utilities, telephone companies
Manufacturing: Chemicals, steel, glassware, pottery
Mining: Bituminous coal, natural gas, petroleum, limestone, salt, sand

▲ **Harpers Ferry** *stands at the confluence of the Potomac and Shenandoah rivers, which divide Virginia, West Virginia, and Maryland. In 1859 abolitionist John Brown raided the federal arsenal here, setting off a course of events that led to the Civil War.*

West Virginia

The only state that separated from another, West Virginia has had a tumultuous history that includes the remarkable mound building by prehistoric peoples, major Revolutionary War engagements, tragic Civil War battles, and the violent struggles of unions to gain a foothold in the coal mines. There's also the impressive natural wealth of the state's many recreational rivers, mysterious valleys, and soaring peaks that make West Virginia the most mountainous state east of the Mississippi River.

THE EARLY DAYS
Some 300 to 400 years ago, the people of the Adena culture inhabited what is now West Virginia. Referred to today as the mound builders, these early Indians had lived in the area since 1000 B.C. Remnants of their civilization, including a number of burial mounds, still exist; one of these earthen structures, Grave Creek Mound near Moundsville, dates back 1,000 to 2,000 years and is the world's tallest conical prehistoric Indian burial mound.

West Virginia's early history was really that of its parent, Virginia, the crown colony chartered by

▶ **Lump coal** *being loaded onto a railroad car near Beckley in 1924. Since the mid-1800s, coal has played a central role in West Virginians' lives.*

James I of England in 1606. When colonists first arrived in Virginia the following year, its western portion was mainly an Indian hunting ground. In 1669 John Lederer, a German physician, was one of the first Europeans to penetrate the remote northwestern portion of the colony, where he found a dwindling number of Indians frequenting the area for its plentiful salt supply. In the early 18th century, some German and Scotch-Irish pioneers decided to settle in western Virginia, but the Indians attacked them for venturing onto their land. Eventually, though, permanent white settlements were established.

A YEARNING FOR SEPARATION
Western Virginia was the site of two key engagements during the Revolutionary War: the Battle of Point Pleasant in 1774, sometimes considered the first skirmish of the war, and the successful defense of Fort Henry against a British and Indian attack in 1782, often thought to be the Revolution's final armed event. During Virginia's first 80 years of statehood, conditions developed in its western counties that sowed the seeds of discontent: the growth of an economy fed by the river systems of the Midwest, rather than by coastal trade; and an agricultural system in which large plantations—and thus slavery—were impractical. Combined with complaints of poor representation in Virginia's legislature, these differences made some of western Virginia's mountain folk yearn for separation.

As early as 1776, in fact, these people had sought the right to break away from Virginia. But it was Virginia's secession from the Union in 1861 that gave the westerners the chance to follow their own course. That year, a reorganized Virginia government loyal to the Union was formed in Wheeling, and two years later a fully autonomous West Virginia—which for a time had been named Kanawha—became the 35th state. Meanwhile, the Civil War raged on. An estimated 632 military actions ravaged the state, and one town, Romney, changed hands 56 times.

THE ERA OF COAL
But West Virginia recovered from the Civil War, and for most of the next 90 years, the huge bituminous-coal reserves in its southern half dominated its economy. Workers came from throughout the South and the East and from such nations as

WEST VIRGINIA TIMELINE
1727 Germans from Pennsylvania settle New Mecklenburg.
1742 Coal is discovered along Coal River streambed.
1774 Settlers defeat Indians at Battle of Point Pleasant.
1776 Western Virginia residents petition Continental Congress for separate statehood.
1836 First railroad comes to Virginia at Harpers Ferry.
1859 Abolitionist John Brown

raids federal arsenal at Harpers Ferry.
1861 Western Virginia refuses to secede from the Union and separates from rest of state.
1863 West Virginia joins the Union as 35th state.
1907 Explosion at Monongah coal mine kills 361 miners.
1921 Battle of Blair Mountain erupts from labor dispute involving coal miners.

1943 Vast salt deposits are discovered in Ohio River valley.
1959 National Radio Astronomy Observatory opens at Green Bank.
1968 Explosions at Farmingham mines kill 78 people and spur new mine-safety laws.
1972 Buffalo Creek flood kills 100 people near Man.
1987 State unemployment rate drops below 10 percent.

Italy, Poland, and Hungary, seeking employment in the huge mining operations that burrowed deep in the earth. The mines were dangerous places where workers could contract black lung or die instantly in a fire or blast—in 1907, for example, 361 perished in an explosion at the Monongah coal mine.

Another hazard soon confronted West Virginia's miners—armed resistance to their efforts to unionize and strike. Between 1912 and 1921, the U.S. Army and the National Guard intervened six times in conflicts between miners and mine owners. After a bloody insurrection at Blair Mountain in 1921, in which federal forces brought in fighter planes and chemical-warfare agents to battle 5,000 striking miners, West Virginia became synonymous with defiance.

NATURAL RICHES

Today few West Virginians focus on the unrest of the past. The state's natural and recreational riches are far more visible. Once covered almost entirely by hardwood trees, West Virginia is still three-quarters forested. The plant life is among the most diverse in the United States, and botanists have spotted such rare species as sundew, bog rosemary, and coltsfoot.

Some of the best river rafting in the East is available in West Virginia. A 15-mile stretch of the New River from Thurmond to Fayette Station offers challenging rapids; the Gauley, Cheat, Tygart Valley, Potomac, Bluestone, and Shenandoah rivers also attract thousands of rafters every year.

Hot water, bubbling from mineral springs, has drawn other visitors to the region for centuries. White Sulphur Springs in southern West Virginia is the best known. As a young surveyor, George Washington partook of the state's curative waters, soothing his weary bones at Berkeley Springs, a spa situated on the Potomac River.

OF PANHANDLES AND MOUNTAINS

Not far from Baltimore and Washington, D.C., West Virginia's eastern panhandle is an area of rolling hills, small towns filled with antique shops, and views of the Potomac and Shenandoah rivers. Immediately to the west lie some of West Virginia's finest attractions: the 900,000-acre, 10-county Monongahela National Forest; Spruce Knob, at 4,861

feet the state's highest peak; and Cass Scenic Railroad State Park, a restored mountain logging town whose company-owned houses still stand and are used as cabins.

West Virginia's northern panhandle, a sliver of land between Ohio and Pennsylvania, contains two cities built around the milling of steel—Wheeling and Weirton, both on the Ohio River. For part of the 19th century, Wheeling was the state's capital, but that distinction now goes to Charleston. Cass Gilbert, designer of the U.S. Supreme Court Building in Washington, D.C., was the architect of West Virginia's capitol, a gold-domed temple that is one of the 20th century's most beautiful classically inspired buildings.

The 60-mile stretch from Charleston west to Huntington is the most heavily populated area in West Virginia. Thanks to nearby deposits of silica, Huntington and the area northward is one of the great glass-making centers in the world, with businesses that produce glass tabletops and sculptures, as well as other items. If you have glass marbles that were manufactured in America, they almost certainly come from here. At the Marble King plant in Paden City, for example, a million marbles a day are produced. Because it can take days for the glass to heat to the proper temperature, the company is open around the clock—an excellent example of West Virginian common sense and resourcefulness.

▲ **Blackwater Falls,** near Davis, cascades 65 feet into a 525-foot-deep gorge. The falls are the main attraction in Blackwater Falls State Park, which is also known for its beautiful forests.

▲ **Most of the glass marbles** made in the United States come from a few factories in the Parkersburg area of West Virginia.

(For map legend, see page 74.)

CITIES AND TOWNS *(For complete index, see page 217.)*

WISCONSIN
1848

▲ *The state flag,* adopted in 1913, displays the state seal. On it, a miner and a sailor hold a shield that shows symbols of Wisconsin's important industries. The badger stands for the state's nickname; 1848 is the year Wisconsin joined the Union.

STATE DATA
State bird: Robin
State flower: Wood violet
State tree: Sugar maple
State motto: Forward
State song: "On, Wisconsin!"
Abbreviations: Wis. or Wisc.; WI (postal)
Origin of the name: From an Indian word, spelled *ouisconsin* by the French, meaning "gathering of the waters" or "wild rushing water"
Nickname: Badger State

AREA AND SIZE
Total area: 56,154 sq. mi.
Rank within U.S.: 26
Extent: 314 mi. north–south; 293 mi. east–west
Highest elevation: Timms Hill, 1,951 ft. above sea level
Lowest elevation: 581 ft. above sea level along the shore of Lake Michigan

POPULATION
Total: 5,326,000
Rank within U.S.: 18
Ethnic breakdown: White: 88.8%; Black: 6.0%; Hispanic: 2.6%; Asian: 1.8%; Indian: 0.8%
Population density: 97.8 people per sq. mi.

CLIMATE

Average monthly temperature in Madison — 100°F / 80°F / 60°F / 40°F / 20°F / 0°F
J F M A M J J A S O N D

Average monthly precipitation in Madison — 10" / 8" / 6" / 4" / 2" / 0"
J F M A M J J A S O N D

ECONOMY
Service industries: Real estate, banking, insurance
Manufacturing: Machinery, dairy products, canned foods, beer, paper products
Agriculture: Dairy cattle, beef cattle, hogs, corn, soybeans, peas

Wisconsin

Lying at the exact geographic heart of North America, Wisconsin is the same distance from the Atlantic and Pacific oceans, the Gulf of Mexico, and the Arctic Sea. Fully a third of the population of the United States lives within 500 miles of Wisconsin, making it a popular destination for travelers as well as a hub of commerce and agriculture. Yet amid its rolling hills, dense forests, and plentiful lakes, the rest of the country can seem pleasantly remote.

AN INDEPENDENT SPIRIT
People have exploited the riches of Wisconsin since at least the Stone Age. In the 17th and 18th centuries, Europeans came in search of furs, but settlement did not begin in earnest until 1822, with the discovery of vast outcroppings of lead. The "lead rush" was on. So eager were the miners to stake their claims that they simply dug shelters in the sides of the hills when the first chill of the harsh Wisconsin winter came on. Derided as "badgers," the nickname stuck. These pioneers became the foundation of Wisconsin statehood and a symbol of the state's fierce and independent spirit.

Wisconsin became a state in 1848. Six years later, outraged over the possible extension of slavery to Wisconsin, its citizens organized a new political movement at Ripon that became known as the Republican Party and soon dominated state politics. In the early 20th century, progressive Republican governors Robert M. La Follette and his son Philip introduced reforms known as the "Wisconsin idea," aimed at bettering the lives of the state's working people. Wisconsin led the nation with such ideas as the minimum wage, aid to dependent children, unemployment pay, workmen's compensation, industrial safety, environmental protection, and direct primaries.

◀ *Apostle Islands National Lakeshore,* comprised of 21 islands and a strip of mainland at Wisconsin's northern tip, is renowned for its magnificent forests, amazing rock formations, and six 19th-century lighthouses. At left, snow-covered birches top the Squaw Bay cliffs.

AMERICA'S DAIRYLAND
Manufacturing accounts for more than a fourth of Wisconsin's gross product, with everything from cars and ships to children's overalls and beer produced. The state is better known, however, as America's Dairyland, serving Americans more fresh butter, milk, and cheese every day than any other state. Dairying began in Wisconsin during the 1870s, when the lead mines had been played out and ill-advised wheat farming had devastated the fragile topsoil. As an alternative to wheat, a newspaperman named William Demster Hoard suggested growing clover and grass, which would thrive in the Wisconsin soil, in order to raise cows for dairy farming. Soon Hoard was even enticing European cheese makers to settle in Wisconsin. Now more than 1.6 million cows dot Wisconsin's landscape. (Not all of its 80,000 farms are dairy farms, however. Wisconsin's farmers also produce more snap beans and sweet corn than do those of any other state, as well as a third of the nation's cranberries.)

NATURE PRESERVED
Wisconsin's other major industry involves the care and feeding of tourists. The state ranks as the top travel destination in the Midwest, attracting more visitors than Yellowstone Park. One hundred years ago, though, no one would have thought of Wisconsin as a traveler's paradise. It was almost denuded of forest, and many of its rivers had become stinking sewers.

Such conditions fostered a strong and enduring conservation movement within the state. (Wisconsin resident John Muir was inspired to found the Sierra Club.) As a result of these efforts, large unspoiled tracts like Horicon Marsh and the Ice Age National Scientific Reserve in southeastern Wisconsin, as well as the North Woods and Lake Superior shore in the north, have been set aside to show visitors what the area must have been like before man came to exploit it.

Glaciers molded most of the state into undulating ridges, low hills, and deep hollows and left behind more than 14,000 lakes, which are now home to 170 species of fish. The south-

▶ *Jersey cows* in Wisconsin. The state has more dairy cows than any other, and well over half of its farm income comes from dairy products. The state also boasts more than 200 cheese factories, which produce some 100 varieties of cheese. Below is an assortment of Wisconsin cheddars.

WISCONSIN TIMELINE

1634 French explorer Jean Nicolet reaches Green Bay shore.
1673 Louis Jolliet and Fr. Jacques Marquette explore upper Mississippi River.
1701 First permanent settlement is established at Green Bay.
1763 England gains Wisconsin area after French and Indian War.
1783 U.S. gains Wisconsin with Northwest Territory.
1832 Black Hawk War ends Indian resistance in Wisconsin.
1836 Wisconsin Territory is established.
1848 Wisconsin joins the Union as 30th state.
1854 Republican Party is founded in Ripon.
1856 Mrs. Carl Schurz opens the country's first kindergarten in Watertown.
1871 Forest fire kills about 1,200 people in six counties.
1872 Wisconsin Dairymen's Association is founded.
1901 Robert M. La Follette, Sr., becomes governor and initiates Progressive era.
1903 Wisconsin is first state to establish primary elections.
1911 Teachers' pensions are established in Wisconsin.
1932 Wisconsin passes first unemployment-compensation act.
1959 St. Lawrence Seaway opens.

west, called the Driftless Area because it was left untouched by the glaciers, is a place of rugged green hills and neat red barns. Here, in the Dells area, the Wisconsin River has carved the exposed sandstone into fantastic shapes.

Outdoor recreation accounts for much of Wisconsin's allure. Each summer hundreds of thousands of people converge on Wittman Field in Oshkosh to attend the Experimental Aircraft Association's annual Fly-in—the largest aviation event in the world. In July logging enthusiasts attend the Lumberjack World Championships in Hayward, while ornithologists, amateur and otherwise, watch bald eagles along the Mississippi. Others visit Door County, a spit of land that juts out into Lake Michigan, offering 250 miles of breathtaking coastline. Every winter, the state is host to the

Birkebinder, the largest cross-country-skiing event in North America, while wilderness enthusiasts gravitate to the far northern lakes to spearfish.

INVENTION CELEBRATED

Other sites highlight Wisconsin's achievements, both great and dubious. Wisconsin is proud of the Yerkes Observatory, near Lake Geneva, which houses the world's largest refracting telescope. The last steam-operated car ferry on the Great Lakes is also notable; capable of carrying 620 passengers, it sails from Manitowoc across to Michigan. And every day during the summer, Circus World at Baraboo throws a three-ring extravaganza in the birthplace of the Ringling Brothers Circus.

Only in Wisconsin can you find such sights as the "Great Wall of China," a floor-to-ceiling exhibit of bathroom fixtures, sponsored by the Kohler Company, and cheeseheads—people who wear plastic wedges of cheese on their heads, especially when their beloved Green Bay Packers are winning.

▲ **The Green Bay Packers,** *renowned for their loyal fans, have played in two recent Super Bowls—in 1997 (shown above), when they won, and in 1998, when they lost. Green Bay is the smallest city in the United States to have a National Football League franchise.*

(For map legend, see page 74.)

0   31
miles

▲ **The state flag,** adopted in 1917, shows the state seal branded onto a buffalo. The seal acclaims equal rights for women. The red border of the flag represents Indians and the blood of the pioneers.

STATE DATA
State bird: Meadowlark
State flower: Indian paintbrush
State tree: Plains cottonwood
State motto: Equal rights
State song: "Wyoming"

Wyoming

Wild and windswept, the high country and the open plains of this Western state have barely been touched by human hands. With just over a half million people, Wyoming ranks last in population of all the states. Lonely though it may seem, every year some 7 million people visit Wyoming for its unrivaled natural wonders.

AN ABUNDANCE OF MOUNTAINS
The Great Plains meet the Rocky Mountains in Wyoming. Like its neighbors Colorado and Montana, the state sits astride the Continental Divide, where rivers on the eastern side eventually drain into the Atlantic Ocean, and those on the western side, into the Pacific. In Wyoming, however, the dividing line splits in two. Look at a topographical map, and you will see mountain ranges bulging in every portion of the state, from the Black Hills in the northeast and the Laramie Mountains in the southeast to the Wind River Range and the Tetons in the west.

Between these ranges lie the high, dry basins and plateaus of sagebrush and short prairie grasses that have cradled much of Wyoming's human history. The state's first residents were Plains Indians, nomadic hunters who followed the

▲ **Castle Geyser,** one of more than 300 geysers and fumaroles in Yellowstone National Park.

superabundant bison herds up and down the grasslands. Theirs was a life that existed in perfect harmony with their surroundings, but white Americans were less favorably disposed.

In the 1840s and 1850s, thousands of settlers traversed the region on the Oregon and Mormon trails; few were tempted to linger, however, warned away by tales of Indian attacks and winters so cruel that even a sunny day could bring a deadly "ground blizzard" of wind-driven snow. By 1869 Wyoming's territorial legislature was so desperate to attract female settlers to the region that it passed the nation's first equal rights laws, guaranteeing women the unprecedented right to vote and hold office. (Wyoming later became the first state to elect a woman governor, Nellie Tayloe Ross, in 1924.)

THE CATTLEMAN'S COMMONWEALTH

It wasn't until the completion of the transcontinental railroad in the southern part of the state in 1869 that white settlers found much use for Wyoming. To ready the animals for fall shipment to eastern stockyards by rail, cattlemen from Texas began to drive their herds north to spend their summers grazing the grasslands of southern and eastern Wyoming. With the herds came a decade of prosperity for the state, and not a few skirmishes between cattlemen, homesteading farmers, rustlers, and sheepherders, whose flocks competed with Texas longhorns for foraging and grazing land. The hostilities reached a peak in 1892, when a group of ranchers banded together to flush out a suspected rustler enclave and killed two men. The U.S. Cavalry was called in, and order was quickly restored, but the incident—known as the Johnson County War—confirmed Wyoming's reputation as a rough-and-tumble vigilante territory.

At the heart of the cattle rancher's enterprise was the cowboy himself, a solitary figure on the horizon, willing to brave hostile Indians, murderous rustlers, and ferocious weather to protect his herd. The cowboy is still king in Wyoming, and ranching remains a major industry, but today's cowhands may well be Latin American vaqueros.

OIL AND OUTLAWS

Since the 1880s Wyoming's economy has ridden cycles of boom and bust as wild as any rodeo ride.

0 — 31 miles

(For map legend, see page 74.)

CITIES AND TOWNS
(For complete index, see page 217.)

Afton **B3**	Lovell **D1**
Buffalo **F1**	Lusk **H3**
Casper **F3**	Lyman **B4**
Cheyenne **H4**	Mills **F3**
Cody **C1**	Newcastle **H2**
Douglas **G3**	Orchard Valley **H4**
Evanston **B4**	Powell **D1**
Evansville **F3**	Rawlins **E4**
Gillette **G1**	Riverton **D2**
Glenrock **G3**	Rock Springs **C4**
Green River **C4**	Saratoga **F4**
Greybull **D1**	Sheridan **F1**
Jackson **B2**	Thermopolis **D2**
Jeffrey City **E3**	Torrington **H3**
Kemmerer **B4**	Wheatland **H3**
Lander **D3**	Worland **E1**
Laramie **G4**	Wright **G2**

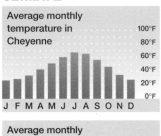

▲ Jackson Lake and the granite peaks of the Teton Range serve as an impressive backdrop to a lush carpet of brightly colored wildflowers.

By century's end, a historically brutal winter, overgrazing, and protracted infighting between competing ranching interests had brought the cattle boom to a screeching halt. No sooner had Wyoming's cattle economy cooled than another source of speculative frenzy took its place: oil. The first successful well was drilled near Lander in 1883; since then, Wyoming's vast petroleum industry—it is the nation's fourth-largest producer—has propelled the state's economy to exuberant highs and despondent lows. Large deposits of coal, uranium, trona, and bentonite round out Wyoming's mining picture.

BEAUTIES OF THE WEST

In recent decades tourism has brought prosperity to the state. From Devil's Tower—a striking buttelike formation in the northeastern corner of the state—to the Teton Range, Wyoming's reputation for untrammeled loveliness is deserved. The federal government owns about half of Wyoming's land, including 10 national forests lying wholly or partially within the state, the National Elk Refuge (winter home to one of North America's largest herds) near Jackson, Grand Teton National Park in the Rockies, and Yellowstone, the oldest U.S. national park.

Roughly half of Wyoming's 7 million annual visitors come to see Yellowstone, which occupies 2,221,773 acres in the northwestern corner of the state. The Old Faithful geyser is the park's most well known attraction, but with molten rock bubbling just one to three miles below the surface of the park (instead of the usual 10 to 30 miles), Yellowstone also contains more geysers, hot springs, and sulfurous steam vents than are found in all the rest of the world. From the first time American fur trapper John Colter laid eyes on it in 1807, Yellowstone's thermal displays have captured the imagination of all who have heard of it; and the park itself remains a slice out of time—merely the most wondrous in a state of natural wonders.

Abbreviations: Wyo.; WY (postal)
Origin of the name: Adapted from two Delaware Indian words meaning "upon the great plain"
Nicknames: Equality State, Cowboy State

AREA AND SIZE
Total area: 97,914 sq. mi.
Rank within U.S.: 9
Extent: 275 mi. north–south; 362 mi. east–west
Highest elevation: Gannett Peak, 13,804 ft. above sea level
Lowest elevation: 3,100 ft. above sea level along the Belle Fourche River in Crook County

POPULATION
Total: 525,000
Rank within U.S.: 50
Ethnic breakdown: White: 89.3%; Hispanic: 6.7%; Indian: 2.3%; Asian: 0.8%; Black: 0.8%
Population density: 5.4 people per sq. mi.

CLIMATE

Average monthly temperature in Cheyenne
100°F 80°F 60°F 40°F 20°F 0°F
J F M A M J J A S O N D

Average monthly precipitation in Cheyenne
10" 8" 6" 4" 2" 0"
J F M A M J J A S O N D

ECONOMY
Service industries: Pipelines, railroads, telephone companies
Mining: Petroleum, coal, natural gas, trona, bentonite clay, uranium
Manufacturing: Chemicals, petroleum products
Agriculture: Beef cattle, milk, sheep, wool, sugar beets, hay, wheat

▼ Wyoming's elk population, one of the largest in the country, numbers more than 100,000.

WYOMING TIMELINE

1807 John Colter explores Yellowstone area.
1812 Robert Stuart discovers South Pass across Rocky Mountains.
1833 Oil is discovered near Wind River Range.
1834 Fort Laramie, the area's first permanent white settlement, is built on Oregon Trail.
1868 Wyoming Territory is created. Coal mining begins.
1869 Women in Wyoming Territory gain right to vote and hold elected office.
1890 Wyoming joins the Union as 44th state.
1891 Yellowstone Timber Land Reserve is designated first national forest.
1892 Cattlemen and homesteaders fight in Johnson County War over cattle-rustling dispute.
1906 Devil's Tower is declared first national monument.
1910 Shoshone Dam is built.
1925 Nellie Tayloe Ross becomes first woman governor in U.S.
1951–52 Uranium is discovered in several areas of Wyoming.
1960 First intercontinental ballistic missile base begins operation near Cheyenne.
1965 Minuteman-missile installation opens near Cheyenne.
1988 One million acres of Yellowstone National Park burn.

Credits and Acknowledgments

Maps, Charts, and Illustrations

10–11 Map by Hammond Incorporated. **12** Maps by Ian Worpole. **12–13** Map by Hammond Incorporated. **14** *top* Illustration by Ian Worpole; *bottom* maps by Ian Worpole. **15** Maps by Hammond Incorporated. **16** Maps by Ian Worpole. **17** Map by Ian Worpole. **18** Map by Ortelius Design. **21** Map by Ian Worpole. **23** Map by Ortelius Design. **25** Map by Ortelius Design. **26** Map by Ortelius Design. **27** Maps by Ian Worpole. **28** Map by Ortelius Design. **29** Map by Ian Worpole. **30** Map by Ian Worpole. **31** Maps by Ian Worpole. **32** Map by Ortelius Design. **33** Maps by Ortelius Design. **34** Map by Ian Worpole. **35** Map by Ortelius Design. **36** Map by Ortelius Design. **37** Map by Ian Worpole. **38** Maps by Ortelius Design. **39** Map by Ortelius Design. **40** Maps by Ortelius Design. **41** Map by Ortelius Design. **43** Map by Ortelius Design. **50** Map by Ian Worpole. **51** Map by Ortelius Design. **53** Map by Ian Worpole. **54** Chart by Ortelius Design. **55** Chart by Ian Worpole. **57** Map by Ortelius Design. **59** Maps by Ortelius Design. **61** Map by Ortelius Design. **62** Map by Ortelius Design. **63** Map by Ortelius Design. **74** Locator map by Ortelius Design; map projection by Ortelius Design; elevation chart by Hammond Incorporated; state map by Hammond Incorporated. **75** Maps by Hammond Incorporated. **76** State map by Hammond Incorporated; locator map by Ortelius Design. **78–79** State map by Hammond Incorporated. **79** Locator map by Ortelius Design. **80** Thematic map by Ian Worpole. **80–81** State map by Hammond Incorporated. **81** Locator map by Ortelius Design. **83** State map by Hammond Incorporated; locator map by Ortelius Design. **84** State map by Hammond Incorporated; locator map by Ortelius Design. **86** Locator map by Ortelius Design. **86–87** State map by Hammond Incorporated. **88–89** State map by Hammond Incorporated. **89** Locator map by Ortelius Design. **90** Map by Hammond Incorporated. **91** Maps by Hammond Incorporated. **92–93** State map by Hammond Incorporated. **93** Locator map by Ortelius Design. **95** State map by Hammond Incorporated; locator map by Ortelius Design. **96** State map by Hammond Incorporated; locator map by Ortelius Design. **98–99** State map by Hammond Incorporated. **99** Locator map by Ortelius Design. **100** Map by Hammond Incorporated. **101** Map by Hammond Incorporated. **102** State map by Hammond Incorporated; locator map by Ortelius Design. **104** Map by Hammond Incorporated. **105** Map by Hammond Incorporated. **106–107** State map by Hammond Incorporated. **107** Locator map by Ortelius Design. **108** State map by Hammond Incorporated; locator map by Ortelius Design. **111** State map by Hammond Incorporated; locator map by Ortelius Design. **112** Metropolitan-area map by Hammond Incorporated; city-street map by Hammond Incorporated; thematic map by Ian Worpole. **115** State map by Hammond Incorporated; locator map by Ortelius Design. **116** Locator map by Ortelius Design. **116–117** State map by Hammond Incorporated. **118** Thematic map by Ian Worpole. **118–119** State map by Hammond Incorporated. **119** Locator map by Ortelius Design. **120–121** State map by Hammond Incorporated. **121** Locator map by Ortelius Design. **122** Locator map by Ortelius Design. **122–123** State map by Hammond Incorporated. **124** Maps by Hammond Incorporated. **125** Map by Hammond Incorporated. **126** State map by Hammond Incorporated; locator map by Ortelius Design. **128–129** State map by Hammond Incorporated. **129** Locator map by Ortelius Design. **131** Maps by Hammond Incorporated. **132–133** State map by Hammond Incorporated. **133** Locator map by Ortelius Design. **134** Maps by Hammond Incorporated. **135** Map by Hammond Incorporated. **137** State map by Hammond Incorporated; locator map by Ortelius Design. **138** State map by Hammond Incorporated; locator map by Ortelius Design; thematic map by Ian Worpole. **139** Map by Hammond Incorporated. **140** State map by Hammond Incorporated; locator map by Ortelius Design. **143** State map by Hammond Incorporated; locator map by Ortelius Design; thematic map by Ian Worpole. **144** Thematic map by Ian Worpole. **144–145** State map by Hammond Incorporated. **145** Locator map by Ortelius Design. **146–147** State map by Hammond Incorporated. **147** Locator map by Ortelius Design. **148** Locator map by Ortelius Design. **148–149** State map by Hammond Incorporated. **150** Map by Hammond Incorporated. **151** State map by Hammond Incorporated; locator map by Ortelius Design. **153** State map by Hammond Incorporated; locator map by Ortelius Design. **155** State map by Hammond Incorporated; locator map by Ortelius Design. **157** State map by Hammond Incorporated; locator map by Ortelius Design. **158–159** State map by Hammond Incorporated. **159** Locator map by Ortelius Design. **160** Map by Hammond Incorporated. **161** Maps by Hammond Incorporated. **162** Locator map by Ortelius Design. **162–163** State map by Hammond Incorporated. **163** Thematic map by Ian Worpole. **164–165** State map by Hammond Incorporated. **165** Locator map by Ortelius Design. **166** Map by Ian Worpole. **167** State map by Hammond Incorporated; locator map by Ortelius Design. **168–169** State map by Hammond Incorporated. **169** Locator map by Ortelius Design. **170–171** State map by Hammond Incorporated. **171** Locator map by Ortelius Design. **172** Locator map by Ortelius Design. **172–173** State map by Hammond Incorporated. **174** Maps by Hammond Incorporated. **176** Map by Ian Worpole. **177** State map by Hammond Incorporated; locator map by Ortelius Design. **179** State map by Hammond Incorporated; locator map by Ortelius Design. **180** Locator map by Ortelius Design. **180–181** State map by Hammond Incorporated. **182–183** State map by Hammond Incorporated. **183** Thematic map by Hammond Incorporated; locator map by Ortelius Design. **184–185** State map by Hammond Incorporated. **185** Locator map by Ortelius Design. **186** Map by Hammond Incorporated. **186–187** State map by Hammond Incorporated. **187** Locator map by Ortelius Design. **188** Maps by Hammond Incorporated. **190** State map by Hammond Incorporated; locator map by Ortelius Design. **193** State map by Hammond Incorporated; locator map by Ortelius Design. **194** Locator map by Ortelius Design. **194–195** State map by Hammond Incorporated. **197** Map by Hammond Incorporated. **198–199** State map by Hammond Incorporated. **199** Locator map by Ortelius Design. **200** *left* Map by Hammond Incorporated; *right* map by Ian Worpole. **201** Map by Hammond Incorporated. **203** State map by Hammond Incorporated; locator map by Ortelius Design. **205** State map by Hammond Incorporated; locator map by Ortelius Design. **206–207** State map by Hammond Incorporated. **207** Locator map by Ortelius Design.

◀ ***Lakes Michigan (left) and Huron,*** *as photographed from the space shuttle* Columbia *in 1991. Clouds form over the warmer land surface, while the skies above the colder lakes remain clear.*

Photographs

1 Marc Muench. **2–3** Brett Baunton/Tony Stone Images. **5** Santi Visalli. **6** Craig Aurness/Woodfin Camp & Associates. **7** Michael Melford. **8–9** Worldsat International, Inc. **13** *top left* © Jeff Gnass; *top center* R. Maiman/Sygma; *top right* Scott T. Smith. **14** *top right* NASA/Photo Resource Hawaii; *bottom right* Worldsat International, Inc./Science Source/Photo Researchers. **15** *top right* © Barrie Rokeach; *center right* Dan Miller/Woodfin Camp & Associates; *bottom right* © Warren Faidley/Weatherstock. **16** *top left* NASA; *top center left* Mark Gibson; *center left* Ryan/Beyer; *bottom left* Richard Kaylin/Tony Stone Images. **17** *left* Edi Ann Otto; *top right* Roger Ressmeyer/Corbis; *center right* C. J. Walker/*The Palm Beach Post*; *bottom right* Corbis-Bettmann. **18** *top left* American Philosophical Society Library; *top right* Hans Reinhard/Bruce Coleman, Inc.; *center right* Jerome Wexler/The National Audubon Society Collection/Photo Researchers; *far right* John Bova/The National Audubon Society Collection/Photo Researchers. **19** *top left* K. H. Switak/The National Audubon Society Collection/Photo Researchers; *center* David and Hayes Norris/The National Audubon Society Collection/Photo Researchers; *center left* John Mitchell/The National Audubon Society Collection/Photo Researchers; *center left center* Gail Jankus/The National Audubon Society Collection/Photo Researchers; *center right center* R. J. Erwin/The National Audubon Society Collection/Photo Researchers; *center right* C. K. Lorenz/The National Audubon Society Collection/Photo Researchers; *bottom left* Frank J. Miller/The National Audubon Society Collection/Photo Researchers; *bottom center* Mitchell P. Gadomski/The National Audubon Society Collection/Photo Researchers; *right* Jeff Foott/Bruce Coleman, Inc. **20** *top left* Natural History Museum, London/Bridgeman Art Library, London/New York; *left center* Stephen J. Kraseman/The National Audubon Society Collection/Photo Researchers; *center* Joe McDonald/Animals Animals; *bottom left* Jeff Lepore/The National Audubon Society Collection/Photo Researchers; *bottom center* Joe McDonald/Animals Animals; *right* Tim Davis/The National Audubon Society Collection/Photo Researchers. **21** *top* Tim Davis/The National Audubon Society Collection/Photo Researchers; *far left* Alan G. Nelson/Animals Animals; *left center* Arthur Morris/Birds as Art; *bottom left* Gerald C. Kelley/The National Audubon Society Collection/Photo Researchers; *top center* Hans Reinhard/Bruce Coleman, Inc.; *center* Brian Skerry; *bottom center* W. T. Davidson/The National Audubon Society Collection/Photo Researchers; *bottom right* Suzanne and Joseph Collins/The National Audubon Society Collection/Photo Researchers; *top right* Donald Specker/Animals Animals; *bottom right* John Chellman/Animals Animals. **22** *top* Fred Bruemmer; *center left* Photo Archives, Denver Museum of Natural History; *bottom left* Arizona State Museum, University of Arizona/Helga Teiwes, Photographer. **23** *left* Alan Kearney/Joe Viesti Associates; *bottom* Ohio Historical Society; *bottom right* William R. Iseminger/Cahokia Mounds State Historic Site. **24** *top left* Herbert Bigford, Sr./Collection, Longyear Museum of Anthropology, Colgate University; *bottom left* British Museum, London. **25** *bottom left* National Museum of American Art, Washington, DC/Art Resource, NY; *bottom center* British Museum, London/Bridgeman Art Library, London/New York; *bottom right* David Muench. **26** *top left* Culver Pictures; *left center* Archive Photos; *bottom* National Maritime Museum, London/Bridgeman Art Library, London/New York. **27** *top left* Culver Pictures; *top right* Isaac Oliver/Victoria and Albert Museum, London/Bridgeman Art Library, London/New York; *center right* Culver Pictures. **28** *top left* Courtesy of the Historical Society of Pennsylvania; *center right* Xavier Della Gatta/Valley Forge Historical Society; *bottom* Library of Congress. **29** *top* National Archives; *bottom right* I. N. Phelps Stokes Collection, Miriam and Ira D. Wallach Division of Art, Prints, and Photographs, The New York Public Library, Astor, Lenox, and Tilden Foundations. **30** *top left* State Historical Society of Iowa; *top right* Kansas Historical Society, Topeka. **31** *top left* Solomon D. Butcher Collection/Nebraska State Historical Society; *left center* Library of Congress; *bottom left* Missouri Historical Society, St. Louis. **32** *left* Culver Pictures; *top right* Corbis-Bettmann; *bottom* Valentine Museum/Cook Collection. **33** *bottom right* Culver Pictures. **34** *top left* The Heard Museum, Fred Harvey Collection; *top* McCord Museum of Canadian History, Montreal; *right* Robert Lindneux/Woolaroc Museum, Bartlesville, OK. **35** © Bob Sacha. **36** *top left* Culver Pictures; *bottom right* Corbis-Bettmann. **37** *top left* Culver Pictures; *top center* AP/Wide World Photos; *bottom left* Culver Pictures; *bottom right* Dorothea Lange/Library of Congress. **38** *top left* Culver Pictures; *bottom left* Culver Pictures. **39** *bottom left* Corbis-Bettmann; *bottom right* National Archives. **40** *top left* Rene Noorbergen/Camera Press London; *center left* Flip Schulke/Black Star; *bottom left* Buffon/Darquenne/Sygma. **41** *top right* C. Hires/G. Merillon/Gamma Liaison; *center right* Alain Nogues/Sygma; *bottom right* NASA. **42** *top left* Private Collection; *center left* Corbis-Bettmann; *bottom* Matt Herron/Take Stock. **43** *left* Marc Riboud/Magnum Photos, Inc.; *bottom right* R. Maiman/Sygma. **44** *top left* Black Star; *top center left* Massachusetts Historical Society; *bottom center left* Corbis-Bettmann; *bottom left* Brown Brothers; *center right* The Granger Collection; *top right* Courtesy of Department of Library Services, American Museum of Natural History; *bottom right* Brown Brothers. **45** *center left* Corbis-Bettmann; *top right* The Granger Collection; *top center right* Archive Photos; *bottom center right* Brown Brothers; *bottom right* FPG International LLC. **46** *top left* Corbis-Bettmann; *top center left* Arizona Historical Society, Tucson; *bottom center left* Culver Pictures; *bottom left* UPI/Corbis-Bettmann; *center right* Witness-Keystone/Sygma; *top right* The Granger Collection. **47** *center left* Black Star; *bottom left* UPI/Corbis-Bettmann; *top right* Bob Adelman/Magnum Photos, Inc.; *center right* Culver Pictures; *bottom right* Corbis-Bettmann. **48** *top left* L'Illustration/Sygma; *top center left* Imapress/Archive Photos; *bottom center left* Dan Connolly/Gamma Liaison; *bottom left* Edgar X. Paxson/Montana Historical Society; *bottom right* Private Collection; *center right* NASA. **49** *top left* Schomburg Center for Research in Black Culture/New York Public Library; *bottom left* Photofest; *top center* Culver Pictures; *top right* Corbis-Bettmann; *center right* Ben Schnall/Archive Photos; *upper bottom right* Rembrandt Peale/Collection of The New-York Historical Society; *center bottom right* Archive Photos; *bottom right* Corbis-Bettmann. **50** *top left* PhotoDisc, Inc.; *center left* Courtesy of the Erie Canal Museum, Syracuse, NY; *bottom* FPG International LLC. **51**

bottom Matt Bradley/Bruce Coleman, Inc.; *center* Alon Reininger/Contact Press Images. **52** *top left* Courtesy of the Washington Apple Commission; *bottom left* Culver Pictures; *center right* Larry Lefever/Grant Heilman Photography. **53** *top left* Hagley Museum and Library; *center left* Comstock, Inc.; *top right* Corbis-Bettmann; *center right* Steve Dunwell/The Image Bank. **54** *top left* National Park Service/Statue of Liberty National Monument; *top right* National Archives/Harmon Foundation. **55** *top left* Gilles Mingasson/Gamma Liaison; *top right* Grantpix/The National Audubon Society Collection/Photo Researchers; *bottom right* William Lopez/NYT Pictures. **56** © Pat O'Hara. **57** *top right* © Jeff Gnass; *center right* David Muench; *bottom right* David Muench. **58** *top left* Lance Nelson/The Stock Market; *bottom left* Holt Studios International/The National Audubon Society Collection/Photo Researchers; *right* A. C. Haralson/Courtesy of Arkansas Department of Parks and Tourism. **59** *top left* Franklin J. Viola/Comstock, Inc.; *bottom left* Alan D. Carey/The National Audubon Society Collection/Photo Researchers; *bottom right* Jay Freis/The Image Bank. **60** *top left* Dan Suzio/The National Audubon Society Collection/Photo Researchers; *bottom left* Comstock, Inc.; *top* Dick Durrance/Woodfin Camp & Associates. **61** *top left* Courtesy of the Indiana Limestone Institute; *center right* Michael Melford. **62** *left* The Spindletop/Gladys City Boomtown Museum, Beaumont, TX; *right* Paul McCormick/The Image Bank. **63** *top right* Leif Skoogfors/Woodfin Camp & Associates; *bottom right* Bob Pizaro/Comstock, Inc. **64** David Muench. **65** *top right* David Barnes/The Stock Market; *top center right* David Muench; *bottom center right* Bob Abraham/The Stock Market; *bottom right* Dan Peha/Joe Viesti Associates. **66** *top left* Trevor Wood/The Image Bank; *center left* Tom Bean/DRK Photo; *bottom left* Bruce Roberts/The National Audubon Society Collection/Photo Researchers; *top right* Scott T. Smith. **67** *center left* Michael Melford; *top right* David Muench; *center right* © Jeff Gnass; *bottom right* David Muench. **68** *top left* Carr Clifton/Minden Pictures, Inc.; *center left* Jeff Foott; *bottom left* David Muench; *center right* David Muench. **69** *top right* B&H Kunz/Okapia/The National Audubon Society Collection/Photo Researchers; *bottom right* Tim Davis/The National Audubon Society Collection /Photo Researchers; *center right* Douglas Peebles; *top left* © Pat O'Hara. **70** *top left* © Pat O'Hara; *center left* © Jeff Gnass; *bottom left* © Pat O'Hara; *top right* © Bill Sherwonit/Alaska Stock. **71** *top right* © Pat O'Hara; *top right* David Muench; *center right* Larry Ulrich/DRK Photo; *bottom right* © Jeff Gnass. **72** *top left* David Muench; *center left* Marc Muench; *bottom right* Tom Bean Photography; *top right* David Muench. **73** *center left* Tom Bean/DRK Photo; *top right* Marc Muench; *center right* Art Gingert/Comstock, Inc.; *bottom right* © Pat O'Hara. **76** John Elk III/Bruce Coleman, Inc. **77** *top center* Dan Brothers/Courtesy of Alabama Bureau of Tourism and Travel; *top left* Dennis Keim; *bottom left* Dennis Keim **78** *top right* © R. E. Johnson/Alaska Stock; *center* © Ray Hafen/Ken Graham Agency; *bottom* Michio Hoshino/Minden Pictures, Inc. **80** © Steve Kaufman/Ken Graham Agency. **81** *left* Michio Hoshino/Minden Pictures, Inc.; *center right* Library of Congress; *bottom right* © Kim Heacox/Ken Graham Agency. **82** *top right* © Carr Clifton; *center left* Adriel Heisey Photography; *bottom center* Bob and Clara Calhoun/Bruce Coleman, Inc. **83** © Barrie Rokeach. **85** *top center* Tom Coker/Ozark Yesteryear Photography; *center right* Lee Foster/Bruce Coleman, Inc.; *bottom center* Allen Smith Collection. **87** *top* Robert Holmes; *center* Darrell Gulin/Tony Stone Images. **88** *center* Inga Spence/Tom Stack & Associates; *bottom left* © Jim Zuckerman/Westlight. **90** *top right* John Elk/Tony Stone Images; *left* Carr Clifton/Minden Pictures, Inc.; *bottom right* © Barrie Rokeach. **91** *top left* Nigel Press/Tony Stone Images; *bottom left* Dave G. Houser/Corbis. **93** *top* Marc Muench; *bottom right* Wendy Shattil/Bob Nozinski/Tom Stack & Associates. **94** *center right* Jack McConnell/McConnell McNamara & Company; *bottom left* Connecticut Historical Society. **95** William Hubbell. **96** Hagley Museum and Library. **97** *top left* © Eric Crossan; *bottom left* © Barrie Rokeach; *bottom right* Lee Snider/Corbis. **98** *bottom center* Randy Wells/Tony Stone Images; *top right* Brian Parker/Tom Stack & Associates; *bottom right* © Warren Morgan/Westlight. **99** Chuck Schmeiser/Unicorn Stock Photos. **100** *bottom* Brian Parker/Tom Stack & Associates; *top right* Aristock/Atlanta. **101** *top left* Index Stock Photography, Inc.; *bottom center* Index Stock Photography, Inc.; *bottom right* Santi Visalli. **102** Manny Rubio/Aristock/Atlanta. **103** *left* Tom Till Photography; *top* Robb Helfrick/Aristock/Atlanta; *bottom right* Mark Gibson. **104** *top left* Flip Schulke/Corbis; *top right* © Bob Krist; *bottom left* Michael Melford; *bottom right* William Henry Jackson/Christopher Cardozo, Inc. **105** *bottom left* David Muench; *bottom right* Gene Ahrens. **106** *bottom left* © Ken Graham/Ken Graham Agency; *center* © Paul Chesley/Photographers/Aspen; *bottom right* Douglas Peebles. **107** David R. Frazier Photo Library. **108** Edward S. Curtis/National Geographic Image Collection. **109** *top* Michael Melford; *center* David R. Frazier Photo Library **110** *top* David R. Frazier Photo Library; *center* David Muench. **111** Chicago Historical Society. **112** Brown Brothers. **113** *top* Mark Segal/Tony Stone Images; *center* Bernard Boutrit/Woodfin Camp & Associates. **114** *bottom right* Corbis-Bettmann; *center left* Tom Till Photography; *top right* Tom Till Photography. **116** *top* James Blank/Bruce Coleman, Inc.; *bottom left* John Elk III/Bruce Coleman, Inc. **117** © Craig Aurness/Westlight. **118** David C. Tomlinson/Tony Stone Images. **119** Kevin Sink/Midwestock. **120** *bottom left* Don & Pat Valenti/Tony Stone Images; *top* Adam Jones. **121** Philip Gould/Corbis. **123** *top* Keith Wood/Tony Stone Images; *center* © Mitchell L. Osborne; *bottom right* Owen Franken/Corbis. **124** *top* Philip Gould/Corbis; *center* UPI/Corbis-Bettmann. **125** *bottom* Nathan Benn/Woodfin Camp & Associates; *right* Bevil S. Knapp/Aristock/Atlanta. **126** Robert Frerck/Woodfin Camp & Associates. **127** *top left* David Muench/Corbis; *bottom* Michael Melford. **128** *center* Paul Souders/Tony Stone Images; *bottom* D. A. Harvey/Woodfin Camp & Associates. **129** Jeff Smith. **130** *top* Sam Abell/National Geographic Image Collection; *bottom* Joseph Sohm/Tony Stone Images. **131** *center right* Adam Woolfitt/Corbis; *top right* Michael Dersin. **132** *center* Richard Nowitz/Corbis; *bottom* Paul Rocheleau. **133** *top right* Dave Stotzer/Cape Ann Photography; *bottom right* NASA/Corbis. **134** Michael Melford. **135** *top* Phil Schermeister/Tony Stone Images; *bottom right* Frank Siteman/Joe Viesti Associates. **136** *top* John and Ann Mahan; *top right* Joe Viesti/Joe Viesti Associates; *bottom center* John and Ann Mahan. **138** *center left* Rolf Peterson; *bottom center* John and Ann Mahan. **139** *top* Macduff Everton/Corbis; *bottom left* Courtesy of the Ford Motor Company; *right* © Michael S. Yamashita. **140** Ryan/Beyer. **141** *bottom left* Craig Blacklock/Blacklock Nature Photography; *top* Ryan/Beyer; *center right* Ryan/Beyer. **142** *top left* C. C. Lockwood/Cactus Clyde Productions; *top right* Garry McMichael/Grant Heilman Photography; *bottom* © Mitchell L. Osborne. **144** *top* Adam Woolfitt/Woodfin Camp & Associates; *bottom* Gregory Foster/Gamma Liaison; *center right* David Muench. **145** Jean Higgins/Aristock/Atlanta. **146** © Paul Chesley/Photographers/Aspen. **147** Annie Griffiths Belt. **148** *bottom* Annie Griffiths Belt; *top right* Michael Busselle/Tony Stone Images. **149** Kenneth Fink/Bruce Coleman, Inc. **150** *center* David Jeffrey/The Image Bank; *top right* David Carriere/Tony Stone Images. **151** Courtesy of New York-New York Hotel & Casino. **152** Kunio Owaki/The Stock Market. **152–153** Comstock, Inc. **153** *bottom left* Farrell Grehan/Corbis. **154** *top* © Jeff Gnass; *bottom* © Walter Chandoha. **155** *left* © Michael S. Yamashita; *bottom right* Corbis-Bettmann. **156** *top* © David Hiser/Photographers/Aspen; *center* © Jerry Jacka; *center left* Bill Patterson/Patterson Graphics; *center right* Girard Foundation Collection, Museum of International Folk Art, Museum of New Mexico, Santa Fe. **157** *bottom* Paul Rocheleau. **158** *center left* Courtesy of Chautauqua Institution Archives; *top right* © Jeff Gnass. **160** *top* Santi Visalli; *center left* Courtesy of George Eastman House; *center right* Steven Mays/Courtesy of Rebus, Inc., NYC. **161** *top left* Mark Gibson; *bottom left* © Jim Marchese/Courtesy of Pellegrini Vineyard. **162** Walter Bibikow/Joe Viesti Associates. **163** Joe Devenney/The Image Bank. **164** Clayton Wolt/Courtesy of North Dakota Tourism Department. **165** *top* Michael Melford/The Image Bank; *bottom* Annie Griffiths Belt/Woodfin Camp & Associates. **166** *top* Richard A. Cooke/Tony Stone Images; *bottom* James Blank/Scenics of America. **167** Brownie Harris/The Stock Market. **168** *center* Laurence Parent; *top right* James Blank/The Stock Market. **169** Western History Collection, University of Oklahoma Library. **170** © Jeff Gnass. **171** *top* Steve Terrill/The Stock Market; *bottom* William H. Mullins/The National Audubon Society Collection/Photo Researchers. **172** UPI/Corbis-Bettmann. **173** *left* Paul Solomon/Woodfin Camp & Associates; *right* George Gerster/Comstock, Inc. **174** *bottom left* Audrey Gibson; *top right* Corbis-Bettmann. **175** *top* Philip E. Davis/Aristock/Atlanta; *bottom* Art Gingert/Comstock, Inc. **176** Norman O. Tomalin/Bruce Coleman, Inc. **177** *left* Museum of Art, Rhode Island School of Design/Gift of Textron, Inc. Photo by Cathy Carver; *bottom* Mark Gibson/The Stock Market. **178** *top* Terry Parke/Transparencies; *bottom* Laurence Parent. **179** *bottom* Nathan Benn/Woodfin Camp & Associates; *top* Tom McHugh/The National Audubon Society Collection/Photo Researchers. **180** Larry Ulrich/Tony Stone Images. **181** *top* Library of Congress; *bottom left* Yale Collection of American Literature/Beinecke Rare Books and Manuscript Library, Yale University; *right* © Jeff Gnass. **182** Edward W. Bower/The Image Bank. **183** *top* Arni Katz/Unicorn Stock Photos; *bottom* Graphic House/Corbis-Bettmann. **184** Joe Viesti/Joe Viesti Associates. **185** *top* Robert Daemmrich/Tony Stone Images; *center* Steven Wilson/Entheos. **186** Lee Foster/Bruce Coleman, Inc. **187** *left* Jim Arndt; *right* Bill Ellzey/Comstock, Inc. **188** *bottom left* Andre Jenny/Aristock/Atlanta; *right* Ken Sherman/Bruce Coleman, Inc. **189** *top* David Muench/Tony Stone Images; *bottom* David Muench; *top right* © David Hiser/Photographers/Aspen; *center right* John Dale/Aristock/Atlanta. **191** *top left* R. Derek Smith/The Image Bank; *bottom* Luis Castaneda/The Image Bank; *center* Stanford University Museum of Art, Gift of David Hewes. **192** *top* Kunio Owaki/The Stock Market; *bottom* Paul Boisvert. **193** *bottom left* Jack Sullivan/Photo Researchers; *bottom right* Phil Schermeister/Corbis. **194** M. Win/Washington Stock. **195** Brian Kenney. **196** *top left* Tom Till Photography; *center left* Appomattox Court House National Historic Park; *bottom left* Morton Beebe/Corbis; *top right* © Robert Llewellyn; *bottom right* © Robert Llewellyn. **197** *top left* © Robert Llewellyn; *bottom* © Robert Llewellyn. **198** Kevin Schafer/Corbis. **199** *top* David Barnes/The Stock Market; *bottom* Buddy Mays/Travel Stock. **200** *top left* Bliss B. Jones/Jones Photo Co.; *bottom* Bill Terry/Joe Viesti Associates. **201** *top left* Terry Donnelly; *bottom left* John Marshall; *top right* Roger Werth/Woodfin Camp & Associates. **202** *top* Richard A. Cooke/Tony Stone Images; *bottom* Hagley Museum and Library. **203** *top right* Gordon Kilgore/Aristock/Atlanta; *center right* Bertram Cohen. **204** *top* John and Ann Mahan; *bottom left* ©1998 Wisconsin Milk Marketing Board; *bottom right* Mark Gibson. **205** Allsport USA/Doug Densiger. **206** Bob Grant/Comstock, Inc. **207** *top* Joe Englander/Joe Viesti Associates; *bottom right* Leonard Lee Rue/Photo Researchers. **208** NASA. **Front endpaper** © Harald Sund. **Back endpaper** Breck P. Kent.

Special Thanks

Edward Allen, Doyle Johnson, Agnes Perez, Economic Research Service, U.S. Department of Agriculture. **William A. Balsley,** Town Historian, Connellsville, Pennsylvania. **Paul Bateman,** The Gold Institute, Washington, D.C. **Louis D. Britsch,** Geologist, U.S. Army Corps of Engineers, New Orleans, Louisiana. **Heidi Christianson,** Rice Council for Market Development, Houston, Texas. **Kirsty Dunn,** Boeing Corporation, Everett, Washington. **Maryke Gillis,** The Nature Conservancy, Vermont Chapter, Montpelier, Vermont. **Ray Hanson,** Iowa Corn Growers Association. **Mike Healy,** Bay Area Rapid Transit, San Francisco, California. **Heidi Helwig,** Bonneville Lock and Dam, Bonneville, Oregon. **Pat Jamieson,** Outdoor Recreation Planner, National Bison Range, Moiese, Montana. **Edward G. Josberger,** Oceanographer, U.S. Geological Survey. **Marty Lane,** Hawaii Volcanoes National Park, Hawaii I., Hawaii. **Stephen G. Martin,** Mississippi Department of Economic and Community Development, Jackson, Mississippi. **Dick Moehl, Diane Werling,** Great Lakes Lighthouse Keepers Association, Dearborn, Michigan. **Bill Mork,** State Climatologist, California Department of Water Resources, Sacramento, California. **Jill Patterson,** Iowa Soybean Promotion Board. **Ronnie Pew,** Country Music Hall of Fame and Museum, Nashville, Tennessee. **Robert Pickering,** Anthropology Department, Denver Museum of Natural History. **Susan Rhyne,** Texas Railroad Commission. **Karsten Rist,** Tropical Audubon Society, Miami, Florida. **Tom Ross,** National Climatic Data Center. **Redge Rothwell,** Game and Fish Office, Cheyenne Bioservices, Cheyenne, Wyoming. **Frances J. Scheid,** Wake County Economic Development, Raleigh, North Carolina. **Pat Ward,** Bagg Bonanza Farm, Mooreton, North Dakota.

General Index

Page numbers in **bold type** refer to illustrations.

Geographic Index

Abbreviations Used in Geographic Index

arch. — archipelago
arpt. — airport
bfld. — battlefield
bor. — borough
Can. — Canada
cap. — capital
cem. — cemetery
coast. — coastal
ctr. — center
des. — desert
fed. — federal
govt. — government
grsld. — grassland
har. — harbor
hist. — historic(al)

int'l — international
intst. — interstate
isl., isls. — island, islands
lab. — laboratory
lag. — lagoon
lakesh. — lakeshore
mem. — memorial
Mex. — Mexico
mil. — military
mon. — monument
mt. — mount
mtn., mts. — mountain, mountains
nat'l — national

pkwy. — parkway
pl. — plain
plat. — plateau
prsv. — preserve
pt. — point
rec. — recreation(al)
ref. — refuge
res. — reservoir, reservation
riv. — river
rsv. — reserve
rvwy. — riverway
seash. — seashore
str. — strait
U.S. — United States
wild. — wildlife, wilderness

Name/map reference/page

Brampton—Cahaba **221**

Brampton, MI **D4**/138
Brampton, ND **H4**/165
Bramwell, WV **B4**/203
Branch, LA **C4**/122
Branch, MI **A4**/137
Branch, MN **F5**/140
Branchport, NY **C3**/159
Branchton, PA **B2**/172
Branchville, CT **B3**/95
Branchville, NJ **C1**/155
Branchville, SC **D3**/179
Branchville, VA **G4**/195
Brandenburg, KY **D3**/121
Brandon, CO **H3**/93
Brandon, FL **F4**/99
Brandon, IA **E2**/117
Brandon, MN **C5**/140
Brandon, MS **C3**/143
Brandon, NE **D3**/148
Brandon, OH **C2**/167
Brandon, SD **J3**/181
Brandon, VT **A3**/193
Brandon, WI **E5**/205
Brandt, SD **J2**/181
Brandy Station, VA **G2**/195
Brandywine, MD **D2**/129
Brandywine, WV **D3**/203
Branford, CT **C3**/95
Branford, FL **F2**/99
Branson, CO **G4**/92
Branson, MO **C5**/145
Brant, MI **C4**/137
Brant Beach, NJ **D4**/155
Brant Lake, NY **G2**/159
Brantford, KS **F1**/119
Brantford, ND **G2**/164
Brantley, AL **C4**/76
Brantwood, WI **C3**/205
Braselton, GA **C1**/102
Brasfield, AR **D3**/84
Brashear, MO **D1**/145
Brasher Falls-Winthrop, NY **F1**/159
Brass Castle, NJ **B2**/155
Brasstown Bald (peak), GA **C1**/102
Braswell, GA **B2**/102
Brattleboro, VT **B4**/193
Brave, PA **A4**/172
Bravo, MI **A5**/137
Brawley, CA **H6**/89
Braxton, MS **C3**/143
Bray, OK **F3**/169
Braymer, MO **C2**/145
Brayton, IA **C3**/117
Brazil, IN **B3**/115
Brazil, MS **B1**/143
Brazil, TN **B2**/182
Brazilton, KS **J3**/119
Brazos (riv.) **G4**/11
Brea, CA **C5**/91
Bread Loaf, VT **B3**/193
Breakabeen, NY **F3**/159
Breaux Bridge, LA **D4**/122
Breckenridge, CO **D2**/92
Breckenridge, MI **C4**/137
Breckenridge, MN **B4**/140
Breckenridge, MO **C2**/145
Breckenridge, OK **F1**/169
Breckenridge, TX **J5**/185
Breda, IA **C2**/117
Breed, WI **E3**/205
Breeden, WV **A4**/203
Breeding, KY **E4**/121
Breedsville, MI **A5**/137
Breese, IL **C5**/111
Breesport, NY **D3**/159
Breezy Point, MN **D4**/140
Breien, ND **E3**/164
Bremen, AL **C2**/76
Bremen, GA **A2**/102
Bremen, IN **C1**/115
Bremen, KS **G1**/119
Bremen, KY **C3**/120
Bremen, ND **F2**/164
Bremen, OH **C3**/167
Bremerton, WA **C2**/198
Bremond, TX **L6**/185
Bremond, TX **K1**/187
Brenham, TX **K2**/187
Brent, AL **B3**/76
Brentford, SD **G1**/181
Brenton, WV **B4**/203
Brentwood, AR **A2**/84
Brentwood, CA **D5**/86
Brentwood, MD **D2**/131
Brentwood, NH **D6**/153
Brentwood, NY **G5**/159
Brentwood, PA **B3**/172
Brentwood, TN **E1**/182
Brethren, MI **A3**/137
Breton, KS **C1**/118
Breton (isls.), LA **F5**/123
Breton (sound), LA **F5**/123
Bretton Woods, NH **D3**/153
Brevard, NC **C2**/162
Brevig Mission, AK **C2**/79
Brevort, MI **B1**/137
Brevort, MI **F3**/138
Brewer, ME **D4**/126
Brewer, MO **G4**/145
Brewers, KY **B4**/120
Brewerton, NY **D2**/159
Brewster, KS **B1**/118
Brewster, MA **G3**/133
Brewster, MN **C7**/140
Brewster, NE **F2**/149
Brewster, NY **G4**/159
Brewster, OH **D2**/167
Brewton, AL **B4**/76
Briarcliff Manor, NY **G4**/159
Briarcliffe Acres, SC **F3**/179
Briartown, OK **H2**/169
Briarwood, ND **J3**/165
Briarwood Beach, OH **D1**/167
Bricelyn, MN **E7**/140
Brices Cross Roads (nat'l bfld. site), MS **D1**/143
Briceville, TN **G1**/183
Brickerville, PA **E3**/173
Bricktown, NJ **D3**/155
Bridal Veil, OR **C2**/170
Bridalveil (falls), CA **F5**/86
Bridge, ID **E7**/108
Bridge, OR **A4**/170
Bridge City, LA **B2**/124
Bridge City, TX **N2**/187
Bridgeboro, GA **C4**/102
Bridgehampton, NY **H5**/159
Bridgeland, UT **E2**/190
Bridgeport, AL **D1**/76
Bridgeport, CA **F4**/87
Bridgeport, CT **B3**/95
Bridgeport, IL **E5**/111
Bridgeport, KS **F2**/119
Bridgeport, MI **D4**/137
Bridgeport, NE **B2**/148
Bridgeport, NJ **B4**/155
Bridgeport, NY **E2**/159
Bridgeport, OH **E2**/167
Bridgeport, OK **E2**/169
Bridgeport, OR **H3**/171
Bridgeport, PA **F3**/173
Bridgeport, PA **A1**/174
Bridgeport, TX **K4**/185
Bridgeport, WA **F1**/198
Bridgeport, WV **C2**/203
Bridger, MT **H4**/147
Bridger, WY **B4**/206
Bridger (mts.), WY **D2**/206
Bridgeton, IN **B3**/115
Bridgeton, MI **B4**/137
Bridgeton, NC **H2**/163
Bridgeton, NJ **B5**/155
Bridgeton, RI **B2**/177
Bridgetown, MD **E1**/129
Bridgetown, OH **A3**/167
Bridgeville, CA **B2**/86
Bridgeville, DE **A3**/96
Bridgeville, PA **A3**/172
Bridgewater, CT **B2**/95
Bridgewater, IA **C3**/117
Bridgewater, MA **F3**/133
Bridgewater, ME **E2**/126
Bridgewater, NH **C4**/153
Bridgewater, NY **E3**/159
Bridgewater, SD **H3**/181
Bridgewater, VA **F2**/195
Bridgewater, VT **B3**/193
Bridgewater Center, VT **B3**/193
Bridgman, MI **A6**/137
Bridgton, ME **B4**/126
Bridport, VT **A3**/193
Brielle, NJ **D3**/155
Brier, WA **B2**/201
Brier Hill, NY **E1**/159
Brierfield, AL **C2**/76
Brigantine, NJ **D5**/155
Briggs, TX **J2**/187
Briggsdale, CO **F1**/92
Brigham City, UT **C1**/190
Bright, IN **E3**/115
Brighton, AL **C2**/76
Brighton, CO **F2**/92
Brighton, FL **G4**/99
Brighton, IA **F3**/117
Brighton, IL **B4**/111
Brighton, MI **D5**/137
Brighton, MO **C4**/145
Brighton, NY **C2**/159
Brighton, OR **B2**/170
Brighton, TN **B2**/182
Brighton, UT **D2**/190
Brightshade, KY **G3**/121
Brightstar, AR **B4**/84
Brightwood, OR **C2**/170
Brightwood, VA **F2**/195
Brill, WI **B3**/205
Brilliant, AL **B1**/76
Brilliant, OH **E2**/167
Brillion, WI **E4**/205
Brimhall (Coyote Canyon), NM **B2**/158
Brimfield, IL **C3**/111
Brimfield, IN **D1**/115
Brimfield, MA **C2**/133
Brimfield, OH **D1**/167
Brimley, MI **G3**/138
Brimson, MN **G3**/140
Brinckerhoff, NY **G4**/159
Bringhurst, IN **C2**/115
Brinkley, AR **D3**/84
Brinktown, MO **D3**/145
Brinnon, WA **C2**/198
Brinsmade, ND **F1**/164
Brinson, GA **B5**/102
Brinton, MI **B4**/137
Briny Breezes, FL **H5**/99
Brisbane, CA **A3**/91
Briscoe, TX **G2**/184
Bristol, CO **H3**/93
Bristol, CT **C2**/95
Bristol, FL **D1**/99
Bristol, GA **D4**/102
Bristol, IN **D1**/115
Bristol, MD **D2**/129
Bristol, ME **C5**/126
Bristol, MI **B3**/137
Bristol, NH **C4**/153
Bristol, PA **G3**/173
Bristol, RI **C3**/177
Bristol, SD **H1**/181
Bristol, TN **J1**/183
Bristol, VA **B4**/194
Bristol, VT **A2**/193
Bristol (mts.), CA **G4**/89
Bristolville, OH **E1**/167
Bristow, IA **E2**/117
Bristow, NE **G1**/149
Bristow, OK **G2**/169
Bristow, VA **G2**/195
Britt, IA **D1**/117
Britt, MN **F3**/140
Britton, MI **D6**/137
Britton, SD **H1**/181
Broad (riv.), SC **C1**/179
Broad Brook, CT **C2**/95
Broad Creek, DE **A3**/96
Broadalbin, NY **F2**/159
Broadbent, OR **A4**/170
Broadhurst, GA **E4**/102
Broadland, SD **G2**/181
Broadus, MT **L4**/147
Broadview, IL **B2**/112
Broadview, MT **H3**/147
Broadview, NM **G3**/157
Broadwater, NE **C2**/148
Broadway, NC **F2**/163
Broadway, NJ **B2**/155
Broadway, OH **B2**/167
Broadwell, IL **C3**/111
Brock, NE **K3**/149
Brockdell, TN **F2**/183
Brocket, ND **G1**/164
Brockhill Beach, DE **B3**/96
Brockport, NY **C2**/158
Brockport, PA **C2**/172
Brockton, MA **E2**/133
Brockton, MT **M1**/147
Brockway, MT **L2**/147
Brockway, PA **C2**/172
Brocton, IL **E4**/111
Brocton, NY **A3**/158
Brodhead, KY **F3**/121
Brodhead, WI **D6**/205
Brodheadsville, PA **F3**/173
Brodnax, VA **F4**/195
Brogan, OR **H3**/171
Brogden, NC **G2**/163
Brokaw, WI **D3**/205
Broken Arrow, OK **H1**/169
Broken Bow, NE **F2**/149
Broken Bow, OK **J3**/169
Broken Bow (lake), OK **J3**/169
Brokeoff (mts.), NM **E5**/157
Bromide, OK **G3**/169
Bronaugh, MO **B4**/145
Bronco, TX **D4**/184
Bronson, FL **F2**/99
Bronson, IA **A2**/116
Bronson, KS **H3**/119
Bronson, MI **B6**/137
Bronson, TX **N6**/185
Bronston, KY **F4**/121
Bronte, TX **G6**/184
Bronwood, GA **B4**/102
Bronx, The (bor.), NY **B1**/161
Bronx, WY **B3**/206
Bronxville, NY **C1**/161
Brook, IN **B2**/115
Brook Park, MN **E5**/140
Brook Park, OH **D1**/167
Brookdale, SC **D3**/179
Brooke, VA **G2**/195
Brookeland, TX **P6**/185
Brooker, FL **F2**/99
Brookfield, CT **B3**/95
Brookfield, GA **C4**/102
Brookfield, IL **B2**/112
Brookfield, MA **C2**/133
Brookfield, MO **C2**/145
Brookfield, NH **D4**/153
Brookfield, NY **E3**/159
Brookfield, OH **E1**/167
Brookfield, VT **B2**/193
Brookfield, WI **E5**/205
Brookgreen Gardens, SC **E3**/179
Brookhaven, MS **H4**/11
Brookhaven, MS **B4**/143
Brookhaven, PA **A3**/174
Brookings, OR **A5**/170
Brookings, SD **J2**/181
Brookland, AR **E2**/84
Brooklawn, NJ **B3**/174
Brooklet, GA **E3**/102
Brooklin, ME **D4**/126
Brookline, MA **E2**/133
Brookline, MA **B2**/134
Brookline, NH **C6**/153
Brooklyn, CT **E2**/95
Brooklyn, GA **B3**/102
Brooklyn, IA **E3**/117
Brooklyn, IN **C3**/115
Brooklyn, KY **D3**/120
Brooklyn, MI **C5**/137
Brooklyn, MS **C4**/143
Brooklyn, PA **F2**/173
Brooklyn, WA **B3**/198
Brooklyn, WI **D6**/205
Brooklyn (bor.), NY **B2**/161
Brooklyn Center, MN **E5**/140
Brooklyn Park, MD **D1**/129
Brooklyn Park, MN **E5**/140
Brookneal, VA **F3**/195
Brookport, IL **D6**/111
Brooks, CA **C4**/86
Brooks, GA **B2**/102
Brooks, KY **E2**/121
Brooks, ME **C4**/126
Brooks, MN **B3**/140
Brooks, MT **G2**/147
Brooks, OR **C2**/170
Brooks, WI **D5**/205
Brooks (isl.), CA **B2**/91
Brooks (range), AK **U10**/10
Brookshire, TX **L3**/187
Brookside, AL **C2**/76
Brookside, DE **A1**/96
Brookston, IN **C2**/115
Brookston, MN **F4**/140
Brooksville, AL **C1**/76
Brooksville, FL **F3**/99
Brooksville, KY **F2**/121
Brooksville, ME **D4**/126
Brooksville, MS **D2**/143
Brooksville, OK **G2**/169
Brooksville, VT **A2**/194
Brookton, GA **C1**/102
Brookton, ME **E3**/126
Brooktondale, NY **D3**/159
Brookview, MD **E2**/129
Brookville, IN **D3**/115
Brookville, KS **F2**/119
Brookville, OH **A3**/167
Brookville, PA **B2**/172
Brookville (lake), IN **E3**/115
Brookwood, AL **B2**/76
Broomall, PA **F4**/173
Broomall, PA **A2**/174
Broomfield, CO **E2**/92
Brooten, MN **C5**/140
Broseley, MO **F5**/145
Brothers, OR **E4**/170
Brotherton, TN **F1**/183
Broughton, OH **A1**/167
Broussard, LA **D4**/122
Browder, KY **C3**/120
Browerville, MN **D4**/140
Brown City, MI **E4**/137
Brown Deer, WI **F5**/205
Brownbranch, MO **D5**/145
Browndell, TX **P6**/185
Browndell, TX **N1**/187
Brownell, KS **D2**/118
Brownfield, ME **B5**/126
Brownfield, MS **D1**/143
Brownfield, TX **E4**/184
Browning, IL **B3**/111
Browning, MO **C1**/145
Browning, MT **C1**/146
Brownington, MO **C3**/145
Brownington, VT **B2**/193
Brownington Village, VT **B2**/193
Brownlee, NE **E1**/149
Brownlee Park, MI **B5**/137
Browns, AL **B3**/76
Browns, IL **E5**/111
Browns Mills, NJ **C4**/155
Browns Point, WA **A5**/201
Browns Spring, MO **C5**/145
Browns Summit, NC **F1**/163
Browns Valley, MN **B5**/140
Brownsboro, OR **C5**/170
Brownsburg, IN **C3**/115
Brownsburg, VA **E3**/195
Brownsdale, MN **F7**/140
Brownson, NE **B2**/148
Brownstown, IL **D5**/111
Brownstown, IN **C4**/115
Brownstown, PA **C3**/172
Brownstown, WA **E3**/198
Brownsville, IN **D3**/115
Brownsville, KY **D3**/120
Brownsville, MD **E1**/129
Brownsville, MN **G7**/140
Brownsville, MS **B3**/143
Brownsville, OR **C3**/170
Brownsville, PA **B3**/172
Brownsville, TN **B2**/182
Brownsville, TX **J7**/187
Brownsville, VT **B3**/193
Brownsville, WI **E5**/205
Brownsville-Bawcomville, LA **C2**/122
Brownton, MN **D6**/140
Brownton, WV **C2**/203
Browntown, VA **F2**/195
Browntown, WI **D6**/205
Brownville, FL **G4**/99
Brownville, ME **C3**/126
Brownville, NE **K3**/149
Brownville, NY **E1**/159
Brownville Junction, ME **C3**/126
Brownwood, TX **J6**/185
Broxton, GA **D4**/102
Brozville, MS **B2**/143
Bruce, FL **C1**/98
Bruce, MS **C2**/143
Bruce, SD **J2**/181
Bruce, WI **B3**/205
Bruce Crossing, MI **B3**/138
Bruceton, TN **C1**/182
Brucetown, VA **F1**/195
Bruceville, IN **B4**/115
Bruceville-Eddy, TX **K6**/185
Bruin, KY **G2**/121
Bruin, PA **B2**/172
Brule, NE **D2**/148
Brule, WI **B2**/205
Brumley, MO **D3**/145
Brundidge, AL **D4**/76
Bruneau, ID **C7**/108
Bruneau (riv.), ID **C8**/108
Bruneau (riv.), NV **E1**/151
Bruning, NE **H3**/149
Bruno, AR **C1**/84
Bruno, MN **F4**/140
Bruno, NE **J2**/149
Brunson, SC **C4**/179
Brunsville, IA **A2**/116
Brunswick, GA **K4**/11
Brunswick, GA **E4**/102
Brunswick, MD **C1**/129
Brunswick, ME **C5**/126
Brunswick, MI **A4**/137
Brunswick, MO **C2**/145
Brunswick, NC **G3**/163
Brunswick, NE **H1**/149
Brunswick, OH **D1**/167
Brunswick, TN **B2**/182
Brusett, MT **J2**/147
Brush, CO **G1**/92
Brushton, NY **F1**/159
Brushy (mts.), VA **C3**/194
Brushy Creek, TX **M6**/185
Brusly, LA **D4**/122
Brussels, IL **B5**/111
Brussels, WI **F4**/205
Brutus, MI **C2**/137
Brutus, MI **G4**/138
Bryan, OH **A1**/167
Bryan, TX **G4**/11
Bryan, TX **K2**/187
Bryans Road, MD **C2**/129
Bryant, AL **D1**/76
Bryant, AR **C3**/84
Bryant, IL **B3**/111
Bryant, IN **E2**/115
Bryant, OK **G2**/169
Bryant, SD **H2**/181
Bryant, WI **D3**/205
Bryant Pond, ME **B4**/126
Bryantsville, KY **F3**/121
Bryantville, MA **F2**/133
Bryce Canyon (nat'l park), UT **C5**/190
Bryceland, LA **C2**/122
Bryn Athyn, PA **C1**/174
Bryn Mawr, PA **F3**/173
Bryn Mawr, PA **A2**/174
Bryson, TX **J4**/185
Bryson City, NC **B2**/162
Buchanan, GA **A2**/102
Buchanan, KY **H2**/121
Buchanan, MI **A6**/137
Buchanan, ND **G2**/164
Buchanan, NY **G4**/159
Buchanan, TN **C1**/182
Buchanan, VA **E3**/194
Buchanan Dam, TX **H2**/187
Buchtel, OH **C3**/167
Buck Creek, IN **C2**/115
Buckatunna, MS **D4**/143
Buckeye, AZ **C4**/83
Buckeye, IA **D2**/117
Buckeye, LA **C3**/122
Buckeye, NM **G5**/157
Buckeye Lake, OH **C3**/167
Buckeystown, MD **C1**/129
Buckfield, ME **B4**/126
Buckhannon, WV **C3**/203
Buckhead, GA **C2**/102
Buckhead Ridge, FL **H4**/99
Buckholts, TX **J2**/187
Buckhorn, MS **C1**/143
Buckhorn, NM **B4**/157
Buckingham, CO **G1**/92
Buckingham, CT **C2**/95
Buckingham, VA **F3**/195
Buckland, AK **D2**/79
Buckland, MA **B1**/132
Buckland, OH **A2**/167
Buckley, IL **D3**/111
Buckley, MI **B3**/137
Buckley, WA **C2**/198
Bucklin, KS **D3**/118
Buckman, MN **D5**/140
Buckner, AR **B4**/84
Buckner, KY **E2**/121
Buckner, MO **B2**/145
Bucks, AL **A4**/76
Bucks Harbor, ME **E4**/126
Buckskin, IN **B4**/115
Bucksport, ME **D4**/126
Bucksport, SC **E3**/179
Bucyrus, KS **J2**/119
Bucyrus, ND **C3**/164
Bucyrus, OH **C2**/167
Bud, WV **B4**/203
Buda, IL **C2**/111
Buda, TX **J2**/187
Budd Lake, NJ **C2**/155
Bude, MS **B4**/143
Buellton, CA **C4**/88
Buena, NJ **C4**/155
Buena, WA **E3**/198
Buena Park, CA **C5**/91
Buena Vista, AR **C4**/84
Buena Vista, CO **D3**/92
Buena Vista, GA **B3**/102
Buena Vista, MS **D2**/143
Buena Vista, NM **E2**/157
Buena Vista, TN **C2**/182
Buena Vista, VA **E3**/195
Bueyeros, NM **G2**/157
Buffalo, AL **D3**/76
Buffalo, IA **G3**/117
Buffalo, IN **C2**/115
Buffalo, KS **H3**/119
Buffalo, MN **E5**/140
Buffalo, MO **C4**/145
Buffalo, MT **G3**/147
Buffalo, ND **H3**/165
Buffalo, NY **L2**/11
Buffalo, NY **B3**/158
Buffalo, OH **D3**/167
Buffalo, OK **D1**/169
Buffalo, SC **C2**/179
Buffalo, SD **B1**/180
Buffalo, TX **L6**/185
Buffalo, WI **B4**/205
Buffalo, WV **B3**/203
Buffalo, WY **F1**/206
Buffalo (nat'l river), AR **B1**/84
Buffalo (riv.), AR **C1**/84
Buffalo Center, IA **D1**/117
Buffalo City, AR **C1**/84
Buffalo City, NC **K2**/163
Buffalo Creek, CO **E2**/92
Buffalo Gap, SD **B3**/180
Buffalo Gap, TX **H5**/185
Buffalo Gap (nat'l grsld.), SD **B3**/180
Buffalo Grove, IL **E1**/111
Buffalo Grove, IL **A1**/112
Buffalo Lake, MN **D6**/140
Buffalo Mills, PA **C4**/172
Buffalo Springs, ND **B3**/164
Buffalo Valley, TN **F1**/183
Buford, GA **B1**/102
Buford, ND **B2**/164
Buford, OH **B3**/167
Buford, WY **G4**/206
Buhl, AL **B2**/76
Buhl, ID **D7**/108
Buhl, MN **F3**/140
Buhler, KS **F2**/119
Buhler, LA **B4**/122
Buies Creek, NC **G2**/163
Bula, TX **E4**/184
Bulan, KY **G3**/121
Bull Run (mts.), NV **D1**/151
Bull Shoals, AR **C1**/84
Bull Shoals (lake), AR **B1**/84
Bull Shoals (lake), MO **C5**/145
Bullard, GA **C3**/102
Bullard, TX **M5**/185
Bullhead, SD **D1**/181
Bullhead City, AZ **A2**/83
Bullion (mts.), CA **G4**/89
Bullock, NC **G1**/163
Bullock, SD **B1**/180
Bulls Gap, TN **H1**/183
Bumble Bee, AZ **C3**/83
Bumpus Mills, TN **D1**/182
Buna, TX **N2**/187
Bunceton, MO **D3**/145
Bunch, OK **J2**/169
Bunche Park, FL **B2**/101
Buncombe, IL **D6**/111
Bunker, MO **E4**/145
Bunker Hill, IL **C4**/111
Bunker Hill, IN **C2**/115
Bunker Hill, KS **E2**/119
Bunker Hill, OR **A4**/170
Bunker Hill, WV **E2**/203
Bunker Hill Monument, MA **D1**/134
Bunker Hill Pavilion, MA **D1**/134
Bunker Hill Village, TX **A3**/188
Bunkerville, NV **F6**/151
Bunkie, LA **C4**/122
Bunkley, MS **B4**/143
Bunn, NC **G2**/163
Bunnell, FL **G2**/99
Buras-Triumph, LA **F5**/122
Burbank, CA **E4**/89
Burbank, CA **A4**/91
Burbank, IL **E2**/111
Burbank, IL **B3**/112
Burbank, OH **D2**/167
Burbank, OK **G1**/169
Burbank, WA **F3**/198
Burchard, NE **J3**/149
Burdell, CA **A1**/91
Burden, KS **G3**/119
Burdett, KS **D2**/118
Burdett, NY **D3**/159
Burdette, AR **F2**/84
Burdette, SD **G2**/181
Burdick, KS **G2**/119
Burdock, SD **B3**/180
Bureau of Engraving and Printing, DC **B5**/131
Bureau of Indian Affairs, DC **B5**/131
Burgaw, NC **H3**/163
Burgess, MO **B4**/145
Burgess, SC **E3**/179
Burgettstown, PA **A3**/172
Burgin, KY **F3**/121
Burgoon, OH **B1**/167
Burien, WA **C2**/198
Burien, WA **B4**/201
Burkburnett, TX **J3**/185
Burke, ID **C2**/108
Burke, NY **F1**/159
Burke, SD **F3**/181
Burke, TX **N6**/185
Burke, VA **G2**/195
Burkes Garden, VA **C3**/194
Burkesville, KY **E4**/121
Burket, IN **D1**/115
Burkett, TX **H6**/185
Burkettsville, OH **A2**/167
Burkeville, TX **P7**/185
Burkeville, TX **N2**/187
Burkeville, VA **F3**/195
Burkittsville, MD **C1**/129
Burleson, TX **K5**/185
Burley, ID **E7**/108
Burley, WA **C2**/198
Burlingame, CA **B3**/91
Burlingame, KS **H2**/119
Burlington, CO **H2**/93
Burlington, CT **C2**/95
Burlington, IA **H2**/11
Burlington, IA **F4**/117
Burlington, IN **C2**/115
Burlington, KS **H2**/119
Burlington, KY **F1**/121
Burlington, MA **E1**/133
Burlington, MA **A1**/134
Burlington, ME **D3**/126
Burlington, MI **B5**/137
Burlington, NC **F1**/163
Burlington, ND **D1**/164
Burlington, NJ **C3**/155
Burlington, OH **C4**/167
Burlington, OK **E1**/169
Burlington, PA **E2**/173
Burlington, VT **M2**/11
Burlington, VT **A2**/193
Burlington, WA **C1**/198
Burlington, WI **E6**/205
Burlington, WV **E2**/203
Burlington, WY **D1**/206
Burlington Flats, NY **E3**/159
Burlington Junction, MO **A1**/144
Burlison, TN **B2**/182
Burna, KY **B3**/120
Burnet, TX **H2**/187
Burnettsville, IN **C2**/115
Burney, CA **D2**/86
Burney, IN **D3**/115
Burneyville, OK **F4**/169
Burnham, IL **C3**/112
Burnham, ME **C4**/126
Burnham, MO **E5**/145
Burnham, PA **D3**/173
Burnips, MI **B5**/137
Burns, CO **D2**/92
Burns, KS **G2**/119
Burns, MS **C3**/143
Burns, OR **F4**/170
Burns, TN **D1**/182
Burns, WY **H4**/207
Burns City, IN **C4**/115
Burns Flat, OK **D2**/169
Burnside, IL **A3**/111
Burnside, KY **F4**/121
Burnside, LA **E4**/122
Burnside, MS **C3**/143
Burnside, PA **C3**/172
Burnstad, ND **F3**/164
Burnsville, AL **C3**/76
Burnsville, MN **E6**/140
Burnsville, MS **D1**/143
Burnsville, NC **C2**/162
Burnsville, VA **E2**/194
Burnsville, WV **C3**/203
Burnt Cabins, PA **D3**/173
Burnt House, WV **C2**/203
Burnt Prairie, IL **D5**/111
Burntfork, WY **B4**/206
Burr, NE **J3**/149
Burr Oak, IA **F1**/117
Burr Oak, KS **E1**/119
Burr Oak, MI **B6**/137
Burr Ridge, IL **B3**/112
Burris, WY **C2**/206
Burrows, IN **C2**/115
Burrsville, MD **E2**/129
Burrton, KS **F2**/119
Burrville, CT **B2**/95
Burrville, UT **D4**/190
Burt, IA **C1**/117
Burt, MI **D4**/137
Burt, ND **C3**/164
Burt, NY **B2**/158
Burt (lake), MI **C2**/137
Burt Lake, MI **C2**/137
Burt Lake, MI **G4**/138
Burton, MI **D5**/137
Burton, NE **F1**/149
Burton, OH **D1**/167
Burton, SC **D4**/179
Burton, TX **K2**/187
Burton, WA **C2**/198
Burton, WA **A5**/201
Burtonsville, MD **D1**/129
Burtonville, KY **G2**/121
Burtrum, MN **D5**/140
Burwell, NE **F2**/149
Busby, MT **K4**/147
Bush, KY **G3**/121
Bush, LA **F4**/122
Bush City, KS **H2**/119
Bushkill, PA **F2**/173
Bushland, TX **E2**/184
Bushnell, FL **F3**/99
Bushnell, IL **B3**/111
Bushnell, NE **B2**/148
Bushnell, SD **J2**/181
Bushong, KS **G2**/119
Bushton, KS **E2**/119
Bushwood, MD **D2**/129
Busick, NC **C2**/162
Bussey, IA **E3**/117
Busti, NY **A3**/158
Butler, AL **A3**/76
Butler, GA **B3**/102
Butler, IL **C4**/111
Butler, IN **E1**/115
Butler, KY **F2**/121
Butler, MD **D1**/129
Butler, MO **B3**/145
Butler, NJ **D2**/155
Butler, OH **C2**/167
Butler, OK **D2**/169
Butler, PA **L2**/11
Butler, PA **B3**/172
Butler, SD **H1**/181
Butler, TN **J1**/183
Butler Springs, AL **C4**/76
Butlerville, AR **D3**/84
Butlerville, IN **D3**/115
Butner, NC **G1**/163
Butte, MT **D3**/147
Butte, ND **E2**/164
Butte, NE **G1**/149
Butte (mts.), NV **E3**/151
Butte City, CA **D3**/86
Butte City, ID **E6**/108
Butte Falls, OR **C5**/170
Butte-Silver Bow County, MT **D3**/146
Butterfield, AR **C3**/84
Butterfield, MN **D7**/140
Butterfield, MO **C5**/145
Butternut, MI **C4**/137
Butternut, WI **C2**/205
Butters, NC **G3**/163
Buttonwillow, CA **D3**/88
Buttzville, NJ **B2**/155
Buxton, ME **B5**/126
Buxton, NC **K2**/163
Buxton, ND **H2**/165
Buxton, OR **B2**/170
Buyck, MN **F2**/140
Buzzards (bay), MA **F3**/133
Buzzards Bay, MA **F3**/133
Byars, OK **F3**/169
Bybee, TN **H1**/183
Byers, CO **F2**/92
Byers, KS **E3**/119
Byers, TX **J3**/185
Byesville, OH **D3**/167
Byfield, MA **F1**/133
Bygland, MN **B3**/140
Byhalia, MS **C1**/143
Bylas, AZ **E4**/83
Byng, OK **G3**/169
Bynum, AL **D2**/76
Bynum, MT **D2**/146
Bynum, NC **F2**/163
Bynum, TX **K6**/185
Bynumville, MO **D2**/145
Byrdstown, TN **F1**/183
Byrnedale, PA **C2**/172
Byromville, GA **C3**/102
Byron, CA **D5**/86
Byron, GA **C3**/102
Byron, IL **C1**/111
Byron, MI **D5**/137
Byron, MN **F6**/140
Byron, NE **H3**/149
Byron, NY **B2**/158
Byron, OK **E1**/169
Byron, WY **D1**/206
Byron Center, MI **B5**/137

C

Caballo, NM **C5**/157
Caballo (res.), NM **C4**/157
Cabazon, CA **G5**/89
Cabery, IL **D3**/111
Cabin Creek, WV **B3**/203
Cabin John, MD **B1**/131
Cabinet (mts.), MT **A1**/146
Cabins, WV **D3**/203
Cabool, MO **D4**/145
Cabot, AR **C3**/84
Cabot, VT **B2**/193
Cabrillo (nat'l mon.), CA **F6**/89
Cache, OK **E3**/169
Cactus, TX **F1**/184
Caddo, OK **G3**/169
Caddo, TX **J5**/185
Caddo (lake), LA **A2**/122
Caddo (mts.), AR **B3**/84
Caddo (nat'l grsld.), TX **L4**/185
Caddo Gap, AR **B3**/84
Caddo Mills, TX **L4**/185
Caddo Valley, AR **B3**/84
Cade, LA **D4**/122
Cades, SC **E3**/179
Cades, TN **C2**/182
Cadet, MO **F4**/145
Cadillac, MI **J2**/11
Cadillac, MI **B3**/137
Cadiz, CA **H4**/89
Cadiz, IN **D3**/115
Cadiz, KY **C4**/120
Cadiz, OH **E2**/167
Cadott, WI **B4**/205
Cadwell, GA **C3**/102
Cadyville, NY **G1**/159
Caesar, MS **C5**/143
Cagle, TN **F2**/183
Cagles Mill (lake), IN **C3**/115
Cahaba, AL **B3**/76

Good Hart—Hale 231

Good Hart, MI F4/138
Good Hope, GA C2/102
Good Hope, IL B3/111
Good Hope, MS C3/143
Good Hope, OH B3/167
Good Thunder, MN D6/140
Goode, VA E3/195
Goodell, IA D2/117
Goodfield, IL C3/111
Goodhue, MN F6/140
Gooding, ID D7/108
Goodings Grove, IL A3/112
Goodland, FL G6/99
Goodland, IN B2/115
Goodland, KS B1/118
Goodland, MN E3/140
Goodlettsville, TN E1/182
Goodman, MO B5/145
Goodman, MS C3/143
Goodman, WI E3/205
Goodnews Bay, AK D4/79
Goodrich, CO F1/92
Goodrich, MI D5/137
Goodrich, ND E2/164
Goodrich, WI C3/205
Goodridge, MN C2/140
Goodspring, TN D2/182
Goodsprings, AL B2/76
Goodsprings, NV E7/151
Goodview, MN G6/140
Goodwater, AL C2/76
Goodwater, OK J4/169
Goodway, AL B4/76
Goodwell, OK B1/168
Goodwin, AR D3/84
Goodwin, SD J2/181
Goodyear, AZ C4/83
Goose (lake) B2/10
Goose Creek, SC D4/179
Goose Lake, IA G3/117
Gordo, AL B2/76
Gordon, AL D4/76
Gordon, GA C3/102
Gordon, KS G3/119
Gordon, LA B4/122
Gordon, NE C1/148
Gordon, OH A3/167
Gordon, PA E3/173
Gordon, TX J5/185
Gordon, WI B2/205
Gordon, WV B4/203
Gordonsburg, TN D2/182
Gordonsville, AL C3/76
Gordonsville, TN F1/183
Gordonsville, VA F2/195
Gordonville, MO G4/145
Gore, OK H2/169
Gore, VA F1/195
Gore (range), CO D2/92
Gore Springs, MS C2/143
Goree, TX H4/185
Goreville, IL D6/111
Gorgas, AL B2/76
Gorham, IL C6/111
Gorham, KS D2/119
Gorham, ME B5/126
Gorham, ND B2/164
Gorham, NH D3/153
Gorman, CA E4/89
Gorman, NC G1/163
Gorman, TN D1/182
Gorman, TX J5/185
Gorum, LA C3/122
Goshen, AL C4/76
Goshen, AR B1/84
Goshen, CT B2/95
Goshen, IN D1/115
Goshen, KY E2/121
Goshen, MA B2/132
Goshen, NH B5/153
Goshen, NJ C5/155
Goshen, NY F4/159
Goshen, OR B4/170
Goshen, UT D3/190
Goshen, VA E3/195
Goshen (Goshen Junction), CA D2/88
Goshen Springs, MS C3/143
Goshute (mts.), NV F2/151
Gosnell, AR F2/84
Gosport, AL B4/76
Gosport, IN C3/115
Goss, MS C4/143
Gossville, NH D5/153
Gotebo, OK E2/169
Gothenburg, NE E3/149
Goudeau, LA C4/122
Gough, GA D2/102
Gould, AR D4/84
Gould, CO D1/92
Gould, OK D3/168
Gould City, MI B1/137
Gould City, MI F3/138
Goulds Mill, VT B3/193
Gouldsboro, ME D4/126
Gouldsboro, PA F2/173
Gouverneur, NY E1/159
Govan, SC C3/179
Gove (Gove City), KS C2/118
Government Camp, OR D2/170
Gowanda, NY B3/158
Gowen, MI B4/137
Gower, MO B2/145
Gowrie, IA C2/117
Grabill, IN E1/115
Grace, ID G7/108
Grace, MS B3/143
Grace City, ND G2/164
Graceham, MD C1/129
Gracemont, OK E2/169
Graceville, FL C1/98
Graceville, MN B5/140
Gracey, KY C4/120
Grady, AL C4/76
Grady, AR D3/84
Grady, NM G3/157
Grady, OK F3/169
Gradyville, KY E3/121
Graeagle, CA E3/86
Graettinger, IA C1/117
Graford, TX J5/185
Grafton, IA D1/117
Grafton, IL B5/111
Grafton, MA D2/133
Grafton, ND H1/165
Grafton, NE H3/149
Grafton, NH C4/153
Grafton, NY G3/159
Grafton, OH C1/167
Grafton, VT B3/193
Grafton, WI F5/205
Grafton, WV C2/203
Grafton Center, NH C4/153
Graham, AL D2/76
Graham, FL F2/99
Graham, GA D4/102
Graham, KY C3/120
Graham, MO A1/144
Graham, NC F1/163
Graham, OK F3/169
Graham, TX J4/185
Grahamsville, NY F4/159
Grahn, KY G2/121
Grainfield, KS C1/118
Graingers, NC H2/163
Grainola, OK G1/169
Grainton, NE D3/148
Grambling, LA C2/122
Gramling, SC B1/179
Grampian, PA C3/172
Gran Quivira, NM D3/157
Granada, CO H3/93
Granada, MN D7/140
Granbury, TX K5/185
Granby, CO E1/92
Granby, CT C2/95
Granby, MA B2/132
Granby, MO B5/145
Granby, VT C2/193
Granby (lake), CO E1/92
Grand (isl.), LA E5/122
Grand (isl.), LA F4/123
Grand (isl.), NY A2/158
Grand (lake), LA C5/122
Grand (lake), OH A2/167
Grand (riv.), MI B5/137
Grand (riv.), MO B1/145
Grand (riv.), SD D1/181
Grand Bay, AL A5/76
Grand Bayou, LA B2/122
Grand Beach, MI A6/137
Grand Blanc, MI D5/137
Grand Calumet (riv.), IL C3/112
Grand Cane, LA B2/122
Grand Canyon (nat'l park), AZ D3/10
Grand Canyon (nat'l park), AZ C1/83
Grand Chenier, LA C5/122
Grand Coteau, LA C4/122
Grand Coulee, WA F2/198
Grand Detour, IL C2/111
Grand Forks, ND H2/165
Grand Glaise, AR D2/84
Grand Gorge, NY F3/159
Grand Gosier (isls.), LA F5/123
Grand Gulf, MS A3/143
Grand Haven, MI A4/137
Grand Hogback (mts.), CO C2/92
Grand Island, NE G3/149
Grand Isle, LA F5/122
Grand Isle, ME D1/126
Grand Isle, VT A2/193
Grand Junction, CO B2/92
Grand Junction, IA C2/117
Grand Junction, MI A5/137
Grand Junction, TN B2/182
Grand Lake, AR D4/84
Grand Lake, CO E1/92
Grand Lake, LA B4/122
Grand Lake o' the Cherokees (lake), OK J1/169
Grand Lake Stream, ME E3/126
Grand Lake Towne, OK H1/169
Grand Ledge, MI C5/137
Grand Marais, MI F3/138
Grand Marais, MN H3/140
Grand Marsh, WI D5/205
Grand Meadow, MN F7/140
Grand Mound, IA G3/117
Grand Mound, WA B3/198
Grand Portage, MN J3/141
Grand Portage (nat'l mon.), MN J3/141
Grand Prairie, TX C2/188
Grand Rapids, MI B5/137
Grand Rapids, MN E3/140
Grand Rapids, ND G3/164
Grand Rapids, OH B1/167
Grand Ridge, FL C1/99
Grand Ridge, IL D2/111
Grand River, IA D4/117
Grand River (nat'l grsld.), SD C1/181
Grand Rivers, KY B3/120
Grand Ronde, OR B2/170
Grand Saline, TX M5/185
Grand Staircase Escalante (nat'l mon.), UT D5/190
Grand Terre (isls.), LA F5/122
Grand Teton (nat'l park), WY B2/206
Grand Tower, IL C6/111
Grand Traverse (bay), MI B2/137
Grand Valley, PA B2/172
Grand View, ID B7/108
Grand View, WI B2/205
Grande Ronde (riv.), OR H2/170
Grandfalls, TX E6/184
Grandfield, OK E3/169
Grandin, MO F5/145
Grandin, ND H2/165
Grandview, AR B1/84
Grandview, IA F3/117
Grandview, IN C5/115
Grandview, MO B3/145
Grandview, OH D3/167
Grandview, TX K5/185
Grandview, WA F3/198
Grandview Park, PA C2/172
Grandview Plaza, KS G1/119
Grandville, MI B5/137
Grandy, MN E5/140
Grandy, NC K1/163
Grange, NH C3/153
Grange City, KY G2/121
Grangeburg, AL D4/76
Granger, IA D3/117
Granger, IN C1/115
Granger, MN F7/140
Granger, MO E1/145
Granger, TX J2/187
Granger, WA E3/198
Granger, WY C4/206
Grangeville, ID B4/108
Grangeville, LA E4/122
Granite, CO D2/92
Granite, MD D1/129
Granite, OK D3/169
Granite, OR G3/170
Granite (mts.), WY E3/206
Granite (peak), MT G4/147
Granite (range), NV A2/151
Granite Canon, WY G4/206
Granite City, IL B5/111
Granite Falls, MN C6/140
Granite Falls, NC D2/162
Granite Falls, WA D1/198
Granite Point, NV B2/152
Granite Quarry, NC E2/162
Granite Shoals, TX H2/187
Graniteville, MA E1/133
Graniteville, SC C3/179
Graniteville-East Barre, VT B2/193
Grannis, AR A3/84
Grano, ND D1/164
Grant, AL C1/76
Grant, CO E2/92
Grant, FL H4/99
Grant, IA C3/117
Grant, MI B4/137
Grant, MT C4/146
Grant, NE D3/148
Grant (range), NV E4/151
Grant City, MO B1/145
Grant Park, IL E2/111
Grant Town, WV C2/203
Grant-Kohrs Ranch (nat'l hist. site), MT D3/146
Grantham, NH B5/153
Granton, WI C4/205
Grants, NM C2/157
Grants Mills, RI C1/177
Grants Pass, OR B5/170
Grantsboro, NC J2/163
Grantsburg, IN C4/115
Grantsburg, WI A3/205
Grantsdale, MT B3/146
Grantsville, MD A1/128
Grantsville, UT C2/190
Grantsville, WV B3/203
Grantville, GA B2/102
Grantville, KS H1/119
Granville, IA B2/116
Granville, IL C2/111
Granville, MA B2/132
Granville, MO D2/145
Granville, ND E1/164
Granville, NY G2/159
Granville, OH C2/167
Granville, TN F1/183
Granville, VT B3/193
Grapeland, MS B2/143
Grapeland, TX M6/185
Grapevine, AR C3/84
Grapevine, TX C1/188
Grasmere, NH C5/153
Grasonville, MD D2/129
Grass Creek, WY D2/206
Grass Lake, MI C5/137
Grass Range, MT H2/147
Grass Valley, CA D3/86
Grass Valley, OR E2/170
Grassflat, PA C2/173
Grasston, MN E5/140
Grassy, MO F4/145
Grassy Butte, ND B2/164
Grassy Key (isl.), FL G7/99
Gratiot, OH C3/167
Gratiot, WI C6/205
Gratis, OH A3/167
Graton, CA C4/86
Grattan, MI B4/137
Gratz, KY F2/121
Gratz, PA E3/173
Gravel Ridge, AR C3/84
Gravel Switch, KY E3/121
Gravelly, AR B3/84
Gravelton, IN D1/115
Graves, GA B4/102
Gravette, AR A1/84
Gravina (isl.), AK C3/81
Gravity, IA C4/117
Grawn, MI B3/137
Gray, GA C2/102
Gray, KY F4/121
Gray, LA E5/122
Gray, ME B5/126
Gray, PA B3/172
Gray, TN J1/183
Gray, VA G4/195
Gray Court, SC B2/179
Gray Hawk, KY G3/121
Gray Horse, OK G1/169
Grayburg, TX M2/187
Grayland, WA A3/198
Grayling, AK D3/79
Grayling, MI C3/137
Grays, AR D2/84
Grays, SC C4/179
Grays Landing, PA B4/172
Grays River, WA B3/198
Grayson, GA C2/102
Grayson, KY H2/121
Grayson, LA C2/122
Grayson, MO B2/145
Grayson, OK H2/169
Graysville, AL C2/76
Graysville, OH D3/167
Graysville, TN F2/183
Grayville, IL E5/111
Greasewood, AZ F2/83
Great (falls), MT E2/147
Great Barrington, MA A2/132
Great Basin (nat'l park), NV F4/151
Great Bend, KS E2/119
Great Bend, ND J3/165
Great Bend, NY E1/159
Great Bend, PA F2/173
Great Cacapon, WV E2/203
Great Egg Harbor (riv.), NJ C4/155
Great Falls, MT E2/147
Great Falls, SC D2/179
Great Meadows-Vienna, NJ C2/155
Great Miami (riv.), OH A2/167
Great Neck, NY C2/161
Great Pee Dee (riv.), SC K4/11
Great Sacandaga (lake), NY F2/159
Great Salt (lake), UT D2/10
Great Salt (lake), UT C1/190
Great Salt Lake (des.), UT D2/10
Great Sand Dunes (nat'l mon.), CO E4/92
Great Smoky (mts.), TN H2/183
Great Smoky Mountains (nat'l park), NC B2/162
Great Smoky Mountains (nat'l park), TN H2/183
Great Valley, NY B3/158
Great Wass (isl.), ME E4/126
Greater Buffalo (int'l arpt.), NY B3/158
Greater Cincinnati (int'l arpt.), KY F1/121
Greater Pittsburgh (int'l arpt.), PA A3/172
Greater Rochester (int'l arpt.), NY C2/159
Greaterville, AZ E6/83
Greece, NY C2/159
Greeley, CO F1/92
Greeley, IA F2/117
Greeley, KS H2/119
Greeley, PA G2/173
Greeley (Greeley Center), NE G2/149
Greeleyville, SC E3/179
Green, KS F1/119
Green, MI B3/138
Green, OH D2/167
Green, OR B4/170
Green (bay), MI D5/138
Green (bay), WI F4/205
Green (mts.), VT B3/193
Green (riv.) D3/10
Green (riv.), KY C3/120
Green Bank, NJ C4/155
Green Bay, VA F3/195
Green Bay, WI E4/205
Green Brook, NJ D2/155
Green Camp, OH B2/167
Green City, MO D1/145
Green Cove Springs, FL G2/99
Green Creek, NJ C5/155
Green Crossing, MS B3/143
Green Forest, AR B1/84
Green Harbor-Cedar Crest, MA F2/133
Green Haven, MD D1/129
Green Hill, RI B4/177
Green Hill, TN E1/182
Green Island, NY G3/159
Green Isle, MN D6/140
Green Lake, MI B5/137
Green Lake, WI E5/205
Green Mountain, IA E2/117
Green Mountain, NC C2/162
Green Mountain Falls, CO E3/92
Green Pond, AL B2/76
Green Pond, NJ D1/155
Green Pond, SC D4/179
Green Ridge, MO C3/145
Green River, UT E4/190
Green River, VT B4/193
Green River, WY C4/206
Green River (lake), KY E3/121
Green Sea, SC F2/179
Green Springs, OH B1/167
Green Sulphur Springs, WV C4/203
Green Valley, AZ E6/83
Green Valley, IL C3/111
Green Valley, MD C1/129
Green Valley, MN C6/140
Greenacres City, FL H5/99
Greenback, TN G2/183
Greenbelt, MD D1/129
Greenbelt, MD D1/131
Greenbelt (nat'l cap. park), MD D1/131
Greenbrier, AL C1/76
Greenbrier, AR C2/84
Greenbrier, TN E1/182
Greenbrier (riv.), WV C4/203
Greenbush, MA F2/133
Greenbush, ME D3/126
Greenbush, MI D3/137
Greenbush, MN B2/140
Greenbush, VA J3/195
Greencastle, IN C3/115
Greencastle, PA D4/173
Greencreek, ID B3/108
Greendale, IN E3/115
Greendell, NJ C2/155
Greene, IA E2/117
Greene, ME B4/126
Greene, ND D1/164
Greene, NY E3/159
Greene, RI B3/177
Greenevers, NC H3/163
Greeneville, TN J1/183
Greenfield, CA B2/88
Greenfield, IA C3/117
Greenfield, IL B4/111
Greenfield, IN D3/115
Greenfield, MA B1/132
Greenfield, ME D3/126
Greenfield, MO C4/145
Greenfield, NH C6/153
Greenfield, OH B3/167
Greenfield, OK E2/169
Greenfield, SD J4/181
Greenfield, TN C1/182
Greenfield, WI E6/205
Greenford, OH E2/167
Greenhorn (mts.), CA E3/89
Greenland, AR A2/84
Greenland, CO F2/92
Greenland, MI B3/138
Greenland, NH E5/153
Greenlawn, NY G5/159
Greenleaf, ID B6/108
Greenleaf, KS G1/119
Greenleafton, MN F7/140
Greenmount, KY F3/121
Greenmount, MD D1/129
Greenough, GA B4/102
Greenport, NY H4/159
Greens Fork, IN D3/115
Greensboro, AL B3/76
Greensboro, FL D1/99
Greensboro, GA C2/102
Greensboro, IN D3/115
Greensboro, MD E2/129
Greensboro, NC F1/163
Greensboro, VT B2/193
Greensboro Bend, VT B2/193
Greensburg, IN D3/115
Greensburg, KS D3/119
Greensburg, KY E3/121
Greensburg, LA E4/122
Greensburg, OH D2/167
Greensburg, PA B3/172
Greentop, MO D1/145
Greentown, IN D2/115
Greentown, OH D2/167
Greenup, IL D4/111
Greenup, KY H2/121
Greenview, CA C1/86
Greenview, IL C3/111
Greenville, AL C4/76
Greenville, CA E2/86
Greenville, FL E1/99
Greenville, GA B2/102
Greenville, IL C5/111
Greenville, IN D4/115
Greenville, KY C3/120
Greenville, ME C3/126
Greenville, MI B4/137
Greenville, MO F4/145
Greenville, MS A2/143
Greenville, NC H2/163
Greenville, NH C6/153
Greenville, OH A2/167
Greenville, PA A2/172
Greenville, RI B2/177
Greenville, SC B2/179
Greenville, TX L4/185
Greenville, UT C4/190
Greenville Junction, ME C3/126
Greenwald, MN D5/140
Greenway, AR E1/84
Greenway, SD F1/181
Greenwell Springs, LA E4/122
Greenwich, CT A3/95
Greenwich, NY G2/159
Greenwich, OH C1/167
Greenwood, AR A2/84
Greenwood, DE A3/96
Greenwood, FL C1/98
Greenwood, IN C3/115
Greenwood, LA B2/122
Greenwood, ME B4/126
Greenwood, MS B2/143
Greenwood, NE J3/149
Greenwood, NY C3/159
Greenwood, SC B2/179
Greenwood, SD G4/181
Greenwood, WI C4/205
Greenwood, WV C2/203
Greenwood (lake), NJ D1/155
Greenwood Lake, NY F4/159
Greenwood Springs, MS D2/143
Greenwood Village, CO E3/92
Greer, AZ F3/83
Greer, ID B3/108
Greer, MO E5/145
Greer, OH C2/167
Greer, SC B2/179
Greers Ferry, AR C2/84
Greers Ferry (lake), AR C2/84
Greggs, GA C4/102
Gregory, MI C5/137
Gregory, SD F3/181
Greilickville, MI B3/137
Grelton, OH B1/167
Grenada, CA C1/86
Grenada, MS C2/143
Grenada (lake), MS C2/143
Grenola, KS G3/119
Grenora, ND B1/164
Grenville, NM G1/157
Grenville, SD H1/181
Gresham, NE H2/149
Gresham, OR C2/170
Gresham, SC E3/179
Gresham, WI E4/205
Gresham Park, GA C3/105
Greshamville, GA C2/102
Gresston, GA C3/102
Gretna, FL D1/99
Gretna, LA C3/124
Gretna, LA E5/122
Gretna, NE J2/149
Gretna, VA E4/195
Grey Eagle, MN D5/140
Greybull, WY D1/206
Greycliff, MT G4/147
Greylock (mt.), MA A1/132
Greystone, CO B1/92
Gridley, CA D3/86
Gridley, IL D3/111
Gridley, KS H2/119
Grier, NM G3/157
Griffin, GA B2/102
Griffin, IN B4/115
Griffith, IN B1/115
Griffin, ND B3/164
Griffithsville, WV B3/203
Griffithville, AR D2/84
Grifton, NC H2/163
Griggs, OK A1/168
Griggsville, IL B4/111
Grigston, KS C2/118
Grimes, AL D4/76
Grimes, CA D3/86
Grimes, IA D3/117
Grimes, OK D2/168
Grimesland, NC H2/163
Grimms Landing, WV B3/203
Grimsley, TN G1/183
Grind Stone City, MI E3/137
Grindstone-Rowes Run, PA B3/172
Grinnell, IA E3/117
Grinnell, KS C1/118
Griswold, IA B3/116
Griswoldville, MA B1/132
Grizzly (isl.), CA C1/91
Grizzly Flats, CA E4/86
Groesbeck, TX L6/185
Groom, TX F2/184
Gross, NE G1/149
Grosse Pointe, MI E5/137
Grosse Pointe Farms, MI E5/137
Grosse Pointe Park, MI E5/137
Grosse Pointe Park, MI C2/139
Grosse Pointe Woods, MI E5/137
Grosse Tete, LA D4/122
Grosvenor Dale, CT E2/95
Groton, CT D3/95
Groton, MA D1/133
Groton, NH C4/153
Groton, NY D3/159
Groton, SD G1/181
Groton, VT B2/193
Grotto, WA D2/198
Grottoes, VA F2/195
Grouse Creek, UT B1/190
Grovania, GA C3/102
Grove, OK J1/169
Grove Beach, CT D3/95
Grove Center, KY B3/120
Grove City, MN D5/140
Grove City, OH B3/167
Grove City, PA A2/172
Grove Hill, AL B4/76
Groveland, CA E5/86
Groveland, FL G3/99
Groveland, MA E1/133
Groveland, NY C3/159
Groveport, OH C3/167
Grover, CO F1/92
Grover, PA E2/173
Grover, SD H2/181
Grover, UT D4/190
Grover, WY B3/206
Grover City, CA C3/88
Grover Hill, OH A1/167
Groves, TX N3/187
Grovespring, MO D4/145
Groveton, NH C2/153
Groveton, TX L1/187
Groveton, TX M6/185
Groveton, VA G2/195
Grovetown, GA D2/102
Growler (mts.), AZ B5/83
Grubbs, AR D2/84
Gruetli-Laager, TN F2/183
Grundy, VA B3/194
Grundy Center, IA E2/117
Gruver, IA C1/117
Gruver, TX F1/184
Grygla, MN C2/140
Guadalupe, CA C4/88
Guadalupe (mts.), NM E5/157
Guadalupe (peak), TX C6/184
Guadalupe (riv.), TX H3/187
Guadalupe Mountains (nat'l park), TX 6C/184
Guadalupita, NM E1/157
Guage, KY G3/121
Gualala, CA B4/86
Guardian, WV C3/203
Guelph, ND G3/164
Guerneville, CA C4/86
Guernsey, WY H3/206
Gueydan, LA C4/122
Guffey, CO E3/92
Guide Rock, NE G3/149
Guild, NH B5/153
Guildhall, VT C2/193
Guilford, CT C3/95
Guilford, ME C3/126
Guilford, NY E3/159
Guilford, VT B4/193
Guilford Courthouse (nat'l mil. park), NC F1/163
Guin, AL B2/76
Guinda, CA C4/86
Guinea, VA G2/195
Guion, AR D2/84
Gulf, NC F2/163
Gulf (coast. pl.), TX H5/187
Gulf Breeze, FL A1/98
Gulf Hammock, FL F2/99
Gulf Hills, MS D5/143
Gulf Islands (nat'l seash.), FL A1/98
Gulf Islands (nat'l seash.), MS D5/143
Gulf Shores, AL B5/76
Gulph Mills, PA A1/174
Gulfport, FL F4/99
Gulfport, IL A3/111
Gulfport, MS C5/143
Gulkana, AK H3/79
Gulliver, MI A2/137
Gulliver, MI E4/138
Gully, MN C3/140
Gulnare, CO F4/92
Gum Springs, AR B3/84
Gumboro, DE B4/96
Gumbranch, GA E4/102
Gun Barrel City, TX L5/185
Gunlock, UT B5/190
Gunnison, CO D3/92
Gunnison, MS B2/143
Gunnison, UT D3/190
Gunnison (riv.), CO B3/92
Gunter, OR B4/170
Gunter, TX L4/185
Guntersville, AL C1/76
Guntersville (lake), AL C1/76
Guntown, MS D1/143
Gurdon, AR B4/84
Gurley, AL C1/76
Gurley, LA D4/122
Gurley, NE C2/148
Gurley, SC F2/179
Gurleyville, CT D2/95
Gurnee, IL E1/111
Gurney, WI C2/205
Gusher, UT F2/190
Gustave, SD B1/180
Gustavus, AK C2/81
Gustavus, OH E1/167
Gustine, CA E5/86
Gustine, TX J6/185
Guston, KY D3/120
Guthrie, KY C4/120
Guthrie, MN D3/140
Guthrie, MO D3/145
Guthrie, OK F2/169
Guthrie, TX G4/184
Guthrie Center, IA C3/117
Guttenberg, IA F2/117
Guttenberg, NJ B2/161
Guy, AR C2/84
Guyandotte (riv.), WV A3/203
Guymon, OK B1/168
Guys, TN C2/182
Guys Mills, PA B2/172
Guysville, OH D3/167
Guyton, GA E3/102
Gwinn, MI D3/138
Gwinner, ND H3/165
Gwynn, VA H3/195
Gwynneville, IN D3/115
Gypsum, CO D2/92
Gypsum, KS F2/119
Gypsum, OH C1/167

H

Habersham, TN G1/183
Hachita, NM B6/157
Hacienda Heights, CA C5/91
Hackberry, AZ B2/83
Hackberry, LA B5/122
Hackensack, MN D4/140
Hackensack, NJ D2/155
Hackensack, NJ B1/161
Hacker Valley, WV C3/203
Hackett, AR A2/84
Hackettstown, NJ C2/155
Hackleburg, AL B1/76
Hacoda, AL C4/76
Hadar, NE H1/149
Haddam, CT C3/95
Haddam, KS F1/119
Haddix, KY G3/121
Haddock, GA C2/102
Haddon Heights, NJ B4/155
Haddon Heights, NJ C3/174
Haddonfield, NJ B4/155
Haddonfield, NJ C3/174
Hadley, KY D3/120
Hadley, MA B2/132
Hadley, MN C6/140
Hadley, PA A2/172
Hadlock-Irondale, WA C1/198
Hadlyme, CT D3/95
Haena, HI B1/106
Hagaman, NY F3/159
Hagan, GA E3/102
Hagarville, AR B2/84
Hagemeister (isl.), AK D4/79
Hagerman, ID D7/108
Hagerman, NM F4/157
Hagerman Fossil Beds (nat'l mon.), ID D7/108
Hagerstown, IN D3/115
Hagerstown, MD C1/129
Hague, FL F2/99
Hague, ND F3/164
Hague, NY G2/159
Hague, VA H2/195
Hahira, GA C5/102
Hahnville, LA E5/122
Haig, NE B2/148
Haigler, NE D3/148
Haiku-Pauwela, HI E3/107
Haile, LA C2/122
Hailesboro, NY E1/159
Hailey, ID D6/108
Haileyville, OK H3/169
Hailstone (nat'l wild. ref.), MT G3/147
Haina, HI F3/107
Haines, AK C2/81
Haines, OR H3/170
Haines City, FL G3/99
Hainesburg, NJ B2/155
Hainesville, NJ C1/155
Halaula, HI F3/107
Halbur, IA C2/117
Haldeman, KY G2/121
Hale, CO H2/93
Hale, IA F2/117
Hale, MI D3/137
Hale, MO C2/145

238 Lynnville—Mayflower Village

Name/map reference/page

Lynnville, TN **D2**/182
Lynnwood, WA **C2**/198
Lynnwood, WA **B2**/201
Lynwood, CA **B5**/91
Lynxville, WI **B5**/205
Lyon, MS **B1**/143
Lyons, CO **E1**/92
Lyons, GA **D3**/102
Lyons, IL **B2**/112
Lyons, IN **B4**/115
Lyons, KS **E2**/119
Lyons, KY **E3**/121
Lyons, MI **C5**/137
Lyons, NE **J2**/149
Lyons, NY **D2**/159
Lyons, OH **A1**/167
Lyons, PA **F3**/173
Lyons, SD **J3**/181
Lyons, WI **E6**/205
Lyons Falls, NY **E2**/159
Lyons Plain, CT **B3**/95
Lysander, NY **D2**/159
Lysite, WY **E2**/206
Lynwood Center, WA **A3**/201
Lytle, TX **H3**/187
Lytton, IA **C2**/117

M

Maalaea, HI **E3**/107
Mabank, TX **L5**/185
Mabel, MN **G7**/140
Maben, MS **C2**/143
Maben, WV **B4**/203
Mabie, WV **D3**/203
Mableton, GA **B2**/102
Mabton, WA **F3**/198
MacArthur, WV **B4**/203
MacBeth, SC **E3**/179
MacClenny, FL **F1**/99
MacClesfield, NC **H2**/163
MacDoel, CA **C1**/86
MacDonaldton, PA **C4**/172
Macedon, NY **C2**/159
Macedonia, IA **B3**/116
Macedonia, IL **D5**/111
Macel, MS **B2**/143
Maceo, KY **D3**/120
MacFarlan, WV **B2**/203
Machesney Park, IL **C1**/111
Machias, ME **E4**/126
Machias, NY **B3**/158
Machias (riv.), ME **E4**/126
Machias Seal (isl.), ME **E4**/126
Machiasport, ME **E4**/126
Machipongo, VA **J3**/195
Mack, CO **B2**/92
Mackay, ID **E6**/108
Mackeys, NC **J2**/163
Mackinac (isl.), MI **C2**/137
Mackinac Island, MI **C2**/137
Mackinaw, IL **C3**/111
Mackinaw (riv.), IL **D3**/111
Mackinaw City, MI **C2**/137
Macks Creek, MO **D4**/145
Macksburg, OH **D3**/167
Macksville, KS **E3**/119
Mackville, KY **E3**/121
Macomb, IL **B3**/111
Macon, GA **C3**/102
Macon, IL **D4**/111
Macon, MO **D2**/145
Macon, MS **D2**/143
Macon, NC **G1**/163
Macon, NE **G3**/149
Macon, OH **B4**/167
Macon, TN **B2**/182
Macungie, PA **F3**/173
Macwahoc, ME **D3**/126
Macy, IN **C2**/115
Macy, NE **J1**/149
Mad (riv.), CA **B2**/86
Madawaska, ME **D1**/126
Madbury, NH **E5**/153
Madden, MS **C3**/143
Maddock, ND **F2**/164
Madeira, OH **A3**/167
Madeira Beach, FL **F4**/99
Madelia, MN **D6**/140
Madeline, CA **E1**/86
Madeline (isl.), WI **C2**/205
Madera, CA **E6**/86
Madera, CA **C2**/88
Madera, PA **C3**/172
Madera Canyon, AZ **E6**/83
Madill, OK **G3**/169
Madison, AL **C1**/76
Madison, AR **E2**/84
Madison, CA **D4**/86
Madison, CT **C3**/95
Madison, FL **E1**/99
Madison, GA **C2**/102
Madison, IN **D4**/115
Madison, KS **G2**/119
Madison, MD **D2**/129
Madison, ME **C4**/126
Madison, MN **B5**/140
Madison, MO **D2**/145
Madison, MS **B3**/143
Madison, NC **F1**/163
Madison, NE **H2**/149
Madison, NH **D4**/153
Madison, NJ **D2**/155
Madison, NY **E3**/159
Madison, OH **D1**/167
Madison, SD **H2**/181
Madison, VA **F2**/195
Madison, WV **B3**/203
Madison (cap.), WI **J2**/11
Madison (cap.), WI **D5**/205
Madison (riv.) **D1**/10
Madison Building, DC **D5**/131
Madison Heights, VA **E3**/195
Madison Junction, WY **B1**/206
Madison Lake, MN **E6**/140
Madisonville, KY **C3**/120
Madisonville, LA **E4**/122
Madisonville, TN **G2**/183
Madisonville, TX **M7**/185
Madisonville, TX **L2**/187
Madras, OR **D3**/170
Madre (lag.), TX **J6**/187
Madre (mts.), CA **C4**/88
Madrid, AL **D4**/76
Madrid, IA **D3**/117
Madrid, NE **D3**/148
Madrid, NY **E1**/159
Maeser, UT **F2**/190
Maeystown, IL **B5**/111
Magalia, CA **D3**/86
Magazine, AR **B2**/84
Magazine (mtn.), AR **B2**/84
Magdalena, NM **C3**/157
Magee, MS **C4**/143
Maggie Valley, NC **B2**/162
Magna, UT **C2**/190
Magnet, NE **H1**/149
Magnetic Springs, OH **B2**/167
Magnolia, AL **B3**/76
Magnolia, AR **B4**/84
Magnolia, DE **B2**/96
Magnolia, IA **B3**6
Magnolia, IL **C2**/111
Magnolia, MN **B7**/140
Magnolia, MS **B4**/143
Magnolia, NC **G3**/163
Magnolia, NJ **C3**/174
Magnolia, TX **L2**/187
Magnolia Springs, AL **B5**/76
Mahaffey, PA **C3**/172
Mahanoy City, PA **E3**/173
Mahaska, KS **F1**/119
Maher, CO **C3**/92
Mahnomen, MN **C3**/140
Mahomet, IL **D3**/111
Mahopac, NY **G4**/159
Mahto, SD **E1**/181
Mahtowa, MN **F4**/140
Mahukona, HI **F3**/107
Mahwah, NJ **D1**/155
Maida, ND **G1**/164
Maiden, NC **D2**/162
Maiden Rock, WI **A4**/205
Maidstone, VT **C2**/193
Maidsville, WV **D2**/203
Maili, HI **C2**/107
Maine, NY **D3**/159
Maine (gulf), ME **C5**/126
Mainesburg, PA **E2**/173
Maineville, OH **A3**/167
Maitland, MO **A1**/144
Maize, KS **F3**/119
Majenica, IN **D2**/115
Majestic, KY **H3**/121
Makaha, HI **C2**/107
Makakilo City, HI **C2**/107
Makanda, IL **C6**/111
Makawao, HI **E3**/107
Makinen, MN **F3**/140
Makoti, ND **D2**/164
Malabar, FL **H3**/99
Malad City, ID **F7**/108
Malaga, NJ **B4**/155
Malaga, NM **F5**/157
Malaga, OH **D3**/167
Malaga, WA **E2**/198
Malakoff, TX **L5**/185
Malaspina (glacier), AK **J4**/79
Malaspina (glacier), AK **A2**/81
Malcolm, AL **A4**/76
Malcolm, NE **J3**/149
Malcom, IA **E3**/117
Malden, IL **C2**/111
Malden, IN **B1**/115
Malden, MA **E2**/133
Malden, MA **B1**/134
Malden, MO **G5**/145
Malden, WA **H2**/199
Malesus, TN **C2**/182
Malheur (lake), OR **G4**/170
Malheur (riv.), OR **G4**/170
Malibu, CA **E4**/89
Malin, OR **D5**/170
Malinta, OH **A1**/167
Mall, The (nat'l cap. park), DC **B5**/131
Mall, The (nat'l cap. park), DC **C2**/131
Mallard, IA **C2**/117
Mallet Creek, OH **D1**/167
Mallory, NY **D2**/159
Mallory, WV **B4**/203
Malmo, MN **E4**/140
Malmo, NE **J2**/149
Malo, WA **G1**/198
Malone, FL **C1**/98
Malone, KY **G3**/121
Malone, MS **C1**/143
Malone, NY **F1**/159
Malone, TX **L6**/185
Malone, WA **B3**/198
Maloneton, KY **H2**/121
Malott, WA **F1**/198
Malta, CO **D2**/92
Malta, ID **E7**/108
Malta, IL **D2**/111
Malta, MT **J1**/147
Malta, OH **D3**/167
Malta Bend, MO **C2**/145
Malvern, AL **D4**/76
Malvern, AR **C3**/84
Malvern, IA **B3**/116
Malvern, OH **D2**/167
Malvern, PA **F3**/173
Malvina, MS **B2**/143
Mamaroneck, NY **G5**/159
Mamaroneck, NY **C1**/161
Mamers, NC **G2**/163
Mamie, NC **K1**/163
Mammoth, AZ **E5**/83
Mammoth, UT **C3**/190
Mammoth Cave (nat'l park), KY **D3**/120
Mammoth Cave (nat'l park), KY **E3**/121
Mammoth Hot Springs, WY **B1**/206
Mammoth Lakes, CA **G5**/87
Mammoth Spring, AR **D1**/84
Mamou, LA **C4**/122
Man, WV **B4**/203
Mana, HI **B1**/106
Manahawkin, NJ **D4**/155
Manalapan, FL **H5**/99
Manalapan, NJ **D3**/155
Manasquan, NJ **D3**/155
Manassa, CO **E4**/92
Manassas, GA **D3**/102
Manassas, VA **G2**/195
Manassas (nat'l bfld. park), VA **G2**/195
Manassas Park, VA **G2**/195
Manawa, WI **E4**/205
Mancelona, MI **B3**/137
Manchaca, TX **J2**/187
Manchaug, MA **D2**/133
Manchester, AL **B2**/76
Manchester, CA **B4**/86
Manchester, CT **C2**/95
Manchester, GA **B3**/102
Manchester, IA **F2**/117
Manchester, IL **B4**/111
Manchester, IN **D3**/115
Manchester, KS **F1**/119
Manchester, KY **G3**/121
Manchester, MA **F1**/133
Manchester, MD **D1**/129
Manchester, ME **C4**/126
Manchester, MI **C5**/137
Manchester, NH **D6**/153
Manchester, NY **C3**/159
Manchester, OH **B4**/167
Manchester, OK **E1**/169
Manchester, PA **E3**/173
Manchester, SD **H2**/181
Manchester, TN **E2**/182
Manchester, VT **A3**/193
Manchester, WA **A4**/201
Manchester Center, VT **A3**/193
Mancos, CO **B4**/92
Mandan, ND **E3**/164
Mandaree, ND **C2**/164
Manderson, WY **E1**/206
Manderson-White Horse Creek, SD **C3**/181
Mandeville, AR **B4**/84
Mandeville, LA **E4**/122
Manfred, ND **F2**/164
Mangham, LA **D2**/122
Mango, FL **F4**/99
Mangum, OK **D3**/169
Manhasset, NY **C2**/161
Manhattan, IL **E2**/111
Manhattan, KS **G1**/119
Manhattan, MT **E4**/147
Manhattan, NV **C4**/151
Manhattan (bor.), NY **B2**/161
Manhattan Beach, CA **E5**/89
Manhattan Beach, CA **A5**/91
Manheim, PA **E3**/173
Manifest, LA **D3**/122
Manila, AR **E2**/84
Manila, UT **F2**/190
Manilla, IA **B3**/116
Manilla, IN **D3**/115
Manistee, MI **A3**/137
Manistee (riv.), MI **B3**/137
Manistique, MI **E4**/138
Manistique (lake), MI **F3**/138
Manito, IL **C3**/111
Manitou, KY **C3**/120
Manitou, ND **C1**/164
Manitou, OK **E3**/169
Manitou Beach, WA **A3**/201
Manitou Beach-Devils Lake, MI **C6**/137
Manitou Springs, CO **F3**/92
Manitowish, WI **C2**/205
Manitowoc, WI **F4**/205
Mankato, KS **E1**/119
Mankato, MN **E6**/140
Manley, NE **J3**/149
Manley Hot Springs, AK **G2**/79
Manlius, IL **C2**/111
Manlius, NY **E2**/159
Manly, IA **D1**/117
Manly, NC **F2**/163
Mannboro, VA **G3**/195
Mannford, OK **G1**/169
Manning, AR **C3**/84
Manning, IA **B3**/117
Manning, KS **C2**/118
Manning, ND **C2**/164
Manning, SC **D3**/179
Mannington, KY **C3**/120
Mannington, WV **C2**/203
Manns Choice, PA **C3**/172
Manns Harbor, NC **K2**/163
Mannsville, KY **E3**/121
Mannsville, NY **D2**/159
Mannsville, OK **G3**/169
Manokotak, AK **E4**/79
Manomet, MA **F3**/133
Manor, GA **D4**/102
Manor, PA **B3**/172
Manor, TX **J2**/187
Manorville, NY **H5**/159
Manquin, VA **G3**/195
Mansfield, AR **A2**/84
Mansfield, GA **C2**/102
Mansfield, IL **D3**/111
Mansfield, IN **B3**/115
Mansfield, LA **B2**/122
Mansfield, MA **E2**/133
Mansfield, MO **D4**/145
Mansfield, OH **C2**/167
Mansfield, PA **D2**/173
Mansfield, SD **G1**/181
Mansfield, TN **C1**/182
Mansfield, TX **B2**/188
Mansfield, WA **F2**/198
Mansfield (mt.), VT **B2**/193
Mansfield Center, CT **D2**/95
Mansfield Depot, CT **D2**/95
Mansfield Hollow (lake), CT **D2**/95
Manson, IA **C2**/117
Manson, WA **E2**/198
Mansura, LA **C3**/122
Mantachie, MS **D1**/143
Mantador, ND **J3**/165
Manteca, CA **D5**/86
Mantee, MS **C2**/143
Manteno, IL **E2**/111
Manteo, NC **K2**/163
Manter, KS **B3**/118
Manti, UT **D3**/190
Mantoloking, NJ **D3**/155
Manton, CA **D2**/86
Manton, MI **B3**/137
Manton, RI **C2**/177
Mantorville, MN **F6**/140
Mantua, AL **B2**/76
Mantua, OH **D1**/167
Mantua, UT **D1**/190
Manuelito, NM **B2**/157
Manvel, ND **H1**/165
Manville, NJ **C2**/155
Manville, WY **H3**/207
Many, LA **B3**/122
Many Farms, AZ **F1**/83
Manzanar (nat'l hist. site), CA **E2**/89
Manzanita, OR **B2**/170
Manzanita, WA **A3**/201
Manzanita, WA **A5**/201
Manzano, NM **D3**/157
Manzano (mts.), NM **D3**/157
Manzanola, CO **G3**/92
Mapes, ND **F2**/164
Maple, WI **B2**/205
Maple City, KS **G3**/119
Maple City, MI **B3**/137
Maple Falls, WA **C1**/198
Maple Grove, MI **B5**/137
Maple Grove, MN **E5**/140
Maple Heights, OH **D1**/167
Maple Hill, KS **G1**/119
Maple Hill, MI **B4**/137
Maple Hill, NC **H3**/163
Maple Lake, MN **D5**/140
Maple Rapids, MI **C4**/137
Maple Shade, NJ **C4**/155
Maple Shade, NJ **C2**/174
Maples, MO **E4**/145
Maplesville, AL **C3**/76
Mapleton, IA **B2**/116
Mapleton, KS **J2**/119
Mapleton, ME **D2**/126
Mapleton, MN **E7**/140
Mapleton, NC **H1**/163
Mapleton, ND **H3**/165
Mapleton, OR **B3**/170
Mapleton, UT **D2**/190
Mapleton Depot, PA **D3**/173
Mapleview, MN **F7**/140
Mapleville, MD **C1**/129
Mapleville, RI **B2**/177
Maplewood, MN **E5**/140
Maplewood, NH **C3**/153
Maplewood, NJ **D2**/155
Maplewood, WA **A5**/201
Maplewood, WI **F4**/205
Mappsville, VA **J3**/195
Maquoketa, IA **G2**/117
Maquam, VT **A2**/193
Maquon, IL **B3**/111
Mar-Mac, NC **G2**/163
Marais des Cygnes (riv.), KS **J2**/119
Marais des Cygnes (riv.), MO **B3**/145
Maramec, OK **G1**/169
Marana, AZ **D5**/83
Marathon, FL **G7**/99
Marathon, IA **C2**/117
Marathon, NY **D3**/159
Marathon, OH **A3**/167
Marathon, TX **C2**/186
Marathon City, WI **D4**/205
Marble, AR **B1**/84
Marble, CO **C2**/92
Marble, MN **E3**/140
Marble, NC **B2**/162
Marble (canyon), AZ **D1**/83
Marble Canyon, AZ **D1**/83
Marble City, OK **J2**/169
Marble Dale, CT **B2**/95
Marble Falls, TX **H2**/187
Marble Hill, MO **G4**/145
Marble Rock, IA **E2**/117
Marble Valley, AL **C2**/76
Marblehead, MA **F1**/133
Marblehead, OH **C1**/167
Marblemount, WA **D1**/198
Marbleton, WY **B3**/206
Marbury, AL **C3**/76
Marbury, MD **C2**/129
Marceline, MO **D2**/145
Marcell, MN **E3**/140
Marcella, AR **D2**/84
Marcella, NJ **D2**/155
Marcellus, MI **B5**/137
Marcellus, NY **D3**/159
Marco, FL **G6**/99
Marco, IN **B4**/115
Marco, LA **C3**/122
Marco (isl.), FL **G6**/99
Marcola, OR **C3**/170
Marcus, IA **B2**/116
Marcus, SD **C2**/181
Marcus, WA **G1**/199
Marcus Hook, PA **F4**/173
Marcy (mt.), NY **G1**/159
Mardela Springs, MD **E2**/129
Mare (isl.), CA **B1**/91
Marengo, IA **E3**/117
Marengo, IL **D1**/111
Marengo, IN **C4**/115
Marengo, OH **C2**/167
Marengo, WI **C2**/205
Marenisco, MI **B3**/138
Marfa, TX **B2**/186
Margaret, TX **H3**/185
Margaretville, NY **F3**/159
Margate, FL **H5**/99
Margate City, NJ **C5**/155
Margerum, AL **A1**/76
Margret, GA **B1**/102
Maria Stein, OH **A2**/167
Mariah Hill, IN **C4**/115
Marianna, AR **E3**/84
Marianna, FL **C1**/98
Marianna, MS **C1**/143
Mariano Lake, NM **B2**/158
Marias (riv.), MT **D1**/146
Mariaville, ME **D4**/126
Maribel, WI **F4**/205
Maricopa, AZ **C4**/83
Maricopa, CA **D3**/88
Maricopa (mts.), AZ **C4**/83
Marie, AR **E2**/84
Marienthal, KS **B2**/118
Marienville, PA **B2**/172
Marietta, GA **B2**/102
Marietta, IL **B3**/111
Marietta, IN **D3**/115
Marietta, MN **B5**/140
Marietta, MS **D1**/143
Marietta, NC **F3**/163
Marietta, OH **D3**/167
Marietta, OK **F4**/169
Marietta, PA **E3**/173
Marietta, SD **B3**/180
Marietta, TX **N4**/185
Marietta-Alderwood, WA **C1**/198
Marina, CA **B2**/88
Marina del Rey, CA **A5**/91
Marine, IL **C5**/111
Marine City, MI **E5**/137
Marine Corps War (nat'l mem.), VA **C2**/131
Marine on Saint Croix, MN **F5**/140
Marineland, FL **G2**/99
Maringouin, LA **D4**/122
Marion, AL **B3**/76
Marion, AR **E2**/84
Marion, CT **C2**/95
Marion, IA **F2**/117
Marion, IL **D6**/111
Marion, IN **D2**/115
Marion, KS **F2**/119
Marion, KY **B3**/120
Marion, LA **C2**/122
Marion, MA **F3**/133
Marion, MI **B3**/137
Marion, MS **D3**/143
Marion, MT **B1**/146
Marion, NC **C2**/162
Marion, ND **G3**/164
Marion, NY **C2**/159
Marion, OH **B2**/167
Marion, OR **C3**/170
Marion, PA **D4**/173
Marion, SC **E2**/179
Marion, SD **H3**/181
Marion, VA **C4**/194
Marion, WI **E4**/205
Marion (lake), SC **D3**/179
Marion Center, PA **B3**/172
Marion Junction, AL **B3**/76
Marionville, MO **C4**/145
Mariposa, CA **F5**/86
Marissa, IL **C5**/111
Mark Center, OH **A1**/167
Mark Twain (lake), MO **D2**/145
Marked Tree, AR **E2**/84
Markesan, WI **E5**/205
Markham, IL **C3**/112
Markham, WA **B3**/198
Markle, IN **D2**/115
Markleeville, CA **F4**/86
Marklesburg (James Creek), PA **C3**/173
Markleton, PA **B4**/172
Markleville, IN **D3**/115
Markleysburg, PA **B4**/172
Marks, MS **B1**/143
Marksville, LA **C3**/122
Markville, MN **F4**/140
Marland, OK **F1**/169
Marlboro, NJ **D3**/155
Marlboro, NY **G4**/159
Marlboro, VT **B4**/193
Marlborough, CT **D2**/95
Marlborough, MA **D2**/133
Marlborough, NH **B6**/153
Marlette, MI **D4**/137
Marlin, TX **L6**/185
Marlin (Krupp), WA **G2**/198
Marlinton, WV **C3**/203
Marlow, AL **B5**/76
Marlow, GA **E3**/102
Marlow, NH **B5**/153
Marlow, OK **F3**/169
Marlow Heights, MD **D3**/131
Marlton, NJ **C4**/155
Marmaduke, AR **E1**/84
Marmarth, ND **B3**/164
Marmet, WV **B3**/203
Marmora, NJ **C5**/155
Marne, IA **B3**/116
Marne, MI **B4**/137
Maroa, IL **D3**/111
Marquam, OR **C2**/170
Marquand, MO **F4**/145
Marquesas Keys (isls.), FL **F7**/99
Marquette, IA **F1**/117
Marquette, KS **F2**/119
Marquette, MI **D3**/138
Marquette, NE **G2**/149
Marquette Heights, IL **C3**/111
Marquez, TX **K1**/187
Marquez, TX **L6**/185
Marrero, LA **E5**/122
Marrero, LA **B3**/124
Marrowbone, KY **E4**/121
Mars, PA **A3**/172
Mars Hill, ME **E2**/126
Mars Hill, NC **C2**/162
Marse, WY **B3**/206
Marseilles, IL **D2**/111
Marseilles, OH **B2**/167
Marsh (isl.), LA **D5**/122
Marsh Hill, PA **E2**/173
Marshall, AR **C2**/84
Marshall, IL **E4**/111
Marshall, IN **B3**/115
Marshall, MI **C5**/137
Marshall, MN **C6**/140
Marshall, MO **C2**/145
Marshall, NC **C2**/162
Marshall, ND **C2**/164
Marshall, OH **B3**/167
Marshall, OK **F1**/169
Marshall, TX **N5**/185
Marshall, VA **G2**/195
Marshall, WI **D5**/205
Marshall (mt.), VA **F2**/195
Marshall Hall, MD **C2**/129
Marshallberg, NC **J3**/163
Marshalls Creek, PA **F2**/173
Marshallton, DE **A1**/96
Marshalltown, IA **E2**/117
Marshallville, GA **C3**/102
Marshallville, OH **D2**/167
Marshes Siding, KY **F4**/121
Marshfield, MA **F2**/133
Marshfield, ME **E4**/126
Marshfield, MO **D4**/145
Marshfield, VT **B2**/193
Marshfield, WI **C4**/205
Marshfield Hills, MA **F2**/133
Marshville, NC **E3**/162
Marsing, ID **B6**/108
Marsland, NE **B1**/148
Marston, MO **G5**/145
Marston, NC **F3**/163
Marstons Mills, MA **G3**/133
Mart, TX **L6**/185
Martel, OH **C2**/167
Martell, CA **E4**/86
Martell, WI **A4**/205
Martelle, IA **F2**/117
Martensdale, IA **D3**/117
Martha, KY **H2**/121
Martha, OK **D3**/169
Martha, TN **E1**/182
Martha Lake, WA **C2**/201
Martha Lake, WA **C2**/198
Martha's Vineyard (isl.), MA **F4**/133
Marthasville, MO **E3**/145
Marthaville, LA **B3**/122
Martin, GA **C1**/102
Martin, KY **H3**/121
Martin, LA **B2**/122
Martin, MI **B5**/137
Martin, ND **E2**/164
Martin, SD **D3**/181
Martin, TN **C1**/182
Martin (lake), AL **D3**/76
Martin Luther King, Jr., Memorial Library, DC **C4**/131
Martin Luther King, Jr. (nat'l hist. site), GA **B3**/105
Martin Van Buren (nat'l hist. site), NY **G3**/159
Martindale, TX **J3**/187
Martinez, CA **C4**/86
Martinez, CA **C1**/91
Martinez, GA **D2**/102
Martins Creek, PA **F3**/173
Martins Ferry, OH **E2**/167
Martinsburg, IA **E3**/117
Martinsburg, IN **C4**/115
Martinsburg, MO **E2**/145
Martinsburg, NE **J1**/149
Martinsburg, NY **E2**/159
Martinsburg, OH **C2**/167
Martinsburg, PA **C3**/173
Martinsburg, WV **F2**/203
Martinsdale, MT **F3**/147
Martinsville, IL **E4**/111
Martinsville, IN **C3**/115
Martinsville, MO **B1**/145
Martinsville, MS **B4**/143
Martinsville, OH **B3**/167
Martinsville, VA **E4**/194
Martinton, IL **E3**/111
Martinville, AR **C2**/84
Marty, SD **G4**/181
Marvel, AL **B2**/76
Marvel, CO **B4**/92
Marvell, AR **E3**/84
Marvin, SD **J1**/181
Marvindale, PA **C2**/172
Marvyn, AL **D3**/76
Marwood, PA **B3**/172
Mary Esther, FL **B1**/98
Mary McLeod Bethune Council House (nat'l hist. site), DC **D2**/131
Marydel, MD **E1**/129
Marydell, MS **C3**/143
Maryhill, WA **E4**/198
Maryland, NY **F3**/159
Maryland City, MD **D1**/129
Maryland Line, MD **D1**/129
Maryneal, TX **G5**/184
Marysvale, UT **C4**/190
Marysville, CA **D3**/86
Marysville, KS **G1**/119
Marysville, MI **E5**/137
Marysville, MT **D3**/146
Marysville, OH **B2**/167
Marysville, PA **E3**/173
Marysville, WA **C1**/198
Maryville, MO **B1**/145
Maryville, TN **H2**/183
Masardis, ME **D2**/126
Masaryktown, FL **F3**/99
Mascot, TN **H1**/183
Mascotte, FL **G3**/99
Mascoutah, IL **C5**/111
Mashpee, MA **G3**/133
Mashulaville, MS **D2**/143
Maskell, NE **J1**/149
Mason, IL **D5**/111
Mason, KY **F2**/121
Mason, MI **C5**/137
Mason, NH **C6**/153
Mason, NV **A4**/151
Mason, OH **A3**/167
Mason, OK **G2**/169
Mason, TN **B2**/182
Mason, TX **G2**/187
Mason, WI **B2**/205
Mason, WV **A2**/203
Mason & Dixon Line **D1**/129
Mason City, IA **D1**/117
Mason City, IL **C3**/111
Mason City, NE **F2**/149
Mason Hall, TN **B1**/182
Masonboro, NC **H3**/163
Masontown, PA **B4**/172
Masontown, WV **D2**/203
Masonville, CO **E1**/92
Masonville, IA **F2**/117
Masonville, KY **C3**/120
Masonville, NY **E3**/159
Mass City, MI **B3**/138
Massac, KY **B3**/120
Massachusetts (bay), MA **F2**/133
Massachusetts (bay), MA **C2**/134
Massapequa, NY **G5**/159
Massbach, IL **B1**/111
Massena, IA **C3**/117
Massena, NY **F1**/159
Massey, MD **E1**/129
Massillon, OH **D2**/167
Mastic, NY **H5**/159
Mastic Beach, NY **H5**/159
Masury, OH **E1**/167
Matador, TX **G3**/184
Matagorda (bay), TX **K4**/187
Matagorda (isl.), TX **K4**/187
Matamoras, PA **G2**/173
Matawan, NJ **D3**/155
Matchwood, MI **B3**/138
Matewan, WV **A4**/203
Matfield Green, KS **G2**/119
Mather, WI **C4**/205
Matherville, IL **B2**/111
Matheson, CO **G2**/92
Mathews, LA **E5**/122
Mathews, VA **H3**/195
Mathiston, MS **C2**/143
Matinicus (isl.), ME **D5**/126
Matlock, WA **B2**/198
Mattamuskeet (lake), NC **J2**/163
Mattapoisett, MA **F3**/133
Mattawa, WA **F3**/198
Mattawamkeag, ME **D3**/126
Mattawan, MI **B5**/137
Mattawana, PA **D3**/173
Matteson, IL **E2**/111
Matthews, IN **D2**/115
Matthews, MO **G5**/145
Matthews, NC **E2**/162
Mattituck, NY **H5**/159
Mattoon, IL **D4**/111
Mattoon, WI **D3**/205
Mattson, MS **B1**/143
Matunuck, RI **B4**/177
Mattydale, NY **D2**/159
Maud, KY **E3**/121
Maud, MS **B1**/143
Maud, OH **A3**/167
Maud, OK **G2**/169
Maud, TX **N4**/185
Maudlow, MT **E3**/147
Maugansville, MD **C1**/129
Maui (isl.), HI **E3**/107
Maui (isl.), HI **Q7**/10
Mauk, GA **B3**/102
Mauldin, SC **B2**/179
Maumee, OH **B1**/167
Maumee (riv.), OH **B1**/167
Maumelle, AR **C3**/84
Mauna Kea (peak), HI **F4**/107
Maunawili, HI **D2**/107
Maunie, IL **D5**/111
Maurepas, LA **E4**/122
Maurepas (lake), LA **E4**/122
Maurice, IA **A2**/116
Maurice, LA **C4**/122
Maurice (riv.), NJ **B5**/155
Mauricetown, NJ **C5**/155
Mauriceville, TX **N2**/187
Maurine, SD **C1**/181
Maury City, TN **B2**/182
Mauston, WI **C5**/205
Maverick, AZ **F4**/83
Max, MN **D3**/140
Max, ND **D2**/164
Max, NE **D3**/148
Max Meadows, VA **D4**/194
Maxbass, ND **D1**/164
Maxeys, GA **C2**/102
Maxie, LA **C4**/122
Maxie, MS **C5**/143
Maxinkuckee, IN **C1**/115
Maxton, NC **F3**/163
Maxville, MT **C3**/146
Maxwell, CA **C3**/86
Maxwell, IA **D3**/117
Maxwell, IN **D3**/115
Maxwell, NE **E2**/149
Maxwell, NM **F1**/157
Maxwell, TN **E2**/182
Maxwelton, WA **A1**/201
May, ID **E5**/108
May, OK **D1**/168
May, TX **J6**/185
Maybee, MI **D5**/137
Maybell, CO **B1**/92
Mayberry, MD **C1**/129
Maybrook, NY **F4**/159
Mayburg, PA **B2**/172
Mayer, AZ **C3**/83
Mayersville, MS **A3**/143
Mayesville, SC **D3**/179
Mayetta, KS **H1**/119
Mayetta, NJ **D4**/155
Mayfield, GA **D2**/102
Mayfield, KS **F3**/119
Mayfield, KY **B4**/120
Mayfield, MI **B3**/137
Mayfield, NY **F2**/159
Mayfield, OK **D2**/168
Mayfield, PA **F2**/173
Mayfield, UT **D3**/190
Mayfield Heights, OH **D1**/167
Mayflower, AR **C3**/84
Mayflower Village, CA **C4**/91

For key to abbreviations, see page 217.

Mayger—Millston 239

Mayger, OR **B1**/170
Mayhew, MS **D2**/143
Mayhill, NM **E5**/157
Mayland, TN **F1**/183
Maylene, AL **C2**/76
Mayna, LA **D3**/122
Maynard, AR **E1**/84
Maynard, IA **F2**/117
Maynard, MA **E2**/133
Maynard, MN **C6**/140
Maynardville, TN **H1**/183
Mayo, FL **E1**/99
Mayo, MD **D2**/129
Mayo, SC **C1**/179
Mayodan, NC **F1**/163
Maypearl, TX **K5**/185
Mays, IN **D3**/115
Mays Landing, NJ **C5**/155
Mays Lick, KY **G2**/121
Maysel, WV **B3**/203
Maysville, GA **C1**/102
Maysville, IA **G3**/117
Maysville, KY **G2**/121
Maysville, MO **B2**/145
Maysville, NC **H3**/163
Maysville, OK **F3**/169
Maytown, KY **G3**/121
Maytown, PA **E3**/173
Mayview, MO **C2**/145
Mayville, MI **D4**/137
Mayville, ND **H2**/165
Mayville, NY **A3**/158
Mayville, OR **E2**/170
Mayville, WI **E5**/205
Maywood, CA **B5**/91
Maywood, IL **B2**/112
Maywood, MO **E2**/145
Maywood, NE **E3**/149
Maywood, NJ **B1**/161
Maza, ND **F1**/164
Mazama, WA **E1**/198
Mazatzal (mts.), AZ **D3**/83
Mazeppa, MN **F6**/140
Mazie, OK **H1**/169
Mazomanie, WI **D5**/205
Mazon, IL **D2**/111
McAdams, MS **C2**/143
McAdoo, PA **F3**/173
McAdoo, TX **F4**/184
McAfee, NJ **C1**/155
McAlester, OK **H3**/169
McAlister, NM **G3**/157
McAlisterville, PA **D3**/173
McAllister, MT **E4**/147
McAlpin, FL **F1**/99
McAndrews, KY **H3**/121
McArthur, CA **D1**/86
McArthur, OH **C3**/167
McAvid, FL **A1**/98
McBain, MI **B3**/137
McBaine, MO **D3**/145
McBean, GA **E2**/102
McBee, SC **D2**/179
McBride, MI **B4**/137
McBride, MO **G4**/145
McBride, MS **B4**/143
McBride, OK **G4**/169
McCabe, MT **M1**/147
McCall, ID **B5**/108
McCall, LA **D4**/122
McCall Creek, MS **B4**/143
McCalla, AL **B2**/76
McCallsburg, IA **D2**/117
McCamey, TX **D1**/186
McCamey, TX **E6**/184
McCammon, ID **F7**/108
McCanna, ND **H1**/165
McCarran (int'l arpt.), NV **E6**/151
McCarthy, AK **J3**/79
McCaskill, AR **B4**/84
McCaulley, TX **G5**/184
McCausland, IA **G3**/117
McCaysville, GA **B1**/102
McClave, CO **H3**/92
McCleary, WA **B2**/198
McClelland, AR **D2**/84
McClellanville, SC **E3**/179
McCloud, CA **C1**/86
McCloud, TN **J1**/183
McClure, IL **C6**/111
McClure, OH **B1**/167
McClure, PA **D3**/173
McClure, VA **B3**/194
McClusky, ND **E2**/164
McColl, SC **E2**/179
McComb, MS **B4**/143
McComb, OH **B1**/167
McConaughy (res.), NE **D2**/148
McCondy, MS **D2**/143
McConnell, TN **C1**/182
McConnells, SC **C2**/179
McConnellsburg, PA **D4**/173
McConnellsville, NY **E2**/159
McConnelsville, OH **D3**/167
McCook, IL **B2**/112
McCook, NE **E3**/149
McCool, MS **C2**/143
McCool Junction, NE **H3**/149
McCordsville, IN **D3**/115
McCorkle, WV **B3**/203
McCormick, SC **B3**/179
McCoy, VA **D3**/194
McCracken, KS **D2**/118
McCrea, PA **D3**/173
McCrory, AR **D2**/84
McCullough, AL **B4**/76
McCullough (range), NV **E7**/151
McCune, KS **H3**/119
McCurtain, OK **J2**/169
McCutchenville, OH **B2**/167
McDade, TX **J2**/187
McDaniel, MD **D2**/129
McDaniels, KY **D3**/120
McDermitt, NV **C1**/151
McDermott, OH **B4**/167
McDonald, KS **B1**/118
McDonald, NC **F3**/163
McDonald, NM **G4**/157
McDonald, OH **E1**/167
McDonald, PA **A3**/172
McDonald, TN **G2**/183
McDonough, GA **B2**/102
McDonough, NY **E3**/159
McDougal, AR **E1**/84
McDowell, KY **H3**/121
McDowell, VA **E2**/195
McDowell, WV **B4**/203
McElhattan, PA **D2**/173
McEwen, TN **D1**/182
McFadden, WY **F4**/206
McFall, MO **B1**/145
McFarlan, NC **F3**/163
McFarland, CA **D3**/88
McFarland, KS **G1**/119
McFarland, MI **D3**/138
McFarland, WI **D5**/205
McGaffey, NM **B2**/157
McGaheysville, VA **F2**/195
McGehee, AR **D4**/84
McGill, NV **F3**/151
McGovern, PA **A3**/172
McGrath, AK **F3**/79
McGrath, MN **E4**/140
McGraw, NY **D3**/159
McGregor, IA **F1**/117
McGregor, MN **E4**/140
McGregor, ND **C1**/164
McGregor, TX **K6**/185
McGrew, NE **B2**/148
McGuffey, OH **B2**/167
McHenry, IL **D1**/111
McHenry, KY **D3**/120
McHenry, MS **C5**/143
McHenry, ND **G2**/164
McIntire, IA **E1**/117
McIntosh, AL **A4**/76
McIntosh, FL **F2**/99
McIntosh, GA **E4**/102
McIntosh, MN **C3**/140
McIntosh, NM **D3**/157
McIntosh, SD **D1**/181
McIntyre, GA **C3**/102
McIvor, MI **D3**/137
McKamie, AR **B4**/84
McKean, PA **A2**/172
McKee, KY **G3**/121
McKee City, NJ **C5**/155
McKees Rocks, PA **A3**/172
McKeesport, PA **B3**/172
McKenna, WA **C3**/198
McKenney, VA **G4**/195
McKenzie, AL **C4**/76
McKenzie, ND **E3**/164
McKenzie, TN **C1**/182
McKenzie (riv.), OR **C3**/170
McKinley, AL **B3**/76
McKinley, MN **F3**/140
McKinley, WY **G3**/206
McKinley (mt.), AK **G3**/79
McKinleyville, CA **A2**/86
McKinney, KY **F3**/121
McKinney, TX **L4**/185
McKinnon, GA **E4**/102
McKinnon, TN **D1**/182
McKinnon, WY **C4**/206
McKittrick, CA **D3**/88
McLain, MS **D4**/143
McLane, PA **A2**/172
McLaughlin, SD **E1**/181
McLaurin, MS **C4**/143
McLean, IL **C3**/111
McLean, NE **H1**/149
McLean, NY **D3**/159
McLean, TX **G2**/184
McLean, VA **B2**/131
McLean, VA **G2**/195
McLeansboro, IL **D5**/111
McLemoresville, TN **C2**/182
McLeod, MT **F4**/147
McLoud, OK **F2**/169
McLoughlin House (nat'l hist. site), OR **C2**/170
McLouth, KS **H1**/119
McMechen, WV **C2**/203
McMillan, MI **F3**/138
McMillan, OK **G3**/169
McMinnville, OR **B2**/170
McMinnville, TN **F2**/183
McMullen, AL **A2**/76
McMurray, PA **A3**/172
McMurray, WA **C1**/198
McNab, AR **B4**/84
McNabb, IL **C2**/111
Mcnair, MS **A4**/143
McNairy, TN **C2**/182
McNary, AZ **F3**/83
McNary, LA **C4**/122
McNary, TX **B6**/184
McNaughton, WI **D3**/205
McNeal, AZ **F6**/83
McNeil, AR **B4**/84
McNeill, MS **C5**/143
McPherson, KS **F2**/119
McQueeney, TX **H3**/187
McRae, AR **D2**/84
McRae, GA **D3**/102
McRoberts, KY **H3**/121
McShan, AL **A2**/76
McSherrystown, PA **D4**/173
McVeigh, KY **H3**/121
McVeytown, PA **D3**/173
McVille, ND **G2**/164
McWilliams, AL **B4**/76
Meacham, OR **G2**/170
Mead, CO **F1**/92
Mead, NE **J2**/149
Mead, OK **G4**/169
Mead (lake) **D3**/10
Meade, KS **C3**/118
Meadow, SD **C1**/181
Meadow, TX **E4**/184
Meadow, UT **C4**/190
Meadow Grove, NE **H1**/149
Meadow Valley, CA **D3**/86
Meadow Valley (mts.), NV **F6**/151
Meadow Vista, CA **D3**/86
Meadowdale, WA **B2**/201
Meadowlands, MN **F3**/140
Meadows, ID **B5**/108
Meadows, NH **D3**/153
Meadville, MO **C2**/145
Meadville, MS **B4**/143
Meadville, PA **A2**/172
Means, KY **G3**/121
Meansville, GA **B2**/102
Mears, MI **A4**/137
Meauwataka, MI **B3**/137
Mebane, NC **F1**/163
Mecca, CA **G5**/89
Mecca, IN **B3**/115
Mechanic Falls, ME **B4**/126
Mechanicsburg, MS **B3**/143
Mechanicsburg, OH **B2**/167
Mechanicsburg, PA **D3**/173
Mechanicsville, CT **E2**/95
Mechanicsville, IA **F3**/117
Mechanicsville, MD **D2**/129
Mechanicsville, PA **E3**/173
Mechanicsville, VA **G3**/195
Mechanicville, NY **G3**/159
Mecklenburg, NY **D3**/159
Mecosta, MI **B4**/137
Medaryville, IN **C1**/115
Medfield, MA **E2**/133
Medford, MA **E2**/133
Medford, MA **B1**/134
Medford, ME **D3**/126
Medford, MN **E6**/140
Medford, NY **G5**/159
Medford, OK **F1**/169
Medford, OR **C5**/170
Medford, WI **C3**/205
Medford Lakes, NJ **C4**/155
Media, IL **B3**/111
Media, PA **F4**/173
Media, PA **A3**/174
Mediapolis, IA **F3**/117
Medical Lake, WA **H2**/199
Medical Springs, OR **H2**/171
Medicine Bow, WY **F4**/206
Medicine Bow (mts.), WY **F4**/206
Medicine Hot Springs, MT **B4**/146
Medicine Lake, MT **M1**/147
Medicine Lodge, KS **E3**/119
Medicine Mound, TX **H3**/185
Medicine Park, OK **E3**/169
Medina, ND **F3**/164
Medina, NY **B2**/158
Medina, OH **D1**/167
Medina, TN **C2**/182
Medina, TX **G3**/187
Medina, WA **C3**/201
Medina (riv.), TX **G5**/10
Medinah, IL **A2**/112
Medix Run, PA **C2**/173
Medon, TN **C2**/182
Medora, IL **B4**/111
Medora, IN **C4**/115
Medora, KS **F2**/119
Medora, ND **B3**/164
Medway, MA **E2**/133
Medway, ME **D3**/126
Meeker, CO **C1**/92
Meeker, LA **C3**/122
Meeker, OH **B2**/167
Meeker, OK **G2**/169
Meeks, GA **D3**/102
Meers, OK **E3**/169
Meeteetse, WY **D1**/206
Megargel, AL **B4**/76
Megargel, TX **J4**/185
Meggett, SC **D4**/179
Mehan, OK **G1**/169
Meherrin, VA **F3**/195
Meherrin (riv.), VA **G4**/195
Mehoopany, PA **E2**/173
Meigs, GA **B4**/102
Meiners Oaks, CA **D4**/88
Meire Grove, MN **D5**/140
Mekinock, ND **H1**/165
Mekoryuk, AK **C3**/79
Melba, ID **B6**/108
Melber, KY **B4**/120
Melbern, OH **A1**/167
Melbeta, NE **B2**/148
Melbourne, AR **D1**/84
Melbourne, FL **H3**/99
Melbourne, IA **D3**/117
Melbourne, MO **C1**/145
Melbourne, WA **B3**/198
Melcher-Dallas, IA **D3**/117
Melder, LA **C3**/122
Meldrim, GA **E3**/102
Melfa, VA **J3**/195
Melhville, MO **F3**/145
Melitota, MD **D1**/129
Mellen, WI **C2**/205
Mellette, SD **G1**/181
Mellott, IN **B2**/115
Mellwood, AR **E3**/84
Melmore, OH **B1**/167
Melrose, FL **F2**/99
Melrose, IA **D4**/117
Melrose, LA **C3**/122
Melrose, MA **E2**/133
Melrose, MA **B1**/134
Melrose, MN **D5**/140
Melrose, MT **D4**/146
Melrose, NM **G3**/157
Melrose, OH **A1**/167
Melrose, OR **B4**/170
Melrose, WI **C4**/205
Melrose Park, IL **B2**/112
Melrude, MN **F3**/140
Melstone, MT **J3**/147
Melvern, KS **H2**/119
Melville, LA **D4**/122
Melville, MT **G3**/147
Melville, ND **F2**/164
Melville, NY **G5**/159
Melville, RI **C3**/177
Melville Landing, VT **A2**/194
Melvin, AL **A4**/76
Melvin, IA **B1**/116
Melvin, IL **D3**/111
Melvin, MI **E4**/137
Melvin, TX **H6**/185
Melvin, TX **G1**/187
Melvin Mills, NH **C5**/153
Melvin Village, NH **D4**/153
Melvina, WI **C5**/205
Melvindale, MI **D5**/137
Melvindale, MI **A3**/139
Memphis, AL **A2**/76
Memphis, IN **D4**/115
Memphis, MI **E5**/137
Memphis, MO **D1**/145
Memphis, MS **B1**/143
Memphis, NE **J2**/149
Memphis, TN **A2**/182
Memphis, TX **G3**/184
Memphis (int'l arpt.), TN **B2**/182
Memphremagog (lake), VT **B2**/193
Mena, AR **A3**/84
Menahga, MN **C4**/140
Menan, ID **G6**/108
Menands, NY **G3**/159
Menard, TX **G2**/187
Menasha, WI **E4**/205
Mendenhall, MS **C4**/143
Mendenhall (glacier), AK **C2**/81
Mendes, GA **E4**/102
Mendham, NJ **C2**/155
Mendocino, CA **B3**/86
Mendon, IL **A3**/111
Mendon, MA **D2**/133
Mendon, MI **B5**/137
Mendon, MO **C2**/145
Mendon, NY **C3**/159
Mendon, OH **A2**/167
Mendon, UT **D1**/190
Mendon, VT **B3**/193
Mendota, CA **C2**/88
Mendota, IL **C2**/111
Mendota, VA **B4**/194
Menemsha, MA **F4**/133
Menifee, AR **C2**/84
Menlo, GA **A1**/102
Menlo, IA **C3**/117
Menlo, KS **C1**/118
Menlo, WA **B3**/198
Menlo Park, CA **C5**/86
Menno, SD **H3**/181
Meno, OK **E1**/169
Menominee, IL **B1**/111
Menominee, MI **D4**/138
Menominee (riv.), WI **F3**/205
Menomonee Falls, WI **E5**/205
Menomonie, WI **B4**/205
Mentasta Lake, AK **J3**/79
Mentmore, NM **B2**/157
Mentone, AL **D1**/76
Mentone, IN **C1**/115
Mentone, TX **D6**/184
Mentor, KS **F2**/119
Mentor, KY **F2**/121
Mentor, MN **B3**/140
Mentor, OH **D1**/167
Mentor-on-the-Lake, OH **D1**/167
Mequon, WI **F5**/205
Mer Rouge, LA **D2**/122
Meramec (riv.), MO **F3**/145
Merced, CA **E5**/86
Merced (riv.), CA **E5**/86
Mercer, ME **C4**/126
Mercer, MO **C1**/145
Mercer, ND **E2**/164
Mercer, OH **A2**/167
Mercer, PA **A2**/172
Mercer, TN **B2**/182
Mercer (isl.), WA **B4**/201
Mercer Island, WA **C2**/198
Mercer Island, WA **C4**/201
Mercersburg, PA **D4**/173
Mercerville-Hamilton Square, NJ **C3**/155
Merchantville, NJ **B4**/155
Merchantville, NJ **C3**/174
Mercier, KS **H1**/119
Mercury, NV **E6**/151
Mercury, TX **H6**/185
Meredith, CO **D2**/92
Meredith, NH **C4**/153
Meredith (lake), TX **F2**/184
Meredith Center, NH **C4**/153
Meredosia, IL **B4**/111
Meriden, CT **C2**/95
Meriden, IA **B2**/116
Meriden, KS **H1**/119
Meriden, NH **B4**/153
Meriden, WY **H4**/207
Meridian, GA **E4**/102
Meridian, ID **B6**/108
Meridian, MS **D3**/143
Meridian, NY **D2**/159
Meridian, OK **F2**/169
Meridian, PA **B3**/172
Meridian, TX **K6**185
Meridian Station, MS **D3**/143
Meridianville, AL **C1**/76
Merigold, MS **B2**/143
Merino, CO **G1**/92
Merkel, TX **G5**/184
Merlin, OR **B5**/170
Mermentau, LA **C4**/122
Merna, NE **F2**/149
Merna, WY **B3**/206
Merom, IN **B3**/115
Merriam, KS **J1**/119
Merrick, NY **G5**/159
Merricourt, ND **G3**/164
Merrifield, ND **H2**/165
Merrill, IA **A2**/116
Merrill, MI **C4**/137
Merrill, MS **D5**/143
Merrill, NY **G1**/159
Merrill, OR **D5**/170
Merrill, WI **D3**/205
Merrillan, WI **C4**/205
Merrillville, IN **B1**/115
Merrimac, KY **E3**/121
Merrimac, MA **F1**/133
Merrimac, WI **D5**/205
Merrimack, NH **D6**/153
Merrimack (riv.), MA **E1**/133
Merrimack (riv.), NH **C5**/153
Merriman, NE **D1**/148
Merrimon, NC **J3**/163
Merrionette Park, IL **C3**/112
Merritt, MI **C3**/137
Merritt, WA **E2**/198
Merritt (isl.), FL **H3**/99
Merritt Island, FL **H3**/99
Merriweather, MI **B3**/138
Merrow, CT **D2**/95
Merry Hill, NC **J1**/163
Merry Oaks, NC **F2**/163
Merryville, LA **B4**/122
Mershon, GA **D4**/102
Mertens, TX **L5**/185
Merton, WI **E5**/205
Mertzon, TX **G6**/184
Mertzon, TX **F1**/186
Merwin, MO **B3**/145
Mesa, AZ **D4**/83
Mesa, CO **B2**/92
Mesa, ID **B5**/108
Mesa, WA **F3**/198
Mesa Verde (nat'l park), CO **B4**/92
Mesabi (range), MN **E3**/140
Mescalero, NM **E4**/157
Mesena, GA **D2**/102
Meservey, IA **D2**/117
Meshoppen, PA **E2**/173
Mesic, NC **J2**/163
Mesick, MI **B3**/137
Mesilla, NM **D5**/157
Mesita, CO **E4**/92
Mesita, NM **C2**/157
Mesquite, NM **D5**/157
Mesquite, NV **F6**/151
Mesquite, TX **L5**/185
Mesquite, TX **E2**/188
Meta, MO **D3**/145
Metairie, LA **E5**/122
Metairie, LA **B2**/124
Metaline, WA **H1**/199
Metaline Falls, WA **H1**/199
Metamora, IL **C3**/111
Metamora, IN **D3**/115
Metamora, MI **D5**/137
Metamora, OH **B1**/167
Metcalfe, MS **A2**/143
Metea, IN **C2**/115
Methow, WA **E1**/198
Methuen, MA **E1**/133
Metlakatla, AK **D3**/81
Metolius, OR **D3**/170
Metropolis, IL **D6**/111
Metropolitan, MI **D4**/138
Metropolitan Oakland (int'l arpt.), CA **B3**/91
Metropolitan Oakland (int'l arpt.), CA **C5**/86
Metter, GA **D3**/102
Mettler, CA **E3**/89
Metuchen, NJ **D2**/155
Metz, IN **E1**/115
Metz, MI **D2**/137
Metz, MI **H4**/138
Metz, MO **B4**/145
Mexia, AL **B4**/76
Mexia, TX **L6**/185
Mexican Hat, UT **F5**/190
Mexican Springs, NM **B2**/157
Mexico, IN **C2**/115
Mexico, KY **B3**/120
Mexico, ME **B4**/126
Mexico, MO **E2**/145
Mexico, NY **D2**/159
Mexico, PA **D3**/173
Mexico (gulf), NAmer. **J4**/11
Mexico Beach, FL **C2**/98
Meyers Chuck, AK **C3**/81
Meyersdale, PA **B4**/172
Mi-Wuk Village, CA **E4**/86
Miami, AZ **E4**/83
Miami, FL **H6**/99
Miami, FL **B3**/101
Miami, IN **C2**/115
Miami, MO **C2**/145
Miami, NM **F1**/157
Miami, OK **J1**/169
Miami, TX **G2**/184
Miami (int'l arpt.), FL **H6**/99
Miami (int'l arpt.), FL **A3**/101
Miami Beach, FL **H6**/99
Miami Beach, FL **C3**/101
Miami Shores, FL **H6**/99
Miami Shores, FL **B2**/101
Miami Springs, FL **A3**/101
Miamisburg, OH **A3**/167
Mica, WA **H2**/199
Micanopy, FL **F2**/99
Micawber, OK **G2**/169
Micco, FL **H4**/99
Miccosukee, FL **D1**/99
Michiana, MI **A6**/137
Michiana Shores, IN **C1**/115
Michie, TN **C2**/182
Michigamme, MI **C3**/138
Michigan, ND **G1**/164
Michigan (lake) **J2**/11
Michigan Center, MI **C5**/137
Michigan City, IN **C1**/115
Michigan City, MS **C1**/143
Michigantown, IN **C2**/115
Michillinda, MI **A4**/137
Mickleton, NJ **B4**/155
Micro, NC **G2**/163
Midas, NV **D1**/151
Middle Bass, OH **C1**/167
Middle Falls, NY **G2**/159
Middle Gate, NV **B3**/152
Middle Granville, NY **G2**/159
Middle Haddam, CT **C2**/95
Middle Hope, NY **F4**/159
Middle Inlet, WI **F3**/205
Middle Loup (riv.), NE **E2**/149
Middle Point, OH **A2**/167
Middle River, MD **D1**/129
Middle River, MN **B2**/140
Middle Valley, NJ **C2**/155
Middleboro, MA **F3**/133
Middlebourne, WV **C2**/203
Middleburg, FL **G1**/99
Middleburg, KY **F3**/121
Middleburg, NC **G1**/163
Middleburg, OH **B2**/167
Middleburg, PA **D3**/173
Middleburg, VA **G2**/195
Middleburg Heights, OH **D1**/167
Middleburgh, NY **F3**/159
Middlebury, CT **B2**/95
Middlebury, IN **D1**/115
Middlebury, VT **A2**/193
Middlebury Center, PA **D2**/173
Middlefield, CT **C2**/95
Middlefield, MA **A2**/132
Middlefield, OH **D1**/167
Middleford, DE **A3**/96
Middleport, NY **B2**/158
Middleport, OH **C3**/167
Middlesboro, KY **G4**/121
Middlesex, NC **G2**/163
Middlesex, NJ **D2**/155
Middlesex, NY **C3**/159
Middlesex, VT **B2**/193
Middleton, ID **B6**/108
Middleton, MA **E1**/133
Middleton, TN **C2**/182
Middleton, WI **D5**/205
Middletown, CA **C4**/86
Middletown, CT **C2**/95
Middletown, DE **A2**/96
Middletown, IA **F4**/117
Middletown, IL **C3**/111
Middletown, IN **D2**/115
Middletown, KY **E2**/121
Middletown, MD **C1**/129
Middletown, MO **E2**/145
Middletown, NC **J2**/163
Middletown, NJ **D3**/155
Middletown, NY **F4**/159
Middletown, OH **A3**/167
Middletown, PA **E3**/173
Middletown, RI **C3**/177
Middletown, VA **F1**/195
Middletown Springs, VT **A3**/193
Middleville, MI **B5**/137
Middleville, NJ **C1**/155
Middleville, NY **F2**/159
Midkiff, WV **A3**/203
Midland, AR **A2**/84
Midland, IN **B3**/115
Midland, LA **C4**/122
Midland, MD **B1**/128
Midland, MI **C4**/137
Midland, NC **E2**/162
Midland, OH **B3**/167
Midland, OR **D5**/170
Midland, PA **A3**/172
Midland, SD **D2**/181
Midland, TX **E6**/184
Midland, VA **G2**/195
Midland, WA **B6**/201
Midland City, AL **D4**/76
Midland Park, NJ **A1**/161
Midlothian, IL **B3**/112
Midlothian, TX **L5**/185
Midlothian, VA **G3**/195
Midnight, MS **B2**/143
Midvale, ID **B5**/108
Midvale, OH **D2**/167
Midvale Corner, WA **B1**/201
Midville, GA **D3**/102
Midway, AL **D3**/76
Midway, DE **B3**/96
Midway, FL **D1**/99
Midway, GA **E4**/102
Midway, KY **F2**/121
Midway, LA **C3**/122
Midway, MS **B3**/143
Midway, PA **D4**/173
Midway, TX **M6**/185
Midway, TX **L1**/187
Midway, UT **D2**/190
Midwest, WY **F2**/206
Midwest City, OK **F2**/169
Mier, IN **D2**/115
Miesville, MN **F6**/140
Mifflin, OH **C2**/167
Mifflin, PA **D3**/173
Mifflinburg, PA **D3**/173
Mifflintown, PA **D3**/173
Mifflinville (Creasy), PA **E2**/173
Miflin, AL **B5**/76
Mikado, MI **D3**/137
Mikana, WI **B3**/205
Mikkalo, OR **E2**/170
Milaca, MN **E5**/140
Milam, TX **P6**/185
Milan, GA **C3**/102
Milan, IL **B2**/111
Milan, IN **D3**/115
Milan, KS **F3**/119
Milan, MI **D5**/137
Milan, MN **C5**/140
Milan, MO **C1**/145
Milan, NH **D2**/153
Milan, NM **C2**/157
Milan, OH **C1**/167
Milan, TN **C2**/182
Milan, WA **H2**/199
Milan, WI **C4**/205
Milano, TX **K2**/187
Milanville, PA **F2**/173
Milbank, SD **J1**/181
Milberger, KS **E2**/119
Milbridge, ME **E4**/126
Milburn, KY **B4**/120
Milburn, NE **F2**/149
Milburn, OK **G3**/169
Mildred, KS **H2**/119
Mildred, MT **M3**/147
Mildred, PA **E2**/173
Miles, IA **G2**/117
Miles, TX **G6**/184
Miles City, MT **L3**/147
Milesburg, PA **D3**/173
Mileston, MS **B2**/143
Milesville, SD **D2**/181
Miley, SC **C4**/179
Milfay, OK **G2**/169
Milford, CA **E2**/86
Milford, CT **B3**/95
Milford, DE **B3**/96
Milford, GA **B4**/102
Milford, IA **B1**/116
Milford, IL **E3**/111
Milford, IN **D1**/115
Milford, KS **F1**/119
Milford, KY **F2**/121
Milford, MA **D2**/133
Milford, ME **D4**/126
Milford, MI **D5**/137
Milford, MO **B4**/145
Milford, NE **H3**/149
Milford, NH **C6**/153
Milford, NJ **B2**/155
Milford, NY **F3**/159
Milford, OH **A3**/167
Milford, PA **G2**/173
Milford, TX **L5**/185
Milford, UT **B4**/190
Milford (lake), KS **F1**/119
Milford Center, OH **B2**/167
Milford Crossroads, DE **A1**/96
Mililani Town, HI **C2**/107
Milk (riv.), U.S., Can. **D1**/10
Mill City, NV **B2**/151
Mill City, OR **C3**/170
Mill Creek, IN **C1**/115
Mill Creek, OK **G3**/169
Mill Creek, PA **D3**/173
Mill Creek, WA **C2**/198
Mill Creek, WA **C2**/201
Mill Creek, WV **D3**/203
Mill Grove, MO **C1**/145
Mill Hall, PA **D2**/173
Mill Iron, MT **M4**/147
Mill River, MA **A2**/132
Mill Run, PA **B4**/172
Mill Shoals, IL **D5**/111
Mill Spring, MO **F4**/145
Mill Springs, KY **F4**/121
Mill Valley, CA **C5**/86
Mill Valley, CA **A2**/91
Mill Village, NH **B5**/154
Mill Village, PA **B2**/172
Mill Village, VT **B2**/193
Mill Village, VT **B3**/193
Milladore, WI **D4**/205
Millarton, ND **G3**/164
Millboro, SD **F3**/181
Millboro, VA **E3**/194
Millbrae, CA **C5**/86
Millbrae, CA **B3**/91
Millbrook, AL **C3**/76
Millbrook, MI **B4**/137
Millbrook, NC **G2**/163
Millbrook, NY **G4**/159
Millburg, MI **A5**/137
Millburn, NJ **D2**/155
Millburne, WY **B4**/206
Millbury, MA **D2**/133
Millbury, OH **B1**/167
Millecoquins, MI **B1**/137
Millcreek, UT **D2**/190
Milldale, CT **C2**/95
Mille Lacs (lake), MN **E5**/140
Milledgeville, GA **C2**/102
Milledgeville, IL **C2**/111
Milledgeville, OH **B3**/167
Milledgeville, TN **C2**/182
Millen, GA **E3**/102
Miller, KS **H2**/119
Miller, MO **C4**/145
Miller, MS **C1**/143
Miller, NE **F3**/149
Miller, OH **C4**/167
Miller, SD **G2**/181
Miller (int'l arpt.), TX **H6**/187
Miller City, OH **A1**/167
Miller Place, NY **H5**/159
Millers, MD **D1**/129
Millers Creek, NC **D1**/162
Millers Falls, MA **C1**/132
Millers Ferry, AL **B3**/76
Millersburg, IA **E3**/117
Millersburg, IN **D1**/115
Millersburg, KY **F2**/121
Millersburg, MI **C2**/137
Millersburg, MI **G4**/138
Millersburg, OH **D2**/167
Millersburg, OR **B3**/170
Millersburg, PA **E3**/173
Millersport, OH **C3**/167
Millerstown, KY **D3**/121
Millerstown, PA **D3**/173
Millersview, TX **H6**/185
Millersville, PA **E4**/173
Millersville, TN **E1**/182
Millerton, LA **B1**/122
Millerton, NY **G4**/159
Millerton, OK **H4**/169
Millerton, PA **E2**/173
Millerville, AL **D2**/76
Millerville, MN **C4**/140
Millett, SC **C3**/179
Millhaven, GA **E3**/102
Millheim, PA **D3**/173
Millhousen, IN **D3**/115
Millican, OR **E4**/170
Milligan, FL **B1**/98
Milligan, NE **H3**/149
Milliken, CO **F1**/92
Millikin, LA **D2**/122
Millington, CT **D3**/95
Millington, IL **D2**/111
Millington, MD **E1**/129
Millington, MI **D4**/137
Millington, NJ **C2**/155
Millington, TN **B2**/182
Millinocket, ME **D3**/126
Millis, MA **E2**/133
Millmont, PA **D3**/173
Millport, AL **A2**/76
Millport, NY **D3**/159
Millport, PA **C2**/173
Millrift, PA **G2**/173
Millry, AL **A4**/76
Mills, NE **F1**/149
Mills, NM **F1**/157
Mills, UT **C3**/190
Mills, WY **F3**/206
Millsboro, DE **B3**/96
Millstadt, IL **B5**/111
Millston, WI **C4**/205

240 Millstone—Mount Sunapee

Name/map reference/page

Millstone, KY **H3**/121
Millstone, NJ **C3**/155
Millstone, WV **B3**/203
Millstone (riv.), NJ **C3**/155
Milltown, AL **D2**/76
Milltown, IN **C4**/115
Milltown, KY **E3**/121
Milltown, NJ **D3**/155
Milltown, WI **A3**/205
Millville, DE **B3**/96
Millville, IN **D3**/115
Millville, MA **D2**/133
Millville, MN **F6**/140
Millville, NJ **B5**/155
Millville, OH **A3**/167
Millville, PA **E2**/173
Millville, RI **B3**/177
Millville, UT **D1**/190
Millwood, GA **D4**/102
Millwood, OH **C2**/167
Millwood, WA **H2**/199
Millwood, WV **B3**/203
Milmay, NJ **C5**/155
Milner, CO **C1**/92
Milner, GA **B2**/102
Milnesand, NM **G4**/157
Milnor, ND **H3**/165
Milo, IA **D3**/117
Milo, KY **H3**/121
Milo, ME **D3**/126
Milo, OK **F3**/169
Milo, OR **B5**/170
Milolii, HI **F4**/107
Milpitas, CA **D5**/86
Milroy, IN **D3**/115
Milroy, MN **C6**/140
Milroy, PA **D3**/173
Milstead, AL **D3**/76
Milton, CT **B2**/95
Milton, DE **B3**/96
Milton, FL **A1**/98
Milton, IA **E4**/117
Milton, IL **B4**/111
Milton, IN **D3**/115
Milton, KS **F3**/119
Milton, KY **E2**/121
Milton, MA **E2**/133
Milton, MA **B3**/134
Milton, NC **F1**/163
Milton, ND **G1**/164
Milton, NH **E5**/153
Milton, NY **G4**/159
Milton, OK **J2**/169
Milton, PA **E2**/173
Milton, TN **E2**/182
Milton, VT **A2**/193
Milton, WA **B6**/201
Milton, WI **E6**/205
Milton, WV **A3**/203
Milton Center, OH **B1**/167
Milton Mills, NH **E5**/153
Milton-Freewater, OR **G2**/170
Miltona, MN **C4**/140
Miltonsburg, OH **D3**/167
Miltonvale, KS **F1**/119
Milwaukee, WI **F5**/205
Milwaukie, OR **C2**/170
Mimbres, NM **C5**/157
Mims, FL **H3**/99
Mims, MS **B1**/143
Mina, NV **B4**/151
Mina, SD **G1**/181
Minam, OR **H2**/170
Minatare, NE **B2**/148
Minburn, IA **C3**/117
Minco, OK **F2**/169
Minden, IA **B3**/116
Minden, LA **B2**/122
Minden, NE **G3**/149
Minden, NV **A4**/151
Minden, TX **N5**/185
Minden, WV **B4**/203
Minden City, MI **E4**/137
Mindenmines, MO **B4**/145
Mineola, IA **B3**/116
Mineola, MO **E3**/145
Mineola, NY **G5**/159
Mineola, TX **M5**/185
Miner, MO **G5**/145
Miner, MT **F4**/147
Mineral, CA **D2**/86
Mineral, OH **C3**/167
Mineral, VA **G2**/195
Mineral, WA **C3**/198
Mineral Bluff, GA **B1**/102
Mineral Center, MN **J3**/140
Mineral City, OH **D2**/167
Mineral Hills, MI **C3**/138
Mineral Point, WI **C6**/205
Mineral Ridge, OH **E1**/167
Mineral Springs, AR **B4**/84
Mineral Springs, NC **E3**/162
Mineral Wells, TX **J5**/185
Mineralwells, WV **B2**/203
Minersville, PA **E3**/173
Minersville, UT **C4**/190
Minerva, KY **G2**/121
Minerva, NY **G2**/159
Minerva, OH **D2**/167
Minerva Park, OH **C2**/167
Minetto, NY **D2**/159
Mineville-Witherbee, NY **G1**/159
Mingo, IA **D3**/117
Mingo, KS **C1**/118
Mingo, WV **C3**/203
Mingo Junction, OH **E2**/167
Mingus, TX **J5**/185
Minidoka, ID **E7**/108
Minier, IL **C3**/111
Minneapolis, KS **F1**/119
Minneapolis, MN **E6**/140
Minneapolis-Saint Paul (Wold-Chamberlain), (int'l arpt.), MN **E6**/140
Minnehaha, WA **C4**/198
Minneiska, MN **G6**/140
Minnekahta, SD **B3**/180
Minneola, KS **C3**/118
Minneota, MN **C6**/140
Minnesota (riv.), MN **B5**/140
Minnesota City, MN **G6**/140
Minnesota Lake, MN **E7**/140
Minnesott Beach, NC **J3**/163
Minnetonka, MN **E6**/140
Minnewaukan, ND **F1**/164
Minnith, MO **F4**/145
Minnora, WV **B3**/203
Minoa, NY **D2**/159
Minocqua, WI **D3**/205
Minong, WI **B2**/205
Minonk, IL **C3**/111
Minooka, IL **D2**/111
Minor Hill, TN **D2**/182
Minortown, CT **B2**/95
Minot, MA **F2**/133
Minot, ME **B4**/126
Minot, ND **D1**/164
Minster, OH **A2**/167
Mint Hill, NC **E2**/162
Minter, AL **C3**/76
Minter City, MS **B2**/143
Minto, AK **G2**/79
Minto, ND **H1**/165
Minturn, AR **D2**/84
Minturn, CO **D2**/92
Minturn, SC **E2**/179
Minute Man (nat'l hist. park), MA **E2**/133
Minuteman (nat'l hist. park), MA **A1**/134
Mio, MI **C3**/137
Mira, LA **B2**/122
Mira Loma, CA **F4**/89
Mirabile, MO **B2**/145
Miramar, FL **H6**/99
Miramar, FL **B2**/101
Miranda, SD **G2**/181
Mirror Lake, NH **D4**/153
Misenheimer, NC **E2**/162
Mishawaka, IN **C1**/115
Mishicot, WI **F4**/205
Mispillion (riv.), DE **B3**/96
Misquamicut, RI **A4**/177
Mission, DE **B3**/96
Mission, OR **G2**/170
Mission, SD **E3**/181
Mission Hill, SD **H4**/181
Mission Ridge, SD **E2**/181
Mission Viejo, CA **F5**/89
Missisquoi (riv.), VT **B2**/193
Mississinewa (lake), IN **D2**/115
Mississippi (delta), LA **J5**/11
Mississippi (delta), LA **F6**/123
Mississippi (nat'l rec. river), MN **F6**/140
Mississippi (sound), AL **A5**/76
Mississippi (sound), MS **D5**/143
Missoula, MT **C3**/146
Missouri (lake), ND **B1**/164
Missouri (riv.) **G2**/10
Missouri Branch, WV **A4**/203
Missouri City, MO **B2**/145
Missouri City, TX **L3**/187
Missouri Valley, IA **B3**/116
Mist, AR **D4**/84
Mist, OR **B2**/170
Misty Fjords (nat'l mon.), AK **D3**/81
Mitchell, AR **C1**/84
Mitchell, GA **D2**/102
Mitchell, IA **E1**/117
Mitchell, IN **C4**/115
Mitchell, LA **B3**/122
Mitchell, NE **B2**/148
Mitchell, OR **E3**/170
Mitchell (isl.), LA **F5**/123
Mitchell (mt.), NC **C2**/162
Mitchellsburg, KY **F3**/121
Mitchellville, AR **D4**/84
Mitchellville, IA **D3**/117
Mitchellville, TN **E1**/182
Mitkof (isl.), AK **C2**/81
Mittie, LA **C4**/122
Mix, LA **D4**/122
Mize, MS **C4**/143
Mizpah, MN **D3**/140
Mizpah, NJ **C5**/155
Moab, UT **F4**/190
Moapa, NV **F6**/151
Mobeetie, TX **G2**/184
Moberly, MO **D2**/145
Mobile, AL **A5**/76
Mobile (bay), AL **A5**/76
Mobile (riv.), AL **A5**/76
Mobjack, VA **H3**/195
Mobridge, SD **E1**/181
Mocanaqua, PA **E2**/173
Moccasin, AZ **C1**/83
Moccasin, MT **G2**/147
Mocksville, NC **E2**/162
Moclips, WA **A2**/198
Modale, IA **A3**/116
Model, CO **F4**/92
Modena, UT **B5**/190
Modena, WI **B4**/205
Modest Town, VA **J3**/195
Modesto, CA **E5**/86
Modesto, IL **C4**/111
Modoc, IN **D2**/115
Modoc, KS **B2**/118
Modoc, SC **B3**/179
Modoc Point, OR **D5**/170
Moenkopi, AZ **D1**/83
Moffat, CO **E4**/92
Moffit, ND **E3**/164
Mogadore, OH **D1**/167
Mogollon, NM **B4**/157
Mogollon (mts.), NM **B4**/157
Mohall, ND **D1**/164
Mohave (lake), NV **F7**/151
Mohawk, MI **C2**/138
Mohawk, NY **E2**/159
Mohawk (mts.), AZ **B5**/83
Mohawk (riv.), NY **M2**/11
Mohegan, CT **D3**/95
Mohegan, RI **B2**/177
Mohler, WA **G2**/199
Mohnton, PA **F3**/173
Mohrsville, PA **F3**/173
Moiese, MT **B2**/146
Moira, NY **F1**/159
Mojave, CA **E3**/89
Mojave (des.), CA **C3**/10
Mokane, MO **E3**/145
Mokelumne (aqueduct), CA **C1**/91
Mokelumne (riv.), CA **E4**/86
Mokelumne Hill, CA **E4**/86
Mokuleia, HI **C2**/107
Molalla, OR **C2**/170
Molena, GA **B2**/102
Molina, CO **B2**/92
Moline, IL **B2**/111
Moline, KS **G3**/119
Moline, MI **B5**/137
Molino, FL **A1**/98
Mollusk, VA **H3**/195
Molokai (isl.), HI **Q7**/10
Molokai (isl.), HI **D2**/107
Molokini (isl.), HI **E3**/107
Molson, WA **F1**/198
Molt, MT **H4**/147
Momence, IL **E2**/111
Momeyer, NC **G2**/163
Mona, UT **D3**/190
Monaca, PA **A3**/172
Monahans, TX **E6**/184
Monango, ND **G3**/164
Monarch, MT **F2**/147
Monarch Mill, SC **C2**/179
Monarda, ME **D3**/126
Monaville, WV **B4**/203
Moncks Corner, SC **D3**/179
Moncure, NC **F2**/163
Mondamin, IA **A3**/116
Mondel, NM **B5**/157
Mondovi, WI **B4**/205
Monero, NM **D1**/157
Monessen, PA **B3**/172
Moneta, VA **E3**/194
Moneta, WY **E2**/206
Monett, MO **C5**/145
Monetta, SC **C3**/179
Monette, AR **E2**/84
Money, MS **B2**/143
Mongo, IN **D1**/115
Monhegan (isl.), ME **C5**/126
Moniac, GA **D5**/102
Monico, WI **D3**/205
Monida, MT **D5**/146
Monie, MD **E2**/129
Monitor, WA **E2**/198
Monitor (range), NV **D4**/151
Monkton, MD **D1**/129
Monkton, VT **A2**/193
Monkton Ridge, VT **A2**/193
Monmouth, IA **G2**/117
Monmouth, IL **B3**/111
Monmouth, ME **B4**/126
Monmouth, OR **B3**/170
Monmouth Beach, NJ **E3**/155
Monmouth Junction, NJ **C3**/155
Mono (lake), CA **G4**/87
Monocacy (nat'l bfld.), MD **C1**/129
Monon, IN **C2**/115
Monona, IA **F1**/117
Monona, WI **D5**/205
Monongah, WV **C2**/203
Monongahela, PA **B3**/172
Monongahela (riv.), PA **B4**/172
Monowi, NE **G1**/149
Monroe, AR **D3**/84
Monroe, CT **B3**/95
Monroe, GA **C2**/102
Monroe, IA **D3**/117
Monroe, IN **E2**/115
Monroe, LA **C2**/122
Monroe, ME **C4**/126
Monroe, MI **D6**/137
Monroe, NC **E3**/162
Monroe, NE **H2**/149
Monroe, NH **B3**/153
Monroe, NY **F4**/159
Monroe, OH **A3**/167
Monroe, OK **J3**/169
Monroe, OR **B3**/170
Monroe, SD **H3**/181
Monroe, TN **F1**/183
Monroe, UT **C4**/190
Monroe, VA **E3**/195
Monroe, WA **D2**/198
Monroe, WI **D6**/205
Monroe (lake), IN **C3**/115
Monroe Bridge, MA **B1**/132
Monroe Center, IL **C1**/111
Monroe City, IN **B4**/115
Monroe City, MO **E2**/145
Monroeton, PA **E2**/173
Monroeville, AL **B4**/76
Monroeville, IN **E2**/115
Monroeville, NJ **B4**/155
Monroeville, OH **C1**/167
Monroeville, PA **B3**/172
Monrovia, AL **C1**/76
Monrovia, CA **C4**/91
Monrovia, IN **C3**/115
Monse, WA **F1**/198
Monsey, NY **F4**/159
Monson, MA **C2**/133
Monson, ME **C3**/126
Mont Alto, PA **D4**/173
Mont Belvieu, TX **M3**/187
Mont Ida, KS **H2**/119
Mont Vernon, NH **C6**/153
Montague, CA **C1**/86
Montague, MA **B1**/132
Montague, MI **A4**/137
Montague, MT **F2**/147
Montague, NC **G3**/163
Montague, NJ **C1**/155
Montague, TX **K4**/185
Montague (isl.), AK **H4**/79
Montague City, MA **B1**/132
Montalba, TX **M6**/185
Montana, AK **G3**/79
Montara, CA **A3**/91
Montauk, NY **J4**/159
Montbrook, FL **F2**/99
Montcalm, WV **B4**/203
Montchanin, DE **A1**/96
Montclair, NJ **D2**/155
Montclair, NJ **A2**/161
Monte Alto, TX **J6**/187
Monte Cristo (mts.), NV **C4**/151
Monte Rio, CA **B4**/86
Monte Vista, CO **D4**/92
Monteagle, TN **F2**/183
Montebello, CA **B5**/91
Montegut, LA **E5**/122
Montello, NV **F1**/151
Montello, WI **D5**/205
Monterey, AL **C4**/76
Monterey, CA **B2**/88
Monterey, IN **C1**/115
Monterey, KY **F2**/121
Monterey, LA **D3**/122
Monterey, MA **A2**/132
Monterey, TN **F1**/183
Monterey, VA **E2**/194
Monterey (bay), CA **B3**/10
Monterey Park, CA **B5**/91
Monterville, WV **C3**/203
Montesano, WA **B3**/198
Montevallo, AL **C2**/76
Montevideo, MN **C6**/140
Monteview, ID **F6**/108
Montezuma, CO **E2**/92
Montezuma, GA **B3**/102
Montezuma, IA **E3**/117
Montezuma, IN **B3**/115
Montezuma, KS **C3**/118
Montezuma, NM **E2**/157
Montezuma, OH **A2**/167
Montezuma, TN **C2**/182
Montezuma Castle (nat'l mon.), AZ **D3**/83
Montezuma Creek, UT **F5**/190
Montfort, WI **C6**/205
Montgomery, GA **E4**/102
Montgomery, IN **B4**/115
Montgomery, LA **C3**/122
Montgomery, MA **B2**/132
Montgomery, MI **C6**/137
Montgomery, MN **E6**/140
Montgomery, MS **B4**/143
Montgomery, NY **F4**/159
Montgomery, OH **A3**/167
Montgomery, PA **E2**/173
Montgomery, TX **L2**/187
Montgomery, VT **B2**/193
Montgomery, WV **B3**/203
Montgomery (cap.), AL **J4**/11
Montgomery (cap.), AL **C3**/76
Montgomery Center, VT **B2**/193
Montgomery City, MO **E3**/145
Montgomery Village, MD **C1**/129
Montgomeryville, PA **F3**/173
Monticello, AR **D4**/84
Monticello, FL **E1**/99
Monticello, GA **C2**/102
Monticello, IA **F2**/117
Monticello, IL **D3**/111
Monticello, IN **C2**/115
Monticello, KY **F4**/121
Monticello, LA **D2**/122
Monticello, ME **E2**/126
Monticello, MN **E5**/140
Monticello, MO **E1**/145
Monticello, MS **B4**/143
Monticello, NM **C4**/157
Monticello, NY **F4**/159
Monticello, OH **A2**/167
Monticello, TX **M4**/185
Monticello, UT **F5**/190
Monticello, VA **F3**/195
Monticello, WI **D6**/205
Montmorenci, IN **B2**/115
Montour, IA **E3**/117
Montour, ID **B6**/108
Montour Falls, NY **D3**/159
Montoursville, PA **E2**/173
Montoya, NM **F2**/157
Montpelier, IA **G3**/117
Montpelier, ID **G7**/108
Montpelier, IN **D2**/115
Montpelier, LA **E4**/122
Montpelier, MS **D2**/143
Montpelier, ND **G3**/164
Montpelier, OH **A1**/167
Montpelier (cap.), VT **M2**/11
Montpelier (cap.), VT **B2**/193
Montreal, MO **D4**/145
Montreal, WI **C2**/205
Montreal (riv.), WI **C2**/205
Montreat, NC **C2**/162
Montrose, AL **B5**/76
Montrose, AR **D4**/84
Montrose, CO **C3**/92
Montrose, GA **C3**/102
Montrose, IA **F4**/117
Montrose, IL **D4**/111
Montrose, LA **C3**/122
Montrose, MI **D4**/137
Montrose, MN **E5**/140
Montrose, MO **C3**/145
Montrose, MS **C3**/143
Montrose, PA **F2**/173
Montrose, SD **H3**/181
Montrose-Ghent, OH **D1**/167
Montross, VA **H2**/195
Montvale, NJ **D1**/155
Montvale, VA **E3**/194
Montville, MA **A2**/132
Montville, NJ **D2**/155
Montville, OH **D1**/167
Monument, CO **F2**/92
Monument, KS **B1**/118
Monument, NM **G5**/157
Monument, OR **F3**/170
Monument Beach, MA **F3**/133
Moodus, CT **D3**/95
Moody, AL **C2**/76
Moody, ME **B5**/126
Moody, MO **E5**/145
Moody, TX **K6**/185
Moodys, OK **J1**/169
Mooers, NY **G1**/159
Mooleyville, KY **D2**/120
Moon, OK **J4**/169
Moorcroft, WY **H1**/206
Moore, ID **E6**/108
Moore, MT **G3**/147
Moore, OK **F2**/169
Moore, TX **G3**/187
Moore, UT **D4**/190
Moore Haven, FL **G5**/99
Moore Park, MI **B5**/137
Moorefield, KY **G2**/121
Moorefield, NE **E3**/149
Moorefield, WV **E2**/203
Mooreland, IN **D3**/115
Mooreland, OK **D1**/169
Moores Bridge, AL **B2**/76
Moores Creek, KY **G3**/121
Moores Creek (nat'l bfld.), NC **G3**/163
Mooresboro, NC **D2**/162
Mooresburg, TN **H1**/183
Moorestown, MI **B3**/137
Moorestown, NJ **C4**/155
Moorestown, NJ **C2**/174
Mooresville, AL **C1**/76
Mooresville, IN **C3**/115
Mooresville, MO **C2**/145
Mooresville, NC **E2**/162
Mooreton, ND **J3**/165
Mooreville, MS **D1**/143
Moorhead, IA **B3**/116
Moorhead, MN **B4**/140
Moorhead, MS **B2**/143
Mooringsport, LA **B2**/122
Moorland, IA **C2**/117
Moorland, MI **B4**/137
Moorman, KY **C3**/120
Moorpark, CA **E4**/89
Moose, WY **B2**/206
Moose Creek, AK **H2**/79
Moose Lake, MN **F4**/140
Moose Pass, AK **G3**/79
Moose River, ME **B3**/126
Moosehead (lake), ME **N1**/11
Mooselookmeguntic (lake), ME **B4**/126
Mooseup Valley, RI **A3**/177
Moosic, PA **F2**/173
Moosup, CT **E2**/95
Moquah, WI **B2**/205
Mora, LA **C3**/122
Mora, MN **E5**/140
Mora, MO **C3**/145
Moraga, CA **C2**/91
Moran, KS **H3**/119
Moran, MI **G4**/138
Moran, MI **C2**/137
Moran, TX **H5**/185
Moran, WY **B2**/206
Moravia, IA **E4**/117
Moravia, NY **D3**/159
Moravian Falls, NC **D1**/162
Moreau (riv.), SD **F1**/10
Moreauville, LA **D3**/122
Morehead, KS **H3**/119
Morehead, KY **G2**/121
Morehead City, NC **J3**/163
Morehouse, MO **G5**/145
Moreland, AR **C2**/84
Moreland, GA **B2**/102
Moreland, ID **F6**/108
Morenci, AZ **F4**/83
Morenci, MI **C6**/137
Moreno Valley, CA **F5**/89
Moretown, VT **B2**/193
Morey, MI **B3**/137
Morgan, GA **B4**/102
Morgan, KY **F2**/121
Morgan, MN **D6**/140
Morgan, MO **D4**/145
Morgan, TX **K5**/185
Morgan, UT **D1**/190
Morgan, VT **B2**/193
Morgan City, LA **D5**/122
Morgan City, MS **B2**/143
Morgan Hill, CA **D5**/86
Morganfield, KY **C3**/120
Morganton, AR **C2**/84
Morganton, GA **B1**/102
Morganton, NC **D2**/162
Morgantown, IN **C3**/115
Morgantown, KY **D3**/120
Morgantown, OH **B3**/167
Morgantown, PA **F3**/173
Morgantown, WV **D2**/203
Morganville, KS **F1**/119
Morganza, LA **D4**/122
Moriah, NY **G1**/159
Moriah Center, NY **G1**/159
Moriarty, NM **D3**/157
Morland, KS **C1**/118
Morley, MI **B4**/137
Morley, MO **G4**/145
Morley, NY **E1**/159
Morley, TN **G1**/183
Mormon Lake, AZ **D3**/83
Morning Sun, IA **F3**/117
Morning View, KY **F2**/121
Morningside, MD **D3**/131
Moro, AR **E3**/84
Moro, OR **E2**/170
Moro Bay, AR **C4**/84
Morocco, IN **B2**/115
Morongo Valley, CA **G4**/89
Moroni, UT **D3**/190
Morral, OH **B2**/167
Morrice, MI **C5**/137
Morrill, KS **H1**/119
Morrill, ME **C4**/126
Morrill, NE **B2**/148
Morrilton, AR **C2**/84
Morris, CT **B2**/95
Morris, GA **B4**/102
Morris, IL **D2**/111
Morris, IN **D3**/115
Morris, MN **C5**/140
Morris, NY **E3**/159
Morris, OK **H2**/169
Morris, PA **D2**/173
Morris Chapel, TN **C2**/182
Morris Plains, NJ **D2**/155
Morris Run, PA **D2**/173
Morrisdale, PA **C3**/173
Morrison, IA **E2**/117
Morrison, IL **C2**/111
Morrison, OK **F1**/169
Morrison, TN **F2**/183
Morrison Bluff, AR **B2**/84
Morrisonville, IL **C4**/111
Morrisonville, NY **G1**/159
Morriston, FL **F2**/99
Morristown, AZ **C4**/83
Morristown, IN **D3**/115
Morristown, MN **E6**/140
Morristown, NJ **D2**/155
Morristown, NY **E1**/159
Morristown, SD **D1**/181
Morristown, TN **H1**/183
Morristown (nat'l hist. park), NJ **C2**/155
Morrisvale, WV **B3**/203
Morrisville, MO **C4**/145
Morrisville, NY **E3**/159
Morrisville, PA **A4**/172
Morrisville, PA **G3**/173
Morrisville, VT **B2**/193
Morro Bay, CA **C3**/88
Morrow, AR **A2**/84
Morrow, GA **B2**/102
Morrow, LA **C4**/122
Morrow, OH **A3**/167
Morrowville, KS **F1**/119
Morse, LA **C4**/122
Morse, TX **F1**/184
Morse, WI **C2**/205
Morse Bluff, NE **J2**/149
Morton, IL **C3**/111
Morton, MN **D6**/140
Morton, MS **C3**/143
Morton, PA **A3**/174
Morton, TX **E4**/184
Morton, WA **C3**/198
Morton, WY **D2**/206
Morton Grove, IL **B1**/112
Mortons Gap, KY **C3**/120
Morven, GA **C5**/102
Morven, NC **E3**/163
Morvin, AL **B4**/76
Mosby, MO **B2**/145
Mosby, MT **J3**/147
Mosca, CO **E4**/92
Moscow, AR **D3**/84
Moscow, IA **F3**/117
Moscow, ID **B3**/108
Moscow, KS **B3**/118
Moscow, KY **A4**/120
Moscow, ME **C3**/126
Moscow, MS **D3**/143
Moscow, OH **A4**/167
Moscow, PA **F2**/173
Moscow, RI **B3**/177
Moscow, TN **B2**/182
Moscow, VT **B2**/193
Moscow Mills, MO **F3**/145
Moseley, VA **G3**/195
Moselle, MO **F3**/145
Moselle, MS **C4**/143
Moses Lake, WA **F2**/198
Mosgrove, PA **B3**/172
Moshannon, PA **C2**/173
Mosheim, TN **J1**/183
Mosher, SD **E3**/181
Mosier, OR **D2**/170
Mosinee, WI **D4**/205
Mosquero, NM **G2**/157
Mosquito Creek (res.), OH **D1**/167
Moss, TN **F1**/183
Moss Bluff, LA **B4**/122
Moss Point, MS **D5**/143
Mossville, IL **C3**/111
Mossy Head, FL **B1**/98
Mossyrock, WA **C3**/198
Motley, MN **D4**/140
Mott, ND **C3**/164
Mottville, MI **B6**/137
Moulton, AL **B1**/76
Moulton, IA **E4**/117
Moulton, TX **J3**/187
Moultonboro, NH **D4**/153
Moultrie, GA **C4**/102
Moultrie (lake), SC **D3**/179
Mound, LA **D2**/122
Mound Bayou, MS **B2**/143
Mound City, IL **C6**/111
Mound City, KS **J2**/119
Mound City, MO **A1**/144
Mound City, SD **E1**/181
Mound Station (Timewell), IL **B3**/111
Mound Valley, KS **H3**/119
Moundridge, KS **F2**/119
Mounds, IL **C6**/111
Mounds, OK **G2**/169
Moundsville, WV **C2**/203
Moundville, AL **B3**/76
Mount Airy, GA **C1**/102
Mount Airy, MD **C1**/129
Mount Airy, NC **E1**/162
Mount Airy, TN **F2**/183
Mount Alto, WV **B3**/203
Mount Alton, PA **C2**/172
Mount Andrew, AL **D4**/76
Mount Angel, OR **C2**/170
Mount Arlington, NJ **C2**/155
Mount Auburn, IA **E2**/117
Mount Auburn, IL **C4**/111
Mount Ayr, IA **C4**/117
Mount Ayr, IN **B2**/115
Mount Baker (nat'l rec. area), WA **D1**/198
Mount Blanchard, OH **B2**/167
Mount Calvary, WI **E5**/205
Mount Carmel, IL **E5**/111
Mount Carmel, LA **B3**/122
Mount Carmel, MS **C4**/143
Mount Carmel, ND **G1**/164
Mount Carmel, OH **A3**/167
Mount Carmel, PA **E3**/173
Mount Carmel, SC **B2**/179
Mount Carmel, TN **J1**/183
Mount Carmel, UT **C5**/190
Mount Carroll, IL **C1**/111
Mount Clare, WV **C2**/203
Mount Clemens, MI **E5**/137
Mount Cobb, PA **F2**/173
Mount Cory, OH **B2**/167
Mount Crawford, VA **F2**/195
Mount Crested Butte, CO **D3**/92
Mount Croghan, SC **D2**/179
Mount Desert (isl.), ME **D4**/126
Mount Desert (Somesville), ME **D4**/126
Mount Dora, FL **G3**/99
Mount Dora, NM **G1**/157
Mount Eaton, OH **D2**/167
Mount Eden, KY **E2**/121
Mount Enterprise, TX **N6**/185
Mount Ephraim, NJ **C3**/174
Mount Erie, IL **D5**/111
Mount Forest, MI **C4**/137
Mount Gilead, NC **E2**/163
Mount Gilead, OH **C2**/167
Mount Gretna, PA **E3**/173
Mount Hermon, LA **E4**/122
Mount Hermon, MA **C1**/132
Mount Holly, AR **C4**/84
Mount Holly, NC **D2**/162
Mount Holly, NJ **C4**/155
Mount Holly, SC **D3**/179
Mount Holly, VT **B3**/193
Mount Holly Springs, PA **D3**/173
Mount Hood, OR **D2**/170
Mount Hope, AL **B1**/76
Mount Hope, KS **F3**/119
Mount Hope, WI **C6**/205
Mount Hope, WV **B4**/203
Mount Horeb, WI **D5**/205
Mount Ida, AR **B3**/84
Mount Ivy, NY **F4**/159
Mount Jackson, VA **F2**/195
Mount Jewett, PA **C2**/172
Mount Joy, PA **E3**/173
Mount Judea, AR **B2**/84
Mount Juliet, TN **E1**/182
Mount Kisco, NY **G4**/159
Mount Laurel, NJ **C4**/155
Mount Lebanon, LA **B2**/122
Mount Lebanon, PA **A3**/172
Mount Liberty, OH **C2**/167
Mount Lookout, WV **C3**/203
Mount Montgomery, NV **B5**/151
Mount Moriah, MO **C1**/145
Mount Morris, IL **C1**/111
Mount Morris, MI **D4**/137
Mount Morris, NY **C3**/159
Mount Morris, PA **A4**/172
Mount Mourne, NC **E2**/162
Mount Nebo, WV **C3**/203
Mount Olive, IL **C4**/111
Mount Olive, MS **C4**/143
Mount Olive, NC **G2**/163
Mount Olivet, KY **F2**/121
Mount Orab, OH **B3**/167
Mount Penn, PA **F3**/173
Mount Pleasant, AR **D2**/84
Mount Pleasant, DE **A1**/96
Mount Pleasant, FL **D1**/99
Mount Pleasant, IA **F4**/117
Mount Pleasant, MI **C4**/137
Mount Pleasant, MS **C1**/143
Mount Pleasant, NC **E2**/162
Mount Pleasant, PA **B3**/172
Mount Pleasant, SC **E4**/179
Mount Pleasant, TN **D2**/182
Mount Pleasant, TX /185
Mount Pleasant, UT **D3**/190
Mount Pocono, PA **F2**/173
Mount Prospect, IL **A1**/112
Mount Pulaski, IL **C3**/111
Mount Rainier, MD **D2**/131
Mount Rainier (nat'l park), WA **D3**/198
Mount Repose, OH **A3**/167
Mount Rogers (nat'l rec. area), VA **C4**/194
Mount Rushmore (nat'l mem.), SD **B3**/180
Mount Saint Helens (nat'l mon.), WA **C3**/198
Mount Salem, KY **F3**/121
Mount Savage, MD **B1**/128
Mount Shasta, CA **C1**/86
Mount Sherman, AR **B1**/84
Mount Sherman, KY **E3**/121
Mount Sinai, NY **G5**/159
Mount Sterling, IL **B4**/111
Mount Sterling, KY **G2**/121
Mount Sterling, OH **B3**/167
Mount Sterling, WI **C5**/205
Mount Storm, WV **D2**/203
Mount Sunapee, NH **B5**/153

For key to abbreviations, see page 217.

242 New Wilmington—Oak Grove

Name/map reference/page

C3/115
New Wilmington, PA **A2**/172
New Winchester, IN **C3**/115
New Winchester, OH **C2**/167
New Windsor, MD **C1**/129
New Windsor, NY **F4**/159
New Woodstock, NY **E3**/159
New York, NY **G5**/159
New York Mills, MN **C4**/140
New York Mills, NY **E2**/159
New Zion, SC **D3**/179
Newald, WI **E3**/205
Newalla, OK **F2**/169
Newark, AR **D2**/84
Newark, CA **C5**/86
Newark, DE **A1**/96
Newark, IL **D2**/111
Newark, MO **E2**/145
Newark, NJ **D2**/155
Newark, NJ **A2**/161
Newark, NY **C2**/159
Newark, OH **C2**/167
Newark, SD **H1**/181
Newark, TX **K4**/185
Newark, VT **C2**/193
Newark (int'l arpt.), NJ **D2**/155
Newark (int'l arpt.), NJ **A2**/161
Newark Museum, NJ **A2**/161
Newark Valley, NY **D3**/159
Newaygo, MI **B4**/137
Newberg, OR **C2**/170
Newbern, AL **B3**/76
Newbern, IN **D3**/115
Newbern, TN **B1**/182
Newberry, FL **F2**/99
Newberry, IN **B4**/115
Newberry, MI **F3**/138
Newberry, SC **C2**/179
Newberry (nat'l mon.), OR **D4**/170
Newborn, GA **C2**/102
Newburg, IA **E3**/117
Newburg, KY **E2**/121
Newburg, MD **D2**/129
Newburg, MO **E4**/145
Newburg, ND **E1**/164
Newburg, PA **D3**/173
Newburg, WI **E5**/205
Newburg, WV **D2**/203
Newburgh, IN **B5**/115
Newburgh, NY **F4**/159
Newbury, MA **F1**/133
Newbury, NH **B5**/153
Newbury, VT **B2**/193
Newburyport, MA **F1**/133
Newcastle, CA **D4**/86
Newcastle, ME **C4**/126
Newcastle, NE **J1**/149
Newcastle, OK **F2**/169
Newcastle, TX **J4**/185
Newcastle, UT **B5**/190
Newcomb, NM **B1**/157
Newcomb, NY **F2**/159
Newcomerstown, OH **D2**/167
Newdale, ID **G6**/108
Newell, AL **D2**/76
Newell, IA **B2**/117
Newell, PA **B3**/172
Newell, SD **B2**/180
Newell, WV **C1**/203
Newellton, LA **D2**/122
Newenham (cape), AK **D4**/79
Newfane, NY **B2**/158
Newfane, VT **B4**/193
Newfield, ME **B5**/126
Newfield, NJ **B4**/155
Newfield, NY **D3**/159
Newfields, NH **E5**/153
Newfolden, MN **B2**/140
Newfound (lake), NH **C4**/153
Newfoundland, KY **G2**/121
Newfoundland, NJ **D1**/155
Newfoundland, PA **F2**/173
Newgulf, TX **L3**/187
Newhalem, WA **D1**/198
Newhalen, AK **F4**/79
Newhall, IA **F3**/117
Newhall, WV **B4**/203
Newhope, AR **B3**/84
Newington, CT **C2**/95
Newington, GA **E3**/102
Newington, NH **E5**/153
Newkirk, NM **F2**/157
Newkirk, OK **F1**/169
Newland, NC **D1**/162
Newlin, TX **G3**/184
Newllano, LA **B3**/122
Newman, CA **D5**/86
Newman, IL **E4**/111
Newman, KY **C3**/120
Newman, MS **B3**/143
Newman Grove, NE **H2**/149
Newmarket, NH **E5**/153
Newnan, GA **B2**/102
Newport, AR **D2**/84
Newport, DE **A1**/96
Newport, IN **B3**/115
Newport, KY **F1**/121
Newport, MD **D2**/129
Newport, ME **C4**/126
Newport, NC **J3**/163
Newport, NE **F1**/149
Newport, NH **B5**/153
Newport, NJ **B5**/155
Newport, NY **E2**/159
Newport, OR **A3**/170
Newport, PA **D3**/173
Newport, RI **C4**/177
Newport, TN **H2**/183
Newport, VT **B2**/193
Newport, WA **H1**/199
Newport Beach, CA **F5**/89
Newport Beach, CA **C6**/91
Newport Center, VT **B2**/193
Newport Hills, WA **C4**/201
Newport News, VA **H4**/195
Newry, ME **B4**/126
Newry, PA **C3**/172
Newry, SC **B2**/179
Newsoms, VA **G4**/195
Newtok, AK **C3**/79
Newton, AL **D4**/76
Newton, GA **B4**/102
Newton, IA **D3**/117
Newton, IL **D5**/111
Newton, KS **F2**/119
Newton, MA **E2**/133
Newton, MA **A2**/134
Newton, MS **C3**/143
Newton, NC **D2**/162
Newton, NH **D6**/153
Newton, NJ **C1**/155
Newton, TX **P7**/185
Newton, TX **N2**/187
Newton, UT **D1**/190
Newton, WV **B3**/203
Newton Falls, NY **F1**/159
Newton Falls, OH **E1**/167
Newton Grove, NC **G2**/163
Newton Hamilton, PA **D3**/173
Newton Junction, NH **D6**/153
Newtown Square, PA **A2**/174
Newtonia, MO **B5**/145
Newtonsville, OH **A3**/167
Newtonville, IN **C4**/115
Newtonville, NJ **C4**/155
Newtown, CT **B3**/95
Newtown, IN **B2**/115
Newtown, KY **F2**/121
Newtown, MO **C1**/145
Newville, AL **D4**/76
Newville, IN **E1**/115
Newville, PA **D3**/173
Newville, WV **C3**/203
Ney, OH **A1**/167
Nez Perce (nat'l hist. park), ID **B3**/108
Nezperce, ID **B3**/108
Niagara, ND **H2**/164
Niagara, WI **F3**/205
Niagara Falls, NY **A2**/158
Niangua, MO **D4**/145
Niantic, CT **D3**/95
Niantic, IL **C4**/111
Niarada, MT **B2**/146
Nibley, UT **D1**/190
Nicasio, CA **C4**/86
Nice, CA **C3**/86
Niceville, FL **B1**/98
Nicholasville, KY **F3**/121
Nicholls, GA **D4**/102
Nichols, IA **F3**/117
Nichols, MN **E4**/140
Nichols, SC **E2**/179
Nichols, WI **E4**/205
Nichols House, MA **E2**/134
Nicholson, GA **C1**/102
Nicholson, MS **C5**/143
Nicholson, PA **F2**/173
Nicholsville, AL **B3**/76
Nicholville, NY **F1**/159
Nickelsville, VA **B4**/194
Nickerson, KS **E2**/119
Nickerson, NE **J2**/149
Nicodemus, KS **D1**/118
Nicodemus (nat'l hist. site), KS **D1**/118
Nicolaus, CA **D4**/86
Nicollet, MN **D6**/140
Nielsville, MN **B3**/140
Nighthawk, WA **F1**/198
Nightmute, AK **C3**/79
Nikishka, AK **G3**/79
Nikolai, AK **F3**/79
Nikolski, AK **F1**/80
Niland, CA **H5**/89
Niles, IL **B1**/112
Niles, KS **F2**/119
Niles, MI **A6**/137
Niles, OH **E1**/167
Nilwood, IL **C4**/111
Nimmons, AR **E1**/84
Nimrod, AR **B3**/84
Nimrod, MN **D4**/140
Nimrod, MT **C1**/146
Ninaview, CO **G4**/92
Ninety Six, SC **B2**/179
Ninety Six (nat'l hist. site), SC **B2**/179
Nineveh, NY **E3**/159
Ninilchik, AK **G3**/79
Ninole, HI **F4**/107
Niobe, ND **C1**/164
Niobe, NY **A3**/158
Niobrara, NE **G1**/149
Niobrara (riv.) **F2**/10
Niota, IL **A3**/111
Niota, TN **G2**/183
Niotaze, KS **G3**/119
Nipomo, CA **C3**/88
Nipton, CA **H3**/89
Nirvana, MI **B4**/137
Niskayuna, NY **G3**/159
Nisland, SD **B2**/180
Nisswa, MN **D4**/140
Nitro, WV **B3**/203
Nitta Yuma, MS **B2**/143
Niumalu, HI **B2**/106
Niverville, NY **G3**/159
Niwot, CO **E1**/92
Nixa, MO **C4**/145
Nixburg, AL **C3**/76
Nixon, NV **A3**/151
Nixon, TX **J3**/187
Noank, CT **D3**/95
Noatak, AK **D2**/79
Noatak (nat'l prsv.), AK **D1**/79
Noatak (riv.), AK **D2**/79
Noble, GA **A1**/102
Noble, IL **D5**/111
Noble, LA **B3**/122
Noble, MO **D5**/145
Noble, OK **F2**/169
Noble Lake, AR **D3**/84
Nobleboro, ME **C4**/126
Noblesville, IN **C2**/115
Nobleton, FL **F3**/99
Nocatee, FL **G4**/99
Nocona, TX **K4**/185
Nod, MS **B3**/143
Nodaway, IA **C4**/117
Nodaway (riv.), MO **A1**/144
Noel, MO **B5**/145
Nogal, NM **E4**/157
Nogales, AZ **E6**/83
Nokesville, VA **G2**/195
Nokomis, AL **B4**/76
Nokomis, IL **C4**/111
Nola, MS **B4**/143
Nolan, WV **A4**/203
Nolanville, TX **K6**/185
Nolanville, TX **J1**/187
Nolensville, TN **E2**/182
Nolin, KY **E3**/121
Nolin River (lake), KY **D3**/120
Noma, FL **C1**/98
Nomans Land (isl.), MA **F4**/133
Nome, AK **C2**/79
Nome, ND **H3**/165
Nome, TX **M2**/187
Nonamesset (isl.), MA **F4**/133
Nondalton, AK **F4**/79
Nonopapa, HI **A2**/106
Nonpareil, NE **B1**/148
Nonquitt, MA **F3**/133
Nooksack, WA **C1**/198
Noonan, ND **B1**/164
Noonday, TX **M5**/185
Noorvik, AK **D2**/79
Nopeming, MN **F4**/140
Nooseneck, RI **B3**/177
Nora, NE **H3**/149
Nora, SD **J4**/181
Nora, VA **B3**/194
Nora Springs, IA **D1**/117
Norbeck, SD **F1**/181
Norborne, MO **C2**/145
Norcatur, KS **C1**/118
Norco, CA **F5**/89
Norco, LA **E4**/122
Norcross, GA **B2**/102
Norcross, ME **D3**/126
Norcross, MN **B5**/140
Norden, NE **E1**/149
Nordland, WA **C1**/198
Nordman, ID **B1**/108
Norene, TN **E1**/182
Norfield, MS **B4**/143
Norfolk, CT **B2**/95
Norfolk, MA **E2**/133
Norfolk, NE **H1**/149
Norfolk, NY **F1**/159
Norfolk, VA **H4**/195
Norfolk (lake), AR **C1**/84
Norfolk (lake), MO **D5**/145
Norfork, AR **C1**/84
Norge, OK **F3**/169
Norge, VA **H3**/195
Norland, FL **B2**/101
Norlina, NC **G1**/163
Norma, ND **D1**/164
Norma, NJ **B5**/155
Norma, TN **G1**/183
Normal, IL **D3**/111
Normalville, PA **B4**/172
Norman, AR **B3**/84
Norman, NC **F2**/163
Norman, NE **G3**/149
Norman, OK **F2**/169
Norman (lake), NC **E2**/162
Norman Park, GA **C4**/102
Normandy, TN **E2**/182
Normandy Beach, NJ **D4**/155
Normandy Park, WA **B5**/201
Normangee, TX **L6**/185
Normangee, TX **K1**/187
Norphlet, AR **C4**/84
Norridge, IL **B2**/112
Norridgewock, ME **C4**/126
Norrie, WI **D4**/205
Norris, IL **B3**/111
Norris, MS **C3**/143
Norris, MT **E4**/147
Norris, SC **B2**/179
Norris, SD **D3**/181
Norris, TN **G1**/183
Norris (lake), TN **H1**/183
Norris City, IL **D6**/111
Norristown, GA **D3**/102
Norristown, PA **F3**/173
Norristown, PA **A1**/174
North, SC **C3**/179
North (isls.), LA **F5**/123
North Acton, MA **E1**/133
North Adams, MA **A1**/132
North Adams, MI **C6**/137
North Amherst, MA **B2**/132
North Andover, MA **E1**/133
North Anson, ME **C4**/126
North Arlington, NJ **A2**/161
North Asheboro, NC **F2**/163
North Ashford, CT **D2**/95
North Atlanta, GA **B2**/102
North Atlanta, GA **C1**/105
North Attleboro, MA **E3**/133
North Augusta, SC **C3**/179
North Baltimore, OH **B1**/167
North Bangor, NY **F1**/159
North Bay, NY **E2**/159
North Bay, WI **F6**/205
North Beach, MD **D2**/129
North Beach Haven, NJ **D4**/155
North Bellingham, MA **E2**/133
North Bend, NE **J2**/149
North Bend, OR **A4**/170
North Bend, PA **D2**/173
North Bend, WA **D2**/198
North Bend, WI **B4**/205
North Bennington, VT **A4**/193
North Bergen, NJ **D2**/155
North Bergen, NJ **B2**/161
North Berwick, ME **B5**/126
North Bloomfield, OH **E1**/167
North Bonneville, WA **D4**/198
North Boston, NY **B3**/158
North Bradley, MI **C4**/137
North Branch, MI **D4**/137
North Branch, MN **F5**/140
North Branch, NH **C5**/153
North Branch, NJ **C2**/155
North Branch Chicago (riv.), IL **C2**/112
North Branford, CT **C3**/95
North Brentwood, MD **D1**/131
North Bridgton, ME **B4**/126
North Brookfield, MA **C2**/133
North Brunswick, NJ **D3**/155
North Buena Vista, IA **G2**/117
North Caldwell, NJ **A1**/161
North Canadian (riv.), OK **G3**/10
North Canton, CT **C2**/95
North Canton, OH **D2**/167
North Cape May, NJ **C6**/155
North Carrollton, MS **C2**/143
North Carver, MA **F3**/133
North Cascades (nat'l park), WA **D1**/198
North Catasauqua, PA **F3**/173
North Charleroi, PA **B3**/172
North Charleston, NH **B5**/154
North Charleston, SC **E4**/179
North Chatham, MA **H3**/133
North Chatham, NH **D3**/153
North Chicago, IL **E1**/111
North Chichester, NH **D5**/153
North Cohasset, MA **F2**/133
North Colebrook, CT **B1**/95
North College Hill, OH **A3**/167
North Collins, NY **B3**/158
North Concord, NC **E2**/162
North Concord, VT **C2**/193
North Conway, NH **D3**/153
North Cove, NC **D2**/162
North Creek, NY **G2**/159
North Crossett, AR **D4**/84
North Danville, VT **B2**/193
North Decatur, GA **C2**/105
North Dighton, MA **E3**/133
North Dorset, VT **A3**/193
North Druid Hills, GA **C2**/105
North Duxbury, VT **B2**/193
North Eagle Butte, SD **D1**/181
North East, MD **E1**/129
North East, PA **B1**/172
North Eastham, MA **H3**/133
North Edwards, CA **F3**/89
North Egremont, MA **A2**/132
North El Monte, CA **C4**/91
North English, IA **E3**/117
North Enid, OK **F1**/169
North Epworth, MI **A4**/137
North Fairfax, VT **A2**/193
North Fairfield, OH **C1**/167
North Falmouth, MA **F3**/133
North Fayston, VT **B2**/193
North Ferrisburg, VT **A2**/193
North Fond du Lac, WI **E5**/205
North Fork, CA **F5**/86
North Fork, ID **E4**/108
North Fork Holston (riv.), VA **B4**/194
North Fork New (mts.), NC **D1**/162
North Fork Salt (riv.), MO **D2**/145
North Fork Shenandoah (riv.), VA **E2**/195
North Fork Village, OH **B3**/167
North Fort Myers, FL **G5**/99
North Foster, RI **A2**/177
North Franklin, CT **D2**/95
North Freedom, WI **D5**/205
North Garden, VA **F3**/195
North Glen Ellyn, IL **A2**/112
North Granby, CT **C2**/95
North Grantham, NH **B4**/154
North Grosvenor Dale, CT **E2**/95
North Groton, NH **C4**/153
North Guam, NM **B2**/158
North Hadley, MA **B2**/132
North Haledon, NJ **D2**/155
North Haledon, NJ **A1**/161
North Hampton, NH **E6**/153
North Hampton, OH **B3**/167
North Hanover, MA **F2**/133
North Harlowe, NC **J3**/163
North Hartsville, SC **D2**/179
North Harwich, MA **G3**/133
North Hatfield, MA **B2**/132
North Haven, CT **C3**/95
North Haven, ME **D4**/126
North Haven, NY **H4**/159
North Haverhill, NH **B3**/153
North Henderson, IL **B2**/111
North Henderson, NC **G1**/163
North Hero, VT **A2**/193
North Hickory, NC **D2**/162
North High Shoals, GA **C2**/102
North Highlands, CA **D4**/86
North Hills, WV **B2**/203
North Hodge, LA **C2**/122
North Hornell, NY **C3**/159
North Hudson, NY **G2**/159
North Hudson, WI **A4**/205
North Hutchinson (isl.), FL **H4**/99
North Hyde Park, VT **B2**/193
North Ironwood, MI **A3**/138
North Java, NY **B3**/158
North Jay, ME **B4**/126
North Judson, IN **C1**/115
North Kansas City, MO **B2**/145
North Kingsville, OH **E1**/167
North Las Vegas, NV **E6**/151
North Lawrence, NY **F1**/159
North Lawrence, OH **D2**/167
North Lewisburg, OH **B2**/167
North Liberty, IA **F3**/117
North Liberty, IN **C1**/115
North Lima, OH **E2**/167
North Limington, ME **B5**/126
North Little Rock, AR **C3**/84
North Logan, UT **D1**/190
North Loup, NE **G2**/149
North Loup (riv.), NE **E1**/149
North Lubec, ME **E4**/126
North Madison, CT **C3**/95
North Madison, OH **D1**/167
North Manchester, IN **D1**/115
North Manitou, MI **B2**/137
North Manitou, MI **F4**/138
North Manitou (isl.), MI **A2**/137
North Manitou (isl.), MI **E4**/138
North Mankato, MN **D6**/140
North Marshfield, MA **F2**/133
North Miami, FL **H6**/99
North Miami, FL **B2**/101
North Miami, OK **J1**/169
North Miami Beach, FL **H6**/99
North Miami Beach, FL **B2**/101
North Middleboro, MA **F3**/133
North Middletown, KY **F2**/121
North Montpelier, VT **B2**/193
North Muskegon, MI **A4**/137
North Myrtle Beach, SC **F3**/179
North New Portland, ME **B4**/126
North Newport, NH **B5**/153
North Newton, KS **F2**/119
North Niles, MI **A6**/137
North Ogden, UT **D1**/190
North Olmsted, OH **D1**/167
North Palm Beach, FL **H5**/99
North Pawlet, VT **A3**/193
North Pembroke, MA **F2**/133
North Perry, OH **D1**/167
North Plain, CT **D3**/95
North Plainfield, NJ **D2**/155
North Plains, OR **C2**/170
North Platte, NE **E2**/149
North Platte (riv.) **E2**/10
North Plymouth, MA **F3**/133
North Pole, AK **H2**/79
North Pomfret, VT **B3**/193
North Port, FL **F4**/99
North Potomac, MD **C1**/129
North Powder, OR **H2**/170
North Pownal, VT **A4**/193
North Prairie, WI **E6**/205
North Providence, RI **C2**/177
North Puyallup, WA **B6**/201
North Raccoon (riv.), IA **C2**/117
North Randolph, VT **B3**/193
North Reading, MA **E1**/133
North Redwood, MN **C6**/140
North Richland Hills, TX **B1**/188
North Richmond, NH **B6**/154
North Ridgeville, OH **C1**/167
North Rim, AZ **C1**/83
North River, NY **F2**/159
North Riverside, IL **B2**/112
North Robinson, OH **C2**/167
North Rose, NY **D2**/159
North Royalton, OH **D1**/167
North Salem, IN **C3**/115
North Salem, NH **D6**/153
North Salt Lake, UT **D2**/190
North San Juan, CA **D3**/86
North Sandwich, NH **D4**/153
North Scituate, MA **F2**/133
North Scituate, RI **B2**/177
North Sea, NY **H5**/159
North Shrewsbury, VT **B3**/193
North Springfield, PA **A2**/172
North Springfield, VA **B3**/131
North Springfield, VT **B3**/193
North Star, OH **A2**/167
North Stonington, CT **E3**/95
North Stratford, NH **C2**/153
North Sutton, NH **C5**/153
North Swansea, MA **E3**/133
North Syracuse, NY **D2**/159
North Terre Haute, IN **B3**/115
North Thetford, VT **B3**/193
North Tonawanda, NY **B2**/158
North Troy, VT **B2**/193
North Truro, MA **G2**/133
North Tunbridge, VT **B3**/193
North Tunica, MS **B1**/143
North Vandergrift-Pleasant View, PA **B3**/172
North Vassalboro, ME **C4**/126
North Vernon, IN **D3**/115
North Wales, PA **F3**/173
North Warren, PA **B2**/172
North Washington, IA **E1**/117
North Waterford, ME **B4**/126
North Weare, NH **C5**/153
North Webster, IN **D1**/115
North Westchester, CT **D2**/95
North Westminster, VT **B3**/193
North Whitefield, ME **C4**/126
North Wildwood, NJ **C6**/155
North Wilkesboro, NC **D1**/162
North Wilton, CT **B3**/95
North Windham, CT **D2**/95
North Windham, ME **B5**/126
North Windham, VT **B3**/193
North Wolcott, VT **B2**/193
North Woodstock, CT **E2**/95
North Woodstock, NH **C3**/153
North York, PA **E4**/173
Northampton, MA **B2**/132
Northampton, PA **F3**/173
Northboro, IA **B4**/116
Northborough, MA **D2**/133
Northbranch, KS **E1**/119
Northbridge, MA **D2**/133
Northbrook, IL **E1**/111
Northbrook, IL **B1**/112
Northbrook, OH **A3**/167
Northeast Harbor, ME **D4**/126
Northfield, CT **B2**/95
Northfield, IL **B1**/112
Northfield, MA **C1**/132
Northfield, ME **E4**/126
Northfield, MN **E6**/140
Northfield, NH **C5**/153
Northfield, NJ **C5**/155
Northfield, TX **G3**/184
Northfield, VT **B2**/193
Northfield, WI **B4**/205
Northfield Center, VT **B2**/194
Northfield Falls, VT **B2**/193
Northgate, ND **C1**/164
Northglenn, CO **F2**/92
Northlake, IL **B2**/112
Northland, MI **D3**/138
Northome, MN **D3**/140
Northport, AL **B2**/76
Northport, ME **D4**/126
Northport, MI **B2**/137
Northport, MI **F4**/138
Northport, NE **B2**/148
Northport, WA **H1**/199
Northport Point, MI **B2**/137
Northridge, OH **B3**/167
Northridge, OH **A3**/167
Northrop, MN **D7**/140
Northumberland, NH **C2**/153
Northumberland, PA **E3**/173
Northvale, NJ **E2**/155
Northview, MO **D4**/145
Northville, CT **B2**/95
Northville, MI **D5**/137
Northville, NY **F2**/159
Northville, SD **G1**/181
Northway, AK **J3**/79
Northwest Harborcreek, PA **B1**/172
Northwood, IA **D1**/117
Northwood, ND **H2**/165
Northwood, NH **D5**/153
Northwood, OH **B1**/167
Northwood Center, NH **D5**/153
Northwye, MO **E4**/145
Norton, KS **D1**/118
Norton, MA **E3**/133
Norton, OH **D1**/167
Norton, TX **G6**/184
Norton, VA **B4**/194
Norton, VT **C1**/193
Norton, WV **D3**/203
Norton (sound), AK **U10**/10
Norton Shores, MI **A4**/137
Nortonville, KS **H1**/119
Nortonville, KY **C3**/120
Nortonville, ND **G3**/164
Norvelt, PA **B3**/172
Norwalk, CA **E5**/89
Norwalk, CA **B5**/91
Norwalk, CT **B3**/95
Norwalk, IA **D3**/117
Norwalk, MI **A3**/137
Norwalk, OH **C1**/167
Norwalk, WI **C5**/205
Norwalk (isls.), CT **B3**/95
Norway, IA **F3**/117
Norway, IN **C2**/115
Norway, KS **F1**/119
Norway, ME **B4**/126
Norway, MI **D4**/138
Norway, OR **A4**/170
Norway, SC **C3**/179
Norwell, MA **F2**/133
Norwich, CT **D2**/95
Norwich, IA **B4**/116
Norwich, KS **F3**/119
Norwich, NY **E3**/159
Norwich, OH **D3**/167
Norwich, VT **B3**/193
Norwood, CO **B3**/92
Norwood, GA **D2**/102
Norwood, LA **D4**/122
Norwood, MA **E2**/133
Norwood, MA **A3**/134
Norwood, MI **B2**/137
Norwood, MN **E6**/140
Norwood, MO **D4**/145
Norwood, NC **E2**/162
Norwood, NY **F1**/159
Norwood, OH **A3**/167
Norwood, VA **F3**/195
Notasulga, AL **D3**/76
Nottawa, MI **B6**/137
Nottingham, AL **C2**/76
Nottingham, NH **D5**/153
Nottinghill, MO **D5**/145
Nottoway, VA **F3**/195
Nottoway (riv.), VA **G4**/195
Notus, ID **B6**/108
Nounan, ID **G7**/108
Novato, CA **C4**/86
Novato, CA **A1**/91
Novelty, MO **D1**/145
Novi, MI **D5**/137
Novice, TX **H6**/185
Novinger, MO **D1**/145
Nowata, OK **H1**/169
Noxapater, MS **C3**/143
Noxen, PA **E2**/173
Noxon, MT **A2**/146
Noyack, NY **H5**/159
Noyes (isl.), AK **C3**/81
Nuberg, GA **D1**/102
Nuckols, KY **C3**/120
Nucla, CO **B3**/92
Nuiqsut, AK **G1**/79
Nulato, AK **E2**/79
Nulato (mts.), AK **D3**/79
Nulltown, IN **D3**/115
Numa, IA **E4**/117
Nunda, NY **C3**/159
Nunda, SD **H2**/181
Nunez, GA **D3**/102
Nunica, MI **A4**/137
Nunivak (isl.), AK **T10**/10
Nunivak (isl.), AK **C3**/79
Nunley, AR **A3**/84
Nunn, CO **F1**/92
Nunnelly, TN **D2**/182
Nuremberg, PA **E3**/173
Nutley, NJ **D2**/155
Nutley, NJ **A2**/161
Nutrioso, AZ **F4**/83
Nutzotin (mts.), AK **J3**/79
Nyack, NY **G4**/159
Nye, MT **G4**/147
Nyssa, OR **J4**/171

O

O'Brien, OR **B5**/170
O'Donnell, TX **F5**/184
O'Fallon, IL **C5**/111
O'Fallon, MO **F3**/145
O'Kean, AR **E1**/84
O'neil, MS **B4**/143
O'Neill, NE **G1**/149
Oacoma, SD **F3**/181
Oahe (lake) **F1**/10
Oahe (lake), SD **E1**/181
Oahu (isl.), HI **Q7**/10
Oahu (isl.), HI **D2**/107
Oak, NE **H3**/149
Oak Bluffs, MA **F4**/133
Oak Brook, IL **A2**/112
Oak City, NC **H2**/163
Oak City, UT **C3**/190
Oak Creek, CO **D1**/92
Oak Creek, WI **F6**/205
Oak Forest, IL **E2**/111
Oak Forest, IL **B3**/112
Oak Grove, IL **B2**/111

For key to abbreviations, see page 217.

Pinaleno (mts.)—Prior Mountains Nat'l Wild Horse Range (nat'l wild. ref.) 245

Pinaleno (mts.), AZ **E5**/83
Pinardville, NH **C6**/153
Pinch, WV **B3**/203
Pinckard, AL **D4**/76
Pinckney, MI **D5**/137
Pinckneyville, IL **C5**/111
Pinckneyville, MS **A4**/143
Pinconning, MI **D4**/137
Pindall, AR **C1**/84
Pine, AZ **D3**/83
Pine, CO **E2**/92
Pine, ID **C6**/108
Pine, MO **E5**/145
Pine (isl.), FL **F5**/99
Pine Apple, AL **C4**/76
Pine Bank, PA **A4**/172
Pine Beach, NJ **D4**/155
Pine Bluff, AR **C3**/84
Pine Bluffs, WY **H4**/207
Pine City, AR **D3**/84
Pine City, MN **F5**/140
Pine City, WA **H2**/199
Pine Forest (range), NV **B1**/151
Pine Grove, AR **C4**/84
Pine Grove, GA **D4**/102
Pine Grove, KY **F2**/121
Pine Grove, LA **E4**/122
Pine Grove, MI **B5**/137
Pine Grove, MS **C1**/143
Pine Grove, PA **E3**/173
Pine Grove, WV **C2**/203
Pine Grove Furnace, PA **D3**/173
Pine Grove Mills, PA **D3**/173
Pine Hill, AL **B4**/76
Pine Hill, KY **F3**/121
Pine Hill, NJ **C4**/155
Pine Island, MN **F6**/140
Pine Island, NY **F4**/159
Pine Knoll Shores, NC **J3**/163
Pine Knot, KY **F4**/121
Pine Level, AL **C3**/76
Pine Level, NC **G2**/163
Pine Log, GA **B1**/102
Pine Meadow, CT **C2**/95
Pine Mountain (Chipley), GA **B3**/102
Pine Nut (mts.), NV **A3**/151
Pine Plains, NY **G4**/159
Pine Prairie, LA **C4**/122
Pine Ridge, AR **B3**/84
Pine Ridge, MS **A4**/143
Pine Ridge, SD **C3**/181
Pine River, MN **D4**/140
Pine Springs, TX **C6**/184
Pine Tree Corners, DE **A2**/96
Pine Valley, CA **G6**/89
Pine Valley, MS **C1**/143
Pine Valley, NJ **C4**/155
Pine Valley, NY **D3**/159
Pine Valley, UT **B5**/190
Pine Valley (mts.), UT **B5**/190
Pine Village, IN **B2**/115
Pinebluff, NC **F2**/163
Pinecliffe, CO **E2**/92
Pinecrest, CA **F4**/86
Pinedale, AZ **E3**/83
Pinedale, NM **B2**/158
Pinedale, WY **C3**/206
Pinehaven, NM **B2**/158
Pinehurst, GA **C3**/102
Pinehurst, ID **B2**/108
Pinehurst, MA **E1**/133
Pinehurst, NC **F2**/163
Pinehurst, TX **L2**/187
Pineland, FL **F5**/99
Pineland, SC **C4**/179
Pineland, TX **P6**/185
Pinellas Park, FL **F4**/99
Pineola, NC **D1**/162
Pineora, GA **E3**/102
Pinesdale, MT **B3**/146
Pinetop-Lakeside, AZ **F3**/83
Pinetops, NC **H2**/163
Pinetta, FL **E1**/99
Pineview, GA **C3**/102
Pineview, NC **F2**/163
Pineville, AR **C1**/84
Pineville, KY **G4**/121
Pineville, LA **C3**/122
Pineville, MO **B5**/145
Pineville, MS **C3**/143
Pineville, NC **E2**/162
Pineville, SC **D3**/179
Pineville, WV **B4**/203
Pinewood, FL **B2**/101
Pinewood, SC **D3**/179
Piney, AR **B2**/84
Piney Flats, TN **J1**/183
Piney Green, NC **H3**/163
Piney Point, MD **D2**/129
Piney Point Village, TX **A4**/188
Piney River, VA **E3**/195
Piney View, WV **B4**/203
Piney Woods, MS **C3**/143
Pingree, ID **F6**/108
Pingree, ND **G2**/164
Pink, OK **F2**/169
Pink Hill, NC **H2**/163
Pinnacle, MT **C1**/146
Pinnacle, NC **E1**/162
Pinnacles (nat'l mon.), CA **B2**/88
Pinnebog, MI **D4**/137
Pinole, CA **C4**/86
Pinole, CA **B1**/91
Pinon, AZ **E1**/83
Pinon, CO **F3**/92
Pinopolis, SC **D3**/179
Pinos Altos, NM **B5**/157
Pinson, TN **C2**/182
Pinson-Clay-Chalkville, AL **C2**/76
Pintada, NM **E3**/157
Pintura, UT **B5**/190
Pioche, NV **F5**/151
Pioneer, LA **D2**/122
Pioneer, OH **A1**/167
Pipe Spring (nat'l mon.), AZ **C1**/83
Piper City, IL **D3**/111
Pipersville, PA **F3**/173
Piperton, TN **B2**/182
Pipestone, MN **B6**/140
Pipestone (nat'l mon.), MN **B6**/140
Pippa Passes, KY **H3**/121
Piqua, KS **H3**/119
Piqua, OH **A2**/167
Pirtleville, AZ **F6**/83
Piru, CA **E4**/89
Piscataquis (riv.), ME **C3**/126
Piscataway, MD **D2**/129
Piscataway, NJ **D2**/155
Piseco, NY **F2**/159
Pisek, ND **H1**/165
Pisgah, AL **D1**/76
Pisgah, IA **B3**/116
Pisgah, MD **C2**/129
Pisgah, OH **A3**/167
Pisgah Forest, NC **C2**/162
Pisinemo, AZ **C5**/83
Pismo Beach, CA **C3**/88
Pistol River, OR **A5**/170
Pit (riv.), CA **D2**/86
Pitkas Point, AK **D3**/79
Pitkin, CO **D3**/92
Pitkin, LA **C4**/122
Pitman, NJ **B4**/155
Pitre (isl.), LA **F4**/123
Pitsburg, OH **A3**/167
Pitt, MN **D2**/140
Pittman Center, TN **H2**/183
Pitts, GA **C4**/102
Pittsboro, IN **C3**/115
Pittsboro, MS **C2**/143
Pittsboro, NC **F2**/163
Pittsburg, CA **D4**/86
Pittsburg, IL **D6**/111
Pittsburg, IN **C2**/115
Pittsburg, KS **J3**/119
Pittsburg, NH **D1**/153
Pittsburg, OK **H3**/169
Pittsburg, TX **N5**/185
Pittsburgh, PA **B3**/172
Pittsfield, IL **B4**/111
Pittsfield, MA **A2**/132
Pittsfield, ME **C4**/126
Pittsfield, NH **D5**/153
Pittsfield, PA **B2**/172
Pittsfield, VT **B3**/193
Pittsford, MI **C6**/137
Pittsford, NY **C2**/159
Pittsford, VT **A3**/193
Pittston, ME **C4**/126
Pittston, PA **F2**/173
Pittstown, NJ **C2**/155
Pittsview, AL **D3**/76
Pittsville, MD **E2**/129
Pittsville, MO **C3**/145
Pittsville, VA **E4**/195
Pittsville, WI **C4**/205
Pittville, CA **D1**/86
Pixley, CA **D3**/88
Pixley, WY **B3**/206
Placentia, CA **C5**/91
Placerville, CA **E4**/86
Placerville, CO **B3**/92
Placerville, ID **C6**/108
Placitas (Placita), NM **D2**/157
Plad, MO **D4**/145
Plain, WI **C5**/205
Plain City, OH **B2**/167
Plain City, UT **C1**/190
Plain Dealing, LA **B2**/122
Plainfield, AR **B4**/84
Plainfield, CT **E2**/95
Plainfield, GA **C3**/102
Plainfield, IA **E2**/117
Plainfield, IN **C3**/115
Plainfield, MA **B1**/132
Plainfield, NH **B4**/153
Plainfield, NJ **D2**/155
Plainfield, OH **D2**/167
Plainfield, VT **B2**/193
Plainfield, WI **D4**/205
Plains, GA **B3**/102
Plains, MT **B2**/146
Plains, PA **F2**/173
Plains, TX **E4**/184
Plains (West Plains), KS **C3**/118
Plainsboro, NJ **C3**/155
Plainview, AR **B3**/84
Plainview, MN **F6**/140
Plainview, NE **H1**/149
Plainview, NY **G5**/159
Plainview, SD **C2**/181
Plainview, TX **F3**/184
Plainville, CT **C2**/95
Plainville, GA **A1**/102
Plainville, IL **A4**/111
Plainville, IN **B4**/115
Plainville, KS **D1**/119
Plainville, MA **E2**/133
Plainwell, MI **B5**/137
Plaisted, ME **D1**/126
Plaistow, NH **D6**/153
Planada, CA **E5**/86
Plankinton, SD **G3**/181
Plano, IL **D2**/111
Plano, TX **L4**/185
Plant, TN **D1**/182
Plant City, FL **F3**/99
Plantation, FL **H5**/99
Plantation, FL **B1**/101
Plantation Key, FL **H7**/99
Plantation Key (isl.), FL **H7**/99
Plantersville, MS **D1**/143
Plantersville, SC **E3**/179
Plaquemine, LA **D4**/122
Plaster City, CA **H6**/89
Platea, PA **A2**/172
Platina, CA **C2**/86
Platinum, AK **D4**/79
Platner, CO **G1**/92
Plato, MN **D6**/140
Plato, MO **D4**/145
Platte, SD **G3**/181
Platte (riv.), NE **G2**/10
Platte Center, NE **H2**/149
Platte City, MO **B2**/145
Plattenville, LA **D5**/122
Platteville, CO **F1**/92
Platteville, WI **C6**/205
Plattsburg, MO **B2**/145
Plattsburgh, NY **G1**/159
Plattsmouth, NE **K2**/149
Plaucheville, LA **D4**/122
Plaza, ND **D1**/164
Plaza, WA **H2**/199
Pleasant City, OH **D3**/167
Pleasant Dale, NE **J3**/149
Pleasant Gap, AL **D2**/76
Pleasant Gap, PA **D3**/173
Pleasant Garden, NC **F2**/163
Pleasant Grove, AL **C2**/76
Pleasant Grove, CA **D4**/86
Pleasant Grove, MS **B1**/143
Pleasant Grove, OH **E2**/167
Pleasant Grove, UT **D2**/190
Pleasant Hill, CA **C5**/86
Pleasant Hill, CA **C2**/91
Pleasant Hill, IA **D3**/117
Pleasant Hill, IL **B4**/111
Pleasant Hill, LA **B3**/122
Pleasant Hill, MO **B3**/145
Pleasant Hill, MS **B4**/143
Pleasant Hill, NC **E1**/162
Pleasant Hill, OH **A2**/167
Pleasant Hill, PA **E4**/173
Pleasant Hill, TN **F2**/183
Pleasant Hills, MD **D1**/129
Pleasant Hills, PA **B3**/172
Pleasant Hope, MO **C4**/145
Pleasant Lake, IN **D1**/115
Pleasant Lake, MA **G3**/133
Pleasant Lake, ND **F1**/164
Pleasant Lane, SC **C3**/179
Pleasant Mills, IN **E2**/115
Pleasant Mount, PA **F2**/173
Pleasant Plain, IA **F3**/117
Pleasant Plain, OH **A3**/167
Pleasant Plains, AR **D2**/84
Pleasant Plains, IL **C4**/111
Pleasant Plains, NJ **D4**/155
Pleasant Prairie, WI **F6**/205
Pleasant Ridge, VA **B3**/131
Pleasant Shade, TN **F1**/183
Pleasant Valley, CT **C2**/95
Pleasant Valley, MO **B2**/145
Pleasant Valley, NY **G4**/159
Pleasant Valley, OR **H3**/171
Pleasant Valley, TX **F4**/184
Pleasant View, TN **D1**/182
Pleasant View, UT **D1**/190
Pleasanton, CA **D5**/86
Pleasanton, KS **J2**/119
Pleasanton, NE **F3**/149
Pleasanton, NM **B4**/157
Pleasantville, IA **D3**/117
Pleasantville, IN **B4**/115
Pleasantville, NJ **C5**/155
Pleasantville, NY **G4**/159
Pleasantville, OH **C3**/167
Pleasantville, PA **B2**/172
Pleasantville, TN **D2**/182
Pleasure Beach, CT **D3**/95
Pleasure Ridge Park, KY **E2**/121
Pleasureville, KY **E2**/121
Plentywood, MT **M1**/147
Pletcher, AL **C3**/76
Plevna, AL **C1**/76
Plevna, KS **E3**/119
Plevna, MO **D2**/145
Plevna, MT **M3**/147
Pliny, WV **A3**/203
Plover, WI **D4**/205
Pluckemin, NJ **C2**/155
Plum, PA **B3**/172
Plum (isl.), MA **F1**/133
Plum Branch, SC **B3**/179
Plum City, WI **A4**/205
Plum Grove, TX **L2**/187
Plum Springs, KY **D3**/120
Plumerville, AR **C2**/84
Plummer, ID **B2**/108
Plummer, MN **B3**/140
Plumsteadville, PA **F3**/173
Plumville, PA **B3**/172
Plumwood, OH **B2**/167
Plush, OR **F5**/170
Plymouth, CA **E4**/86
Plymouth, DE **A2**/96
Plymouth, IA **D1**/117
Plymouth, IL **B3**/111
Plymouth, IN **C1**/115
Plymouth, MA **F3**/133
Plymouth, ME **C4**/126
Plymouth, MN **E5**/140
Plymouth, NC **J2**/163
Plymouth, NE **J3**/149
Plymouth, NH **C4**/153
Plymouth, OH **C2**/167
Plymouth, PA **F2**/173
Plymouth, UT **C1**/190
Plymouth, VT **B3**/193
Plymouth, WA **F4**/198
Plymouth, WI **F5**/205
Plymouth (bay), MA **F3**/133
Plymouth Meeting, PA **B1**/174
Plymouth Township, MI **D5**/137
Plympton, MA **F3**/133
Plymptonville, PA **C2**/172
Poca, WV **B3**/203
Pocahontas, AR **E1**/84
Pocahontas, IA **C2**/117
Pocahontas, IL **C5**/111
Pocahontas, MO **G4**/145
Pocahontas, MS **B3**/143
Pocahontas, TN **C2**/182
Pocahontas, VA **C3**/194
Pocasset, MA **F3**/133
Pocasset, OK **F2**/169
Pocatalico, WV **B3**/203
Pocatello, ID **F7**/108
Pocola, OK **J2**/169
Pocomoke (sound), MD **E3**/129
Pocomoke (sound), VA **J3**/195
Pocomoke City, MD **E2**/129
Pocono Lake, PA **F2**/173
Pocono Pines, PA **F2**/173
Poe, IN **D2**/115
Poestenkill, NY **G3**/159
Point, LA **C2**/122
Point, TX **M5**/185
Point Arena, CA **B4**/86
Point au Fer (isl.), LA **D5**/122
Point Baker, AK **C2**/81
Point Clear, AL **B5**/76
Point Harbor, NC **K1**/163
Point Hope, AK **C1**/79
Point Lay, AK **D1**/79
Point Marion, PA **B4**/172
Point of Rocks, MD **C1**/129
Point Pleasant, MO **G5**/145
Point Pleasant, NJ **D3**/155
Point Pleasant, PA **F3**/173
Point Pleasant, WV **A3**/203
Point Pleasant Beach, NJ **D3**/155
Point Reyes (nat'l seash.), CA **B4**/86
Point Reyes Station, CA **C4**/86
Point Roberts, WA **B1**/198
Point Washington, FL **B1**/98
Pointe aux Pins, MI **C2**/137
Pointe aux Pins, MI **G4**/138
Points, WV **E2**/203
Poipu, HI **B2**/106
Pokagon, MI **A6**/137
Polacca, AZ **E2**/83
Poland, IN **C3**/115
Poland, ME **B4**/126
Poland, NY **E2**/159
Poland, OH **E1**/167
Poland Spring, ME **B4**/126
Polar, WI **E3**/205
Polaris, MT **C4**/146
Polebridge, MT **B1**/146
Polk, MO **C4**/145
Polk, NE **H2**/149
Polk, OH **C2**/167
Polk, PA **B2**/172
Polk City, FL **G3**/99
Polk City, IA **D3**/117
Polkton, NC **E2**/162
Polkville, MS **C3**/143
Polkville, NC **D2**/162
Pollard, AL **B4**/76
Pollard, AR **E1**/84
Pollock, ID **B4**/108
Pollock, LA **C3**/122
Pollock, MO **C1**/145
Pollock, SD **E1**/181
Pollock Pines, CA **E4**/86
Pollocksville, NC **H2**/163
Polo, IL **C2**/111
Polo, MO **B2**/145
Polonia, WI **D4**/205
Polson, MT **B2**/146
Polvadera, NM **D3**/157
Pomaria, SC **C2**/179
Pomerene, AZ **E6**/83
Pomeroy, IA **C2**/117
Pomeroy, OH **C3**/167
Pomeroy, WA **H3**/199
Pomfret, CT **E2**/95
Pomfret, MD **C2**/129
Pomfret, VT **B3**/193
Pomona, CA **F4**/89
Pomona, KS **H2**/119
Pomona, MD **D1**/129
Pomona, MO **E5**/145
Pomona, NJ **C5**/155
Pomona Park, FL **G2**/99
Pomonkey, MD **C2**/129
Pompano Beach, FL **H5**/99
Pompey, NY **D3**/159
Pompeys Pillar, MT **J4**/147
Pompton Lakes, NJ **D2**/155
Ponca, AR **B1**/84
Ponca, NE **J1**/149
Ponca City, OK **F1**/169
Ponce de Leon, FL **C1**/98
Ponce Inlet, FL **H2**/99
Poncha Springs, CO **D3**/92
Ponchatoula, LA **E4**/122
Pond Creek, OK **F1**/169
Pond Eddy, PA **G2**/173
Ponder, TX **K4**/185
Ponderay, ID **B1**/108
Ponderosa, NM **D2**/157
Pondosa, CA **D1**/86
Ponemah, MN **D2**/140
Ponemah, NH **C6**/153
Poneto, IN **D2**/115
Ponkapoag, MA **B3**/134
Ponset, CT **C3**/95
Pontchartrain (lake), LA **H4**/11
Pontiac, IL **D3**/111
Pontiac, MI **D5**/137
Pontiac, MO **D5**/145
Pontiac, SC **D2**/179
Pontoosuc, IL **A3**/111
Pontotoc, MS **D1**/143
Pontotoc, OK **G3**/169
Pontotoc, TX **H2**/187
Pony, MT **E4**/146
Ponzer, NC **J2**/163
Poole, KY **C3**/120
Poole (isl.), ME **D1**/129
Pooler, GA **E3**/102
Poolesville, MD **C1**/129
Poolville, NY **E3**/159
Pope, MS **C1**/143
Popes Creek, MD **D2**/129
Poplar, MT **L1**/147
Poplar, WI **B2**/205
Poplar Bluff, MO **F5**/145
Poplar Branch, NC **K1**/163
Poplar Creek, MS **C2**/143
Poplar Grove, IL **D1**/111
Poplar Tent, NC **E2**/162
Poplar-Cotton Center, CA **D2**/88
Poplarville, KY **F3**/121
Poplarville, MS **C5**/143
Poquetanuck, CT **D3**/95
Poquonock Bridge, CT **D3**/95
Poquoson, VA **H3**/195
Porcupine, SD **C3**/181
Porcupine (riv.), U.S., Can. **W10**/10
Port Alexander, AK **C2**/81
Port Allegany, PA **C2**/173
Port Allen, LA **D4**/122
Port Alsworth, AK **F3**/79
Port Angeles, WA **B1**/198
Port Arthur, TX **N3**/187
Port Austin, MI **E3**/137
Port Barre, LA **D4**/122
Port Blakely, WA **A3**/201
Port Bolivar, TX **M3**/187
Port Byron, NY **D2**/159
Port Carbon, PA **E3**/173
Port Charlotte, FL **F5**/99
Port Chester, NY **G4**/159
Port Clarence, AK **C2**/79
Port Clinton, OH **C1**/167
Port Clinton, PA **E3**/173
Port Clyde, ME **C5**/126
Port Deposit, MD **D1**/129
Port Dickinson, NY **E3**/159
Port Edwards, WI **D4**/205
Port Elizabeth, NJ **C5**/155
Port Ewen, NY **G4**/159
Port Gamble, WA **C2**/198
Port Gamble, WA **A2**/201
Port Gibson, MS **B4**/143
Port Graham, AK **G4**/79
Port Heiden, AK **E4**/79
Port Henry, NY **G1**/159
Port Hope, MI **E4**/137
Port Hudson, LA **D4**/122
Port Hueneme, CA **D4**/88
Port Huron, MI **E5**/137
Port Inland, MI **B2**/137
Port Jefferson, NY **G5**/159
Port Jefferson, OH **A2**/167
Port Jefferson Station, NY **G5**/159
Port Jervis, NY **F4**/159
Port Kent, NY **G1**/159
Port Leyden, NY **E2**/159
Port Lions, AK **F4**/79
Port Madison, WA **A3**/201
Port Mahon, DE **B2**/96
Port Matilda, PA **C3**/173
Port Monmouth, NJ **D3**/155
Port Morris, NJ **C2**/155
Port Neches, TX **N3**/187
Port Norris, NJ **B5**/155
Port Orange, FL **H2**/99
Port Orchard, WA **C2**/198
Port Orford, OR **A5**/170
Port Penn, DE **A1**/96
Port Reading, NJ **D2**/155
Port Republic, NJ **D4**/155
Port Richey, FL **F3**/99
Port Royal, KY **E2**/121
Port Royal, PA **D3**/173
Port Royal, SC **D4**/179
Port Royal, VA **G2**/195
Port Saint Joe, FL **C2**/98
Port Saint Lucie, FL **H4**/99
Port Salerno, FL **H4**/99
Port Sanilac, MI **E4**/137
Port Sheldon, MI **A5**/137
Port Sulphur, LA **F5**/122
Port Tobacco Village, MD **C2**/129
Port Townsend, WA **C1**/198
Port Trevorton, PA **E3**/173
Port Vincent, LA **E4**/122
Port Washington, NY **G5**/159
Port Washington, OH **D2**/167
Port Washington, WI **F5**/205
Port Wentworth, GA **E3**/102
Port William, OH **B3**/167
Port Wing, WI **B2**/205
Portage, IN **B1**/115
Portage, ME **D2**/126
Portage, MI **B5**/137
Portage, OH **B1**/167
Portage, PA **C3**/172
Portage, UT **C1**/190
Portage, WI **D5**/205
Portage Des Sioux, MO **F3**/145
Portage Lakes, OH **D1**/167
Portageville, MO **G5**/145
Portageville, NY **B3**/158
Portal, AZ **F6**/83
Portal, GA **E3**/102
Portal, ND **C1**/164
Portales, NM **G3**/157
Porter, IN **B1**/115
Porter, ME **B5**/126
Porter, MN **B6**/140
Porter, OH **C4**/167
Porter, OK **H2**/169
Porter, WA **B3**/198
Porterdale, GA **C2**/102
Porterfield, WI **F3**/205
Portersville, AL **D1**/76
Portersville, PA **A3**/172
Porterville, CA **D2**/89
Porterville, MS **D3**/143
Porthill, ID **B1**/108
Portia, AR **D1**/84
Portis, KS **E1**/119
Portland, AR **D4**/84
Portland, CT **C2**/95
Portland, FL **B1**/98
Portland, IN **E2**/115
Portland, ME **B5**/126
Portland, MI **C5**/137
Portland, ND **H2**/165
Portland, NY **A3**/158
Portland, OH **D3**/167
Portland, OR **C2**/170
Portland, PA **F3**/173
Portland, TN **E1**/182
Portland (int'l arpt.), OR **C2**/170
Portland Jetport (int'l arpt.), ME **B5**/126
Portlock, AK **G4**/79
Portola, CA **E3**/86
Portsmouth, IA **B3**/116
Portsmouth, NH **E5**/153
Portsmouth, OH **C4**/167
Portsmouth, RI **C3**/177
Portsmouth, VA **H4**/195
Portsmouth (isl.), NC **J2**/163
Portville, NY **B3**/158
Porum, OK **H2**/169
Posen, IL **C3**/112
Posen, MI **D2**/137
Posen, MI **H4**/138
Poseyville, IN **B4**/115
Possession, WA **B1**/201
Post, TX **F4**/184
Post Falls, ID **B2**/108
Post Mills, VT **B3**/193
Poston, AZ **A4**/83
Postville, IA **F1**/117
Potato Creek, SD **D3**/181
Poteau, OK **J2**/169
Poth, TX **H3**/187
Potholes (res.), WA **F3**/198
Potlatch, ID **B3**/108
Potlatch, WA **B2**/198
Potomac, IL **E3**/111
Potomac, MD **C1**/129
Potomac, MD **B1**/131
Potomac (riv.), MD **C1**/129
Potomac (riv.), VA **H2**/195
Potomac Heights, MD **C2**/129
Potosi, MO **F4**/145
Potosi, TX **H5**/185
Potosi, WI **C6**/205
Potrero, CA **G6**/89
Potsdam, MN **F6**/140
Potsdam, NY **F1**/159
Potter, KS **H1**/119
Potter, NE **B2**/148
Potter, WI **E4**/205
Potter Hill, RI **A4**/177
Pottersdale, PA **C2**/173
Pottersville, MO **D5**/145
Pottersville, NJ **C2**/155
Pottersville, NY **G2**/159
Potterville, MI **C5**/137
Potts Camp, MS **C1**/143
Pottsboro, TX **L4**/185
Pottstown, PA **F3**/173
Pottsville, AR **B2**/84
Pottsville, PA **E3**/173
Pottsville, TX **J6**/185
Potwin, KS **F3**/119
Poughkeepsie, AR **D1**/84
Poughkeepsie, NY **G4**/159
Poulan, GA **C4**/102
Poulsbo, WA **C2**/198
Poultney, VT **A3**/193
Pound, VA **B3**/194
Pound, WI **E3**/205
Pounding Mill, VA **C3**/194
Poverty Point (nat'l mon.), LA **D2**/122
Poway, CA **F6**/89
Powder (riv.) **E1**/10
Powder River, WY **F2**/206
Powder Springs, GA **B2**/102
Powder Springs, TN **H1**/183
Powderhorn, CO **C3**/92
Powderly, KY **C3**/120
Powderly, TX **M4**/185
Powderville, MT **L4**/147
Powe, MO **F5**/145
Powell, NE **H3**/149
Powell, OH **B2**/167
Powell, PA **E2**/173
Powell, TN **G1**/183
Powell, TX **L5**/185
Powell, WY **D1**/206
Powell (lake) **D3**/10
Powell (riv.), TN **H1**/183
Powells Crossroads, TN **F2**/183
Powells Point, NC **K1**/163
Powellsville, NC **J1**/163
Powellton, WV **B3**/203
Powellville, MD **E2**/129
Powelton, GA **D2**/102
Power, MT **E2**/147
Powers, MI **D4**/138
Powers, OR **A5**/170
Powers Lake, ND **C1**/164
Powersville, MO **C1**/145
Powhatan, LA **B3**/122
Powhatan, VA **G3**/195
Powhatan Point, OH **E3**/167
Powhattan, KS **H1**/119
Pownal, VT **A4**/193
Pownal Center, VT **A4**/193
Poy Sippi, WI **E4**/205
Poyen, AR **C3**/84
Poygan (lake), WI **E4**/205
Poynette, WI **D5**/205
Poynor, MO **F5**/145
Poynor, TX **M5**/185
Prague, NE **J2**/149
Prague, OK **G2**/169
Prairie, AL **B3**/76
Prairie City, IA **D3**/117
Prairie City, IL **B3**/111
Prairie City, OR **G3**/170
Prairie City, SD **C1**/180
Prairie Creek, IN **B3**/115
Prairie Dog Town Fork (riv.), TX **F3**/184
Prairie du Chien, WI **B5**/205
Prairie du Rocher, IL **B5**/111
Prairie du Sac, WI **D5**/205
Prairie Farm, WI **B3**/205
Prairie Grove, AR **A2**/84
Prairie Home, MO **D3**/145
Prairie Point, MS **D2**/143
Prairie Rose, ND **J3**/165
Prairie View, KS **D1**/118
Prairie View, TX **L2**/187
Prairie Village, KS **J2**/119
Prairieburg, IA **F2**/117
Prairieton, IN **B3**/115
Prairieville, LA **E4**/122
Prairieville, MI **B5**/137
Pratt, KS **E3**/119
Pratt, WV **B3**/203
Prattsburg, GA **B3**/102
Prattsburg, NY **C3**/159
Prattsville, AR **C3**/84
Prattsville, NY **F3**/159
Prattville, AL **C3**/76
Pray, MT **F4**/147
Preakness (mts.), NJ **A1**/161
Preble, IN **D2**/115
Preble, NY **D3**/159
Prentice, WI **C3**/205
Prentiss, ME **D3**/126
Prentiss, MS **C4**/143
Prescott, AR **B4**/84
Prescott, AZ **C3**/83
Prescott, IA **C3**/117
Prescott, KS **J2**/119
Prescott, MI **D3**/137
Prescott, OR **C1**/170
Prescott, WA **G3**/199
Prescott, WI **A4**/205
Prescott Valley, AZ **C3**/83
Presho, SD **E3**/181
President, PA **B2**/172
Presidential Lake Estates, NJ **C4**/155
Presidio, TX **B3**/186
Presque Isle, ME **D2**/126
Presque Isle, MI **D2**/137
Presque Isle, MI **H4**/138
Presque Isle, WI **D2**/205
Preston, GA **B3**/102
Preston, IA **G2**/117
Preston, ID **G7**/108
Preston, KS **E3**/119
Preston, KY **G2**/121
Preston, MD **E2**/129
Preston, MN **F7**/140
Preston, MO **C4**/145
Preston, MS **D3**/143
Preston, NE **K3**/149
Preston, NV **E4**/151
Preston, OK **H2**/169
Preston Hollow, NY **F3**/159
Prestonsburg, KY **H3**/121
Prestonville, KY **E2**/121
Pretty Boy (res.), MD **D1**/129
Pretty Prairie, KS **E3**/119
Prewitt, NM **B2**/157
Pribilof (isls.), AK **B4**/78
Price, MD **E1**/129
Price, ND **E2**/164
Price, UT **E3**/190
Price, WI **B4**/205
Price (riv.), UT **E3**/190
Pricedale, MS **B4**/143
Priceville, AL **C1**/76
Prichard, AL **A5**/76
Prichard, MS **B1**/143
Prichard, WV **A3**/203
Priddy, TX **J6**/185
Pride, LA **E4**/122
Pridgen, GA **D4**/102
Priest (lake), ID **B1**/108
Priest River, ID **B1**/108
Primehook Beach, DE **B3**/96
Primghar, IA **B1**/116
Primm Springs, TN **D2**/182
Primrose, GA **B2**/102
Primrose, NE **G2**/149
Primrose, RI **B2**/177
Prince Frederick, MD **D2**/129
Prince of Wales (isl.), AK **C3**/81
Prince William (sound), AK **H3**/79
Princes Lake, IN **C3**/115
Princess Anne, MD **E2**/129
Princeton, AL **C1**/76
Princeton, CA **C3**/86
Princeton, IA **G3**/117
Princeton, ID **B3**/108
Princeton, IL **C2**/111
Princeton, IN **B4**/115
Princeton, KS **H2**/119
Princeton, KY **C3**/120
Princeton, LA **B2**/122
Princeton, MA **D2**/133
Princeton, ME **E3**/126
Princeton, MI **D3**/138
Princeton, MN **E5**/140
Princeton, MO **C1**/145
Princeton, NC **G2**/163
Princeton, NJ **C3**/155
Princeton, SC **B2**/179
Princeton, TX **L4**/185
Princeton, WI **D5**/205
Princeton, WV **B4**/203
Princeton Junction, NJ **C3**/155
Princeville, HI **B1**/106
Princeville, IL **C3**/111
Princeville, NC **H2**/163
Prineville, OR **E3**/170
Prineville (res.), OR **E3**/170
Pringle, SD **B3**/180
Prinsburg, MN **C6**/140
Prior Lake, MN **E6**/140
Prior Mountains Nat'l Wild Horse Range (nat'l wild. ref.), MT **H4**/147

246 Pritchardville—Ridley

Name/map reference/page

Pritchardville, SC **D4**/179
Pritchett, CO **H4**/92
Procious, WV **B3**/203
Proctor, CO **H1**/92
Proctor, MT **B2**/146
Proctor, OK **J2**/169
Proctor, PA **E2**/173
Proctor, TX **J6**/185
Proctor, VT **A3**/193
Proctor, WV **C2**/203
Proctorsville, VT **B3**/193
Proctorville, NC **F3**/163
Proctorville, OH **C4**/167
Progress, MS **B4**/143
Promise City, IA **D4**/117
Promontory, UT **C1**/190
Prompton, PA **F2**/173
Prophetstown, IL **C2**/111
Prospect, AL **B2**/76
Prospect, CT **C3**/95
Prospect, KY **E2**/121
Prospect, ME **D4**/126
Prospect, NY **E2**/159
Prospect, OH **B2**/167
Prospect, OR **C5**/170
Prospect, PA **A3**/172
Prospect, VA **F3**/195
Prospect Harbor, ME **D4**/126
Prospect Heights, IL **A1**/112
Prospect Hill, NC **F1**/163
Prospect Park, NJ **A1**/161
Prospect Park, PA **C2**/173
Prospect Park, PA **A3**/174
Prosper, MI **B3**/137
Prosperity, PA **A3**/172
Prosperity, SC **C2**/179
Prosperity, WV **B4**/203
Prosser, NE **G3**/149
Prosser, WA **F3**/198
Protection, KS **D3**/118
Protivin, IA **E1**/117
Provencal, LA **B3**/122
Providence, AL **B3**/76
Providence, KY **C3**/120
Providence, UT **D1**/190
Providence (cap.), RI **M2**/11
Providence (cap.), RI **C2**/177
Providence (mts.), CA **H4**/89
Providence (riv.), RI **C2**/177
Providence Forge, VA **G3**/195
Provincetown, MA **G2**/133
Provo, AR **A3**/84
Provo, SD **B3**/180
Provo, UT **D2**/190
Prudence (isl.), RI **C3**/177
Prudenville, MI **C3**/137
Prudhoe (bay), AK **G1**/79
Prudhoe Bay, AK **G1**/79
Prue, OK **G1**/169
Prunedale, CA **B2**/88
Pryor, CO **F4**/92
Pryor, MT **H4**/147
Pryorsburg, KY **B4**/120
Pryse, KY **G3**/121
Pu'uhonua o Honaunau (nat'l hist. park), HI **F4**/107
Puako, HI **F4**/107
Puckett, MS **C3**/143
Pueblo, CO **F3**/92
Pueblo West, CO **F3**/92
Puget (sound), WA **B1**/10
Puhi, HI **B2**/106
Pukalani, HI **E3**/107
Pukoo, HI **E2**/107
Pukwana, SD **F3**/181
Pulaski, GA **E3**/102
Pulaski, IA **E4**/117
Pulaski, IL **C6**/111
Pulaski, KY **F3**/121
Pulaski, MS **C3**/143
Pulaski, NY **D2**/159
Pulaski, OH **A1**/167
Pulaski, PA **A2**/172
Pulaski, TN **D2**/182
Pulaski, VA **D3**/194
Pulaski, WI **E4**/205
Pulehu, HI **E3**/107
Pullman, MI **A5**/137
Pullman, WA **H3**/199
Pulteney, NY **C3**/159
Pumpkin Center, NC **H3**/163
Pumpville, TX **E3**/186
Punaluu, HI **F4**/107
Pungo, NC **J2**/163
Pungoteague, VA **J3**/195
Punta Gorda, FL **F5**/99
Punxsutawney, PA **C3**/172
Purcell, MO **B4**/145
Purcell, OK **F2**/169
Purcellville, VA **G1**/195
Purdin, MO **C2**/145
Purdum, NE **E1**/149
Purdy, MO **C5**/145
Purdy, VA **G4**/195
Pure Air, MO **D1**/145
Purgatoire (riv.), CO **F3**/10
Purgitsville, WV **E2**/203
Purvis, MS **C4**/143
Puryear, TN **C1**/182
Put-in-Bay, OH **C1**/167
Putnam, AL **A3**/76
Putnam, CT **E2**/95
Putnam, GA **B3**/102
Putnam, IL **C2**/111
Putnam, OK **E2**/169
Putnam, TX **H5**/185
Putnam Lake, NY **G4**/159
Putnamville, IN **C3**/115
Putney, GA **B4**/102
Putney, SD **G1**/181
Putney, VT **B4**/193
Puuanahulu, HI **F4**/107
Puuiki, HI **E3**/107
Puukohola Heiau (nat'l hist. site), HI **F3**/107
Puunene, HI **E3**/107
Puuwai, HI **A2**/106
Puxico, MO **F5**/145
Puyallup, WA **C2**/198
Puyallup, WA **B6**/201
Pyatt, AR **C1**/84
Pyland, MS **C2**/143
Pymatuning (res.), PA **A2**/172
Pyote, TX **D6**/184
Pyramid, KY **H3**/121
Pyramid (lake), NV **C2**/10
Pyrites, NY **E1**/159
Pyriton, AL **D2**/76

Q

Quabbin (res.), MA **C2**/133
Quaddick, CT **E2**/95
Quail, TX **G3**/184
Quaker City, NH **B5**/154
Quaker City, OH **D3**/167
Quaker Farms, CT **B3**/95
Quaker Hill, CT **D3**/95
Quakertown, NJ **C2**/155
Quakertown, PA **F3**/173
Quality, KY **D3**/120
Quamba, MN **E5**/140
Quanah, TX **H3**/185
Quantico, MD **E2**/129
Quantico, VA **G2**/195
Quapaw, OK **J1**/169
Quarryville, PA **E4**/173
Quartz Hill, CA **E4**/89
Quartz Mountain, OR **E5**/170
Quartzsite, AZ **A4**/83
Quasqueton, IA **F2**/117
Quay, NM **G3**/157
Quay, OK **G1**/169
Quealy, WY **C4**/206
Quebeck, TN **F2**/183
Quechee, VT **B3**/193
Quecreek, PA **B3**/172
Queen, PA **C3**/172
Queen Anne, MD **E2**/129
Queen City, MO **D1**/145
Queen City, TX **N4**/185
Queen Creek, AZ **D4**/83
Queens (bor.), NY **B2**/161
Queenstown, MD **D2**/129
Queets, WA **A2**/198
Quemado, NM **B3**/158
Quenemo, KS **H2**/119
Questa, NM **E1**/157
Quick, WV **B3**/203
Quidnick, RI **B3**/177
Quijotoa, AZ **C5**/83
Quilcene, WA **C2**/198
Quimby, IA **B2**/116
Quimby, ME **D2**/126
Quimby, MI **B5**/137
Quinault, WA **B2**/198
Quinault (riv.), WA **B2**/198
Quinby, SC **E2**/179
Quinby, VA **J3**/195
Quincy, FL **D1**/99
Quincy, IL **A4**/111
Quincy, IN **C3**/115
Quincy, KS **H3**/119
Quincy, KY **G2**/121
Quincy, MA **F2**/133
Quincy, MA **C3**/134
Quincy, MI **C6**/137
Quincy, NH **C4**/153
Quincy, OH **B2**/167
Quincy, WA **F2**/198
Quincy-East Quincy, CA **E3**/86
Quinebaug (riv.), CT **E2**/95
Quinebaug (riv.), MA **D3**/133
Quinhagak, AK **D4**/79
Quinlan, OK **D1**/169
Quinlan, TX **L5**/185
Quinn, SD **C3**/181
Quinn Canyon (range), NV **E5**/151
Quinnipiac (riv.), CT **C3**/95
Quinter, KS **C1**/118
Quinton, KY **F4**/121
Quinton, NJ **B4**/155
Quinton, OK **H2**/169
Quinton, VA **G3**/195
Quinttown, NH **B4**/154
Quinwood, WV **C3**/203
Quitaque, TX **F3**/184
Quitman, AR **C2**/84
Quitman, GA **C5**/102
Quitman, LA **C2**/122
Quitman, MS **D3**/143
Quitman, TX **M5**/185
Quito, MS **B2**/143
Qulin, MO **F5**/145
Quogue, NY **H5**/159
Quonochontaug, RI **B4**/177

R

R. S. Kerr (res.), OK **H2**/169
Rabun, AL **B4**/76
Raccoon (riv.), OH **C3**/167
Raccourci (lake), LA **E5**/122
Raceland, KY **H2**/121
Raceland, LA **E5**/122
Racepond, GA **D4**/102
Racine, MN **F7**/140
Racine, MO **B5**/145
Racine, OH **D4**/167
Racine, WI **F6**/205
Racine, WV **B3**/203
Raco, MI **G3**/138
Racola, MO **F3**/145
Radcliff, KY **E3**/121
Radcliff, OH **C3**/167
Radcliffe, IA **D2**/117
Radersburg, MT **E3**/147
Radford, VA **D3**/194
Radiant, VA **F2**/195
Radisson, WI **B3**/205
Radium, CO **D2**/92
Radium, KS **E2**/119
Radium Springs, NM **D5**/157
Radnor, IN **C2**/115
Radnor, OH **B2**/167
Radnor, WV **A3**/203
Radom, IL **C5**/111
Raeford, NC **F3**/163
Raeville, NE **G2**/149
Ragan, NE **F3**/149
Ragan, WY **B4**/206
Ragland, AL **C2**/76
Ragley, LA **B4**/122
Rago, KS **E3**/119
Ragsdale, IN **B4**/115
Rahway, NJ **D2**/155
Raiford, FL **F1**/99
Railroad (range), NV **E4**/151
Rainbow, CA **F5**/89
Rainbow, CT **C2**/95
Rainbow Bridge (nat'l mon.), UT **E5**/190
Rainbow City, AL **C2**/76
Rainelle, WV **C4**/203
Rainier, OR **C1**/170
Rainier (mt.), WA **B1**/10
Rainier (mt.), WA **D3**/198
Rains, SC **E2**/179
Rainsboro, OH **B3**/167
Rainsburg, PA **C4**/172
Rainsville, AL **D1**/76
Rainsville, NM **E2**/157
Rainy (riv.), U.S., Can. **D2**/140
Rake, IA **D1**/117
Raleigh, FL **F2**/99
Raleigh, MS **C3**/143
Raleigh, ND **D3**/164
Raleigh (cap.), NC **L3**/11
Raleigh (cap.), NC **G2**/163
Raleigh-Durham (int'l arpt.), NC **G2**/163
Ralls, TX **F4**/184
Ralph, AL **B2**/76
Ralph, MI **D3**/138
Ralph, SD **B1**/180
Ralphton, PA **B3**/172
Ralston, NE **J2**/149
Ralston, NJ **C2**/155
Ralston, OK **G1**/169
Ralston, PA **E2**/173
Ralston, TN **C1**/182
Ralston, WA **G3**/199
Ralston, WY **D1**/206
Ramah, CO **F2**/92
Ramah, NM **B2**/157
Ramer, AL **C3**/76
Ramer, TN **C2**/182
Ramey, PA **C3**/173
Ramhurst, GA **B1**/102
Ramon, NM **F3**/157
Ramona, CA **G5**/89
Ramona, KS **F2**/119
Ramona, OK **H1**/169
Ramona, SD **H2**/181
Rampart, AK **G2**/79
Ramsay, MT **D4**/146
Ramseur, NC **F2**/163
Ramsey, IL **C4**/111
Ramsey, IN **C4**/115
Ramsey, NJ **D1**/155
Ranburne, AL **D2**/76
Ranchester, WY **E1**/206
Rancho Cucamonga (Cucamonga), CA **F4**/89
Rancho Mirage, CA **G5**/89
Rancho Palos Verdes, CA **E5**/89
Rancho Palos Verdes, CA **A6**/91
Rancho Santa Fe, CA **F5**/89
Ranchos de Taos, NM **E1**/157
Rancocas, NJ **C4**/155
Rand, CO **D1**/92
Randall, IA **D2**/117
Randall, KS **E1**/119
Randall, MN **D4**/140
Randallstown, MD **D1**/129
Randle, WA **D3**/198
Randleman, NC **F2**/163
Randlett, OK **E3**/169
Randlett, UT **F2**/190
Randolph, AL **C3**/76
Randolph, AZ **D5**/83
Randolph, IA **B4**/116
Randolph, KS **G1**/119
Randolph, MA **E2**/133
Randolph, ME **C4**/126
Randolph, MN **E6**/140
Randolph, NE **H1**/149
Randolph, NH **D3**/153
Randolph, NJ **C2**/155
Randolph, NY **B3**/158
Randolph, OH **D1**/167
Randolph, UT **D1**/190
Randolph, VA **F4**/195
Randolph, VT **B3**/193
Randolph, WI **D5**/205
Randolph Center, VT **B3**/193
Random Lake, WI **F5**/205
Rangeley, ME **B4**/126
Rangeley (lake), ME **B4**/126
Rangely, CO **B1**/92
Ranger, GA **B1**/102
Ranger, NC **A2**/162
Ranger, TX **J5**/185
Ranger, WV **A3**/203
Ranier, MN **E2**/140
Rankin, IL **E3**/111
Rankin, TX **F6**/184
Rankin, TX **E1**/186
Ransom, IL **D2**/111
Ransom, KS **D2**/118
Ransomville, NY **B2**/158
Rantoul, IL **D3**/111
Rantoul, KS **H2**/119
Rapelje, MT **G4**/147
Raphine, VA **E3**/195
Rapid City, MI **B3**/137
Rapid River, MI **E4**/138
Rapids, NY **B2**/158
Rapids City, IL **B2**/111
Rappahannock (riv.), VA **G2**/195
Raquette (riv.), NY **F1**/159
Raquette Lake, NY **F2**/159
Rarden, OH **B4**/167
Raritan, IL **B3**/111
Raritan, NJ **C2**/155
Raritan (riv.), NJ **C2**/155
Rat (isls.), AK **S11**/10
Rat (isls.), AK **C2**/80
Ratcliff, AR **B2**/84
Ratcliff, TX **M6**/185
Rathbun (lake), IA **D4**/117
Rathdrum, ID **B2**/108
Ratio, AR **E3**/84
Raton, NM **F1**/157
Rattan, OK **H3**/169
Rattlesnake, NM **B1**/158
Rattlesnake Wilderness (nat'l rec. area), MT **C2**/146
Raub, ND **C2**/164
Rauch, MN **E3**/140
Rauville, SD **H2**/181
Ravalli, MT **B2**/146
Ravanna, AR **A4**/84
Raven, VA **C3**/194
Ravena, NY **G3**/159
Ravendale, CA **E2**/86
Ravenden, AR **D1**/84
Ravenden Springs, AR **D1**/84
Ravenel, SC **D4**/179
Ravenna, KY **G3**/121
Ravenna, MI **B4**/137
Ravenna, NE **G2**/149
Ravenna, OH **D1**/167
Ravenwood, VA **B3**/131
Ravenswood, WV **B3**/203
Ravenwood, MO **B1**/145
Ravia, OK **G3**/169
Ravine, PA **E3**/173
Ravinia, SD **G3**/181
Rawlings, MD **B1**/128
Rawlings, VA **G4**/195
Rawlins, WY **E4**/206
Rawson, ND **B2**/164
Rawson, OH **B2**/167
Ray, MN **E2**/140
Ray, ND **B1**/164
Ray, OH **C3**/167
Ray City, GA **C4**/102
Ray Hubbard (lake), TX **L5**/185
Ray Roberts (lake), TX **K4**/185
Raybon, GA **E4**/102
Rayland, OH **E2**/167
Rayle, GA **D2**/102
Raymer, CO **G1**/92
Raymond, CA **F5**/86
Raymond, IA **E2**/117
Raymond, ID **G7**/108
Raymond, IL **C4**/111
Raymond, KS **E2**/119
Raymond, ME **B5**/126
Raymond, MN **C5**/140
Raymond, MS **B3**/143
Raymond, MT **M1**/147
Raymond, NE **J3**/149
Raymond, NH **D5**/153
Raymond, SD **H2**/181
Raymond, WA **B3**/198
Raymondville, MO **E4**/145
Raymondville, NY **F1**/159
Raymore, MO **B3**/145
Rayne, LA **C4**/122
Raynesford, MT **F2**/147
Raynham, MA **E3**/133
Raynham, NC **F3**/163
Raynham Center, MA **E3**/133
Rays Crossing, IN **D3**/115
Raystown (lake), PA **C3**/173
Raytown, MO **B2**/145
Rayville, LA **D2**/122
Rayville, MO **B2**/145
Raywick, KY **E3**/121
Rea, MO **B1**/145
Reader, AR **B4**/84
Reader, WV **C2**/203
Readfield, ME **C4**/126
Reading, KS **H2**/119
Reading, MA **E1**/133
Reading, MA **B1**/134
Reading, MI **C6**/137
Reading, MN **C7**/140
Reading, OH **A3**/167
Reading, PA **F3**/173
Readington, NJ **C2**/155
Readland, AR **D4**/84
Readlyn, IA **E2**/117
Reads Landing, MN **F6**/140
Readstown, WI **C5**/205
Readsville, MO **E3**/145
Ready, KY **D3**/120
Reagan, OK **G3**/169
Reagan, TN **C2**/182
Reagan, TX **L6**/185
Reagan, TX **K1**/187
Reamstown, PA **E3**/173
Reardan, WA **H2**/199
Reasnor, IA **D3**/117
Reaville, NJ **C3**/155
Rebecca, GA **C4**/102
Recluse, WY **G1**/206
Rector, AR **E1**/84
Red (lakes), MN **H1**/11
Red (riv.) **G4**/10
Red Bank, NJ **D3**/155
Red Bank, NJ **B3**/174
Red Bank, SC **C3**/179
Red Bank, TN **F2**/183
Red Banks, MS **C1**/143
Red Bay, AL **A1**/76
Red Bay, FL **C1**/98
Red Beach, ME **E3**/126
Red Bluff, CA **C2**/86
Red Boiling Springs, TN **F1**/183
Red Bud, IL **C5**/111
Red Cedar (riv.), WI **B3**/205
Red Cliff, CO **D2**/92
Red Cliff, WI **C2**/205
Red Cloud, NE **G3**/149
Red Creek, NY **D2**/159
Red Devil, AK **E3**/79
Red Feather Lakes, CO **E1**/92
Red Hill, NM **B3**/158
Red Hill, PA **F3**/173
Red Hill Patrick Henry (nat'l mem.), VA **F3**/195
Red Hook, NY **G4**/159
Red House, NV **C2**/151
Red House, VA **F3**/195
Red House, WV **B3**/203
Red Jacket, WV **A4**/203
Red Lake, MN **C3**/140
Red Lake (riv.), MN **B3**/140
Red Lake Falls, MN **B3**/140
Red Level, AL **C4**/76
Red Lick, MS **B4**/143
Red Lion, DE **A1**/96
Red Lion, NJ **C4**/155
Red Lion, OH **A3**/167
Red Lion, PA **E4**/173
Red Lodge, MT **G4**/147
Red Mill (lake), DE **B3**/96
Red Mountain, CA **F3**/89
Red Oak, IA **B3**/116
Red Oak, MI **C3**/137
Red Oak, NC **H1**/163
Red Oak, OK **H3**/169
Red Oaks Mill, NY **G4**/159
Red River, NM **E1**/157
Red River Hot Springs, ID **C4**/108
Red River of the North (riv.), U.S., Can. **A3**/140
Red River of the North (riv.), U.S., Can. **H2**/165
Red Rock, TX **J3**/187
Red Rock (lake), IA **E3**/117
Red Rock Lakes (nat'l wild. ref.), MT **E5**/147
Red Springs, NC **F3**/163
Red Wing, CO **E4**/92
Red Wing, MN **F6**/140
Redan, GA **B2**/102
Redbush, KY **H3**/121
Redby, MN **D3**/140
Redcrest, CA **B2**/86
Reddell, LA **C4**/122
Redden, DE **B3**/96
Reddick, FL **F2**/99
Redding, CA **C2**/86
Redding, CT **B3**/95
Redding, IA **C4**/117
Redding Ridge, CT **B3**/95
Reddington, IN **D3**/115
Redfern, SD **B2**/180
Redfield, AR **C3**/84
Redfield, IA **C3**/117
Redfield, KS **J3**/119
Redfield, NY **E2**/159
Redfield, SD **G2**/181
Redford, MI **D5**/137
Redford, TX **B3**/186
Redgranite, WI **D4**/205
Redhouse, KY **F3**/121
Redig, SD **B1**/180
Redington, NE **B2**/148
Redkey, IN **D2**/115
Redland, MD **C1**/129
Redlands, CA **F4**/89
Redlands, CO **B2**/92
Redman, MI **E4**/137
Redmon, IL **E4**/111
Redmond, OR **D3**/170
Redmond, UT **D3**/190
Redmond, WA **C2**/198
Redmond, WA **C3**/201
Redondo, WA **B5**/201
Redondo Beach, CA **E5**/89
Redondo Beach, CA **A5**/91
Redowl, SD **C2**/181
Redrock, NM **B5**/157
Redstone, CO **C2**/92
Redstone, MT **M1**/147
Redstone, NH **D3**/153
Redvale, CO **B3**/92
Redwater, TX **N4**/185
Redway, CA **B2**/86
Redwine, KY **G2**/121
Redwood, MS **B3**/143
Redwood, NY **E1**/159
Redwood (nat'l park), CA **A1**/86
Redwood City, CA **C5**/86
Redwood Falls, MN **C6**/140
Ree Heights, SD **F2**/181
Reece, KS **G3**/119
Reece City, AL **C1**/76
Reed, AR **D4**/84
Reed, KY **C3**/120
Reed, ME **D3**/126
Reed, OK **D3**/168
Reed City, MI **B4**/137
Reed Creek, GA **D1**/102
Reeder, ND **C3**/164
Reedley, CA **D2**/88
Reedsburg, OH **C2**/167
Reedsburg, WI **C5**/205
Reedsport, OR **A4**/170
Reedsville, OH **D3**/167
Reedsville, WI **F4**/205
Reedsville, WV **D2**/203
Reedville, VA **H3**/195
Reedy, WV **B3**/203
Reelsville, IN **C3**/115
Reeman, MI **A4**/137
Reese, MI **D4**/137
Reese (riv.), NV **C3**/151
Reeseville, WI **E5**/205
Reesville, OH **B3**/167
Reeves (Reaves School), LA **B4**/122
Reevesville, SC **D3**/179
Reform, AL **A2**/76
Reform, MS **C2**/143
Refuge, MS **A2**/143
Refugio, TX **J4**/187
Regan, ND **E2**/164
Regent, ND **C3**/164
Reggio, LA **F5**/122
Regina, NM **D1**/157
Register, GA **E3**/102
Rehoboth, MA **E3**/133
Rehoboth, NM **B2**/157
Rehoboth, VA **F4**/195
Rehoboth (bay), DE **B3**/96
Rehoboth Beach, DE **B3**/96
Reid, MD **C1**/129
Reidland, KY **B3**/120
Reids Grove, MD **E2**/129
Reidsville, GA **D3**/102
Reidsville, NC **F1**/163
Reily, OH **A3**/167
Reinbeck, IA **E2**/117
Reinersville, OH **D3**/167
Reinerton-Orwin-Muir, PA **E3**/173
Reisterstown, MD **D1**/129
Reklaw, TX **N6**/185
Reliance, MD **E2**/129
Reliance, SD **F3**/181
Reliance, TN **G2**/183
Reliance, WY **C4**/206
Rembert, SC **D2**/179
Rembrandt, IA **B2**/116
Remer, MN **E3**/140
Remerton, GA **C5**/102
Remington, IN **B2**/115
Remington, VA **G2**/195
Remlap, AL **C2**/76
Remote, OR **B4**/170
Remsen, IA **B2**/116
Remsen, NY **E2**/159
Rena Lara, MS **B1**/143
Rencona, NM **E2**/157
Rend (lake), IL **C5**/111
Rendon, TX **B2**/188
Rendville, OH **C3**/167
Renfroe, AL **C2**/76
Renfroe, GA **B3**/102
Renfrow, OK **F1**/169
Renick, MO **D2**/145
Renner, SD **J3**/181
Rennert, NC **F3**/163
Renno, SC **C2**/179
Reno, NV **A3**/151
Reno, OH **D3**/167
Reno, TX **K5**/185
Reno, TX **M4**/185
Renova, MS **B2**/143
Renovo, PA **D2**/173
Renshaw, MS **B3**/143
Rensselaer, IN **B2**/115
Rensselaer, NY **G3**/159
Rensselaer Falls, NY **E1**/159
Rentiesville, OK **H2**/169
Renton, WA **C2**/198
Renton, WA **C4**/201
Rentz, GA **D3**/102
Renville, MN **C6**/140
Renwick, IA **D2**/117
Replete, WV **C3**/203
Repton, AL **B4**/76
Republic, KS **F1**/119
Republic, MI **D3**/138
Republic, MO **C4**/145
Republic, OH **B1**/167
Republic, PA **B4**/172
Republic, WA **G1**/198
Republican (riv.) **F2**/10
Republican City, NE **F3**/149
Republican Grove, VA **E4**/195
Requa, CA **A1**/86
Resaca, GA **B1**/102
Reserve, KS **H1**/119
Reserve, LA **E4**/122
Reserve, MT **M1**/147
Reserve, NM **B4**/157
Reserve, WI **B3**/205
Rest Haven, GA **C1**/102
Reston, VA **G2**/195
Retsof, NY **C3**/159
Reubens, ID **B3**/108
Reva, SD **B1**/180
Revere, MA **E2**/133
Revere, MA **B2**/134
Revere, MN **C6**/140
Revere, MO **E1**/145
Revere, ND **G2**/164
Revillagigedo (isl.), AK **D3**/81
Revillo, SD **J1**/181
Rew, PA **C2**/172
Rewey, WI **C6**/205
Rex, NC **F3**/163
Rexburg, ID **G6**/108
Rexford, KS **C1**/118
Rexford, MT **A1**/146
Rexton, MI **B1**/137
Rexton, MI **F3**/138
Rexville, NY **C3**/159
Reydell, AR **D3**/84
Reydon, OK **D2**/168
Reyno, AR **E1**/84
Reynolds, GA **B3**/102
Reynolds, IL **B2**/111
Reynolds, IN **C2**/115
Reynolds, MO **E4**/145
Reynolds, ND **H2**/165
Reynolds, NE **H3**/149
Reynoldsburg, OH **C3**/167
Reynoldsville, PA **C2**/172
Rhame, ND **B3**/164
Rhems, SC **E3**/179
Rhine, GA **C4**/102
Rhinebeck, NY **G4**/159
Rhinecliff, NY **G4**/159
Rhinelander, WI **D3**/205
Rhode (isl.), RI **C3**/177
Rhodes, IA **D3**/117
Rhodes, MI **C4**/137
Rhodes Point, MD **D3**/129
Rhyolite, NV **D6**/151
Rialto, CA **F4**/89
Rib Lake, WI **C3**/205
Ribera, NM **E2**/157
Rice, CA **J4**/89
Rice, KS **F1**/119
Rice, MN **D5**/140
Rice, TX **L5**/185
Rice, WA **G1**/199
Rice City, RI **A3**/177
Rice Lake, WI **B3**/205
Riceboro, GA **E4**/102
Ricetown, KY **G3**/121
Riceville, IA **E1**/117
Riceville, PA **B2**/172
Riceville, TN **G2**/183
Rich, MS **B1**/143
Rich Creek, VA **D3**/194
Rich Hill, MO **B3**/145
Rich Mountain, AR **A3**/84
Rich Square, NC **H1**/163
Richards, MO **B4**/145
Richardson, KY **H3**/121
Richardson, TX **E1**/188
Richardsville, KY **D3**/120
Richardton, ND **C3**/164
Richboro, PA **F3**/173
Richburg, NY **B3**/158
Richburg, SC **C2**/179
Richelieu, KY **D3**/120
Richey, MS **B2**/143
Richey, MT **L2**/147
Richfield, ID **D6**/108
Richfield, KS **B3**/118
Richfield, MN **E6**/140
Richfield, NC **E2**/162
Richfield, OH **D1**/167
Richfield, PA **D3**/173
Richfield, UT **C4**/190
Richfield Springs, NY **F3**/159
Richford, NY **D3**/159
Richford, VT **B2**/193
Richgrove, CA **D3**/88
Richland, GA **B3**/102
Richland, IA **F3**/117
Richland, IN **D3**/115
Richland, KS **H2**/119
Richland, MI **B5**/137
Richland, MO **D4**/145
Richland, MT **K1**/147
Richland, NE **H2**/149
Richland, NJ **C5**/155
Richland, NY **D2**/159
Richland, OR **H3**/171
Richland, TX **L6**/185
Richland, WA **F3**/198
Richland Center, WI **C5**/205
Richland Hills, TX **B1**/188
Richland Springs, TX **J6**/185
Richland Springs, TX **H1**/187
Richlands, NC **H3**/163
Richlands, VA **C3**/194
Richlandtown, PA **F3**/173
Richmond, AL **B3**/76
Richmond, AR **A4**/84
Richmond, CA **C5**/86
Richmond, CA **B2**/91
Richmond, IA **F3**/117
Richmond, IL **D1**/111
Richmond, IN **E3**/115
Richmond, KS **H2**/119
Richmond, KY **F3**/121
Richmond, LA **D2**/122
Richmond, MA **A2**/132
Richmond, ME **C4**/126
Richmond, MI **E5**/137
Richmond, MN **D5**/140
Richmond, MO **C2**/145
Richmond, NH **B6**/153
Richmond, OH **E2**/167
Richmond, TX **L3**/187
Richmond, UT **D1**/190
Richmond, VT **B2**/193
Richmond (cap.), VA **L3**/11
Richmond (cap.), VA **G3**/195
Richmond (nat'l bfld. park), VA **G3**/195
Richmond Beach-Innis Arden, WA **B2**/201
Richmond Dale, OH **C3**/167
Richmond Furnace, MA **A2**/132
Richmond Hill, GA **E4**/102
Richmondville, NY **F3**/159
Richton, MS **D4**/143
Richvale, CA **D3**/86
Richville, MI **D4**/137
Richville, MN **C4**/140
Richville, NY **E1**/159
Richwood, LA **C2**/122
Richwood, MN **C4**/140
Richwood, NJ **B4**/155
Richwood, OH **B2**/167
Richwood, WI **E5**/205
Richwood, WV **C3**/203
Richwoods, MO **F3**/145
Rickardsville, IA **G2**/117
Rickman, TN **F1**/183
Rico, CO **B4**/92
Riddle, ID **B7**/108
Riddle, OR **B5**/170
Riddlesburg, PA **C3**/173
Riddleton, TN **E1**/182
Riddleville, GA **D3**/102
Riderwood, AL **A3**/76
Ridge, MD **D2**/129
Ridge, MT **L4**/147
Ridge, NY **H5**/159
Ridge Farm, IL **E4**/111
Ridge Manor, FL **F3**/99
Ridge Spring, SC **C3**/179
Ridgecrest, CA **F3**/89
Ridgecrest, LA **D3**/122
Ridgefield, CT **B3**/95
Ridgefield, NJ **B1**/161
Ridgefield, WA **C4**/198
Ridgefield Park, NJ **D2**/155
Ridgefield Park, NJ **B1**/161
Ridgeland, MS **B3**/143
Ridgeland, SC **D4**/179
Ridgeland, WI **B3**/205
Ridgeley, WV **E2**/203
Ridgely, MD **E2**/129
Ridgely, TN **B1**/182
Ridgetop, TN **E1**/182
Ridgeview, SD **E1**/181
Ridgeville, GA **E4**/102
Ridgeville, IN **D2**/115
Ridgeville, SC **D3**/179
Ridgeville Corners, OH **A1**/167
Ridgeway, IA **F1**/117
Ridgeway, MN **G7**/140
Ridgeway, MO **C1**/145
Ridgeway, NC **G1**/163
Ridgeway, OH **B2**/167
Ridgeway, SC **D2**/179
Ridgeway, VA **E4**/194
Ridgeway, WI **D5**/205
Ridgeway, WV **E2**/203
Ridgewood, NJ **D2**/155
Ridgewood, NJ **A1**/161
Ridgway, CO **C3**/92
Ridgway, IL **D6**/111
Ridgway, PA **C2**/172
Ridley, TN **D2**/182

For key to abbreviations, see page 217.

Tyler—Wales 253

Tyler, WA **H2**/199
Tyler Park, VA **B2**/131
Tylersburg, PA **B2**/172
Tylersville, PA **D3**/173
Tylertown, MS **B4**/143
Tyndall, SD **H4**/181
Tyner, IN **C1**/115
Tyner, KY **G3**/121
Tyngsboro, MA **E1**/133
Tyonek, AK **G3**/79
Tyringham, MA **A2**/132
Tyro, KS **H3**/119
Tyro, MS **C1**/143
Tyro, VA **E3**/195
Tyrone, CO **F4**/92
Tyrone, GA **B2**/102
Tyrone, KY **F2**/121
Tyrone, MO **E4**/145
Tyrone, NM **B5**/157
Tyrone, OK **B1**/168
Tyrone, PA **C3**/173
Tyronza, AR **E2**/84
Tysons Corner, VA **G2**/195

U

U.S.S. Arizona (nat'l mem.), HI **D2**/107
Ubly, MI **E4**/137
Uchee, AL **D3**/76
Ucon, ID **G6**/108
Ucross, WY **F1**/206
Udall, KS **F3**/119
Uehling, NE **J2**/149
Uhland, TX **J3**/187
Uhrichsville, OH **D2**/167
Uinta (mts.), UT **E2**/190
Ukiah, CA **B3**/86
Ukiah, OR **G2**/170
Ukolnoi (isl.), AK **D5**/79
Ulah, NC **F2**/163
Ulak (isl.), AK **D2**/80
Ulen, MN **B3**/140
Ullin, IL **C6**/111
Ulm, AR **D3**/84
Ulm, MT **E2**/147
Ulm, WY **F1**/206
Ulmer, SC **C3**/179
Ulster, PA **E2**/173
Ulupalakua, HI **E3**/107
Ulysses, KS **B3**/118
Ulysses, KY **H3**/121
Ulysses, NE **H2**/149
Ulysses, PA **D2**/173
Ulysses S. Grant (nat'l hist. site), MO **F3**/145
Umapine, OR **G2**/170
Umatilla, FL **G3**/99
Umatilla, OR **F2**/170
Umbagog (lake), ME **A4**/126
Umbagog (lake), NH **D2**/153
Umbarger, TX **E3**/184
Umiat, AK **F1**/79
Umnak (isl.), AK **B5**/78
Umnak (isl.), AK **F1**/80
Umpqua, OR **B4**/170
Umpqua (riv.), OR **B2**/10
Unadilla, GA **C3**/102
Unadilla, NE **J3**/149
Unadilla, NY **E3**/159
Unaka, NC **A2**/162
Unaka (mts.), NC **C1**/162
Unaka (mts.), TN **J1**/183
Unalakleet, AK **D3**/79
Unalaska, AK **C5**/78
Unalaska, AK **G1**/80
Unalaska (isl.), AK **U11**/10
Unalaska (isl.), AK **C5**/78
Unalaska (isl.), AK **G1**/80
Uncasville-Oxoboxo Valley, CT **D3**/95
Uncertain, TX **N5**/185
Underhill, VT **B2**/193
Underhill, WI **E4**/205
Underhill Center, VT **B2**/193
Underwood, IA **B3**/116
Underwood, IN **D4**/115
Underwood, MN **C4**/140
Underwood, ND **D2**/164
Underwood, WA **D4**/198
Underwood-Petersville, AL **B1**/76
Uneeda, WV **B3**/203
Unga (isl.), AK **D5**/79
Unger, WV **E2**/203
Unicoi, TN **J1**/183
Unicoi (mts.), NC **A2**/162
Unicoi (mts.), TN **G2**/183
Unimak (isl.), AK **C5**/79
Union, AL **B3**/76
Union, AR **D1**/84
Union, CT **D2**/95
Union, IA **D2**/117
Union, KY **F2**/121
Union, ME **C4**/126
Union, MI **B6**/137
Union, MO **E3**/145
Union, MS **B4**/143
Union, MS **C3**/143
Union, ND **H1**/164
Union, NE **K3**/149
Union, NJ **D2**/155
Union, OH **A3**/167
Union, OR **H2**/170
Union, SC **C2**/179
Union, WV **C4**/203
Union Beach, NJ **D3**/155
Union Bridge, MD **C1**/129
Union Center, SD **C2**/181
Union Center, WI **C5**/205
Union Church, MS **B4**/143
Union City, CA **C5**/86
Union City, CA **C3**/91
Union City, GA **B2**/102
Union City, IN **E2**/115
Union City, MI **B5**/137
Union City, NJ **D2**/155
Union City, NJ **B2**/161
Union City, OH **A2**/167
Union City, OK **F2**/169
Union City, PA **B2**/172
Union City, TN **B1**/182
Union Creek, OR **C5**/170
Union Dale, PA **F2**/173
Union Furnace, OH **C3**/167
Union Gap, WA **E3**/198
Union Grove, AL **C1**/76
Union Grove, NC **E1**/162
Union Grove, WI **E6**/205
Union Hall, VA **E4**/194
Union Hill, NY **C2**/159
Union Level, VA **F4**/195
Union Mills, IN **C1**/115
Union Mills, MD **C1**/129
Union Mills, NC **D2**/162
Union Park, FL **G3**/99
Union Pier, MI **A6**/137
Union Point, GA **C2**/102
Union Springs, AL **D3**/76
Union Springs, NY **D3**/159
Union Star, KY **D3**/120
Union Star, MO **B2**/145
Union Station, DC **D4**/131
Union Village, RI **B2**/177
Union Village, VT **B3**/193
Uniondale, IN **D2**/115
Uniondale, NY **G5**/159
Uniontown, AL **B3**/76
Uniontown, AR **A2**/84
Uniontown, KS **J3**/119
Uniontown, KY **C3**/120
Uniontown, MD **C1**/129
Uniontown, OH **D2**/167
Uniontown, PA **B4**/172
Uniontown, WA **H3**/199
Unionville, GA **C4**/102
Unionville, IA **E4**/117
Unionville, IN **C3**/115
Unionville, MI **D4**/137
Unionville, MO **C1**/145
Unionville, NC **E2**/162
Unionville, NV **B2**/151
Unionville, NY **F4**/159
Unionville, TN **E2**/182
Unionville, VA **G2**/195
Unionville Center, OH **B2**/167
Uniopolis, OH **A2**/167
United Nations, NY **C4**/161
United Nations, NY **B2**/161
United States Air Force Academy, CO **E2**/92
United States Botanic Gardens, DC **D5**/131
United States Capitol, DC **D5**/131
United States Capitol, DC **C2**/131
United States Census Bureau, MD **D3**/131
United States Chamber of Commerce, DC **B4**/131
United States Holocaust Memorial Museum, DC **B5**/131
United States Merchant Marine Academy, NY **C2**/161
United States Ski Hall Of Fame, MI **D3**/138
United States Supreme Court, DC **D5**/131
United States Weather Bureau, MD **D3**/131
Unity, ME **C4**/126
Unity, NH **B5**/153
Unity, OR **G3**/170
Unity, WI **C4**/205
Unityville, PA **E2**/173
Unityville, SD **H3**/181
Universal, IN **B3**/115
Universal City, TX **H3**/187
University, MS **C1**/143
University City, MO **F3**/145
University Heights, IA **F3**/117
University Park, IA **E3**/117
University Park, MD **D1**/131
University Park, NM **D5**/157
University Park, TX **D1**/188
University Place, WA **C2**/198
University Place, WA **A6**/201
Upalco, UT **E2**/190
Upham, ND **E1**/164
Upland, IN **D2**/115
Upland, KS **F1**/119
Upland, NE **G3**/149
Upland, PA **F4**/173
Upland, PA **A3**/174
Upper Arlington, OH **B2**/167
Upper Darby, PA **F4**/173
Upper Darby, PA **B3**/174
Upper Fairmount, MD **E2**/129
Upper Falls, MD **D1**/129
Upper Frenchville, ME **D1**/126
Upper Greenwood Lake, NJ **D1**/155
Upper Jay, NY **G1**/159
Upper Klamath (lake), OR **D5**/170
Upper Lake, CA **C3**/86
Upper Macopin, NJ **D1**/155
Upper Marlboro (Marlboro), MD **D2**/129
Upper Matecumbe Key (isl.), FL **G7**/99
Upper Nutria, NM **B2**/158
Upper Red (lake), MN **D2**/140
Upper Saddle River, NJ **D1**/155
Upper Sandusky, OH **B2**/167
Upper Saranac (lake), NY **F1**/159
Upper Stepney, CT **B3**/95
Upper Tract, WV **D3**/203
Upper Tygart, KY **G2**/121
Upperglade, WV **C3**/203
Upperville, VA **G2**/195
Upsala, MN **D5**/140
Upson, WI **C2**/205
Upton, KY **E3**/121
Upton, MA **D2**/133
Upton, ME **A4**/126
Upton, UT **B4**/190
Upton, WY **H1**/206
Upton-West Upton, MA **D2**/133
Urania, LA **C3**/122
Uravan, CO **B3**/92
Urban, PA **E3**/173
Urban, WA **C1**/198
Urbana, AR **C4**/84
Urbana, IA **F2**/117
Urbana, IL **D3**/111
Urbana, IN **D2**/115
Urbana, MD **C1**/129
Urbana, MO **C4**/145
Urbana, OH **B2**/167
Urbancrest, OH **B3**/167
Urbandale, IA **D3**/117
Urbanette, AR **B1**/84
Urbank, MN **C4**/140
Urbanna, VA **H3**/195
Uriah, AL **B4**/76
Urich, MO **B3**/145
Ursa, IL **A3**/111
Ursina, PA **B4**/172
Ursine, NV **F5**/151
Usk, WA **H1**/199
Usquepaug, RI **B4**/177
Usta, SD **C1**/181
Utah (lake), UT **C2**/190
Ute, IA **B2**/116
Ute Park, NM **E1**/157
Utica, IN **D4**/115
Utica, KS **C2**/118
Utica, KY **C3**/120
Utica, MI **D5**/137
Utica, MN **G7**/140
Utica, MO **C2**/145
Utica, MS **B3**/143
Utica, MT **F3**/147
Utica, NE **H3**/149
Utica, NY **E2**/159
Utica, OH **C2**/167
Utica, OK **G4**/169
Utica, PA **B2**/172
Utica, SC **B2**/179
Utica, SD **H4**/181
Utleyville, CO **G4**/92
Utopia, TX **G3**/187
Uvada, UT **A5**/190
Uvalda, GA **D3**/102
Uvalde, TX **G3**/187
Uxbridge, MA **D2**/133
Uyak, AK **F4**/79

V

Vaca, Key (isl.), FL **G7**/99
Vacaville, CA **D4**/86
Vacherie, LA **E4**/122
Vaden, AR **C4**/84
Vader, WA **C3**/198
Vadito, NM **E1**/157
Vado, NM **D5**/157
Vaiden, MS **C2**/143
Vail, AZ **E5**/83
Vail, CO **D2**/92
Vail, IA **B2**/116
Vails, NJ **B2**/155
Vails Gate, NY **F4**/159
Val Verda, UT **D2**/190
Val Verde, CA **E4**/89
Valatie, NY **G3**/159
Valders, WI **F4**/205
Valdese, NC **D2**/162
Valdez, AK **H3**/79
Valdez, CO **F4**/92
Valdez, NM **E1**/157
Valdosta, GA **C5**/102
Vale, NC **D2**/162
Vale, OR **H4**/171
Vale, SD **B2**/180
Vale, TN **C1**/182
Valeda, KS **H3**/119
Valeene, IN **C4**/115
Valencia, NM **D3**/157
Valencia, PA **B3**/172
Valencia Heights, SC **D3**/179
Valentine, AZ **B2**/83
Valentine, NE **E1**/149
Valentine, TX **B2**/186
Valentines, VA **G4**/195
Valhermoso Springs, AL **C1**/76
Valier, IL **C5**/111
Valier, MT **D1**/146
Valier, PA **B3**/172
Valinda, CA **C5**/91
Valle Vista, CA **G5**/89
Vallecitos, NM **D1**/157
Vallejo, CA **C4**/86
Vallejo, CA **B1**/91
Valles Mines, MO **F3**/145
Valley, AL **D3**/76
Valley, MS **B3**/143
Valley, NE **J2**/149
Valley, WA **H1**/199
Valley, WI **C5**/205
Valley Center, CA **F5**/89
Valley Center, KS **F3**/119
Valley City, ND **G3**/164
Valley City, OH **D1**/167
Valley Falls, KS **H1**/119
Valley Falls, NY **G3**/159
Valley Falls, OR **E5**/170
Valley Falls, RI **C2**/177
Valley Falls, SC **C1**/179
Valley Farms, AZ **D5**/83
Valley Forge, PA **F3**/173
Valley Forge, TN **J1**/183
Valley Forge (nat'l hist. park), PA **F3**/173
Valley Grove, WV **C1**/203
Valley Head, AL **D1**/76
Valley Head, WV **C3**/203
Valley Hill, NC **C2**/162
Valley Lee, MD **D2**/129
Valley Mills, TX **K6**/185
Valley Park, MS **B3**/143
Valley Spring, TX **H2**/187
Valley Springs, AR **C1**/84
Valley Springs, SD **J3**/181
Valley Station, KY **E2**/121
Valley Stream, NY **G5**/159
Valley Stream, NY **C2**/161
Valley View, KY **F3**/121
Valley View, PA **E3**/173
Valley View, TX **K4**/185
Valleyford, WA **H2**/199
Valliant, OK **H3**/169
Vallonia, IN **C4**/115
Valmeyer, IL **B5**/111
Valmora, NM **F2**/157
Valmy, NV **C2**/151
Valmy, WI **F4**/205
Valona, GA **E4**/102
Valparaiso, FL **B1**/98
Valparaiso, IN **B1**/115
Valparaiso, NE **J2**/149
Valsetz, OR **B3**/170
Value, MS **C3**/143
Van, PA **B2**/172
Van, TX **M5**/185
Van, WV **B4**/203
Van Alstyne, TX **L4**/185
Van Buren, AR **A2**/84
Van Buren, IN **D2**/115
Van Buren, ME **E1**/126
Van Buren, MO **E5**/145
Van Buren, OH **B1**/167
Van Etten, NY **D3**/159
Van Horn, TX **C6**/184
Van Horn, TX **B1**/186
Van Horne, IA **E2**/117
Van Lear, KY **H3**/121
Van Meter, IA **D3**/117
Van Tassell, WY **H3**/207
Van Vleck, TX **L3**/187
Van Vleet, MS **D2**/143
Van Wert, GA **A2**/102
Van Wert, IA **D4**/117
Van Wert, OH **A2**/167
Van Wyck, SC **D2**/179
Vananda, MT **J3**/147
Vanatta, OH **C2**/167
Vance, AL **B2**/76
Vance, MS **B1**/143
Vance, SC **D3**/179
Vanceboro, ME **E3**/126
Vanceboro, NC **H2**/163
Vanceburg, KY **G2**/121
Vancleave, MS **D5**/143
Vancourt, TX **G6**/184
Vancouver, WA **C4**/198
Vandalia, IL **C5**/111
Vandalia, MI **B6**/137
Vandalia, MO **E2**/145
Vandalia, MT **K1**/147
Vandalia, OH **A3**/167
Vandemere, NC **J2**/163
Vandenberg Village, CA **C4**/88
Vander, NC **G2**/163
Vanderbilt, MI **G4**/138
Vanderbilt, MI **C2**/137
Vanderbilt, PA **B3**/172
Vanderbilt, TX **K4**/187
Vanderbilt Mansion (nat'l hist. site), NY **G4**/159
Vandercook Lake, MI **C5**/137
Vandergrift, PA **B3**/172
Vanderpool, TX **G3**/187
Vandervoort, AR **A3**/84
Vandiver, AL **C2**/76
Vandling, PA **F2**/173
Vanduser, MO **G5**/145
Vanleer, TN **D1**/182
Vanlue, OH **B2**/167
Vanndale, AR **E2**/84
Vanoss, OK **G3**/169
Vanport, PA **A3**/172
Vansant, VA **B3**/194
Vantage, WA **F3**/198
Vanzant, MO **D5**/145
Vardaman, MS **C2**/143
Varna, IL **C2**/111
Varnado, LA **F4**/122
Varner, KS **E3**/119
Varney, WV **A4**/203
Varnville, SC **C4**/179
Varysburg, NY **B3**/158
Vashon, WA **A5**/201
Vashon (isl.), WA **A5**/201
Vashon Heights, WA **A4**/201
Vass, NC **F2**/163
Vassalboro, ME **C4**/126
Vassar, KS **H2**/119
Vassar, MI **D4**/137
Vaucluse, SC **C3**/179
Vaughan, MS **B3**/143
Vaughan, NC **G1**/163
Vaughan, WV **B3**/203
Vaughn, MT **E2**/147
Vaughn, NM **E3**/157
Vaughn, WA **C2**/198
Vaughnsville, OH **A2**/167
Vayland, SD **G2**/181
Vealmoor, TX **F5**/184
Veazie, ME **D4**/126
Veblen, SD **H1**/181
Veedersburg, IN **B2**/115
Vega, TX **E2**/184
Veguita, NM **D3**/157
Velarde, NM **E1**/157
Velma, OK **F3**/169
Velpen, IN **B4**/115
Velva, ND **E1**/164
Venango, NE **C3**/148
Venango, PA **A2**/172
Venedocia, OH **A2**/167
Venedy, IL **C5**/111
Veneta, OR **B3**/170
Venetie, AK **H2**/79
Venice, FL **F4**/99
Venice, IL **B5**/111
Venice, UT **C4**/190
Venice, WA **A3**/201
Ventnor City, NJ **D5**/155
Ventura, IA **D1**/117
Ventura (San Buenaventura), CA **D4**/88
Venturia, ND **F4**/164
Venus, FL **G4**/99
Venus, PA **B2**/172
Venus, TX **K5**/185
Vera, OK **H1**/169
Vera, TX **H4**/185
Verbena, AL **C3**/76
Verda, KY **G4**/121
Verda, LA **C3**/122
Verde (riv.), AZ **C3**/83
Verdel, NE **G1**/149
Verden, OK **E2**/169
Verdery, SC **B2**/179
Verdi, NV **A3**/151
Verdigre, NE **G1**/149
Verdigris, OK **H1**/169
Verdigris (riv.), KS **H3**/119
Verdon, NE **K3**/149
Verdon, SD **G1**/181
Verdugo (mts.), CA **A4**/91
Verdunville, WV **A4**/203
Verendrye, ND **E1**/164
Vergas, MN **C4**/140
Vergennes, IL **C6**/111
Vergennes, VT **A2**/193
Veribest, TX **G6**/184
Vermilion, IL **E4**/111
Vermilion, OH **C1**/167
Vermilion (lake), MN **E3**/140
Vermilion (range), MN **F3**/140
Vermilion (riv.), IL **D2**/111
Vermillion, KS **G1**/119
Vermillion, MN **F6**/140
Vermillion (riv.), SD **H3**/181
Vermont, IL **B3**/111
Vermontville, MI **B5**/137
Vernal, UT **F2**/190
Verndale, MN **C4**/140
Vernon, AL **A2**/76
Vernon, AZ **F3**/83
Vernon, CA **B5**/91
Vernon, CO **H2**/93
Vernon, CT **D2**/95
Vernon, DE **A3**/96
Vernon, FL **C1**/98
Vernon, IL **C5**/111
Vernon, IN **D4**/115
Vernon, KY **E4**/121
Vernon, MI **C5**/137
Vernon, OK **H2**/169
Vernon, TX **H3**/185
Vernon, UT **C2**/190
Vernon, VT **B4**/193
Vernon Center, MN **D7**/140
Vernon Hill, VA **E4**/195
Vernon Hills, IL **E1**/111
Vernon Valley, NJ **D1**/155
Vernonia, OR **B2**/170
Vero Beach, FL **H4**/99
Verona, IL **D2**/111
Verona, KY **F2**/121
Verona, MO **C5**/145
Verona, MS **D1**/143
Verona, ND **G3**/164
Verona, NJ **D2**/155
Verona, NJ **A1**/161
Verona, NY **E2**/159
Verona, VA **E2**/195
Verona, WI **D6**/205
Versailles, CT **D2**/95
Versailles, IL **B4**/111
Versailles, IN **D3**/115
Versailles, KY **F2**/121
Versailles, MO **D3**/145
Versailles, OH **A2**/167
Vershire, VT **B3**/193
Veseli, MN **E6**/140
Vesper, KS **E1**/119
Vesper, WI **D4**/205
Vesta, MN **C6**/140
Vesta, VA **D4**/194
Vestaburg, MI **C4**/137
Vestavia Hills, AL **C2**/76
Vesuvius, VA **E3**/195
Vetal, SD **D3**/181
Veteran, WY **H4**/207
Vevay, IN **D4**/115
Veyo, UT **B5**/190
Vian, OK **J2**/169
Viborg, SD **H3**/181
Viburnum, MO **E4**/145
Vicco, KY **G3**/121
Vichy, MO **E3**/145
Vici, OK **D1**/169
Vick, AR **C4**/84
Vick, LA **C3**/122
Vickery, OH **C1**/167
Vicksburg, AZ **B4**/83
Vicksburg, IN **B3**/115
Vicksburg, MI **B5**/137
Vicksburg, MS **B3**/143
Vicksburg (nat'l mil. park), MS **B3**/143
Victor, CA **D4**/86
Victor, CO **E3**/92
Victor, IA **E3**/117
Victor, ID **G6**/108
Victor, MT **B3**/146
Victor, NY **C3**/159
Victoria, AR **E2**/84
Victoria, IL **B2**/111
Victoria, KS **D2**/119
Victoria, MI **B3**/138
Victoria, MO **F3**/145
Victoria, MS **C1**/143
Victoria, TX **J4**/187
Victoria, VA **F4**/195
Victorville, CA **F4**/89
Victory, NY **D2**/159
Victory, VT **C2**/193
Victory, WI **B5**/205
Victory Gardens, NJ **C2**/155
Vida, MT **L2**/147
Vida, OR **C3**/170
Vidal, CA **J4**/89
Vidalia, GA **D3**/102
Vidalia, LA **D3**/122
Vidor, TX **M2**/187
Vidrine, LA **C4**/122
Vienna, GA **C3**/102
Vienna, IL **D6**/111
Vienna, IN **D4**/115
Vienna, LA **C2**/122
Vienna, MD **E2**/129
Vienna, MO **E3**/145
Vienna, SD **H2**/181
Vienna, VA **G2**/195
Vienna, WV **B2**/203
Vietnam Veterans Memorial, DC **A5**/131
Vieux Carré (French Quarter), LA **E2**/124
View Park-Windsor Hills, CA **A5**/91
Viking, MN **B2**/140
Vilano Beach, FL **G2**/99
Vilas, CO **H4**/93
Vilas, NC **D1**/162
Vilas, SD **H2**/181
Vilbig (lakes), TX **C2**/188
Vildo, TN **B2**/182
Villa Grove, CO **E3**/92
Villa Grove, IL **D4**/111
Villa Park, CA **C6**/91
Villa Park, IL **A2**/112
Villa Ranchaero, SD **B2**/180
Villa Rica, GA **B2**/102
Villa Ridge, MO **F3**/145
Village, AR **B4**/84
Village Mills, TX **M2**/187
Villanova, PA **A2**/174
Villanow, GA **A1**/102
Villanueva, NM **E2**/157
Villard, MN **C5**/140
Villas, NJ **C5**/155
Ville Platte, LA **C4**/122
Villegreen, CO **G4**/92
Villisca, IA **C4**/117
Vilonia, AR **C2**/84
Vimy Ridge, AR **C3**/84
Vina, AL **A1**/76
Vina, CA **C3**/86
Vinalhaven, ME **D4**/126
Vinalhaven (isl.), ME **D4**/126
Vincennes, IN **B4**/115
Vincent, AL **C2**/76
Vincent, CA **E4**/89
Vincent, CA **C4**/91
Vincent, IA **C2**/117
Vincent, OH **D3**/167
Vincentown, NJ **C4**/155
Vinco, PA **C3**/172
Vine Grove, KY **E3**/121
Vine Hill, CA **C1**/91
Vinegar Bend, AL **A4**/76
Vineland, MN **E4**/140
Vineland, NJ **B5**/155
Vineyard Haven, MA **F4**/133
Vining, KS **F1**/119
Vining, MN **C4**/140
Vinings, GA **A1**/105
Vinita, OK **H1**/169
Vinland, KS **H2**/119
Vinson, OK **D3**/168
Vinton, IA **E2**/117
Vinton, LA **B4**/122
Vinton, OH **C4**/167
Vinton, TX **A6**/184
Vintondale, PA **C3**/172
Viola, AR **D1**/84
Viola, DE **A2**/96
Viola, IA **F2**/117
Viola, ID **A3**/108
Viola, IL **B2**/111
Viola, KS **F3**/119
Viola, KY **B4**/120
Viola, MN **F6**/140
Viola, TN **F2**/183
Viola, WI **C5**/205
Violet, LA **F5**/122
Violet Hill, AR **D1**/84
Virden, IL **C4**/111
Virden, NM **A5**/157
Virgelle, MT **F1**/147
Virgie, KY **H3**/121
Virgil, KS **G3**/119
Virgil, SD **G2**/181
Virgin, UT **B5**/190
Virgin (riv.), NV **G5**/151
Virgin (riv.), UT **B5**/190
Virginia, ID **F7**/108
Virginia, IL **B4**/111
Virginia, MN **F3**/140
Virginia, NE **J3**/149
Virginia (isl.), FL **C3**/101
Virginia (mts.), NV **A2**/151
Virginia Beach, VA **J4**/195
Virginia City, MT **E4**/146
Virginia City, NV **A3**/151
Virginia Dale, CO **E1**/92
Viroqua, WI **C5**/205
Visalia, CA **D2**/88
Visalia, KY **F2**/121
Vista, CA **F5**/89
Vista, MO **C4**/145
Vivian, LA **B2**/122
Vivian, SD **E3**/181
Vixen, LA **C2**/122
Vliets, KS **G1**/119
Voca, TX **H6**/185
Voca, TX **G1**/187
Vogel Center, MI **B3**/137
Volant, PA **A2**/172
Volborg, MT **L4**/147
Volcano, CA **E4**/86
Volcano, HI **F4**/107
Volga, IA **F2**/117
Volga, SD **J2**/181
Volin, SD **H4**/181
Volney, MI **A4**/137
Volney, VA **C4**/194
Voltaire, ND **E1**/164
Volunteer, SD **B2**/180
Voluntown, CT **E2**/95
Vona, CO **H2**/92
Vonore, TN **G2**/183
Voorheesville, NY **G3**/159
Voss, ND **H1**/165
Vossburg, MS **D4**/143
Voyageurs (nat'l park), MN **F2**/140
Vredenburgh, AL **B4**/76
Vulcan, MO **F4**/145
Vya, NV **A1**/151

W

Wabash, AR **E3**/84
Wabash, IN **D2**/115
Wabash, OH **A2**/167
Wabash (riv.) **J3**/11
Wabasha, MN **F6**/140
Wabasso, FL **H4**/99
Wabasso, MN **C6**/140
Wabaunsee, KS **G1**/119
Wabbaseka, AR **D3**/84
Wabeno, WI **E3**/205
Wabuska, NV **A3**/151
Waccamaw (riv.), SC **F3**/179
Wachapreague, VA **J3**/195
Wachusett (res.), MA **D2**/133
Waco, GA **A2**/102
Waco, KY **F3**/121
Waco, NC **D2**/162
Waco, NE **H3**/149
Waco, TX **K6**/185
Waconda (lake), KS **E1**/119
Waconia, MN **E6**/140
Waddington, NY **E1**/159
Waddy, KY **E2**/121
Wade, MS **D5**/143
Wade, NC **G2**/163
Wade, OK **G4**/169
Wade Hampton, SC **B2**/179
Wadena, IA **F2**/117
Wadena, MN **C4**/140
Wadesboro, LA **E4**/122
Wadesboro, NC **E3**/162
Wadestown, WV **C2**/203
Wadesville, IN **B4**/115
Wadeville, NC **F2**/163
Wadhams, NY **G1**/159
Wadley, AL **D2**/76
Wadley, GA **D3**/102
Wadsworth, AL **C3**/76
Wadsworth, NV **A3**/151
Wadsworth, OH **D1**/167
Waelder, TX **J3**/187
Wagarville, AL **A4**/76
Wagener, SC **C3**/179
Waggaman, LA **A3**/124
Waggoner, IL **C4**/111
Wagner, MT **H1**/147
Wagner, SD **G3**/181
Wagon Mound, NM **F1**/157
Wagoner, OK **H2**/169
Wagontire, OR **F4**/170
Wagram, NC **F3**/163
Wah Wah (mts.), UT **B4**/190
Wahalak, MS **D3**/143
Wahiawa, HI **C2**/107
Wahkiacus, WA **D4**/198
Wahkon, MN **E4**/140
Wahoo, NE **J2**/149
Wahpeton, IA **B1**/116
Wahpeton, ND **J3**/165
Wahsatch, UT **D1**/190
Waialee, HI **C2**/107
Waialua, HI **C2**/107
Waianae, HI **C2**/107
Waianae (range), HI **C2**/107
Waihee-Waiehu, HI **E3**/107
Waikane, HI **D2**/107
Waikii, HI **F4**/107
Waikoloa Village, HI **F4**/107
Wailua, HI **B1**/106
Wailuku, HI **E3**/107
Wailuku (riv.), HI **F4**/107
Waimanalo, HI **D2**/107
Waimanalo Beach, HI **D2**/107
Waimea, HI **B2**/106
Waimea (riv.), HI **B2**/106
Waimea Falls, HI **C2**/107
Wainiha, HI **B1**/106
Wainwright, AK **D1**/79
Wainwright, OK **H2**/169
Waiohinu, HI **F4**/107
Waipahu, HI **C2**/107
Waipio, HI **F3**/107
Waipio Acres, HI **C2**/107
Waite, ME **E3**/126
Waite Park, MN **D5**/140
Waites, MS **C1**/143
Waiteville, WV **C4**/203
Waits River, VT **B2**/193
Waitsburg, WA **G3**/199
Waitsfield, VT **B2**/193
Waka, TX **F1**/184
Wakarusa, IN **C1**/115
Wakarusa, KS **H2**/119
Wake Forest, NC **G2**/163
Wake Village, TX **N4**/185
Wakeeney, KS **D1**/118
Wakefield, KS **F1**/119
Wakefield, LA **D4**/122
Wakefield, MA **E1**/133
Wakefield, MA **B1**/134
Wakefield, MI **B3**/138
Wakefield, NE **J1**/149
Wakefield, NH **D4**/153
Wakefield, OH **B4**/167
Wakefield, VA **H4**/195
Wakefield-Peacedale, RI **B4**/177
Wakelee, MI **B6**/137
Wakeman, OH **C1**/167
Wakenda, MO **C2**/145
Wakita, OK **F1**/169
Wakonda, SD **H3**/181
Wakpala, SD **E1**/181
Wakulla, FL **D1**/99
Walbridge, OH **B1**/167
Walcott, AR **E1**/84
Walcott, IA **G3**/117
Walcott, ND **J3**/165
Walcott, WY **F4**/206
Walden, CO **D1**/92
Walden, GA **C3**/102
Walden, KY **F4**/121
Walden, NY **F4**/159
Walden Heights, VT **B2**/193
Waldenburg, AR **E2**/84
Waldheim, LA **E4**/122
Waldo, AR **B4**/84
Waldo, FL **F2**/99
Waldo, KS **E1**/119
Waldo, ME **C4**/126
Waldo, OH **B2**/167
Waldo, WI **F5**/205
Waldoboro, ME **C4**/126
Waldorf, MD **D2**/129
Waldorf, MN **E7**/140
Waldport, OR **A3**/170
Waldron, AR **A3**/84
Waldron, IN **D3**/115
Waldron, KS **E3**/119
Waldron, MI **C6**/137
Waldron, MO **B2**/145
Waldron, WA **B1**/198
Waldrup, MS **C4**/143
Waldwick, NJ **D2**/155
Wales, AK **B2**/79

▶ **Endpaper:** *Although serene on a calm day, the waters off North Carolina's Cape Hatteras National Seashore have been dubbed the Graveyard of the Atlantic.*